1,000,000 Books

are available to read at

---◆---

www.ForgottenBooks.com

---◆---

Read online
Download PDF
Purchase in print

ISBN 978-0-243-89071-2
PIBN 10804884

1 MONTH OF
FREE
READING

at
www.ForgottenBooks.com

By purchasing this book you are eligible for one month membership to ForgottenBooks.com, giving you unlimited access to our entire collection of over 1,000,000 titles via our web site and mobile apps.

To claim your free month visit:
www.forgottenbooks.com/free804884

CONGREGATIONAL
CHURCH· HYMNAL

OR,

Hymns of Worship, Praise, and Prayer,

FOR CONGREGATIONAL CHURCHES.

EDITED FOR

THE CONGREGATIONAL UNION OF ENGLAND AND WAL

BY

· GEORGE S. BARRETT, B.A., D.D.

PART I.—HYMNS.

LONDON:

MEMORIAL HALL, FARRINGDON STRE

NOTE.—The verses enclosed within brackets may be omitted if the hymn be thought too long for public worship.

Medium 16mo. Brevior.—6.1906.

ALEXANDER & SHEPHEARD, LTD., Printers, Norwich St., Fetter Lane, London.

NOTE.

THE Editor of this Hymnal, and the Committee of the Congregational Union of England and Wales, beg to tender grateful acknowledgments to the following Authors or owners of Copyright Hymns or Translations for permission kindly given to use them in this book:—

Rev. Canon Baynes, 488;
Rev. A. G. W. Blunt, 625;
The late Rev. J. E. Bode, 380;
Rev. Canon Bright, 555, 679;
Mrs. Bubier, 372;
The Archbishop of Canterbury, 713;
Mrs. Charles, 269, 489;
Rev. Dr. Conder, 74o;
Mrs. G. W. Conder, 757;
Miss F. E. Cox, 154, 349;
Rev. T. G. Crippen, 470, 658;
Rev. W. H. Davison, 617;
Rev. R. Dawson, 725;
Rev. E. A. Dayman, 508;
Sir E. Denny, 111, 575;
Miss E. O. Dobree, 604;
The late Bishop of Ely, 102;
Rev. Archdeacon Farrar, 741;
Mrs. Faussett, 350;
Mr. C. L. Ford, 483;
The late Rev. W. Gaskell, 379;
Mrs. Godwin, 261;
Rev. S. C. Hamerton, 740;
Mr. W. E. Hickson, 653;
Mr. E. Hodder, 761;
Mrs. E. P. Hood, 73, 752;
Rev. J. P. Hopps, 766;
Mr. T. Hughes, 403;
Miss Ingelow, 127;

Miss Irons, 268;
Rev. J. Julian, 79;
The Bishop of Lichfield, 150, 505;
Miss Livock, 677;
Dr. G. Macdonald, 680;
Rev. Dr. Martineau, 137;
Mr. G. Massey, 665;
Miss Matheson, 756;
Mr. A. Midlane, 758;
Mrs. G. Moultrie, 214, 645;
Mrs. Mudie, 308;
Miss C. M. Noel, 75;
Rev. G. Phillimore, 672;
Rev. F. Pott, 616;
Rev. G. R. Prynne, 190;
The late Rev. W. B. Robertson, 472
Rev. R. H. Robinson, 703;
Mrs. W. Robinson, 274;
Mr. W. H. Scott, 750;
The Representatives of the late Dean Stanley, 133;
Mr. A. Strahan, 185;
Dr. Thomas, 256;
Rev. H. Twells, 520;
Mr. G. Watson, 592;
Rev. B. Waugh, 749;
The Dean of Wells, 622;
Mr. W. Whiting, 639;
Mr. H. H. Wyatt, 648;

And to the following Authors or Translators for the Hymns bearing their names, which are too numerous to specify in detail :—

Mrs. C. F. Alexander; The Representatives of the late Dean Alford; E. S. A.; Rev. S. Baring-Gould; The Bishop of Bedford; Rev. Dr. Bonar; Miss Borthwick, for Hymns from the Land of Luther; The Representatives of the late Sir J. Bowring; Bishop A. C. Coxe, of Western, New York; Mr. W. C. Dix; Mrs. Downton, for Hymns by the late Rev. H. Downton; Rev. J. Ellerton; The Bishop of Exeter; The Rev. Canon Furse, for the hymns of the late Rev. Dr. Monsell; Mr. Redland Furse; Mr. T. H. Gill; Rev. J. Hamilton; Miss Havergal, for the hymns of the late Miss F. R. Havergal; The Proprietors of "Hymns Ancient and Modern"; Rev. Dr. Littledale; H. L. L.; Mrs. Lynch; Rev. W. T. Matson; The Rev. H. A. Mills, for the use of the late Rev. E. Caswall's hymns; The Representatives of the late Dean Milman; Cardinal Newman; Mr. F. T. Palgrave; Rev. T. B. Pollock; Mr. G. Rawson; Rev. S. J. Stone; Rev. G. Thring; Rev. L. Tuttiett; Miss A. L. Waring; Rev. Chr. Wordsworth, for the hymns of the late Bishop of Lincoln.

And to the following Publishers for leave to use hymns which are their Copyrights, and which in some cases have been purchased:—

Messrs. G. Bell & Sons, for the use of Miss Procter's hymns; The Proprietors of Mrs. A. Cross's "Hymns on the Holy Communion," for Hymns 482 and 514, taken from that work; Messrs. J. T. Hayes, for Dr. Irons' hymn, 430; Messrs. Longman, for the use of the translations by Miss Winkworth from the "Lyra Germanica"; Messrs. Macmillan, for Hymn 100, from Lord Tennyson's "In Memoriam"; Messrs. J. Masters, for certain of Mrs. Alexander's and of the late Dr. Neale's hymns; Messrs. Morgan & Scott, for Dr. Bonar's hymn, 239; Messrs. Novello, for the use of the following hymns by the late Dr. Neale, published in the Hymnal noted, 85, 135; Messrs. Oliphant, Anderson, & Ferrier, for the use of the late Rev. R. M. McCheyne's hymn, 305; Messrs. Parker, for the use of the hymns of the Rev. J. Keble, from "The Christian Year," and of the Rev. J. Williams; Messrs. Richardson, for the hymns of the late Rev. F. W. Faber; The R. T. S., for Mr. T. Kelly's and Miss Elliott's hymns.

All further acknowledgments will be found in the full Preface to the Crown 8vo. Edition of the Hymns, and to the Editions of the Hymns with Tunes.

GENERAL TABLE OF CONTENTS.

ALPHABETICAL INDEX TO HYMNS.

	NO.
A charge to keep I have	314
A few more years shall roll	408
A little child the Saviour came	472
A safe stronghold our God is still	343
A thousand years have come and gone	89
A voice upon the midnight air	137
Abide with me! fast falls the eventide	684
According to Thy gracious word	496
Across the sky the shades of night	722
Again, as evening's shadow falls	523
All faded is the glowing light	182
All glory, laud, and honour	135
All hail the power of Jesu's name	63
All people that on earth do dwell	531
All that I was, my sin, my guilt	281
All that's good, and great, and true	736
All things are Thine; no gift have we	612
All ye that pass by	148
Almighty God, Whose only Son	577
And can it be, that I should gain	280
And didst Thou love the race that loved not Thee	127
And now the wants are told, that brought	555
And wilt Thou pardon, Lord	262
Angels, from the realms of glory	91
Angel voices, ever singing	616
Another year is dawning	723
Approach, my soul, the mercy-seat	561
Arise, O King of grace, arise	445
Around the throne of God in heaven	775
Art thou weary, art thou languid	236
As helpless as a child who clings	334
As to His earthly parents' home	750
As with gladness men of old	98
At even, ere the sun was set	520
At the name of Jesus	75
At Thy feet, O Christ, we lay	679
Awake, and sing the song	78
Awake, awake, O Zion	584
Awake, my soul, and with the sun	668
Awake, my soul, in joyful lays	131
Awake, my soul, stretch every nerve	396
Awake, our souls; away, our fears	397
Before Jehovah's awful throne	532
Begin, my tongue, some heavenly theme	55
Begone, unbelief	331
Behold! how glorious is yon sky	436
Behold! the Eternal King and Priest	490
Behold the glories of the Lamb	81
	NO.
Behold! the Mountain of the Lord	581
Behold the throne of grace	562
Behold us, Lord, a little space	556
Behold what wondrous grace	288
Beneath the shadow of the cross	302
Beyond, beyond that boundless sea	8
Beyond the glittering starry skies	168
Birds have their quiet nest	287
Blessèd city, heavenly Salem	607
Blest are the pure in heart	319
Blest day of God, most calm, most bright	510
Bread of heaven! on Thee I feed	493
Bread of the world, in mercy broken	494
Break, new-born Year, on glad eyes break	719
Brief life is here our portion *Part I.*	435
Brightest and best of the sons of the morning	100
Brightly gleams our banner	746
By Christ redeemed, in Christ restored	478
Calm me, my God, and keep me calm	345
Captain and Saviour of the host	423
Children of the Heavenly King	444
Christ for the world we sing!	587
Christ, from Whom all blessings flow	447
Christ the Lord is risen again!	156
Christ the Lord is risen to-day	151
Christ to the young man said, "Yet one thing more"	459
Christ, Whose glory fills the skies	674
Christian! dost thou see them	305
"Christian! seek not yet repose"	304
Christian, work for Jesus	621
Christians, awake, salute the happy morn	88
Come, dearest Lord, descend, and dwell	369
Come, Holy Ghost, and through each heart	209
Come, Holy Ghost, in love	213
Come, Holy Ghost, our hearts inspire	220
Come, Holy Ghost, our souls inspire	463
Come, Holy Spirit, come	218
Come, Holy Spirit, heavenly Dove	205
Come, Holy Spirit, heavenly Dove	208
Come in, thou blessèd of the Lord	456
Come! kingdom of our God	573
Come, labour on!	389

INDEX OF FIRST LINES

OF ALL VERSES EXCEPT THE FIRST.

HYMNS.

I.

The Eternal God.

1.—HIS GLORY, WORSHIP, AND PRAISE.

1   10.10.11.11.

f O WORSHIP the King,
　All-glorious above ;
O gratefully sing
　His power and His love ;
Our Shield and Defender,
　The Ancient of days,
Pavilioned in splendour,
　And girded with praise.

f O tell of His might,
　O sing of His grace,
Whose robe is the light,
　Whose canopy, space ;
His chariots of wrath
　The deep thunder-clouds form ;
And dark is His path
　On the wings of the storm.

[*mf* The earth with its store
　Of wonders untold,
Almighty ! Thy power
　Hath founded of old ;
Hath stablished it fast
　By a changeless decree,
And round it hath cast,
　Like a mantle, the sea.]

mf Thy bountiful care
　What tongue can recite !
It breathes in the air,
　It shines in the light,
It streams from the hills,
　It descends to the plain,
p And sweetly distils
　In the dew and the rain.

p Frail children of dust,
　And feeble as frail,
cres In Thee do we trust,
　Nor find Thee to fail ;
mf Thy mercies how tender,
　How firm to the end,
Our Maker, Defender,
　Redeemer, and Friend !

f O measureless might !
　Ineffable love !
While angels delight
　To hymn Thee above,
dim The humbler creation,
　Though feeble their lays,
cres With true adoration
　Shall lisp to Thy praise.

R. Grant.

2   6.6.8.4.6.6.8.4.

PART I.

f　THE God of Abraham praise,
　Who reigns enthroned above ;
Ancient of everlasting days,
p　　And God of love :
f　Jehovah, Great I AM !
　By earth and heaven confest ;
p I bow and bless the sacred Name,
　For ever blest.

mf　The God of Abraham praise,
　At Whose supreme command
From earth I rise and seek the jo
　At His right hand :
I all on earth forsake,
　Its wisdom, fame, and pow

cres And Him my only Portion make,
    My Shield and Tower.
f   The God of Abraham praise,
    Whose all-sufficient grace
Shall guide me all my happy days,
    In all my ways.
He calls a worm His friend,
    He calls Himself my God,
And He shall save me to the end
    Through Jesu's blood.
mf He by Himself hath sworn,
    I on His oath depend ;
I shall, on eagles' wings upborne,
    To heaven ascend :
cres I shall behold His face,
    I shall His power adore,
f And sing the wonders of His grace
    For evermore.

6.6.8.4.6.6.8.4.
PART II.
mf The goodly land I see,
    With peace and plenty blessed ;
A land of sacred liberty
    And endless rest :
There milk and honey flow,
    And oil and wine abound ;
And trees of life for ever grow,
    With mercy crowned.
mf There dwells the Lord our King,
    The Lord our righteousness ;
f Triumphant o'er the world and sin,
    The Prince of peace
On Sion's sacred height
    His kingdom still maintains,
cres And glorious, with His saints in
    light,
f   For ever reigns.
Before the great Three-One,
    They all exulting stand,
f And tell the wonders He hath done
    Through all their land.

dim The listening spheres attend,
cres And swell the growing fame,
f And sing, in songs which never end
    The wondrous Name.

6.6.8.4.6.6.8.4.
PART III.
mf   The God Who reigns on high
    The great archangels sing,
f And " Holy, holy, holy " cry,
    " Almighty King !
mf   Who was, and is the same,
    And evermore shall be ;
f Jehovah—Father—great I AM,
    We worship Thee."
mf   Before the Saviour's face
    The ransom'd nations bow ;
O'erwhelm'd at His almighty
    grace,
    For ever new :
He shows His prints of love,—
cres They kindle to a flame, [above
f And sound, through all the world
    His wondrous Name.
f   The whole triumphant host
    Give thanks to God on high :
Hail, Father, Son, and Holy Ghost
    They ever cry :
Hail, Abraham's God and mine
    (I join the heavenly lays ;)
All might and majesty are Thine,
ff   And endless praise.
T. Olivers, Part III., *v.* 2, *l.* 8 *altd*

3
                  L.M.
mf WE praise, we worship Thee, O God
    Thy sovereign power we sound
    abroad :
All nations bow before Thy throne
    And Thee the Eternal Father own
f Loud hallelujahs to Thy name
    Angels and seraphim proclaim ;

The heavens and all the powers on
high
With rapture constantly do cry,—
p "O, holy, holy, holy Lord,
*cres*Thou God of Hosts, by all adored ;
f Earth and the heavens are full of
Thee,
. Thy light,Thy power, Thy majesty."

Apostles join the glorious throng,
And swell the loud immortal song ;
Prophets enraptured hear the
sound,
And spread the hallelujah round.

f Victorious martyrs join their lays
And shout the omnipotence of grace,
While all Thy Church, through all
the earth,
Acknowledge and extol Thy worth.

f Glory to Thee, O God most high !
Father, we praise Thy majesty ;
The Son, the Spirit, we adore ;
One Godhead, blest for evermore.
McAll's Coll., 1824, *v.* 6, *l.* 1 *altd.*

4   8.7.8.7.

f PRAISE the Lord, ye heavens adore
Him ;   [height ;
Praise Him, angels, in the
Sun and moon, rejoice before Him ;
Praise Him, all ye stars of light.

f Praise the Lord, for He hath spoken;
Worlds His mighty voice obeyed :
Laws which never shall be broken,
For their guidance He hath
made.

f Praise the Lord, for He is glorious :
Never shall His promise fail.
*cres*God hath made His saints victorious ;
Sin and death shall not prevail.

f Praise the God of our salvation.
Hosts on high His power pr
claim ;
ff Heaven and earth, and all creatic
Laud and magnify His name.
Foundling Coll., c. 1801—180

5   L.M.

mf LORD of all being, throned afar,
Thy glory flames from sun and sta
Centre and soul of every sphere
Yet to each loving heart how nea

mf Sun of our life, Thy quickening r
Sheds on our path the glow of da
Star of our hope, Thy softeni
light   -   [nigh
Cheers the long watches of th

p Our midnight is Thy smile wit
drawn ;   [dawı
*cres*Our noontide is Thy gracio
Our rainbow arch, Thy mercy
sign ;   [Thir
f All, save the clouds of sin, a

mf Lord of all life, below, above,
Whose light is truth, Who
warmth is love,
Before Thy ever-blazing throne
We ask no lustre of our own.

p Grant us Thy truth to make us fre
And kindling hearts that burn f
Thee,
*cres*Till all Thy living altars claim
mf One holy light, one heavenly flam
O. W. Holmes.

6   C.M.

f FILL Thou my life, O Lord my G
In every part with praise,
That my whole being may pre
Thy being and Thy ways.

f Not for the lip of praise alone,
　Nor e'en the praising heart,
　I ask, but for a life made up
　　Of praise in every part.

mf Praise in the common things of life,
　Its goings out and in ;
　Praise in each duty and each deed,
dim 　However small and mean.

mf Fill every part of me with praise :
　Let all my being speak
　Of Thee, and of Thy love, O Lord,
dim 　Poor though I be, and weak.

f So shalt Thou, Lord, from me, e'en
　Receive the glory due ;　[me,
　And so shall I begin on earth
　The song for ever new.

mf So shall no part of day or night
　From sacredness be free ;
f But all my life, in every step,
　Be fellowship with Thee.
　　　　　　　　H. Bonar.

7　　　　　　　　C.M.

f LONG as I live I'll bless Thy name,
　My King, my God of love ;
　My work and joy shall be the same
　In the bright world above:

f Great is the Lord, His power
　　unknown,
　And let His praise be great :
　I'll sing the honours of Thy throne,
　Thy works of grace repeat.

f Thy grace shall dwell upon my
　　tongue,
　And while my lips rejoice,
　The men that hear my sacred song
　Shall join their cheerful voice.

f Fathers to sons shall teach Thy
　　name,
　And children learn Thy ways ;

Ages to come Thy truth proclaim,
　And nations sound Thy praise.

mf Thy glorious deeds of ancient date
　Shall through the world be
　　known ;　　　　[state,
f Thine arm of power, Thy heavenly
　With public splendour shown.

mf The world is governed by Thy
　　hands,
　Thy saints are ruled by love ;
f And Thine eternal kingdom stands,
　Though rocks and hills remove.
　　　　I. Watts, v. 6, l. 1. altd.

8　　　　　　C.M., 6 lines.

mf BEYOND, beyond that boundless sea,
　Above that dome of sky,　[flee,
　Farther than thought itself can
　Thy dwelling is on high ;
dim Yet dear the awful thought to me,
　That Thou, my God, art nigh :

mp Art nigh, and yet my labouring
　　Feels after Thee in vain,　[mind
　Thee in these works of power to
　Or to Thy seat attain ;　　[find,
　Thy messenger, the stormy wind ;
　Thy path, the trackless main :

f These speak of Thee with loud
　　acclaim ;
　They thunder forth Thy praise,
　The glorious honour of Thy name,
　The wonders of Thy ways :
dim But Thou art not in tempest-flame,
　Nor in day's glorious blaze.

f We hear Thy voice when thunders
　　roll
　Through the wide fields of air ;
　The waves obey Thy dread control ;
dim 　Yet still Thou art not there.
　Where shall I find Him, O my soul,
　Who yet is everywhere ?

mp O ! not in circling depth or height,
But in the conscious breast ;
Present to faith, though veiled
    from sight,
There doth His Spirit rest.
O come, Thou Presence Infinite !
And make Thy creature blest.

J. Conder.

9
          7s.

mf LET us with a gladsome mind
Praise the Lord, for He is kind :
f For His mercies aye endure,
Ever faithful, ever sure.

mf Let us blaze His name abroad,
For of gods He is the God :
f For His mercies aye endure,
Ever faithful, ever sure.

mf He, with all-commanding might,
Filled the new-made world with
f For His mercies aye endure, [light :
Ever faithful, ever sure.

[*mf* He the golden·tressèd sun
Caused all day his course to run :
f For His mercies aye endure,
Ever faithful, ever sure.

mf And the moon to shine by night
'Mong her spangled sisters bright :
f For His mercies aye endure,
Ever faithful, ever sure.].

mf All things living He doth feed ;
His full hand supplies their need :
f For His mercies aye endure.
Ever faithful, ever sure.

mf He His chosen race did bless,
In the wasteful wilderness :
f For His mercies aye endure,
Ever faithful, ever sure.

p He hath, with a piteous *eye*,
Looked *upon our misery :*

f For His mercies aye endure,
Ever faithful, ever sure.

mf Let us therefore warble forth
His high majesty and worth :
f For His mercies aye endure,
Ever faithful, ever sure.

J. Milton, altd. .

10
        8.7.8.7.4.7.

mf PRAISE, my soul, the King of
   heaven ;
To His feet thy tribute bring ;
Ransomed, healed, restored, for-
   given,   [sing ?
Who like thee His praise should
ff   Praise Him ! praise Him !
Praise the everlasting King !

mf Praise Him for His grace and
   favour·
To our fathers in distress ;
Praise Him still the same for ever,
Slow to chide, and swift to
   bless :
ff   Praise Him ! praise Him !
Glorious in His faithfulness !

p Father-like He tends and spares us ;
Well our feeble frame He
   knows ;
In His hands He gently bears us,
Rescues us from all our foes :
ff   Praise Him ! praise Him !
Widely as His mercy flows !

f Angels, help us to adore Him,
Ye behold Him face to face ;
Sun and moon, bow down before
   Him ;
Dwellers all in time and space,
ff   Praise Him ! praise Him !
Praise with us the God of
   grace !

H. F. Lyte

11
4.4.6.4.4.6, or C.M.

f MY God, my King,
Thy praise I'll sing,
My heart is all Thine own :
My highest powers,
My choicest hours,
I yield to Thee alone.

f My voice, awake
Thy part to take ;
My soul, the concert join ;
Till all around
Shall catch the sound,
And mix their hymns with mine.

p But man is weak
Thy praise to speak ;
Your God, ye angels sing ;
'Tis yours to see,
More near than we,
The glories of our King.

cres His truth and grace
Fill time and space,
As large His honours be ;
cres Till all that live
Their homage give,
f And praise my God with me.

H. F. Lyte.

12
88.88.88.

mf I'LL praise my Maker with my
breath,
dim And when my voice is lost in death,
cres Praise shall employ my nobler
powers ;   [past,
My days of praise shall ne'er be
While life and thought and being
Or immortality endures.   [last,

f Happy the man whose hopes rely
On Israel's God ; He made the sky
And earth and seas, with all
their train :   ·

His truth for ever stands secure ;
He saves the oppressed, He feeds
the poor,   [vain.
And none shall find His promise

mp The Lord hath eyes to give the
blind ;
The Lord supports the sinking
mind ;
He sends the labouring con-
science peace ;
He helps the stranger in distress,
The widow and the fatherless,
And grants the prisoner sweet
release.   ●

f I'll praise Him while He lends me
breath ; ·
And when my voice is lost in death,
Praise shall employ my nobler
powers ;   [past,
My days of praise shall ne'er be
While life and thought and being
Or immortality endures.   [last,

I. Watts.

13
8.7.8.7.4.7.

f GOD the Lord is King—before Him,
Earth, with all thy nations,
wait !
Where the cherubim adore Him,
Sitteth He in royal state :
p   He is holy ;
cres Blessed, only Potentate !

f God the Lord is King of glory,
Zion, tell the world His fame ;
Ancient Israel, the story
Of His faithfulness proclaim :
p   He is holy ;
Holy is His awful name.

mp In old times when dangers
darkened,   [seer,
When, invoked by priest and

*cres*To His people's cry He hearkened ;
    Answered them in all their fear ;
p   He is holy ;   [near.
cres As they called, they found Him

mp Laws divine to them were spoken
    From the pillar of the cloud ;
*cres*Sacred precepts, quickly broken !
f   Fiercely then His vengeance
      flowed :
p   He is holy ;   [bowed.
    To the dust their hearts were

mp But their Father God forgave them
    When they sought His face
    once more ;
*cres*Ever ready was to save them,
    Tenderly did He restore ;
p   He is holy ;
cres We, too, will His grace implore.

mp God in Christ is all forgiving,
    Waits His mercy to fulfil :
*cres*Come, exalt Him, all the living ;
f   Come, ascend His Zion, still !
p   He is holy ;
cres Worship at His holy hill.
               G. Rawson.

14   L.M.

mf GIVE to our God immortal praise,
    Mercy and truth are all His ways :
*cres*Wonders of grace to God belong,
    Repeat His mercies in your song.

mf Give to the Lord of lords renown ;
    The King of kings with glory
    crown :
*cres*His mercies ever shall endure,
    When lords and kings are known
    no more.

mf He built the earth, He spread the
    sky,   [high :
    And fixed the starry lights on

*cres*Wonders of grace to God belon
    Repeat His mercies in your son

mf He fills the sun with morning lig
    He bids the moon direct the nig
*cres*His mercies ever shall endure,
    When suns and moons shall sh
    no more.

p He sent His Son with power to s
    From guilt and darkness and
    grave :
*cres*Wonders of grace to God belon
    Repeat His mercies in your son

mf Through this vain world He gui
    our feet,
    And leads us to His heavenly se
*cres*His mercies ever shall endure,
    When this vain world shall be
    more.   *I. Watts*

15   8.8.6.8.8.6

f LORD God, by Whom all chang
    wrought,   [broug
    By Whom new things to birth
    In Whom no change is known
    Whate'er Thou dost, whate'er Th
    art,   [pa
    Thy people still in Thee h
    Still, still Thou art our own.

[*mp*Ancient of Days ! we dwell
    Out of Thine own eternity [Th
    Our peace and joy are wrough
    We rest in our eternal God,
    And make secure and sweet abe
    With Thee, Who changest not

mp Each steadfast promise we posse
    Thine everlasting truth we bles
    Thine everlasting love ;   [cla
*cres*The unfailing Helper close
    The everlasting Arms we grasp
f   Nor from the Refuge move.

mp Spirit Who makest all things new,
Thou leadest onward ; we pursue
The heavenly march sublime.
cres 'Neath Thy renewing fire we glow,
And still from strength to strength
we go,
f From height to height we climb.

mf Darkness and dread we leave
behind,
New light, new glory still we find,
New realms divine possess ;
cres New Births of Grace, new raptures
bring :
Triumphant, the new song we sing,
f The great Renewer bless.

mf To Thee we rise, in Thee we rest ;
We stay at home, we go in quest,
Still Thou art our abode.
cres The rapture swells, the wonder
grows,
As full on us new life still flows
f From our unchanging God.
T. H. Gill.

16   C.M., double.

f THOU wast, O God! and Thou
wast blest
Before the world begun ;
Of Thine eternity possessed
Before time's glass did run.
Thou needest none Thy praise to
sing.
As if Thy joy could fade ;
Couldst Thou have needed any-
thing,
Thou couldst have nothing made.

[*mf* Great and good God! it pleasèd
Thee
Thy Godhead to declare ;
And what Thy goodness did decree,
Thy greatness did prepare.

f Thou spak'st, and heaven and ear
appeared,
And answered to Thy call ;
As if their Maker's voice th
heard,
Which is the creature's all.]
f To whom, Lord! should I sir
but Thee ?
The Maker of my tongue !
Lo ! other lords would seize on n
But I to Thee belong.
mf As waters haste unto their sea,
And earth unto its earth,
So let my soul return to Thee,
From Whom it had its birth.

p But I am fallen on the night,
And cannot come to Thee ;
cres Yet speak the word, let there
light ;
It shall enlighten me :   [Lo]
mf And let Thy word, most migh
Thy fallen creature raise :
Oh, make me o'er again, and I
f Shall sing my Maker's praise.
J. Mason.

17   C.:

f THOUSANDS of thousands sta]
around
Thy throne, O God most high
Ten thousand times ten thousa]
sound
dim Thy praise—but who am I ?

mf Thy brightness unto them appea
Whilst I Thy footsteps trace ;
A sound of God comes to my ea
But they behold Thy Face.

mp How great a being, Lord, is Thi]
Which doth all beings keep !
Thy knowledge is the only line
To sound so vast a deep.

mf Thy arm of might, most mighty King,   [break :
Both rocks and hearts doth
My God, Thou canst do everything
But what should show Thee weak.

mp Most pure and holy are Thine eyes,
Most holy is Thy name ;
Thy saints, and laws, and penalties
Thy holiness proclaim.

mf Great is Thy truth, and shall prevail
To unbelievers' shame ;
Thy truth and years do never fail,
Thou ever art the same.

J. Mason.

18   S.M.

mf MY God, how wonderful Thou art :
Thy majesty how bright !
How beautiful Thy mercy-seat,
In depths of burning light !

p How dread are Thine eternal years.
O everlasting Lord !
By prostrate spirits. day and night.
Incessantly adored.

[*mf* How beautiful, how beautiful
The sight of Thee must be ;—
Thine endless wisdom, boundless
And awful purity !]   [power,

O how I fear Thee, Living God !
With deepest, tenderest fears ;
And worship Thee with trembling
And penitential tears.   [hope

nf Yet may I love Thee, too, O Lord.
Almighty as Thou art ;
For Thou hast stooped to ask of me
dim The love of my poor heart.

p No earthly father loves like Thee,
No mother half so mild

Bears and forbears as Thou has
With me, Thy sinful child. [don

mf Father of Jesus, love's reward !
What rapture will it be
p Prostrate before Thy throne to lie
cres And gaze, and gaze on Thee !

F. W. Faber.

19   C.M.

f GREAT God, how infinite art Thou
dim What worthless worms are we !
cres Let the whole race of creatures bow
f   And pay their praise to Thee.

f Thy throne eternal ages stood,
. Ere seas or stars were made ;
Thou art the ever-living God,
Were all the nations dead.

mf Nature and time quite naked lie
To Thine immense survey,
From the formation of the sky
To the great burning day.

mf Eternity, with all its years,
Stands present in Thy view ;
To Thee there's nothing old appears
Great God, there's nothing new

mp Our lives through various scene
are drawn,
And vexed with trifling cares ;
cres While Thine eternal thought move
Thine undisturbed affairs.   [o

Great God. how infinite art Thou
dim What worthless worms are we !
cres Let the whole race of creatures bow
f   And pay their praise to Thee.

I. Watts.

20   8.6.8.8.6.

f ETERNAL Light ! Eternal Light !
How pure the soul must be,

When, placed within Thy searching
   sight,   [delight,
It shrinks not, but with calm
   Can live and look on Thee !

mf The spirits that surround Thy
   throne
   May bear the burning bliss ;
But that is surely theirs alone,
*dim*Since they have never, never
   known
p   A fallen world like this.

p O ! how shall I, whose native sphere
   Is dark, whose mind is dim,
Before the Ineffable appear,
And on my naked spirit bear
   The uncreated beam ?

mf There is a way for man to rise
   To that sublime abode :—
An offering and a sacrifice,
A Holy Spirit's energies,
   An Advocate with God :—

f These, these prepare us for the sight
   Of Holiness above :
The sons of ignorance and night
*cres*May dwell in the Eternal Light
ff   Through the Eternal Love !
             T. Binney.

21   8.7.8.7.
mf ROUND the Lord in glory seated,
   Cherubim and Seraphim
Filled His temple and repeated
   Each to each the alternate
   hymn :—

f "Lord, Thy glory fills the heaven,
   Earth is with its fulness stored ;
Unto Thee be glory given,
   Holy, Holy, Holy Lord ! "

*f Heaven is still with glory ringing,
   Earth takes up the angels' cry,*

mf "Holy, Holy, Holy," singing,
   "Lord of Hosts, Thou Lord most
   High."

mf With His seraph-train before Him,
   With His holy Church below,
Thus unite we to adore Him,
   Bid we thus our anthem flow :—

f "Lord, Thy glory fills the heaven,
   Earth is with its fulness stored ;
Unto Thee be glory given,
rall Holy, Holy, Holy Lord ! "
             R. Mant.

22   L.M., with refrain.
f WIDE as His vast dominion lies,
Make the Creator's name be known :
Loud as His thunder shout His
   praise,
And sound it lofty as His throne.
Each of His works His name dis-
   plays,   [praise.
But they can ne'er fulfil His

f The Lord ! how absolute He reigns !
Let every angel bend the knee,
Sing of His love in heavenly strains,
And speak how fierce His terrors be.
Each of His works His name dis-
   plays,   [praise.
But they can ne'er fulfil His

f High on a throne His glories dwell.
An awful throne of shining bliss,
Fly through the world, O sun
   and tell   [His
How dark thy beams compared to
Each of His works His name
   displays,   [praise.
But they can ne'er fulfil His

[*f* Awake, ye tempests, and His fame
In sounds of dreadful praise declare;
And the sweet whisper of His name
Fill every gentler breeze of air.

Each of His works His name displays,   [praise.
But they can ne'er fulfil His

f Let clouds and winds and waves
agree
To join their praise with blazing
fire ;
Let the firm earth and rolling sea
In this eternal song conspire.
Each of His works His name
displays,
But they can ne'er fulfil His
praise.]

f Jehovah ! 'tis a glorious word !
O may it dwell on every tongue !
But saints who best have known
the Lord
Are bound to raise the noblest
song.
Each of His works His name
displays,   [praise.
But they can ne'er fulfil His

I. Watts.

23   8.7.8.7.

f GOD, my King, Thy might cor
fessing,
Ever will I bless Thy name ;
Day by day Thy throne addressing
Still will I Thy praise proclain

mf Nor shall fail from memory
treasure,   [wrought-
Works by love and merc
Works of love surpassing measur
Works of mercy passing though

mp Full of kindness and compassion,
Slow of anger, vast in love ;
God is good to all creation ; [prov
All His works His goodne

mf All Thy works, O Lord, shall ble
Thee.
Thee shall all Thy saints adore
cres King supreme shall they confe
Thee,   [powe
f   And proclaim Thy sovereig

R. Mant.

2.—HIS WORKS IN CREATION.

24   C.M.

f PRAISE ye the Lord, immortal
choirs
That fill the worlds above ;
Praise Him Who formed you of
His fires,
And feeds you with His love.

f Shine to His praise, ye crystal skies,
The floor of His abode ;   [eyes
Or veil in shades your thousand
Before your brighter God.

f Thou restless globe of golden light,
Whose beams create our days,
Join with the silver queen of night,
To own your borrowed rays.

f Thunder and hail, and fire an
storms,
The troops of His command.
Appear in all your dreadful form
And speak His awful hand.

f Shout to the Lord, ye surging sea
In your eternal roar ;   [prais
Let wave to wave resound H
And shore reply to shore.

mf Thus while the meaner creatur
sing,
cres Ye mortals, catch the sound ;
f Echo the glories of your King
Through all the nations round

I. Watts, vv. 1, 2 altd.

25 C.M.

f THE Lord our God is clothed with
The winds obey His will ; [might.
He speaks, and in His heavenly
height
The rolling sun stands still.

f Rebel, ye waves, and o'er the land
With threatening aspect roar ;
The Lord uplifts His awful hand,
And chains you to the shore.

f Ye winds of night, your force com-
Without His high behest, [bine ;
Ye shall not, in the mountain pine,
Disturb the sparrow's nest.

f His voice sublime is heard afar ;
In distant peals it dies ;
He yokes the whirlwind to His car,
And sweeps the howling skies.

f Ye sons of earth, in reverence bend ;
Ye nations, wait His nod ;
*res*And bid the choral song ascend
f   To celebrate our God.
H. K. White.

26 C.M.

f THERE is a book, who runs may
read,
Which heavenly truth imparts,
And all the lore its scholars need,
Pure eyes and Christian hearts.

f The works of God, above, below,
Within us and around,
Are pages in that book, to show
How God Himself is found.

f The glorious sky, embracing all,
Is like the Maker's love,
Wherewith encompassed, great and
small
In peace and order move.

f One Name, above all glorious
names,
With its ten thousand tongues
The everlasting sea proclaims,
Echoing angelic songs.

f The raging fire, the roaring wind,
Thy boundless power display ;
p But in the gentler breeze we find
pp   Thy Spirit's viewless way.

Two worlds are ours : 'tis only sin
Forbids us to descry   [within,
The mystic heaven and earth
Plain as the sea and sky.

mf Thou Who hast given me eyes to see,
And love this sight so fair,
Give me a heart to find out Thee,
And read Thee everywhere.
J. Keble.

27 7s., 6 lines.

mf FOR the beauty of the earth,
For the beauty of the skies,
For the love which from our birth
Over and around us lies :
f Father, unto Thee we raise
This, our sacrifice of praise.

mf For the beauty of each hour
Of the day and of the night,
Hill and vale, and tree and flower,
Sun and moon, and stars of light
f Father, unto Thee we raise
This, our sacrifice of praise.

mf For the joy of human love,
Brother, sister, parent, child,
Friends on earth, and friends above:
For all gentle thoughts and mild :
f Father, unto Thee we raise
This, our sacrifice of praise.

mf For each perfect gift of Thine
To our race so freely given,

Graces, human and Divine,
Flowers of earth, and buds of
heaven :
f Father, unto Thee we raise
This, our sacrifice of praise.

mf For Thy Church that evermore
Lifteth holy hands above,
Offering up on every shore
Its pure sacrifice of love :
f Father, unto Thee we raise
This, our sacrifice of praise.

F. S. Pierpoint, altd.

28 7s., 6 lines.

f O GIVE thanks to Him Who made
Morning light and evening shade ,
Source and Giver of all good,
Nightly sleep and daily food ;
Quickener of our wearied powers ;
Guard of our unconscious hours.

f O give thanks to nature's King,
Who made every breathing thing :
His, our warm and sentient frame,
His, the mind's immortal flame,
O, how close the ties that bind
Spirits to the Eternal Mind !

f O give thanks with heart and lip,
For we are His workmanship,
And all creatures are His care :
Not a bird that cleaves the air
Falls unnoticed ; but who can
Speak the Father's love to man ?

f O give thanks to Him Who came
*dim*In a mortal, suffering frame—
Temple of the Deity—
Came, for rebel man to die ;
  * In the path Himself has trod,
 ⸝ Leading back His saints *to* God.

J Conder.

29 7.6.7.6.

f THE Lord is King, and weareth,
A robe of glory bright ;
He clothed with strength appeareth,
And girt with powerful might.

mf The earth He hath so grounded
That moved it cannot be :
His throne long since was founded ;
More old than time is He.

f The waters highly flowèd,
And raised their voice, O Lord ;
The seas their fury showèd,
And loud their billows roared.

ff But God in strength excelleth
Strong seas and powerful deeps ;
*dim*With Him all pureness dwelleth,
cres And firm His truth He keeps.

G. Wither.

30 L.M.

f THE Lord is King ; He wrought
His will
In heaven above, in earth below ;
His wonders the wide ocean fill,
The caverned deeps His judgment
show.

f The Lord is King ; the word stands
fast ;
Nature abides, for He is strong ;
The perfect note He gave, shall last
Till cadence of her even-song.

f The Lord is King ; ye worlds,
rejoice !
The waves of power, that from
His shrine
Thrill out in silence, have no
choice :
They harm not till He gives the
sign.

f The Lord is King ; (*dim*) hush,
　　wayward heart !
Earth's wisdom fails, earth's daring
　　faints ; 　　　　　[departs,
*cres*There seek Him whence He ne'er
　　And own Him greatest in His
　　saints.

f Thou, Lord, art King ; crowned
　　priests are we,
To cast cur crowns before the
　　Throne.
By us the creature worships Thee,
Yet we but bring Thee of Thine
　　own.

f To the Great Maker. to the Son,
Himself vouchsafing to be made,
To the Good Spirit, Three in One,
All praise by all His works be paid.

J. Keble.

31　　　　　6.6.6.6.4.4.4.4.

f YE boundless realms of joy,
Exalt your Maker's fame.
His praise your song employ
Above the starry frame ;
　　Your voices raise,
　　Ye cherubim,
　　And seraphim,
　　To sing His praise.

mf Thou moon, that rul'st the night,
And sun, that guid'st the day ;
Ye glittering stars of light,
To Him your homage pay ;
　　His praise declare,
　　Ye heavens above,
　　And clouds that move
　　In liquid air.

f Let them adore the Lord,
And praise His holy Name,
By Whose Almighty Word
They all from nothing came :

cres And all shall last,
From changes free
His firm decree
Stands ever fast.

f To God, the Father. Son,
And Spirit ever Blest,
Eternal Three in One,
All worship be addressed
As heretofore
It was, is now,
And shall be so
For evermore.

N. Tate and N.

32　　　　　　{

mf THOU art, O God, the
　　light
Of all this wondrous wor
Its glow by day. its smile
Are but reflections cau
　　Thee ;
*cres*Where'er we turn Th
f And all things fair and l
　　Thine.

mp When day, with farew
　　delays
Among the opening clou
And we can almost think
Through golden vist
　　heaven ;—
*cres*Those hues, that mark
So soft, so radiant, Lord,

mp When night, with wings
　　gloom,
O'ershadows all the earth
Like some dark, beaute
　　whose plume
Is sparkling with un
*cres*That sacred gloom, th
　　Divine,
So grand, so countless,

mp When youthful Spring around us breathes,
Thy Spirit warms her fragrant sigh,
And every flower that Summer wreathes

Is born beneath that kindlir eye ;—
cres Where'er we turn, Thy glories shin
f And all things fair and bright a Thine.　　*T. Moore.*

3.—*HIS GOODNESS IN PROVIDENCE.*

33　　　　　　　C.M.

f THE mercies of my God and King
My tongue shall still pursue.
O happy they who, while they sing
Those mercies, share them too.

f As bright and lasting as the sun,
As lofty as the sky,　　　|run,
From age to age Thy truth shall
And chance and change defy.

f The covenant of the King of kings
Shall stand for ever sure :
Beneath the shadow of Thy wings
Thy saints repose secure.

f Thine is the earth. and Thine the
Created at Thy will :　　[skies,
The waves at Thy command arise,
At Thy command are still.

f In earth below, in heaven above,
Who, who is Lord like Thee ?
O spread the gospel of Thy love.
Till all, Thy glories see.

　　　　　H. F. Lyte.

34　　　6.7.6.7.6.6.6.6.

f Now thank we all our God.
With hearts, and hands. and voices,
Who wondrous things hath done,
In Whom His world rejoices ;
p Who, from our mother's arms,
Hath blessed us on our way
cres With countless gifts of love,
　And still is ours to-day
f Oh may this bounteous God
Through all our life be near us,

With ever joyful hearts
dim And blessèd peace to cheer us ;
mf And keep us in His grace,
And guide us when perplexed,
cres And free us from all ills
In this world and the next.

ff All praise and thanks to God
The Father, now be given,
The Son, and Him Who reigns
With Them in highest heaven,
The One eternal God,
Whom heaven and earth adore
For thus it was, is now,
And shall be evermore.

　　M. Rinckart, tr. by Catherir
　　　　　Winkworth.

35　　　　　　　C.M.

mf MY Shepherd will supply my need
Jehovah is His name ;
In pastures fresh He makes me fee
Beside the living stream.

mp He brings my wandering spiri
When I forsake His ways. [bac
And leads me, for His mercy's sake
In paths of truth and grace.

p When I walk through the shades o
Thy presence is my stay : [death
cres A word of Thy supporting breatl
Drives all my fears away.

mf Thy hand, in sight of all my fo
Doth still my table spread ;
My cup with blessings overflo
Thine oil anoints my head.

mf The sure provisions of my God
Attend me all my days ;
O may Thy house be mine abode,
And all my work be praise !

mp There would I find a settled rest,
While others go and come ;
No more a stranger or a guest,
But like a child at home.

I. Watts.

36 C.M.

mf THE God of love my Shepherd is,
To watch me and to feed :
I shall not want, for I am His,
He careth for my need.

p His gentle goodness leadeth me,
And makes me down to lie
cres In greenest pastures fearlessly
p The quiet waters by.

cres And so restoreth He my soul :
p And when I go astray
cres He brings me back with sweet
control
f Into the rightful way.

p When darkness comes and death is
near,
I feel my Shepherd's rod,
cres And so I quite forget my fear,
dim And lean upon my God.

f Thy bounties, amid all my foes,
My life, my spirit bless,
My cup of comfort overflows
dim With tender faithfulness.

f Goodness and mercy, peace and
love,
Shall fill my earthly days ;
Till the eternal house above
Shall witness to my praise.

G. Rawson.

37

mf THE King of love my She
Whose goodness failetl
I nothing lack if I am H
And He is mine, for ev

mf Where streams of living w
My ransomed soul He
And, where the verdant
grow,
With food celestial fee

p Perverse and foolish oft I
cres But yet in love He sou
dim And on His shoulder ger
f And home, rejoicing, br

p In death's dark vale I fea
cres With Thee, dear Lord, t
Thy rod and staff my con
Thy Cross before to gu

mf Thou spread'st a table in
Thy Unction grace bes
f And O what transport of
From Thy pure chalice

mf And so through all the
days
Thy goodness faileth n
cres Good Shepherd, may I
praise
Within Thy house for (

H. W.

38

f OUR God, our help in ag
Our hope for years to (
Our shelter from the stor
And our eternal home

f Under the shadow of Thy
Thy saints have dwelt
Sufficient is Thine arm al
And our defence is sur

mf Before the hills in order stood,
  Or earth received her frame,
f From everlasting Thou art God,
  To endless years the same.

f A thousand ages in Thy sight
  Are like an evening gone ;
*dim*Short as the watch that ends the
  night
  Before the rising sun.

p Time, like an ever-rolling stream,
  Bears all its sons away ,
*dim*They fly, forgotten, as a dream
p   Dies at the opening day.

f Our God, our help in ages past,
  Our hope for years to come,
  Be Thou our guard while troubles
  And our eternal home.   [last,
          I. Watts.

39   C.M.

mf I **WORSHIP** Thee, sweet will of
  God !
  And all Thy ways adore,
  And every day I live I seem
  To love Thee more and more.

mf I love to kiss each print where
  Thou
  Hast set Thine unseen feet ·
  I cannot fear Thee, blessèd will,
  Thine empire is so sweet.

mf I have no cares, O blessèd will !
  For all my cares are Thine ;
 • I live in triumph, Lord, for Thou
  Hast made Thy triumph mine.

mf He always wins who sides with
  God,
  To him no chance is lost ;
  God's will is *sweetest to him* when
  It triumphs at his cost.

mf Ill, that He blesses, is our good,
  And unblest good is ill ;
  And all is right that seems most
  wrong,
  If it be His sweet will.
          F. W. Faber.

40   C.M.

f LIFT up to God the voice of praise,
  Whose breath our souls inspired ;
  Loud and more loud the anthem
  raise,
  With grateful ardour fired.

f Lift up to God the voice of praise,
  Whose tender care sustains
*dim*Our feeble frame, encompassed
  round
  With death's unnumbered pains.

f Lift up to God the voice of praise,
  Whose goodness. passing thought,
  Loads every minute as it flies
  With benefits unsought.

f Lift up to God the voice of praise,
  From Whom salvation flows ;
  Who sent His Son our souls to save
dim From everlasting woes.

f Lift up to God the voice of praise,
  For hope's transporting ray,
  That lights through darkest shades
  of death
  To realms of endless day.
          R. Wardlaw.

41   L.M.

f HIGH in the heavens, Eternal God,
  Thy goodness in full glory shines ;
  Thy truth shall break through
  every cloud
  That veils and darkens Thy desi

f For ever firm Thy justice stands,
  As mountains their foundations
    keep ;
  Wise are the wonders of Thy hands :
  Thy judgments are a mighty deep.

mf Thy providence is kind and large,
  Both man and beast Thy bounty
    share ;
  The whole creation is Thy charge,
  But Saints are Thy peculiar care.

p My God, how excellent Thy grace,
  Whence all our hope and comfort
    spring !
dim The sons of Adam in distress
  Fly to the shadow of Thy wing.

mf From the provisions of Thy house
  We shall be fed with sweet repast ;
  Where mercy like a river flows,
  And brings salvation to our taste.

mf Life, like a fountain rich and free,
  Springs from the presence of the
    Lord ;
f And in Thy light our souls shall see
  The glories promised in Thy word.
                              I. Watts.

42
                          8.4.8.4.8.4.
mf My God, I thank Thee, Who hast
  The earth so bright,   [made
  So full of splendour and of joy,
    Beauty and light ;
  So many glorious things are here,
    Noble and right.

mf I thank Thee, too, that Thou hast
  Joy to abound ;   [made
  So many gentle thoughts and deeds
    Circling us round ;
That in the darkest spot of earth
Some love is found.

mf I thank Thee more that all my joy
p   Is touched with pain ;
  That shadows fall on brightest
    That thorns remain ; [hours,
mf So that earth's bliss may be my
  And not my chain.   [guide,

[*p* For Thou Who knowest, Lord, how
  Our weak heart clings,   [soon
  Hast given us joys, tender and true,
    Yet all with wings,
cres So that we see, gleaming on high,
  Diviner things.]

f I thank Thee, Lord, that Thou hast
  The best in store ;   [kept
mf I have enough, yet not too much,
  To long for more ;
  A yearning for a deeper peace
    Not known before.

mf I thank Thee, Lord, that here our
  Though amply blest,   [souls,
  Can never find, although they seek,
    A perfect rest,—
dim Nor ever shall, until they lean
rall   On Jesus' breast.
              Adelaide Anne Procter.

43
                                 C.M.
mf O God, my strength and fortitude,
  Of force I must love Thee ;
  Thou art my castle and defence,
    In my necessity.

f The Lord Jehovah is my God,
  My rock, my strength, my
    wealth.
  My strong Deliverer, and my trust,
  My spirit's only health.

p In my distress I sought my God,
  I sought Jehovah's face ;
cres My cry before Him came ; He
  heard
  Out of His holy place.

*cres*The Lord descended from above,
 And bowed the heavens most high ;
 And underneath His feet He cast
 The darkness of the sky.

f On cherub and on cherubim
 Full royally He rode, [winds
ff And on the wings of mighty
 Came flying all abroad.

f The voice of God did thunder high.
 The lightnings answered keen.
 The channels of the deep were bared,
 The world's foundations seen.

p And so delivered He my soul ;
 Who is a rock but He ?
*cres*He liveth—blessèd be my rock !
 My God exalted be !

  T. Sternhold and G. Rawson.

44   8.7.8.7.

mp GOD is love : His mercy brightens
 All the path in which we rove ;
*cres*Bliss He wakes, and woe He lightens ;
 f God is wisdom, God is love.

mp Chance and change are busy ever ;
 Man decays and ages move ;
*cres*But His mercy waneth never ;
 f God is wisdom, God is love.

mp E'en the hour that darkest seemeth
 Will His changeless goodness prove ; [streameth ;
*cres*From the gloom His brightness
 f God is wisdom, God is love.

mp He with earthly cares entwineth
 Hope and comfort from above
*cres*Everywhere His glory shineth ;
 f God is wisdom, God is love.

     J. Bowring.

45   8.7.8 7.8.8.7.

f LORD, Thou hast been our dwellin
 In every generation ; [pla
 Thy people still have known T
  grace,
 And blessed Thy consolation ;
 Through every age Thou hear
  our cry ;
 Through every age we found Th
  nigh,
 Our strength and our salvatic
mp Our cleaving sins we oft have we
 And oft Thy patience provèd ;
*cres*But still Thy faith we fast ha
  kept,
 Thy Name we still have lovèd
 And Thou hast kept and loved
  well, ·
 Hast granted us in Thee to dwe
 f Unshaken, unremovèd.

mp Lord, nothing from Thine arms
  love
 Shall Thine own people sever
*cres*Our Helper never will remove,
 Our God will fail us never.
f Thy people, Lord, have dwelt
  Thee ;   [
 Our dwelling-place Thou still w
 ff For ever and for ever.

     T. H. Gill.

46   C.M.

f O GOD of Bethel, by Whose han
 Thy people still are fed ;
dim Who through this weary pilgri
 Hast all our fathers led, [a
mf Our vows, our prayers, we n
  present
 Before Thy throne of grace ;
 God of our fathers, be the God
 Of their succeeding race.

Through each perplexing path of
    life
Our wandering footsteps guide :
Give us, each day, our daily bread,
    And raiment fit provide.

O spread Thy covering wings
    around,
    Till all our wanderings cease,
*dim*And at our Father's loved abode
p   Our souls arrive in peace.

mp Such blessings from Thy gracious
    hand
    Our humble prayers implore,
f And Thou shalt be our chosen God
    And portion evermore.

P. Doddridge and J. Logan.

47   •   ·   C.M.

mp GOD moves in a mysterious way
    His wonders to perform ;
f He plants His footsteps in the sea,
    And rides upon the storm.

mp Deep in unfathomable mines
    Of never-failing skill,
*cres*He treasures up His bright designs,
    And works His sovereign will.

mp Ye fearful saints, fresh courage
    take ;
    The clouds ye so much dread
*cres*Are big with mercy, and shall
    break
    In blessings on your head.

mp Judge not the Lord by feeble sense,
    But trust Him for His grace ;
    Behind a frowning Providence
cres He hides a smiling face.

mf His purposes will ripen fast,
    Unfolding every hour ;
    The bud may have a bitter taste,
    But sweet will be the flower.

Blind unbelief is sure to
    And scan His work in
f God is His own interpret
    And He will make it p
        W.

48   L.M.,

f SING to the Lord a joyfu
    Lift up your hearts, yo
    raise,
    To us His gracious gifts
    To Him our songs of
      praise.
    For He is Lord of he
      earth,
    Whom angels serve a
      adore,
    The Father, Son, and H
    To Whom be praise for

f For life and love, for rest
    For daily help and night
    Sing to the Lord, for He
    And praise His Name, for
    For He is, etc.

f For strength to those wh
    wait,
    His truth to prove, His w
    Praise ye our God, for He
    Trust in His Name, for It
    For He is, etc.

f For joys untold that from
    Cheer those who love I
    employ,
    Sing to our God, for He
    Exalt His Name, for It is
    For He is, etc.

f For life below, with all i
    And for that life, more
    high,
    That inner life which ov
    Shall ever shine, and n

Sing to the Lord of heaven and
   earth,   [adore.
Whom angels serve and saints
The Father, Son, and Holy Ghost,
To Whom be praise for evermore.
          J. S. B. Monsell.

49   C.M.

mf THROUGH all the changing scenes
   In trouble and in joy, [of life,
*cres*The praises of my God shall still
   My heart and tongue employ.

Of His deliverance I will boast,
   Till all that are distressed,
From mine example comfort take,
   And soothe their griefs to rest.

f O magnify the Lord with me,
   With me exalt His Name ;
p When in distress to Him I called,
cres He to my rescue came.

mf O make but trial of His love,
   Experience will decide
How blest are they, and only they,
   Who in His truth confide !

*cres*Fear Him, ye saints, and you will
   then
-Have nothing else to fear ;
Make but His service your delight,
Your wants shall be His care.
         N. Tate and N. Brady.

50   L.M

f THE Lord is King ! lift up 1
   voice,
O earth, and all ye heavens, rejoi(
From world to world the joy sh
   ring.
The Lord Omnipotent is King.

f The Lord is King ! who then sh
   dare
Resist His will, distrust His car
Or murmur at His wise decrees,
Or doubt His royal promises?

mf The Lord is King ! Child of 1
   dust,
The Judge of all the earth is ju;
Holy and true are all His ways
Let every creature speak His prai

f He reigns ! ye saints, exalt y(
   strains ;
Your God is King, your Fati
   reigns ;
And He is at the Father's side,
*dim*The Man of Love, the Crucified.

f O, when His wisdom can mistak
His might decay. His love forsal
Then may His children cease
   sing,
The Lord Omnipotent is King.
         J. Conder.

4.—HIS GRACE IN REDEMPTION.

51   C.M.

f PRAISE to the Holiest in the
   height,
And in the depth be praise ;
In all His words most wonderful,
Most sure in all His ways !

mf Oh, loving wisdom of our God !
dim When all was sin and shame,

*cres*A second Adam to the fight
   And to the rescue came.

mf Oh, wisest love ! that flesh a1
   blood,
Which did in Adam fail,
Should strive afresh against th
   foe,
Should strive and should pr

f And that a higher gift than grace
   Should flesh and blood refine,
   God's presence, and His very Self,
   And essence all-divine !

f Oh, generous love ! that He, Who
   In man for man the foe, [smote
p The double agony in man
   For man should undergo ;

p And in the garden secretly,
   And on the Cross on high,
   Should teach His brethren and
dim To suffer and to die ! [inspire
            J. H. Newman.

52   C.M.

f O LORD, our Lord, how wondrous
   Is Thine exalted Name ! [great
   The glories of Thy heavenly state
   Let men and babes proclaim.

mf When I behold Thy works on high,
   The moon that rules the night,
   And stars that well adorn the sky—
   Those moving worlds of light ;

mp Lord, what is man or all his race,
   Who dwells so far below,
   That Thou shouldst visit him with
   And love his nature so ?— [grace,
mp That Thine eternal Son should bear
   To take a mortal form ;
   Made lower than His angels are,
dim To save a dying worm ?

f Let Him be crowned with majesty
   Who bowed His head to death ;
   And be His honours sounded high
   By all things that have breath.

ff Jesus, our Lord, how wondrous
   Is Thine exalted Name ? [great
   The glories of Thy heavenly state
   Let the whole earth proclaim.
            I. Watts.

53   7s.

f I WILL praise Thee every day,
   Now Thine anger's turned away;
   Comfortable thoughts arise
   From the bleeding sacrifice.

mf Here, in the fair gospel-field,
   Wells of free salvation yield
   Streams of life, a plenteous store,
   And my soul shall thirst no more.

mf Jesus is become at length
   My salvation and my strength ;
   And His praises shall prolong,
   While I live, my pleasant song.

f Praise ye, then, His glorious Name ;
   Publish His exalted fame !
   Still His worth your praise exceeds :
   Excellent are all His deeds.

f Raise again the joyful sound ;
   Let the nations roll it round !
   Zion, shout ! for this is He :
   God the Saviour dwells in thee.
           W. Cowper.

54   S.M.

f   MY soul repeat His praise
      Whose mercies are so great,
dim Whose anger is so slow to rise,
      So ready to abate.

f   High as the heavens are raised
      Above the ground we tread,
   So far the riches of His grace
      Our highest thoughts exceed,
mp   His power subdues our sins ;
      And His forgiving love,
   Far as the east is from the west,
      Doth all our guilt remove.

      The pity of the Lord
      To those that fear His Name,
   Is such as tender parents feel ;
      He knows our feeble frame.

v Our days are as the grass,
  Or like the morning flower ;
If one sharp blast sweep o'er the
  It withers in an hour. [field,

~es But Thy compassions, Lord.
  To endless years endure,
f And children's children ever find
  Thy words of promise sure.

      I. Watts.

55   C.M.

f BEGIN my tongue, some heavenly
  theme,
  And speak some boundless thing,
  The mighty works, or mightier
  Of our eternal King. [Name,

f Tell of His wondrous faithfulness,
  And sound His power abroad,
  Sing the sweet promise of His grace
  And the performing God.

mf Engraved as in eternal brass,
  The mighty promise shines ;
  Nor can the powers of darkness
  Those everlasting lines. [rase

f His very word of grace is strong
  As that which built the skies ;
  The voice that rolls the stars along
  Speaks all the promises.

v Oh ! might I hear Thy heavenly
  tongue
  But whisper, "Thou art mine" ;
*cres*Those gentle words should raise
  my song
  To notes almost divine.

mf How would my leaping heart
  rejoice,
  And think my heaven secure !
f I'd trust the all-creating voice,
  And faith desires no more.

      I. Watts.

56   L.M.

f O LOVE of God ! how strong and
  Eternal and yet ever new ; [true,
  Uncomprehended and unbought,
  Beyond all knowledge and all
  thought.

[*f* O love of God, how deep and great !
  Far deeper than man's deepest hate:
  Self-fed, self-kindled, like the light,
  Changeless, eternal, infinite.

mp O heavenly love, how precious still,
  In days of weariness and ill !
p In nights of pain and helplessness,
*cres*To heal, to comfort, and to bless !]

mp O wide-embracing, wondrous love,
  We read thee in the sky above ;
  We read thee in the earth below,
*cres*In seas that swell and streams that
  flow.

mp We read thee best in Him Who
  came
  To bear for us the cross of shame ;
*cres*Sent by the Father from on high,
f Our life to live, our death to die.

mf We read thy power to bless and
  save
*dim*E'en in the darkness of the grave ;
*cres*Still more in resurrection light
f We read the fulness of thy might.

mf O love of God ! our shield and stay
  Through all the perils of our way ;
f Eternal love, in thee we rest,
  For ever safe, for ever blest !

      H. Bonar.

57   8.7.8.7.4.7.

mf MIGHTY God, while angels bless
  Thee,
  May a mortal sing Thy Name

Lord of men as well as angels,
Thou art every creature's theme.
Hallelujah !
Hallelujah, Amen.

[Lord of every land and nation,
Ancient of eternal days, •
Sounded through the wide creation
Be Thy just and lawful praise.
Hallelujah !
Hallelujah, Amen.]

mf For the grandeur of Thy nature—
Grand beyond a seraph's thought;
For created works of power,
Works with skill and kindness
Hallelujah ! [wrought;
Hallelujah, Amen.

For Thy providence that governs
Through Thine empire's wide
domain,
Wings an angel, guides a sparrow;
Blessèd be Thy gentle reign.
Hallelujah !
Hallelujah, Amen.

mf But Thy rich, Thy free redemption,
Dark through brightness all
along,
Thought is poor, and poor expres-
sion ;
Who dare sing that awful song ?
Hallelujah !
Hallelujah, Amen.

[Brightness of the Father's glory,
Shall Thy praise unuttered lie ?
Fly, my tongue, such guilty silence,
Sing the Lord Who came to die.
Hallelujah !
Hallelujah, Amen.]

mf From the highest throne of glory,
p   To the cross of deepest woe,
All to ransom guilty captives,—

cres Flow my praise, for
Hallelujah !
Hallelujah, Ar

f Go—return, immortal
Leave Thy footstoo
throne,
Thence return and rei{
Be the kingdom all '
Hallelujah !
Hallelujah, An

R. Robinson, v. 1

58

f GOD is love ; by Him t
Hang the glorious o
In their language glad
Speaking to us day a
Their great story
God is Love, and Goc

f And the teeming earth
In that message fron
With ten thousand thou
Telling back from hil
Her glad story,
God is Might, and Gc

f With these anthems of
Mingling in harmoni
Christian songs of Chrisl
To the world with bl
Tell their story ;
God is Love, and God

mf Through that preciou
sought us,
Wandering from His
With that precious life
cres Then let all our futur
f   Tell this story :
Love is Life—our live

f Gladsome is the theme an
Praise to Christ ou
Head :

Christ, the risen Christ, victorious,
Earth and hell hath captive led.
    Welcome story !   [dead.
Love lives on, and Death is
mf Up to Him let each affection
    Daily rise, and round Him move
*cres*Our whole lives. one resurrection
    To the life of life above ;
f   Their glad story,
    God is Life ; and God is Love.
              J. S. B. Monsell.

59   L.M., with refrain.

f GREAT God of wonders! all Thy
    ways
Are matchless, godlike, and divine ;
But the fair glories of Thy grace
More godlike and unrivalled shine.
f Who is a pardoning God like
    Thee ?   [free ?
    Or who has grace so rich and
mf Crimes of such horror to forgive,
Such guilty, daring worms to
    spare,—
This is Thy grand prerogative,
And none shall in the honour
    share.
f Who is a pardoning God like
    Thee ?   [free ?
    Or who has grace so rich and
mp Angels and men, resign your claim
To pity, mercy, love, and grace ;
*cres*These glories crown Jehovah's
    name
With an incomparable blaze.
ff Who is a pardoning God like
    Thee ?   [free ?
    Or who has grace so rich and
mp In wonder lost, with trembling
    joy
We take the pardon of our God—
*cres*Pardon for crimes of deepest dye,

A pardon bought with Jesus' blood.
ff Who is a pardoning God like
    Thee ?
    Or who has grace so rich and
    free ?
mf O may this strange, this matchless
    grace,
This godlike miracle of love,
f Fill the wide earth with grateful
    praise,
And all the angelic hosts above.
ff Who is a pardoning God like
    Thee ?   [free ?
    Or who has grace so rich and
              S. Davies.

60   S.M.

f GRACE, 'tis a charming sound,
Harmonious to the ear :
Heaven with the echo shall resound,
And all the earth shall hear.
mf Grace first contrived the way
To save rebellious man ;
And all the steps that grace display,
Which drew the wondrous plan.
mf Grace taught my wandering feet
To tread the heavenly road ;
And new supplies each hour I
    meet,
While pressing on to God.
f Grace all the work shall crown
Through everlasting days :
It lays in heaven the topmost stone,
And well deserves the praise.
             P. Doddridge.

61   C.M.

f THY ceaseless, unexhausted love,
Unmerited and free,
Delights our evil to remove,
And help our misery.

mf Thou waitest to be gracious still ;
Thou dost with sinners bear ;
That, saved, we may Thy goodness feel,
And all Thy grace declare.

mf Thy goodness and Thy truth to me,
To every soul, abound,
A vast, unfathomable sea,
Where all our thoughts are drowned.

mf Its streams the whole creation reach,
So plenteous is the store ;
Enough for all, enough for each,
Enough for evermore.

mf Faithful, O Lord, Thy mercies are,
A rock that cannot move :
A thousand promises declare
Thy constancy of love.

f Throughout the universe it rei
Unalterably sure ;   [remι
And while the truth of
The goodness must endure.

C. Wesle

62   C.1

mf SALVATION ! O the joyful sou
'Tis pleasure to our ears ;
A sovereign balm for every woι
A cordial for our fears.

mp Buried in sorrow and in sin,
At hell's dark door we lay ;
*cres*But we arise by grace Divine
To see a heavenly day.

f Salvation ! let the echo fly
The spacious earth around,
While all the armies of the skγ
Conspire to raise the sound.

I. Watt

II.
The Lord Jesus Christ.
1.—HIS GODHEAD, PRAISE, AND GLORY.

63   C.M.

f ALL hail the power of Jesu's name !
dim Let angels prostrate fall ;
*cres*Bring forth the royal diadem,
f   To crown Him Lord of all.

mf Crown Him, ye martyrs of your God,
Who from His altar call ;
*cres*Extol the Stem-of-Jesse's rod,
f   And crown Him Lord of all.

mf Ye seed of Israel's chosen race,
Ye ransomed of the fall,
*cres*Hail Him Who saves you by His grace,
f   And crown Him Lord of all.

p Sinners ! whose love can ne'er foι
The wormwood and the gall,
*cres*Go—spread your trophies at feet,
f   And crown Him Lord of all.

ff Let every kindred, every tribe,
On this terrestrial ball,
To Him all majesty ascribe,
And crown Him Lord of all !

mf O that with yonder sacred thro
We at His feet may fall ;
*cres*Join in the everlasting song,
ff   And crown Him Lord of all.

E. Perronet, v. 5 altd. J. Ripι
and v. 6 J. Rippon.

64   6.6.4.6.6.6.4.

f GLORY to God on high !
  Let praises fill the sky ;
    Praise ye His Name :
  Angels His Name adore,
p Who all our sorrows bore ;
cres And saints cry evermore,
ff   Worthy the Lamb !
f All they around the throne
  Cheerfully join in one,
    Praising His Name ;
p We who have felt His blood
  Sealing our peace with God,
cres Spread His dear fame abroad ;
ff   Worthy the Lamb !
[*f* To Him our hearts we raise,
  None else shall have our praise ;
    Praise ye His Name :
  Him our exalted Lord,
  Him as below adored,
  We praise with one accord,
ff   Worthy the Lamb !]
f Join all the ransomed race
  Our Lord and God to bless,
    Praise ye His Name :
  In Him we will rejoice,
  Making a cheerful noise,
  And say with heart and voice,
ff   Worthy the Lamb !
p Though we must change our place,
  Our souls will never cease
cres   Praising His Name :
  To Him we'll tribute bring,
  Laud Him our gracious King,
  And, without ceasing. sing,
ff   Worthy the Lamb !
               J. Allen.

65   C.M., double.

f JESUS is God ! The solid earth,
  The ocean broad and bright,

The countless stars like golden dust,
  That strew the skies at night,
The wheeling storm, the dreadful
  fire,
  The pleasant wholesome air,
The summer's sun, the winter's
  frost,
  His own creations were.

f Jesus is God ! The glorious bands
  Of golden angels sing
Songs of adoring praise to Him,
  Their Maker and their King.
He was true God in Bethlehem's
  crib,
  On Calvary's cross true God ;
He Who in heaven eternal reigned,
  In time on earth abode.

f Jesus is God ! Oh could I now
  But compass land and sea,
To teach and tell this single truth,
  How happy should I be !
Oh, had I but an angel's voice
  I would proclaim so loud !
Jesus, the good, the beautiful,
  Is everlasting God !

mp Jesus is God ! Let sorrow come,
  And pain, and every ill ;
cres All are worth while, for all are
    means
  His glory to fulfil.
Worth while a thousand years of
  To speak one little word,   [life,
f If by that "I believe" we own
  The Godhead of our Lord.
      F. W. Faber, v. 4, l. 7 altd.

66   L.M.

f Go, worship at Immanuel's feet ;
  See, in His face what wonders meet
Earth is too narrow to express
  His worth, His glory, or His gr

mf The whole creation can afford
But some faint shadows of my Lord;·
Nature, to make His beauties
known,
Must mingle colours not her own.

mf Oh ! let me climb those higher skies
Where storms and darkness never
rise ! 　　　　　[abroad,
There He displays His ˙ powers
And shines and reigns, th' incar-
nate God.

mf Nor earth, nor seas, nor sun, nor
stars,
Nor heaven His full resemblance
bears :
His beauties we can never trace,
f Till we behold Him face to face.
　　　　　　　　　　I. Watts.

67　　　　　　10.10.7.

f SING Alleluia forth in duteous
praise, 　　　　　[raise
*cres*O citizens of heaven, and sweetly
ff 　　　　An endless Alleluia.

f Ye next who stand before th'
Eternal Light, 　　　[height
*cres*In hymning choirs re-echo to the
ff 　　　　An endless Alleluia.

f The Holy City shall take up your
strain, 　　　　[wake again
*cres*And, with glad songs resounding,
ff 　　　　An endless Alleluia.

f In blissful answering strains ye
thus rejoice 　　　[ful voice,
*cres*To render to the Lord, with thank-
ff 　　　　An endless Alleluia.

mf Ye who have gained at length
your palms in bliss, [still be this,
*cres*Victorious ones, your chant shall
ff 　　　*An endless Alleluia.*

mf There, in one grand acclaim. for
ever ring 　　[of your King,
*cres*The strains which tell the honour
ff 　　　　An endless Alleluia.

[*p* This is the rest for weary ones
brought back, [none shall lack,
*cres*This is the food and drink which
ff 　　　　An endless Alleluia.

ff While Thee, by Whom were all
things made, we praise 　[lays,
For ever, and tell out in sweetest
An endless Alleluia !]]

ff Almighty Christ, to Thee our
voices sing 　　　　[bring
Glory for evermore ; to Thee we
An endless Alleluia.

Latin, 5th century (?), tr. by J. Ellerton.

68　　　　　　　L.M.

f JESUS, Thou everlasting King,
Accept the tribute which we bring ;
Accept the well-deserved renown,
And wear our praises as Thy crown.

mf Let every act of worship be
Like our espousals, Lord, to Thee ;
Like the dear hour when from
above
We first received Thy pledge of
love.

mf The gladness of that happy day,
Our hearts would wish it long to
stay :
Nor let our faith forsake its hold,
Nor comfort sink, nor love grow
cold.

mf Let every moment as it flies,
Increase Thy praise, improve our
joys, 　　　　　　[Name
f Till we are raised to sing Thy
At the great supper of the Lamb.

mf O that the months would roll away,
And bring that coronation day !
cres The King of Grace shall fill the throne,
f With all His Father's glories on.

I. Watts.

69　　　　　　　L.M.

f WHAT equal honours shall we bring
To Thee, O Lord our God, the Lamb,
When all the notes that angels sing
Are far inferior to Thy Name ?

f Worthy is He that once was slain,
The Prince of Peace that groaned and died ;
Worthy to rise and live and reign
At His Almighty Father's side.

f Power and dominion are His due
Who stood condemned at Pilate's bar ;
Wisdom belongs to Jesus too,
Though He was charged with madness here.

mf All riches are His native right,
Yet He sustained amazing loss ;
f To Him ascribe eternal might,
Who left His weakness on the cross.

f Honour immortal must be paid,
Instead of scandal and of scorn ;
While glory shines around His head,
And a bright crown without a thorn.

f Blessings for ever on the Lamb,
Who bore the curse for wretched men ;
Let angels sound His sacred Name,
·And every creature say, Amen.

I. Watts.

70　　　　　　　C.M.

f MY Saviour, my Almighty Friend,
When I begin Thy praise, [end,
Where will the growing numbers
The numbers of Thy grace ?

mf Thou art my everlasting trust,
Thy goodness I adore ;
And since I knew Thy graces first,
I speak Thy glories more.

mf My feet shall travel all the length
Of the celestial road, [strength,
f And march with courage in Thy
To see my Father, God.

p When I am filled with sore distress
For some surprising sin, [ness,
cres I'll plead Thy perfect righteous-
And mention none but Thine.

mf How will my lips rejoice to tell
The victories of my King ! [hell,
cres My soul, redeemed from sin and
f Shall Thy salvation sing.

f Awake, awake, my tuneful powers ;
With this delightful song
I'll entertain the darkest hours,
Nor think the season long.

I. Watts.

71　　　　6.5., 8 lines.

mf SAVIOUR, Blessèd Saviour,
Listen while we sing ;
Hearts and voices raising
Praises to our King.
cres All we have we offer,
All we hope to be,
Body, soul, and spirit,
All we yield to Thee.

p Farther, ever farther
From Thy wounded Side,
Heedlessly we wandered,
Wandered far and wide ;

cres Till Thou cam'st in mercy,
Seeking young and old,
p Lovingly to bear them,
Saviour, to Thy fold.

np Nearer, ever nearer,
Christ, we draw to Thee,
Deep in adoration
Bending low the knee.
Thou, for our redemption,
Cam'st on earth to die;
f Thou, that we might follow,
Hast gone up on high.

[*cres* Great, and ever greater,
Are Thy mercies here;
True and everlasting
Are the glories there;
Where no pain nor sorrow,
Toil nor care, is known;
Where the angel-legions
Circle round Thy throne.

p Dark, and ever darker,
Was the wintry past;
f Now a ray of gladness
O'er our path is cast;
Every day that passeth,
Every hour that flies,
Tells of love unfeignèd,
Love that never dies.

mf Clearer still, and clearer,
Dawns the light from heaven,
In our sadness bringing
News of sins forgiven;
cres Life has lost its shadows,
Pure the light within;
Thou hast shed Thy radiance
On a world of sin.]

f Brighter still, and brighter,
Glows the western sun,
*dim Shedding all its gladness
O'er our work that's done;*

p Time will soon be over,
Toil and sorrow past;
May we, Blessèd Saviour,
Find a rest at last!

cres Onward, ever onward,
Journeying o'er the road
Worn by saints before us,
Journeying on to God;
Leaving all behind us,
May we hasten on,
Backward never looking
Till the prize is won.

f Higher then, and higher,
Bear the ransomed soul,
Earthly toils forgotten,
Saviour, to its goal;
ff Where, in joys unthought o
Saints with angels sing,
Never weary, raising
Praises to their King.

G. Thri

72 C.

f O FOR a thousand tongues to
My great Redeemer's praise
The glories of my God and Ki
The triumphs of His grace.

mf My gracious Master and my G
Assist me to proclaim,
cres To spread through all the
abroad
The honours of Thy Name.

p Jesus, the Name that charm
fears,
That bids our sorrows cease.
'Tis music in the sinner's ears
'Tis life and health and pea

mf He breaks the power of canc
He sets the prisoner free;
His blood can make the fo
His blood availed for me. [c

He speaks, and, listening to· His
   voice,
New life the dead receive ;
The   mournful,   broken   hearts
   rejoice,
   The humble poor believe.
f Hear Him, ye deaf ; His praise, ye
   dumb,
   Your loosened tongues employ ;
Ye blind, behold your Saviour come;
   And leap, ye lame, for joy.]
f Look unto Him, ye nations ; own
   Your God, ye fallen race ; [alone ;
Look, and be saved through faith
   Be justified by grace.
                              C. Wesley.

73   6.5., 12 lines.
f Sing a hymn to Jesus,
   When the heart is faint ;
Tell it all to Jesus,
   Comfort or complaint ;
p If the work is sorrow,
   If the way is long,
   If thou dread'st the morrow.
Tell it Him in song ;
Though thy heart be aching
   For the crown and palm,
ve Keep thy spirit waking
   With a thankful psalm.

mp Jesus, we are lowly,
   Thou art very high ;
We are all unholy,
   Thou art purity.
We are frail and fleeting,
   Thou art still the same,
All life's joys are meeting
   In Thy blessèd Name.
ve Sing a hymn to Jesus,
   When thy heart is faint :
Tell it all to Jesus,
   Comfort or complaint.]

mf All begins in Jesus,
   And in Him I see
All the eternal Godhead
   Coming down to me.
cres I climb to His brightness,
   Up my steps of praise ;
And a sudden lightness
   Gilds my darkened days.
cres So I sing to Jesus,
   When my heart is faint ;
So I tell to Jesus,
   Comfort or complaint.
mp All His words are music,
   Though they make me weep,
Infinitely tender,
   Infinitely deep.
Time can never render
   All in Him I see ;
Infinitely tender,
   Human Deity.
cres Sing a hymn to Jesus,
   When thy heart is faint ;
Tell it all to Jesus,
   Comfort or complaint.
mp Jesus, let me love Thee,
   Infinitely sweet !
What are the poor odours
   I bring to Thy feet ?
cres Yet I love Thee, love Thee ;
   Come into my heart !
And ere long remove me
   To be where Thou art.
f Thus I sing to Jesus,
   When my heart is faint ;
So I tell to Jesus,
   Comfort or complaint.
                              E. P. Hood.

74   C.M.
f Come, let us join our cheerful
   songs
   With angels round the throne

f And that a higher gift than grace
 Should flesh and blood refine,
 God's presence, and His very Self,
 And essence all-divine !

f Oh, generous love ! that He, Who
 In man for man the foe, [smote
p The double agony in man
 For man should undergo ;

p And in the garden secretly,
 And on the Cross on high,
 Should teach His brethren and
dim To suffer and to die ! [inspire
J. H. Newman.

52 C.M.

f O LORD, our Lord, how wondrous
 Is Thine exalted Name ! [great
 The glories of Thy heavenly state
 Let men and babes proclaim.

mf When I behold Thy works on high,
 The moon that rules the night,
 And stars that well adorn the sky—
 Those moving worlds of light ;

mp Lord, what is man or all his race,
 Who dwells so far below,
 That Thou shouldst visit him with
 And love his nature so ?— [grace,

mp That Thine eternal Son should bear
 To take a mortal form ;
 Made lower than His angels are,
dim To save a dying worm ?

f Let Him be crowned with majesty
 Who bowed His head to death ;
 And be His honours sounded high
 By all things that have breath.

ff Jesus, our Lord, how wondrous
 Is Thine exalted Name ? [great
 The glories of Thy heavenly state
 Let the whole earth proclaim.
I. Watts.

53 7s.

f I WILL praise Thee every day,
 Now Thine anger's turned away;
 Comfortable thoughts arise
 From the bleeding sacrifice.

mf Here, in the fair gospel-field,
 Wells of free salvation yield
 Streams of life, a plenteous store,
 And my soul shall thirst no more.

mf Jesus is become at length
 My salvation and my strength ;
 And His praises shall prolong,
 While I live, my pleasant song.

f Praise ye, then, His glorious Name ;
 Publish His exalted fame !
 Still His worth your praise exceeds :
 Excellent are all His deeds.

f Raise again the joyful sound ;
 Let the nations roll it round !
 Zion, shout ! for this is He :
 God the Saviour dwells in thee.
W. Cowper.

54 S.M.

f My soul repeat His praise
 Whose mercies are so great,
dim Whose anger is so slow to rise,
 So ready to abate.

f High as the heavens are raised
 Above the ground we tread,
 So far the riches of His grace
 Our highest thoughts exceed,

mp His power subdues our sins ;
 And His forgiving love,
 Far as the east is from the west,
 Doth all our guilt remove.

 The pity of the Lord
 To those that fear His Name,
 Is such as tender parents feel ;
 He knows our feeble frame.

v Our days are as the grass,
  Or like the morning flower ;
If one sharp blast sweep o'er the
  It withers in an hour. [field,
cres But Thy compassions, Lord.
  To endless years endure,
f And children's children ever find
  Thy words of promise sure.

I. Watts.

55 C.M.

f BEGIN my tongue, some heavenly
    theme,
  And speak some boundless thing,
The mighty works, or mightier
  Of our eternal King. [Name,

f Tell of His wondrous faithfulness,
  And sound His power abroad,
Sing the sweet promise of His grace
  And the performing God.

mf Engraved as in eternal brass,
  The mighty promise shines ;
Nor can the powers of darkness
  Those everlasting lines. [rase

f His very word of grace is strong
  As that which built the skies ;
The voice that rolls the stars along
  Speaks all the promises.

v Oh ! might I hear Thy heavenly
    tongue
  But whisper, "Thou art mine" ;
cres Those gentle words should raise
    my song
  To notes almost divine.

mf How would my leaping heart
    rejoice,
  And think my heaven secure !
f I'd trust the all-creating voice,
  And faith desires no more.

I. Watts.

56 L.M.

f O LOVE of God ! how strong an
  Eternal and yet ever new ; [tru
Uncomprehended and unbought,
  Beyond all knowledge and a
•   thought.

[*f* O love of God, how deep and great
  Far deeper than man's deepest hat
Self-fed, self-kindled, like the ligh
  Changeless, eternal, infinite.

mp O heavenly love, how precious stil
  In days of weariness and ill !
p In nights of pain and helplessnes
cres To heal, to comfort, and to bless

mp O wide-embracing, wondrous lov
  We read thee in the sky above ;
We read thee in the earth below,
cres In seas that swell and streams tha
    flow.

mp We read thee best in Him Wh
    came
  To bear for us the cross of shame
cres Sent by the Father from on high
f Our life to live, our death to die.

mf We read thy power to bless an
    save
dim E'en in the darkness of the grave
cres Still more in resurrection light
f We read the fulness of thy migh

mf O love of God ! our shield and sta
  Through all the perils of our way
f Eternal love, in thee we rest,
  For ever safe, for ever blest !

H. Bonar.

57 8.7.8.7.4.7.

mf MIGHTY God, while angels b
    Thee,
  May a mortal sing Thy Na

Lord of men as well as angels,
Thou art every creature's theme.
Hallelujah !
Hallelujah, Amen.

[Lord of every land and nation,
Ancient of eternal days,
Sounded through the wide creation
Be Thy just and lawful praise.
Hallelujah !
Hallelujah, Amen.]

mf For the grandeur of Thy nature—
Grand beyond a seraph's thought;
For created works of power,
Works with skill and kindness
Hallelujah ! [wrought;
Hallelujah, Amen.

For Thy providence that governs
Through Thine empire's wide
domain,
Wings an angel, guides a sparrow ;
Blessèd be Thy gentle reign.
Hallelujah !
Hallelujah, Amen.

mf But Thy rich, Thy free redemption,
Dark through brightness all
along,
Thought is poor, and poor expres-
sion ;
Who dare sing that awful song ?
Hallelujah !
Hallelujah, Amen.

[Brightness of the Father's glory,
Shall Thy praise unuttered lie ?
Fly, my tongue, such guilty silence,
Sing the Lord Who came to die.
Hallelujah !
Hallelujah, Amen.]

mf From the highest throne of glory,
p   To the cross of deepest woe,
All to ransom guilty captives,—

cres Flow my praise, for e
Hallelujah !
Hallelujah, Am

f Go — return, immortal S
Leave Thy footstool,
throne,
Thence return and reig
Be the kingdom all T
Hallelujah !
Hallelujah, Am

R. Robinson, v. 1,

58   8

f GOD is love ; by Him u
Hang the glorious or
In their language glad
Speaking to us day a
Their great story
God is Love, and God

f And the teeming earth
In that message from
With ten thousand thou
Telling back from hil
Her glad story,
God is Might, and Gc

f With these anthems of
Mingling in harmoni
Christian songs of Chris
To the world with bl
Tell their story ;
God is Love, and God

mf Through that preciou
sought us,
Wandering from His
With that precious life
cres Then let all our futur
f   Tell this story :
Love is Life—our liv

f Gladsome is the theme a
Praise to Christ ou
Head :

Christ, the risen Christ, victorious,
 Earth and hell hath captive led.
  Welcome story !   [dead.
 Love lives on, and Death is
Up to Him let each affection
 Daily rise, and round Him move
*f*Our whole lives. one resurrection
 To the life of life above ;
  Their glad story,
 God is Life ; and God is Love.

J. S. B. Monsell.

9   L.M., with refrain.

GREAT God of wonders! all Thy
  ways
Are matchless, godlike, and divine ;
But the fair glories of Thy grace
More godlike and unrivalled shine.
f Who is a pardoning God like
   Thee ?   [free ?
 Or who has grace so rich and

*f*Crimes of such horror to forgive,
 Such guilty, daring worms to
  spare,—
This is Thy grand prerogative,
And none shall in the honour
  share.
f Who is a pardoning God like
   Thee ?   [free ?
 Or who has grace so rich and

p Angels and men, resign your claim
 To pity, mercy, love, and grace ;
*cr*These glories crown Jehovah's
  name
With an incomparable blaze.
f Who is a pardoning God like
   Thee ?   [free ?
 Or who has grace so rich and

p In wonder lost, with trembling
  joy
We take the *pardon of our God—*
*cr*Pardon for crimes of deepest dye,

A pardon bought with Jesus' blood.
ff Who is a pardoning God like
   Thee ?
 Or who has grace so rich and
  free ?

mf O may this strange, this matchless
  grace,
This godlike miracle of love,
f Fill the wide earth with grateful
  praise,
And all the angelic hosts above.
ff Who is a pardoning God like
   Thee ?   [free ?
 Or who has grace so rich and

S. Davies.

60   S.M.

f GRACE, 'tis a charming sound,
  Harmonious to the ear :
Heaven with the echo shall resound,
 And all the earth shall hear.

mf Grace first contrived the way
  To save rebellious man ;
And all the steps that grace display,
 Which drew the wondrous plan.

mf Grace taught my wandering feet
  To tread the heavenly road ;
And new supplies each hour I
  meet,
 While pressing on to God.

f Grace all the work shall crown
  Through everlasting days :
It lays in heaven the topmost stone,
 And well deserves the praise.

P. Doddridge.

61   C.M.

f THY ceaseless, unexhausted love,
  Unmerited and free,
Delights our evil to remove,
 And help our misery.

mf Thou waitest to be gracious still ;
Thou dost with sinners bear ;
That, saved, we may Thy goodness
feel,
And all Thy grace declare.

mf Thy goodness and Thy truth to me,
To every soul, abound,
A vast, unfathomable sea,
Where all our thoughts are
drowned.

mf Its streams the whole creation
reach,
So plenteous is the store ;
Enough for all, enough for each,
Enough for evermore.

mf Faithful, O Lord, Thy mercies are,
A rock that cannot move :
A thousand promises declare
Thy constancy of love.

f Throughout the universe it reig
Unalterably sure ;   [rema
And while the truth of (
The goodness must endure.

C. Wesley

62   C.M

mf SALVATION ! O the joyful sour
'Tis pleasure to our ears ;
A sovereign balm for every wou
A cordial for our fears.

mp Buried in sorrow and in sin,
At hell's dark door we lay ;
cres But we arise by grace Divine
To see a heavenly day.

f Salvation ! let the echo fly
The spacious earth around,
While all the armies of the sky
Conspire to raise the sound.

I. Watts

II.
The Lord Jesus Christ.
1.—HIS GODHEAD, PRAISE, AND GLORY.

63   C.M.
f ALL hail the power of Jesu's name !
dim Let angels prostrate fall ;
cres Bring forth the royal diadem,
f   To crown Him Lord of all.

nf Crown Him, ye martyrs of your
God,
Who from His altar call ;
cres Extol the Stem-of-Jesse's rod,
f   And crown Him Lord of all.

mf Ye seed of Israel's chosen race,
Ye ransomed of the fall,
cres Hail Him Who saves you by His
grace,
f   And crown Him Lord of all.

p Sinners ! whose love can ne'er for
The wormwood and the gall,
cres Go—spread your trophies at]
feet,
f   And crown Him Lord of all.

ff Let every kindred, every tribe,
On this terrestrial ball,
To Him all majesty ascribe,
And crown Him Lord of all !

mf O that with yonder sacred thro1
We at His feet may fall ;
cres Join in the everlasting song,
ff   And crown Him Lord of all.

*E. Perronet, v. 5 altd. J. Ripp
and v. 6 J. Rippon.*

6.6.4.6.6.6.6.4.

ɔ God on high !
ɩes fill the sky ;
se ye His Name :
Iis Name adore,
our sorrows bore ;
ɩts cry evermore,
thy the Lamb !

around the throne
ly join in one,
ising His Name ;
have felt His blood
ɔur peace with God,
His dear fame abroad ;
thy the Lamb !

our hearts we raise,
ɩe shall have our praise ;
ise ye His Name :
· exalted Lord,
below adored,
se with one accord,
rthy the Lamb !]

the ransomed race
d and God to bless,
ise ye His Name :
we will rejoice,
a cheerful noise,
· with heart and voice,
rthy the Lamb !

we must change our place,
ls will never cease
ɩising His Name :
we'll tribute bring,
im our gracious King,
thout ceasing sing,
rthy the Lamb !

J. Allen.

C.M., double.

s God ! *The solid earth,*
ɩean broad and bright,

The countless stars like golden dust,
That strew the skies at night,
The wheeling storm, the dreadful
fire,
The pleasant wholesome air,
The summer's sun, the winter's
frost,
His own creations were.

f Jesus is God ! The glorious bands
Of golden angels sing
Songs of adoring praise to Him,
Their Maker and their King.
He was true God in Bethlehem's
crib,
On Calvary's cross true God ;
He Who in heaven eternal reigned,
In time on earth abode.

f Jesus is God ! Oh could I now
But compass land and sea,
To teach and tell this single truth,
How happy should I be !
Oh, had I but an angel's voice
I would proclaim so loud !
Jesus, the good, the beautiful,
Is everlasting God !

mp Jesus is God ! Let sorrow come,
And pain, and every ill ;
cres All are worth while, for all are
means
His glory to fulfil.
Worth while a thousand years of
To speak one little word, [life,
f If by that "I believe" we own
The Godhead of our Lord.

F. W. Faber, v. 4, l. 7 altd.

66 L.M.

f Go, worship at Immanuel's feet ;
See, in His face what wonders meet ;
Earth is too narrow to express
His worth, His glory, or His grace

mf The whole creation can afford
But some faint shadows of my Lord;
Nature, to make His beauties
known,
Must mingle colours not her own.

mf Oh! let me climb those higher skies
Where storms and darkness never
rise! [abroad,
There He displays His powers
And shines and reigns, th' incar-
nate God.

mf Nor earth, nor seas, nor sun, nor
stars,
Nor heaven His full resemblance
bears :
His beauties we can never trace,
f Till we behold Him face to face.

I. Watts.

67 10.10.7.

f SING Alleluia forth in duteous
praise, [raise
cres O citizens of heaven, and sweetly
ff An endless Alleluia.

f Ye next who stand before th'
Eternal Light, [height
cres In hymning choirs re-echo to the
ff An endless Alleluia.

f The Holy City shall take up your
strain, [wake again
cres And, with glad songs resounding,
ff An endless Alleluia.

f In blissful answering strains ye
thus rejoice [ful voice,
cres To render to the Lord, with thank-
ff An endless Alleluia.

mf Ye who have gained at length
your palms in bliss, [still be this,
cres Victorious ones, your chant shall
ff An endless Alleluia.

mf There, in one grand a
ever ring [of
cres The strains which tell
ff An endless

[*p* This is the rest for
brought back, [none
cres This is the food and d
ff An endless

ff While Thee, by Whor
things made, we prai
For ever, and tell out
An endless

ff Almighty Christ, to
voices sing
Glory for evermore ; t
An endless

Latin, 5th century (?), tr. by

68

f JESUS, Thou everlastin
Accept the tribute whic
Accept the well-deserve
And wear our praises as

mf Let every act of worshi
Like our espousals, Lor
Like the dear hour
above
We first received Thy
love.

mf The gladness of that h
Our hearts would wisl
stay :
Nor let our faith forsal
Nor comfort sink, nor
cold.

mf Let every moment as it
Increase Thy praise, i
joys,
f Till we are raised t
At the great supper of

mf O that the months would roll away,
And bring that coronation day !
cres The King of Grace shall fill the throne,
f With all His Father's glories on.

I. Watts.

69 L.M.

f WHAT equal honours shall we bring
To Thee, O Lord our God, the Lamb,
When all the notes that angels sing
Are far inferior to Thy Name ?

f Worthy is He that once was slain,
The Prince of Peace that groaned and died ;
Worthy to rise and live and reign
At His Almighty Father's side.

f Power and dominion are His due
Who stood condemned at Pilate's bar ;
Wisdom belongs to Jesus too,
Though He was charged with madness here.

mf All riches are His native right,
Yet He sustained amazing loss ;
f To Him ascribe eternal might,
Who left His weakness on the cross.

f Honour immortal must be paid,
Instead of scandal and of scorn ;
While glory shines around His head,
And a bright crown without a thorn.

f Blessings for ever on the Lamb,
Who bore the curse for wretched men ;
Let angels sound His sacred Name,
And every creature say, Amen.

I. Watts.

70 C.M.

f MY Saviour, my Almighty Friend,
When I begin Thy praise, [end,
Where will the growing numbers
The numbers of Thy grace ?

mf Thou art my everlasting trust,
Thy goodness I adore ;
And since I knew Thy graces first,
I speak Thy glories more.

mf My feet shall travel all the length
Of the celestial road, [strength,
f And march with courage in Thy
To see my Father, God.

p When I am filled with sore distress
For some surprising sin, [ness,
cres I'll plead Thy perfect righteous-
And mention none but Thine.

mf How will my lips rejoice to tell
The victories of my King ! [hell,
cres My soul, redeemed from sin and
f Shall Thy salvation sing.

f Awake, awake, my tuneful powers ;
With this delightful song
I'll entertain the darkest hours,
Nor think the season long.

I. Watts.

71 6.5., 8 lines.

mf SAVIOUR, Blessèd Saviour,
Listen while we sing ;
Hearts and voices raising
Praises to our King.

cres All we have we offer,
All we hope to be,
Body, soul, and spirit,
All we yield to Thee.

p Farther, ever farther
From Thy wounded Side,
Heedlessly we wandered,
Wandered far and wide ;

cres Till Thou cam'st in mercy,
Seeking young and old,
p Lovingly to bear them,
Saviour, to Thy fold.

mp Nearer, ever nearer,
Christ, we draw to Thee,
Deep in adoration
Bending low the knee.
Thou, for our redemption,
Cam'st on earth to die ;
f Thou, that we might follow,
Hast gone up on high.

{*cres* Great, and ever greater,
Are Thy mercies here ;
True and everlasting
Are the glories there ;
Where no pain nor sorrow,
Toil nor care, is known ;
Where the angel-legions
Circle round Thy throne.

p Dark, and ever darker,
Was the wintry past ;
f Now a ray of gladness
O'er our path is cast ;
Every day that passeth,
Every hour that flies,
Tells of love unfeignèd,
Love that never dies.

mf Clearer still, and clearer,
Dawns the light from heaven,
In our sadness bringing
News of sins forgiven ;
cres Life has lost its shadows,
Pure the light within ;
Thou hast shed Thy radiance
On a world of sin.]

f Brighter still, and brighter,
Glows the western sun,
dim Shedding all its gladness
O'er our work that's done ;

p Time will soon be over,
Toil and sorrow past ;
May we, Blessèd Saviour
Find a rest at last !

cres Onward, ever onward,
Journeying o'er the ro
Worn by saints before us
Journeying on to God
Leaving all behind us,
May we hasten on,
Backward never looking
Till the prize is won.

f Higher then, and higher
Bear the ransomed sou
Earthly toils forgotten,
Saviour, to its goal ;
ff Where, in joys unthougl
Saints with angels sin
Never weary, raising
Praises to their King.
G. T

72

f O FOR a thousand tongues
My great Redeemer's pr
The glories of my God and
The triumphs of His gr

mf My gracious Master and m
Assist me to proclaim,
cres To spread through all tl
abroad
The honours of Thy Nar

p Jesus, the Name that cha
fears,
That bids our sorrows ce
'Tis music in the sinner's e
'Tis life and health and

mf He breaks the power of (
He sets the prisoner free
His blood can make the
His blood availed for me

f He speaks, and, listening to· His voice,
New life the dead receive ;
The mournful, broken hearts rejoice,
The humble poor believe.

f Hear Him, ye deaf ; His praise, ye dumb,
Your loosened tongues employ ;
Ye blind, behold your Saviour come;
And leap, ye lame, for joy.]

f Look unto Him, ye nations ; own
Your God, ye fallen race ; [alone;
Look, and be saved through faith
Be justified by grace.

C. Wesley.

'3   6.5., 12 lines.

f SING a hymn to Jesus,
When the heart is faint ;
Tell it all to Jesus,
Comfort or complaint ;

p If the work is sorrow,
If the way is long,
If thou dread'st the morrow.
Tell it Him in song ;
Though thy heart be aching
For the crown and palm,

cs Keep thy spirit waking
With a thankful psalm.

mp Jesus, we are lowly,
Thou art very high ;
We are all unholy,
Thou art purity.
We are frail and fleeting,
Thou art still the same,
All life's joys are meeting
In Thy blessèd Name.

cs Sing a hymn to Jesus,
When thy heart is faint :
Tell it all to Jesus,
Comfort or complaint.]

mf All begins in Jesus,
And in Him I see
All the eternal Godhead
Coming down to me.

cres I climb to His brightness,
Up my steps of praise ;
And a sudden lightness
Gilds my darkened days.

cres So I sing to Jesus,
When my heart is faint ;
So I tell to Jesus,
Comfort or complaint.

mp All His words are music,
Though they make me weep,
Infinitely tender,
Infinitely deep.
Time can never render
All in Him I see ;
Infinitely tender,
Human Deity.

cres Sing a hymn to Jesus,
When thy heart is faint ;
Tell it all to Jesus,
Comfort or complaint.

mp Jesus, let me love Thee,
Infinitely sweet !
What are the poor odours
I bring to Thy feet ?

cres Yet I love Thee, love Thee ;
Come into my heart !
And ere long remove me
To be where Thou art.

f Thus I sing to Jesus,
When my heart is faint ;
So I tell to Jesus,
Comfort or complaint.

E. P. Hood.

74   C.M.

f COME, let us join our cheerful songs
With angels round the throne

Ten thousand thousand are their
tongues,
But all their joys are one.

f Worthy the Lamb that died,—they
cry,—
To be exalted thus :
Worthy the Lamb, — our lips
reply,—

p For He was slain for us.

mf Jesus is worthy to receive
Honour and power divine ;

*cres*And blessings more than we can
give,
Be, Lord, for ever Thine.

f Let all that dwell above the sky,
And air and earth and seas,
Conspire to lift Thy glories high,
And speak Thine endless praise.

f The whole creation join in one,
To bless the sacred Name
Of Him that sits upon the throne,
And to adore the Lamb.
I. Watts.

75   6.5., 8 lines.

mf AT the name of Jesus
Every knee shall bow,

*cres*Every tongue confess Him
King of glory now.

mf 'Tis the Father's pleasure
We should call Him Lord,

*cres*Who from the beginning
Was the mighty Word :—

mf Mighty and mysterious
In the highest height,
God from everlasting,
Very Light of light.
In the Father's bosom.
With the Spirit blest,

*dim*Love, in Love Eternal,

p Rest, in perfect rest.

mf At His voice creation
Sprang at once to sight,
All the angel faces,
All the hosts of light ;

*cres*Throne and dominations,
Stars upon their way,
All the heavenly orders
In their great array.

p Humbled for a season,
To receive a Name
From the lips of sinners
Unto whom He came,

*cres*Faithfully He bore it
Spotless to the last,
Brought it back victorious
When from death He pas

f Bore it up triumphant
With its human light,
Through all ranks of creati
To the central height ;
To the Throne of Godhead,
To the Father's breast,
Filled it with the glory
Of that perfect rest.

[*mf*In your hearts enthrone H
There let Him subdue
All that is not holy,
All that is not true :

*cres*Crown Him as your Captai
In temptation's hour,
Let His will enfold you
In its light and power.]

f Brothers, this Lord Jesus
Shall return again,
With His Father's glory,
With His angel-train ;

ff For all wreaths of empire
Meet upon His brow,
And our hearts confess Hi
King of glory now.
Caroline M.

76   10.10.11.11.
f   YE servants of God,

And publish ab
   His wonderful name ;
The name all-victorious
   Of Jesus extol ,
His kingdom is glorious
   And rules over all.

f

Almighty to save ;
   And still He is nigh,
His presence we have ;
   The great congregation

f   Salvation to God,
   Who sits on the throne,—
Let all cry aloud,
   And honour the Son ;
The praises of Jesus
   The angels proclaim.
Fall down on their faces,
   And worship the Lamb.

f   Then let us adore,
   And give Him His right,—
All glory and power,
   All wisdom and might

With angels above,
And thanks never ceasing,
   For infinite love.
           C. Wesley.

77   8.6.8.6.8.8.
f THOU art the Everlasting Word,
   The Father's only Son ;
God, manifestly seen and heard,
   And Heaven's Beloved One.

ff Worthy, O Lamb of God, art Thou,
   That every knee to Thee should
   bow.
f In Thee, most perfectly expressed,
   The Father's glories shine :
Of the full Deity possessed ;
   Eternally divine.
ff Worthy, O Lamb of God, art Thou,
   That every knee to Thee should
   bow.
[*f* True Image of the Infinite,
   Whose Essence is concealed ;
Brightness of Uncreated Light ;
   The heart of God revealed.
ff Worthy, O Lamb of God, art Thou,
   That every knee to Thee should
   bow.]
But the high mysteries of Thy
   Name
An angel's grasp
The Father only—glorious claim—
   The Son can comprehend.
ff Worthy, O Lamb of God, art Thou,
   That every knee to Thee should
   bow.
mp Yet, loving Thee, on whom His love
   Ineffable doth rest,
cres Thy glorious worshippers above,
   As one with Thee are blest.
ff Worthy, O Lamb of God, art Thou,
   That every knee to Thee should
   bow.
f Throughout the universe of bliss
   The centre Thou, and sun,
The eternal theme

ff Worthy, O Lamb of God, art Thou,
   That every knee to Thee should
   bow.
           J. Conder.

78 S.M.

f Awake, and sing the song
   Of Moses and the Lamb :
   Wake every heart and every tongue.
   To praise the Saviour's name.
p   Sing of His dying love ;
cres Sing of His rising power ;
   Sing how He intercedes above,
   For those whose sins He bore.
mf   Sing, till we feel our hearts
   Ascending with our tongues ;
cres Sing, till the love of sin departs,
   And grace inspires our songs.
mp   Ye pilgrims on the road
   To Zion's city, sing :
cres Rejoice ye in the Lamb of God,
   In Christ the eternal King.
sf   Soon shall we hear Him say,—
   Ye blessed children. come ;
p   Soon will He call us hence away,
cres And take His wanderers home.
f   There shall each raptured tongue
   His endless praise proclaim ;
   And sing in sweeter notes the song
   Of Moses and the Lamb.

W. Hammond, altd. M. Madan, A. M.
   Tvplady, and W. J. Hall.

79 6.5., 12 lines.

f Hark ! the voice eternal
   Robed in majesty,
   Calling into being
   Earth and sea and sky ;
   Hark ! in countless numbers
   All the angel-throng
   Hail Creation's morning
   With one burst of song.
cres   High in regal glory,
   'Mid eternal light,
f   Reign, O King Immortal,
   Holy, Infinite.

mf Bright the world and glorious,
   Calm both earth and sea,
   Noble in its grandeur
   Stood man's purity :
dim Came the great transgression,
   Came the saddening fall,
p Death and desolation
   Breathing over all.
cres   Still in regal glory,
   'Mid eternal light.
   Reigned the King Immortal
   Holy, Infinite.

mf Long the nations waited,
   Through the troubled night,
   Looking, longing, yearning
   For the promised light.
cres Prophets saw the morning
   Breaking far away,
   Minstrels sang the splendour
   Of that opening day.
f   Whilst in regal glory,
   'Mid eternal light,
   Reigned the King Immortal
   Holy, Infinite.

f Brightly dawned the Advent
   Of the new-born King,
   Joyously the watchers
   Heard the angels sing.
dim Sadly closed the evening
   Of His hallowed life,
p As the noontide darkness
   Veiled the last dread strife.
cres   Lo ! again in glory,
   'Mid eternal light,
   Reigns the King Immortal,
   Holy, Infinite.

mf Lo ! again He cometh,
   Robed in clouds of Light,
   As the Judge Eternal,
   Armed with power and might.
   Nations to His footstool
   Gathered then shall be :

rth shall yield her treasures,
\nd her dead, the sea.
  Till the trumpet soundeth,
    'Mid eternal light,
  Reign, Thou King Immortal,
    Holy, Infinite.

u ! Lord and Master.
?rophet, Priest, and King.
Thy feet triumphant
Iallowed praise we bring.
ine the pain and weeping,
Ihine the victory ;
wer, and praise, and honour,
3e, O Lord, to Thee.
  High in regal glory,
    'Mid eternal light,
  Reign, O King Immortal,
    IIoly, Infinite. *J. Juli..n.*

6s., 6 lines.

IEN morning gilds the skies,
' heart awaking cries,
lay Jesus Christ be praised ! ''
ike at work and prayer
Jesus I repair :
/lay Jesus Christ be praised ! ''

ien sleep her balm denies,
' silent spirit sighs,
/lay Jesus Christ be praised ! ''
ien evil thoughts molest,
th this I shield my breast,
May Jesus Christ be praised ! ''

es sadness fill my mind ?
solace here I find,
lay Jesus Christ be praised ! "
fades my earthly bliss ?
y comfort still is this,
lay Jesus Christ be praised ! "

heaven's eternal bliss
e loveliest strain is this,
lay Jesus Christ be praised ! "

p The powers of darkness fear
cres When this sweet chant they hear,
  " May Jesus Christ be praised ! "

f To God, the Word, on high,
The hosts of angels cry,
  " May Jesus Christ be praised ! ''
Let mortals, too, upraise
Their voice in hymns of praise :
  " May Jesus Christ be praised ! "

ff Let earth's wide circle round
In joyful notes resound,
  " May Jesus Christ be praised ! "
Let air and sea and sky,
From depth to height, reply,
  " May Jesus Christ be praised ! "

mf Be this, while life is mine,
My canticle divine,
f " May Jesus Christ be praised ! "
Be this the eternal song
Through all the ages on,
cres " May Jesus Christ be praised ! ''
German, 19th century, tr. E. Caswall.

81   C.M.

f BEHOLD the glories of the Lamb,
  Amidst His Father's throne :
Prepare new honours for His Name,
  And songs before unknown.

mf Let elders worship at His feet,
  The Church adore around,
With vials full of odours sweet ;
p   And harps of sweetest sound.

mf Now to the Lamb that once was
    slain
  Be endless blessings paid ;
f Salvation, glory, joy remain
  For ever on Thy head.

mf Thou hast redeemed our souls with
    blood,
cres Hast set the prisoners free;

Hast made us kings and priests to God,
f   And we shall reign with Thee.
mf The worlds of nature and of grace
Are put beneath Thy power ;
Then shorten these delaying days,
And bring the promised hour.
I. Watts.

82   L.M.

f Now to the Lord a noble song !
Awake, my soul ; awake, my tongue ;
Hosanna to the Eternal Name,
And all His boundless love proclaim.

mf See where it shines in Jesus' face,
The brightest image of His grace :
God, in the person of His Son,
Has all His mightiest works outdone.

mf The spacious earth and s
flood
Proclaim the wise and]
God ;
And Thy rich glories from
Sparkle in every rolling s

cres But in His looks a glory s
The noblest labour of Thy
The radiant lustre of His
Outshines the wonders of 1

p Grace ! 'tis a sweet, a c
theme ;
My thoughts rejoice a
Name :
Ye angels, dwell upon the
Ye heavens, reflect it to the

mp O may I live to reach the
Where He unveils His love
cres Where all His beauties you
f And sing His Name to harp
I.

2.—HIS INCARNATION AND BIRTH.

83   Irregular.

f   O COME, all ye faithful,
Joyful and triumphant,
O come ye, O come ye to Bethlehem;
Come and behold Him,
Born the King of Angels .
p   O come, let us adore Him,
cres   O come, let us adore Him,
mf O come, let us adore Him, Christ the Lord.

f   True God of true God,
Light of Light eternal,
Lo, He abhors not the Virgin's womb.
Son of the Father,
Begotten not created :

p   O come, let us adore F
cres   O come, let us adore F
mf O come, let us adore Him
the Lord.

f   Sing. choirs of Angels
Sing in exultation,
Sing, all ye citizens of
Sing ye, " All glory
To God in the Highes
p   O come, let us adore F
cres   O come, let us adore F
mf O come, let us adore Him
the Lord.

f   Yea, Lord, we hail Th
Born this happy morn
Jesu, to Thee be glory giv

Word of the Father
Now in flesh appearing :
O come, let us adore Him,
O come, let us adore Him,
me, let us adore Him,(*f*) Christ
　the Lord.

onaventura (1221-1274), *tr. F:
Oakeley* (1802-1880), *altd.*

　　　　　　7s., 8 lines.
K ! the herald angels sing,—
y to the new-born King ;
e on earth, and mercy mild ;
and sinners reconciled.
ul, all ye nations, rise ;
the triumph of the skies :
ι the angelic host proclaim,—
st is born in Bethlehem.

st, by highest heaven adored,
st, the everlasting Lord ;
· in time behold Him come,
)ring of a virgin's womb !
:d in flesh the Godhead see :
the Incarnate Deity !
sed as Man with men to
'ell,
s our Immanuel.

　the heaven-born Prince of
ace !
the Sun of Righteousness !
t and life to all He brings,
ι with healing in His wings.
　He lays His glory by :
ι, that man no more may
);
ι to raise the sons of earth ;
ι to give them second birth.

*Wesley, altd. by G. Whitefield
and M. Madan.*

85　　　　　　　8.7.8.7.8.7.*l.*

OF the Father, sole begotten,
　Ere the worlds began to be,
He the Alpha and Omega,
　He the source, the ending He,
Of the things that are, that have
　　been,
　And that future years shall see,
　　Evermore and evermore !

mf He is here, Whom seers in old time
　Chanted of, while ages ran ;
Whom the writings of the Prophets
　Promised since the world began :
Then foretold, now manifested,
　Praise Him, every child of man,
　　Evermore and evermore !

ff Praise Him, O ye heaven of heavens!
　Praise Him, angels in the height !
Praise Him, every power and king-
　　dom,
　Praise Him in His boundless
　　might :
Let no tongue of man be silent,
　Let each heart and voice unite,
　　Evermore and evermore !

mf Thee let age and Thee let manhood,
　Thee let choirs of infants sing ;
mp Thee the matrons and the maidens,
　And the children answering :
*cres*Let their guileless song re-echo,
　And their heart its praises bring,
　　Evermore and evermore !

ff Laud and honour to the Father,
　Laud and honour to the Son,
Laud and honour to the Spirit.
　Ever Three and ever One
Consubstantial, Co-eternal,
　While unending ages run,
　　Evermore and evermore !
Prudentius, tr. J. M. Neale, *altd.*

86   Irregular.

mf THOU didst leave Thy throne and
     · Thy kingly crown   [me:
     When Thou camest to earth for
p But in Bethlehem's home there
     was found no room
     For Thy holy nativity,   [Jesus,
cres   O come to my heart, Lord
dim   There is room in my heart for
       Thee.

f Heaven's arches rang when the
     angels sang,
     Proclaiming Thy royal degree ;
mf But of lowly birth cam'st Thou,
     Lord, on earth,
p   And in great humility :
. *cres*   O come to my heart, Lord
       Jesus,
dim   There is room in my heart for
       Thee.

mf The foxes found rest, and the
     bird its nest
     In the shade of the cedar tree ;
p But Thy couch was the sod, O
     Thou Son of God,
     In the deserts of Galilee : [Jesus,
cres   O come to my heart, Lord
dim   There is room in my heart for
       Thee.

mf Thou camest, Lord, with the living
     word   [free ;
     That should set Thy children
p But with mocking scorn, and with
     crown of thorn,
pp   They bore Thee to Calvary :
cres   O come to my heart, Lord
       Jesus,
dim   Thy cross is my only plea.

mf When heaven's arch shall ring,
     and hér choirs shall sing
   At Thy coming to victory,

cres Let Thy voice call me
     saying, " Yet there i
     There is room at My
     Thee " :   [Lor
f   And my heart shall
     When Thou comest and
     for me.

           Emily E. S. E

87

f HARK the glad sound, the
     comes,
     The Saviour promised lo
     Let every heart prepare a
     And every voice a song.

f He comes the prisoners to
     In Satan's bondage held
     The gates of brass before Hi
     The iron fetters yield.

mf He comes from thickest film
     To clear the mental ray,
     And on the eyeballs of the
     To pour celestial day. '

p He comes the broken heart
     The bleeding soul to cure
cres And with the treasures
     To enrich the humble p

f Our glad hosannas, Prince
     Thy welcome shall proc
ff And heaven's eternal arch
     With Thy belovèd Name

           P. Dodd

88   10s., 6

f CHRISTIANS, awake, sa
     happy morn,   [w
     Whereon the Saviour of
     Rise to adore the mystery
     Which hosts of angels
     from above

With them the joyful tidings first
  begun   [Son.
Of God incarnate and the Virgin's
mf Then to the watchful shepherds it
  was told,   [voice : "Behold,
Who heard the angelic herald's
I bring good tidings of a Saviour's
  birth   [earth :
To you and all the nations upon
This day hath God fulfilled His
  promised word,   [the Lord."
This day is born a Saviour, Christ

f He spake, and straightway the
  celestial choir,   [conspire :
In hymns of joy, unknown before,
The praises of redeeming love they
  sang,   [Alleluias rang :
And heaven's whole orb with
p God's highest glory was their
  anthem still,   [good will."
" Peace upon earth, and unto men

O ! may we keep and ponder in
  our mind   [mankind ;
God's wondrous love in saving lost
p Trace we the Babe, Who hath
  retrieved our loss,   [cross ;
From His poor manger to His bitter
*cres*Tread in His steps, assisted by His
  grace,   [takes place.
Till man's first heavenly state again

f Then may we hope, the angelic
  thrones among,   [song ;
To sing, redeemed, a glad triumphal
He that was born upon this joyful
  day,   [play ;
Around us all His glory shall dis-
Saved by His love, incessant we
  shall sing,   [King.
Eternal praise to heaven's Almighty

*J. Byrom, v. 3, l. 6, v. 4, l. 1,
v. 5, l. 6 altd.*

89   C.M., double.

mf A THOUSAND years have come and
  gone,
And near a thousand more,
Since happier light from heaven
  shone
Than ever shone before ;
*cres*And in the hearts of old and young
A joy most joyful stirred,
f That sent such news from tongue
  to tongue
As ears had never heard.

Then angels on their starry way
Felt bliss unfelt before,
For news that men should be as
  they
To darkened earth they bore ;
p So toiling men and spirits bright
A first communion had,
*cres*And in meek mercy's rising light
Were each exceeding glad.

f And we are glad, and we will sing,
As in the days of yore ;
Come all, and hearts made ready
  bring
To welcome back once more
The day when first on wintry earth
A summer change began,
And, dawning in a lowly birth,
Uprose the Light of man.

p For trouble such as men must bear
From childhood to fourscore,
He shared with us, that we might
  share
His joy for evermore ;
*cres*And twice a thousand years of
  grief,
Of conflict and of sin,   [sheaf
f May tell how large the harvest
His patient love shall win.

             T. T. Lynch

90 C.M.

f JOY to the world! the Lord is
   come;
   Let earth receive her King;
   Let every heart prepare Him room,
   And heaven and nature sing.

f Joy to the earth! the Saviour
   reigns;
   Let men their songs employ;
   While fields and floods, rocks, hills,
     and plains,
   Repeat the sounding joy.

p No more let sins and sorrows grow,
   Nor thorns infest the ground;
*cres*He comes to make His blessings
    flow
   Far as the curse is found.

f He rules the world with truth and
   grace,
   And makes the nations prove
   The glories of His righteousness,
   And wonders of His love.

               I. Watts.

91 8.7.8.7.4.7.

f ANGELS, from the realms of glory,
   Wing your flight o'er all the
    earth;
   Ye who sang creation's story
    Now proclaim Messiah's birth;
     Come and worship; [King.
   Worship Christ, the new-born

mf Shepherds in the field abiding,
    Watching o'er your flocks by
     night,
*cres*God with man is now residing,
    Yonder shines the infant-light;
f   Come and worship;
   *Worship Christ, the new-born
   King.*

mf Sages, leave your contemp
   Brighter visions beam af
   Seek the great Desire of N
   Ye have seen His natal s
f   Come and worship;
   Worship Christ, the n

mf Saints, before the altar ben
p   Watching long in hope a
*cres*Suddenly the Lord descend
   In His temple shall appe
f   Come and worship;
   Worship Christ, the n

mp Sinners wrung with t
   pentance,
   Doomed for guilt to endle
*cres*Justice now revokes your s
   Mercy calls you,—brea
   chains;
f   Come and worship;
   Worship Christ, the n
   King.   *J. Montgo*

92 8

f HARK, an awful voice is sou
   "Christ is nigh," it seem
   "Cast away the dreams of d
   O ye children of the day.

   Startled at the solemn war
   Let the earth-bound soul
   Christ, her Sun, all sloth dis
   Shines upon the mornin

mf Lo, the Lamb so long expe
   Comes with pardon dow
   heaven;
*dim*Let us haste, with tears of
   One and all to be forgive

mf So when next He comes wit
p   Wrapping all the earth i
*cres*May He then, as our defen
   On the clouds of heaven

ry, virtue, merit,
ther and the Son,
·eternal Spirit,
rnal ages run.
ntury, tr. E. Caswall.

C.M., double.

n the midnight clear,
ious song of old,
s bending near the earth
their harps of gold :
the earth, goodwill to
[King " ;
eaven's all - gracious
n solemn stillness lay
he angels sing.

h the cloven skies they

ceful wings unfurled,
ir heavenly music floats
he weary world :
ıd and lowly plains
d on heavenly wing,
'er its Babel sounds
èd angels sing.

e woes of sin and strife
d has suffered long,
he angel-strain have

ısand years of wrong ;
war with man hears not
song which they bring—
noise, ye men of strife,
· the angels sing.

ath life's crushing load,
ırms are bending low,
ong the climbing way
ıry steps and slow,—
or glad and golden hours
iftly on the wing *;*
le the weary road,
the angels sing.

mf For lo ! the days are hastening on,
By prophet-bards foretold,
cres When with the ever-circling years
Comes round the age of gold ;
f When peace shall over all the earth
Its ancient splendours fling,
ff And the whole world send back
the song
pp Which now the angels sing.

E. H. Sears.

94 7.6.7.6., double.

f HAIL to the Lord's anointed ;
Great David's greater Son !
Hail, in the time appointed,
His reign on earth begun !
He comes to break oppression,
To set the captive free, ·
To take away transgression,
And rule in equity.

[*mf* He comes with succour speedy
To those that suffer wrong ;
To help the poor and needy,
And bid the weak be strong ;
cres To give them songs for sighing,
Their darkness turn to light.
dim Whose souls condemned and dying,
mf Were precious in His sight.]

p He shall come down like showers
Upon the fruitful earth ;
cres And love, joy, hope, like flowers,
Spring in His path to birth :
mf Before Him, on the mountains,
Shall peace, the herald, go,
cres And righteousness, in fountains,
From hill to valley flow.

[*mf* Arabia's desert ranger
To Him shall bow the knee :
The Ethiopian stranger
His glory come to see :

8*

*cres*With offerings of devotion,
 Ships from the isles shall meet,
 To pour the wealth of ocean
 In tribute at His feet.]
mf Kings shall fall down before Him,
 And gold and incense bring ;
 All nations shall adore Him,
 His praise all people sing :
*cres*For He shall have dominion
 O'er river, sea. and shore,
 Far as the eagle's pinion,
 Or dove's light wing can soar.

p For Him shall prayer unceasing
 And daily vows ascend ;
*cres*His kingdom still increasing,—
 A kingdom without end.
mf The mountain dews shall nourish
 A seed in weakness sown,
*cres*Whose fruit shall spread and
  flourish,
 And shake like Lebanon.

f O'er every foe victorious,
 He on His throne shall rest ;
 From age to age more glorious,
 All blessing and all blest.
*cres*The tide of time shall never
 His covenant remove ;
 His Name shall stand for ever ;
rall That Name to us is—Love.
    J. Montgomery.

95
     7s., with refrain.
f SING, O sing, this blessèd morn,
 Unto us a child is born,
 Unto us a Son is given, [heaven.
 God Himself comes down from
 Sing, O sing, this blessèd morn,
 Jesus Christ to-day is born.

f God with us, Immanuel,
 Deigns for ever now to dwell,
 And on Adam's fallen race

Sheds the fulness of His ⸗
 Sing, O sing, this blessè⸗
 Jesus Christ to-day is b⸗
f God comes down that man
 Lifted by Him to the skie⸗
 Christ is Son of Man that
 Sons of God in Him may
 Sing, O sing, this blessè⸗
 Jesus Christ to-day is b⸗

f O renew us, Lord, we pra⸗
 With Thy spirit day by da⸗
 That we ever one may be
 With the Father and with
 Sing, O sing, this blessè⸗
 Jesus Christ to-day is b⸗
    C. Words⸗

96

mf GOD from on high hath h⸗
 Let sighs and sorrows cea⸗
 The skies unfold, and lo !
 Descends the gift of Peac⸗

[Hark ! on the midnight ai⸗
Celestial voices swell !
The hosts of heaven procl⸗
God comes on earth to dw⸗

Haste with the shepherds
 The mystery of Grace ;
mf A manger-bed, a Child,
 Is all the eye can trace.

Is this the Eternal Son,
 Who on the starry throne,
 Before the world began,
 Was with the Father one ?

*cres*Yes, Faith can pierce the
 Which shrouds His glory ⸗
 And hails Him Lord and (⸗
 To Whom all creatures bo⸗

[Faith sees the sapphire th⸗
 Where angels evermore

*dim*Adoring, tremble still,
p And trembling, still adore.]

mf O Child ; Thy silence speaks,
And bids us not refuse
To bear what flesh would shun,
To spurn what flesh would choose.

*cres*Fill us with holy love,
Heal Thou our earthly pride ;
Be born within our hearts,
And ever there abide.

C. *Coffin, tr. J. R. Woodford.*

97   8.8.8.8.8.8.6.8.

LIFT up your heads, ye mighty
gates,
Behold the King of glory waits,
The King of kings is drawing near,
The Saviour of the world is here ;
Life and salvation doth He bring,
Wherefore rejoice, and gladly sing
f   Praise, O my God, to Thee !
Creator, wise is Thy decree !

· The Lord is just, a helper tried,
Mercy is ever at His side,
His kingly crown is holiness,
His sceptre, pity in distress,
The end of all our woe He brings ;
Wherefore the earth is glad and
sings
f   Praise, O my God, to Thee !
O Saviour, great Thy deeds shall be !

Oh, blest the land, the city blest,
Where Christ the ruler is confest !
O, happy hearts and happy homes
To whom this King in triumph
comes !
The cloudless Sun of joy He is,
Who bringeth pure delight and
bliss ;
ff   Praise, O my God, to Thee !
Comforter, for Thy comfort free !

Fling wide the portals of your heart
Make it a temple set apart
From earthly use for heaven's
employ,
Adorned with prayer, and love, and
joy ;
So shall your Sovereign enter in,
And new and nobler life begin.
ff   Praise, O my God, be Thine,
For word, and deed, and grace
Divine.

Redeemer, come ! I open wide
My heart to Thee; here, Lord, abide!
Let me Thy inner presence feel,
Thy grace and love in me reveal,
Thy Holy Spirit guide us on
Until our glorious goal is won !
ff   Eternal praise and fame,
Be offered, Saviour, to Thy Name !

G. *Weissel, tr. Catherine Winkworth.*

3.—HIS MANIFESTATION TO THE GENTILES.

98   7s., 6 lines.

f As with gladness men of old
Did the guiding star behold,
As with joy they hailed its light,
Leading onward, beaming bright ;
f So, most gracious Lord, may we
Evermore be led to Thee.

mf As with joyful steps they sped,
Saviour, to Thy lowly bed,
There to bend the knee before
Thee Whom heaven and earth
adore :
p So may we with willing feet
Ever seek the mercy-seat.

mf As they offered gifts most rare
At Thy cradle rude and bare ;
So may we with holy joy,
Pure, and free from sin's alloy,
f All our costliest treasures bring,
Christ, to Thee, our Heavenly King.

p Holy Jesus, every day
Keep us in the narrow way ;
*cres*And, when earthly things are past,
Bring our ransomed souls at last
f Where they need no star to guide,
Where no clouds Thy glory hide.

ff In the heavenly country bright
Need they no created light ;
Thou, its Light, its Joy, its Crown,
Thou, its Sun which goes not down ;
There for ever may we sing
Hallelujahs to our King.

W. C. Dix.

99　　　6.5., 12 lines.

f FROM the eastern mountains
Pressing on they come,
Wise men in their wisdom
To His humble home ;
Stirred by deep devotion,
Hastening from afar,
Ever journeying onward,
Guided by a Star.
Light of Life that shinedst,
Ere the world began ;
Draw Thou near and lighten
Every heart of man.

η There their Lord and Saviour
Meek and lowly lay,
Wondrous Light that led them
Onward on their way,
*cres*Ever now to lighten
Nations from afar,
As they journey homeward
By that guiding Star.
Light of Life, etc.]

f Thou Who in a manger
Once hast lowly lain,
Who dost now in glory
O'er all kingdoms reign,
Gather in the heathen
Who in lands afar
Ne'er have seen the brightness
Of Thy guiding Star.
Light of Life, etc.

p Gather in the outcasts,
Who have gone astray,
*cres*Throw Thy radiance o'er them
Guide them on their way.
*dim*Those who never knew Thee,
Or have wandered far,
Guide them by the brightness
Of Thy guiding Star.
Light of Life, etc.

*cres*Onward through the darkness
Of the lonely night,
Shining still before them
With Thy kindly light,
Guide them, Jew and Gentile,
Homeward from afar.
Young and old together,
By Thy guiding Star.
Light of Life, etc.

f Until every nation,
Whether bond or free,
'Neath Thy starlit banner,
Jesu, follows Thee
O'er the distant mountains
To that heavenly home,
Where nor sin nor sorrow
Evermore shall come.
Light of Life that shinedst
Ere the world began ;
Draw Thou near, and ligh
Every heart of man.

G. Thris

lOO   11.10.11.10.

nf BRIGHTEST and best of the sons of
   the morning,
   Dawn on our darkness, and lend
   us Thine aid :
   Star of the East, the horizon
   adorning,   [deemer is laid.
dim Guide where our Infant Re-

p Cold on His cradle the dewdrops
   are shining,
   Low lies His head with the
   beasts of the stall ;
cres Angels adore Him, in slumber re-
   clining,   [of all.
f   Maker, and Monarch, and Saviour

mf Say, shall we yield Him, in costly
   devotion,   [Divine ;
   Odours of Edom and offerings
   Gems of the mountain, and pearls
   of the ocean, [from the mine ?
   Myrrh from the forest, or gold

   Vainly we offer each ample obla-
   tion ;
   Vainly with gifts would His
   favour secure ;
   Richer, by far, is the heart's adoration ;   [the poor.
   Dearer to God are the prayers of

f Brightest and best of the sons of
   the morning,
   Dawn on our darkness, and lend
   us Thine aid :

   Star of the East, the horizon
   adorning,
dim Guide where our Infant Redeemer is laid.

               R. Heber.

101   C.M.

mf THE race that long in darkness
   pined
   Have seen a glorious light ;
   The people dwell in day, who dwelt
dim In death's surrounding night.

f To hail Thy rise, Thou better Sun,
   The gathering nations come,
   Joyous as when the reapers bear
   The harvest-treasures home.

   To us a Child of Hope is born,
   To us a Son is given ;
   Him shall the tribes of earth obey,
   Him all the hosts of heaven.

   His Name shall be the Prince of
   Peace,
   For evermore adored,
cres The Wonderful, the Counsellor,
   The great and mighty Lord.

ff His power increasing still shall
   spread,
   His reign no end shall know :
   Justice shall guard His throne
   above,
   And Peace abound below.

              J. Morrison.

4.—HIS CHILDHOOD.

102   S.M.

mf WITHIN the Father's house
   The Son hath found His home :
   And to His temple suddenly
   The Lord of Life hath come.

   The doctors of the law
   Gaze on the wondrous Child,
   And marvel at His gracious
   words
   Of wisdom undefiled.

p Yet not to them is given
The mighty truth to know,
To lift the fleshly veil which hides
Incarnate God below.

The secret of the Lord
Escapes each human eye,
And faithful pondering hearts
await
cres The full Epiphany.

Lord, visit Thou our souls,
And teach us by Thy grace

dim Each dim revealing of Thyself
With loving awe to trace;
f Till from our darkened sight
The cloud shall pass away,
And on the cleansèd soul shall burst
The everlasting day;
ff Till we behold Thy face,
And know, as we are known,
Thee, Father, Son, and Holy Ghost
Co-equal Three in One.

J. R. Woodford.

5.—HIS TEMPTATION.

103 C.M.

mf WITH joy we meditate the grace
Of our High Priest above;
p His heart is made of tenderness,
It overflows with love.

Touched with a sympathy within,
He knows our feeble frame;
He knows what sore temptations
mean,
For He has felt the same.

mf But spotless, innocent, and pure,
The great Redeemer stood,
f While Satan's fiery darts He bore,
And did resist to blood.

p He, in the days of feeble flesh,
Poured out His cries and tears;
And in His measure feels afresh
What every member bears.

mf He'll never quench the smoking flax,
But raise it to a flame;
dim The bruisèd reed He never breaks,
Nor scorns the meanest name.

mf Then let our humble faith address
His mercy and His power;
cres We shall obtain delivering grace
In the distressing hour.

I. Watts, v. 1, l. 4 altd.

104 C.M.

mf LORD, Thou in all things like was
made
To us, yet free from sin;
p Then how unlike to us, O Lord,
Replies the voice within.

mp Our faith is weak;—O Light of
light!
cres Clear Thou our clouded view;
That, Son of Man, and Son of God,
We give Thee honour due.

p O Son of Man! Thyself hast proved
Our trials and our tears; [repose,
Life's thankless toil, and scant
Death's agonies and fears.

f O Son of God! in glory raised,
Thou sittest on Thy throne:
Thence, by Thy pleadings, and
Thy grace,
Still succouring Thine own.

mf Brother and Saviour, Friend and
Judge!
To Thee, O Christ, be given
To bind upon Thy crown the names
Most blest in earth and heaven.

J. Anstice.

6.—*HIS HUMAN LIFE AND HUMILIATION.*

105 8.7.8.7., double.

p WHO is this, so weak and helpless,
  Child of lowly Hebrew maid,
Rudely in a stable sheltered,
  Coldly in a manger laid?
f 'Tis the Lord of all creation,
  Who this wondrous path hath
    trod;
He is God from everlasting,
  And to everlasting, God.

p Who is this, a Man of sorrows
  Walking sadly life's hard way,
Homeless, weary, sighing, weeping
  Over sin and Satan's sway?
f 'Tis our God, our glorious Saviour,
  Who above the starry sky
Now for us a place prepareth,
  Where no tear can dim the eye.

p Who is this—behold Him shedding
  Drops of blood upon the ground?
Who is this—despised, rejected,
  Mocked, insulted, beaten, bound?
f 'Tis our God, Who gifts and graces
  On His Church now poureth
    down;
Who shall smite in holy vengeance
  All His foes beneath His throne.

p Who is this that hangeth dying,
  While the rude world scoffs and
    scorns,
Numbered with the malefactors,
  Torn with nails and crowned
    with thorns?
f 'Tis the God Who ever liveth
  'Mid the shining ones on high,
In the glorious golden city
  Reigning everlastingly.

W. W. How.

106 L.M.

mf O WHO like Thee, so calm, so bright,
  Thou Son of man, Thou Light of
    light!
O who like Thee did ever go
So patient through a world of woe!

mp O who like Thee so humbly bore
  The scorn, the scoffs of men before;
So meek, forgiving, Godlike, high,
So glorious in humility!

[*p* And all Thy life's unchanging years,
  A man of sorrows and of tears,
The cross, where all our sins were
    laid, [weighed;
Upon Thy bending shoulders

pp And death that sets the prisoners
    free,
Was pang, and scoff, and scorn to
    Thee; [glowed,
cres Yet love through all Thy torture
  And mercy with Thy life-blood
    flowed.]

mf O wondrous Lord, our souls would
    be [Thee,
Still more and more conformed to
Would lose the pride, the taint of
    sin [within;
That burns these fevered veins

mp And learn of Thee, the lowly One,
  And like Thee, all our journey run,
Above the world, and all its mirth,
Yet weeping still with weeping
    earth.

f Oh in this light be mine to go,
  Illuming all my way of woe;
And give us ever on the road
To trace Thy footsteps, O my G

A. C. Cox

107　　　　　　L.M.

mf THOU Son of God and Son of man,
　Beloved, adored Immanuel ;
　Who didst, before all time began,
　In glory with Thy Father dwell ;—

f We sing Thy love, Who didst in
　　time,
　For us humanity assume ;
dim To answer for the sinner's crime,
p To suffer in the sinner's room.

f The ransomed Church Thy glory
　　sings ;　　　　　[obey ;
　The hosts of Heaven Thy will
　And, Lord of lords and King of
　　kings,
　We celebrate Thy blessèd sway.

p A servant's form didst Thou
　　sustain ;
　And with delight the law obey ;
dim And then endure amazing pain,
　Whilst all our sorrows on Thee lay.

mf Blest Saviour ! we are wholly
　　Thine ;
　So freely loved, so dearly bought :
　Our souls to Thee would we
　　resign,—
　To Thee would subject every
　　thought.
　　　　　　　J. Ryland.

108　　　　　　C.M.

p O ! MEAN may seem this house of
　　clay,
　Yet 'twas the Lord's abode ;
　Our feet may mourn this thorny
　　way,
cres Yet here Immanuel trod.

　This fleshly robe the Lord did
　　wear;
　This watch the Lord did keep ;

dim These burdens sore the Lord did
　　bear.
p　These tears the Lord did weep.

cres Our very frailty brings us near
　　Unto the Lord of Heaven ;
　To every grief, to every tear
　　Such glory strange is given.

　But not this fleshly robe alone
　　Shall link us, Lord, to Thee ;
　Not only in the tear and groan
　　Shall the dear kindred be ;—

f We shall be reckoned for Thine own
　　Because Thy heaven we share,
　Because we sing around Thy throne,
　　And Thy bright raiment wear.

ff O mighty grace, our life to live,
　　To make our earth divine !
　O mighty grace, Thy heaven to give,
　　And lift our life to Thine.
　　　　　　　T. H. Gill.

109　　　　　　L.M.

mf STRONG Son of God, immortal
　　Love,　　　　　[face.
　Whom we, that have not seen Thy
　　By faith, and faith alone, embrace,
　Believing where we cannot prove ;

p Thou wilt not leave us in the dust :
　Thou madest man, he knows not
　　why :
　He thinks he was not made to die :
　And Thou hast made him : Thou
　　art just.

[*mf* Thou seemest human and divine,
　The highest, holiest manhood,
　　Thou :
　Our wills are ours, we know not
　　how :
　Our wills are ours, to make them
　　Thine.

p Our little systems have their day :
  They have their day and cease to be:
  They are but broken lights of Thee,
cres And Thou, O Lord, art more than
  they.]
mf We have but faith : we cannot
  know :
  For knowledge is of things we see.
cres And yet we trust it comes from
  Thee :
  A beam in darkness . let it grow.

mf Let knowledge grow from more to
  more,
dim But more of reverence in us dwell :
cres That mind and soul, according well,
  May make one music as before,
f But vaster. (*dim*) We are fools and
  slight,
  We mock Thee when we do not fear.
  But help Thy foolish ones to bear ;
  Help Thy vain world to bear Thy
  light.   *A. Tennyson.*

7.—*HIS EXAMPLE.*

110   C.M.

p LORD. as to Thy dear cross we flee,
  And plead to be forgiven.
  So let Thy life our pattern be,
cres And form our souls for Heaven.

p Help us. through good report and ill,
  Our daily cross to bear,
  Like Thee. to do our Father's will,
  Our brethren's griefs to share.

[*mf* Let grace our selfishness expel,
  Our earthliness refine,
  And kindness in our bosoms dwell,
  As free and true as Thine.

If joy shall at Thy bidding fly,
  And grief's dark day come on,
  We. in our turn, would meekly cry,
  Father ! Thy will be done !]

Should friends misjudge, or foes
  defame,
  Or brethren faithless prove,
  Then like Thine own, be all our aim
  To conquer them by love.

Kept peaceful in the midst of strife,
  Forgiving and forgiven,
cres O may we lead the pilgrim's life,
f   And follow Thee to Heaven !
          J. H. Gurney.

111   C.M.

mf WHAT grace, O Lord, and beauty
  shone
  Around Thy steps below ;
  What patient love was seen in all
  Thy life and death of woe.

p For, ever on Thy burdened heart
  A weight of sorrows hung ;
  Yet no ungentle murmuring word
  Escaped Thy silent tongue.

Thy foes might hate. despise, revile.
  Thy friends unfaithful prove ,
  Unwearied in forgiveness still,
  Thy heart could only love.

mf O give us hearts to love like Thee,
  Like Thee, O Lord. to grieve,
dim Far more for others' sins, than all
  The wrongs that we receive.

One with Thyself, may every eye,
  In us, Thy brethren, see
  The gentleness and grace that
  spring
  From union, Lord, with Thee.
          E. Denny

112   L.M.

mf How shall I follow Him I serve?
How shall I copy Him I love?
Nor from those blessèd footsteps
   swerve,
Which lead me to His seat above!

p Privations, sorrows, bitter scorn,
The life of toil, the mean abode,
The faithless kiss, the crown of
   thorn,—
Are these the consecrated road?

[*mf* 'Twas thus He suffered, though a
   Son,
Foreknowing, choosing, feeling all;
cres Until the perfect work was done,
dim And drunk, the bitter cup of gall.]

p Lord, should my path through
   suffering lie,
Forbid it I should e'er repine ;
Still let me turn to Calvary,
dim Nor heed my griefs, remembering
   Thine.

O let me think how Thou didst leave
Untasted every pure delight,
To fast, to faint, to watch, to grieve,
The toilsome day, the homeless
   night :—

p To faint, to grieve, to die for me!
Thou camest not Thyself to please :
cres And, dear as earthly comforts be,
Shall I not love Thee more than
   these ?

mf Yes! I would count them all but
   loss,
To gain the notice of Thine eye :
p Flesh shrinks and trembles at the
   cross,
f But Thou canst give the victory.
            J. Conder.

113

mf TEACH me, O Lord, Thy
And give me an obedien
That in Thy service I m
My soul's delight from ·

Guide me, O Saviour,
   hand,
And so control my tho
   deeds,
That I may tread the ɩ
   leads
cres Right onward to the bl·

p Help me, O Saviour, her
The sacred footsteps Thoɩ
And meekly walking wiɩ
To grow in goodness,
   grace.

mf Guard me, O Lord, that I
Forsake the right, or do t
cres Against temptation
   strong,
And round me spread Tl
   ing care.

f Bless me in every task, (
Begun, continued, done
Fulfil Thy perfect work
And Thine abounding gɩ
            W. T.

114   6.6.1

p THOU Who didst stooɩ
To drain the cup of ʍ
Wearing the form
   mortality ;
Thy blessèd labours dɩ
cres Thy crown of victory
Hast passed from earth·
Thy home on high,

p It was no path of flowers,
    Through this dark world of ours.
    Belovèd of the Father, Thou didst
      tread ;
    And shall we in dismay
    Shrink from the narrow way,
    When clouds and darkness are
      around it spread ?

f O Thou, Who art our life,
    Be with us through the strife ;
*dim*Thy holy head by earth's fierce
    storms was bowed.
    Raise Thou our eyes above,
    To see a Father's love,
    Beam like the bow of promise
      through the cloud.

p E'en through the awful gloom
    Which hovers o'er the tomb,
*cres*That light of love our guiding
    star shall be ;
    Our spirits shall not dread
    The shadowy path to tread,
    Friend, Guardian, Saviour, which
      doth lead to Thee.
          Sarah E. Miles.

115   L.M.

mf MY dear Redeemer and my Lord,
    I read my duty in Thy word ;
*cres*But in Thy life the law appears
    Drawn out in living characters.

mf Such was Thy truth, and such Thy
    zeal,
    Such deference to Thy Father's will
    Such love, and meekness so divine,
    I would transcribe and make them
    mine.

p Cold mountains and the midnight
    air   [prayer ;
    Witnessed the fervour of Thy
    The desert Thy temptations knew,
*cres*Thy conflict and Thy victory too.

mf Be Thou my pattern ; make me
    bear
    More of Thy gracious image here ;
*cres*Then God, the Judge, shall own
    my name
    Amongst the followers of the
    Lamb.
          I. Watts.

8.—HIS MIRACLES.

116   C.M.

f JESU, if still Thou art to-day
    As yesterday the same,
    Present to heal, in me display
    The virtue of Thy Name.

    Now, Lord, to Whom for help I call,
    Thy miracles repeat ;
p With pitying eyes, behold me fall
    A leper at Thy feet.

    Thou seest me deaf to Thy com-
      mand,—
    Open, O Lord, *my ear ;*

*cres*Bid me stretch out my withered
    hand,
    And lift it up in prayer.

p Silent (alas ! Thou know'st how
    long),
    My voice I cannot raise ; [tongue,
*cres*But O ! when Thou shalt loose my
f The dumb shall sing Thy praise.

[*p* Blind from my birth to guilt and
    Thee,
    And dark I am within ;
    The love of God I cannot see,
    The sinfulness of sin.

cres But Thou, they say, art passing by ;
O let me find Thee near !
Jesu. in mercy hear my cry,
Thou Son of David, hear !]

Behold me waiting in the way
For Thee, the heavenly light ;
cres Command me to be brought, and say,
f   "Sinner, receive thy sight !"

C. Wesley.

117   C.M., double.

mf O WHERE is He that trod the sea ?
Oh, where is He that spake,—
And demons from their victims flee,
The dead their slumbers break ;
The palsied rise in freedom strong,
The dumb men talk and sing,
dim And from blind eyes, benighted long,
cres Bright beams of morning spring.

mf O where is He that trod the sea ?
Oh, where is He that spake.—
And piercing words of liberty,
The deaf ears open shake ;
dim And mildest words arrest the haste
Of fever's deadly fire,
cres And strong ones heal the weak who waste
Their life in sad desire.

mf O where is He that trod the sea ?
'Tis only He can save ;
To thousands hungering wearily,
A wondrous meal He gave :
f Full soon, celestially fed,
Their rustic fare they take ;
dim 'Twas springtide when He blest the bread,
f   And harvest when He brake.

p O where is He that trod the sea ?
cres *My soul ! the Lord is here :*

f Let all thy fears be hushed in thee ;
To leap, to look, to hear
Be thine : thy needs He'll satisfy :
Art thou diseased or dumb ?
Or dost thou in thine hunger cry !
"I come," saith Christ, " I come.'

T. T. Lynch.

118   8.8.8.3.

mf FIERCE raged the tempest o'er the deep,   [keep :
Watch did Thine anxious servants
p But Thou wast wrapped in guileless sleep.
pp   Calm and still.

mf "Save, Lord, we perish," was their cry,
cres "O save us in our agony ;"
f Thy word above the storm rose high,
pp   " Peace, be still."

mf The wild winds hushed ; the angry deep
dim Sank, like a little child, to sleep ;
p The sullen billows ceased to leap,
f   At Thy will.

mf So, when our life is clouded o'er,
cres And storm winds drift us from the shore.
Say, lest we sink to rise no more
pp   " Peace, be still."

G. Thring.

119   C.M.

p HEAL us, Immanuel ! hear our prayer ;
We wait to feel Thy touch ;
Deep-wounded souls to Thee repair,
And, Saviour, we are such.

Our faith is feeble, we confess ;
We faintly trust Thy word ;

But wilt Thou pity us the less ?
res Be that far from Thee, Lord.

Remember him who once applied
 With trembling for relief :—
" Lord, I believe," with tears He
 cried,—
 " O help my unbelief ! "

nf She, too, who touched Thee in the
 press,
 And healing virtue stole, [peace,
dim Was answered,—" Daughter, go in
res Thy faith hath made thee
 whole."

Concealed amid the gathering
 throng,
 She would have shunned Thy
  view ;
mf And if her faith was firm and
 strong,
dim Had strong misgivings too.

Like her, with hopes and fears we
 come,
 To touch Thee, if we may :
cres Oh ! send us not despairing home :
p Send none unhealed away.

   W. Cowper, v. 1, l. 1 altd.

9.—*HIS LOVE, TENDERNESS, AND SYMPATHY.*

120   6.6.6.6.4.4.4.4.

f MY song is love unknown ;
 My Saviour's love to me ;
dim Love to the loveless shown,
 That they might lovely be.
  Oh, who am I,
  That for my sake
  My Lord should take
  Frail flesh, and die ?

mf He came from His blessed throne
 Salvation to bestow :
 But men made strange. and none
 The longed-for Christ would know,
  But oh ! my Friend ;
  My Friend indeed,
  Who at my need
  His life did spend.

f Sometimes they strew His way,
 And His sweet praises sing ;
 Resounding all the day,
 Hosannas to their King.
dim Then " Crucify ! "
  Is all their breath,
p And for His death
  They thirst and cry.]

[*mp* Why, what hath my Lord done ?
 What makes this rage and spite ?
cres He made the lame to run,
 He gave the blind their sight.
  Sweet injuries !
  Yet they at these
  Themselves displease,
  And 'gainst Him rise.

They rise and needs will have
 My dear Lord made away ;
 A murderer they save,
 The Prince of life they slay.
  Yet cheerful He
  To suff'ring goes,
  That He His foes
  From thence might free.]

p In life, no house, no home
 My Lord on earth might have :
 In death, no friendly tomb,
 But what a stranger gave.
  What may I say ?
  Heav'n was His home ;
  But mine the tomb
  Wherein He lay.

mf Here might I stay and sing,
  No story so divine ;
f Never was love, dear King !
dim Never was grief like Thine.
f   This is my Friend,
    In Whose sweet praise
    I all my days
    Could gladly spend.
              S. Crossman.

121   8.8.6.8.8.6.

mf O LOVE divine, how sweet Thou art!
  When shall I find my willing heart
  All taken up by Thee ?
cres I thirst, I faint, I die to prove
  The greatness of redeeming love,
  The love of Christ to me !

  Stronger His love than death or
    hell ;
  Its riches are unsearchable :
  The firstborn sons of light
  Desire in vain its depths to see ;
dim They cannot reach the mystery,
  The length and breadth and
    height.
p God only knows the love of God :
  O that it now were shed abroad
  In this poor stony heart !
cres For love I sigh, for love I pine ;
  This only portion, Lord, be mine,
  Be mine this better part.
              C. Wesley.

122   8.7.8.7., double.

f LOVE divine all loves excelling,
  Joy of heaven, to earth come
    down ;
  Fix in us Thy humble dwelling ;
  All Thy faithful mercies crown.
  Jesus, Thou art all compassion ;
  Pure, unbounded love Thou art .
cres *Visit us with Thy salvation ;*
  Enter every longing heart.

mf Come, almighty to deliver,
  Let us all Thy grace receive ;
  Suddenly return, and never,
  Never more Thy temples leave.
f Thee we would be always blessing,
  Serve Thee as Thy hosts above;
  Pray, and praise Thee without
    ceasing ;
  Glory in Thy precious love.

cres Finish, then, Thy new creation ;
  Pure, unspotted may we be :
  Let us see Thy great salvation
  Perfectly restored in Thee :
ff Changed from glory into glory,
  Till in heaven we take our place;
  Till we cast our crowns before Thee,
  Lost in wonder, love, and praise.
              C. Wesley.

123   88.88.88.

mf JESU ! Thy boundless love to me
  No thought can reach, no tongue
    declare ;
  O knit my thankful heart to Thee,
  And reign without a rival there :
cres Thine wholly, Thine alone, I am ;
  Lord, with Thy love my heart
    inflame.

mf O grant that nothing in my soul
  May dwell, but Thy pure love alone:
  O may Thy love possess me whole,
  My joy, my treasure, and my crown:
f All coldness from my heart remove ;
  My every act, word, thought, be
    love !

mf O Love ! how cheering is thy ray !
  All pain before thy presence flies ;
p Care, anguish, sorrow, melt away,
cres Where'er thy healing beams arise :
f O Jesu ! nothing may I see,
  Nothing desire, or seek, but Thee !

[Still let Thy love point out my
   way !
How wondrous things Thy love
   hath wrought !
Still lead me, lest I go astray ;
Direct my word, inspire my
   thought ;
And if I fall, soon may I hear
Thy voice, and know that love is
   near.]

p In suffering be Thy love my peace ;
cres In weakness be Thy love my power;
p And when the storms of life shall
   cease,
pp O Jesu, in that solemn hour,
In death, as life, be Thou my guide,
And save me, Who for me hast
   died.

   P. Gerhardt, tr. J. Wesley, v. 2,
   l. 5, v. 5, l. 4 altd.

124   88.88.88.

mf THOU hidden Source of calm repose;
Thou all-sufficient Love divine ;
My help and refuge from my foes,
Secure I am, if Thou art mine :
And lo ! from sin, and grief, and
   shame
dim I hide me, Jesus, in Thy Name.

f Thy mighty Name salvation is,
And keeps my happy soul above ;
Comfort it brings, and power, and
   peace,
And joy and everlasting love :
To me, with Thy dear Name, are
   given
Pardon and holiness and heaven.

mp Jesus, my all in all Thou art,
My rest in toil, mine ease in pain ;
p The medicine of my broken heart ;
In war, *my peace ; in loss, my gain;*

cres My smile beneath the tyrant's
   frown ;
In shame, my glory and my crown :
f In want, my plentiful supply ;
In weakness, mine almighty power;
In bonds, my perfect liberty ;
My light in Satan's darkest hour ;
cres In grief, my joy unspeakable ;
ff My life in death ; my heaven in
   hell.   *C. Wesley.*

125   C.M.

mp THERE'S not a grief, however light,
Too light for sympathy !
There's not a care, however slight,
Too slight to bring to Thee !

Thou Who hast trod the thorny road
Wilt share each small distress ;
For He Who bore the greater load
Will not refuse the less.

There's not a secret sigh we breathe,
But meets the ear Divine ;
And every cross grows light beneath
The shadow, Lord, of Thine.

Life's woes without,—sin's strife
   within,
The heart would overflow ;[sin,—
cres But for that love which died for
That love which wept with woe.

All human sympathy but cheers,
   When it is learned from Thee,
Alas for grief !—but for those tears
Which fell at Bethany !

   Jane Crewdson.

126   C.M.

   PART I.

mf JESUS, the very thought of Thee
With sweetness fills my breast ;
cres But sweeter far Thy face to see,
p   And in Thy presence rest.

f Nor voice can sing, nor heart can
frame,
Nor can the memory find,
A sweeter sound than Thy blest
Name,
O Saviour of mankind !

p O hope of every contrite heart !
O joy of all the meek !   [art !
To those who fall, how kind Thou
cres How good to those who seek.

f But what to those who find ? Ah,
this
Nor tongue nor pen can show :
The love of Jesus, what it is
None but His loved ones know.

mf O Jesus, Light of all below !
Thou Fount of life and fire !
Surpassing all the joys we know,
And all we can desire !

f Jesus, my only joy be Thou
As Thou my prize wilt be ;
Jesus, be Thou my glory now,
And through Eternity.
Bernard of Clairvaux, tr. E. Caswall.

PART II.   C.M.

f O JESUS, King most wonderful !
Thou conqueror renowned !
p Thou sweetness most ineffable !
In Whom all joys are found !

mf When once Thou visitest the heart,
Then truth begins to shine ;
Then earthly vanities depart ;
Then wakens love divine.

f Jesus ! Thy mercies are untold,
Through each returning day ;
Thy love exceeds a thousandfold
Whatever we can say.

mf May every heart confess Thy Name,
And ever Thee adore ;

cres And seeking Thee, itself i
To seek Thee more and

f Thee may our tongues
bless ;
Thee may we love alone
cres And ever in our lives exp
The image of Thine ow

p Grant me, while here on
stay,
Thy love to feel and kn
cres And when from hence I p
To me Thy glory show.
Bernard of Clairvaux, tr. E.

127   10.1

mf AND didst Thou love the
loved not Thee,
And didst Thou take to I
human brow ?
Dost plead with man's
the marvellous sea ?
Art Thou his kinsma

O God, O kinsman loved,
enough !
O Man, with eyes majest
Whose feet have toiled a
pathways rough,
Whose lips drawn

By that one likeness whic
and Thine,
By that one nature which c
By th at high heaven where
Thou dost shine,
To draw us sinners in

p By Thy last silence in the ju
hall,   [dea
By long foreknowledge
By darkness, by the wc
and the gall,
I pray Thee visit me.

mf Come, lest. this heart should, cold
   and cast away,   [tain—
dim Die ere the great adored she enter-
p Lest eyes which never saw Thine
   earthly day   [reign.
   Should miss Thy heavenly
             Jean Ingelow.

128
          L.M., with refrain.

mf JESU, my Lord, my God. my all,
   Hear me, blest Saviour, when I call ;
   Hear me, and from Thy dwelling-
     place
   Pour down the riches of Thy grace :
cres   Jesu, my Lord, I Thee adore ;
f   Oh, make me love Thee more
     and more.

p Jesu, too late I Thee have sought ;
cres How can I love Thee as I ought ?
   And how extol Thy matchless fame,
   The glorious beauty of Thy Name ?
f   Jesu, my Lord, I Thee adore ;
     Oh, make me love Thee more
     and more.

p Jesu, what didst Thou find in me
   That Thou hast dealt so lovingly ?
cres How great the joy that Thou hast
     brought,
   So far exceeding hope or thought ;
f   Jesu, my Lord, I Thee adore ;
     O make me love Thee more
     and more.

f Jesu, of Thee shall be my song ;
   To Thee my heart and soul belong ;
   All that I have or am is Thine,
   And Thou, blest Saviour, Thou art
     mine :
ff   Jesu, my Lord, I Thee adore ;
     Oh, make me love Thee more
     and more.
             H. Collins.

129
               C.M.

f O MYSTERY of Love Divine,
   That thought and thanks o'er-
     powers !
   Lord Jesus ! was our portion Thine,
    And is Thy portion ours ?
p Emmanuel ! didst Thou take our
     place
   To set us in Thine own ?
cres Didst Thou our low estate embrace
   To lift us to Thy throne ?
p Didst Thou fulfil each righteous
     deed,
   God's perfect will express,
f That we, the unfaithful ones,
     might plead
   Thy perfect faithfulness ?
p On Thy pure soul did dread and
     gloom
   In that drear garden rise ? [bloom
f Are ours the brightness and the
   Of Thine own Paradise ?
p For Thee the Father's hidden face ?
   For Thee the bitter cry ?
f For us the Father's endless grace,
   The song of victory ?
p Our load of sin and misery
   Didst Thou, the Sinless, bear ?
f Thy spotless robe of purity
   Do we, the sinners, wear ?
mf Lord Jesus ! is it even so ?
   Have we been lovèd thus ?
   What love can we on Thee bestow
   Who hast exchanged with us ?
f Thou, Who our very place didst
     take,
   Dwell in our very heart ! [make,
   Thou, Who Thy portion ours dost
   Thyself—Thyself impart.
             T. H. Gill.

130
7s.

f Now begin the heavenly theme :
Sing aloud in Jesus' Name ;
Ye who Jesus' kindness prove,
Triumph in redeeming love.

Ye, who see the Father's grace
Beaming in the Saviour's face,
As to Canaan on ye move,
Praise and bless redeeming love.

p Mourning souls, dry up your
tears ;
*cres*Banish all your guilty fears ;
f See your guilt and curse remove,
Cancelled by redeeming love.

p Ye, alas ! who long have been
Willing slaves of death and sin,
*cres*Now from bliss no longer rove ;
Stop and taste redeeming love.

f Welcome, all by sin oppressed :
Welcome to His sacred rest :
Nothing brought Him from above,
Nothing but redeeming love.

ff Hither, then, your music bring ;
Strike aloud each joyful string :
Mortals, join the hosts above,
Join to praise redeeming love.
— *Langford.*

131
L.M.

f Awake, my soul, in joyful lays,
And sing thy great Redeemer's
praise ;
He justly claims a song from me,
His loving-kindness is so free !

mp He saw me ruined in the fall,
Yet loved me, notwithstanding
all ;
*cres*He saved me from my lost estate :
His loving-kindness is so great !

p Often I feel my sinful l
Prone from my Jesus t
And though I oft have l
f His loving-kindness cha

p So when I pass deatl
vale,
And all the powers of r
O may my last expiring
*cres*His loving-kindness sin

f Then shall I mount
away
To the bright world of e
Then shall I sing with
prise
His loving-kindness in 1

f Then with the golden ha
And with their anthe
mine ;
And loudly sound, on e
The loving-kindness of
S.

132

mf My blessèd Saviour, is T
So great, so fr'll, so fr
Behold, I give my love,
My life, my all to The

f I love Thee for that glori
In Thy great self I se
p I love Thee for that
cross
Thou hast endured for

mf No man of greater love c
Than for His friend to
But for Thy foes, Lord, 1
slain :
cres What love with Thine

J. Stennett, v. 3, l.

10.—*HIS TRANSFIGURATION.*

133   L.M., double.

mf O MASTER, it is good to be ‚[Thee,
High on the mountain here with
Here, in an ampler, purer air,
Above the stir of toil and care ;
dim Of hearts distract with doubt and
grief,
Believing in their unbelief,
p Calling Thy servants all in vain
To ease them of their bitter pain.

mf O Master, it is good to be   [three
With Thee and with Thy faithful
Here, where the Apostle's heart of
rock   [shock ;
Is nerved against temptation's
Here, where the Son of Thunder
learns   [word that burns ;
The thought that breathes, and
Here, where on eagles' wings we
move   [is Love.
With Him Whose last best creed

f O Master, it is good to be   [Thee ;
Entranced, enwrapt alone with
And watch Thy glistering raiment
glow   [snow ;
Whiter than Hermon's whitest
The human lineaments that shine
Irradiant with a light divine,
Till we too change from grace to
grace,
Gazing on that transfigured face.

mf O Master, it is good to be   [Thee ;
Here on the Holy Mount with
When darkling in the depths of
night,
When dazzled with excess of light,
dim We bow before the Heavenly Voice
That bids bewildered souls rejoice,
p Though love wax cold and faith
be dim,   [Him!"
cres "This is My Son! oh, hear ye
        A. P. Stanley.

11.—*HIS ENTRY INTO JERUSALEM.*

134   L.M.

f RIDE on! ride on in majesty !
Hark ! all the tribes Hosanna cry.
mp O Saviour meek, pursue Thy road
With palms and scattered garments
strewed.

f Ride on! ride on in majesty !
p In lowly pomp ride on to die !
cres O Christ ! Thy triumphs now begin
O'er captive Death and conquered
Sin.

f Ride on! ride on in majesty !
dim The wingèd squadrons of the sky
Look down with sad and wondering eyes
p To see the approaching Sacrifice.

f Ride on! ride on in majesty !
mf Thy last and fiercest strife is nigh ;
The Father on His sapphire throne
Expects His own anointed Son.

f Ride on! ride on in majesty !
p In lowly pomp ride on to die !
pp Bow Thy meek Head to mortal
pain !   [reign !
ff Then take, O God ! Thy power, and
        H. H. Milman, v. 1, l. 3 altd.

135   7.6.7.6., with chorus.

f ALL glory, laud, and honour,
To Thee, Redeemer, King \
To Whom the lips of children
Made sweet hosannas ring.

Thou art the King of Israel,
Thou David's royal Son,
Who in the Lord's Name comest,
The King and Blessèd One.
    All glory, etc.

ff The company of angels
Are praising Thee on high,
And mortal men, and all things
Created, make reply,
    All glory, etc.

f The people of the Hebrews
With palms before Thee went;
Our praise and prayer and anthems
Before Thee we present.
    All glory, etc.

mf To Thee before Thy Passion
They sang their hymns of prais
To Thee, now high exalted,
Our melody we raise,
    All glory, etc.

*cres*Thou didst accept their praises;
Accept the prayers we bring,
Who in all good delightest,
Thou good and gracious King.

All glory, laud, and honour,
To Thee, Redeemer, King
To Whom the lips of childre
Made sweet hosannas ring
Theodulph of Orleans, tr. J. M.
Neale, altd.

12.—*HIS AGONY IN GETHSEMANE.*

136   8.6.8.6.8.8.

p HE knelt. the Saviour knelt, and
    prayed,
When but His Father's eye[shade,
Looked through the lonely garden's
    On that dread agony:
The Lord of all, above, beneath,
Was bowed with sorrow unto death.

The sun set in a fearful hour:
The stars might well grow dim,
When this mortality had power
So to o'ershadow him!
That He, Who gave man's breath
    might know
The very depths of human woe.

He knew them all—the doubt, the
    strife,
The faint, perplexing dread;
The mists that hang o'er parting
    life
All gathered round His head:
And the Deliverer knelt to pray,
Yet passed it not, that cup, away.

It passed not, though the storm
    wave
Had sunk beneath His tread;
It passed not, though to Him the
    grave
Had yielded up its dead: [high
*cres*But there was sent Him from or
f A gift of strength for man to die.

mf And was His mortal hour beset
With anguish and dismay?
How may we meet our conflict yet
In the dark narrow way?
How but through Him, that path
    Who trod?
*cres*Save, or we perish, Son of God!
    Felicia D. Hemans.

137   L.M.

p A VOICE upon the midnight air,
Where Kedron's moonlit waters
    stray,
Weeps forth in agony of prayer,
"O Father\ take this cup away."

Ah! Thou Who sorrowest unto
   death,
*cres*We con_{quer} in Thy mortal fra ;
And ear_{th to} r all her children saith,
  O God ! take not this cup away.

p O Lord of sorrow ! meekly die :
  Thou'lt heal or hallow all our woe;
Thy Name refresh the mourner's
   sigh,
  Thy peace revive the faint and low.

mf Great Chief of faithful souls, arise ;
  None else can lead the martyr-band,

Who teach the brave how peril flies,
  When faith, unarmed, uplifts the
   hand.

f O King of Earth ! the Cross ascend;
  O'er climes and ages 'tis Thy throne ;
Where'er Thy fading eye may bend,
  The desert blooms, and is Thine own.

mf Thy parting blessing, Lord, we pray;
  Make but one fold below, above ;
dim And when we go the last lone way,
cres O give the welcome of Thy love.
    J. Martineau's Selection, 1840.

13.—*HIS PASSION AND DEATH.*

138   7.6.7.6., double.

mp O SACRED Head ! now wounded,
  With grief and shame weighed
   down ;
dim Now scornfully surrounded
  With thorns, Thy only crown ;
f O sacred Head ! what glory,
  What bliss till now was Thine !
I read the wondrous story,
cres I joy to call Thee mine.

f O noblest brow, and dearest ! ·
  In other days, the world
All feared when Thou appearedst ;
  What shame on Thee is hurled !
p How art Thou pale with anguish,
  With sore abuse and scorn ;
How does that visage languish
  Which once was bright as morn !

mf What Thou, my Lord, hast suffered
  Was all for sinners' gain ;
p Mine, mine was the transgression,
  But Thine the deadly pain.
Lo ! here I fall, my Saviour !
  'Tis I deserve Thy place ;
Look on me with Thy favour,
  Vouchsafe to me Thy grace.

mf What language shall I borrow
  To thank Thee, dearest Friend,
For this, Thy dying sorrow,
  Thy pity without end !
cres O make me Thine for ever !
  And should I fainting be,
Lord, let me never, never
  Outlive my love to Thee.

p Be near when I am dying.
  O show Thy cross to me !
cres And for my succour flying,
  Come, Lord, to set me free.
These eyes, new faith receiving,
  From Jesus shall not move,
p For he who dies believing,
  Dies safely through Thy love.
  Paul Gerhardt, tr. J. W. Alexander,
     v. 1, *l.* 7 altd.

139   L.M.

mf WHEN I survey the wondrous cross
  On which the Prince of glory died,
My richest gain I count but loss,
  And pour contempt on all my pride.

cres Forbid it, Lord, that I should boast
  Save in the death of Christ my God

All the vain things that charm me
    most,
I sacrifice them to His blood.

pp See from His head, His hands, His
    feet,   [down ;
Sorrow and love flow mingled
*cres*Did e'er such love and sorrow meet,
Or thorns compose so rich a crown ?

mf Were the whole realm of nature
    mine,
That were a present far too small ;
f Love so amazing, so divine.
Demands my soul, my life, my all !

I. Watts.

140   6.5.6.5.

mf GLORY be to Jesus,
    Who, in bitter pains,
    Poured for me the life-blood
    From His sacred veins !

Grace and life eternal
    In that blood I find,
    Blest be His compassion,
    Infinitely kind !

Blest through endless ages
    Be the precious stream,
    Which from endless torments
    Doth the world redeem !.

[Abel's blood for vengeance
    Pleaded to the skies ;
cres But the blood of Jesus
    For our pardon cries.]

p Oft as it is sprinkled
    On our guilty hearts,
mf Satan in confusion
    Terror-struck departs ;

Oft as earth exulting
cres Wafts its praise on high,
Angel hosts rejoicing
Make their glad reply.

f Lift ye, then, your voices ;
    Swell the mighty flood ;
cres Louder still and louder,
    Praise the precious blood.

Italian, tr. E. Caswall.

141   6.8.6.4.

mp Lo ! on the inglorious tree
    The Lord, the Lord of glory hangs;
p Forsaken now is He,
    And pierced with pangs.

A shameful death He dies,
*cres*Uplifted with transgressors twain;
    A Lamb for sacrifice,
p   By sinners slain.

Full is His cup of woe ;
    In death His drooping head
    declines ;
    'Tis done ! He cries ; and now
pp   His soul resigns.

mp O come, my soul, and gaze [thorn ;
    On that great grief, that crown of
cres In deep and dread amaze
p   There look and mourn.

For thee He shed His blood ;
    Weep, till with woe thine eyes
    grow dim ;
    To that accursèd wood
    Thou hast nailed Him.

mf To Thee, the mighty Lord,
f Who washed in blood our sins away
ff Our boundless gratitude
    Its thanks would pay.

Latin, 9th century, tr. W. J. Blew, ultd

142   L.M.

p O COME and mourn with m
    awhile :
    O come ye to the Saviour's side :
    O come, together let us mourn ;
pp Jesus, our Lord, is crucified.

mp Have we no tears to shed for Him,
　While soldiers scoff and Jews
　　deride?
　Ah! look how patiently He hangs;
pp Jesus, our Lord, is crucified.

mf Seven times He spoke, seven words
　of love; 　　　　　[cried
　And all three hours His silence
　For mercy on the souls of men:
pp Jesus, our Lord, is crucified.

[*cres*Oh break, oh break, hard heart
　of mine!
p Thy weak self-love and guilty pride
　His Pilate and His Judas were:
pp Jesus, our Lord, is crucified.]

　Come, let us stand beneath the
　　Cross;
　The fountain opened in His side
　Shall purge our deepest stains
　　away:
pp Jesus, our Lord, is crucified.

*cres*A broken heart, a fount of tears,—
　Ask, and they will not be denied;
　A broken heart love's offering is:
　Jesus, our Lord, is crucified.

f O love of God! O sin of man!
　In this dread act your strength is
　　tried;
f And victory remains with love;
*dim*For He, our Lord, is crucified.

*F. W. Faber, v. 1, ll. 2, 3; v. 5, ll. 2,
3; v. 6, l. 3, and last line of each
v. altd.*

143　　　　　　　　　S.M.

mf　NOT all the blood of beasts,
　On Jewish altars slain,
　Could give the guilty conscience
　　peace,
　Or wash away the stain:

cres But Christ. the heavenly Lamb,
　Takes all our sins away;
　A sacrifice of nobler name,
　And richer blood than they.

mp　My faith would lay her hand
　On that dear head of Thine,
　While like a penitent I stand,
　And there confess my sin.

　My soul looks back to see
　The burdens thou didst bear
　When hanging on th' accursèd tree,
　And hopes her guilt was there.

cres　Believing, we rejoice
　To see the curse remove;
f We bless the Lamb with cheerful
　　voice,
　And sing His bleeding love.
　　　　　　　　　　　I. Watts.

144　　　　　　　　8.7.8.7.

mf IN the cross of Christ I glory;
　Towering o'er the wrecks of
　　time,
　All the light of sacred story
　Gathers round its head sublime.

p When the woes of life o'ertake me,
　Hopes deceive, and fears annoy,
*cres*Never shall the cross forsake me:
　Lo! it glows with peace and joy

　When the sun of bliss is beaming
　Light and love upon my way:
　From the cross the radiance stream-
　　ing
　Adds more lustre to the day.

　Bane and blessing, pain and
　　pleasure,
　By the cross are sanctified;
p Peace is there, that knows no
　　measure,
cres Joys, that through all time abi

f In the cross of Christ I glory ;
　Towering o'er the wrecks of time,
All the light of sacred story
　Gathers round its head sublime.
J. Bowring.

145　　　　　7s., 6 lines.

mf THRONED upon the awful tree,
　King of grief, I watch with Thee :
*dim*Darkness veils Thine anguished
　　face,
None its lines of woe can trace,
None can tell what pangs unknown
pp Hold Thee silent and alone.

p Silent through those three dread
　　hours,
*cres*Wrestling with the evil powers,
*dim*Left alone with human sin,
　Gloom around Thee and within,
　Till the appointed time is nigh,
pp Till the Lamb of God may die.

mf Hark ! that cry that peals aloud
　Upward through the whelming
　　cloud !
*cres*Thou, the Father's only Son,
　Thou, His own Anointed One,
　Thou dost ask Him—"Can it be ?
*dim*Why hast Thou forsaken Me ? "

p Lord, should fear and anguish roll
　Darkly o'er my sinful soul,
　Thou, Who once was thus bereft
*cres*That Thine own might ne'er be
　　left—
　Teach me by that bitter cry
mf In the gloom to know Thee nigh.
J. Ellerton.

146　　　　　8.7.8.7.4.7.

f HARK! the voice of love and mercy
　Sounds aloud from Calvary ;

See, it rends the rocks asu
　Shakes the earth and
　　sky ;
p　　It is finished !
cres Hear the dying Saviou

mf It is finished !—O what p
　Do those gracious word
　Heavenly　　blessings
　　measure,
　Flow to us from Christ t
p　　It is finished !
cres Saints, the dying words

mf Finished, all the types and
　Of the ceremonial law
　Finished, all that G
　　promised ;
　Death and hell no more
p　　It is finished !
cres Saints, from hence your
　　draw.

f Tune your harps anew, ye
　Join to sing the glorio
*cres*All on earth, and all in h
　Join to praise Immanu
ff　　Hallelujah !
　Glory to the bleeding I
J.

147

mf NATURE with open volun
　To　spread　her　Maker'
　　abroad ;
　And every labour of His
　Shows something worthy

f But in the grace that resc
　His brightest form of glo
　He e, on the Cross,'tis fair
　In precious blood, and
　　lines.

O the sweet wonders of that cross,
*dim*Where Christ my Saviour loved
   and died !
*cres*Her noblest life my spirit draws
From His dear wounds and bleeding side.
f I would for ever speak His Name,
In sounds to mortal ears unknown ;
ff With angels join to praise the
   Lamb,
And worship at His Father's
   throne.
       I. Watts, v. 3, l. 2 altd.

148   5.5.11.5.5.11.

mf   ALL ye that pass by,
    To Jesus draw nigh :
To you is it nothing that Jesus
   should die?
    Your ransom and peace,
    Your surety He is :
*dim*Come, see if there ever was sorrow
   like His.

    He dies to atone
    For sins not His own ;
Your debt He hath paid, and your
   work He hath done.

Ye all may receive
The peace He did leave,
Who made intercession, "My
   Father, forgive ! "
For you and for me
He prayed on the tree : [free.
The prayer is accepted, the sinner is
   That sinner am I,
   Who on Jesus rely,
And come for the pardon God can-
   not deny.
cres My pardon I claim,
    For a sinner I am,
A sinner believing in Jesus' Name.
    He purchased the grace
    Which now I embrace :
O Father, Thou know'st He hath
   died in my place.
f His death is my plea;
    My Advocate see,
And hear the blood speak that hath
   answered for me.
    My ransom He was
    When He bled on the cross ;
And by losing his life He hath
   carried my cause.
            C. Wesley.

14.—HIS BURIAL AND DESCENT INTO HADES.

149   7s., 3 lines.

p WEEPING as they go their way,
Their dear Lord in earth to lay,
*cres*Late at even !—who are they?

These are they who watched to see
Where He hung in agony,
Dying on the accursèd tree.

f All is over—in the tomb
Sleeps He, 'mid its silent gloom,
Till the dawn of *Easter* come.

pp All is over—fought the fight ;
Heaviness is for a night,
Joy comes with the morning light.

*cres*Leave we in the grave with Him,
Sins that shame and doubts that dim
If our souls would rise with Him.

f Glory to the Lord Who gave
His pure Body to the grave,
Us from sin and death to save.
     W. S. Raymond, v. 3, l. 2 altd.
          G. Thring.

150   8.7.8.7.

p It is finished ! Blessèd Jesus,
  Thou hast breathed Thy latest
    sigh,
Teaching us, the sons of Adam.
  How the Son of God can die.

Lifeless lies the broken Body,
  Hidden in its rocky bed,
Laid aside like folded garment :
  Where is now the Spirit fled ?

cres In the gloomy realms of darkness
  Shines a light unknown before,
For the Lord of dead and living
  Enters at the open door.

See ! He comes, a willing Victim.
  Unresisting hither led ;

Passing from the C₁
  To the mansions (

f Lo ! the heavenly
    Him
As He draws His
All amazed they sta
  At the gracious w₁

For Himself proclai₁
  Of His own Incar
And the death He d
  Victor in that awf

p Jesus, Lord of dead
  Let Thy mercy res
Grant me, too, when
  Rest in Paradise w

             W. D

15.—HIS RESURRECTION.

151   7s.

f Christ the Lord is risen to-day,
Sons of men and angels say :
Raise your joys and triumphs high.
Sing, ye heavens, and earth reply.

Love's redeeming work is done,
Fought the fight, the battle won :
Lo ! our Sun's eclipse is o'er ;
Lo ! He sets in blood no more.

f Vain the stone, the watch, the seal ;
Christ hath burst the gates of hell !
Death in vain forbids His rise ;
Christ hath opened Paradise !

Lives again our glorious King :
Where, O Death, is now thy sting ?
p Once He died, our souls to save :
cres Where thy victory, O Grave ?

mf Soar we now where Christ has led,
Following our exalted Head ;

cres Made like Him, like
  Ours the cross, the g₁

ff Hail the Lord of
    Heaven !
Praise to Thee by bo₁
Thee we greet trium₁
Hail, the Resurrectio

152   1

f "Welcome, happy m
  to age shall say ;
Hell to-day is vanqui₁
  is won to-day ;
Lo ! the Dead is liv
  evermore !
Him, their true Cre
  works adore !

ff   "Welcome, happ
    age to age shal

[Earth with joy confesses, clothing
  her for Spring,
All good gifts returned with her
  returning King :
Bloom in every meadow, leaves on
  every bough,   [triumph now.
ff Speak His sorrows ended, hail His
    Hell to-day is vanquished ;
    Heaven is won to-day !

Months in due succession, days of
  lengthening light,
Hours and passing moments praise
  Thee in their flight ;
Brightness of the morning, sky and
  fields and sea,   [praise to Thee.
ff Vanquisher of darkness, bring their
    "Welcome, happy morning !"
    age to age shall say.]

Maker and Redeemer, Life and
  Health of all,
Thou from Heaven beholding
  human nature's fall,
Of the Father's Godhead true and
  only Son,   [put on.
ff Manhood to deliver, manhood didst
    Hell to-day is vanquished ;
    Heaven is won to-day !

p Thou, of Life the Author, death
    didst undergo,
Tread the path of darkness, saving
  strength to show ;
cres Come, then, True and Faithful,
    now fulfil Thy word ;
'Tis Thine own third morning !
  Rise, O buried Lord !
ff   "Welcome, happy morning !"
    age to age shall say.

f Loose the souls long prisoned,
    bound with Satan's chain ;
All that now is fallen raise to life
  again ;

Show Thy face in brightness, bid
  the nations see ;
Bring again our daylight : day
  returns with Thee !
ff   Hell to-day is vanquished !
    Heaven is won to-day !

V. Fortunatus, tr. J. Ellerton.

153   L.M.

f LIGHT'S glittering morn bedecks
    the sky ;   [cry ;
Heaven thunders forth its victor-
The glad earth shouts her triumph
  high,   [reply ;
And groaning hell makes wild

While He, the King, the mighty
  King,
Despoiling death of all its sting,
And trampling down the powers
  of night,
Brings forth His ransomed saints
  to light.

[mf His tomb of late the threefold
    guard
Of watch and stone and seal had
  barred ;
cres But now, in pomp and triumph
    high,
He comes from death to victory.]

The pains of hell are loosed at last :
The days of mourning now are past;
An angel robed in light hath said,
ff "The Lord is risen from the dead."

p Jesu, the King of Gentleness,
Do Thou Thyself our hearts possess,
cres That we may give Thee all our days
The tribute of our grateful praise.

mf O Lord of all, with us abide
  In this our joyful Easter-tide ;

From every weapon death can wield
Thine own redeemed for ever shield.

ff All praise be Thine, O risen Lord,
From death to endless life restored ;
All praise to God the Father be
And Holy Ghost eternally.

Latin, 6th century, tr. J. M. Neale,
altd.

154   7.8.7.8.7.7.

f   JESUS lives ! no longer now
Can thy terrors, Death, appal me ;
Jesus lives ! by this I know
From the grave He will recall me ;
Brighter scenes at death com-
mence ;
This shall be my confidence.

mf   Jesus lives ! to Him the Throne
High o'er heaven and earth is given;
I may go where He is gone,
Live and reign with Him in heaven:
God through Christ forgives
offence ;
cres   This shall be my confidence.

mp   Jesus lives ! for me He died ;
cres Hence will I, to Jesus living,
Pure in heart and act abide,
Praise to Him and glory giving :
Freely God doth aid dispense ;
This shall be my confidence.

f   Jesus lives ! my heart knows well
Nought from me His love shall
sever ;
Life, nor Death, nor powers of
hell,
Part me now from Christ for ever :
God will be a sure Defence ;
This shall be my confidence.

f   *Jesus lives ! henceforth is death*
Entrance-gate of life immortal ;

` This shall calm my tr
breath,
p When I pass its gloomy p(
Faith shall cry, as fails ea
Lord, Thou art my confi

C. F. Gellert, tr. F. 1

155   7.6.7.6., (

f THE Day of Resurrection
Earth, tell it out abroad
The Passover of gladness,
The Passover of God :
From Death to Life Etern
From earth unto the sk
ff Our Christ hath brought `
With hymns of victory.

mf Our hearts be pure from (
That we may see aright
The Lord in rays eternal
Of Resurrection-Light ;
cres And, listening to His acc
May hear, so calm and
His own "All hail !" and
May raise the victor st1

f Now let the heavens be j(
Let earth her song begi
Let the round world keep
And all that is therein :
Invisible and visible,
Their notes let all thin(
ff For Christ the Lord is ris
Our joy that hath no e

J. Damascenus, tr. J. M.

156

f CHRIST the Lord is risen
Christ hath broken every
Hark, the angels shout f(
Singing evermore on hig`
Hallelujah.

ho gave for us His life,
:or us endured the strife,
· Paschal Lamb to-day !
o sing for joy and say :
    Hallelujah.

ho bore all pain and loss
)rtless upon the cross,
in glory now on high,
; for us and hears our cry :
    Hallelujah.

hose path no records tell,
lescended into hell,
the strong man armed hath
nd,
in highest heaven is crowned:
    Hallelujah.

ho slumbered in the grave,
lted now to save ;
hrough Christendom it rings
the Lamb is King of kings !
    Hallelujah.

our Paschal Lamb indeed,
, to-day Thy people feed ;
)ur sins and guilt away,
we all may sing for aye,
    Hallelujah.
    Weisse, tr. C. Winkworth.

L.M.
'or a tune of lofty praise
·at Jehovah's equal Son !
:, my voice, in heavenly lays,
oud the wonders He hath
:.

how He left the worlds of
t,   [a ove ;
the bright robes He bwore
swift and joyful was His
it,
igs of everlasting love.

p Deep in the shades of gloomy death
  The almighty Captive prisoner lay ;
f The almighty Captive left the earth,
  And rose to everlasting day.

Lift up your eyes, ye sons of light.
Up to His throne of shining grace ;
See what immortal glories sit
Round the sweet beauties of His face.

ff Amongst a thousand harps and songs,
  Jesus, the God, exalted reigns ;
  His sacred Name fills all their tongues,
  And echoes through the heavenly plains.
      I. Watts.

158   6.6.6.6.4.4.4.4.

mf YES ! the Redeemer rose ;
  The Saviour left the dead,
  And o'er our hellish foes
  High raised His conquering head ;
    In wild dismay,
    The guards around
    Fell to the ground,
    And sank away.

p Lo ! the angelic bands
  In full assembly meet,
  To wait His high commands,
  And worship at His feet ;
    Joyful they come,
    And wing their way
    From realms of day
    To such a tomb.

f Then back to Heaven they fly,
  And the glad tidings bear.
  Hark ! as they soar on high,
  What music fills the air !

Their anthems say,—
Jesus, Who bled,
Hath left the dead ;
He rose to-day.

Ye mortals, catch the sound.
Redeemed by Him from hell ;
And send the echo round
The globe on which you dwell :
Transported, cry,—
Jesus, Who bled,
Hath left the dead,
No more to die.

ff All hail ! triumphant Lord,
Who sav'st us with Thy blood ;
Wide be Thy Name adored,
Thou rising, reigning God !
With Thee we rise,
With Thee we reign,
And empires gain
Beyond the skies.

P. Doddridge.

159 8.8.8.5.

mf HAIL, holy day, most blest, most
dear !   [and drear,
When death's dark region, sad

Those strange mysterious s
did hear,
cres "The Lord is risen."

f The Holy Captive's bonds are
To Him the keys of death are
Be glad, O earth, and sho
heaven,
"The Lord is risen."

mp Shall this triumphant
inspire
Each angel's song, each se
lyre,
cres And I not sing with such a
f . "The Lord is risen" ?

p Yet not for them His life He
He did not die their souls to
It is for man that from the
cres "The Lord is risen."

p For man He left His gl
throne,
For man to death's dark
went down ;
cres And now to heaven, for man
f "The Lord is risen."

Charlotte El

16.—HIS ASCENSION.

160 7s.

f HAIL the day that sees Him rise
To His throne above the skies ;
p Christ, awhile to mortals given,
f Re-ascends His native heaven.

ff There the glorious triumph waits ;
Lift your heads, eternal gates ;
Wide unfold the radiant scene ;
Take the King of Glory in.

f Him though highest heaven receives
p Still He loves the earth He leaves;

f Though returning to His thr
p Still He calls mankind His o

mp See ! He lifts His hands abov
See ! He shows the prints of
Hark ! His gracious lips bes
Blessings on His Church bel

Still for us His death He ple
Prevalent He intercedes,
cres Near Himself prepares our
f Firstfruits of the human ra

Lord, though parted from our
   sight
f High above yon azure height,
   Grant our hearts may thither rise,
Following Thee above the skies.
         C. Wesley, v. 1, *l.* 2, *v.* 2, *l.* 1,
            v. 5, *l.* 4, *v.* 6, *l.* 4 *altd.*

161   6.6.6.6.8.8.

f GOD is gone up on high,
     With a triumphant noise :
     The clarions of the sky
     Proclaim the angelic joys.
f Join all on earth, rejoice and sing ;
   Glory ascribe to glory's King.

f God in the flesh below,
     For us He reigns above :
     Let all the nations know
     Our Jesus' conquering love.
f Join all on earth, rejoice and
        sing ;
   Glory ascribe to glory's King.

f All power to our great Lord
     Is by the Father given ;
     By angel-hosts adored,
     He reigns supreme in heaven :
f Join all on earth, rejoice and
        sing ;
   Glory ascribe to glory's King.

f High on His holy seat,
     He bears the righteous sway ;
     His foes beneath His feet
     Shall sink and die away :
f Join all on earth, rejoice and sing ;
   Glory ascribe to glory's King.

f His foes and ours are one,—
     Satan, the world, and sin ;
     But He shall tread them down,
     And bring His kingdom in :
f Join all on earth, rejoice and sing ;
   Glory ascribe to glory's King.

mf Till all the earth, renewed
      In righteousness divine,
cres With all the hosts of God
      In one great chorus join ;
ff Join all on earth, rejoice and sing ;
   Glory ascribe to glory's King.
                              C. Wesley.

162   S.M., double.

f   THOU hast gone up on high !
      Triumphant o'er the grave,
   And captive led captivity,
      Thy ransomed ones to save.
      Thou hast gone up on high !
dim Oh ! help us to ascend,
cres And there with Thee continually
      In heart and spirit blend.

f   Thou art gone up on high !
      To mansions in the skies,
   And round Thy throne unceasingly
      The songs of praise arise.
p   But we are lingering here,
      With sin and care oppressed ;
   Oh ! let the Comforter be near,
      To lead us to our rest.

[*f*   Thou art gone up on high !
dim But Thou didst first come down,
p Through earth's most bitter agony,
      To pass unto Thy crown.
   And girt with griefs and fears
      Our onward course must be,
   But only let that path of tears
      Lead us at last to Thee.]

f   Thou art gone up on high !
      But Thou shalt come again,
   With all the bright ones of the sky
      Attendant on Thy train.
   Oh ! by Thy saving power,
      So make us live and die, [hour,
   That we may stand, in that dread
      At Thy right hand on high.
                              Emma Toke.

4

163 C.M.

f THE golden gates lift up their
heads,
The doors are open wide ;
The King of Glory is gone in
⁄ Unto His Father's side.

mf Thou art gone up before us, Lord,
To make for us a place, ⌈art,
That we may be where now Thou
And look upon God's face.

cres And ever on our earthly path
A gleam of glory lies ;
A light still breaks behind the
cloud
That veiled Thee from our eyes.

f Lift up our hearts, lift up our
minds,
Let Thy dear grace be given,
dim That, while we linger yet below,
cres Our treasure be in Heaven.

f That, where Thou art at God's
right hand,
Our hope, our love may be ;
Dwell now in us, that we may
dwell
For evermore in Thee.

C. Frances Alexander.

164 6.6.6.6.

f THOU hast gone up again,
Thou Who didst first come down,
Thou hast gone up to reign,
Gone up, from Cross to Crown.

Beyond the opening sky
No more Thy face we see ;
Yet draw our souls on high,
That we may dwell with Thee.

Up to those regions blest,
Where faith has fullest sway ;

Up to T
Up to T
[*mf* Up to
Up to t
Unvex
dim Where

cres Up, up
Fount
f Up to t
ff All its

mp Not no
Or futu
Lord, l
To mal

p Here h
Here b
cres So sha
And st

165

f OUR L
Our Je
The po
Dragg

mf There
And a
ff Lift u
gate
Ye eve

f Loose
And
scer
ff He cl
Recei

mp Who i
f The L
The
o'er
And

uf Lo! His triumphal chariot waits,
And angels chant the solemn lay;
ff Lift up your heads, ye heavenly
gates;
Ye everlasting doors, give way.

mp Who is the King of Glory? who?
ff The Lord, of boundless power
possessed,
The King of saints and angels too;
God over all, for ever blest!

C. Wesley.

166
8.7.8.7.8.8.7.

uf LET God arise, and let His foes
Be scattered now before Him;
Let all on Him with joy repose,
p In worship who adore Him.
cres Before the Lord let them rejoice,
f And in His praise lift up their
voice
Who rideth on the heavens.

f When Thou, O God, Thy flock
didst guide,
Earth shook at Thy descending:

When Thou on Sinai didst abide,
The rocks beneath were rending.
Thou, Lord, didst send a plenteous
rain,
And didst Thy heritage sustain,
Their weariness refreshing.

f Thou hast gone up, O God, on high,
With angel hosts attending;
Thou captive ledd'st captivity,
To Heaven's high throne
ascending.
Thou hast received gifts for men,
That God might dwell with them
again;
dim E'en with our race rebellious.

f Blest be the Lord for all His love,
The God of our salvation;
He daily blesseth from above
His own—His ransomed nation.
ff The Father, Son, and Spirit bless,
One God of Power and Holiness;
Eternal be our praises.

Tr. New Congregational Hymn Book,
1859, v. 1, l. 4 altd.

17.—HIS REIGN.

67
S.M., double.

f CROWN Him with many crowns,
The Lamb upon His throne;
Hark! how the heavenly anthem
drowns
All music but its own.
Awake, my soul, and sing
Of Him Who died for thee,
cres And hail Him as thy chosen King
Through all eternity.

f Crown Him, the Lord of Love!
p Behold His Hands and Side,
Rich Wounds, yet visible above
In beauty glorified;

pp No angel in the sky
Can fully bear that sight,
But downward bends his burning
eye
At mysteries so bright.

[*mf* Crown Him, the Lord of Peace:
Whose power a sceptre sways
From pole to pole—that wars may
cease,
dim Absorbed in prayer and praise:
cres His reign shall know no end,
And round His pierced Feet
Fair flowers of paradise extend
Their fragrance ever sweet.]

ff Crown Him, the Lord of Heaven,
　　One with the Father known,
　　And the blest Spirit, through Him
　　　given,
　　From yonder glorious throne !
f　All hail ! Redeemer, hail !
p　For Thou hast died for me :
ff Thy praise shall never, never fail
　　Throughout eternity.

Y. Bridges.

168
C.M.

mf BEYOND the glittering starry skies,
　　Far as the eternal hills, [light.
　　There, in the boundless worlds of
　　Our Great Redeemer dwells.

　　Legions of angels round His throne
　　In countless armies shine ;
　　At His right hand, with golden
　　　harps,
　　They offer songs divine.

f Hail, Prince !—they cry,—for ever
　　hail !
　　Whose unexampled love [realms
　　Moved Thee to quit these glorious
　　And royalties above.

p Whilst He did condescend on earth
　　To suffer rude disdain,
cres They cast their honours at His feet,
　　And waited in His train.]

　　Through all His travels here below,
　　They did His steps attend ;
p Oft gazed and wondered where at
　　last
　　The scene of love would end.

pp They saw His heart, transfixed with
　　wounds,
　　With love and grief run o'er :
f They saw Him break the bars of
　　death,
　　Which none e'er brake before.

They brought His ch
　above,
　To bear Him to His t
ff Spread their triumph
　and cried,—
　The glorious work is

J. Fanch, v. 1, l.
v. 7, l. 3 a

169
6

f REJOICE, the Lord is
　Your Lord and King
　Mortals, give thanks
　And triumph evermo
ff Lift up your heart, lif
　Rejoice ; again I say, r

f　Jesus, the Saviour, re
　　The God of truth and
p　When He had purged
cres　He took His seat abov
ff Lift up your heart, li
　Rejoice ; again I say, r

f　His kingdom cannot
　　He rules o'er earth a
　　The keys of death an
　　Are to our Jesus give
ff Lift up your heart, li
　Rejoice ; again I say, r

f　He sits at God's righ
　　Till all His foes subr
　　And bow to His com
　　And fall beneath His
ff Lift up your heart, li
　Rejoice ; again I say,

cres Rejoice in glorious h
　Jesus, the Judge, sha
　And take His servan
　To their eternal hom
f We soon shall hear the
ff The trump of God sha
　Rejoice.

170   C.M.

p THE head that once was crowned
    with thorns
f Is crowned with glory now :
    A royal diadem adorns
    The mighty Victor's brow.

The highest place that heaven
    affords
Is His, is His by right :
The King of kings, and Lord of
    lords,
And heaven's eternal Light.

f The joy of all who dwell above,
    The joy of all below
To whom He manifests His love,
    And grants His name to know :

p To them the cross, with all its
    shame,
cres With all its grace, is given ;
f Their name an everlasting name,
    Their joy the joy of heaven.

f They suffer with their Lord below :
f They reign with Him above ;
mf Their profit and their joy, to know
    The mystery of His love.

The cross He bore is life and health,
    Though shame and death to
    Him ;   [wealth,
f His people's hope, His people's
    Their everlasting theme.

                        T. Kelly.

171   -   8.7.8.7.4.7.

f LOOK, ye saints, the sight is
    glorious :
See the Man of Sorrows now,
From the fight returned victorious :
    Every knee to Him shall bow.
f   Crown Him, crown Him :
    Crowns become the Victor's brow.

f Crown the Saviour, angels ! crown
    Him,
    Rich the trophies Jesus brings ;
In the seat of power enthrone Him,
    While the vault of heaven rings.
ff   Crown Him, crown Him :
    Crown the Saviour, King of
    kings !

p Sinners in derision crowned Him.
    Mocking thus the Saviour's
    claim ;
f Saints and angels crowd around
    Him,
    Own His title, praise His Name.
ff   Crown Him, crown Him :
    Spread abroad the Victor's fame.

f Hark, those bursts of acclamation !
    Hark, those loud triumphant
    chords !
Jesus takes the highest station :
    O what joy the sight affords !
ff   Crown Him, crown Him,
    Kings of kings, and Lord of
    lords !
                        T. Kelly.

172   C.M.

f O THE delights, the heavenly joys,
    The glories of the place
Where Jesus sheds the brightest
    beams
Of His o'erflowing grace.

mf Sweet majesty and awful love
    Sit smiling on His brow.
And all the glorious ranks above
dim At humble distance bow.

Princes to His imperial Name
    Bend their bright sceptres down,
f Dominions, thrones, and powers
    rejoice
    To see Him wear the crown.

Archangels sound His lofty praise
Through every heavenly street,
And lay their highest honours
down
dim Submissive at His feet.

p His head, the dear majestic head,
That cruel thorns did wound,
f See what immortal glories shine.
And circle it around.

This is the Man, th' exalted Man,
Whom we unseen adore ;
ff But when our eyes behold His face,
Our hearts shall love Him more.

I. Watts.

173   8.7.8.7., double.

mf HAIL, Thou once despisèd Jesus.
Hail, Thou Galilean King !
Thou didst suffer to release us,
Thou didst free salvation bring :
p Hail, Thou agonizing Saviour,
Bearer of our sin and shame ;
*cres*By Thy merits we find favour ;
Life is given through Thy Name !

mf Paschal Lamb, by God appointed,
All our sins were on Thee laid ;
*cres*By Almighty Love anointed,
Thou hast full atonement made :
f All Thy people are forgiven
Through the virtue of Thy blood ;
Opened is the gate of heaven ; [God.
p   Peace is made 'twixt man and

f Jesus, hail ! enthroned in glory,
There for ever to abide ;
All the heavenly hosts adore Thee,
Seated at Thy Father's side.
*cres*There for sinners Thou art plead-
ing ;   [pare ;
There Thou dost our place pre-
Ever for us interceding,
Till in glory we appear.

f Worship, honour, powei
ing,
Thou art worthy to i
Loudest praises, withou
Meet it is for us to g
ff Help, ye bright angelic
Bring your sweetest, r
Help to sing our Saviot
Help to chant Imman

J. ɹ

174   9.6.9

mp OH, show me not my Sav
As on the Cross He b
*cres*Nor in the tomb, a Caṛ
f   For He has left the d
Then bid me not that for
For my Redeemer ow
ff Who, to the highes
ascended,
In glory fills the thro

p Weep not for Him ai
station !
Weep only for thy sii
*cres*View where He lay w
tion ;
'Tis there our hope be
Yet stay not there, t
feeding
Amid the scenes He t
Look up and see Him i
At the right hand of

[*f* Still in the shameful Cɪ
dim Where His dear blood
For there the great Pro
Abolished all my guil
Yet what, 'mid conflict a
tion,
Shall strength and suc
f He lives, the Captain of
Therefore His servan'

, He death's dark king
ted,
ercame the grave ;
ie triumph He completed,
t, He reigns to save.
  happy myriads bow
e Him :
es, the Judge of men ;
s shall see Him and adore
:
sus ! own me then.

J. Conder.

8.7.8.7., double.

in long-expected Jesus,
  set Thy people free ;

From our fears and sins release us ;
  Let us find our rest in Thee.
f Israel's strength and consolation,
  Hope of all the earth Thou art :
Dear desire of every nation,
  Joy of every longing heart.
cres Born Thy people to deliver ;
  Born a child, and yet a King ;
Born to reign in us for ever ;
  Now Thy gracious kingdom
    bring ;
mf By Thine own Eternal Spirit,
  Rule in all our hearts alone : ·
f By Thine all-sufficient merit,
  Raise us to Thy glorious throne.

C. Wesley.

—HIS SECOND ADVENT AND JUDGMENT.

L.M., with refrain.

) come. Emmanuel,
im captive Israel,
rns in lonely exile here,
Son of God appear.
joice : Emmanuel
e to thee, O Israel.

[hou Rod of Jesse, free
i from Satan's tyranny ;
ths of hell Thy people
    [grave.
  them victory o'er the
ijoice : Emmanuel
e to thee, O Israel.]

[hou Day-spring, come
er
i by Thine advent here ;
the gloomy clouds of
    [flight.
's dark shadows put to
ijoice : Emmanuel
i *to thee, O Israel.*

mf O come, Thou Key of David, come,
  And open wide our heavenly home ;
  Make safe the way that leads on
    high,
  And close the path to misery.
ff Rejoice, rejoice : Emmanuel
  Shall come to thee, O Israel.

mf O come, O come. Thou Lord of
    might,
  Who to Thy tribes, on Sinai's height,
  In ancient times didst give the law
  In cloud, and majesty, and awe.
ff Rejoice, rejoice : Emmanuel
  Shall come to thee, O Israel.

*Latin, 12th century, tr. by J. M. Neale,
altd. by Compilers of "Hymns
Ancient and Modern."*

177   6.6.6.6., double.

f LIFT up your heads, rejoice,
  Redemption draweth nigh ,

*dim*Now breathes a softer air,
  Now shines a milder sky;
*cres*The early trees put forth
  Their new and tender leaf:
*dim*Hushed is the moaning wind
  That told of winter's grief.

f Lift up your heads, rejoice,
  Redemption draweth nigh;
mf Now mount the laden clouds,
  Now flames the darkening sky;
  The early scattered drops
  Descend with heavy fall,
  And to the waiting earth
  The hidden thunders call.

f Lift up your heads, rejoice,
  Redemption draweth nigh;
mf O, note the varying signs
  Of earth, and air, and sky;
  The God of Glory comes,
*dim*In gentleness and might,
  To comfort and alarm.
*cres*To succour and to smite.

mf He comes the wide world's King,
  He comes the true heart's Friend.
*cres*New gladness to begin,
  And ancient wrong to end;
  He comes to fill with light
  The weary waiting eye:
f Lift up your heads, rejoice,
  Redemption draweth nigh.

                    T. T. Lynch.

178   L.M.

mf WHEN Christ came down on earth
  of old,
  He took our nature poor and low;
  He wore no form of angel mould,
  But shared our weakness and our
  woe.

mf But when He cometh b� [...]
  more,
  There shall be set the gre [...]
*cres*And earth and heaven ⸀ [...]
  before
  The face of Him that sits [...]

mp O Son of God, in glory cr⸀ [...]
  The Judge ordained of q⸀ [...]
  dead;
  O Son of Man, so pitying [...]
  For a^{ll} t^{h}e tears Thy peop [...]

mp Be with us in that awful [...]
  And by Thy crown and [...]
  grave,
  By all Thy love, and all Th [...]
*cres*In that great day of judgm [...]

              C. Frances Alex [...]

179   8.7.⸀ [...]

f Lo! He comes with clouds [...]
  ing,
  Once for favoured sinne [...]
  Thousand thousand saints a [...]
  Swell the triumph of H [...]
ff   Hallelujah! [...]
  God appears, on earth t [...]

mp Every eye shall now behol [...]
  Robed in dreadful maje⸀ [...]
p Those who set at nought [...]
  Him,
  Pierced and nailed Hin [...]
pp   Deeply wailing,
  Shall the true Messiah s [...]

mp Every island, sea, and mo⸀ [...]
  Heaven and earth shall fl [...]
p All who hate Him mu⸀ [...]
  founded,
  Hear the trump procl⸀ [...]
  day;
ff   Come to judgme⸀ [...]
  Come to judgment, com⸀ [...]

f Now Redemption, long expected,
　See in solemn pomp appear !
All His saints, by man rejected,
　Now shall meet Him in the air.
　　Hallelujah !
　See the day of God appear !

ff Yea, Amen ! let all adore Thee,
　High on Thine eternal throne :
Saviour, take the power and glory,
Claim the kingdom for Thine
　own :
　　O, come quickly,
　Hallelujah ! come, Lord, come !

*Variation by M. Madan from
C. Wesley, and J. Cennick.*

180　　　　　88.88.88.

mp O QUICKLY come, dread Judge of
　all ;
For, awful though Thine advent be,
All shadows from the truth will
　fall,
And falsehood die, in sight of
　Thee :
cres O quickly come : for doubt and
　fear
Like clouds dissolve when Thou art
　near.

mp O quickly come, great King of all ;
　Reign all around us, and within ;
Let sin no more our souls enthral,
Let pain and sorrow die with sin :
cres O quickly come : for Thou alone
Canst make Thy scattered people
　one.

mp O quickly come, true Life of all ;
For death is mighty all around ;
On every home His shadows fall,
On every heart His mark is found :
O quickly come : for grief and pain
Can never cloud Thy glorious reign.

mp O quickly come, true Light of all ;
　For gloomy night broods o'er our
　way ;
And weakly souls begin to fall
With weary watching for the day :
cres O quickly come : for round Thy
　throne
No eye is blind, no night is known.

L. Tuttiett.

181　　　　8.7.8.7.8.8.7.

mf GREAT God, what do I see and
　hear ?
The end of things created :
The Judge of all men doth appear,
On clouds of glory seated !
ff The trumpet sounds, the graves
　restore
The dead which they contained
　before ;
dim Prepare, my soul, to meet Him.

mf The dead in Christ shall first arise,
　At the last trumpet's sounding ;
cres Caught up to meet Him in the
　skies,
f With joy their Lord surrounding :
No gloomy fears their souls dismay ;
His presence sheds eternal day
On those prepared to meet Him.

mf Far over space, through distant
　spheres,
The lightnings are prevailing ;
The ungodly rise, but all their
　tears
And sighs are unavailing :
p The day of grace is past and gone,
Trembling they stand before His
　throne,
All unprepared to meet Him.

mf Great God, what do I see and hear ?
　The end of things created :

cres The Judge of all men doth appear,
f   On clouds of glory seated !
p Low at His cross I view the day
   When heaven and earth shall pass
      away,
cres And thus prepare to meet Him.

   v. 1 Anon. based on B. Ringwaldt ;
   vv. 2, 3 W. B. Collyer, v. 2 altd.
   T. Cotterill, v. 3 altd. Anon.

182   C.M.

f ALL faded is the glowing light
   That once from heaven shone,
   When startled shepherds in the
      night
   The angels came upon.

mf O. shine again. ye angel host,
   And say that He is near ;
   Though but a simple few at most
   Believe He will appear.

mp Ye heavens, that have been growing
      dark,
   Now also are ye dumb ; ["Hark,
   When shall the listeners say,
   They're singing—He will come"?

mf Lord, come again, O, come again,
   Come even as Thou wilt ;
   But not anew to suffer pain,
   And strive with human guilt.

mf O, come again, Thou mighty King,
   Let earth Thy glory see ;
   And et us hear the angels sing,
   "He comes with victory."

                        T. T. Lynch.

183   C.M.

mf THE Lord will come and not be slow
   His footsteps cannot err ;
   Before Him righteousness shall go,
   His royal harbinger.

mf Mercy and truth that long were
      missed,
   Now joyfully are met ;
dim Sweet peace and righteousness
      have kissed,
   And hand in hand are set.

mf Truth from the earth, like to a
      flower,
   Shall bud and blossom then ;
   And Justice, from her heavenly
      bower,
   Look down on mortal men.

mp Rise, Lord, judge Thou the earth
      in might,
   This longing earth redress ;
cres For Thou art He Who shall by
      right
   The nations all possess.

mf The nations all whom Thou hast
      made
   Shall come, and all shall frame
dim To bow them low before Thee, Lord,
   And glorify Thy Name.

f For great Thou art, and wonders
      great
   By Thy strong hand are done ;
   Thou, in Thine everlasting seat,
   Remainest God alone.

Cento from J. Milton, v. 4, l. 2 altd.

19.—HIS NAMES, MEDIATORIAL TITLES, AND OFFICES.

184   6.6.6.6.8.8.

mf   JOIN all the glorious names
      Of wisdom love. and   wer

   That ever mortal knew,
   That angels ever bore :
All are too mean to speak His worth,
Too mean to set my Saviour forth.

mf But oh ! what gentle terms,
What condescending ways
Doth our Redeemer use
To teach His heavenly grace !
*cres*Mine eyes with joy and wonder see
What forms of love He bears for me.

mf Great Prophet of my God,
My tongue would bless Thy
Name :
By Thee the joyful news
Of our salvation came,
*cres*The joyful news of sins forgiven,
Of hell subdued, and peace with
heaven.

f Be Thou my Counsellor,
My Pattern, and my Guide,
And through this desert land,
Still keep me near Thy side :
p O let my feet ne'er run astray,
Nor rove, nor seek the crooked way.

[*mf* I love my Shepherd's voice,
His watchful eye small keep
My wandering soul among
The thousands of His sheep :
*cres*He feeds His flock, He calls their
names,
His bosom bears the tender lambs.]

mf Jesus, my great High Priest,
p Offered His blood, and died ;
cres My guilty conscience seeks
No sacrifice beside :
f His powerful blood did once atone,
And now it pleads before the throne.

mf My dear almighty Lord,
My Conqu'ror and my King,
Thy sceptre and Thy sword,
Thy reigning grace I sing :
*dim*Thine is the power ; behold, I sit
In willing bonds beneath Thy feet.

I. Watts.

185   L.M.

mf ONE Lord there is, all lords above ;
His name is Truth, His name is
Love,
His name is Beauty, it is Light,
His will is Everlasting Right.

mf But ah ! to Wrong, what is His
name ?
This Lord is a consuming flame
To every wrong beneath the sun :
He is one Lord, the Holy One.

f Lord of the Everlasting Name,
Truth, Beauty, Light, Consuming
Flame !
*dim*Shall I not lift my heart to Thee,
And ask Thee, Lord, to rule in me ?

p If I be ruled in other wise,
My lot is cast with all that dies ;
With things that harm, and things
that hate ;   [gate—
And roam by night and miss the

mf The happy gate, which leads to
where
Love is like sunshine in the air,
*cres*And Love and Law are both the
same,
f Named with an Everlasting Name.

W. B. Rands.

186   9.9.9.9.

mf REST of the weary, Joy of the sad ;
p Hope of the dreary, *f* Light of the
glad :   [to the end ;
Home of the stranger, Strength
*cres*Refuge from danger, Saviour and
Friend.

mp Pillow where lying, love rests its
head ;   [dead ;
p Peace of the dying, *f* Life of the

*cres*Path of the lowly, Prize at the end :
  Breath of the holy, Saviour and
  Friend.

mp When my feet stumble, to Thee
  I'll cry,
  Crown of the humble, *f* Cross of
  the high ;
*cres*When my steps wander, over me
  bend,
  Truer and fonder, Saviour and
  Friend.

mf Ever confessing Thee, I will raise
*cres*Unto Thee blessing, glory, and
  praise ;   [end,
  All my endeavour, world without
f Thine to be ever, Saviour and
  Friend.

J. S. B. Monsell.

187   C.M.

mf How sweet the name of Jesus
  sounds
  In a believer's ear !   [wounds,
p It soothes his sorrows, heals his
cres And drives away his fear.

p It makes the wounded spirit whole,
  And calms the troubled breast :
  'Tis manna to the hungry soul,
  And to the weary, rest.

mf Dear name ! the rock on which I
  build ;
  My shield and hiding-place,
  My never-failing treasury, filled
  With boundless stores of grace.

f Jesus, my Shepherd, Guardian,
  Friend ;
  My Prophet, Priest, and King ;
  My Lord, my Life, my Way, my
  End,
  Accept the praise I bring.

mp Weak is the effort of my heart.
  And cold my warmest thought;
*cres*But when I see Thee as Thou art,
  I'll praise Thee as I ought :

mf Till then, I would Thy love proclaim
  With every fleeting breath ;
  And may the music of Thy name
dim Refresh my soul in death.

J. Newton, v. 4, l. 1 altd.

188   L.M.

mf O CHRIST, our true and only Light
  Illumine those who sit in night,
*cres*Let those afar now hear Thy voice,
  And in Thy fold with us rejoice.

p And all who else have strayed
  from Thee,
  Oh gently seek ! Thy healing be
  To every wounded conscience given.
*cres*And let them also share Thy
  heaven.

p Oh make the deaf to hear Thy
  word,   [dear Lord,
*cres*And teach the dumb to speak,
  Who dare not yet the faith avow,
p Though secretly they hold it now.

mp Shine on the darkened and the cold,
  Recall the wanderers from Thy
  fold,
*cres*Unite those now who walk apart,
  Confirm the weak and doubting
  heart.

f So they with us may evermore
  Such grace with wondering thanks
  adore,
ff And endless praise to Thee be given
  By all Thy Church in earth and
  heaven.

J. Heermann, tr. Catherine Winkworth.

189   7.6.7.6.

nf O JESUS, ever present,
  O Shepherd, ever kind.
  Thy very Name is music
  To ear, and heart, and mind.

nf It woke our wondering childhood
  To muse on things above ;
  It drew our harder manhood
  With cords of mighty love.

p How oft to sure destruction
  Our feet had gone astray,
  Wert Thou not, patient Shepherd,
  The Guardian of our way.

p How oft in darkness fallen,
  And wounded sore by sin,
  Thy Hand has gently raised us,
  And healing balm poured in.

mf Thy Voice, in life so mighty,
  In death shall make us bold :
  O bring us all together
  To Thine eternal fold.

nf O Shepherd good ! we follow
  And trust in Thee for all,
  To guide us and to feed us,
  And raise us when we fall.
                          L. Tuttiett.

190   6.5.6.5.

p JESU, meek and gentle,
  Son of God most High,
  Pitying, loving Saviour,
  Hear Thy children's cry.

mf Pardon our offences,
  Loose our captive chains,
  Break down every idol
  Which our soul detains.

f Give us holy freedom,
  · Fill our hearts with love,

Draw us, holy Jesu,
  To the realms above.

mf Lead us on our journey,
  Be Thyself the Way
  Through earth's passing darkness
  To Heaven's endless day.

p Jesu, meek and gentle,
  Son of God most High,
  Pitying, loving Saviour,
  Hear Thy children's cry.
                      G. R. Prynne.

191   C.M.

PART I.

[*f* IMMORTAL Love, for ever full,
  For ever flowing free,
  For ever shared, for ever whole,
  A never-ebbing sea !

mf Our outward lips confess the Name
  All other names above ;
  Love only knoweth whence it cam
  And comprehendeth love.]

mf We may not climb the heavenly
        steeps
  To bring the Lord Christ down :
  In vain we search the lowest deeps,
  For Him no depths can drown.

mp But warm, sweet, tender even yet
  A present help is He ;
  And faith has still its Olivet,
  And love its Galilee.

mp The healing of His seamless dress
  Is by our beds of pain ;   [press,
  We touch Him in life's throng and
  And we are whole again.

mp Through Him the first fond prayers
          are said
  Our lips of childhood frame,
dim The last low whispers of our dead
  Are burdened with His Name.

mf O Lord and Master of us all !
  Whate'er our name or sign.
  We own Thy sway, we hear Thy call.
  We test our lives by Thine.

PART II.   C.M.

mf O LORD and Master of us all !
  Whate'er our name or sign,
  We own Thy sway, we hear Thy call,
  We test our lives by Thine.

mf Thou judgest us : Thy purity
  Doth all our lusts condemn ;
  The love that draws us nearer Thee
  Is hot with wrath to them.

mp Our thoughts lie open to Thy sight :
  And, naked to Thy glance,
  Our secret sins are in the light
  Of Thy pure countenance.

mp Yet, weak and blinded though we
    be,
  Thou dost our service own ;
cres We bring our varying gifts to Thee,
  And Thou rejectest none.

mf To Thee our full humanity,
  Its joys and pains belong ;
  The wrong of man to man on Thee
  Inflicts a deeper wrong.

mf Deep strike Thy roots, O heavenly
    Vine,
  Within our earthly sod,
  Most human, and yet most divine,
  The flower of man and God.

PART III.   C.M.

p WE faintly hear, we dimly see,
  In differing phrase we pray ;
cres But, dim or clear, we own in Thee
f   The Light. the Truth, the Way !

p Apart from Thee all gain is loss,
  All labour vainly done ;
  The solemn shadow of Thy Cross
  Is better than the sun.

mf Alone, O Love ineffable !
  Thy saving Name is given ;
p To turn aside from Thee is hell,
f   To walk with Thee is heaven !

mf Our Friend, our Brother, and our
    Lord,
  What may Thy service be ?
  Nor name. nor form, nor ritual
    word.
  But simply following Thee.

mp Thy litanies, sweet offices
  Of love and gratitude ;
cres Thy sacramental liturgies
  The joy of doing good.

f The heart must ring Thy Christmas
    bells.
  Thy inward altars raise,
  Its faith and hopes Thy canticles,
  And its obedience praise !
            J. G. Whittier.

192   8.7.8.7., double.

mf LIGHT of those whose dreary
    dwelling
  Borders on the shades of death,
  Come, and by Thy love's revealing,
  Dissipate the clouds beneath.
  The new heaven and earth's
    Creator,
  In our deepest darkness rise,
  Scattering all the night of nature,
  Pouring eyesight on our eyes.

mp Still we wait for Thine appearing :
  Life and joy Thy beams impart,
  Chasing all our fears, and cheering
  Every poor, benighted heart.
  Come and manifest the favour
  God hath for our ransomed race ;
cres Come, Thou universal Saviour,
  Come and bring the gospel grace

mp Save us in Thy great compassion,
 O Thou mild, pacific Prince;
Give the knowledge of salvation;
 Give the pardon of our sins.
cres By Thine all-restoring merit,
 Every burdened soul release;
Every weary, wandering spirit
p Guide into Thy perfect peace.
C. Wesley.

193   7s., 6 lines.

f GOD the Father's only Son,
Yet with Him in Glory One,
One in wisdom, One in might,
Absolute and Infinite :
dim Jesu ! I believe in Thee,
Thou art Lord and God to me.

[*mf* Preacher of eternal peace,
Christ, anointed to release,
Setting wide the dungeon door,
Unto sinners chained before :
dim Jesu ! I believe in Thee,
Prophet sent from God to me.

mp Low in sad Gethsemane,
High on dreadful Calvary,
In the Garden, on the Cross,
Making good our utter loss :
dim Jesu ! I believe in Thee,
Priest and Sacrifice for me.]

mf Ruler of Thy ransomed race,
And Protector by Thy grace,
Leader in the way we wend,
And Rewarder at the end :
dim Jesu ! I believe in Thee,
Christ, the King of kings to me.

mp Light revealed through clouds of pain,
That the blind might see again ;
Love, content in death to lie,
That the dead might never die :
dim Jesu ! I believe in Thee,
Light, and Love, and Life to me.

mf All that I am fain to know,
 While I watch and wait below ;
cres All that I would find above,
 All of everlasting love,
f Jesu ! I believe in Thee
 Thou art all in all to me.
S. J. Stone.

194   8.8.8.6.

mf O THOU, the contrite sinner's Friend,
Who loving, lov'st them to the end,
On this alone my hopes depend,
dim That Thou wilt plead for me !

mf When, weary in the Christian race,
Far off appears my resting-place,
And, fainting, I mistrust Thy grace,
dim Then, Saviour, plead for me !

p When I have erred and gone astray
Afar from Thine and wisdom's way,
And see no glimmering guiding ray,
 Still, Saviour, plead for me !

p When Satan, by my sins made bold,
Strives from Thy cross to loose my hold,
cres Then with Thy pitying arms enfold,
f And plead, O plead for me !

pp And when my dying hour draws near.
Darkened with anguish, guilt, and fear,
cres Then to my fainting sight appear,
f Pleading in heaven for me !

mf When the full light of heavenly day
Reveals my sins in dread array,
cres Say Thou hast washed them all away ;
f O say, Thou plead'st for me !
Charlotte Elliott.

195 L.M.

mf WHERE high the heavenly Temple
stands,   [hands,
The house of God not made with
A great High Priest our nature
wears,
The Guardian of mankind appears.

mf He who for men their Surety stood,
p And poured on earth His precious
Blood,
*cres*Pursues in heaven His mighty
plan,
f The Saviour and the Friend of man.

f Though now ascended up on high,
mf He bends on earth a Brother's eye;
Partaker of the human name,
*dim*He knows the frailty of our frame.

p Our Fellow-sufferer yet retains
A fellow-feeling of our pains ;
And still remembers in the skies
pp His tears, His agonies, and cries.

p In every pang that rends the heart
The Man of Sorrows had a part ;
mf He sympathises with our grief,
And to the sufferer sends relief.

*cres*With boldness, therefore, at the
Throne,
*dim*Let us make all our sorrows known;
mf And ask the aid of heavenly power
To help us in the evil hour.
M. Bruce.

196 8.7.8.7.7.7.

mf ONE there is above all others
Well deserves the name of Friend,
His is love beyond a brother's,
Costly, free, and knows no end :
cres They who once His kindness
prove,
f Find it everlasting love.

mf Which of all our friends to save us
Could, or would, have shed his
blood ?
p But our Jesus died to have us
Reconciled in Him to God :
cres This was boundless love indeed !
f Jesus is a Friend in need.

mp When He lived on earth abasèd,
Friend of sinners was His name ;
*cres*Now, above all glory raisèd,
He rejoices in the same :
Still He calls them brethren,
friends,
And to all their wants attends.

p Oh for grace our hearts to soften !
Teach us, Lord, at length to love ;
We, alas ! forget too often
What a Friend we have above :
cres But, when home our souls are
brought,
f We shall love Thee as we ought.
J. Newton.

197 7.6.7.6.7.7.

f JESUS, Sun and Shield art Thou ;
Sun and Shield for ever !
Never canst Thou cease to shine,
Cease to guard us never.
Cheer our steps as on we go,
Come between us and the foe.

f Jesus, Bread and Wine art Thou,
Wine and bread for ever !
Never canst Thou cease to feed,
Or refresh us never.
Feed we still on bread divine,
Drink we still this heavenly wine !

mp Jesus, Love and Life art Thou,
Life and love for ever !
Ne'er to quicken shalt Thou cease,
Or to love us never.
All of life and love we need
Is in Thee, in Thee indeed.

p Jesus, Peace and Joy art Thou,
    Joy and peace for ever !
Joy that fades not, changes not,
    Peace that leaves us never.
Joy and peace we have in Thee,
    Now and through eternity.

f Jesus, Song and Strength art Thou,
    Strength and song for ever !
Strength that never can decay,
    Song that ceaseth never.
Still to us this strength and song
Through eternal days prolong.

                   H. Bonar.

198   7s., 6 lines.

mf SON of God, to Thee I cry ;
    By the wondrous mystery
    Of Thy dwelling here on earth,
    By Thy pure and holy birth,
*cres*Lord, Thy presence let me see,
    Manifest Thyself to me.

p Lamb of God, to Thee I cry ;
    By Thy bitter agony,
pp By Thy pangs, to us unknown,
    By Thy Spirit's parting groan,
*cres*Lord, Thy presence let me see,
    Manifest Thyself to me.

mf Prince of Life, to Thee I cry ;
    By Thy glorious majesty,
    By Thy triumph o'er the grave,
    By Thy power to help and save,
*cres*Lord, Thy presence let me see,
    Manifest Thyself to me.

f Lord of glory, God most high,
    Man exalted to the sky,
    With Thy love my bosom fill ;
    Prompt me to perform Thy will ;
*cres*Then Thy glory I shall see,
    Thou wilt bring me home to Thee.

                R. Mant, altd.

199   7.7.7.5.

LORD of mercy and of might,
Of mankind the life and light,
Maker, Teacher, Infinite :
p   Jesus, hear and save !

Strong Creator, Saviour mild,
Humbled to a mortal child,
Captive, beaten, bound, reviled :
p   Jesus, hear and save !

f Throned above celestial things.
Borne aloft on angels' wings,
Lord of lords, and King of kings :
p   Jesus, hear and save !

Soon to come to earth again,
Judge of angels and of men ;
Hear us now, and hear us then :
p   Jesus, hear and save !

                  R. Heber.

200   7s., 8 lines.

p SAVIOUR, when in dust to Thee,
Low we bend the adoring knee ;
When, repentant, to the skies
Scarce we lift our weeping eyes ;
O ! by all the pains and woe,
Suffered once for man below,
*cres*Bending from Thy throne on high,
pp Hear our solemn litany.

mf By Thy helpless infant years,
By Thy life of want and tears,
By Thy days of sore distress
In the savage wilderness,
By the dread mysterious hour
Of the insulting tempter's power ;
*cres*Turn, O turn a favouring eye,
pp Hear our solemn litany.

mf By the sacred griefs that wept
O'er the grave where Lazarus slept :
By the boding tears that flowed
Over Salem's loved abode ;

By the anguished sigh that told
Treachery lurked within Thy fold ;
*cres*From Thy seat above the sky,
pp Hear our solemn litany.

p By Thine hour of dire despair,
By Thine agony of prayer ;
By the cross, the nail, the thorn,
Piercing spear and torturing scorn ;
*cres*By the gloom that veiled the skies
O'er the dreadful sacrifice,

*dim*Listen to our humble cry ;
pp Hear our solemn litany.

pp By Thy deep expiring groan ;
*cres*By the sad sepulchral stone ;
By the vault whose dark abode
Held in vain the rising God ;
f O ! from earth to heaven restored,
ff Mighty re-ascended Lord,
*dim*Listen, listen to the cry
pp Of our solemn litany.

R. Grant.

III.

The Holy Spirit.

1.—*HIS MANIFESTATION AT PENTECOST.*

201   C.M.

f WHEN God of old came down from
        heaven,
In power and wrath He came ;
Before His feet the clouds were
        riven,
Half darkness and half flame.

[*f* Around the trembling mountain's
        base
The prostrate people lay ;
*dim*A day of wrath and not of
        grace ;
A dim and dreadful day.]

p But, when He came the second
        time,
He came in power and love ;
Softer than gale at morning prime
Hovered His holy Dove.

[*f* The fires, that rushed on Sinai
        down
In sudden torrents dread,
p Now gently light, a glorious crown
On every sainted head.]

f And, as on Israel's awe-struck
        ear
The voice exceeding loud,
ff The trump, that angels quake to
        hear,
Thrilled from the deep dark
        cloud ;

mf So, when the Spirit of our God
        Came down, His flock to find,
*cres*A voice from heaven was heard
        abroad,
A rushing, mighty wind.

f It fills the Church of God, it fills
        The sinful world around ;
p Only in stubborn hearts and wills
        No place for it is found.

mf Come, Lord ! come, Wisdom, Love
        and Power ;
Open our ears to hear !
*cres*Let us not miss the accepted hour ;
f   Save, Lord, by love or fear !

J. Keble.

202   8.6.8.4.

p OUR blest Redeemer, ere He
    breathed
  His tender, last farewell,
A Guide, a Comforter bequeathed
    With us to dwell.

[*mf* He came in semblance of a dove,
  With sheltering wings outspread,
p The holy balm of peace and love
    On earth to shed.]

f He came in tongues of living flame
  To teach, convince, subdue ;
  All-powerful as the wind He came—
p   As viewless too.

mf He came sweet influence to impart,
  A gracious, willing guest,

While He can find one humble heart
p   Wherein to rest.

p And His that gentle voice we hear,
  Soft as the breath of even,
That cheeks each fault, that calms
    each fear,
pp   And speaks of Heaven.

cres And every virtue we possess,
  And every victory won,
mf And every thought of holiness,
    Are His alone.

p Spirit of purity and grace,
  Our weakness pitying see ;
cres O make our hearts Thy dwelling-
    place,
f   And worthier Thee.
            Harriet Auber.

2.—*HIS OPERATION IN THE HEART.*

203   7s., 6 lines.

mf GRACIOUS Spirit, dwell with me—
  I myself would gracious be ;
  And, with words that help and heal,
  Would Thy life in mine reveal ;
cres And, with actions bold and meek,
  Would for Christ my Saviour speak.

mf Truthful Spirit, dwell with me—
  I myself would truthful be ;
  And, with wisdom kind and clear,
  Let Thy life in mine appear ;
  And, with actions brotherly,
  Speak my Lord's sincerity.

p Tender Spirit, dwell with me—
  I myself would tender be ;
  Shut my heart up like a flower,
  At temptation's darksome hour ;
cres Open it when shines the sun,
  And His love by fragrance own.

p Silent Spirit, dwell with me—
  I myself would quiet be :
  Quiet as the growing blade,
  Which through earth its way hath
    made,
  Silently, like morning light,
  Putting mists and chills to flight.

f Mighty Spirit, dwell with me—
  I myself would mighty be :
  Mighty so as to prevail,
  Where unaided man must fail ;
cres Ever, by a mighty hope,
  Pressing on and bearing up.

p Holy Spirit, dwell with me—
  I myself would holy be :
cres Separate from sin, I would
  Choose and cherish all things good ;
mf And whatever I can be
  Give to Him Who gave me Thee.
            T. T. Lynch.

204
7s.

mf HOLY SPIRIT, Truth Divine !
Dawn upon this soul of mine ;
Word of God, and inward Light,
Wake my spirit, clear my sight.

mf Holy Spirit, Love Divine !
Glow within this heart of mine ;
Kindle every high desire ;
Perish self in Thy pure fire !

mf Holy Spirit, Power Divine !
Fill and nerve this will of mine ;
By Thee may I strongly live,
Bravely bear, and nobly strive !

mf Holy Spirit, Right Divine !
King within my conscience reign ;
Be my Lord, and I shall be
Firmly bound, for ever free.

p Holy Spirit, Peace Divine !
Still this restless heart of mine ;
Speak to calm this tossing sea,
Stayed in Thy tranquillity.

mf Holy Spirit, Joy Divine !
Gladden Thou this heart of mine ;
In the desert ways I sing
f Spring, O Well, for ever spring !
S. Longfellow.

205
C.M.

mf COME, Holy Spirit, heavenly Dove,
With all Thy quickening powers !
Kindle a flame of sacred love
In these cold hearts of ours.

mf Look how we grovel here below,
Fond of these trifling toys ;
Our souls can neither fly nor go
To reach eternal joys !

*p In vain we tune our formal songs,
In vain we strive to rise ;*

Hosannas languish on our tongues,
And our devotion dies.

p Dear Lord, and shall we ever lie
At this poor dying rate ?
Our love so faint, so cold to Thee,
And Thine to us so great !

mf Come, Holy Spirit, heavenly Dove,
With all Thy quickening powers !
Come, shed abroad a Saviour's love,
And that shall kindle ours.
I. Watts.

206
C.M.

mf LORD ! am I precious in Thy sight ?
Lord ! would'st Thou have me
Thine ?
What ! may I grieve, may I delight
The Majesty Divine ?

mp O Holy Spirit ! dost Thou mourn
When I from Thee depart ?
cres Dost Thou rejoice when I return
And give Thee back my heart ?

mf O sweet, strange height of Grace
Divine
My sin Thy grief to make,
And this poor faithfulness of mine
For Thy delight to take !

mp Strange height of sin to spurn the
love
That yearns to make me blest,
And drive away the Heavenly Dove
That fain would be my guest !

mf O happy Heaven where Thine
embrace
I never more shall leave,
Nor ever cast away Thy grace,
Nor once Thy Spirit grieve !

ιf Let me, dear Lord, each grace possess [bright,
That makes Thy Heaven more
*res*And bring the humble holiness
f　That gives my God delight.
T. H. Gill.

207　　　　　　　　　C.M.
f ENTHRONED on high, Almighty Lord,
The Holy Ghost send down ;
Fulfil in us Thy faithful word,
And all Thy mercies crown.

mf Though on our heads no tongues of fire
Their wondrous powers impart,
*dim*Grant, Saviour, what we more desire,
Thy Spirit in our heart.

mp Spirit of life and light and love,
Thy heavenly influence give :
*cres*Quicken our souls, born from above,
In Christ, that we may live.

mf To our benighted minds reveal
The glories of His grace ;
And bring us where no clouds conceal
The brightness of His face.

mf His love within us shed abroad,
Life's ever-springing well,
Till God in us, and we in God,
In love eternal dwell.
T. Haweis.

208　　　　　　　　　L.M.
mf COME, Holy Spirit, heavenly Dove,
My sinful maladies remove !
Be Thou my Light, be Thou my Guide,
O'er *every thought and step* preside.

mf The light of truth to me display ;
That I may know and choose my way ;
Plant holy fear within mine heart,
That I from God may ne'er depart.

mf Conduct me safe, conduct me far
From every sin and hurtful snare ;
Lead me to God, my final Rest,
In His enjoyment to be blest.

mp Lead me to Christ, the Living Way,
Nor let me from His pastures stray :
*cres*Lead me to Heaven, the seat of bliss,
ff Where pleasure in perfection is.

mf Lead me to holiness, the road [God ;
That I must take to dwell with
Lead to Thy Word, that rules must give,
And sure directions how to live.

mf Thus I, conducted still by Thee,
Of God a child beloved shall be,
*cres*Here to His family pertain,
f Hereafter with Him ever reign.
S. Browne.

209　　　　　　　　　L.M.
f COME, Holy Ghost, and through each heart
In Thy full flood of glory pour ;
Who, with the Son and Father, art
One Godhead blessed for evermore.

f So shall voice, mind, and strength conspire
Thy praise eternal to resound :
So shall our hearts be set on fire,
And kindle every heart around.

mf Father of mercies, hear our cry,
Hear us, O sole-begotten Son :
Who with the Holy Ghost Most High,
f Reignest while endless ages run.
Ambrose, tr. E. Caswo

3.—*HIS INFLUENCE IN THE CHURCH AND IN THE WORLD.*

210   88.88.88.

mf CREATOR Spirit ! by Whose aid
  The world's foundations first were laid,
Come, visit every pious mind ;
Come, pour Thy joys on human kind ;
p From sin and sorrow set us free,
*cres*And make Thy temples worthy Thee.

mf O source of uncreated light,
  The Father's promised Paraclete !
Thrice holy fount, thrice holy fire,
*cres*Our hearts with heavenly love inspire ;
f Come, and Thy sacred unction bring
To sanctify us, while we sing.

mf Thou strength of His almighty hand,   [earth command,
Whose power does heaven and
Refine and purge our earthly parts;
But, O, inflame and fire our hearts !
And, lest our feet should step astray,
Protect, and guide us in the way.

f Plenteous of grace, descend from high,
Rich in Thy sevenfold energy !
Make us eternal truths receive,
And practise all that we believe.
Give us Thyself, that we may see
The Father and the Son by Thee.

f Immortal honour, endless fame,
Attend the Almighty Father's Name :
The Saviour Son be glorified,
p Who for lost man's redemption died:
*cres*And equal adoration be,
  Eternal Paraclete, to Thee.

Gregory the Great, paraphr. J. Dryden.

211   L.M.

mf COME, O Creator Spirit blest !
And in our souls take up Thy rest;
Come, with Thy grace and heavenly aid,
To fill the hearts which Thou hast made.

mp Great Paraclete ; to Thee we cry :
*cres*O highest gift of God most high !
O fount of life | O fire of love !
And sweet anointing from above !

mf The sacred sevenfold grace is Thine,
Dread Finger of the hand divine !
The promise of the Father Thou !
Who dost the tongue with power endow.

mf Our senses touch with light and fire;
Our hearts with charity inspire ;
And with endurance from on high
*dim*The weakness of our flesh supply.

mf Far back our enemy repel,
*dim*And let Thy peace within us dwell;
So may we, having Thee for guide,
Turn from each hurtful thing aside.

mf O may Thy grace on us bestow
The Father and the Son to know,
*cres*And evermore to hold confessed
Thyself of each the Spirit blest.

Gregory the Great, tr. E. Caswall.

212   7.7.7.

mf HOLY SPIRIT ! Lord of light !
From the clear celestial height
Thy pure beaming radiance give :

mf Come, Thou Father of the poor !
Come, with treasures which endure!
Come, Thou Light of all that live !

*mp*Thou, of all consolers best,
　Thou the soul's delightsome guest,
　Dost refreshing peace bestow ;

mp Thou in toil art comfort sweet ;
　Pleasant coolness in the heat ;
　Solace in the midst of woe.]

mf Light immortal ! light divine.!
　Visit Thou these hearts of Thine,
　And our inmost being fill :

p If Thou take Thy grace away,
　Nothing pure in man will stay ;
　All his good is turned to ill.

[*mp*Heal our wounds ; our strength
　　renew ;
　On our dryness pour Thy dew ;
　Wash the stains of guilt away :]

mp Bend the stubborn heart and will ;
　Melt the frozen, warm the chill ;
　Guide the steps that go astray.

mf Thou, on those who evermore
　Thee confess and Thee adore,
　In Thy sevenfold gifts, descend :

p Give them comfort when they die,
*cres*Give them life with Thee on high,
f Give them joys that never end.
Robert II. of France, tr. E. Caswall.

213　　　　　　6.6.4.6.6.6.4.

mf COME, Holy Ghost in love,
　Shed on us from above
　　Thine own bright ray :
　Divinely good Thou art ;
　Thy sacred gifts impart
　To gladden each sad heart :
cres　　O come to-day.

mf Come, tenderest friend and best,
　Our most delightful Guest,
　　With soothing power :

p Rest, which the weary know.
　Shade, 'mid the noontide glow.
　Peace, when deep griefs o'erflow,
cres　　Cheer us this hour.

mf Come, Light serene and still,
　Our inmost bosoms fill ;
　　Dwell in each breast :
　We know no dawn but Thine ;
*cres*Send forth Thy beams divine,
　On our dark souls to shine,
　　And make us blest.

mf Exalt our low desires.
p Extinguish passion's fires,
　　Heal every wound ;
　Our stubborn spirits bend,
　Our icy coldness end,
*cres*Our devious steps attend,
　　While heavenward bound.

f Come, all the faithful bless :
　Let all who Christ confess
　　His praise employ ;
　Give virtue's rich reward ;
　Victorious death accord,
*cres*And, with our glorious Lord,
ff　　Eternal joy.
　　　Robert II. of France, paraphr.
　　　　　R. Palmer.

214　　　　　　　　P.M.

mp　　COME Thou, O come ;
　　Sweetest and kindliest,
　　Giver of tranquil rest
　　Unto the weary soul ;
　　In all anxiety
　　With pow'r from heav'n on high
pp　　　　Console

mf　　Come Thou, O come ;
　　Help in the hour of need,
*dim*Strength of the broken reed,
　　Guide of each lonely one ;

Orphans' and widows' stay,
Who tread in life's hard way
pp   Alone.
f   Come Thou, O come ;
Glorious and shadow-free, ·
Star of the stormy sea,
Light of the tempest-tost ;
Harbour our souls to save
*dim*When hope upon the wave
pp   Is lost.
ff   Come Thou, O come ;
Joy in life's narrow path,
*dim*Hope in the hour of death,
Come, Blessèd Spirit, come ;
Lead Thou us tenderly,
Till we shall find with Thee
pp   Our home.
Latin, 9th century, tr. G. Moultrie.

215   6.5., 12 lines.
mf HEAR us, Thou that broodedst
O'er the watery deep,
Waking all creation
From its primal sleep ;
Holy Spirit, breathing
Breath of life divine,
Breathe into our spirits,
Blending them with Thine.
ff   Light and Life Immortal !
Hear us as we raise
Hearts, as well as voices,
Mingling prayer and praise.

[*mf* When the sun ariseth
In a cloudless sky,
May we feel Thy presence,
Holy Spirit, nigh ;
Shed Thy radiance o'er us,
Keep it cloudless still,
Through the day before us,
Perfecting Thy will.
ff   Light and Life Immortal !
        etc.]

mf When the fight is fiercest
In the noontide heat,
Bear us, Holy Spirit,
To our Saviour's feet,
There to find a refuge
Till our work is done,
There to fight the battle
.Till the battle's won.
ff   Light and Life Imm
p If the day be falling
Sadly as it goes,
Slowly in its sadness
Sinking to its close,
*cres*May Thy love in mercy
Kindling ere it die,
Cast a ray of glory
O'er our evening sky.
ff   Light and Life Imm
mf Morning, noon, and evening
Whensoe'er it be,
Grant us, gracious Spirit,
Quickening life in Thee ;
Life, that gives us, living,
Life of heavenly love ;
Life, that brings us, dying,
Life, from heaven above.
ff   Life and Light Immorta
Hear us as we raise
Hearts, as well as voice
Mingling prayer and
        G. Th

216   7.7
mf GRACIOUS Spirit, Holy Gho
Taught by Thee, we covet n
Of Thy gifts at Pentecost,
Holy, heavenly love.
mp Love is kind, and suffers lon
Love is meek, and thinks no v
*cres*Love, than death itself
strong :
Therefore give us love.

p Prophecy will fade away,
  Melting in the light of day ;
*cres*Love will ever with us stay :
  Therefore give us love.

mp Faith will vanish into sight ;
  Hope be emptied in delight ;
*cres*Love in heaven will shine more
  bright :
  Therefore give us love.

mf Faith and hope and love we see
  Joining hand in hand agree ;
*cres*But the greatest of the three,
  And the best, is love.

p From the overshadowing
  Of Thy gold and silver wing,
*cres*Shed on us, who to Thee sing,
f   Holy, heavenly love.
                  C. Wordsworth.

217   7.7.7.5.

mf COME to our poor nature's night,
  With Thy blessèd inward light,
  Holy Ghost, the Infinite ;
p   Comforter Divine.

p We are sinful—cleanse us, Lord ;
  Sick and faint—Thy strength
  afford ;
*cres*Lost,—until by Thee restored,
  Comforter Divine.

[*p* Orphans are our souls, and poor ;
*cres*Give us from Thy heavenly store
f Faith, love, joy, for evermore,
p   Comforter Divine.

mp Like the dew Thy peace distill ;
  Guide, subdue our wayward will,
p Things of Christ unfolding still,
  Comforter Divine.]

p Gentle, awful, holy Guest,
  Make *Thy temple in each breast—*

There Thy presence be confessed ;
  Comforter Divine.

p With us, for us, intercede,
  And with voiceless groanings, plead
  Our unutterable need,
  Comforter Divine.

mf In us, " Abba, Father," cry ;
*cres*Earnest of the bliss on high ;
f Seal of immortality ;
  Comforter Divine.

mf Search for us the depths of God ;
*cres*Upwards by the starry road
f Bear us to Thy high abode ;
dim   Comforter Divine.
                  G. Rawson.

218   S.M.

mf COME, Holy Spirit, come ;
  Let Thy bright beams arise,
  Dispel the darkness from our minds,
  And open all our eyes.

mf Revive our drooping faith,
  Our doubts and fears remove,
  And kindle in our breasts the flame
  Of never-dying love.

p Convince us of our sin,
  Then lead to Jesus' blood,
  And to our wondering view reveal
  The secret love of God.

mf 'Tis Thine to cleanse the heart,
  To sanctify the soul,
  To pour fresh life in every part,
  And new-create the whole.

f Dwell therefore in our hearts,
  Our minds from bondage free ;
*cres*Then we shall know, and praise,
  and love
ff The Father, Son, and Thee !
                  J. Har

219   S.M., double.

mf   LORD God, the Holy Ghost,
In this accepted hour,
As on the day of Pentecost,
cres   Descend in all Thy power !
We meet with one accord
In our appointed place,
And wait the promise of our Lord,
The Spirit of all grace.

f   Like mighty rushing wind
Upon the waves beneath,
Move with one impulse every mind,
One soul, one feeling breathe ;
p   The young, the old, inspire
With wisdom from above, [fire
*cres*And give us hearts and tongues of
To pray, and praise, and love.

p   Spirit of Light, explore
And chase our gloom away,
*cres*With lustre shining more and more
Unto the perfect day !
mf . Spirit of Truth, be Thou
In life and death our Guide !
*cres*O Spirit of Adoption, now
May we be sanctified !

        J. Montgomery.

220   C.M.

mf COME, Holy Ghost, our hearts
inspire ;
Let us Thine influence prove,
Source of the old prophetic fire,
Fountain of light and love.

mf Come, Holy Ghost, for moved by
Thee
The prophets wrote and spoke ;
Unlock the truth, Thyself the
Key,
Unseal the sacred book.

mp Expand Thy wings, celestial Dove,
Brood o'er our nature's night ;
On our disordered spirits move,
cres And let there now be light.

mf God, through Himself, we then
shall know,
If Thou within us shine,
*cres*And sound, with all Thy saints
below.
The depths of love divine.

        C. Wesley.

IV.

The Most Holy Trinity.

1.—*ADORATION.*

221   7s., 6 lines.

p HOLY, Holy, Holy Lord,
God of Hosts, Eternal King,
*cres*By the heavens and earth adored,
f Angels and archangels sing,
ff Chanting everlastingly,
To the Blessèd Trinity.

mf Since by Thee were all things
made,
And in Thee do all things live,
Be to Thee all honour paid,
f Praise to Thee let all things give,
ff Singing everlastingly
To the Blessèd Trinity.

mp Cherubim and seraphim
dim Veil their faces with their wings ;
Eyes of angels are too dim
To behold the King of kings,
ff While they sing eternally
To the Blessèd Trinity.

mf Thee Apostles, Prophets Thee,
dim Thee the noble Martyr band,
Praise with solemn jubilee ;
Thee the Church in every land,
ff Singing everlastingly
To the Blessèd Trinity.

mf To the Father ; to the Son,
dim Who for us vouchsafed to die ;
And to God the Holy One,
Who the Church doth sanctify ;
ff Sing we too with glad accord,
Holy, Holy, Holy Lord.

C. Wordsworth, v. 5, ll. 5, 6 altd.

222   11.12.12.10.

p HOLY, Holy, Holy, (*cres*) Lord
God Almighty !
Early in the morning our songs
shall rise to Thee. [Mighty,
p Holy,Holy,Holy,(*cres*)Merciful and
f   God in Three Persons, Blessèd
Trinity !

p Holy, Holy, Holy ! (*cres*) all the
saints adore Thee,
Casting down their golden crowns
around the glassy sea ;
Cherubim and seraphim falling
down before Thee,
Who wert, and art, and evermore shalt be.

p Holy, Holy, Holy, though the
darkness hide Thee,
Though the eye of sinful man Thy
glory may not see ;

mf Only Thou art holy : there is none
beside Thee   [purity.
Perfect in power, in love, and

p   Holy, Holy, Holy, (*cres*) Lord
God Almighty !
f All Thy works shall praise Thy
Name, in earth and sky and
sea ;
Holy, Holy, Holy, (*cres*) Merciful
and Mighty,   [Trinity !
p   God in Three Persons, Blessèd

R. Heber.

223   7s., 8 lines.

p HOLY, Holy, Holy Lord   [earth.
God of Hosts, when heaven and
Out of darkness, at Thy word,
Issued into glorious birth,
cres All Thy works before Thee stood,
And Thine eye beheld them good ;
While they sang with sweet accord,
dim Holy, Holy, Holy Lord.

mf Holy, Holy, Holy, Thee
One Jehovah evermore,
Father, Son, and Spirit, we,
p Dust and ashes, would adore :
Lightly by the world esteemed,
From that world by Thee redeemed,
f Sing we here with glad accord,
dim Holy, Holy, Holy Lord.

mf Holy, Holy, Holy, all   [sing :
cres Heaven's triumphant choirs shall
When the ransomed nations fall
At the footstool of their King,
f Then shall saints and seraphim,
Hearts and voices swell one hymn,
Round the Throne with full accord,
Holy, Holy, Holy Lord.

J. Montgomery.

2.—*INVOCATION.*

224 C.M.

mp MOST ancient of all mysteries!
  Before Thy throne we lie;
  Have mercy now, most Merciful,
  Most holy Trinity!

[*mp*When heaven and earth were yet
  unmade,
  When time was yet unknown,
  Thou in Thy bliss and majesty
  Didst live and love alone!]

mf How wonderful creation is,
  The work that Thou didst bless,
  And, oh! what then must Thou be
  like,
  Eternal Loveliness?

mf How beautiful the Angels are,
  The Saints how bright in bliss:
  But with Thy beauty, Lord! com-
  pared,
  How dull, how poor is this!

mp O listen, then, Most Pitiful!
  To Thy poor creature's heart;
*cres*It blesses Thee that Thou art
  God,
  That Thou art what Thou art!

mp Most ancient of all mysteries!
  Still at Thy throne we lie;
  Have mercy now, most Merciful,
  Most holy Trinity!
                  F. W. Faber.

225 L.M.

mf FATHER of heaven! Whose love
  profound
  A ransom for our souls hath found,
p Before Thy throne we sinners bend:
cresTo us Thy pardoning love extend.

mf Almighty Son! Incarna
  Our Prophet, Priest,
  Lord,
p Before Thy throne we sinners
*cres*To us Thy saving grace exte

mf Eternal Spirit! by Whose b
  The soul is raised from si
  death,
p Before Thy throne we sinners
*cres*To us Thy quickening power
  tend.

mf Jehovah! Father, Spirit, Son!
*cres*Mysterious Godhead! Three
  One!
p Before Thy throne we sinners
*cres*Grace, pardon, life to us extend.
                  E. Cooper.

226 7.7.7.5.

mf THREE in One, and One in
  Ruler of the earth and sea,
  Hear us, while we lift to Thee
  Holy chant and psalm.

mf Light of Lights! with morni
  shine,
  Lift on us Thy light divine;
  And let charity benign
p   Breathe on us her balm.

  Light of Lights! when falls t
  even,
  Let it sink on sins forgiven!
  Fold us in the peace of heaven,
  Shed a vesper calm.

mf Three in One, and One in Three
  Darkling here we worship Thee
*cres*With the saints hereafter we
  Hope to bear the palm.
                  G. Rorison

27   6.6.4.6.6.6.6.4.

COME, Thou Almighty King,
Help us Thy Name to sing,
  Help us to praise :
Father all-glorious,
O'er all victorious,
Come and reign over us,
  Ancient of days.

Come, Thou Incarnate Word,
Gird on Thy mighty sword,
  Our prayer attend :
Come, and Thy people bless,
And give Thy word success ;
Spirit of holiness,
  On us descend.

Come, Holy Comforter,
Thy sacred witness bear,
  In this glad hour :
Thou Who almighty art,
Now rule in every heart,
And ne'er from us depart,
  Spirit of power !

To the Great One in Three,
Eternal praises be,
  Hence evermore :
His sovereign majesty,
May we in glory see,
And to eternity
  Love and adore.

Whitfield's Leaflet, 1757.

28   8.7.8.7.3.

LORD, I hear of showers of blessing
  Thou art scattering, full and free;
Showers, the thirsty land refresh-
  ing :
 Let some droppings fall on me,
    Even me.

p Pass me not, O gracious Father !
  Sinful though my heart may
    be ;
  Thou might'st leave me, but the
    rather
cres Let Thy mercy light on me,
p   Even me.

p Pass me not, O tender Saviour !
  Let me love and cling to Thee ;
cres I am longing for Thy favour ;
  When Thou comest, call for me,
p   Even me.

p Pass me not, O mighty Spirit !
  Thou canst make the blind to
    see ;
  Witnesser of Jesus' merit,
cres Speak the word of power to me,
p   Even me.

[*p* Have I long in sin been sleeping,
  Long been slighting, grieving
    Thee ?
  Has the world my heart been
    keeping ?
cres Oh ! forgive and rescue me.
p   Even me.]

mf Love of God, so pure and changeless,
  Blood of Christ. so rich and free.
  Grace of God, so strong and bound-
    less,
cres Magnify them all in me,
p   Even me

p Pass me not, this lost one bringing ;
  Satan's slave, Thy child shall
    be ;
cres All my heart to Thee is springing ;
p   Blessing others, oh ! bless me,
                     Even me.

Elizabeth Codner, v. 2., l. 3 altd.

V.

The Holy Scriptures.

229   C.M.

mf LAMP of our feet, whereby we trace
   Our path when wont to stray ;
   Stream, from the fount of heavenly
     grace :
   Brook, by the traveller's way :

mf Bread of our souls, whereon we
     feed ;
   True manna from on high; ⌊read
   Our guide and chart, wherein we
   Of realms beyond the sky :

mf Pillar of fire, through watches dark,
   Or radiant cloud by day :
   When waves would whelm our
     tossing bark,
   Our anchor and our stay :

mf Word of the ever living God,
   Will of His glorious Son, [trod,
   Without thee how could earth be
   Or heaven itself be won !

mp Yet to unfold thy hidden worth,
   Thy mysteries to reveal, [forth,
   That Spirit which first gave thee
   Thy volume must unseal.

mf And we, if we aright would learn
   The wisdom it imparts,
   Must to its heavenly teaching turn,
   With simple, childlike hearts.
            B. Barton.

230   8.6.8.4.

f To Thee, O God, we render thanks,
   That Thou to us hast given
A light that shineth on our path,—
A light from heaven :—

mf That Thou into the hearts of men
   Didst breathe Thy breath Divine,
   And mad'st their lips the source
     from whence
   Flowed words of Thine :—

   The words that speak of lives that
     live,
   And life beyond the grave,
   Of Him Who came that life to
     give,—
   Those lives to save :—

p Of Him Who lowly came as man,—
cres To come as man again
f On clouds of glory throned on high,
   As Judge of men.

mf Who lived on earth, on earth Who
     died,
   To set His servants free,
   And left this message as their
     guide,—
p   "Remember Me."

mp Then teach us humbly so to tread
   The path that Saviour trod,
cres Till by His quickening spirit led,
f   We meet our God.
            G. Thring.

231   C.M.

mf THE Spirit breathes upon the word,
   And brings the truth to sight :
   Precepts and promises afford
   A sanctifying light.

mf A glory gilds the sacred page
   Majestic, like the sun :
   It gives a light to every age ;
   It gives, but borrows none.

mf The hand that gave it still supplies
 The gracious light and heat ;
cres His truths upon the nations rise ;
 They rise, but never set.

f Let everlasting thanks be Thine,
 For such a bright display
As makes a world of darkness shine
 With beams of heavenly day.

mf My soul rejoices to pursue
 The steps of Him I love,
cres Till glory breaks upon my view
 In brighter worlds above.
     W. Cowper.

232   7.6.7.6., double.

f O WORD of God incarnate !
 O Wisdom from on high !
O Truth unchanged, unchanging !
 O Light of our dark sky !
We praise Thee for the radiance
 That from the hallowed page,
A lantern to our footsteps,
 Shines on from age to age.

mf The Church from her dear Master
 Received the gift divine,
And still that light she lifteth
 O'er all the earth to shine.
It is the golden casket,
 Where gems of truths are stored ;
It is the heaven-drawn picture
 Of Christ the living Word.

mf It floateth like a banner
 Before God's hosts unfurled ;
It shineth like a beacon
 Above the darkling world :
It is the chart and compass
 That o'er life's surging sea,
'Mid mists and rocks and quick-
  sands,
 Still guides, O Christ, to Thee

mp O make Thy Church, dear Saviour,
 A lamp of burnished gold,
To bear before the nations
 Thy true light as of old ;
O teach Thy wandering pilgrims
 By this their path to trace,
cres Till clouds and darkness ended,
f They see Thee face to face !
     W. W. How.

233   C.M.

mf LORD, I have made Thy word my
  choice,
 My lasting heritage ; [rejoice,
cres There shall my noblest powers
 My warmest thoughts engage.

mf I'll read the histories of Thy love,
 And keep Thy laws in sight ;
While through the promises I rove,
cres With ever fresh delight.

f 'Tis a broad land of wealth un-
  known,
 Where springs of life arise,
Seeds of immortal bliss are sown,
 And hidden glory lies.

p The best relief that mourners have ;
 It makes our sorrows blest ;
cres Our fairest hope beyond the grave,
p And our eternal rest.
     I. Watts.

234   L.M.

mf O GOD ! Who didst Thy will unfold
 In wondrous ways to saints of old,
 By dream, by oracle, or seer,
 Wilt Thou not still Thy people hear?

mf What though no answering voice
  is heard ?
 Thine oracles, the written word,
 Counsel and guidance still impart
 Responsive to the upright heart.

mf What though no more by dreams is
    shown   [known ?
    That future things to God are
    Enough the promises reveal ;
    Wisdom and love the rest conceal.

mf Faith asks no signal from the skies
    To show that prayers accepted rise ;
    Our Priest is in the holy place,
    And answers from the throne of
      grace.

mf Lord, with this grace our hearts
    inspire ;
    Answer our sacrifice by fire ;
f And by Thy mighty acts declare
    Thou art the God Who heareth
    prayer.   *J. Conder.*

235   6.6.6.6., Trochaic.

mf LORD, Thy Word abideth,
    And our footsteps guideth ;
    Who its truth believeth
    Light and joy receiveth.

p When our foes are near us,
cres Then Thy Word doth cheer us ;
    Word of consolation,
    Message of salvation.

p When the storms are o'er us,
    And dark clouds before us,
cres Then its light directeth
    And our way protecteth.

mf Who can tell the pleasure,
    Who recount the treasure,
    By Thy Word imparted
    To the simple-hearted ?

    Word of mercy, giving
    Succour to the living ;
    Word of life, supplying
p Comfort to the dying !

mf Oh, that we discerning
    Its most holy learning,
    Lord, may love and fear Thee,
    Evermore be near Thee !

            H. W. Baker.

VI.

The Gospel and its Invitations.

236   8.5.8.3.

p ART thou weary, art thou languid,
    Art thou sore distrest ? [coming,
cres " Come to Me," saith One, " and
p   Be at rest."

mf Hath He marks to lead me to Him,
    If He be my guide ? [prints,
dim " In His feet and hands are wound-
p   And His side."

mf Is there diadem, as Monarch,
    That His brow adorns ?
cres " Yea, a crown, in very surety :
p   But of thorns."

mf If I find Him, if I follow,
    What His guerdon here ?
p " Many a sorrow, many a labour,
    Many a tear."

f If I still hold closely to Him,
    What hath He at last ?
f " Sorrow vanquished, labour ended,
cres   Jordan past."

mf If I ask Him to receive me,
    Will He say me nay ?
f " Not till earth and not till heaven
    Pass away."

mf Finding, following, keeping, struggling,
 Is He sure to bless?
f Saints, apostles, prophets, martyrs,
ff   Answer, "Yes."
Stephen the Sabaite, tr. J. M. Neale,
  v. 7, l. 3 altd.

237   7s.

f WELCOME, welcome! sinner, hear;
 Hang not back through shame or
  fear;
 Doubt not, nor distrust the call;
 Mercy is proclaimed to all.

mf Welcome to the offered peace:
 Welcome, prisoner, to release:
 Burst thy bonds; be saved; be free;
 Rise and come; He calleth thee.

mp Welcome, weeping penitent,
 Grace has made thy heart relent;
 Welcome, long-estrangèd child:
 God in Christ is reconciled.

mf Welcome to the cleansing fount,
 Springing from the sacred mount;
 Welcome to the feast divine,
 Bread of life, and living wine.

mp All ye weary and distressed,
 Welcome to relief and rest.
cres All is ready; hear the call,
f There is ample room for all.
     J. Conder.

238   6.4.6.4.

mf TO-DAY, the Saviour calls;
 Ye, wanderers, come!
cres O ye benighted souls,
 Why longer roam?

mf To-day, the Saviour calls;
cres O listen now;
 Within these sacred walls
 To Jesus bow.

mf To-day, the Saviour calls;
 For refuge fly:
p The storm of vengeance falls,
pp Ruin is nigh.

mf The Spirit calls to-day;
cres Yield to His power;
p O grieve Him not away,
cres 'Tis mercy's hour.
   S. Smith and T. Hastings.

239   10.10.10.

mf "YET there is room!"—The Lamb's
 bright hall of song, [along;
 With its fair glory, beckons thee
p Room! room! still room!—O enter,
 enter now!

p Day is declining, and the sun is
 low; [makes haste to go;
 The shadows lengthen, — light
 Room! room! still room!—O enter,
 enter now!

f The bridal hall is filling for the
 feast; [groom's guest;
 Pass in, pass in, and be the Bride-
 Room! room! still room!—O enter,
 enter now!

[*f* It fills, it fills, that hall of jubilee!
 Make haste! make haste!—'tis not
 too full for thee; [enter now!
 Room! room! still room!—O enter,

mf "Yet there is room!" Still open
 stands the gate, [late;
 The gate of love,—it is not yet too
 Room! room! still room!—O enter,
 enter now!]

f Pass in, pass in! That banquet is
 for thee, [free;
 That cup of everlasting love is
 Room! room! still room!—O enter
 enter now!

b

f All heaven is there, all joy! Go
   in, go in;
The angels beckon thee the prize
   to win;
Room! room! still room!—O enter,
   enter now!

ff Louder and louder sounds the
   loving call!
Come, lingerer, come!—enter that
   festal hall!
Room! room! still room!—O enter,
   enter now!

p Ere night that gate may close, and
   seal thy doom;
Then the last, low, long cry—"No
   room, no room!"
pp No room! no room!—O woeful
   cry—"No room!"

H. Bonar.

240   8.7.8.7.4.7.

p COME, ye sinners, poor and
   wretched,
Weak and wounded, sick and
   sore;
mf Jesus ready stands to save you,
Full of pity joined with power.
   He is able;
   He is willing: doubt no more.

mf Ho! ye needy, come, and welcome,
God's free bounty glorify;
True belief and true repentance,
cres Every grace that brings us nigh,
   Without money,
   Come to Jesus Christ and buy.

mf Let not conscience make you linger,
Nor of fitness fondly dream;
All the fitness He requireth
cres Is to feel your need of Him:
   This He gives you;
   'Tis the Spirit's rising beam.

[*mp*Come, ye weary, heavy-laden,
Bruised and broken by the fall;
If you tarry till you're better,
You will never come at all.
   Not the righteous,
   Sinners, Jesus came to call.]

mf Lo! the incarnate God, ascended,
Pleads the merit of His blood.
Venture on Him, venture wholly,
Let no other trust intrude:
   None but Jesus
   Can do helpless sinners good.

f Saints and angels joined in concert,
Sing the praises of the Lamb;
While the blissful seats of heaven
Sweetly echo with His name.
ff   Hallelujah!
   Sinners here may sing the same

J. Hart.

241   C.M., double.

f THE Lord is rich and merciful,
The Lord is very kind;
Oh, come to Him, come now to Him,
With a believing mind.   [thee,
p His comforts, they shall strengthen
cres Like flowing waters cool;
And He shall for thy spirit be
A fountain ever full.

f The Lord is glorious and strong,
Our God is very high;
Oh, trust in Him, trust now in Him
And have security.
He shall be to thee like the sea,
And thou shalt surely feel.
His wind, that bloweth healthily,
Thy sicknesses to heal.

f The Lord is wonderful and wise,
As all the ages tell;
Oh, learn of Him, learn now of Him,
Then with thee it is well.

And with His light thou shalt be
 blest,
Therein to work and live ;
And He shall be to thee a rest
 When evening hours arrive.
T. T. Lynch.

242   7.6.7.6., double.

p O JESU, Thou art standing
. Outside the fast-closed door,
In lowly patience waiting
 To pass the threshold o'er ;
f Shame on us, Christian brothers,
 His name and sign who bear,
Oh shame, thrice shame upon us,
p To keep Him standing there.

O Jesu, Thou art knocking,
 And lo ! that hand is scarred,
And thorns Thy brow encircle,
 And tears Thy face have marred :
*cres*Oh love that passeth knowledge
 So patiently to wait !
*dim*Oh sin that hath no equal
p So fast to bar the gate !

O Jesu, Thou art pleading
 In accents meek and low,
" I died for you My children,
cres And will ye treat Me so ? "
*mf*O Lord, with shame and sorrow,
 We open now the door ;
Dear Saviour, enter, enter,
 And leave us nevermore.
W. W. How.

243   8.7.8.7.

*mp*WAS there ever kindest shepherd
 Half so gentle, half so sweet,
As the Saviour Who would have us
 Come and gather at His feet ?

*mf*It is God : His love looks mighty,
 But *is mightier than it seems* :

'Tis our Father : and His fondness
 Goes far out beyond our dreams.

*mf*There's a wideness in God's mercy,
 Like the wideness of the sea :
There's a kindness in His justice
 Which is more than liberty.

f For the love of God is broader
 Than the measures of man's
  mind,
And the Heart of the Eternal
 Is most wonderfully kind.

*dim*But we make His love too narrow
 By false limits of our own ;
And we magnify His strictness
 With a zeal He will not own.

*mf*There is plentiful redemption
 In the blood that has been shed ;
There is joy for all its members
 In the sorrows of the Head.

*mp*If our love were but more simple,
 We should take Him at His word;
*cres*And our lives would be all sunshine
 In the sweetness of our Lord.
F. W. Faber.

244   7s.

*mf*TIME is earnest, passing by ;
 Death is earnest, drawing nigh :
Sinner, wilt thou trifling be ?
 Time and death appeal to thee.

*mf*Life is earnest : when 'tis o'er,
 Thou returnest nevermore ;
Soon to meet eternity,
 Wilt thou never serious be ?

p God is earnest : kneel and pray,
 Ere thy season pass away ;
 Ere He set His judgment throne ;
 Ere the day of grace be gone.

mf Christ is earnest, bids thee come ;
Paid, thy spirit's priceless sum ;
Wilt thou spurn the Saviour's love,
Pleading with thee from above ?

mf O be earnest, do not stay ;
dim Thou mayest perish, e'en to-day.
cres Rise, thou lost one, rise and flee ;
Lo ! thy Saviour waits for thee.

S. Dyer.

245
S.M.

mf TO-MORROW, Lord, is Thine,
Lodged in Thy sovereign hand ;
And if its sun arise and shine,
It shines by Thy command.

mf The present moment flies,
And bears our life away :
O make Thy servants truly wise,
That they may live to-day.

mf Since on this wingèd hour
Eternity is hung,
Waken by Thine almighty power
The agèd and the young.

mf One thing demands our care ;
O be it still pursued,
dim Lest, slighted once, the season fair
p Should never be renewed.

mf To Jesus may we fly,
cres Swift as the morning light,
dim Lest life's young golden beams should die
p In sudden, endless night.

P. Doddridge.

246
L.M.

mp RETURN, O wanderer, return,
And seek an injured Father's face ;

Those warm desires that in thee burn
Were kindled by reclaiming grace.

mp Return, O wanderer, return,
And seek a Father's melting heart ;
Whose pitying eyes thy grief discern,
Whose hand can heal thy inward smart.

mp Return, O wanderer, return,
He heard thy deep repentant sigh ;
He saw thy softened spirit mourn,
When no intruding ear was nigh.

mp Return, O wanderer, return,
cres Thy Saviour bids thy spirit live ;
Go to His bleeding feet, and learn
f How freely Jesus can forgive.

W. B. Collyer.

247
7.6.7.6., double.

mf "Come unto Me, ye weary,
p And I will give you rest."
O blessèd voice of Jesus,
cres Which comes to hearts oppressed!
mf It tells of benediction,
Of pardon, grace, and peace,
f Of joy that hath no ending,
Of love which cannot cease.

mf "Come unto Me, dear children,
And I will give you Light."
p O loving voice of Jesus,
cres Which comes to cheer the night !
p Our hearts were filled with sadness,
And we had lost our way,
f But morning brings us gladness,
And songs the break of day.

mf "Come unto Me, ye fainting,
And I will give you Life."
O peaceful voice of Jesus,
cres Which comes to end our strife

mf The foe is stern and eager,
The fight is fierce and long,
f But Thou hast made us mighty,
And stronger than the strong.

mf "And whosoever cometh
I will not cast Him out."

O patient love of Jesus
cres Which drives away our doubt;
mf Which calls us very sinners,
p Unworthy though we be
cres Of love so free and boundless,
rall To come, dear Lord, to Thee !
W. C. Dix.

VII.
The Christian Life.
1.—*REPENTANCE AND CONFESSION.*

248   L.M.

p SHOW pity, Lord ; O Lord, forgive,
Let a repenting rebel live ;
cres Are not Thy mercies large and free?
May not a sinner trust in Thee ?

mp My sins, though great, do not sur-
pass
The power and glory of Thy grace:
cres Great God, Thy nature hath no
bound,
So let Thy pardoning love be found.

p O wash my soul from every sin,
And make my guilty conscience
clean ;
Here, on my heart, the burden lies.
And past offences pain mine eyes.

p My lips, with shame, my sins con-
fess   [grace :
Against Thy law, against Thy
Lord, should Thy judgment grow
severe,   [clear.
I am condemned, but Thou art

mp Yet save a trembling sinner, Lord,
Whose hope, still hovering round
Thy word,   [there,
cres Would light on some sweet promise
Some sure support against despair.
    •   *I. Watts, v. 2, l. 1 altd.*

249   S.M.

mf HELP me, my God, to speak
True words to Thee each day ;
Real let my voice be when I praise,
And trustful when I pray.

mf Thy words are true to me, ·
Let mine to Thee be true ;
The speech of my whole heart and
soul,
However low and few.

mp True words of grief for sin,
Of longing to be free,
Of groaning for deliverance,
And likeness, Lord, to Thee.

mf True words of faith and hope,
Of godly joy and grief ;
cres Lord, I believe, Oh hear my cry,
dim Help Thou my unbelief.
     H. Bonar.

250   L.M.

p WITH broken heart and contrite
sigh,
A trembling sinner, Lord, I cry ;
cres "Thy pardoning grace is rich and
free,
p O God, be merciful to me."

mp I smite upon my troubled breast,
  With deep and conscious guilt
    oppressed ;
Christ and His cross my only plea,
p " O God, be merciful to me."

p Far off I stand with tearful eyes,
  Nor dare uplift them to the skies ;
*cres*But Thou dost all my anguish see,
p " O God, be merciful to me."

mp Nor alms, nor deeds that I have
    done,
  Can for a single sin atone :
*cres*To Calvary alone I flee,
p " O God, be merciful to me."

mf And when redeemed from sin and
    hell,
  With all the ransomed throng I
    dwell,
*cres*My raptured song shall ever be,
ff " God has been merciful to me."

C. Elven.

251
7.6.7.6., double.

p O JESU, Lord, most merciful,
  Low at Thy Cross we lie ;
O sinner's Friend most pitiful,
  Hear our bewailing cry.
We come to Thee with mourning,
  We come to Thee in woe ;
With contrite hearts returni)
  And tears that overflow.

mf O gracious Intercessor !
  O Priest within the Veil !
Plead for each lost transgressor,
  The Blood that cannot fail.
*dim*We spread our sins before Thee,
  We tell them one by one ;
*cres*O, for Thy Name's great glory,
  Forgive all we have done.

p O by Thy Cross and Passion,
  Thy Tears and Agony,
And Crown of cruel fashion,
  And Death on Calvary ;
By all that untold suffering
  Endured by Thee alone ;
*cres*O Priest ! O Spotless Offering !
f Plead, for Thou didst atone.

f And in these hearts now broken
  Re-enter Thou and reign ;
And say, by that dear token,
  We are absolved again.
And build us up, and guide us,
  And guard us day by day ;
And in Thy presence hide us,
  And keep our souls alway.

J. Hamilton.

252
7.7.7.

p LORD, in this Thy mercy's day,
  Ere it pass for aye away,
  On our knees we fall and pray ;

Holy Jesus, grant us tears,
  Fill us with heart-searching fears.
  Ere that awful doom appears.

mf Lord, on us Thy Spirit pour,
  Kneeling lowly at the door,
  Ere it close for evermore.

pp By Thy night of agony,
  By Thy supplicating cry,
  By Thy willingness to die,

By Thy tears of bitter woe
  For Jerusalem below,
  Let us not Thy love forego.

p 'Neath Thy wings let us have place,
*cres*Lest we lose this day of grace,
mf Ere we shall behold Thy face.

I. Williams, v. 3, ll. 1, 2 altd.

253
7s.

mp SINFUL, sighing to be blest,
Bound, and longing to be free,
Weary, waiting for my rest,
"God be merciful to me!"

mp Goodness, I have none to plead,
Sinfulness in all I see;
I can only bring my need:
"God be merciful to me!"

p Broken heart and downcast eyes
Dare not lift themselves to Thee,
cres Yet Thou canst interpret sighs:
"God be merciful to me!"

mp From this sinful heart of mine
To Thy bosom I would flee;
I am not my own, but Thine:
"God be merciful to me!"

f There is One beside the throne,
And my only hope and plea
Are in Him, and Him alone:
"God be merciful to me!"

f He my cause will undertake,
My Interpreter will be;
He's my all, and for His sake,
"God be merciful to me!"

J. S. B. Monsell.

254
L.M.

mp HEAR, gracious God! a sinner's cry,
For I have nowhere else to fly;
My hope, my only hope's in Thee:
O God, be merciful to me!

mp To Thee I come. a sinner poor,
And wait for mercy at Thy door;
Indeed, I've nowhere else to flee:
O God, be merciful to me!

p To Thee I come, a sinner weak,
And scarce know how to pray or
speak;

From fear and weakness set me
free:
O God, be merciful to me!

p To Thee I come, a sinner vile;
Upon me, Lord, vouchsafe to smile
Mercy alone I make my plea:
O God, be merciful to me!

p To Thee I come, a sinner great,
And well Thou knowest all my
state;
cres Yet full forgiveness is with Thee:
O God, be merciful to me!

p To Thee I come, a sinner lost,
Nor have I aught wherein to
trust;   [would be;
cres But where Thou art, Lord, I
dim O God, be merciful to me!

S. Medley.

255
C.M.

mp LOVE me, O Lord, forgivingly,
O ever be my Friend;
And still, when Thou reprovest me,
Reproof with pity blend.

mp O pity me when weak I fall;
And as, with saddened eyes,
I upwards look, O let Thy call
Come, strengthening me to rise.

mp My sins, dispersed by mercy bright,
Like clouds again grow black;
O change the winds that bring
such night,
And drive the darkness back.

mp This striving weather, let it cease;
cres Then fervent, fruitful days
Shall yield both promise and
increase,
And make my growth Thy praise.

T. T. Lynch.

256
4.6.4.6.4.6.4.6.

mp SHOW pity, Lord,
For we are frail and faint ;
We fade away,
O list to our complaint !
We fade away
Like flowers in the sun ;
cres We just begin,
dim And then our work is done.

mp Show pity, Lord,
Our souls are sore distressed ;
As troubled seas,
Our natures have no rest ;
cres As troubled seas
That surging, beat the shore,
We throb and heave,
Ever and evermore.

mp Show pity, Lord,
Our grief is in our sin ;
We would be cleansed ;
O make us pure within !
We would be cleansed,
For this we cry to Thee,
cres Thy word of love
Can make the conscience free.

mf Show pity, Lord,
Inspire our hearts with love ;
That holy love
Which draws the soul above ;
cres That holy love
Which makes us one with Thee,
And with Thy saints,
Through all eternity.
D. Thomas.

257
C.M.

p O LORD, turn not Thy face away
From them that lowly lie,
Lamenting sore their sinful life
With tears and bitter cry.

mf Thy mercy-gates are open wide
To them that mourn their sin ;
cres O shut them not against us, Lord,
But let us enter in.

p We need not to confess our fault,
For surely Thou canst tell ; [are,
What we have done, and what we
Thou knowest very well :

mf Wherefore, to beg and to entreat,
With tears we come to Thee,
cres As children that have done amiss
p Fall at their father's knee.

mf And need we then, O Lord, repeat
The blessing which we crave,
When Thou dost know, before we
speak,
The thing that we would have ?

mf Mercy, O Lord, mercy we ask,
This is the total sum ;
For mercy, Lord, is all our prayer ;
cres O let Thy mercy come !
Variation by R. Heber from
J. Marckant.

258
C.M.

p How sad our state by nature is !
Our sin, how deep it stains !
And Satan binds our captive minds
Fast in his slavish chains.

cres But there's a voice of sovereign
grace
Sounds from the sacred word ;
Ho ! ye despairing sinners, come,
And trust upon the Lord.

f My soul obeys the Almighty call,
And runs to this relief ;
I would believe Thy promise, Lord,
O help my unbelief !

mp To the dear fountain of Thy blood,
Incarnate God, I fly ;

Here let me wash my guilty soul
From crimes of deepest dye.

mp A guilty, weak, and helpless worm,
On Thy kind arms I fall ; [ness,
cres Be Thou my strength and righteous-
My Jesus, and my All.

I. Watts, v. 4, l. 2 altd.

259
7.7.7.7.8.8.

mp FROM the deeps of grief and fear,
Lord, to Thee my soul repairs :
From Thy heaven bow down
Thine ear ;
Let Thy mercy meet my prayers.
O if Thou mark'st what's done
amiss, [bliss ?
What soul so pure, can see Thy

mf But with Thee sweet mercy
stands,
Sealing pardons, working fear :
Wait, my soul, wait on His
hands ;
Wait, mine eye, O wait, mine ear :
If He His eye or tongue affords,
Watch all His looks, catch all His
words.

mp As a watchman waits for day,
Looks for light, and looks again :
When the night grows old and
For relief he calls amain : [grey,
So look, so wait, so long mine eyes,
To see my Lord, my Sun, arise.

mf Wait, ye saints, wait on our Lord ;
From His tongue sweet mercy
flows :
Trust His cross, wait on His word ;
On that tree redemption grows.
f He will redeem His Israel
From sin and wrath, from death
and hell.

P. Fletcher. v. 3, l. 4, v. 4, l. 3 altd.

260
S.M.

mp OPPRESSED with sin and woe,
A burdened heart I bear ;
Opposed by many a mighty foe,
But I will not despair.

mp With this polluted heart
I dare to come to Thee,—
Holy and mighty as Thou art,—
For Thou wilt pardon me.

mp I feel that I am weak,
And prone to every sin ;
cres But Thou Who giv'st to those who
seek,
Wilt give me strength within.

p Far as the earth may be
From yonder starry skies ;
Remoter still am I from Thee :
cres Yet Thou wilt not despise.

mf I need not fear my foes ;
I need not yield to care ;
I need not sink beneath my woes,
For Thou wilt answer prayer.

mf In my Redeemer's name,
I give myself to Thee ;
And, all unworthy as I am,
My God will cherish me

Annie Bronte.

261
8.4.8.4.8.8.8.

mf MY Saviour, 'mid life's varied scene,
Be Thou my stay :
Guide me, through each perplexing
path,
To perfect day ;
dim In weakness and in sin I stand,
cres Still faith can clasp Thy mighty
hand,
And follow at Thy dear comman

mp My Saviour, I have nought to bring
   Worthy of Thee ;
dim A broken heart Thou wilt not
   spurn,
    Accept of me.
I need Thy righteousness divine,
cres I plead Thy promises as mine,
dim I perish if I am not Thine.

mp My Saviour, wilt Thou turn away
   From such a cry ?
My Refuge, wilt Thou me forget,
   And must I die ?   [light
Faith trembles ; but her glance of
Has pierced through regions dark
   as night,
And entered into realms of light.

mf My Saviour, 'mid heaven's glorious
   throng,
   I see Thee there,   [love
Pleading with all Thy matchless
   And tender care :
Not for the angel forms around,
But for lost souls in fetters bound,
That they may hear salvation's
   sound.

mf My Saviour, thus I find my rest
   Alone with Thee ;
Beneath Thy wing I have no fear
   Of what may be.
cres Strengthened with Thy all-glorious
   might,
I shall be conqueror in the fight,
f Then give to Thee my crown of
   light.
       Elizabeth A. Godwin.

262   S.M.

p AND wilt Thou pardon, Lord,
   A sinner such as I ?   [record
*Although Thy book his crimes
Of such a crimson dye ?*

So deep are they engraved,—
So terrible their fear,   [saved.
The righteous scarcely shall be
And where shall I appear ?

cres My soul, make all things known
   To Him Who all things sees ;
That so the Lamb may yet atone
   For thine iniquities.

mf O Thou Physician blest,
   Make clean my guilty soul !
dim And me, by many a sin oppressed,
cres Restore, and keep me whole !

f I know not how to praise
   Thy mercy and Thy love :
But deign Thy servant to upraise,
   And I shall learn above !
    Joseph of the Studium, tr.
      . *J. M. Neale.*

263   8.7.8.7.8.8.7.

mf OUT of the depths I cry to Thee,
   Lord God, O hear my wailing !
Thy gracious ear incline to me,
   And make my prayer availing !
dim On my misdeeds in mercy look,
   O deign to blot them from Thy
    book,
p Or who can stand before Thee ?

mf Thy sovereign grace and boundless
   love
   Make Thee, O Lord, forgiving ;
My purest thoughts and deeds but
   Sin in my heart is living : [prove
None guiltless in Thy sight appear,
All who approach Thy throne must
   fear,
p And humbly trust Thy mercy.

mf Thou canst be merciful while just,
   This is my hope's foundation ;
On Thy redeeming grace I trust,
   Grant me, then, Thy salvation.

*cres*Shielded by Thee I stand secure,
Thy word is firm, Thy promise sure,
And I rely upon Thee.

mp Like those who watch for midnight's hour
  To hail the dawning morrow,
*cres*I wait for Thee, I trust Thy power,
Unmoved by doubt or sorrow
So thus let Israel hope in Thee,
And he shall find Thy mercy free,
And Thy redemption plenteous.

mf Where'er the greatest sins abound,
By grace they are exceeded ;
Thy helping hand is always found
cres With aid where aid is needed :
Thy hand, the only hand to save,
Will rescue Israel from the grave,
And pardon his transgression.

M. Luther, tr. New Congregational Hymn Book, 1859.

264   S.M.

p OUT of the deep I call
To Thee, O Lord, to Thee ;
Before Thy throne of grace I fall,
Be merciful to me.

p Out of the deep I cry,
The woeful deep of sin,
Of evil done in days gone by,
Of evil now within.

p Out of the deep of fear
And dread of coming shame,
From morning watch till night is near
cres I plead the Precious Name.

mf Lord, there is mercy now,
As ever was, with Thee ;
Before Thy throne of grace I bow,
Be merciful to me.

H. W. Baker.

2.—FAITH IN JESUS: PARDON AND JUSTIFICATION.

265   8.8.8.6.

p JUST as I am—without one plea,
But that Thy blood was shed for me,
*cres*And that Thou bidst me come to Thee,
p   O Lamb of God, I come.

p Just as I am—and waiting not
To rid my soul of one dark blot ;
*cres*To Thee, Whose blood can cleanse each spot,
p   O Lamb of God, I come.

p Just as I am—though tossed about
With many a conflict, many a doubt,
*cres*Fightings and fears within, without,
p   O Lamb of God, I come.

[*p* Just as I am,—poor, wretched, blind ;
*cres*Sight, riches, healing of the mind.
Yea, all I need, in Thee to find,
p   O Lamb of God, I come.]

p Just as I am—(*cres*) Thou wilt receive,
Wilt welcome, pardon, cleanse, relieve ;
mf Because Thy promise I believe,
    O Lamb of God, I come.

p Just as I am—(*cres*) Thy love unknown
Has broken every barrier down ;
mf Now, to be Thine, yea, Thine alone
    O Lamb of God, I come.

[*p* Just as I am—(*cres*) of that free love
The breadth, length, depth, and height to prove,
*cres*Here for a season, (*f*) then above,
O Lamb of God, I come.]

Charlotte Elliott.

266   10.10.10.10.

p WEARY of earth and laden with my sin, [enter in ;
I look at heaven and long to
*cres*But there no evil thing may find a home, [me "come."
And yet I hear a voice, that bids

p So vile I am, how dare I hope to stand [land ?
In the pure glory of the promised
Before the whiteness of that throne appear ? [draw me near.
*cres*Yet there are hands stretched out to

p The while I fain would tread the heavenly way,
Seems evil ever with me day by day;
*cres*Yet on mine ears the gracious tidings fall, [loosed from all."
f "Repent, confess, and thou art

f It is the voice of Jesus that I hear,
His are the hands outstretched to draw me near. [all atone,
And His the Blood, that can for
And set me faultless there before the Throne.

[*mf*O great Absolver, grant my soul may wear [prayer,
The lowliest garb of penitence and
*cres*That in the Father's courts my glorious dress [righteousness.
f May be the garment of Thy

mf Yea, Thou will answer for me, righteous Lord ; [great reward ;
Thine all the merits, mine the
p Thine the sharp thorns, and mine the golden crown ;
f Mine the life won, and Thine the life laid down.

mf Nought can I bring, dear Lord, for all I owe, [bestow ;
Yet let my full heart what it can
Like that sweet word let my devotion prove, [love.
*cres*Forgiven greatly, how I greatly

S. J. Stone.

267   S.M.

p NOT what these hands have done
Can save this guilty soul ;
Not what this toiling flesh has borne
Can make my spirit whole.

p Not what I feel or do
Can give me peace with God ;
*dim*Not all my prayers, and sighs, and tears,
pp Can bear my awful load.

mf Thy work alone, O Christ,
Can ease this weight of sin ;
Thy blood alone, O Lamb of God,
Can give me peace within.

mf Thy love to me, O God,
Not mine, O Lord, to Thee,
p Can rid me of this dark unrest,
cres And set my spirit free.

mf Thy grace alone, O God,
To me can pardon speak ;
Thy power alone, O Son of God,
Can this sore bondage break.

I bless the Christs of God,
I rest on love divine :   [heart.
And with unfaltering lip and
I call this Saviour mine.
H. Bonar.

68   8.8.8.6.
DRAWN to the Cross which Thou
    hast blessed   [tressed,
With healing gifts for souls dis-
To find in Thee my Life, my Rest,
    Christ Crucified, I come.

Stained with the sins which I have
    wrought   [thought,
In word and deed and secret
*pre*For pardon which Thy Blood hath
    bought,
p   Christ Crucified, I come.

Weary of selfishness and pride,
False pleasures gone, vain hopes
    denied,   [hide.
Deep in Thy wounds my shame to
p   Christ Crucified, I come.

*mp*Thou knowest all my griefs and
    fears,   [years ;
Thy grace abused, my misspent
Yet now to Thee, for cleansing tears,
p   Christ Crucified, I come.

*mf*I would not, if I could, conceal
The ills which only Thou canst heal ;
*pre*So to the Cross, where sinners kneel,
p   Christ Crucified, I come.

*mp*Wash me, and take away each stain,
Let nothing of my sin remain ;
For cleansing, though it be through
    pain,
p   Christ Crucified, I come.

*mp*And then for work to do for Thee,
Which shall so sweet a service be,
That angels well might envy me,
p   Christ Crucified, I come.

mp A life of labour, prayers, and love,
Which shall my heart's conversion
    prove,
Till to a glorious Rest above,
p   Christ Crucified, I come.

*mf*To share with Thee Thy Life
    Divine,   [mine,
Thy Righteousness, Thy Likeness
Since Thou hast made my nature
    Thine.
p   Christ Crucified, I come.]

mf To be what Thou wouldst have me
    be,
Accepted, sanctified in Thee, [in me.
*cres*Through what Thy grace shall work
dim   Christ Crucified, I come.
Genevière Irons.

269   7s.
mp NEVER further than Thy Cross ;
    Never higher than Thy feet ;
    Here earth's precious things seem
        dross ;   [sweet.
    Here earth's bitter things grow

mp Gazing thus, our sin we see,
    Learn Thy love while gazing thus—
    Sin, which laid the Cross on Thee,
    Love, which bore the Cross for us.

mf Here we learn to serve and give,
    And, rejoicing, self deny ;
    Here we gather love to live,
    Here we gather faith to die.

mf Symbols of our liberty
    And our service here unite ;
    Captives by Thy Cross set free,
    Soldiers of Thy Cross, we fight.

mf Pressing onwards as we can,
    Still to this our hearts must tend—
    Where our earliest hopes began,
    There our last aspirings end,

mf Till amid the Hosts óf light
    We in Thee redeemed, complete,
f Through Thy Cross made pure and
      white,
    Cast our crowns before Thy feet.
               Elizabeth Charles.

270   L.M.

mf No more, my God, I boast no more
    Of all the duties I have done ;
    I quit the hopes I held before,
    To trust the merits of Thy Son.

mf Now, for the love I bear His name,
    What was my gain I count my loss ;
    My former pride I call my shame,
    And nail my glory to His Cross.

mf Yes, and I must and will esteem
    All things but loss for Jesus' sake ;
    O may my soul be found in Him,
    And of His righteousness partake.

mf The best obedience of my hands
    Dares not appear before Thy throne;
    But faith can answer Thy demands
    By pleading what my Lord has
      done.   *I. Watts.*

271   6.6.4.6.6.6.4.

mf   MY faith looks up to Thee,
    Thou Lamb of Calvary,
      Saviour Divine :
p   Now hear me while I pray ;
    Take all my guilt away ;
cres O let me from this day
      Be wholly Thine.

mf   May Thy rich grace impart
    Strength to my fainting heart,
      My zeal inspire :
p   As Thou hast died for me,
cres O may my love to Thee
    Pure, warm, and changeless be,
f   A living fire.

p   While life's dark maze I tread,
    And griefs around me spread,
      Be Thou my Guide ;
cres Bid darkness turn to day,
    Wipe sorrow's tears away,
dim Nor let me ever stray
p   From Thee aside.

p   When ends life's transient dream,
    When death's cold, sullen stream
      Shall o'er me roll,
cres Blest Saviour, then, in love,
    Fear and distrust remove ;
    O bear me safe above—
f   A ransomed soul.
              Ray Palmer.

272   C.M.

mf THERE is a fountain filled with
      blood
    Drawn from Emmanuel's veins ;
    And sinners, plunged beneath that
      flood,
    Lose all their guilty stains.

mf The dying thief rejoiced to see
    That fountain in his day ;
p And there have I, as vile as he,
cres Washed all my sins away.

p Dear dying Lamb ! Thy precious
    Blood
    Shall never lose its power, [God
cres Till all the ransomed Church of
    Be saved, to sin no more.

mf E'er since, by faith, I saw the stream
    Thy flowing wounds supply,
cres Redeeming love has been my theme,
f   And shall be till I die.

f Then in a nobler, sweeter song,
    I'll sing Thy power to save,
dim When this poor lisping, stammer-
      ing tongue
p   Lies silent in the grave.

[*mf* Lord, I believe Thou hast prepared,
Unworthy though I be,
cres For me a blood-bought free reward,
f A golden harp for me.

f 'Tis strung, and tuned for endless years,
And formed by power divine,
To sound in God the Father's ears
No other name but Thine.]
W. Cowper.

273 7s., 6 lines.

mf ROCK of Ages, cleft for me,
Let me hide myself in Thee;
Let the water and the blood,
From Thy riven side which flowed,
cres Be of sin the double cure—
dim Cleanse me from its guilt and power.

p Not the labours of my hands
Can fulfil Thy law's demands.
Could my zeal no respite know,
Could my tears for ever flow,
cres All for sin could not atone;
f Thou must save, and Thou alone.

p Nothing in my hand I bring;
Simply to Thy Cross I cling;
Naked, come to Thee for dress;
Helpless, look to Thee for grace:
cres Foul, I to the Fountain fly;
f Wash me, Saviour, or I die.

mf While I draw this fleeting breath,
pp When mine eyes shall close in death,
cres When I soar through tracts unknown,
See Thee on Thy judgment-throne,
pp Rock of Ages, cleft for me,
pp Let me hide myself in Thee.
A. M. Toplady, v. 4, l. 2 altd.

274 7s., 6 lines.

mp WEARY with my load of sin,
All diseased and faint within,
See me, Lord, Thy grace entreat,
See me prostrate at Thy feet;
Here before Thy Cross I lie,
dim Here I live or here I die.

mp I have tried and tried in vain
Many ways to ease my pain;
Now all other hope is past,
Only this is left at last:
Here before Thy Cross I lie,
dim Here I live or here I die.

mp If I perish, be it here,
With the Friend of sinners near;
Lord, it is enough—I know
Never sinner perished so:
dim Here before Thy Cross I lie,
cres Here I cannot, cannot die.
George Wade-Robinson.

275 7s., 8 lines.

mf JESU, Lover of my soul,
Let me to Thy bosom fly,
cres While the nearer waters roll,
While the tempest still is high!
p Hide me, O my Saviour, hide,
Till the storm of life is past;
cres Safe into the haven guide;
dim O receive my soul at last!

mf Other refuge have I none;
Hangs my helpless soul on Thee;
p Leave, ah! leave me not alone,
Still support and comfort me!
cres All my trust on Thee is stayed,
All my help from Thee I bring:
dim Cover my defenceless head
With the shadow of Thy wing!

mf Thou, O Christ, art all I want;
More than all in Thee I find:

Raise the fallen, cheer the faint,
Heal the sick, and lead the blind !
p Just and holy is Thy Name ;
I am all unrighteousness ;
False and full of sin I am,
*cres*Thou art full of truth and grace.

mf Plenteous grace with Thee is found,
Grace to cover all my sin ;
*cres*Let the healing streams abound ;
Make and keep me pure within ;
f Thou of life the Fountain art,
Freely let me take of Thee ;
Spring Thou up within my heart !
Rise to all eternity !
C. Wesley.

276 C.M.

p WHEN wounded sore the stricken
soul
Lies bleeding and unbound,
*cres*One only hand, a piercèd hand,
mf Can salve the sinner's wound.

p When sorrow swells the laden
breast,
And tears of anguish flow,
*cres*One only heart, a broken heart,
mf Can feel the sinner's woe.

p When penitence has wept in vain
Over some foul dark spot,
*cres*One only stream, a stream of blood,
mf Can wash away the blot.

'Tis Jesus' blood that washes white,
His hand that brings relief,
*cres*His heart that's touched with all
our joys,
p And feeleth for our grief.

mf Lift up Thy bleeding hand, O Lord ;
Unseal that cleansing tide ;
We have no shelter from our sin
p But in Thy wounded side.
C. Frances Alexander.

277 6.6.6.6.8J

mp I BRING my sins to Thee,
The sins I cannot count,
That all may cleansèd be
In Thy once opened Fount.
*cres*I bring them, Saviour, all to Th
The burden is too great for me.

mp My heart to Thee I bring,
The heart I cannot read ;
A faithless, wandering thing
An evil heart indeed.
I bring it, Saviour, now to The
That fixed and faithful it may

p To Thee I bring my care,
The care I cannot flee ;
Thou wilt not only share,
But bear it all for me.
O loving Saviour, now to Thee
I bring the load that wearies n

p I bring my grief to Thee,
The grief I cannot tell ;
No words shall needed be,
Thou knowest all so well.
I bring the sorrow laid on me,
O suffering Saviour, now to Th

f My joys to Thee I bring,
The joys Thy love hath givel
That each may be a wing
To lift me nearer heaven.
I bring them, Saviour, all to Tl
For Thou hast purchased all for

mf My life I bring to Thee,
I would not be my own ;
O Saviour, let me be
Thine ever, Thine alone.
f My heart, my life, my all I bri
To Thee, my Saviour and my Ki
Frances R. Harergo

278   88.88.88.

mf WE saw Thee not when Thou didst
   come
  To this poor world of sin and death,
  Nor e'er beheld Thy cottage home
  In that despisèd Nazareth ;
f But we believe Thy footsteps trod
  Its streets and plains, Thou Son of
   God.

mf We did not see Thee lifted high,
  Amid that wild and savage crew ;
dim Nor heard Thy meek, imploring
   cry,
f "Forgive, they know not what
  they do !"
  Yet we believe the deed was done,
dim Which shook the earth, and veiled
  the sun.

mf We stood not by the empty tomb,
  Where late Thy sacred body lay ;

cres Nor sat within that upper room,
  Nor met Thee in the open way ;
f But we believe that angels said,
  "Why seek the living with the
  dead ?"

mf We did not mark the chosen few,
  When Thou didst through the
   clouds ascend,   [ing view.
  First, lift to heaven their wonder-
p Then to the earth all prostrate
  bend ;
f Yet we believe that mortal eyes
  Beheld that journey to the skies.

  And now that Thou dost reign on
   high,   [bless,
  And thence Thy waiting people
mf No ray of glory from the sky
  Doth shine upon our wilderness ;
ff But we believe Thy faithful word,
  And trust in our redeeming Lord.
            J. H. Gurney.

3.—JOY AND PEACE IN BELIEVING.

279   C.M., double.

p I HEARD the voice of Jesus say,
  "Come unto Me and rest ; [down
cres Lay down, thou weary one, lay
  Thy head upon My breast."
p I came to Jesus as I was,
  Weary, and worn, and sad ;
cres I found in Him a resting-place,
ff And He has made me glad.

p I heard the voice of Jesus say,
mf "Behold, I freely give
cres The living water ; thirsty one,
  Stoop down, and drink, and live."
p I came to Jesus, and I drank
  Of that life-giving stream ;
cres My thirst was quenched, my soul re-
f And now I live in Him. [vived,

p I heard the voice of Jesus say,
mf "I am this dark world's Light ;
cres Look unto Me, thy morn shall rise,
  And all thy day be bright."
p I looked to Jesus, and I found
cres In Him my Star, my Sun ;
  And in that light of life I'll walk,
dim Till travelling days are done.
            H. Bonar.

280   88.88.88.

mf AND can it be, that I should gain
  An interest in the Saviour's blood?
  Died He for me, who caused His
  pain?
  For me, who Him to death pursue

f Amazing love! how can it be
That Thou, my God, shouldst die
for me?

mf 'Tis mystery all! The Immortal
dies!   [design?
Who can explore His strange
In vain the firstborn seraph tries
To sound the depths of love divine!
f 'Tis mercy all! let earth adore,
Let angel-minds inquire no more.

mf He left His Father's throne above,
(So free, so infinite His grace!)
Emptied Himself of all but love,
And bled for Adam's helpless race
: 'Tis mercy all, immense and free,
For, O my God, it found out me!

mf Long my imprisoned spirit lay
Fast bound in sin and nature's
night;
cres Thine eye diffused a quickening
ray,
I woke, the dungeon flamed with
light;
f My chains fell off, my heart was
free,
I rose, went forth, and followed
Thee.

mf No condemnation now I dread,
Jesus, and all in Him, is mine;
Alive in Him, my living Head,
And clothed in righteousness divine,
f Bold I approach the eternal throne,
And claim the crown, through
Christ, my own.

C. Wesley.

281   C.M.
p ALL that I was, my sin, my guilt,
My death, was all mine own;
cres All that I am I owe to Thee,
My gracious God, alone.

p The evil of my former state
Was mine, and only mine;
cres The good in which I now rejoice
Is Thine, and only Thine.

p The darkness of my former night,
The bondage—all was mine;
cres The light of life in which I walk,
The liberty is Thine.

mp Thy grace first made me feel my
sin,
It taught me to believe;
cres Then, in believing, peace I found,
f   And now I live, I live.

mf All that I am, e'en here on earth,
All that I hope to be,
cres When Jesus comes and glory dawns,
I owe it, Lord, to Thee.

H. Bonar.

282   C.M.
mf WE praise and bless Thee, gracious
Lord,
Our Saviour kind and true,
For all the old things passed away,
For all Thou hast made new.

p The old security is gone
In which so long we lay;
cres The sleep of death Thou hast
dispelled,
The darkness rolled away.

f New hopes, new purposes, desires,
And joys, Thy grace has given;
Old ties are broken from the earth,
New ones attach to heaven.

p But yet how much must be
destroyed,
How much renewed must be,
Ere we can fully stand complete
In likeness, Lord, to Thee!

mf Thou, only Thou, must carry on
  The work Thou hast begun ;
  Of Thine own strength Thou must
    impart,
  In Thine own ways to run.

f So shall we faultless stand at last
  Before Thy Father's throne,
  The blessedness for ever ours,
  The glory all Thine own !

  C. J. P. Spitta, tr. H. L. L.

283   8.7.8.7., double.

f I'VE found a Friend ; oh, such a
    Friend !
  He loved me ere I knew Him !
  He drew me with the cords of love,
  And thus He bound me to Him :
  And round my heart still closely
    twine   [sever ;
  Those ties which nought can
  For I am His, and He is mine,
  For ever and for ever.

f I've found a Friend ; oh, such a
    Friend !
dim He bled, He died to save me ;
  And not alone the gift of life,
  But His own self He gave me.
  Nought that I have my own I call,
    I hold it for the Giver : [my all,
cres My heart, my strength, my life,
  Are His, and His for ever.

f I've found a Friend ; oh, such a
    Friend !
  So kind, and true, and tender,
  So wise a Counsellor and Guide,
  So mighty a Defender.   [well,
mf From Him, Who loves me now so
  What power my soul can sever?
cres Shall life ?—or death ?—or earth ?
  —or hell ?
f No ! I am *His for ever !*   *Anon.*

284   L.M.

mp LORD, I was blind : I could not see
  In Thy marred visage any grace ;
cres But now the beauty of Thy face
f In radiant vision dawns on me.

mp Lord, I was deaf : I could not hear
  The thrilling music of Thy voice ;
cres But now I hear Thee and rejoice,
f And all Thy uttered words are dear.

mp Lord, I was dumb : I could not
    speak
  The grace and glory of Thy Name ;
cres But now, as touched with living
    flame,
f My lips Thine eager praises wake.

p Lord, I was dead : I could not stir
  My lifeless soul to come to Thee ;
cres But now, since Thou hast
    quickened me,
f I rise from sin's dark sepulchre,

f Lord, Thou hast made the blind
    to see,   [speak,
  The deaf to hear, the dumb to
ff The dead to live ; and lo, I break
  The chains of my captivity.

  W. T. Matson.

285   10.10.

mf PEACE, perfect peace, in this dark
    world of sin ?
p The blood of Jesus whispers peace
    within.

mf Peace, perfect peace, by thronging
    duties pressed ?
p To do the will of Jesus, this is rest.

mf Peace, perfect peace, with sorrows
    surging round ?
p On Jesus' bosom nought but calm
  is found.

mf Peace, perfect peace, with loved
    ones far away?   [they.
cres In Jesus' keeping we are safe, and

mf Peace, perfect peace, our future all
    unknown?   [throne.
cres Jesus we know, and He is on the

p Peace, perfect peace, death shadow-
    ing us and ours?
    Jesus has vanquished death and
    all its powers.

p It is enough : earth's struggles
    soon shall cease, [perfect peace.
cres And Jesus call us to heaven's
                   E. H. Bickersteth.

286   · 88.88.88.

Now I have found the ground
    wherein
Sure my soul's anchor may remain ;
The wounds of Jesus, for my sin
Before the world's foundation
    slain ;
Whose mercy shall unshaken stay
When heaven and earth are fled
    away.

[*mf* Father, Thine everlasting grace
    Our scanty thought surpasses far ;
dim Thy heart still melts with tender-
    ness ;
    Thine arms of love still open are,
cres Returning sinners to receive,
    That mercy they may taste and
    live.]

mp O Love ! Thou bottomless abyss !
    My sins are swallowed up in Thee :
cres Covered is my unrighteousness,
    Nor spot of guilt remains on me :
    While Jesus' Blood, through earth
    and skies,
Mercy, free boundless mercy, cries !

mf With faith I plunge me in this sea ;
    Here is my hope, my joy, my rest :
    Hither, when hell assails, I flee,
    I look into my Saviour's breast :
cres Away, sad doubt, and anxious fear !
    Mercy is all that's written there !

p Though waves and storms go o'er
    my head ;
    Though strength, and health, and
    friends be gone ;   [dead ;
    Though joys be withered all and
    Though every comfort be with-
    drawn ;
cres On this my steadfast soul relies ;
mf Father ! Thy mercy never dies.

mf Fixed on this ground will I remain,
dim Though my heart fail and flesh
    decay :
cres This anchor shall my soul sustain,
    When earth's foundations melt
    away :   [prove,
mf Mercy's full power I then shall
f Loved with an everlasting love.
          J. Wesley, from J. A. Rothe.

287   6.10.6.10.

mf BIRDS have their quiet nest,
    Foxes their holes, and man his
    peaceful bed ;
    All creatures have their rest,
dim But Jesus had not where to lay
    His head.

mp And yet He came to give
    The weary and the heaven-laden
    rest ;
cres To bid the sinner live,
dim And soothe our griefs to slumber
    on His breast.

p I, who once made Him grieve ;
    I, who once bade His gentle spirit
    mourn ;

Whose hand essayed to weave
For His meek·brow the cruel crown
  of thorn !

p What then, am I, my God,
Permitted thus the paths of peace
  to tread ?
Peace purchased by the blood
Of Him Who had not where to lay
  His head.

p O why should I have peace ?
*cres*Why, but for that unchanged,
  undying love,
Which would not, could not cease,
f Until it made me heir of joys above.

mf Yes, but for pardoning grace
I feel I never should in glory see

The brightness of that face
*dim*That once was pale and agonised
  for me.

mp Let the birds seek their nest,
Foxes their holes, and man his
  peaceful bed ;
cres Come, Saviour, in my breast
*dim*Deign to repose Thine oft-rejected
  head.]

mp Come ! give me rest, and take
The only rest on earth Thou lovest,
  —within
A heart, that for Thy sake
p Lies bleeding, broken, penitent for
  sin.
         J. S. B. Monsell.

4.—THE SPIRIT OF ADOPTION.

288   S.M.

f BEHOLD what wondrous grace
  The Father hath bestowed
On sinners of a mortal race,
To call them sons of God !

mf Nor doth it yet appear
How great we must be made ;
*cres*But when we see our Saviour
  here,
We shall be like our Head.

mf A hope so much divine
May trials well endure ;
May purge our souls from sense and
  sin,
As Christ the Lord is pure.

mp If in my Father's love
I share a filial part,
Send down Thy Spirit like a dove,
To rest upon my heart.

mp We would no longer lie
Like slaves beneath the throne ;
*cres*My faith shall Abba, Father, cry,
And Thou the kindred own.
         I. Watts.

289   C.M.

mf MY God, my Father, blissful name !
O may I call Thee mine ?
May I with sweet assurance claim
A portion so divine ?

mf This only can my fears control,
And bid my sorrows fly.
What harm can ever reach my soul
Beneath my Father's eye ?

mp Whate'er Thy providence denies
I calmly would resign, (mine ;
For Thou art just, and good. and
O bend my will to Thine.

mp Whate'er Thy sacred will ordains,
    O give me strength to bear !
    And let me know my Father reigns,
    And trust His tender care.
mp Thy sovereign ways are all un-
      known
    To my weak, erring sight ;

cres Yet let my soul adoring
    That all Thy ways are
mf My God, my Father, be
    My solace and my sta;
f O wilt Thou seal my hun
    And drive my fears av
        Ann I

5.—LOVE TO GOD.

290
                7s.

mf HARK, my soul, it is the Lord :
    'Tis thy Saviour ; hear His word.
    Jesus speaks, and speaks to thee,—
p Say, poor sinner, lov'st thou Me ?

mf I delivered thee when bound,
    And, when bleeding, healed thy
      wound ;
cres Sought thee wandering, set thee
      right :
    Turned thy darkness into light.

mf Can a woman's tender care
    Cease towards the child she bare ?
p Yes, she may forgetful be,
cres Yet will I remember thee.

mf Mine is an unchanging love,
    Higher than the heights above :
    Deeper than the depths beneath :
cres Free and faithful, strong as death.

f Thou shalt see My glory soon,
p When the work of grace is done ;
cres Partner of My throne shalt be ;
pp Say, poor sinner, lov'st thou Me ?

mf Lord, it is my chief complaint,
    That my love is weak and faint ;
cres Yet I love Thee, and adore ;
f O for grace to love Thee more.
            W. Cowper.

291

mf MY God, I love Thee,—n
    I hope for heaven the;
    Nor because they who lov
p   Are lost eternally.

mf Thou, O my Jesus, Thou
    Upon the Cross embrac
    For me didst bear the
dim   And manifold disgrac

mp And griefs and torment
      less,
    And sweat of agony,
dim And death itself—and al
    Who was Thine enemy

cres Then why, O blessèd Je
    Should I not love The
    Not for the sake of winni;
    Or of escaping hell ;

mp Not with the hope o;
      aught ;
    Not seeking a reward ;
    But as Thyself hast love
    O ever-loving Lord.

mf E'en so I love Thee, and
cres   And in Thy praise wi
f Solely because Thou art
    And my eternal King.
    F. Xavier, tr. E. Caswall, c.

292 C.M., double.

mf WHEN I had wandered from His fold,
His love the wand'rer sought;
When slave-like into bondage sold,
His blood my freedom bought:
cres Therefore that life, by Him redeemed,
Is His through all its days,
And as with blessings it hath teemed,
So let it teem with praise:
f For I am His, and He is mine,
The God Whom I adore!
cres My Father, Saviour, Comforter,
ff Now and for evermore!

mf When I forgat His tender love,
And my affections set
Not upon holy things above,
He did not me forget,
dim But gently chastening, gently tried
To draw me back to bliss,
And hide me in His wounded side;
cres Therefore I'm tenfold His: [etc.
f For I am His, and He is mine,

p When, sunk in sorrow, I despaired
And changed my hopes for fears,
He bore my griefs, my burden shared,
And wiped away my tears;
cres Therefore the joy by Him restored
To Him by right belongs,
And to my gracious loving Lord
mf I'll sing through life my songs:
f For I am His, and He is mine, etc.

mp When I beneath my cross lay down,
And could no further move,
cres He raised me up, He showed the crown,
p And whispered, "I am Love":

cres Therefore that Love my song shall be,
And to my glorious King,
mf Through time and through eternity,
cres My life His praise shall sing:
f For I am His and He is mine,
The God Whom I adore!
cres My Father, Saviour, Comforter,
ff Now and for evermore!

J. S. B. Monsell.

293 88.88.88.

mf THOU hidden Love of God, Whose height, [knows;
Whose depth unfathomed, no man
I see from far Thy beauteous light,
dim Inly I sigh for Thy repose:
p My heart is pained, nor can it be
At rest, till it finds rest in Thee.

mf 'Tis mercy all, that Thou hast brought [Thee:
My mind to seek her peace in
Yet while I seek, but find Thee not, [see:
No peace my wandering soul shall
p O when shall all my wanderings end,
And all my steps to Thee-ward tend!

mf Is there a thing beneath the sun
That strives with Thee my heart to share?
cres Ah! tear it thence, and reign alone,
The Lord of every motion there;
p Then shall my heart from earth be free,
When it hath found repose in Thee.

mf O Love, Thy sovereign aid impart,
To save me from low-thoughted care; [heart.
Chase this self-will through all m
Through all its latent mazes the

Make me Thy duteous child, that I
Ceaseless may "Abba, Father" cry !

mf Each moment draw from earth
    away   [call ;
My heart, that lowly waits Thy
Speak to my inmost soul, and say,
"I am thy Love, thy God, thy
    All."   [voice,
To feel Thy power, to hear Thy
To taste Thy love, be all my choice.

      G. Tersteegen, tr. J. Wesley.

294   8.6.8.6.8.8.8.8.

mf MY heart to Thee I give for aye,
  O Jesu, sweetest, best ;
Thy heart to me give Thou, I pray,
  O Jesu, loveliest.
Our hearts alone Thou dost require,
Our hearts alone Thou dost desire :
*cres*Make me love Thee as Thou dost
    me,
  O Jesu, Fount of Charity.

mp What for Thy grace can I repay,
  God, Who for me wast born ?
What for Thy love before Thee lay,
  Man, Who didst suffer scorn?
"Thy heart," Thou sayest, "give
    Me here " :
 'Take Thou my heart, O Jesu dear,
*cres*Make me love Thee as Thou dost
    me,
  O Jesu, Fount of Charity.

mf For me Thy heart is open wide,
  That I may entrance find,
And there my own within it hide,
  And close in union bind.
Thou, Jesu blest, by love possest,
Thyself didst give, that I might live:
*cres*Make me love Thee as Thou dost
    me,
  O Jesu, Fount of Charity.

mf Here is the heart's true
    found,
  And here is rest secure, [
  And here is love's most
  And here salvation sure.
In this cleft Rock, once ren
  And in this heart's protecting
*cres*May I confide, may I abide,
  O Jesu, Saviour glorified.

Latin, 9th century, tr. R. F. Litt

295

mf O THOU Who camest from
  The pure celestial fire to impart,
Kindle a flame of sacred love
  On the mean altar of my heart.

mf There let it for Thy glory burn,
  With inextinguishable blaze ;
And trembling, to its source
  In humble prayer and f
    praise.

mp Jesus, confirm my heart's desire
  To work and speak and think
    Thee ;
Still let me guard the holy fire,
  And still stir up Thy gift in me.

mf Ready for all Thy perfect will,
  My acts of faith and love repeat,
Till death Thy endless mercies
  And make the sacrifice complete.

        C. Wesley.

296   7.6.7.6., double.

mf To Thee, O dear, dear Saviour !
  My spirit turns for rest,
My peace is in Thy favour,
  My pillow on Thy breast ;
Though all the world deceive me,
  I know that I am Thine,
And Thou wilt never leave me,
  O blessèd Saviour mine.

mf In Thee my trust abideth,
On Thee my hope relies,
O Thou Whose love provideth
For all beneath the skies ;
O Thou Whose mercy found me,
From bondage set me free,
And then for ever bound me
With threefold cords to Thee.

mp My grief is in the dulness
With which this sluggish heart
Doth open to the fulness
Of all Thou wouldst impart ;
*cres*My joy is in Thy beauty
Of holiness divine,
My comfort in the duty
That binds my life to Thine.

[*mp*Alas, that I should ever
Have failed in love to Thee,
The only one Who never
Forgot or slighted me !
*cres*O for a heart to love Thee
More truly as I ought,
And nothing place above Thee
. In deed, or word, or thought.]

f O for that choicest blessing
Of living in Thy love,
And thus on earth possessing
The peace of heaven above ;
mf O for the bliss that by it
The soul securely knows,
*dim*The holy calm and quiet
p Of faith's serene repose.

J. S. B. Monsell.

297 888.888.

mf O GOD, of good the unfathomed
sea ! [Thee ?
Who would not give his heart to
Who would not love Thee with his
might ?
O Jesu, Lover of mankind,

Who would not his whole soul and
mind,
With all his strength, to Thee
unite ?

[*f* Thou shin'st with everlasting rays ;
Before the insufferable blaze
*dim*Angels with both wings veil their
eyes ;
*cres*Yet free as air Thy bounty streams
On all Thy works ; Thy mercy's
beams
Diffusive as Thy sun's arise .

mf Astonished at Thy frowning brow,
Earth, hell, and heaven's strong
pillars bow ;
f Terrible majesty is Thine ! [press
Who then can that vast love ex-
Which bows Thee down to me, who
less
*dim*Than nothing am, till Thou art
mine ?]

mf Fountain of good ! all blessing
flows [knows ;
From Thee ; no want Thy fulness
What but Thyself canst Thou de-
sire ?
Yet, self-sufficient as Thou art,
Thou dost desire my worthless
heart ;
This, only this, dost Thou require.

f O God, of good the unfathomed
sea ! [Thee ?
Who would not give his heart to
Who would not love Thee with his
might ?
O Jesu, Lover of mankind, [mind,
ff Who would not his whole soul and
With all his strength, to Thee
. unite ?

J. Scheffler, tr. J. Wesley

298 ·   88.88.88.

f THEE will I love, my strength,
   my tower,
Thee will I love, my joy, my crown,
Thee will I love with all my power,
In all Thy works, and Thee alone ;
Thee will I love, till the pure fire
Fill my whole soul with chaste
   desire.

p In darkness willingly I strayed,
   I sought Thee, yet from Thee I
   roved ;
Far wide my wandering thoughts
   were spread,   [loved ;
Thy creatures more than Thee I
And now if more at length I see,
'Tis through Thy light, and comes
   from Thee.]

f I thank Thee, uncreated Sun,
   That Thy bright beams on me have
   shined ;
I thank Thee, Who hast overthrown
My foes, and healed my wounded
   mind ;
I thank Thee, Whose enlivening
   voice
Bids my freed heart in Thee rejoice.

f Give to mine eyes refreshing tears,
Give to my heart chaste, hallowed
   fires,
Give to my soul, with filial fears,
The love that all heaven's host
   inspires,   [might,
That all my powers, with all their
In Thy sole glory may unite.

f Thee will I love, my joy, my crown;
   Thee will I love, my Lord, my God;
mf Thee will I love, beneath Thy
   frown,

Or smile, Thy sceptre, or Thy rod
p What though my flesh and hear
   decay ?
cres Thee shall I love in endless day.

       J. Scheffler, tr. J. Wesley.

299   6.6.6.6.8.8.

f WHOM should we love like Thee
   Our God, our Guide, our King,
   The tower to which we flee,
   The rock to which we cling ?
ff O for a thousand tongues to show
   The mercies which to Thee we owe

mf The storm upon us fell,
   The floods around us rose ;
   The depths of death and hell
   Seemed on our souls to close.
dim To God we cried in strong despair
cres He heard, and came to help our
   prayer.

mf He came the King of kings,
   He bowed the sable sky ;
   And on the tempest's wings
   Walked down serene from high.
The earth beneath His footsteps
   shook,   [rebuke
The mountains quaked at His

mf Above the storm He stood,
dim And awed it to repose ;
   He drew us from the flood,
   And scattered all our foes.
cres He set us in a spacious place,
mf And there upholds us by His grace.

f Whom should we love like Thee,
   Our God, our Guide, our King,
   The tower to which we flee,
   The rock to which we cling ?
ff O for a thousand tongues to show
   The mercies which to Thee we owe.

       H. F. Lyte.

6.—LOVE TO MAN.

300   7s.

mf FATHER, to Thy sinful child
  Though Thy law is reconciled,
dim By Thy pardoning grace I live ;
  Daily still I cry,—Forgive.

[*mf* Though my ransomed price He paid
  Upon Whom my guilt was laid,
dim Humbly at Thy mercy-seat,
  Full remission I entreat.]

mp Lord, forgive me, day by day,
  Debts I cannot hope to pay ;
  Duties I have left undone ;
  Evils I have failed to shun ;

mp Trespasses in word or thought ;
  Deeds from evil motive wrought ;
  Cold ingratitude, distrust ;
  Thoughts unhallowed or unjust.

mp Pardon, Lord ! and are there those
  Who my debtors are, or foes ?
  I, who by forgiveness live,
  Here their trespasses forgive.

[*mp* May I feel beneath my wrongs
  Vengeance unto God belongs,
  Nor a worse requital dare
  Than the meek revenge of prayer.]

mp Much forgiven, may I learn
  Love for hatred to return ;
cres Then assured my heart shall be,
f Thou, my God, hast pardoned me.
                          J. Conder.

301   C.M.

mf O GOD ! Whose thoughts are
    br¹ghtest light,
  Whose love runs always clear,
  To Whose kind wisdom sinning
    souls
  Amidst their sins are dear !

mp Sweeten my bitter-thoughted heart
  With charity like Thine,
  Till self shall be the only spot
  On earth which does not shine.

mp Hard-heartedness dwells not with
    souls
  Round whom Thine arms are
    drawn ;
dim And dark thoughts fade away in
    grace,
  Like cloud-spots in the dawn.

mf But they have caught the way of
    God,
  To Whom self lies displayed
  In such clear vision as to cast
  O'er others' faults a shade.

mf All bitterness is from ourselves,
  All sweetness is from Thee ;
  O God ! for evermore be Thou
  Fountain and fire in me !

    F. W. Faber, v. 5, l. 3 altd.

302   C.M.

mp BENEATH the shadow of the Cross,
  As earthly hopes remove,
  His new commandment Jesus gives,
  His blessèd word of love.

mf O bond of union, strong and deep !
  O bond of perfect peace !
  Not e'en the lifted Cross can harm,
  If we but hold to this.

mf Then, Jesus, be Thy spirit ours,
  And swift our feet shall move
dim To deeds of pure self-sacrifice
  And the sweet tasks of love.

            S. Longfellow.

7.—*CONSECRATION AND HOLINESS.*

303 6.4.6.4.10.10.

mf I LIFT my heart to Thee,
  Saviour Divine!
For Thou art all to me,
  And I am Thine.
Is there on earth a closer bond than
    this,   [am His"?
That "my Belovèd's mine, and I

mf Thine am I by all ties;
  But chiefly Thine,
That through Thy sacrifice
  Thou, Lord, art mine.
By Thine own cords of love, so
    sweetly wound
Around me, I to Thee am closely
    bound.

mp To Thee, Thou bleeding Lamb,
  I all things owe;
All that I have and am,
  And all I know.
All that I have is now no longer
    mine,   [am Thine.
And I am not mine own; Lord, I

mf How can I, Lord, withhold
  Life's brightest hour
From Thee; or gathered gold,
  Or any power?
Why should I keep one precious
    thing from Thee,
When Thou hast given Thine own
    dear Self for me?

mp I pray Thee, Saviour, keep
  Me in Thy love,
pp Until death's holy sleep
  Shall me remove
cres To that fair realm where, sin and
    sorrow o'er,   [evermore.
f Thou and Thine own are One for
            C. E. Mudie

304 C.M.

f O FOR a heart to praise my God;
  A heart from sin set free;
  A heart that always feels Thy bl
dim So freely spilt for me.

mf A heart resigned, submissive, me
  My dear Redeemer's throne;
  Where only Christ is heard to sp
  Where Jesus reigns alone.

mp A humble, lowly, contrite heart,
  Believing, true, and clean, [p
  Which neither life nor death c
  From Him that dwells within.

mp A heart in every thought renew
  And filled with love divine;
  Perfect and right, and pure
    good;
  •A copy, Lord, of Thine.

mf Thy nature, gracious Lord, impar
  Come quickly from above;
cres Write Thy new name upon
    heart,
  Thy new best name of Love.
            C. Wesley.

305 7s., 6 lines.

mf WHEN this passing world is done,
  When has sunk yon glaring sun,
  When we stand with Christ on high
  Looking o'er life's history,
p Then, Lord, shall I fully know,
cres Not till then, how much I owe.

mf When I stand before the throne,
  Dressed in beauty not my own,
  When I see Thee as Thou art,
  Love Thee with unsinning heart,
p Then, Lord, shall I fully know,
cres Not till then, how much I owe.

mf When the praise of heaven I
    hear,
*cres*Loud as thunders to the ear,
    Loud as many waters' noise,
    Sweet as harp's melodious voice,
p Then, Lord, shall I fully know,
*cres*Not till then, how much I owe.

mf E'en on earth, as through a glass,
    Darkly let Thy glory pass ;
    Make forgiveness feel so sweet ;
    Make Thy Spirit's help so meet ;
p E'en on earth, Lord, make me
    know
*cres*Something of how much I owe.

    R. M. M'Cheyne, v. 1, ll. 3 4 altd.

306 S.M.

f   DEAR Lord and Master mine,
      Thy happy servant see ;
      My Conqueror, with what joy divine
      Thy captive clings to Thee !

nf I love Thy yoke to wear,
      To feel Thy gracious bands—
      Sweetly restrainèd by Thy care,
      And happy in Thy hands.

nf No bar would I remove,
      No bond would I unbind :
      Within the limits of Thy love
      Full liberty I find.

nf I would not walk alone,
      But still with Thee, my God.
      At every step my blindness own,
      And ask of Thee the road.

mp The weakness I enjoy
      That casts me on Thy breast ;
*cres*The conflicts that Thy strength
      employ
      Make me divinely blest.

mp Dear Lord and Master mine,
      Still keep Thy servant true !
      My Guardian and my Guide Divine
cres Bring, bring Thy pilgrim
      through !

mf My Conqueror and my King,
      Still keep me in Thy train, [bring
f   And with Thee Thy glad captive
      When Thou return'st to reign !

                    T. H. Gill.

307 L.M., with refrain.

mf O LOVE, Who formedst me to wear
    The image of Thy Godhead here ;
    Who soughtest me with tender care
    Through all my wand'rings wild
    and drear ;
*cres*O Love, I give myself to Thee,
f Thine ever, only Thine to be.

mf O Love, Who once in time wast
    slain,   [bitter woe ;
    Pierced through and through with
    O Love, Who wrestling thus didst
    gain
    That we eternal joy might know ;
*cres*O Love, I give myself to Thee,
f Thine ever, only Thine to be.

[*mf*O Love, of Whom is truth and light,
    The Word and Spirit, life and
    power ;   [that smite,
    Whose heart was bared to them
    To shield us in our trial hour ;
*cres*O Love. I give myself to Thee,
f Thine ever, only Thine to be.]

mf O Love, Who lovest me for aye,
    Who for my soul dost ever plead ;
    O Love, Who didst my ransom pay,
    Whose power sufficeth in my stead:
*cres*O Love, I give myself to Thee,
f Thine ever, only Thine to be.

mf O Love, Who once shalt bid me rise
From out this dying life of ours ;
O Love, Who once above yon skies
Shalt set me in the fadeless bowers;
cres O Love, I give myself to Thee,
f Thine ever, Thine alone to be.
J. Scheffler, tr., Catherine Winkworth.

308 C.M.

mf O JESUS CHRIST, grow Thou in me,
And all things else recede ;
My heart be daily nearer Thee,
From sin be daily freed.

mf Each day let Thy supporting might
My weakness still embrace ;
My darkness vanish in Thy light,
Thy life my death efface.

mf In Thy bright beams which on me
fall
Fade every evil thought ;
That I am nothing, Thou art all,
I would be daily taught.

mp Make this poor self grow less and
less,
Be Thou my life and aim ;
O make me daily, through Thy
grace,
More worthy of Thy Name.

mp Daily more filled with Thee my
heart,
Daily from self more free ;
Thou, to Whom prayer did strength
impart,
Of my prayer Hearer be.

mf Let faith in Thee and in Thy might
My every motive move,
f Be Thou alone my soul's delight,
My passion and my love.
J. C. Lavater, tr. H. B. Smith.

309

mf MY gracious Lord, I own
To every service I can pe
And call it my supreme c
To hear Thy dictates, an

mf What is my being but fo
Its sure support, its nobl
Thy ever-smiling face to
And serve the cause c
Friend ?

mp I would not breathe fo
joy,
Or to increase my worldl
Nor future days or powei
To spread a sounding nam

mf 'Tis to my Saviour I wou
To Him Who for my ranf
Nor could untainted Ede:
Such bliss as blossoms at

mf His work my hoary age sl
When youthful vigour is
dim And my last hour of life
cres His love hath animating
P. Dod

310

mf TAKE my life, and let it l
Consecrated, Lord, to The
Take my moments and m
Let them flow in ceaseless

mf Take my hands, and let the
At the impulse of Thy lov
Take my feet, and let thei
Swift and beautiful for T

mf Take my voice, and let me
Always, only, for my Kinj
Take my lips, and let ther
Filled with messages from

mf Take my silver and my gold,
Not a mite would I withhold ;
Take my intellect, and use
Every power as Thou shalt choose.

mf Take my will, and make it Thine ;
p It shall be no longer mine ;
cres Take my heart, it is Thine own ;
It shall be Thy royal throne.

mf Take my love, my Lord I pour
At Thy feet its treasure store ;
cres Take myself, and I will be
f Ever, only, all for Thee.

Frances R. Havergal.

311   7s.

mf HOLY Lamb, who Thee receive,
Who in Thee begin to live,
Day and night they cry to Thee,—
As Thou art, so let us be.

mp Jesu, see my panting breast !
See, I pant in Thee to rest !
Gladly would I now be clean :
Cleanse me, Lord, from every sin.

mp Fix, O fix my wavering mind !
To Thy Cross my spirit bind ;
Earthly passions far remove ;
Swallow up my soul in love.

p Dust and ashes though we be,
Full of sin and misery,
cres Thine we are, Thou Son of God !
Take the purchase of Thy blood !

mp Jesu, when Thy light we see,
All our soul's athirst for Thee :
When Thy quickening power we prove,
All our *heart dissolves in love.*

mf Boundless wisdom, power divine,
Love unspeakable, are Thine :
f Praise by all to Thee be given,
Sons of earth, and hosts of heaven !

A. Dober, tr. J. Wesley.

312   6.4.6.4.7.6.7.4.

mf I NEED Thee every hour,
Most gracious Lord ;
No tender voice like Thine
Can peace afford.
cres I need Thee, O I need Thee ;
Every hour I need Thee ;
f O bless me now, my Saviour,
I come to Thee !

mf I need Thee every hour ;
Stay Thou near by ;
Temptations lose their power
When Thou art nigh.
I need Thee, etc.

mp I need Thee every hour,
In joy or pain ;
Come quickly and abide,
Or life is vain.
I need Thee, etc.

mf I need Thee every hour ;
Teach me Thy will ;
And Thy rich promises
In me fulfil.
I need Thee, etc.

mf I need Thee every hour,
Most Holy One ;
cres O make me Thine indeed,
Thou blessèd Son !
cres I need Thee, O I need Thee ;
Every hour I need Thee ;
f O bless me now, my Saviour,
I come to Thee !

Annie S. Hawks

313   S.M.

f   LORD, in the strength of grace,
    With a glad heart and free,
    Myself, my residue of days,
    I consecrate to Thee.

f   Thy ransomed servant, I
    Restore to Thee Thine own,
    And from this moment live or die
    To serve my God alone.
                C. Wesley.

314   S.M.

mf   A CHARGE to keep I have,
    A God to glorify ;
    A never-dying soul to save,
    And fit it for the sky ;

mf   To serve the present age,
    My calling to fulfil ;—
    O may it all my powers engage
    To do my Master's will.

mf   Arm me with jealous care,
    As in Thy sight to live ;
    And O ! Thy servant, Lord, prepare
    A strict account to give :

mf   Help me to watch and pray,
    And on Thyself rely,
dim Assured, if I my trust betray,
p   I shall for ever die.
                C. Wesley.

315   8.7.8.8.7.

p OH the bitter shame and sorrow.
    That a time could ever be
    When I let the Saviour's pity
    Plead   in   vain,   and   proudly
      answered :
mf   " All of self, and none of Thee ! "

p Yet He found me : I beheld Him
    Bleeding on the accursèd tree :
    Heard Him pray, "Forgive them
      Father ! "
dim And my wistful heart said faintly,
pp   "Some of self, and some of
      Thee ! "

mf Day by day, His tender mercy,
    Healing, helping, full and free,
    Sweet and strong, and ah ! so
      patient,
    Brought   me   lower,   while   I
      whispered,
p   " Less of self, and more of Thee ! '

f Higher than the highest heaven,
    Deeper than the deepest sea,
    Lord, Thy love at last has con-
      quered ;
cres Grant me now my soul's desire,
ff   "None of self, and all of Thee ! "
                T. Monod.

8.—CHARACTER AND VIRTUES.

316   7s.

mf JESUS, cast a look on me ;
    Give me sweet simplicity,
    Make me poor and keep me low,
    Seeking only Thee to know ;
mf Weanèd from my lordly self,
    Weanèd from the miser's pelf,

Weanèd from the scorner's ways,
Weanèd from the lust of praise.

mf All that feeds my busy pride,
    Cast it evermore aside ;
    Bid my will to Thine submit ;
    Lay me humbly at Thy feet.

Make me like a little child,
Of my strength and wisdom spoiled,
Seeing only in Thy light,
Walking only in Thy might,

Leaning on Thy loving breast,
Where a weary soul may rest ;
Feeling well the peace of God
Flowing from Thy precious Blood.

In this posture let me live,
And hosannas daily give ;
In this temper let me die
And hosannas ever cry !

J. Berridge.

17   6.5.6.5., double.

PURER yet and purer
I would be in mind,
Dearer yet and dearer
Every duty find ;
Hoping still and trusting
God without a fear,
Patiently believing
He will make all clear.

Calmer yet and calmer
In the hours of pain,
Surer yet and surer
Peace at last to gain ;
Suffering still and doing,
To His will resigned,
And to God subduing
Heart and will and mind.

Higher yet and higher
Out of cloud and night,
Nearer yet and nearer
Rising to the light —
Light serene and holy,
Where my soul may rest,
Purified and lowly,
Sanctified and blest.

mf Swifter yet and swifter
Ever onward run,
cres Firmer yet and firmer
Step as I go on ;
Oft these earnest longings
Swell within my breast,
Yet their inner meaning
Ne'er can be expressed.

J. W. von Goethe, tr. Anon.

318   L.M.

f So let our lips and lives express
The holy gospel we profess ;
So let our works and virtues shine,
To prove the doctrine all divine.

f Thus shall we best proclaim abroad
The honours of our Saviour God,
When the salvation reigns within,
And grace subdues the power of sin.

mf Our flesh and sense must be denied,
Passion and envy, lust and pride ;
While justice, temperance, truth,
and love,
Our inward piety approve.

mf Religion bears our spirits up
While we expect that blessèd hope—
cres The bright appearing of the Lord,
And faith stands leaning on His
word.

I. Watts.

319   S.M.

mf BLEST are the pure in heart,
For they shall see our God ;
The secret of the Lord is theirs ;
Their soul is Christ's abode.

mf The Lord, Who left the heavens
Our life and peace to bring,
dim To dwell in lowliness with men,
Their Pattern and their King ;

mf He to the lowly soul
Doth still Himself impart,
And for His dwelling and His throne
Chooseth the pure in heart.

p Lord, we Thy presence seek ;
May ours this blessing be ;
Give us a pure and lowly heart,
A temple meet for Thee.
J. Keble and W. J. Hall.

[SEE ALSO SECTION VII. 16.]

9.—DISCIPLINE AND COMFORT.

320   6.4.6.4.6.6.4.

mf NEARER, my God, to Thee—
Nearer to Thee,
p E'en though it be a cross
That raiseth me ;
cres Still all my song shall be,
Nearer, my God, to Thee—
dim Nearer to Thee.

p Though like the wanderer,
The sun gone down,
Darkness be over me,
My rest a stone ;
cres Yet in my dreams, I'd be
Nearer, my God, to Thee—
dim Nearer to Thee.

mf There let the way appear,
Steps unto heaven ;
All that Thou send'st to me
In mercy given :
Angels to beckon me
cres Nearer, my God, to Thee—
dim Nearer to Thee.

f Then with my waking thoughts,
Bright with Thy praise,
Out of my stony griefs
Bethel I'll raise,
p So by my woes to be
cres Nearer, my God, to Thee—
dim Nearer to Thee.

f Or if on joyful wing,
Cleaving the sky,

Sun, moon, and stars forgot,
Upwards I fly,
cres Still all my song shall be,
Nearer, my God, to Thee—
dim Nearer to Thee.
Sarah F. Adams.

321   S.M.

mf THOU say'st, "Take up thy cross,
O man, and follow Me : "
The night is black, the feet are slack,
Yet we would follow Thee.

mp But O, dear Lord, we cry,
That we Thy Face could see !
Thy blessèd Face one moment's space ;
Then might we follow Thee !

mp Dim tracts of time divide
Those golden days from me ;
Thy voice comes strange o'er year of change ;
How can we follow Thee ?

mp Comes faint and far Thy voice
From vales of Galilee ;
Thy vision fades in ancient shades ;
How should we follow Thee ?

mp Ah, sense-bound heart and blind!
Is nought but what we see ?
Can time undo what once was true ?
Can we not follow Thee ?

mf Within our heart of hearts ·
      In nearest nearness be :
*cres*Set up Thy throne within Thine
      own :—
f   Go, Lord : we follow Thee.

F. T. Palgrave.

322   8.7.8.7.

mf JESUS calls us o'er the tumult
     Of our life's wild, restless sea ;
     Day by day His sweet voice
     soundeth,
     Saying, (*p*) "Christian, follow
     Me."

p Jesus calls us (*cres*) from the wor-
    ship
    Of the vain world's golden store,
    From each idol that would keep us,
    Saying, (*p*) "Christian, love Me
    more."

mf In our joys and in our sorrows,
     Days of toil and hours of ease,
     Still He calls, in cares and plea-
     sures,
cres "Christian, love Me more than
      these."

p Jesus calls us ! (*cres*) By Thy
    mercies,
    Saviour, may we hear Thy call,
f Give our hearts to Thy obedience,
    Serve and love Thee best of all.

C. Frances Alexander.

323   8.8.8.6., Trochaic.

f Lo ! the storms of life are breaking,
    Faithless fears our hearts are
    shaking ;
    For our succour undertaking,
    Lord and Saviour, help us.

mp Lo ! the world from Thee rebelling,
     Round Thy Church, in pride, is
     swelling ;   [ing,
     With Thy word their madness quell-
dim Lord and Saviour, help us.

f On Thine own command relying,
    We our onward task are plying,
    Unto Thee for safety sighing,
dim Lord and Saviour, help us.

p By Thy birth, Thy cross, Thy
    passion,
    By Thy tears of deep compassion,
cres By Thy mighty intercession,
dim Lord and Saviour, help us.

H. Alford.

324   C.M.

mf O THOU from Whom all goodness
     flows,
     I lift my soul to Thee ;
dim In all my sorrows, conflicts, woes,
p Good Lord, remember me.

mp When on my aching, burdened heart
     My sins lie heavily,   [impart ;
cres Thy pardon speak, new peace
p Good Lord, remember me.

mp When trials sore obstruct my way,
     And ills I cannot flee,
cres O let my strength be as my day ;
p Good Lord, remember me.

mp When worn with pain, disease, and
     grief,
     This feeble body see ;   [relief ;
     Grant patience, rest, and kind
p Good Lord, remember me.

mp If for Thy sake upon my name
     Shame and reproach shall be,
     All hail reproach, and welcom
     shame ;
p Good Lord, remember me.

pp When, in the solemn hour of death,
 I wait Thy just decree,
 Be this the prayer of my last breath,
p Good Lord, remember me.
mf And when before Thy throne I stand,
 And lift my soul to Thee,
cres Then with the saints at Thy right hand,
p Good Lord, remember me.

 T. Haweis and T. Cotterill.

325   10.4.10.4.

mf I DO not ask, O Lord, that life may be
 A pleasant road ;
 I do not ask that Thou wouldst take from me
 Aught of its load :

mf I do not ask that flowers should always sprin.
 Beneath my feet ;   [sting
 I know too well the poison and the
 Of things too sweet.

mf For one thing only, Lord, dear Lord, I plead ;
 Lead me aright,
dim Though strength should falter, and though heart should bleed,
cres Through Peace to Light.

 I do not ask, O Lord, that Thou
. shouldst shed
 Full radiance here ;
p Give but a ray of peace, that I may tread
 Without a fear.

mp I do not ask my cross to understand,
 My way to see ;   [hand,
cres Better in darkness just to feel Thy
 And follow Thee.

. Joy is like restless day, but pe
 divine
p Like quiet night :
cres Lead me, O Lord, till perfect shall shine,
. f Through Peace to Light.

 Adelaide A. Procte

326   5.5.3.

mp THROW away Thy rod,
 Throw away Thy wrath,
 O my God ;
 Take the gentle path.

mp For my heart's desire
 Unto Thine is bent ;
 I aspire
 To a full consent.

mp Though I fail, I weep,
 Though I halt in pace,
 Yet I creep
 To the throne of grace.

mp Then let wrath remove,
 Love will do the deed ;
cres For with love
 Stony hearts will bleed.

mp Throw away Thy rod :
 Though man frailties hath,
cres Thou art God ;
 Throw away Thy wrath.

 G. Herber

327   C.M

mf THOU, Lord, art Love, and ev
 where
 Thy Name is brightly shown
 Beneath, on earth—Thy foots
 fair,
 Above, in heaven—Thy thro

mf Thy ways are Love—though they
    transcend
    Our feeble range of sight,
    They wind through darkness to
    their end
cres In everlasting light.

mp Thy thoughts are Love, and Jesus is
    The loving voice they find ;
    His Love lights up the vast abyss
    Of the Eternal Mind.

mp Thy chastisements are Love—more
    deep
  . They stamp the seal Divine,
    And by a sweet compulsion keep
    Our spirits nearer Thine.

mp Thy heaven is the abode of Love !
    O blessèd Lord, that we [remove,
    May there, when time's dim shades
    Be gathered home to Thee !

mf Then with Thy resting saints to fall
    Adoring round Thy throne,
cres When all shall love Thee, Lord,
    and all
f   Shall in Thy love be one.

                  J. D. Burns.

328   8.7.8.7., double.

mf JESUS, I my cross have taken,
    All to leave and follow Thee ;
p Destitute, despised, forsaken,
cres Thou, from hence, my all shalt be:
    Perish every fond ambition,
    All I sought, and hoped, and
    known ;
mf Yet how rich is my condition !
    God and Heaven are still my own!

[*mf* Let the world despise and leave me,
    They have left my Saviour too ;
    Human *hearts and looks* deceive me;
    Thou art not, like man, untrue :

And, while Thou shalt smile upon
    me,
    God of wisdom, love, and might,
    Foes may hate, and friends may
    shun me
f Show Thy face, and all is bright !

p Man may trouble and distress me,
    'Twill but drive me to Thy breast;
    Life with trials hard may press
    me,
    Heaven will bring me sweeter
    rest !
cres O ! 'tis not in grief to harm me,
    While Thy love is left to me !
    O ! 'twere not in joy to charm me
    Were that joy unmixed with
    Thee !]

mf Take, my soul, thy full salvation ;
    Rise o'er sin, and fear, and
    care ;
    Joy to find, in every station,
    Something still to do or bear.
p Think what Spirit dwells within
    thee !
cres What a Father's smile is thine !
    What a Saviour died to win thee !
    Child of Heaven, shouldst thou
    repine ?

f Haste then on from grace to glory,
    Armed by faith, and winged by
    prayer ;
    Heaven's eternal day's before thee,
    God's own hand shall guide thee
    there !
p Soon shall close thy earthly mission,
    Swift shall pass thy pilgrim
    days ;
cres Hope soon change to glad fruition,
f   Faith to sight, and prayer to
    praise !

                  H. F. Lyte.

329   7.7.7.6.

mf In the dark and cloudy day,
    When earth's riches flee away,
    And the last hope will not stay,
p   My Saviour, comfort me.

mp When the hoard of many years
    Like a fleet cloud disappears,
    And the future's full of fears,
p   My Saviour, comfort me.

mp When the secret idol's gone
    That my poor heart yearned upon,
*dim*Desolate, bereft, alone,
p   My Saviour, comfort me.

mp Thou Who wast so sorely tried,
    In the darkness crucified,
*cres*Bid me in Thy love confide :
p   My Saviour, comfort me.

mf Not unduly let me grieve,
    Meekly the kind stripes receive,
    Let me humbly still believe:
p   My Saviour, comfort me.

mf So shall it be good for me
    Much afflicted now to be,
    If Thou wilt but tenderly,
    My Saviour, comfort me.

G. Rawson.

330   7s.

p When our heads are bowed with
    woe,
    When our bitter tears o'erflow ;
    When we mourn the lost, the dear,
*dim*Jesu, Son of Mary, hear !

p Thou our throbbing flesh hast worn,
    Thou our mortal griefs hast borne,
    Thou hast shed the human tear:
*dim*Jesu, Son of Mary, hear !

[*p* Thou hast bowed the dying head :
    Thou the blood of life hast shed ;
    Thou hast filled a mortal bier :
*dim*Jesu, Son of Mary, hear !]

p When the heart is sad within
    With the thought of all its sin ;
    When the spirit shrinks with fear,
*dim*Jesu, Son of Mary, hear !

p Thou the shame, the grief, hast
    known,   [own;
*cres*Though the sins were not Thine
    Thou hast deigned their load to
    bear:
*dim*Jesu, Son of Mary, hear !

H. H. Milman.

10.—*TRUST IN GOD, RESIGNATION, SUBMISSION, PEACE.*

331   10.10.11.11.

f   Begone, unbelief ;
    My Saviour is near,
    And for my relief
    Will surely appear.
    By prayer let me wrestle,
    And He will perform ;
With Christ in the vessel,
I smile at the storm.

mp   Though dark be my way,
    Since He is my Guide,
    'Tis mine to obey,
    'Tis His to provide ;
    Though cisterns be broken,
    And creatures all fail,
    The word He hath spoken
    Shall surely prevail.

f His love in time past
   Forbids me to think,
He'll leave me at last
   In trouble to sink :
Each sweet Ebenezer
   I have in review
Confirms His good pleasure
   To help me quite through.]

   Why should I complain
   Of want or distress,
Temptation or pain ?
   He told me no less :
The heirs of salvation,
   I know from His word,
Through much tribulation
   Must follow their Lord.

ɔ How bitter that cup,
   No heart can conceive,
Which He drank quite up,
   That sinners might live !
His way was much rougher
   And darker than mine ;
Did Jesus thus suffer,
   And shall I repine ?

f Since all that I meet
   Shall work for my good,
The bitter is sweet,
   The medicine food ;
Though painful at present,
   'Twill cease before long ;
f And then, O how pleasant
   The conqueror's song !
            J. Newton.

32   11.10.11.6.

f STILL will we trust, though earth
   seem dark and dreary,
And the heart faint beneath His
   chastening rod ;
Though rough and steep our pathway, worn and weary,
   Still will we trust in God.

mf Our eyes see dimly till by faith
   anointed,
And our blind choosing brings
   us grief and pain ;
Through Him alone Who hath our
   way appointed,
   We find our peace again.

mp Choose for us, God ! nor let our
   weak preferring
Cheat our poor souls of good
   Thou hast designed ;
. Choose for us, God ! Thy wisdom
   is unerring,
   And we are fools and blind.

mf Let us press on, in patient self-
   denial,   .
Accept the hardship, shrink not
   from the loss ;   [trial,
Our portion lies beyond the hour of
   Our crown beyond the cross.
          W. H. Burleigh.

333   8.8.6.8.8.6.

f O LORD, how happy should we be
   If we could cast our care on Thee,
dim If we from self could rest,
   And feel at heart that One above,
cres In perfect wisdom, perfect love,
   Is working for the best !

mp How far from this our daily life,
   Ever disturbed by anxious strife,
   By sudden wild alarms !
cres Oh, could we but relinquish all
   Our earthly props, and simply fall
   On Thine almighty arms !

p Could we but kneel and cast our load,
   E'en while we pray, upon our God,
cres Then rise with lightened cheer.
f Sure that the Father, Who is nigh
   To still the famished raven's cry
   Will hear in that we fear !

mp We cannot trust Him as we should :
So chafes weak nature's restless
    mood
To cast its peace away ;
*cres*Yet birds and flowerets round us
    preach,
And all the present evil teach
Sufficient for the day.

cp Lord, make these faithless hearts
    of ours
Such lessons learn from birds and
    flowers ;
Make them from self to cease,
*cres*Leave all things to a Father's will,
*dim*And taste, before Him lying still,
p E'en in affliction, peace.

J. Anstice, v. 4, l. 2 altd.

334 C.M., double.

mp As helpless as a child who clings
Fast to his father's arm,
And casts his weakness on the
    strength
That keeps him safe from harm,
*cres*So I, my Father, cling to Thee,
And thus I every hour
Would link my earthly feebleness
To Thine almighty power.

mf As trustful as a child who looks
Up in his mother's face,
And all his little griefs and tears
Forgets in her embrace,
*cres*So I to Thee, my Saviour, look,
And in Thy face divine,
Can read the love that will sustain
As weak a faith as mine.

mp As loving as a child who sits
Close by his parent's knee,
And knows no want while he can
    have
That sweet society.

*cres*So, sitting at Thy feet, my heart
Would all its love outpour,
And pray that Thou wouldst teach
    me, Lord,
f To love Thee more and more.

J. D. Burns.

335 88.88.88.

mp HE sendeth sun, He sendeth shower,
Alike they're needful for the flower;
And joys and tears alike are sent
To give the soul fit nourishment :
p As comes to me, or cloud or sun,
Father, Thy will, not mine, be done.

mp Can loving children e'er reprove
With murmurs those they trust
    and love ?
*cres*My Father, I would ever be
A trusting, loving child to Thee :
p As comes to me, or cloud or sun,
Father, Thy will, not mine, be done.

mp O ne'er will I at life repine,
Enough that Thou hast made it
    mine ; [death,
*dim*When falls the shadow cold of
*cres*I yet will sing, with parting breath,
As comes to me, or shade or sun,
Father, Thy will, not mine, be done.

Sarah F. Adams, v. 2, ll. 2, 3 altd.

336 8.6.8.8.6.

mf DEAR Lord and Father of mankind,
Forgive our feverish ways !
Reclothe us in our rightful mind ;
In purer lives Thy service find,
In deeper reverence, praise.

mp In simple trust like theirs who
Beside the Syrian sea, [heard,
The gracious calling of the Lord,
*cres*Let us, like them, without a word
Rise up and follow Thee.

mp O Sabbath rest by Galilee !
O calm of hills above,
Where Jesus knelt to share with
thee
The silence of eternity,
Interpreted by love !

p With that deep hush subduing all
Our words and works that drown
The tender whisper of Thy call,
As noiseless let Thy blessing fall
As fell Thy manna down.

p Drop Thy still dews of quietness,
Till all our strivings cease :
cres Take from our souls the strain and
stress ;
And let our ordered lives confess
The beauty of Thy peace.

mp Breathe through the pulses of
desire
Thy coolness and Thy balm ;
Let sense be dumb, its heats expire :
Speak through the earthquake,
wind. and fire,
O still small voice of calm !

J. G. Whittier.

337   7s.

mf THOUGH Thou slay me, I will trust,
Thou art God, but I am dust ;
Though Thou grieve, Thy grace
I'll prove,
I am loveless, Thou art love.

mp Though Thou seem to turn away,
cres I will nearer to Thee stay ;
mp Though Thy silence wound me sore,
cres I will follow Thee the more.

mp Though Thy face I cannot see,
cres Well I know 'tis turned to me ;
mp Though the clouds exclude its light,
cres Well I know its beams are bright.

mp Though the children's bread denied,
cres Still I linger by Thy side ;
mp Though Thy fulness Thou refuse,
cres Still the crumbs I may not lose.

mf Any sorrow I can bear,
Save the sorrow of despair ;
Anything Thou ask'st resign,
Save the bliss of being Thine.

mf Nothing that mine eyes can see
Shall disturb my faith in Thee ;
Love to wait can well afford
For the leisure of the Lord.

J. S. B. Monsell.

338   8.8.8.4.

mf MY God, my Father, while I stray
Far from my home, on life's rough
way,
cres O teach me from my heart to say,
dim   " Thy will be done ! "

p Though dark my path and sad
my lot,
Let me " be still," and murmur not,
cres Or breathe the prayer divinely
taught,
dim   " Thy will be done ! "

p If Thou shouldst call me to resign
What most I prized,—it ne'er was
mine ;
I only yield Thee what was Thine :
pp   " Thy will be done ! "

mf Let but my fainting heart be blest
With Thy sweet Spirit for its guest,
My God, to Thee I leave the rest :
p   " Thy will be done ! "

mf Renew my will from day to day ;
Blend it with Thine ; and take
away
All that now makes it hard to say,
p   " Thy will be done !"   6a.

mf Then, when on earth I breathe no
more, [before,
The prayer oft mixed with tears
*cres*I'll sing upon a happier shore,—
f "Thy will be done!"
Charlotte Elliott.

339 C.M.

mf LORD, it belongs not to my care
Whether I die or live;
To love and serve Thee is my share,
And this Thy grace must give.

mp If life be long, I will be glad,
That I may still obey;
If short, yet why should I be sad
To soar to endless day?

*mp*Christ leads me through no darker
rooms
Than He went through before;
He that unto God's Kingdom comes
Must enter by this door.

mp Come, Lord, when grace hath made
Thy blessèd face to see; [me meet
For if Thy work on earth be sweet,
What will Thy glory be?

mf Then I shall end my sad complaints
And weary sinful days, [saints
*cres*And join with the triumphant
f That sing Jehovah's praise.

mf My knowledge of that life is small;
The eye of faith is dim; [all,
*cres*But 'tis enough that Christ knows
f And I shall be with Him.
R. Baxter, v. 1, l. 1, v. 2, l. 4 altd.

340 PART I. S.M.

mf COMMIT thou all thy griefs
And ways into His hands,
To His sure Truth and tender care,
Who earth and Heaven com-
mands,

[*mf* Who points the
course,
Whom winds and
He shall direct thy w
He shall prepare t

mf Thou on the Lord
So safe shalt thou
Fix on His Work thy
So shall thy work

mf No profit canst the
By self-consuming
To Him commend t
dim Attends the softes

mf Thy everlasting T
Father! Thy cease
Sees all Thy childrei
knows
What best for eacl

mf Thou everywhere
And all things ser
Thy every act pure b
Thy path unsullied
J. Wesley, from F

PART II.

mf GIVE to the winds
Hope, and be undi
God hears thy sigh
thy tears,
God shall lift up t

mp Through waves ar
storms,
He gently clears t
*cres*Wait thou His time
night
f Soon end in joyous

[*mf* What though thou
Yet heaven and ea
*cres*Proclaim, God sitteth
And ruleth all thii

to His sovereign sway
ose and to command ;
thou wondering own, His

rise, how strong His hand !
eest our weakness, Lord !
arts are known to Thee :
Thou up the sinking hand,
m the feeble knee !

, in life, in death,
eadfast Truth declare,
lish, with our latest breath,
ve and guardian care !

esley, from P. Gerhardt.

C.M.

er, it is good for me
ist and not to trace,
it with deep humility
hy revealing grace.

hen Thy way is in the sea
trange to mortal sense,
hee in the m$_y$ster$_y$,
t Thy providence.

, see the secret things
s my dark abode ;
it reach with earthly wings
eights and depths of God.

and patience! wait a while!
oubting, not in fear ;
n in heaven my Father's
le
render all things clear.

ou shalt end Time's short
ose,
n uncertain night ;
t the grand apocalypse,
l the perfect light.

G. Rawson.

342 L.M.

mf O BLESSÈD life ! the heart at rest
When all without tumultuous
seems, [deems
That trusts a higher will, and
That higher will, not mine, the best.

mf O blessèd life ! the mind that sees,
Whatever change the years may
b
A n$\ldots$ still in everything,
And shining through all mysteries.

mf O blessèd life ! the soul that soars,
*dim*When sense of mortal sight is dim,
Beyond the sense—beyond to Him
*cres*Whose love unlocks the heavenly
doors.

mf O blessèd life ! heart, mind, and
soul [free
From self-born aims and wishes
In all—at one with Deity,
And loyal to the Lord's control.

mf O life ! how blessèd, how divine !
High life, the earnest of a higher !
*cres*Saviour, fulfil my deep desire,
f And let this blessèd life be mine.

W. T. Matson.

343 8.7.8.7.6.6.6.6.7

f A SAFE stronghold our God is still
A trusty shield and weapon ;
He'll help us clear from all the ill
That hath us now o'ertaken.
mf The ancient prince of hell
Hath risen with purpose fell ;
Strong mail of craft and power
He weareth in this hour ;
On earth is not his fellow.

f With force of arms we nothing can.
p Full soon were we down-ridden

*cres*But for us fights the proper Man,
f   Whom God Himself hath bidden.
     Ask ye, Who is this same?
,ff   Christ Jesus is His Name.
     The Lord Sabaoth's Son ;
   .   He, and no other one,
     Shall conquer in the battle.

f And were this world all devils o'er,
    And watching to devour us,
    We lay it not to heart so sore ;
    Not they can overpower us.
     And let the prince of ill
     Look grim as e'er he will, .
     He harms us not a whit ;
     For why? his doom is writ ;
ff   A word shall quickly slay him.

mf God's word, for all their craft and
     force,
    One moment shall not linger,
    But, spite of hell, shall have its
     course ;
    'Tis written by His finger.
p   And, though they take our life,
     Goods, honour, children, wife,
cres   Yet is their profit small ;
     These things shall vanish all,
f   The city of God remaineth.
       M. Luther, tr. T. Carlyle.

344   6.6.6.6

p THY way, not mine, O Lord,
    However dark it be !
    Lead me by Thine own hand,
    Choose out the path for me.

p Smooth let it be or rough,
    It will be still the best ;
    Winding or straight, it leads
*cres*Right onward to Thy rest.

p I dare not choose my lot ;
  I would not, if I might ;

mf Choose Thou for me, my God ;
    So shall I walk aright.

mf Take Thou my cup, and it
    With joy or sorrow fill,
    As best to Thee may seem ;
    Choose Thou my good and ill ;

mf Choose Thou for me my friends,
    My sickness or my health ;
*dim*Choose Thou my cares for me,
    My poverty or wealth.

mf Not mine, not mine the choice,
    In things or great or small ;.
*cres*Be Thou my guide, my strength,
f My wisdom, and my all !
         H. Bonar.

345   C.M.

mp CALM me, my God, and keep me
    calm,
    While these hot breezes blow ;
    Be like the night-dew's cooling
    balm
    Upon earth's fevered brow.

mp Calm me, my God, and keep me
    calm,
    Soft resting on Thy breast ;
    Soothe me with holy hymn and
    psalm,
    And bid my spirit rest.

mp Yes, keep me calm, though loud
    and rude
    The sounds my ear that greet,
    Calm in the closet's solitude,
    Calm in the bustling street ;

mp Calm in the hour of buoyant health,
    Calm in my hour of pain ;
    Calm in my poverty or wealth,
    Calm in my loss or gain ;

[*mp*Calm in the sufferance of wrong,
    Like Him Who bore my shame,

Calm 'mid the threatening, taunting throng,
Who hate Thy holy Name ;
mf Calm when the great world's news with power
My listening spirit stir ;
Let not the tidings of the hour
E'er find too fond an ear.]

mp Calm as the ray of sun or star
Which storms assail in vain ;
cres Moving unruffled through earth's war,
The eternal calm to gain.

H. Bonar.

346   C.M., 6 lines.

mf FATHER, I know that all my life
Is portioned out for me,
The changes that are sure to come,
I do not f^{e}ar to se^e ;
cres I ask Thee for a present mind
Intent on pleasing Thee.

mf I ask Thee for a thoughtful love,
Through constant watching wise,
To meet the glad with joyful smiles,
dim To wipe the weeping eyes ;
A heart at leisure from itself,
p To soothe and sympathise.

[*mf* I would not have the restless will
That hurries to and fro,
Seeking for some great thing to do,
Or secret thing to know ;
dim I would be treated as a child,
And guided where I go.

mf Wherever in the world I am,
In whatsoe'er estate,
I have a fellowship with hearts
To keep and cultivate ;
A work of lowly love to do
For Him on Whom I wait.]

mf I ask Thee for the daily strength
To none that ask denied ;
A mind to blend with outward life,
While keeping at Thy side :
Content to fill a little space,
If Thou be glorified.

p Briers beset our daily path,
That call for patient care ;
There is a cross in every lot,
An earnest need for prayer :
cres But lowly hearts that lean on Thee
Are happy anywhere.

mf In service which Thy will appoints,
There are no bonds for me ;
My inmost heart is taught "the truth"
That makes Thy children "free":
cres A life of self-renouncing love
f Is one of liberty.

Anna L. Waring, altd.

347   C.M., double.

mf MY heart is resting, O my God,
I will give thanks and sing ;
My heart is at the secret source
Of every precious thing :
p Now the frail vessel Thou hast made
No hand but Thine shall fill ;
The waters of the earth have failed,
cres And I am thirsty still.

mf I thirst for springs of heavenly life,
And here all day they rise—
I seek the treasure of Thy love,
And close at hand it lies ;
And a "new song" is in my mouth
To long-loved music set—
cres Glory to Thee for all the grace
dim I have not tasted yet.

*cres*Glory to Thee for strength with-
    held,
dim For want and weakness known—
    The fear that sends me to Thy
      breast,
    For what is most my own.
mf I have a heritage of joy
    That yet I must not see ;
p The hand that bled to make it mine
cres Is keeping it for me.

mf My heart is resting, O my God,
    My heart is in Thy care—
*cres*I hear the voice of joy and health
f   Resounding everywhere. [soul,
mf "Thou art my portion," saith my
    Ten thousand voices say ;
*cres*The music of their glad Amen,
f   Will never die away.
                Anna L. Waring.

348   C.M.

mf WE bless Thee for Thy peace, O God,
    Deep as the unfathomed sea,
    Which falls like sunshine on the
      road
    Of those who trust in Thee.

mp We ask not, Father, for repose
    Which comes from outward rest,
    If we may have through all life's
      woes
    Thy peace within our breast.

mf That peace which suffers and is
      strong,
    Trusts where it cannot see,
    Deems not the trial-way too long,
    But leaves the end with Thee.

mf That peace which flows serene and
      deep,
    A river in the soul   [keep—
Whose banks a living verdure
God's sunshine o'er the whole.

mp O Father, give our hearts this
    Whate'er the outward be,
*cres*Till all life's discipline shall
    And we go home to Thee.

349   6.5.6.5.

mf OH ! let him whose sorrow
    No relief can find,
*cres*Trust in God, and borrow
    Ease for heart and mind.

p Where the mourner weeping
    Sheds the secret tear,
mf God His watch is keeping,
    Though none else be near.

mf God will never leave thee,
    All thy wants He knows,
    Feels the pains that grieve thee,
    Sees thy cares and woes.

f Raise thine eyes to heaven
    When thy spirits quail,
    When, by tempests driven,
    Heart and courage fail.

p When in grief you languish,
cres He will dry the tear,
mf Who His children's anguish
    Soothes with succour near.

p All thy woe and sadness,
    In this world below,
*cres*Balance not the gladness
    Thou in heaven shalt know,—

mf When thy gracious Saviour,
    In the realms above,
    Crowns thee with His favour,
f   Fills thee with His love.
    H. S. Oswald, tr. Frances E. Cox.

350   8.8.8.4.

mf O LAMB of God ! that tak'st a
    Our sin, and bidd'st our
      cease,

Turn Thou, oh, turn this night to day,
p　　Grant us Thy peace !

mf The troubled world hath war without ;
The restless wayward heart within
dim Hath fear and weariness and doubt,
And death and sin.

mp And there are needs that none can know
And tears no eye but Thine can see ;
Hopes nought can satisfy below ;
We look to Thee.

mp Probe deep the wound if so Thou wilt, 　　　[dross :
If pain must wake us.　Purge our
Help us to lay our load of guilt
Beneath Thy Cross ;

mp That we, amid the toil and strife,
And storms that never end below,
Through all the chance and change of life,
Thy peace may know :

mf The peace that is not ours, but Thine,— 　.　[thus !—
cres O safe and true and deathless
f 'Gainst which all storms in vain combine,
p　　Grant, grant to us !

Alessie Faussett.

351　　　　　　　　　L.M.

mf O LOVE divine, that stooped to share
Our sharpest pang, our bitterest tear, 　　　[care :
On Thee we cast each earthborn
We smile at pain while Thou art near !

mp Though long the weary way we tread, 　　　[year ;
And sorrow crown each lingering
cres No path we shun, no darkness dread, 　　　[art near.
Our hearts still whispering, Thou

mp When drooping pleasure turns to grief, 　　　[fear ;
dim And trembling faith is changed to
The murmuring wind, the quivering leaf,
Shall softly tell us, Thou art near !

mp On Thee we fling our burdening woe,
O Love divine, for ever dear ;
cres Content to suffer, while we know,
Living and dying, Thou art near !

O. W. Holmes.

352　　　　　　　　8.8.8.6.

mf O HOLY Saviour, Friend unseen,
The faint, the weak, on Thee may lean : 　　　[scene,
Help me, throughout life's varying
By faith to cling to Thee !

mf Blest with communion so divine,
Take what Thou wilt, shall I repine,
When, as the branches to the vine,
My soul may cling to Thee ?

mf What though the world deceitful prove, 　　　[remove ?
And earthly friends and joys
cres With patient uncomplaining love
dim　Still would I cling to Thee !

mp Though faith and hope awhile be tried,
I ask not, need not, aught beside.
How safe, how calm, how satisfi
The souls that cling to Thee !

mf They fear not life's rough storms
 to brave,   [save ;
Since Thou art near, and strong to
Nor shudder e'en at death's dark
 wave ;
Because they cling to Thee !

mf Blest is my lot, whate'er befall :
What can disturb me, who appal.
While, as my strength, my rock,
 my all,
Saviour ! I cling to Thee ?
    Charlotte Elliott.

353   C.M., 6 lines.

mf Go not far from me, O my strength,
 Whom all my times obey ;
Take from me anything Thou wilt,
 But go not Thou away,—
And let the storm that does Thy
 work
Deal with me as it may.

mp On Thy compassion I repose,
 In weakness and distress ;
I will not ask for greater ease,
 Lest I should love Thee less.
cres Oh ! 'tis a blessèd thing for me
 To need Thy tenderness.

mf Thy love has many a lighted path
 No outward eye can trace ;
And my heart sees Thee in the deep,
 With darkness on its face,
And commures with Thee 'mid
 the storm,
 As in a secret place.

mp When I am feeble as a child,
 And flesh and heart give way,
cres Then on Thy everlasting strength
 With passive trust I stay,
*f And the rough wind becomes a song,
 And darkness shines like day.*

mf There is no death for me to fear,
 For Christ, my Lord, hath died ;
There is no curse in this my pain,
 For He was crucified ;
And it is fellowship with Him
 That keeps me near His side.

mf My heart is fixed, O God, my
 strength,—
 My heart is strong to bear ;
cres I will be joyful in Thy love,
dim And peaceful in Thy care. [sake,
Deal with me, for my Saviour's
 According to His prayer.
    Anna L. Waring.

354   7s., 6 lines.

p QUIET, Lord, my froward heart ;
Make me teachable and mild,
Upright, simple, free from art ;
Make me as a weanèd child :
From distrust and envy free,
mf Pleased with all that pleases Thee.

mf What Thou shalt to-day provide,
Let me as a child receive ;
What to-morrow may betide,
Calmly to Thy wisdom leave.
'Tis enough that Thou wilt care :
dim Why should I the burden bear ?

mf As a little child relies
On a care beyond his own ;
Knows he's neither strong nor wise;
Fears to stir a step alone ;
cres Let me thus with Thee abide,
As my Father, Guard, and Guide.

mf Thus preserved from Satan's wiles,
Safe from dangers, free from fears,
May I live upon Thy smiles,
Till the promised hour appears,
cres When the sons of God shall prove
All their Father's boundless love.
    J. Newton.

11.—ASPIRATION AND HOPE.

55   L.M.

p LET me be with Thee where Thou
   art,
   My Saviour, my eternal Rest ;
res Then only will this longing heart
   Be fully and for ever blest.

f Let me be with Thee where Thou
   art,
   Thy unveiled glory to behold ;
im Then only will this wayward heart
   Cease to be treacherous, faithless,
   cold.

f Let me be with Thee where Thou
   art,
   Where spotless saints Thy Name
   adore ;
im Then only will this sinful heart
   Be evil and defiled no more.

f Let me be with Thee where Thou
   art,
p Where none can die, whence none
   remove ;
res There neither life nor death will
   part
   Me from Thy presence and Thy
   love.
          *Charlotte Elliott, v. 2, l. 3, v. 4,
          ll. 2, 3 altd.*

56   8.8.6.8.8.6.

f COME on, my partners in distress,
   My comrades through the wilder-
   ness,
   Who still your sorrows feel ;
   Awhile forget your griefs and fears,
   And look beyond this vale of tears,
   To that celestial hill.

mf Beyond the bounds of time and
      space,   [place,
   Look forward to that heavenly
   The saints' secure abode :
f On faith's strong eagle-pinions rise,
   And force your passage to the skies,
   And scale the mount of God.

[*mp* Who suffer with our Master here,
   We shall before His face appear,
   And by His side sit down :
   To patient faith the prize is sure,
   And all that to the end endure
   The cross, shall wear the crown.

mf Thrice blessèd, bliss-inspiring hope!
   It lifts the fainting spirit up ;
   It brings to life the dead :
f Our conflicts here shall soon be past,
   And we in joy ascend at last,
   Triumphant with our Head.]

f That great mysterious Deity
   We soon with open face shall see ;
   The beatific sight   [with praise,
ff Shall fill heaven's sounding courts
   And wide diffuse the golden blaze
   Of everlasting light.

f The Father shining on His throne,
   The glorious co-eternal Son,
   The Spirit, one and seven,
   Conspire our rapture to complete ;
dim And, lo ! we fall before His feet,
pp   And silence heightens heaven.

mp In hope of that ecstatic pause,
   Jesus, we now sustain the cross,
dim And at Thy footstool fall ;
cres Till Thou our hidden life reveal,
   Till Thou our ravished spirits fill,
ff   And God is all in all !
          C. Wesley, v. 1, l. 3, v. 3, l. 5

357 C.M., double.

mf THE roseate hues of early dawn.
   The brightness of the day,
   The crimson of the sunset sky,
p   How fast they fade away !
*cres*O for the pearly gates of heaven,
   O for the golden floor ;
f O for the Sun of Righteousness
   That setteth nevermore !

mp The highest hopes we cherish here,
   How fast they tire and faint !
   How many a spot defiles the robe
   That wraps an earthly saint !
*cres*O for a heart that never sins,
   O for a soul washed white,
f O for a voice to praise our king,
   Nor weary day or night !

mf Here faith is ours, and heavenly
      hope,
   And grace to lead us higher ;
*cres*But there are perfectness and peace,
   Beyond our best desire.
f O by Thy love and anguish, Lord,
   O by Thy life laid down,
*dim*Grant that we fall not from Thy
      grace,
pp   Nor cast away our crown !

                C. Frances Alexander.

358 S.M., double.

mf JESU, my strength, my hope,
   On Thee I cast my care,
   With humble confidence look up,
   And know, Thou hear'st my
      prayer.
   Give me on Thee to wait
   Till I can all things do,
   On Thee, almighty to create !
   Almighty to renew !

[*mp*I want a godly fear,
   A quick-discerning eye,
   That looks to Thee when sin is near
   And sees the Tempter fly ;
   A spirit still prepared,
   And armed with jealous care,
   For ever standing on its guard,
   And watching unto prayer.

mp I want a heart to pray,
   To pray and never cease,
   Never to murmur at Thy stay,
   Or wish my sufferings less ;
   This blessing, above all,
   Always to pray, I want,
   Out of the deep on Thee to call,
   And never, never faint.]

mf I want a true regard,
   A single, steady aim,
   Unmoved by threat'ning or reward,
   To Thee and Thy great Name ;
*cres*A jealous, just concern
   For Thine immortal praise ;
f A pure desire that all may learn
   And glorify Thy grace.

mf I rest upon Thy word ;
   Thy promise is for me ;
*cres*My succour and salvation, Lord,
   Shall surely come from Thee.
mp But let me still abide,
cres Nor from my hope remove,
   Till Thou my patient spirit guide
   Into Thy perfect love !

                C. Wesley.

359 L.M.

mf O THOU, to Whose all-searching
      sight
   The darkness shineth as the light,
   Search, prove my heart ; it pants
      for Thee ;   [free !
   O, burst these bands, and set it

mf Wash out its stains, refine its dross ;
  Nail my affections to the cross ;
  Hallow each thought ; let all
    within   [clean.
  Be clean, as Thou, my Lord, art

mp If in this darksome wild I stray,
  Be Thou my Light, be Thou my
    Way ;
*cres*No foes, no violence I fear,
  No fraud, while Thou, my God, art
    near.

mp When rising floods my soul o'erflow,
p When sinks my heart in waves of
    woe,

*cres*Jesu, Thy timely aid impart,
  And raise my head, and cheer my
    heart.

mf Saviour ! where'er Thy steps I see,
*cres*Dauntless, untired, I follow Thee :
  O let Thy hand support me still,
  And lead me to Thy holy hill !

mf If rough and thorny be the way,
  My strength proportion to my day ;
*cres*Till toil, and grief, and pain shall
    cease
  Where all is calm and joy and peace.
  N. L. von Zinzendorf, v. 4 J. A.
  Freylinghausen, tr. J. Wesley.

12.—*JOY IN GOD.*

360   S.M.

f COME, we that love the Lord,
  And let our joys be known ;
  Join in a song with sweet accord,
  And thus surround the throne.

[*mf* The sorrows of the mind
  Be banished from the place :
  Religion never was designed
  To make our pleasures less.

mp Let those refuse to sing
  That never knew our God ;
*cres*But children of the heavenly King
  May speak their joys abroad.]

mf The men of grace have found
  Glory begun below ;
  Celestial fruits on earthly ground,
  From faith and hope may grow.

mf The hill of Zion yields
  A thousand sacred sweets,
  Before we reach the heavenly fields,
  Or walk the golden streets.

[*mf* There shall we see His face,
  And never, never sin :
  There, from the rivers of His grace
  Drink endless pleasures in.]

f Then let our songs abound,
  And every tear be dry ;
*cres*We're marching through Im-
    manuel's ground
ff To fairer worlds on high.

  I. Watts, v. 3, l. 3 altd.

361   S.M.

mf MY God, my life, my love,
  To Thee, to Thee I call,
  I cannot live if Thou remove,
  For Thou art all in all.

mf To Thee, and Thee alone,
  The angels owe their bliss ;
  They sit around Thy gracious
    throne,
  And dwell where Jesus is.

mp Not all the harps above
Can make a heavenly place.
If God His residence remove
Or but conceal His face.

mp Nor earth, nor all the sky,
Can one delight afford,
No, not a drop of real joy,
Without Thy presence, Lord.

mf Thou art the sea of love,
Where all my pleasures roll,
The circle where my passions move,
And centre of my soul.

I. Watts.

362 7.6.7.6., double.

mf SOMETIMES a light surprises
The Christian while he sings :
*cres*It is the Lord Who rises
With healing in His wings.
p When comforts are declining,
He grants the soul, again,
*cres*A season of clear shining,
To cheer it after rain.

mf In holy contemplation
We sweetly then pursue
The theme of God's salvation,
And find it ever new.
*cres*Set free from present sorrow
We cheerfully can say,
mf E'en let the unknown morrow
Bring with it what it may,—

mf It can bring with it nothing,
But He will bear us through :
Who gives the lilies clothing,
Will clothe His people too.
Beneath the spreading heavens
No creature but is fed ;
*And He Who feeds the ravens
Will give His children bread.*

p Though vine nor fig-tree neither
Their wonted fruit shall bear ;
Though all the field should wither,
Nor flocks nor herds be there ;
*cres*Yet, God the same abiding,
His praise shall tune my voice ;
f For while in Him confiding,
I cannot but rejoice.

W. Cowper.

363 L.M.

mf O HAPPY day that fixed my choice
On Thee, my Saviour and my God :
Well may this glowing heart rejoice,
And tell its raptures all abroad.

mf O happy bond, that seals my vows
To Him Who merits all my love :
Let cheerful anthems fill His house,
While to that sacred shrine I move.

p 'Tis done ! the great transaction's
done ;
*cres*I am my Lord's and He is mine :
mf He drew me, and I followed on,
Charmed to confess the voice divine.

mf Now rest, my long-divided heart·
Fixed on this blissful centre, rest :
With ashes who would grudge to
part, [feast ?
When called on angels' bread to
f High heaven, that heard the solemn
vow,
That vow renewed shall daily hear :
p Till in life's latest hour I bow,
*cres*And bless in death a bond so dear.

P. Doddridge.

364 C.M.

mf O LORD, I would delight in Thee,
And on Thy care depend ;
To Thee in every trouble flee,
My best, my only Friend.

mf When all created streams are dried,
Thy fulness is the same :
May I with this be satisfied,
And glory in Thy Name !

mp No good in creatures can be found,
But may be found in Thee ;
cres I must have all things, and abound,
While God is God to me.

mp Oh ! that I had a stronger faith,
To look within the veil !
To credit what my Saviour saith,
Whose word can never fail :

cres He that has made my heaven
secure,
Will here all good provide ;
While Christ is rich, can I be poor?
What can I want beside ?

mf O Lord, I cast my care on Thee ;
I triumph and adore :　　　[be
cres Henceforth my great concern shall
f　　To love and please Thee more.
　　　　　　　　　　J. Ryland.

365　　　　　　　C.M.

f MY God, the spring of all my joys,
The life of my delights,
The glory of my brightest days,
And comfort of my nights !

mp In darkest shades if He appear,
My dawning is begun !
cres He is my soul's sweet morning star,
f　　And He my rising sun.

mf The opening heavens around me
shine
With beams of sacred bliss,
dim While Jesus shows His heart is
mine,
p　　And whispers,—I am His.

mf My soul would leave this heavy clay
At that transporting word ;

f Run up with joy the shining way
To embrace my dearest Lord :

ff Fearless of hell and ghastly death,
I'd break through every foe ;
The wings of love and arms of faith
Should　bear　me　conqueror
through.
　　　　　　　　　　I. Watts.

366　　　　　　　C.M.

f REJOICE, believer, .n the Lord,
Who makes your cause His own :
The hope that's built upon His
word
Can ne'er be overthrown.

mf Though many foes beset your road,
And feeble is your arm,
Your life is hid with Christ in God,
Beyond the reach of harm.

mp Weak as you are you shall not faint :
Or fainting, shall not die :
cres Jesus, the strength of every saint,
Will aid you from on high.

mp Though　unperceived　by　mortal
sense,
Faith sees Him always near,
cres A Guide, a glory, a defence :
Then what have you to fear ?

mf As surely as He overcame,
And triumphed once for you,
f So surely you that love His Name
Shall in Him triumph too.
　　　　　　　　　　J. Newton.

367　　　　　　　S.M.

mf　YOUR harps, ye trembling saints,
Down from the willows take ;
Loud to the praise of Love divin
Bid every string awake.

mf Though in a foreign land,
We are not far from home ;
And nearer to our house above,
We every moment come.

[*f* His Grace will to the end
Stronger and brighter shine ;
Nor present things, nor things to
come,
Shall quench the spark divine.]

p When we in darkness walk,
Nor feel the heavenly flame,

*cres*Then is the time to trust our God,
And rest upon His Name.

mf Soon shall our doubts and fears
Subside at His control ;
*cres*His loving-kindness shall break
through
The midnight of the soul.

mf Blest is the man, O God,
That stays himself on Thee !
*cres*Who wait for Thy salvation, Lord,
f Shall Thy salvation see !
A. M. Toplady.

13.—COMMUNION WITH GOD.

368 S.M.

mf WITH Thee, my Lord, my God,
I would desire to be :
By day, by night, at home, abroad,
I would be still with Thee.

mp With Thee, when dawn comes
in,
And calls me back to care ;
Each day returning to begin
With Thee, my God, in prayer.

mf With Thee, amid the crowd
That throngs the busy mart ;
To hear Thy voice, 'mid clamour
loud,
dim Speak softly to my heart.

mp With Thee, when day is done,
And evening calms the mind ;
The setting as the rising sun
With Thee my heart would find.

mp With Thee, when darkness brings
The signal of repose,
Calm in the shadow of Thy wings
Mine eyelids I would close.

mf With Thee, in Thee, by faith
Abiding I would be :
*cres*By day, by night, in life, in death,
I would be still with Thee.
J. D. Burns, v. 3, l. 3 altd.

369 L.M.

mf COME, dearest Lord, descend and
dwell
By faith and love in every breast ;
Then shall we know and taste and
feel.
f The joys that cannot be expressed.

mf Come, fill our hearts with inward
strength,
Make our enlargèd souls possess
And learn the height, and breadth,
and length
Of Thine unmeasurable grace.

f Now to the God Whose power can do
More than our thoughts or wishes
know,
Be everlasting honours done
By all the Church, through Christ
His Son. *I. Watts.*

370 C.M.

f WALK in the light ! so shalt thou
   know
   That fellowship of love
   His Spirit only can bestow,
   Who reigns in light above.

mf Walk in the light ! and sin abhorred
   Shall ne'er defile again ;
   The blood of Jesus Christ thy Lord
   Shall cleanse from every stain.

mf Walk in the light ! and thou shalt
   find
   Thy heart made truly His
   Who dwells in .cloudless light
   enshrined,
   In Whom no darkness is.

mf Walk in the light ! and thou shalt
   own
   Thy darkness passed away,
cres Because that light hath on thee
   shone,
   In which is perfect day.

mf Walk in the light ! and e'en the
   tomb
   No fearful shade shall wear ;
cres Glory shall chase away its gloom,
   For Christ hath conquered there.

mf Walk in the light ! and thine
   shall be
   A path, though thorny, bright ;
cres For God, by grace, shall dwell in
   thee,
f   And God Himself is Light.

                              B. Barton.

371 6.4.6.4.6.6.4.

mf WALKING with Thee, my God,
      Saviour benign,
   Daily confer on me
   Converse divine :

   Jesus, in Thee restored,
   Brother and blessèd Lord,
      Let it be mine.

mf Walking with Thee. my God,
      Like as a child
   Leans on his father's strength,
      Crossing the wild ;
   And by the way is taught
   Lessons of holy thought,
      Faith undefiled.

mf Darkness and earthly mists,
      How do they flee,
   Far underneath my feet,
      Walking with Thee :
f   Pure is that upper air,
   Cloudless the prospect there,
      Walking with Thee.

mp Walking in reverence
      Humbly with Thee,
cres Yet from all abject fear
      Lovingly free :
f   E'en as a friend with friend,
   Cheered to the journey's end,
      Walking with Thee.

mf Then Thy companions here
      Walking with Thee,
cres Rise to a higher life,
      Soul liberty :
dim They are not, here to love,
   But to the home above,
      Taken by Thee.

p   Gently translated, they
      Pass out of sight,
   Gone as the morning stars
      Flee with the night :
   Taken to endless day,
dim So may I fade away
      Into Thy light.

                              G. Rawson

372   C.M.

mf I WOULD commune with Thee, my
    E'en to Thy seat I come ; [God,
    I leave my joys. I leave my sins,
    And seek in Thee my home.

mf I stand upon the mount of God,
    With sunlight in my soul ;
    I hear the storms in vales beneath,
    I hear the thunders roll ;

mp But I am calm with Thee, my God,
    Beneath these glorious skies ;
    And to the height on which I stand
    Nor storms nor clouds can rise.

f O this is life ! O this is joy !
    My God, to find Thee so !
    Thy face to see, Thy voice to hear,
    And all Thy love to know.
                G. B. Bubier.

373   C.M.

mf TALK with us, Lord. Thyself reveal,
    While here o'er earth we rove ;
    Speak to our hearts, and let us feel
    The kindling of Thy love.

mf With Thee conversing, we forget
    All time and toil and care ;
*dim*Labour is rest, and pain is sweet,
    If Thou, my God, art here.

mf Here, then, my God, vouchsafe to
    stay,
    And bid my heart rejoice ;
*cres*My bounding heart shall own Thy
    sway,
    And echo to Thy voice.

mf Let this mine every hour employ,
    Till I Thy glory see,
*cres*Enter into my Master's joy,
    And find my heaven in Thee.
                C. Wesley.

374   88.88.88.

mf COME, O Thou Traveller unknown,
    Whom still I hold, but cannot see,
    My company before is gone,
    And I am left alone with Thee ;
f With Thee all night I mean to stay
ff And wrestle till the break of day

[*mp* I need not tell Thee who I am,
    My misery or sin declare ;
    Thyself hast called me by my name;
    Look on Thy hands, and read it
    there !
f But Who, I ask Thee, Who art
    Thou ?
ff Tell me Thy Name, and tell me
    now.]

mf Wilt Thou not yet to me reveal
    Thy new, unutterable Name ?
*cres*Tell me, I still beseech Thee, tell :
    To know it now, resolved I am :
f Wrestling, I will not let Thee go,
ff Till I Thy Name, Thy Nature know.

mp Yield to me now, for I am weak,
    But confident in self-despair ;
    Speak to my heart, in blessings
    speak,
    Be conquered by my instant prayer!
f Speak, or Thou never hence shalt
    move,
ff And tell me, if Thy Name is Love ?

f 'Tis Love ! 'tis Love ! Thou diedst
    for me !
    I hear Thy whisper in my heart !
    The morning breaks, the shadows
    flee ;
    Pure universal Love Thou art !
f To me, to all, Thy mercies move ;
ff Thy Nature, and Thy Name, is
    Love !

mf My prayer hath power with God ;
   the grace
Unspeakable I now receive ;
Through faith I see Thee face to
   face,
I see Thee face to face, and live :
f In vain I have not wept and strove:
ff Thy Nature, and Thy Name, is Love.

mf I know Thee, Saviour, Who Thou
   art ;
Jesus, the feeble sinner's Friend !
Nor wilt Thou with the night depart.
But stay, and love me to the end !
f Thy mercies never shall remove.
ff Thy Nature, and Thy Name, is Love!
   C. Wesley, v. 5, *l.* 5 *altd.*

14.—SERVICE AND REWARD.

375   6.5., 12 lines.

f WHO is on the Lord's side ?
Who will serve the King ?
Who will be His-helpers
Other lives to bring ?
Who will leave the world's side ?
Who will face the foe ?
Who is on the Lord's side ?
Who will for Him go ?
p   By Thy call of mercy,
cres   By Thy grace divine,
We are on the Lord's side,
f   Saviour, we are Thine!

[*mf* Not for weight of glory,
Nor for crown and palm,
Enter we the army,
Raise the warrior psalm ;
p But for love that claimeth
Lives for whom He died,
cres He whom Jesus nameth
Must be on His side.
f   By Thy love constraining,
By Thy grace divine,
We are on the Lord's side,
Saviour, we are Thine !]

mf Jesus, Thou hast bought us.
Not with gold or gem,
p But with Thine own life-blood,
cres For Thy diadem.
With Thy blessing filling
Each **who** **comes** to Thee,

Thou hast made us willing,
Thou hast made us free.
f   By Thy grand redemption
By Thy grace divine,
We are on the Lord's side,
Saviour, we are Thine !

mf Fierce may be the conflict,
Strong may be the foe, ·
cres But the King's own army
None can overthrow.
Round His standard ranging,
Victory is secure !
For His truth unchanging
Makes the triumph sure.
f   Joyfully enlisting
By Thy grace divine,
We are on the Lord's side,
Saviour, we are Thine !

mf Chosen to be soldiers
In an alien land,
"Chosen, callèd, faithful,"
For our Captain's band,
In the service royal,
Let us not grow cold :
f Let us be right loyal,
Noble, true, and bold.
mf   Master, Thou wilt keep us,
By Thy grace divine,
cres   Always on the Lord's side,
f   Saviour, always Thine !
    Frances R. Havergal.

376   C.M., 6 lines.

mp DISMISS me not Thy service, Lord,
But train me for Thy will ;
For even I, in fields so broad,
Some duties may fulfil ;
And I will ask for no reward,
Except to serve Thee still.

mf How many serve, how many more
May to the service come :
To tend the vines, the grapes to
store,
Thou dost appoint for some ;
Thou hast Thy young men at the
war,
Thy little ones at home.

mf All works are good, and each is best
As most it pleases Thee ;
Each worker pleases when the rest
He serves in charity ;
And neither man nor work unblest
Wilt Thou permit to be.

mf Our Master all the work hath done
He asks of us to-day ;
Sharing His service, every one
Share too His Sonship may :
Lord, I would serve and be a son ;
Dismiss me not, I pray.
         T. T. Lynch.

377   L.M.

mf O MASTER, let me walk with Thee
In lowly paths of service free ;
Tell me Thy secret ; help me bear
The strain of toil, the fret of care.

mp Help me, the slow of heart to move
By some clear winning word of love;
Teach me the wayward feet to stay,
And guide them in the homeward
way.

mp Teach me Thy patience ; still with
Thee
In closer, dearer company,
cres In work that keeps faith sweet
and strong,
f In trust that triumphs over wrong.

mf In hope that sends a shining ray
Far down the future's broadening
way ;
dim In peace that only Thou canst give,
With Thee, O Master, let me live !
         W. Gladden.

378   C.M.

mf OH, it is hard to work for God,
To rise and take His part
Upon this battle-field of earth,
And not sometimes lose heart !

mp He hides Himself so wondrously,
As though there were no God :
He is least seen when all the power
Of ill are most abroad.

[*mp* Or He deserts us at the hour
The fight is all but lost ;
And seems to leave us to ourselves
Just when we need Him most.

mf It is not so, but so it looks ;
dim And we lose courage then ; [kept
And doubts will come if God hath
His promises to men.]

mf Ah ! God is other than we think ;
His ways are far above, [reached
Far beyond reason's height, and
Only by childlike love.

mf Workman of God ! oh, lose not
heart,
But learn what God is like ;
And, in the darkest battle-field,
Thou shalt know where to strike.

f Thrice blest is he to whom is given
   The instinct that can tell
That God is on the field, when He
   Is most invisible.

ff For right is right, since God is God ;
   And right the day must win ;
nf To doubt would be disloyalty,
   To falter would be sin.

               F. W. Fiber.

379   C.M.

mp THOUGH lowly here our lot may be,
   High work have we to do ;
In faith and trust to follow Him
   Whose lot was lowly too.

p Our days of darkness we may bear,
   Strong in a Father's love,
*cres*Leaning on His almighty arm,
   And fixed our hopes above.

mp Our lives enriched with gentle
     thoughts
   And loving deeds may be,
cres A stream that still the nobler grows
   The nearer to the sea.

mf To duty firm, to conscience true,
   However tried and pressed.
In God's clear sight high work we
    do,
   If we but do our best.

mf Thus may we make the lowliest lot
   With rays of glory bright:
*cres*Thus may we turn a crown of
    thorns
   Into a crown of light.

             Lord Houghton.

380   7.6.7.6., double.

mf O JESUS, I have promised
   To serve Thee *to the end ;*

Be Thou for ever near me,
   My Master and my Friend .
*cres*I shall not fear the battle
   If Thou art by my side,
mf Nor wander from the pathway
   If Thou wilt be my Guide.

mf O let me feel Thee near me.
   The world is ever near :
I see the sights that dazzle,
   The tempting sounds I hear :
p My foes are ever near me,
   Around me and within ;
*cres*But, Jesus, draw Thou nearer,
   And shield my soul from sin.

p O let me hear Thee speaking,
   In accents clear and still,
Above the storms of passion,
   The murmurs of self-will.
mf O speak ! to reassure me,
   To hasten or control ;
*cres*O speak ! and make me listen,
   Thou Guardian of my soul.

mf O Jesus ! Thou hast promised,
   To all who follow Thee,
That where Thou art in glory
   There shall Thy servant be ;
*cres*And, Jesus, I have promised
   To serve Thee to the end ;
*dim*O give me grace to follow
   My Master and my Friend !

p O let me see Thy footmarks,
   And in them plant mine own :
   My hope to follow duly
   Is in Thy strength alone.
*cres*O guide me, call me, draw me,
   Uphold me to the end :
f And then in heaven receive me,
   My Saviour and my Friend\

            J. E. Bode

381   C.M., double.

mf How blessèd from the bonds of sin
    And earthly fetters free,
    In singleness of heart and aim,
    Thy servant, Lord, to be !
    The hardest toil to undertake
    With joy at Thy command,
*dim*The meanest office to receive
    With meekness at Thy hand.

mf With willing heart and longing
     eyes,
    To watch before Thy gate,
    Ready to run the weary race,
    To bear the heavy weight ;
p No voice of thunder to expect,
    But follow calm and still,
*cres*For love can easily divine
    The One Belovèd's will.

mf Thus may I serve Thee, gracious
     Lord !
    Thus ever Thine alone,
    My soul and body given to Thee,
    The purchase Thou hast won.
p Through evil or through good
     report,   .
    Still keeping by Thy side,
*cres*By life or death, in this poor
    flesh,
    Let Christ be magnified.

mf How happily the working days
    In this dear service fly,
p How rapidly the closing hour,
    The time of rest draws nigh !
*cres*When all the faithful gather
    home,
    A joyful company,
' *f* And ever where the Master is,
    Still His blest servants be.

       C. J. Spitta, tr. H. L. L.

382   4.10.10

f   COME, labour on !
mf Who dares stand idle on the
     plain ?   [golden
    While all around him wa
    And to each servant does the
     say,
    " Go, work to-day ! "

f   Come, labour on !
mf Claim the high calling ang
     not share,—   [nes
    To young and old the gospe
    Redeem the time ; its ho
     swiftly fl ,
p   The night draws nigh.

f   Come, labour on !
mf The labourers are few, the
     wide,   [blanks su
    New stations must be fill
    From voices distant far, or
     home,
    The call is, " Come ! "

f   Come, labour on !
mf The enemy is watching, nig
     day,   [seed
p To sow the tares, to snat
    While we in sleep our dut
     forgot,
    He slumbered not.

f   Come, labour on !
mf The toil is pleasant, the rev
     sure,   [e
    Blessèd are those who to t
*cres*How full their joy, how dee
    rest shall be,
p   O Lord, with Thee !

       H. .

    [SEE ALSO SECTION VIII. 3 (3).]

EMPTATIONS, DECLENSIONS, AND RECOVERY.

8.7.8.7.4.7.

Lord, we kneel before Thee,
from heaven Thy gracious
;
ir waiting souls adore Thee,
l of helpless sinners, hear !
ɣ Thy mercy,
ver us, good Lord !

the depth of nature's
dness,
the hardening power of sin,
  malice and unkindness,
the pride that lurks within,
y Thy mercy,
ver us, good Lord ‹

mptation sorely presses,
  day of Satan's power,
mes of deep distresses,
h dark and trying hour,
ɣ Thy mercy,
ɤer us, good Lord !

e world around is smiling,
  time of wealth and ease,
joys our hearts beguiling,
  day of health and peace,
ɤ Thy mercy,
ɤer us, good Lord !

eary night of sickness,
  time of grief and pain,
ə feel our mortal weak-

the creature's help is vain,
· Thy mercy,
·er us, good Lord ;

emn hour of dying,
ıwful judgment-day,

*cres*May our souls, on Thee relying,
  Find Thee still our hope and stay
p   By Thy mercy,
cres O deliver us, good Lord !
                              J. J. Cummins.

384   L.M.

mp STAY, Thou insulted Spirit, stay,
  Though I have done Thee such
    despite ;
  Nor cast the sinner quite away,
  Nor take Thine everlasting flight.

mp Though I have steeled my stubborr
    heart,
  And shaken off my guilty fears ; ●
  And vexed, and urged Thee to
    depart,
  For many long rebellious years ;

*dim*Though I have most unfaithful
    been
  Of all whoe'er Thy grace received ;
*cres*Ten thousand times Thy goodness
    seen,
*dim*Ten thousand times Thy goodness
    grieved ;

mp Yet, O ! the chief of sinners spare,
  In honour of my great High
    Priest ;
  Nor, in Thy righteous anger, swear
  To exclude me from Thy people's
    rest.

mf Now, Lord, my weary soul release;
*cres*Upraise me with Thy gracious
    hand ;
  And guide into Thy perfect peace,
  And bring me to the promised land.
                              C. Wesley.

385   C.M.

mf O HELP us, Lord, each hour of need,
Thy heavenly succour give ;
Help us in thought and word and
    deed,
Each hour, on earth, we live.

p O help us, when our spirits bleed
With contrite anguish sore ;
And when our hearts are cold and
    dead,
O help us, Lord, the more.

mf O help us, through the prayer of
    faith,
More firmly to believe ;
*cres*For still the more the servant hath,
The more shall he receive.

p O help us, Jesus, from on high,
We know no help but Thee ;
*cres*O help us so to live and die,
f   As Thine in heaven to be.

         H. H. Milman.

386   C.M.

p O FOR a closer walk with God,
A calm and heavenly frame ;
*cres*A light to shine upon the road
That leads me to the Lamb.

p Where is the blessedness I knew,
When first I saw the Lord ?
Where is the soul-refreshing view
Of Jesus and His word?

mp What peaceful hours I once enjoyed!
How sweet their memory still !
p But they have left an aching void
The world can never fill.

mp Return, O holy Dove, return,
Sweet messenger of rest ; [mourn,
*cres*I hate the sins that made Thee
dim And drove Thee from my breast.

mf The dearest idol I have know
Whate'er that idol be,
*cres*Help me to tear it from Thy t.
And worship only Thee.

mf So shall my walk be close wit
Calm and serene my fram
So purer light shall mark th
That leads me to the Laml

         W. Cou

387   6.5.6.5., dou

mf IN the hour of trial,
Jesu ! plead for me,
Lest by base denial
I depart from Thee ;
When Thou seest me waver,
With a look recall,
Nor, for fear or favour,
Suffer me to fall.

mf With forbidden pleasures
Should this vain world ch:
Or its tempting treasures
Spread, to work me harm
p Bring to my remembrance
Sad Gethsemane,
Or, in dark resemblance,
Cross-crowned Calvary.

p Should Thy mercy send me
Sorrow, toil, and woe ;
Or should pain attend me
On my path below ;
*cres*Grant that I may never
Fail Thy hand to see ;
Grant that I may ever
Cast my care on Thee.

pp When my last hour cometh,
Fraught with strife and p
mf When my dust returneth
To the dust again ;

ıy truth relying
ough that mortal strife,
take me. dying,
ternal life.

mery, altd. Frances A. Hutton.

L.M.

! and shall it ever be,
·tal man ashamed of Thee?
ncd of Thee, Whom angels
se,
: glories shine through end-
days?

ıed of Jesus! sooner far
ening blush to own a star;
.eds the beams of light divine
ıis benighted soul of mine.

ıed of Jesus! just as soon
idnight be ashamed of noon;
ıidnight with my soul till He,
: Morning Star, bid darkness

ıed of Jesus! that dear
nd
'hom my hopes of heaven
:nd!
when I blush, be this my
ne,
no more revere His Name.

ıed of Jesus! yes, I may
I've no guilt to wash away;
ır to wipe, no good to crave,
.rs to quell, no soul to save.

hen—nor is my boasting
—
en I boast a Saviour slain;
h! may this my glory be,
Jhrist is not ashamed of me!

Grigg, altd. by B. Francis.

389 C.M.

mf COME, let us to the Lord our God
With contrite hearts return;
Our ?od is gracious, nor will leave
The desolate to mourn.

[*mf* His voice commands the tempest
forth,
And stills the stormy wave;
And though His arm be strong to
smite
'Tis also strong to save.]

p Long hath the night of sorrow
reigned;
cres The dawn shall bring us light;
f God shall appear, and we shall rise
With gladness in His sight.

mf Our hearts, if God we seek to know
Shall know Him and rejoice;
cres His coming like the morn shall be,
Like morning songs His voice.

mp As dew upon the tender herb,
Diffusing fragrance round;
As showers that usher in the spring,
And cheer the thirsty ground:

f So shall His presence bless our souls,
And shed a joyful light: [away
That hallowed morn shall chase
The sorrows of the night.

J. Morrison.

390 7s., double.

mp DEPTH of mercy! can there be
Mercy still reserved for me?
Can my God His wrath forbear?
Me, the chief of sinners, spare?
I have long withstood His grace,
Long provoked Him to His face;
Would not hearken to His calls;
Grieved Him by a thousand falls.

mf Kindled His relentings are ;
   Me He still delights to spare ;
   Cries,—"How shall I give thee up?"
   Lets the lifted thunder drop.
   There for me the Saviour stands :
   ·Shows IIis wounds, and spreads
     His hands.
*cres*God is love ! I know, 1 feel ;
   Jesus pleads, and loves me still.

mp Jesus, answer from above :
   Is not all Thy nature love ?
   Wilt Thou not the wrong forget ?
   Suffer me to kiss Thy feet ?
*cres*If I rightly read Thy heart,
   If Thou all compassion art,
   Bow Thine ear, in mercy bow ;
   Pardon and accept me now.

mp Pity from Thine eye let fall ;
   By a look my soul recall ;
   Now, the stone to flesh convert,
   Cast a look, and break my heart.
   Now incline me to repent ;
   Let me now my fall lament :
   Now, my foul revolt deplore ;
   Weep, believe, and sin no more.

               C. Wesley.

391   C.M.

p LONG have I sat beneath the sound
   Of Thy salvation, Lord ; [found,
   But still how weak my faith is
   And knowledge of Thy word !

Oft I frequent Thy holy place,
   And hear almost in vain !
How small a portion of Thy grace
   My memory can retain !

How cold and feeble is my love !
   How negligent my fear !
How low my hope of joys above !
   How few affections there !

mf Great God ! Thy sovereign power
     impart,
   To give Thy word success ;
   Write Thy salvation in my heart,
   And make me learn Thy grace.

mf Show my forgetful feet the way
   That leads to joys on high ;
   There knowledge grows without
     decay,
   And love shall never die.

               I. Watts.

16.—CONFLICT : COURAGE : VICTORY.

392   C.M., double.

mf THE Son of God goes forth to
     war,
   A kingly crown to gain ;
   His blood-red banner streams afar :
cres Who follows in His train ?
p Who best can drink His cup of woe,
   Triumphant over pain,
   Who patient bears His cross below,
mf   He follows in His train.

f The martyr first, whose eagle eye
   Could pierce beyond the grave,

Who saw his Master in the sky,
   And called on Him to save :
p Like Him, with pardon on His
     tongue,
   In midst of mortal pain,
   He prayed for them that did the
     wrong :
cres Who follows in His train ?

mf A glorious band, the chosen few
   On whom the Spirit came,
*cres*Twelve valiant saints, their hope
     they knew,
   And mocked the cross and flame :

p They met the tyrant's brandished
    steel,
    The lion's gory mane,
    They bowed their necks, the death
    to feel !
cres Who follows in their train ?

mf A noble army—men and boys,
    The matron and the maid,
cres Around the Saviour's throne re-
    joice,
    In robes of light arrayed :
f They climbed the steep ascent of
    heaven,
dim Through peril, toil, and pain :
cres O God, to us may grace be given
    To follow in their train.

                  R. Heber.

393   6.5., 12 lines.

f   ONWARD, Christian soldiers,
    Marching as to war,
    With the cross of Jesus,
    Going on before.
    Christ, the royal Master,
    Leads against the foe ;
    Forward into battle,
    See His banners go.
ff   Onward, Christian soldiers,
      Marching as to war,
      With the cross of Jesus,
      Going on before.

f   At the sign of triumph
    Satan's host doth flee ;
    On, then, Christian soldiers,
    On to victory !
    Hell's foundations quiver
    At the shout of praise ;
cres Brothers, lift your voices,
    Loud your anthems raise.
    Onward, etc.

f   Like a mighty army
    Moves the Church of God :
mf Brothers, we are treading
    Where the saints have trod.
    We are not divided,
    All one body we,
cres One in hope and doctrine,
    One in charity.
    Onward, etc.

p   Crowns and thrones may perish,
    Kingdoms rise and wane,
cres But the Church of Jesus
    Constant will remain.
f   Gates of hell can never
    'Gainst that Church prevail ;
    We have Christ's own promise,
    And that cannot fail.
    Onward, etc.

f   Onward, then, ye people,
    Join our happy throng,
    Blend with ours your voices
    In the triumph-song ;
cres Glory, praise, and honour,
    Unto Christ, the King,
mf This through countless ages
    Men and angels sing.
ff   Onward, Christian soldiers,
      Marching as to war,
      With the cross of Jesus,
      Going on before.

            S. Baring-Gould.

394   7.7.7.3.

mf "CHRISTIAN ! seek not yet repose,
    Cast thy dreams of ease away,
    Thou art in the midst of foes :
p   "Watch and pray."

mf Principalities and powers,
    Mustering their unseen array,
    Wait for thine unguarded hour
p   "Watch and pray."

1. f Gird thy heavenly armour on,
  Wear it ever night and day ;
*cres*Ambushed lies the evil one :
p   " Watch and pray."

f Hear the victors who o'ercame ;
p Still they mark each warrior's way;
*res*All with one sweet voice exclaim,
  v   " Watch and pray.

mf Hear, above all, hear thy Lord,
  Him thou lovest to obey ;
p Hide within thy heart His word,
  " Watch and pray."

mf Watch, as if on that alone
  Hung the issue of the day ;
  Pray that help may be sent down .
f   " Watch and pray."
  Charlotte Elliott, v. 1, l. 2 altd.

395   6.5.6.5., double.

mp CHRISTIAN ! dost thou see them
  On the holy ground,
  How the powers of darkness
  Compass thee around ?
f Christian ! up and smite them,
  Counting gain but loss ;
  Smite them by the merit
  Of the Holy Cross.

mp Christian ! dost thou feel them,
  How they work within,
  Striving, tempting, luring,
  Goading into sin ?
f Christian ! never tremble ;
  Never be downcast ;
  Gird thee for the conflict,
  Watch and pray and fast.

mp Christian ! dost thou hear them,
  How they speak thee fair ?
"Always fast and vigil ?
Always watch and prayer ? "

f Christian ! say but boldly,
  " While I breathe I pray ; "
  Peace shall follow battle,
  Night shall end in day.

p " Well I know thy trouble,
  O My servant true ;
pp Thou art very weary,—
  I was weary too :
*cres*But that toil shall make thee
  Some day all Mine own ;
mf And the end of sorrow
f   Shall be near My Throne."
  Andrew of Crete, tr. J. M. Neale,
  v. 1, ll. 3, 4, v. 2, ll. 6, 7, 8 altd.

396   C.M.

f AWAKE, my soul, stretch every
  nerve,
  And press with vigour on ;   •
  A heavenly race demands thy zeal
  And an immortal crown.

f A cloud of witnesses around
  Hold thee in full survey ;
  Forget the steps already trod,
  And onward urge thy way.

f 'Tis God's all-animating voice
  That calls thee from on high ;
  'Tis His own hand presents the prize
  To thine aspiring eye ;—

f That prize, with peerless glories
  bright,
  Which shall new lustre boast,
  When victors' wreaths and mon-
  archs' gems
p   Shall blend in common dust.

f Blest Saviour, introduced by Thee,
  Have I my race begun ;   [feet
  And crowned with victory, at Thy
  I'll lay my honours down.
  P. Doddridge.

397   L.M.

f AWAKE, our souls; away our fears ;
  Let every trembling thought be
    g°ne ;
  Awake, and run the heavenly race,
  And put a cheerful courage on.

mf True, 'tis a strait and thorny
    road,
  And mortal spirits tire and faint ;
  But they forget the mighty God
  That feeds the strength of every
    saint :—

f The Mighty God Whose matchless
    power
  Is ever new and ever young, [years
  And firm endures, while endless
  Their everlasting circles run.

mf From Thee, the overflowing spring,
  Our souls shall drink a fresh supply,
  While such as trust their native
    strength   [die.
dim Shall melt away, and droop, and

mf Swift as an eagle cuts the air,
  We'll mount aloft to Thine abode ;
cres On wings of love our souls shall
    fly,
f Nor tire amidst the heavenly road.

               I. Watts.

398   L.M.

f STAND up, my soul, shake off thy
    fears,
  And gird the gospel armour on :
  March to the gates of endless joy,
  Where thy great Captain-Saviour's
    gone.

f Hell and thy sins resist thy course,
  But hell and sin are **vanquished**
    foes;

Thy Jesus nailed them to the cross.
And sung the triumph when He
  rose.

mf Then let my soul march boldly on,
  Press forward to the heavenly gate ;
dim There peace and joy eternal reign.
cres And glittering robes for conquerors
  wait.

f There I shall wear a starry crown.
  And triumph in almighty grace.
ff While all the armies of the skies
  Join in my glorious Leader's praise.

               I. Watts.

399   S.M.

mf YE servants of the Lord,
  Each in His office wait,
  Observant of His heavenly word,
p   And watchful at His gate.

f Let all your lamps be bright,
  And trim the golden flame ;
  Gird up your loins, as in His sight,
p   For awful is His Name.

mf Watch ;—'tis your Lord's com-
    mand ;
p   And while we speak, He's near :
mf Mark the first signal of His hand,
  And ready all appear.

cres O happy servant he,
  In such a posture found !
  He shall his Lord with rapture see,
  And be with honour crowned.

f   Christ shall the banquet spread
  With His own royal hand,
  And raise that favoured servant's
    head
  Amidst the angelic band.

               P. Doddridge.

400   7s.

vf MUCH in sorrow, oft in woe,
  Onward, Christians, onward go ;
*res*Fight the fight, and, worn with
    strife,
  Steep with tears the Bread of Life.

f Onward, Christians, onward go ;
  Join the war, and face the foe ;
  Faint not ! much doth yet remain;
p Dreary is the long campaign.

f 'Shrink not, Christians ! will ye
    yield ?
  Will ye quit the painful field ?
  Will ye flee in danger's hour ?
  Know ye not your Captain's
    power ?

mf Let your drooping hearts be glad ;
  March, in heavenly armour clad ;
  Fight, nor think the battle long ;
f Victory soon shall tune your song.

p Let not sorrow dim your eye,
*cres*Soon shall every tear be dry ;
mf Let not woe your course impede ;
f Great your strength, if great your
    need.

f Onward then to battle move ;
  More than conquerors ye shall
    prove ;
*res*Though opposed by many a foe,
ff Christian soldiers, onward go.

    Fragment by H. K. White, completed
      by Fanny F. Maitland.

401   S.M., double.

f SOLDIERS of Christ, arise,
  And put your armour on,
  Strong in the strength which God
    supplies
  Through His eternal Son ;

  Strong in the Lord of hosts,
  And in His mighty power,
  Who in the strength of Jesus trusts
    Is more than conqueror.

f Stand then in His great might,
  With all His strength endued ;
  But take, to arm you for the fight,
    The panoply of God ;—
mf That having all things done,
  And all your conflicts passed,
*cres*Ye may o'ercome through Christ
    alone,
  And stand entire at last.

mf Leave no unguarded place,
  No weakness of the soul,
  Take every virtue, every grace,
    And fortify the whole.
f To keep your armour bright,
  Attend with constant care,
  Still walking in your Captain's
    sight,
  And watching unto prayer.

mf From strength to strength go
    on,
  Wrestle, and fight, and pray,
  Tread all the powers of darkness
    down,
f And win the well-fought day.
mf Still let the Spirit cry,
  In all His soldiers, " Come,"
*cres*Till Christ the Lord descend from
    high,
  And take the conquerors home.

        C. Wesley.

402   7.6.7.6.. double.

mf STAND up ! stand up for Jesus,
  Ye soldiers of the cross ;
  Lift high His royal banner,
  It must not suffer loss.

f From victory unto victory
   His army shall He lead,
  ·Till every foe is vanquished,
   And Christ is Lord indeed.

[*mf* Stand up ! stand up for Jesus,
   The solemn watchword hear ;
  If while ye sleep He suffers,
   Away with shame and fear !
  Where'er you meet with evil—
   Within you, or without—
*cres*Charge ! for the God of Battles,
   And put the foe to rout.]

mf Stand up ! stand up for Jesus !
   The trumpet call obey ;
  Forth to the mighty conflict,
   In this His glorious day !
  Ye that are men now serve Him
   Against unnumbered foes ;
f Your courage rise with danger,
   And strength to strength oppose.

mf Stand up ! stand up for Jesus !
   Stand in His strength alone ;
p The arm of flesh will fail you,
   Ye dare not trust your own.
  Put on the Gospel armour,
   Each piece put on with prayer !
  Where duty calls, or danger,
   Be never wanting there.

[*mf* Stand up ! stand up for Jesus !
   Each soldier to his post ;
  Close up the broken column,
   And shout through all the host.
f Make good the loss so heavy,
   In those that still remain ;
  And prove to all around you
   That death itself is gain.]

mf Stand up ! stand up for Jesus !
   The strife will not be long ;
  This day the noise of battle,
   The next the victor's song.

f To him that overcometh
   A crown of life shall be ;
  He, with the King of glory,
   Shall reign eternally.

              G. Duffield.

403   C.M.

mf O GOD of Truth, Whose living Word
   Upholds whate'er hath breath,
  Look down on Thy creation, Lord,
   Enslaved by sin and death.

mf Set up Thy standard, Lord, that we
   Who claim a heavenly birth, [lies
  May march with Thee to smite the
   That vex Thy groaning earth.

mf Ah ! would we join that blest array,
   And follow in the might
  Of Him, the Faithful and the True,
   In raiment clean and white !

mf We fight for truth, we fight for God,
   Poor slaves of lies and sin !
  He who would fight for Thee on
   earth
   Must first be true within.

mp Then, God of Truth, for Whom we
   long,
  Thou Who wilt hear our prayer,
  Do Thine own battle in our hearts,
   And slay the falsehood there.

f Still smite ! still burn ! till naught
   is left
  But God's own truth and love ;
  Then, Lord, as morning dew come
   down,
   Rest on us from above.

mf Yea, come ! then, tried as in the fire,
   From every lie set free,
cres Thy perfect truth shall dwell in
f   And we shall live in Thee.
                   T. Hug)

17.—*PILGRIMAGE.*

404   6.5., 12 lines.

nf FORWARD ! be our watchword,
    Steps and voices joined ;
    Seek the things before us,
    Not a look behind ;
    Burns the fiery pillar
    At our army's head ;
    Who shall dream of shrinking,
    By our Captain led ?
  f   Forward through the desert,
      Through the toil and fight ;
    Jordan flows before us,
      Sion beams with light.

[*mf*Forward, when in childhood
    Buds the infant mind ;
    All through youth and manhood,
    Not a thought behind ;
    Speed through realms of nature,
    Climb the steps of grace ;
    Faint not, till in glory
    Gleams our Father's face.
  f   Forward, all the lifetime,
      Climb from height to height;
    Till the head be hoary,
    Till the eve be light.

mf Forward, flock of Jesus,
    Salt of all the earth,
    Till each yearning purpose
    Spring to glorious birth ;
 p Sick, they ask for healing,
    Blind, they grope for day ;
*cres*Pour upon the nations
    Wisdom's loving ray.
  f   Forward, out of error,
      Leave behind the night ;
    Forward through the darkness,
    Forward into light.]

mf Glories upon glories
    Hath our God prepared,

By the souls that love **Him**
    One day to be shared ;
 p Eye hath not beheld them,
    Ear hath never heard ;
    Nor of these hath uttered
    Thought or speech a word ;
  f   Forward, ever forward,
      Clad in armour bright ;
    Till the veil be lifted.
    Till our faith be sight.

mf Far o'er yon horizon
    Rise the city towers,
    Where our God abideth,—
    That fair home is ours :
    Flash the streets with jasper,
    Shine the gates with gold :
    Flows the gladdening river,
    Shedding joys untold.
  f   Thither, onward thither,
      In the Spirit's might ;
    Pilgrims to your country,
    Forward into light.

ff To the Eternal Father
    Loudest anthems raise :
    To the Son and Spirit
    Echo songs of praise :
    To the Lord of Glory,
    Blessèd Three in One,
    Be by men and angels
    Endless honour done.
 p   Weak are earthly praises,
      Dull the songs of night :
cres   Forward into triumph,
  f   Forward into light !

                H. Alford.

405   L.M.

mf JESUS, my all, to Heaven is gone ;
    He that I placed my hopes upon·

His track I see ; and I'll pursue
The narrow way till Him I view.

mf The way the holy prophets went,
The road that leads from banish-
ment,
The King's highway of holiness,
I'll go ; for all the paths are peace.

mp This is the way I long have sought,
And mourned because I found it
not ;
My grief, my burden, long have
been
Because I could not cease from sin.

mp The more I strove against its
power,
I sinned and stumbled but the more;
cres Till late I heard my Saviour say,
"Come hither, soul ! for I'm the
Way !"

f Lo ! glad I come ; and Thou, dear
Lamb,
Shalt take me to Thee, as I am :
Nothing but sin I Thee can give ;
Yet help me, and Thy praise I'll
live !

mf Now I will tell to sinners round
What a dear Saviour I have found ;
I'll point to Thy redeeming blood,
And say,"Behold the Way to God !"

J. Cennick.

406   6.6.8.6.4.7.

mf FROM Egypt lately come,
Where death and darkness reign,
We seek our new, our better home,
Where we our rest shall gain.
f   Hallelujah !
We are on our way to God.

mf To Canaan's sacred bound
We haste with songs of joy ;
Where peace and liberty are found
And sweets that never cloy.
f   Hallelujah !
We are on our way to God.

mp Our toils and conflicts cease,
On Canaan's happy shore ;
We there shall dwell in endless
peace
And never hunger more.
f   Hallelujah !
We are on our way to God.

mf There, in celestial strains,
Enraptured myriads sing ;
There love in every bosom reigns,
For God Himself is King.
f   Hallelujah !
We are on our way to God.

mf We soon shall join the throng ;
Their pleasures we shall share ;
And sing the everlasting song,
With all the ransomed there.
f   Hallelujah !
We are on our way to God.

mp How sweet the prospect is !
It cheers the pilgrim's breast :
We're journeying through the
wilderness,
cres But soon shall gain our rest.
f   Hallelujah !
We are on our way to God.

T. Kelly.

407   7.6.7.6.

f O HAPPY band of pilgrims,
If onward ye will tread,
With Jesus as your Fellow,
To Jesus as your Head ;

mf O happy, if ye labour
    As Jesus did for men ;
    O happy, if ye hunger
    As Jesus hungered then.

mp The Cross that Jesus carried,
    He carried as your'due ;
cres The Crown that Jesus weareth,
    He weareth it for you.

mp The trials that beset you,
    The sorrows ye endure,
    The manifold temptations
    That death alone can cure,—

mf What are they but His jewels,
    Of right celestial worth ?
    What are they but the ladder
    Set up to heaven, on earth ?

f O happy band of pilgrims,
    Look upward to the skies,
    Where such a light affliction
    Shall win you such a prize.

Joseph of the Studium, tr. J. M. Neale.

408   S.M., double.

mf A FEW more years shall roll,
    A few more seasons come, [rest
dim And we shall be with those that
    Asleep within the tomb.
cres   Then, O my Lord, prepare
    My soul for that great day ;
dim   O ! wash me in Thy precious
    Blood,
p   And take my sins away.

[*mf* A few more suns shall set
    O'er these dark hills of time.
p And we shall be where suns are not,
    A far serener clime :
cres   Then, O my Lord. prepare
    My soul for that blest day :
dim   O ! wash me in Thy precious
    Blood.
p   And take my sins away.

mf A few more storms shall be
    On this wild rocky shore,
    And we shall be where tem
      cease,
    And surges swell no more :
cres   Then, O my Lord, prepare
    My soul for that calm day·
dim   O ! wash me in Thy p
    Blood,
p   And take my sins away.]

p A few more struggles here,
    A few more partings o'er,
    A few more toils, a few more
    And we shall weep no more :
cres   Then, O my Lord, prepa
    My soul for that bright d
dim   O ! wash me in Thy preci
    Blood,
p   And take my sins away.

mf A few more Sabbaths here
    Shall cheer us on our way,
    And we shall reach the endles
      rest,
    The eternal Sabbath-day :
cres   Then, O my Lord, prepare
    My soul for that sweet day ;
dim   O ! wash me in Thy precious
    Blood,
p   And take my sins away.

p 'Tis but a little while,
    And He shall come again,
cres Who died that we might live, Who
      lives
    That we with Him may reign :
cres   Then, O my Lord, prepare
    My soul for that glad day
dim   O ! wash me in Thy precious
    Blood,
p   And take my sins away.

H. Bonar.

409   8.7.8.7., double.

mf THROUGH the night of doubt and
     sorrow,
     Onward goes the pilgrim band,
Singing songs of expectation,
     Marching to the Promised Land ;
Clear before us through the dark-
     ness
     Gleams and burns the guiding
     Light ;
Brother clasps the hand of brother,
     Stepping fearless through the
     night.

p One the Light of God's own
     Presence
     O'er His ransomed people shed,
*cres*Chasing far the gloom and terror,
     Brightening all the path we
     tread :
mf One the object of our journey,
     One the faith which never tires,

One the earnest looking forward,
     One the hope our God inspires :
f One the strain that lips of thousands
     Lift as from the heart of one ;
p One the conflict, one the peril,
cres One the march in God begun :
ff One the gladness of rejoicing
     On the far eternal shore,
Where the One Almighty Father
     Reigns in love for evermore.

mf Onward therefore, pilgrim brothers,
     Onward with the Cross our aid !
p Bear its shame, and fight its battle,
     Till we rest beneath its shade.
mf Soon shall come the great awaking,
cres Soon the rending of the tomb ;
f Then the scattering of all shadows,
     And the end of toil and gloom.

     *B. S. Ingemann, tr. S. Baring-
     Gould, altd. by Compilers of
     Hymns Ancient and Modern.*

18.—DIVINE GUIDANCE AND PROTECTION.

410   5.5.8.8.5.5.

mf JESUS, still lead on,
     Till our rest be won ;
p And although the way be cheerless
*cres*We will follow, calm and fearless ;
mf   Guide us by Thy hand
     To our Fatherland.

p   If the way be drear,
     If the foe be near,
Let not faithless fears o'ertake us,
*cres*Let not faith and hope forsake us ;
     For, through many a foe,
     To our home we go.

p   When we seek relief
     From a long-felt grief ; [tions,
     When oppressed by new tempta-

*cres*Lord, increase and perfect patience;
     Show us that bright shore,
     Where we weep no more.

mf   Jesus, still lead on
     Till our rest be won ;
Heavenly Leader, still direct us,
Still support, console, protect us,
cres   Till we safely stand
f   In our Fatherland.

     N. L. v. Zinzendorf, tr. H. L. L.

411   L.M.

mf O GRANT us light, that we may
     know
     The wisdom Thou alone canst giv

                       7º

*cres*That truth may guide where'er
  we go,
And virtue bless where'er we live.

mf O grant us light, that we may see
  Where error lurks in human lore,
*cres*And turn our doubting minds to
  Thee,
And love Thy simple word the more.

mp O grant us light, that we may learn
  How dead is life from Thee apart ;
*cres*How sure is joy for all who turn
  To Thee an undivided heart.

mp O grant us light, in grief and pain,
  To lift our burdened hearts above ;
*cres*And count the very Cross a gain,
f And bless our Father's hidden love.

mp O grant us light, that we may trace
  A pledge of life in seeming death ;
And own the grave a resting-place,
  Nor dread at last to sleep beneath.

mf O grant us light. when soon or late
  All earthly scenes shall pass away,
*cres*In Thee to find the open gate
f To deathless home and endless day.

L. Tuttiett.

412   88.88.88.

mf LEADER of faithful souls, and guide
  Of all who travel to the sky,
Come, and with us, even us, abide,
  Who would on Thee alone rely :
On Thee alone our spirits stay,
While held in life's uneven way.

mf Strangers and pilgrims here below,
  This earth, we know, is not our
  place :   [woe.
And hasten through this vale of
And, restless to behold Thy face,
*cres*Swift to our heavenly country move
Our everlasting home above.

mp Through Thee, Who all our sins
  hast borne.
Freely and graciously forgiven,
*cres*With songs to Zion we return,
  Contending for our native heaven;—
f That palace of our glorious King,
  We find it nearer while we sing.

mf Raised by the breath of love divine,
  We urge our way with strength
  renewed :
. The Church of the firstborn to join,
  We travel to the mount of God ;
*cres*With joy upon our heads arise,
f And meet our Captain in the skies.

C. Wesley.

413   8.7.8.7.4.4.7.

mf LEAD us, heavenly Father, lead us
  O'er the world's tempestuous sea ;
Guard us, guide us, keep us, feed us,
  For we have no help but Thee ;
cres   Yet possessing
    Every blessing,
f   If our God our Father be.

p Saviour, breathe forgiveness o'er us;
  All our weakness Thou dost know;
Thou didst tread this earth before us,
  Thou didst feel its keenest woe ;
    Lone and dreary,
    Faint and weary,
Through the desert Thou didst go.

mf Spirit of our God, descending,
  Fill our hearts with heavenly joy,
Love with every passion blending,
  Pleasure that can never cloy :
cres   Thus provided,
    Pardoned, guided,
f   Nothing can our peace destroy.

J. Edmeston.

414
10.4.10.4.10.10.

mf LEAD, kindly Light, amid the
encircling gloom,
cres Lead Thou me on :
p The night is dark, and I am far
from home,
Lead Thou me on : [to see
*cres*Keep Thou my feet ; I do not ask
. The distant scene ; (*p*) one step
enough for me.

mf I was not ever thus, nor prayed
that Thou
Shouldst lead me on :
I loved to choose and see my path ;
(*p*) but now,
Lead Thou me on :
*cres*I loved the garish day, and, spite
of fears,
Pride ruled my will ; (*p*) remember
not past years.

mf So long Thy power hath blest me,
(*cres*) sure it still
Will lead me on,
O'er moor and fen, o'er crag and
torrent, till
The night is gone,
f And with the morn those angel
faces smile,
*dim*Which I have loved long since,
(*p*) and lost awhile.
J. H. Newman.

415
8.7.8.7.4.7.ʲ

mf GUIDE me, O Thou Great Jehovah!
Pilgrim through this barren land;
p I am weak, but Thou art mighty,
f Hold me with Thy powerful
hand :
Bread of heaven !
dim Feed me till I want no more.

mf Open Thou the crystal fountain,
. Whence the healing stream doth
flow :
Let the fiery, cloudy pillar
Lead me all my journey through :
cres Strong Deliverer ! [shield.
f Be Thou still my strength and
p When I tread the verge of Jordan,
Bid my anxious fears subside ;
*cres*Death of deaths, and hell's
destruction !   '
Land me safe on Canaan's side :
ff Songs of praises
I will ever give to Thee.
. *Welsh of W. Williams, v. 1 tr.*
P. Williams ; vv. 2, 3 tr. W.
Williams.

416
7s.

mf HEAVENLY Father ! to Whose eye
Future things unfolded lie.
Through the desert where I stray,
Let Thy counsels guide my way.

mp Lead me not, for flesh is frail,
Where fierce trials would assail :
Leave me not, in darkened hour,
To withstand the tempter's power.

mf Lord ! uphold me day by day ;
Shed a light upon my way ;
Guide me through perplexing
snares ;
Care for me in all my cares.

mf Help Thy servant to maintain
A profession free from stain ;
That my sole reproach may be
Following Christ and fearing Thee.

p Should Thy wisdom, Lord, decree
Trials long and sharp for me,
Pain or sorrow, care or shame,
*cres*Father ! glorify Thy Name

mp Let me neither faint nor fear,
　　Feeling still that Thou art near ;
cres In the course my Saviour trod,
　　Tending still to Thee, my God.

J. Conder.

417　　　　8.7.8.7., double.

mf COME, Thou fount of every blessing,
　　Tune my heart to sing Thy grace :
　　Streams of mercy, never ceasing,
　　Call for songs of loudest praise.
mf Teach me some melodious measure,
　　Sung by flaming tongues above :
cres O ! the vast, the boundless treasure
　　Of my Lord's unchanging love.

mf Here I raise mine Ebenezer ;
　　Hither, by Thy help, I'm come,
　　And I hope, by Thy good pleasure,
　　Safely to arrive at home.
p Jesus sought me when a stranger,
　　Wandering from the fold of God ;
cres He, to rescue me from danger,
　　Interposed His precious blood.

f O ! to grace how great a debtor
　　Daily I'm constrained to be !
　　Let that grace, Lord, like a fetter,
　　Bind my wandering heart to Thee.
mp Prone to wander ; Lord, I feel it ;
　　Prone to leave the God I love,
cres Take my heart, O take and seal it,
　　Seal it from Thy courts above.

*R. Robinson, v. 1, ll. 5, 7, 8, v. 3. l. 7
altd.*

418　　　　S.M.

f To God the only wise,
　　Our Saviour and our King,
　Let all the saints below the skies
　　Their humble praises bring.

mf 'Tis His almighty l
　　His counsel and Hi:
　　Preserve us safe from ɛ
　　And every hurtful ɪ

mf He will present our
　　Unblemished and c
cres Before the glory of ʜ
　　With joys divinely ɪ

mf Then all the chosen
　　Shall meet around t
　　Shall bless the conduct
　　And make His won

f To our Redeemer, G
　　Wisdom and power
　　Immortal crowns of ɪ
　　And everlasting son

419

f GOD is our refuge, trie
　　Amid a stormy wor
　　We will not fear thoɪ
　　And hills in ocean ɪ

f The waves may roar, tʜ
　　shake,
　　Our comforts shall
　　The Lord His saints
　　sake ;
dim The Lord will give

mp A gentle stream of hɕ
　　To us shall ever floɪ
　　It issues from His Th
cres It cheers His Churc

mf When earth and hel
　　came,
　　He spake, and q
cres The Lord of Hosts is s
f The God of grace is

19.—THE MINISTRY OF ANGELS.

420   L.M.

mp THEY come, God's messengers of
   love,   [above,
They come from realms of peace
From homes of never-fading light,
From heavenly mansions ever
   bright.

mp They come to watch around us here,
To soothe our sorrow, calm our fear ;
They come to speed us on our way ;
God willeth them with us to stay.

mp But chiefly at its journey's end
'Tis theirs the spirit to befriend,
And whisper to the faithful heart,
" O Christian soul, in peace depart."

p Blest Jesu, Thou Whose groans and
   tears
Have sanctified frail nature's fears,
When to the earth in sorrow
   weighed   [aid,—
Thou didst not scorn Thine angels'

mp An angel-guard to us supply,
p When on the bed of death we lie ;
cres And in Thine own Almighty Arms
O shield us in the last alarms.

mf To God the Father, God the Son,
. And God the Spirit, Three in One,
cres From all above, and all below,
f Let joyful praise unceasing flow.
          R. Campbell, altd.

421   11.10.11.10.9.11.

mf HARK ! hark ! my soul ! angelic
   songs are swelling
O'er earth's green fields and
   ocean's wave-beat shore :
How sweet the truth those blessèd
   strains are telling [no more.
Of that new life when sin shall be

p Angels of Jesus,
   Angels of light,
f Singing to welcome
   The pilgrims of the night !

mf Onward we go, for still we hear
     them singing,
p "Come, weary souls ! for Jesus
   bids you come ! "·
mf And through the dark its echoes
   sweetly ringing, [home.
The music of the Gospel leads us
   Angels of Jesus, etc.

pp Far, far away, like bells at evening
   pealing, [land and sea,
cres The voice of Jesus sounds o'er
p And laden souls by thousands
   meekly stealing,
cres Kind Shepherd ! turn their weary
   steps to Thee.
   Angels of Jesus, etc.

mf Rest comes at length ; though life
   be long and dreary,
The day must dawn, and darksome night be past ;
All journeys end in welcomes to
   the weary,
cres And heaven, the heart's true
   home, will come at last.
   Angels of Jesus, etc.

mf Angels ! sing on : your faithful
   watches keeping,
Sing us sweet fragments of the
   songs above ;
Till morning's joy shall end the
   night of weeping,
cres And life's long shadows break
   in cloudless love.
   Angels of Jesus, etc.
    F. W. Faber, c. 5, ll. 3, 4 altd.

20.—DEATH.

422   6.6.8.6.8.8.

mp FRIEND after friend departs;
  Who hath not lost a friend ?
There is no union here of hearts,
  That finds not here an end :
Were this frail world our only rest,
Living or dying, none were blest.

mp Beyond the flight of time,
  Beyond this vale of death,
There surely is some blessèd clime
  Where life is not a breath,
Nor life's affections transient fire,
Whose sparks fly upwards to expire.

mf There is a world above,
  Where parting is unknown ;
A whole eternity of love,
  Formed for the good alone :
And faith beholds the dying here
Translated to that happier sphere.

p Thus star by star declines
  Till all are passed away, [shines
*cres*As morning high and higher
mf To pure and perfect day ;
Nor sink those stars in empty
   night ;
*cres*They hide themselves (*f*) in
  heaven's own light.

           J. Montgomery.

423   C.M.

mf CAPTAIN and Saviour of the host
  Of Christian chivalry,   [true,
*cres*We bless Thee for our comrade
  Now summoned up to Thee.

mp We bless Thee for his every step
  In faithful following Thee,
*cres*And for his good fight fought so
  well,
  And crowned with victory.

mp We thank Thee that the waywo
  sleeps
p The sleep in Jesus blessed ;
*cres*The purified and ransomed soul
p Hath entered into rest.

mp We bless Thee that his huml
  love
  Hath met with such regard ;
*cres*We bless Thee for his blessedne
mf And for his rich reward.

           G. Rawsn.

424   6.6.4., double

mp LOWLY and solemn be
  Thy children's cry to Thee,
    Father divine ;
  A hymn of suppliant breath,
  Owning that life and death
    Alike are Thine.

mp O Father, in that hour,
  When earth all succouring pow
    Shall disavow,
  When spear and shield and cro
  In faintness are cast down,
    Sustain us, Thou !

mp By Him Who bowed to take
  The death-cup for our sake,
    The thorn, the rod ;
  From Whom the last dismay
  Was not to pass away ;
    Aid us, O God.

mp Tremblers beside the grave,
  We call on Thee to save,
    Father divine !
*cres*Hear, hear our suppliant breatl
  Keep us, in life and death,
    Thine, only Thine.

          Felicia D. Heman

425   88.88.88.

mf GOD of the living, in Whose eyes
Unveiled Thy whole creation lies;
All souls are Thine;—we must not say
That those are dead who pass away;
From this our world of flesh set free,
We know them living unto Thee.

mp Released from earthly toil and strife,
With Thee is hidden still their life;
Thine are their thoughts, their works, their powers.
All Thine, and yet most truly ours;
For well we know, where'er they be,
Our dead are living unto Thee.

[*mp* Not spilt like water on the ground,
Not wrapped in dreamless sleep profound,
Not wandering in unknown despair
Beyond Thy voice, Thine arm, Thy care;
Not left to lie like fallen tree:
cres Not dead, but living unto Thee.]

mf Thy word is true, Thy will is just.
To Thee we leave them, Lord, in trust; [gave
And bless Thee for the love which
Thy Son to fill a human grave,
That none might fear that world to see
Where all are living unto Thee.

mf O Breather into man of breath.
O Holder of the keys of death,
O Giver of the life within, [sin;
Save us from death, the death of
cres That body, soul, and spirit be,
For ever living unto Thee!

J. Ellerton.

[SEE ALSO SECTION XI. 2.]

21.—*THE REST AFTER DEATH.*

426   S.M., double.

f "FOR ever with the Lord!"
p Amen, so let it be;
cres Life from the dead is in that word,
'Tis immortality:
p Here in the body pent,
Absent from Him I roam,
cres Yet nightly pitch my moving tent
A day's march nearer home.

[*mf* My Father's house on high,
Home of my soul, how near.
At times, to faith's far-seeing eye,
• Thy golden gates appear:
p Ah! then my spirit faints
cres To reach the land I love,
f The bright inheritance of saints,
Jerusalem above.

f I hear at morn and even,
At noon and midnight hour,
cr. The choral harmonies of heaven
Earth's Babel tongues o'erpower
p Then, then I feel that He,
Remembered or forgot,
cres The Lord is never far from me,
Though I perceive Him not.]

f "For ever with the Lord!"
Father. if 'tis Thy will,
The promise of that faithful word
E'en here to me fulfil.
cres Be Thou at my right hand,
Then can I never fail;
Uphold Thou me, and I shall stand;
f Fight, and I must prevail.

p   So when my latest breath
     Shall rend the veil in twain.
*cres*By death I shall escape from
         death,
     And life eternal gain.
f   Knowing as I am known,
     How shall I love that word,
     And oft repeat before the throne,
     "For ever with the Lord!"

f   The trump of final doom
     Will speak the self-same word,
*cres*And Heaven's voice thunder
         through the tomb,
ff "For ever with the Lord!'
ff That resurrection-word,
     That shout of victory, [Lord!"
     Once more, "For ever with the
     Amen, so let it be.

                    J. Montgomery.

427   9s.

mf LIGHT after darkness, gain after
       loss ;   [after cross ;
     Strength after weakness, crown
     Sweet after bitter, hope after fears,
     Home after wandering, praise after
         tears.   *np*

mf Sheaves after sowing, sun after
       rain,
     Sight after mystery, peace after
       pain ;
     Joy after sorrow, calm after blast,
*dim*Rest after weariness. sweet rest at
       last.

f Near after distant, gleam after
       gloom ;   [tomb ;
     Love after loneliness, life after
     After long agony, rapture of bliss :
     Right was the pathway leading to
       this.

              Frances R. Havergal.

428   8.6.8.6

p O PARADISE ! O Paradis
     Who doth not crave fo
     Who would not seek tl
       land,
     Where they that loved
mf   Where loyal hearts s
     Stand ever in the lig
     All   rapture   throu
       through,
     In God's most holy s

p O Paradise ! O Paradise !
     The world is growing
     Who would not be at res
     Where love is never co
mf   Where loyal hearts

mf O Paradise ! O Paradise !
p   'Tis weary waiting her
*cres*I long to be where Jesus
     To feel, to see Him nea
mf   Where loyal hearts

mf O Paradise ! O Paradise
p   I want to sin no more,
*cres*I want to be as pure on
     As on thy spotless shor
mf   Where loyal hearts s
     Stand ever in the lig
     All   rapture   throu
       through,
     In God's most holy
                         F. W.

429

p WHEN the day of toil is
     When the race of life is
     Father, grant Thy weari
pp   Rest for evermore !

p When the strife of sin is
     When the toe within is

*res*Be Thy gracious word fulfilled,
p   Peace for evermore !

uf When the darkness melts away
    At the breaking of the day,
*res*Bid us hail the cheering ray ;—
f   Light for evermore !

p When the heart by sorrow tried
    Feels at length its throbs subside,
*res*Bring us, where all tears are dried.
f   Joy for evermore !

p When for vanished days we yearn.
    Days that never can return,
*cres*Teach us in Thy love to learn
f   Love for evermore !

pp When the breath of life is flown,
    When the grave must claim its own,
*cres*Lord of life ! be ours Thy crown—
f   Life for evermore !

J. Ellerton.

22.—THE RESURRECTION.

430   6.6.6.6.6.4.

mf No sorrow, and no sighing,
    O world of peace undying !
    There shall true life begin,
    No curse, no pain, no sin,
    Above, around, within ;
f   We shall be changed.

mf Transformed, from light to light,
    From grace, to glory's height ;
    To more than angels knew
    Of perfect, pure, and true,—
    For all things shall be new ;
f   We shall be changed.

mf Eternal life, with God,
    " Christ's joy " in spheres untrod !
    When shall time's shadows fly,
    And morning fill the sky,
    When shall the Lord draw nigh,
f   And we be changed !

mf We shall be like our Lord,
    Our nature all restored
    In Him Who is our Head,
    The First-Born from the dead.
f By Him to glory led ;
    The same, yet changed.

W. J. Irons.

431   L.M., with refrain.

mf WE sing His love, Who once was slain ;
    Who soon o'er death revived again,
    That all His saints through Him might have
    Eternal conquests o'er the grave.
ff   Soon shall the trumpet sound, and we
    Shall rise to immortality.

mp The saints who now in Jesus sleep,
    His own almighty power shall keep,
*cres*Till dawns the bright illustrious day
    When death itself shall die away.
ff   Soon, etc.

f How loud shall our glad voices sing,
    When Christ His risen saints shall bring,
    From beds of dust and silent clay,
    To realms or everlasting day !
ff   Soon, etc.

f When Jesus we in glory meet,
    Our utmost joys shall be complete :
    When landed on that heavenly shore,

Death and the curse shall be no
more.
ff Soon, etc.

mf Hasten, dear Lord, the glorious
day,
And this delightful scene display,

When all Thy saints fr[c
shall rise,
Raptured in bliss beyond·
ff Soon shall the trump[e
and we
Shall rise to immortali[

[SEE ALSO SECTION XI. 2.]   *1*

23.—*THE FINAL GLORY OF HEAVEN.*

432   6.6.6.6.4.4.4.4.

mf JERUSALEM on high,
My song and city is,
My home whene'er I die,
The centre of my bliss.
f   O happy place !
When shall I be,
My God, with Thee,
To see Thy face ?

mf Thy walls, sweet city ! thine
With pearls are garnishèd,
Thy gates with praises shine,
Thy streets with gold are spread.
f   O happy place ! etc.

mf There dwells my Lord, my King,
p Judged here unfit to live ;
cres There angels to Him sing,
And lowly homage give.
f   O happy place ! etc.

[*mf* The patriarchs of old
There from their travels cease :
The prophets there behold
Their longed-for Prince of Peace.
f   O happy place etc.]

mf The Lamb's apostles there
I might with joy behold :
The harpers I might hear
Harping on harps of gold.
f   O happy place ! etc.

p No tears from any eyes ·
Drop in that holy choir :
But death itself there di[e
and sighs themselves ex[
f   O happy place ! etc.

mf Sweet place : sweet place
The court of God most h[i
The heaven of heavens, t[
Of spotless majesty !
f   O happy place !
When shall I be,
My God, with Thee,
To see Thy face ?
              S. Cr

433

f THERE is a land of pure
Where saints immortal[
Infinite day excludes the[
And pleasures banish [

f There everlasting spring
And never-withering f[
p Death, like a narrow sea[
This heavenly land fr[

mf Sweet fields beyond th[e
flood
Stand dressed in living[
So to the Jews old Cana[
While Jordan rolled b[

p But timorous mortals start and
    shrink
    To cross this narrow sea,
And linger, shivering on the brink,
And fear to launch away.

mf O could we make our doubts
    remove,
    Those gloomy doubts that rise;
*cres*And see the Canaan that we love
    With unbeclouded eyes:

*mf*Could we but climb where Moses
    stóod,
    And view the landscape o'er,
f Not Jordan's stream, nor death's
    cold flood
Should fright us from the shore.

I. Watts.

434   C.M.

mf JERUSALEM, my happy home,
    Name ever dear to me;
When shall my labours have an end
In joy and peace in thee?

mf When shall these eyes thy heaven-
    built walls
And pearly gates behold.
*res*Thy bulwarks with salvation
    strong,
And streets of shining gold?

mf There happier bowers than Eden
    bloom,
    Nor sin nor sorrow know;
*res*Blest seats, through rude and
    stormy scenes,
I onward press to you.

p Why should I shrink at pain and
    woe,
    Or feel at death dismay?
*cres*I've Canaan's goodly land in view,
f And realms of endless day.

mf Apostles, martyrs, propnets there,
    Around my Saviour stand;
And soon my friends in Christ below
Will join the glorious band.

mf Jerusalem, my happy home,
    My soul still pants for thee;
*cres*Then shall my labours have an end,
f When I thy joys shall see.

B., circ. 1801.

435   7.6.7.6., double.

PART I.

p BRIEF life is here our portion;
    Brief sorrow, short-lived care;
*cres*The life that knows no ending,
    The tearless life, is there:
mf O happy retribution!
    Short toil, eternal rest;
For mortals and for sinners
A mansion with the blest!

mf There grief is turned to pleasure
    Such pleasure, as below
No human voice can utter,
No human heart can know:
p And now we fight the battle,
cres But then shall wear the crown
Of full and everlasting
And passionless renown.

mf And there is David's fountain,
    And life in fullest glow,
And there the light is golden,
    And milk and honey flow;
The light that hath no evening,
    The health that hath no sore,
The life that hath no ending,
    But lasteth evermore.

f 'Midst power that knows no limit,
    And wisdom free from bound,
*cres*The beatific vision
    Shall glad the saints around.

mp For He Whom now we trust in
   Shall then be seen and known ;
cres And they that know and see Him
   Shall have Him for their own.

f Yes ! God, our King and Portion,
   In fulness of His grace
cres We then shall see for ever,
   And worship face to face.
p In mercy, Jesu, bring us
   To that dear land of rest,
cres Where Thou art with the Father
   And Spirit ever blest.

         7.6.7.6., double.
PART II.
mf For thee, O dear, dear country,
   Mine eyes their vigils keep ;
   For very love, beholding
p   Thy happy name, they weep.
cres The mention of thy glory
   Is unction to the breast,
dim And medicine in sickness,
   And love, and life, and rest.

mf O one, O only mansion,
   O paradise of joy,
   Where tears are ever banished,
   And smiles have no alloy !
   Thine ageless walls are bonded
   With amethyst unpriced ;
   The saints build up its fabric ;
   The corner-stone is Christ.

The Cross is all thy splendour,
   The Crucified thy praise,
   His laud and benediction
   Thy ransomed people raise :
   Jesus, the Crown of Beauty,
   True God and Man they sing ;
   Their never-failing portion,
   Their glorious Lord and King.

mf Thou hast no shore, fair ocean !
   Thou hast no time, bright day !

p Dear fountain of refreshment
   To pilgrims far away !
cres Upon the Rock of Ages
   They raise thy holy tower ;
f Thine is the victor's laurel,
   And thine the golden dower.

The only art thou needest,
   Thanksgiving for thy lot :
   The only joy thou seekest,
   The life where death is not.
p In mercy, Jesu, bring us
   To that dear land of rest,
mf Where Thou art with the Father
   And Spirit ever blest.

     v. 3, *ll.* 5, 7, 8 *altd.*
        7.6.7.6., double.
PART III.
mf Jerusalem the golden,
   With milk and honey blest,
dim Beneath thy contemplation
p   Sink heart and voice oppressed.
cres I know not, oh, I know not
   What social joys are there,
f What radiancy of glory,
   What light beyond compare.

f They stand, those halls of Sion,
   All jubilant with song,
   And bright with many an angel,
   And all the martyr-throng ;
   The Prince is ever in them,
   The daylight is serene,
   The pastures of the blessèd
   Are decked in glorious sheen.

mf There is the throne of David ;
   And there, from care released,
f The song of them that triumph,
   The shout of them that feast ;
mf And they, who with their Leader
   Have conquered in the fight,
   For ever and for ever
   Are clad in robes of white.

nf Jerusalem the glorious !
　　The joy of the elect !
　　O dear and future vision
　　That eager hearts expect ;
cres Ev'n now by faith I see thee,
　　Ev'n here thy walls discern :
　　To thee my thoughts are kindled,
　　And strive, and pant, and yearn.
f O mine, O golden Sion !
　　O lovelier far than gold !
　　O sweet and blessèd country,
　　Shall I thy joys behold ?
p In mercy, Jesu, bring us
　　To that dear land of rest,
nf Where Thou art with the Father
　　And Spirit ever blest.

Cento from Bernard of Cluny, tr.
　J. M. Neale. v. 5, l. 4 altd.

436　　　　8.8.7.8.8.7.8.8.8.
mf BEHOLD ! how glorious is yon sky !
　　Lo ! there the righteous never die,

But dwell in peace for ever ;
Then who would wear this earthly
　　clay,
When bid to cast life's chains away
And win Thy gracious favour ?
p　　Holy, Holy, oh ! forgive us ;
And receive us, Heavenly Father,
When　around　Thy　throne　we
　　gather.

mf Confiding in Thy sacred word,
　　Our Saviour is our hope, O Lord,
　　The guiding star before us ;
　　Our Shepherd, leading us the way,
　　If from Thy paths our footsteps
　　　stray,
　　To Thee He will restore us ;
p　　Holy, Holy, ever hear us,
　　And receive us, while we gather
　　Round　Thy　throne,　Almighty
　　　Father !

Tr. New Congregational Hymn
　Book, 1859.

VIII.
The Church of Christ.
1.—*ITS CHARACTER, UNITY, AND PRIVILEGES.*

437　　　　8.7.8.7.8.8.7.
mf WE come unto our fathers' God :
　　Their Rock is our Salvation :
　　The Eternal Arms, their dear abode,
　　We make our habitation :
cres We bring Thee, Lord, the praise
　　they brought ;
　　We seek Thee as Thy saints have
　　　sought
　　In every generation.
mf The Fire Divine, their steps that
　　　led,
　　Still goeth bright before us ;

cres The Heavenly Shield, around them
　　　spread,
　　Is still high holden o'er us :
　　The grace those sinners that sub-
　　　dued,　　　　　[renewed,
　　The strength those weaklings that
　　　Doth vanquish, doth restore us.

mp The cleaving sins that brought
　　　them low
　　Are still our souls oppressing ;
dim The tears that from their eyes did
　　　flow,
p　　Fall fast, our shame confessing

As with Thee, Lord, prevailed
 their cry,   [high
*res*So our strong prayer ascends on
And bringeth down Thy blessing.

f Their joy unto their Lord we bring;
Their song to us descendeth :
The Spirit Who in them did sing
To us His music lendeth.

His song in them, in us, is one ;
*cres*We raise it high, we send it on—
ff The song that never endeth !

mf Ye saints to come, take up the strain—
The same sweet theme endeavour!
*cres*Unbroken be the Golden Chain !
Keep on the song for ever !

f Safe in the same dear dwelling-place,
Rich with the same eternal grace,
Bless the same boundless Giver !

T. H. Gill.

438   S.M.

mf I LOVE Thy kingdom, Lord,
The house of Thine abode,
The Church our blest Redeemer saved
With His own precious blood.

I love Thy Church, O God ;
Her walls before Thee stand ;
Dear as the apple of Thine eye,
And graven on Thy hand.

mp For her my tears shall fall,
For her my prayers ascend,
To her my cares and toils be given,
Till toils and cares shall end.

mf Beyond my highest joy.
I prize her heavenly ways ; [vows.
Her sweet communion, solemn
Her hymns of love and praise.

mp Jesus, Thou Friend divine,
Our Saviour and our King,
Thy hand from every snare and sin
Shall great deliverance bring.

mf Sure as Thy truth shall last,
To Zion shall be given
*cres*The highest glories earth can yield
And brighter bliss of heaven.

T. Dwight.

439   S.M., double.

mf FAR down the ages now,
Her journey well-nigh done,
The pilgrim Church pursues her way,
 In haste to reach the crown.

The story of the past
Comes up before her view ;
How well it seems to suit her still
Old, and yet ever new !

mp 'Tis the same story still,
Of sin and weariness ;
*cres*Of grace and love still flowing down
To pardon and to bless :

dim No wider is the gate,
No broader is the way,
No smoother is the ancient path,
That leads to light and day.

mp No sweeter is the cup,
Nor less our lot of ill ;
'Twas tribulation ages since,
'Tis tribulation still :

mf No slacker grows the fight,
No feebler is the foe,
*cres*No less the need of armour tried
Of shield and spear and bow.

mf Thus onward still we press, .
Through evil and through good
Through pain and poverty and want,
Through peril and through blood

cres Still faithful to our God,
 And to our Captain true ;
f We follow where He leads the way,
 The Kingdom in our view.
 H. Bonar.

440 11.11.11.5.

mf LORD of our life, and God of our
 salvation, [every nation,
 Star of our night, and Hope of
*cres*Hear and receive Thy Church's
 supplication,
f Lord God Almighty.

See round Thine ark the hungry
 billows curling ; [unfurling :
See how Thy foes their banners are
Lord, while their darts of venom
 they are hurling,
 Thou canst preserve us.

mf Lord. Thou canst help when earthly
 armour faileth ;
 Lord, Thou canst save when sin
 itself assaileth ;
*cres*Lord. o'er Thy Rock nor death nor
 hell prevaileth :
dim Grant us Thy peace, Lord.

p Peace in our hearts our evil
 thoughts assuaging,
 Peace in Thy Church where brothers
 are engaging, [is waging :
 Peace where the world its busy war
 Calm Thy foes raging.

mf Grant us Thy help till backward
 they are driven,
 Grant them Thy truth that they
 may be forgiven,
p Grant peace on earth. and, after
 we have striven,
pp Peace in Thy heaven.
 **M. A. *von Loewenstern* (1594-1648),
 tr. *Pusey* (1799-1855).**

441 8.7.8.7., double.

f GLORIOUS things of thee are
 spoken,
 Zion, city of our God ;
He, Whose word cannot be broken,
 Formed thee for His own abode :
On the Rock of Ages founded,
 What can shake thy sure repose ?
With salvation's walls surrounded,
 Thou mayst smile at all thy foes.

[*f* See, the streams of living waters,
 Springing from eternal love,
Well supply thy sons and daughters,
 And all fear of want remove :
Who can faint, while such a river
 Ever flows their thirst to assuage ;
Grace, which, like the Lord the
 giver,
 Never fails from age to age ?]

mf Blest inhabitants of Zion,
 Washed in the Redeemer's blood ;
Jesus, Whom their souls rely on,
 Makes them kings and priests to
 God.
'Tis His love His people raises
 Over self to reign as kings ;
And as priests. His solemn praises
 Each for a thankoffering brings.

mf Saviour, if of Zion's city
 I, through grace, a member am,
Let the world deride or pity,
 I will glory in Thy Name :
*dim*Fading is the worldling's pleasure,
 All his boasted pomp and show ;
*cres*Solid joys and lasting treasure
f None but Zion's children know.
 J. Newton.

442 6.6.6.6.8.8.

mf ONE sole baptismal sign,
 One Lord below, above.

One faith, one hope divine,
One only watchword, love :
*cres*From different temples though it
    rise,
One song ascendeth to the skies.

mf Our Sacrifice is one ;
One Priest before the throne,
The slain, the risen Son,
Redeemer, Lord alone :
*dim*And sighs from contrite hearts
    that spring,
Our chief, our choicest offering.

p O may that holy prayer,
His tenderest and His last,
His constant, latest care
Ere to His throne He passed,
*cres*No longer unfulfilled remain,
The world's offence, His people's
    stain !

mf Head of Thy Church beneath,
The catholic, the true,
On all her members breathe,
Her broken frame renew :
*cres*Then shall Thy perfect will be
    done,   [as one.
When Christians love and live
                                G. Robinson.

443   7.6.7.6., double.
mf THE Church's one foundation
Is Jesus Christ her Lord ;

She is His new creation
By water and the word :   [her
From heaven He came and sought
To be His holy bride ;
*dim*With His own blood He bought her,
And for her life He died.

mf Elect from every nation,
Yet one o'er all the earth,
Her charter of salvation
One Lord, one Faith, one Birth.
p One Holy Name she blesses,
Partakes one Holy Food,
And to one hope she presses
With every grace endued.

p 'Mid toil, and tribulation,
And tumult of the war,
She waits the consummation
Of peace for evermore ;
*cres*Till with the vision glorious
Her longing eyes are blest,
·f And the great Church victorious
dim Shall be the Church at rest.

mf Yet she on earth hath union
With God the THREE in ONE,
p And mystic sweet communion
With those whose rest is won :
f O happy ones and holy !
·p Lord, give us grace that we,
Like them the meek and lowly,
cres On high may dwell with Thee.
                                S. J. Stone.

2.—CHURCH MEETINGS.

(1) GENERAL HYMNS.

444   7s.
f CHILDREN of the Heavenly King,
As ye journey, sweetly sing ;
Sing your Saviour's worthy praise,
Glorious in His works and ways !

mf We are travelling home to
    God,
In the way the Fathers trod ;
They are happy now ; and we
Soon their happiness shall see.

f Shout, ye little flock, and blest !
   You on Jesus' Throne shall rest ;
   There your seat is now prepared,
   There your kingdom and reward.

f Lift your eyes, ye sons of Light !
   Zion's city is in sight :
   There our endless home shall be,
   There our Lord we soon shall see.

nf Fear not, brethren ; joyful stand
   On the borders of your land ;
*cres*Jesus Christ, your Father's Son,
   Bids you undismayed go on.

mf Lord ! obediently we go,
   Gladly leaving all below :
*cres*Only Thou our Leader be,
   f And we still will follow Thee !

              J. Cennick.

445   C.M.

mf ARISE, O King of grace, arise,
   And enter to Thy rest :   [eyes
 Lo ! Thy Church waits with longing
   Thus to be owned and blest.

mf Enter with all Thy glorious train,
   Thy Spirit and Thy word ;
 All that the ark did once contain
   Could no such grace afford.

mf Here, Mighty God, accept our vows,
   Here let Thy praise be spread ;
 Bless the provisions of Thy house,
   And fill Thy poor with bread.

nf Here let the Son of David reign,
   Let God's Anointed shine,
 Justice and truth His court main-
   tain,
 With love and power divine.

f Here let Him hold a lasting throne ;
   And as His kingdom grows,

Fresh honours shall adorn His
   crown, .
 And shame confound His foes.

              I. Watts.

446   7s.

mf JESUS, Lord, we look to Thee,
   Let us in Thy Name agree :
 Show Thyself the Prince of Peace ;
   Bid all strife for ever cease.

mf Make us of one heart and mind,
   Courteous, pitiful, and kind,
*dim*Lowly, meek, in thought and word,
   Altogether like the Lord.

mp Let us for each other care.
   Each the other's burden bear ;
 To Thy Church the pattern give ;
   Show how true believers live.

mp Free from anger and from pride,
   Let us thus in God abide ;
 All the depths of love express,
   All the heights of holiness !

mf Let us then with joy remove :
   To the family above ;
 On the wings of angels fly ;
   Show how true believers die !

             C. Wesley.

447   7s.

mf CHRIST, from Whom all blessings
   flow,
 Perfecting the saints below,
 Hear us, who Thy nature share,
 Who Thy mystic body are.

mf Join us, in one spirit join,
   Let us still receive of Thine ;
 Still for more on Thee we call ;
 Thou who fillest all in all.

mf Closer knit to Thee, our Head ;
 Nourish us, O Christ, and feed \

Let us daily growth receive,
More and more in Jesus live.

mp Sweetly may we all agree,
Touched with softest sympathy ;
Kindly for each other care ;
Every member feel its share.

mf Fill us with the Father's love ;
Never from our souls remove :
Dwell in us, and we shall be
Thine through all eternity.

C. Wesley.

448 L.M.

mf HEAD of the Church, our risen
Lord,
Who by Thy Spirit dost preside
O'er the whole body ; by Whose
word
They all are ruled and sanctified :

mp Our prayers and intercessions
hear
For all Thy family at large,
That each in his appointed sphere
His proper service may discharge.

mf So, through the grace derived from
Thee,
In Whom all fulness dwells above,
May Thy whole Church united be,
And edify itself in love.

J. Conder, adapted from Gelasius.

449 8.7.8.7.8.7.

f HALLELUJAH ! song of gladness
Song of everlasting joy ;
Hallelujah ! song the sweetest
That can angel-hosts employ ;
Hymning in God's holy presence
Their high praise eternally.

f Hallelujah ! Church victorious,
Thou mayest lift this joyful
strain ;
Hallelujah ! songs of triumph
Well befit the ransomed train
We our song must raise with sadness,
While in exile we remain.

mf Hallelujah ! strains of gladness
Suit not souls with anguish torn
dim Hallelujah ! notes of sadness
Best befit our state forlorn ;
For, in this dark world of sorrow
We with tears our sin must
mourn.

mf But our earnest supplication,
Holy God, we raise to Thee ;
Bring us to Thy blissful presence
Make us all Thy joys to see ;
cres Then to Thee our Hallelujah
f Singing everlastingly.

*Latin, 13th century, tr. J. Chandler
and others.*

(2) RECEPTION OF MEMBERS.

450 L.M.

mf JESUS, Thy sovereign grace we
bless, [success ;
That crowns Thy gospel with
Subjecting rebels to Thy throne,
And gathering to Thy fold Thine
own.

mf Those who have now Thy truth
confessed
As their own faith and hope and
rest,
We, in Thy Name, with love
embrace
As fellow-heirs of heavenly grace

ring members, may they share
oys and griefs which others
r ;
active in their stations prove,
l the offices of love.

ι all temptations them defend,
keep them steadfast to the end;
abiding in Thy love,
. they join the Church above.

W. H. Bathurst.

C.M.

NESS, ye men and angels, now :
fore the Lord we speak ;
im we make our solemn vow.
vow we dare not break ;

, long as life itself shall last,
irselves to Christ we yield ;
from His cause will we depart,
ever quit the field.

rust not in our native strength,
it on His grace rely,   [Lord
, with returning wants, the
ill all our need supply.

ide our doubtful feet aright,
id keep us in Thy ways ;
while we tur^n ^{o}ur vo^{ws} to prayers,
irn Thou our prayers to praise.

B. Beddome.

L.M.

DRED in Christ, for His dear
ke,
arty welcome here receive ;
we together now partake
joys which only He can give.

eu and us by grace 'tis given
know the Saviour's precious
ame ;

And shortly we shall meet in
heaven,   [same.
Our hope, our way, our end the
May He by Whose kind care we
meet,
Send His good Spirit from above ;
Make our communications sweet,
And cause our hearts to burn with
love.

mp Forgotten be each worldly theme,
When Christians meet together
thus :
We only wish to speak of Him [us.
Who lived and died and reigns for

We'll talk of all He did and said
And suffered for us here below ;
The path He marked for us to tread,
And what He's doing for us now.

mf Thus, as the moments pass away,
We'll love and wonder and adore :
cres And hasten on the glorious day
f When we shall meet to part no
more.

J. Newton.

453   C.M.

mf COME in, thou blessèd of the Lord;
Stranger nor foe art thou ;
We welcome thee with warm
accord,
Our friend, our brother now.

mf The cup of blessing which we bless
The heavenly bread we brake,
Our Saviour's blood and righteous-
ness,
Freely with us partake.

mp In weal or woe, in joy or care,
Thy portion shall be ours. [share ;
Christians their mutual burdens
They lend their mutual powers

mf Come with us; we will do thee good,
As God to us hath done; [stood,
Stand but in Him, as those have
'Whose faith the victory won.

p And when, by turns, we pass away
As star by star grows dim,
cres May each, translated into day,
mf Be lost and found in Him.

J. Montgomery.

3.—*ITS MINISTERS.*
(1) FOR A CHURCH SEEKING A PASTOR.

454　　　　　　　　L.M.

mp ETERNAL Shepherd, God most
High,
In mercy hearken as we cry,
And send us in our time of need
A pastor wise, Thy flock to lead.

mp Be his, like Thee, O Jesu meek,
To heal the bruised, to stay the
weak,　　[and strong,
And, in Thy might made brave
To war with sin, to right the
wrong.

mp So leading where Thyself hast
trod,
So guiding with Thy staff and rod,
May he Thy sheep in safety bring
To those bright pastures of the
King.

mf And when at last, O gracious
Lord,
Thou shalt bestow his full reward,
cres Let those whom he hath led aright
Be jewels in his crown of light.

R. F. Littledale.

(2) ORDINATION OR RECOGNITION OF MINISTERS.

455　　　　　　　・L.M.

mf WE bid thee welcome in the name
Of Jesus our exalted Head;
Come as a Servant: so He came;
And we receive thee in His stead.

mf Come as a Shepherd: guard and
keep　　　　[sin;
This fold from hell and earth and
Nourish the lambs, and feed the
sheep;
The wounded heal, the lost bring in.

mf Come as a Watchman: take thy
star'd
Upon thy tower amidst the sky;
And when the sword comes on the
land,
Call us to fight, or warn to fly.

mp Come as an Angel, hence to guide
A band of pilgrims on their way;
That, safely walking at thy side,
We fail not, faint not, turn, nor
stray.

mp Come as a Teacher, sent from God,
Charged His whole counsel to declare:　　　　[rod.
cres Lift o'er our ranks the prophet's
While we uphold thy hands with
prayer.

J. Montgomery.

456　　　　7.6.7.6., double.

mf LORD of the living harvest,
That whitens o'er the plain,
Where angels soon shall gather
Their sheaves of golden grain.

ıe hands to labour,
arts to trust and love,
 with them to hasten
ɡdom from above.
ɾs in Thy vineyard,
ɔut, Christ, to be
 bear the burden
ɾ days for Thee.
other wages,
ıou shalt call us home,
ɘ shared the travail
akes Thy kingdom come.
ıou Holy Spirit,
ɔur souls with light ;
ɑ spotless raiment,
clean and white ;
ɣ sacred temple
us, where we stand,
fy Thy people
out this happy land.
, God the Father,
us, God the Son,
, God the Spirit,
ı Three in One !
royal priesthood,
ıtly to adore,
 with Thy fulness,
ı for evermore.
Monsell, v. 3, l. 5 altd.

L.M.

r on : spend, and be

do the Father's will ;
ıy the Master went ;
the servant tread it still ?

on, 'tis not for nought ;
ɣ loss is heavenly gain ;
 thee, love thee, praise
 ;   [men ?
er · praises :—what are

mf Go, labour on : enough while here
 If He shall praise thee, if He deign
 Thy willing heart to mark and
 cheer ;
No toil for Him shall be in vain.

[Go, labour on while it is day, [on ;
 The world's dark night is hastening
*cres*Speed, speed thy work, cast sloth
 away :   ‾
*dim*It is not thus that souls are won.]

p Men die in darkness at thy side,
 Without a hope to cheer the tomb ;
f Take up the torch and wave it wide,
 The torch that lights time's thickest
 gloom.

mf Toil on, faint not, keep watch and
 pray ;
 · Be wise the erring soul to win ;.
 Go forth into the world's highway,
 Compel the wanderer to come in.

Toil on, and in thy toil rejoice :
 For toil comes rest, for exile home ;
*cres*Soon shalt thou hear the Bridegroom's voice,   [come."
f The midnight peal, "Behold I
                          H. Bonar.

458   C.M.

f THOU Who Thyself didst sanctify.
 And set Thyself apart,
 Thy servant's purpose ratify,
 The purpose of his heart. ·

mf In reverence he himself would yield
 To be Thy soldier true,
 In the high places of the field
 Thy glorious work to do.

mf Captain Divine ! his name enrol :
 In token, let him feel   [soul,
 The fire from heaven within his
 The ever-burning zeal !

: him his armour, all of light ;
nd with unfaltering breath,
d, make him Thy great battle
   fight,
And faithful be to death !

e that o'ercometh, Lord, with
   Thee
The morning star shall own,
'he robe and palm of victory,
And the immortal crown.
       · *G. Rawson.*

59   10.6.10.6.

f CHRIST to the young man said,
   "Yet one thing more ;
If thou would'st perfect be,
Sell all thou hast and give it to
   the poor,
And come and follow Me !"

mp Within this temple Christ again,
   unseen,
Those sacred words hath said ;
And His invisible hands to-day
   have been
Laid on a young man's head.

mp And evermore beside him on his way
The unseen Christ shall move.
That he may lean upon His arm,
   and say,   [prove ?"
"Dost Thou, dear Lord, ap-
mp Beside him at the marriage-feast
   shall be,
To make the scene more fair ;
Beside him in the dark Gethsemane
Of pain and midnight prayer.

p O holy trust ! O endless sense of rest!
Like the belovèd John   [breast,
cres To lay his head upon the Saviour's
And thus to journey on !
      H. W. Longfellow.

460   L.M

mf REAPER ! behold the fields
   white   [wor
With the great harvest of
Soldier ! seek thou the thick
   fight,   ·
Thy Captain's standard is unfur

mf Wise to win souls,—exhort, repro
And watch the flock redeemed
   blood ;
Warn with thy tears, preach
   deep love
The gospel of the grace of God

mp Toil on, in the appointed way,
The precious fruit shall s
   appear ;   [d
Work thou thy work whilst it
The shadows lengthen—night
   near.

mf Soon shalt thou hear the Mast
   voice,   [com
The welcome cry, " Beho
Within the pearly gates rejoi
And rest thee in thy heavenly]
      G. Rau

461

mf O GOD! Thy children gather
Thy blessing now await
Thy servant, girded for hi
Stands at the temple ga

mp A holy purpose in his hea
Has deepened calm and
Now from his childhood's
He comes to do Thy w

mp O Father ! keep his sou'
To every hope of goo
cres And may his life of lo
Man's true brother

np O Father ! keep His spirit quick
To every form of wrong ;
And in the ear of sin and self
May his rebuke be strong !

np O give him, in Thy holy work,
Patience to wait Thy time ;
And, toiling still with man, to breathe
The soul's serener clime !

np And grant him many hearts to lead
Into Thy perfect rest ·   [work ;
*cres*Bless Thou him, Father, and his
Bless ! and they shall be blest !

S. Longfellow, v. 1, l. 2 altd.

462   S.M.

mf Sow in the morn thy seed,
At eve hold not thine hand ;
To doubt and fear give thou no heed,
Broadcast it o'er the land.

[*mf* Beside all waters sow,
The highway furrows stock,
Drop it where thorns and thistles grow,
Scatter it on the rock.]

np The good, the fruitful ground,
Expect not here nor there,
O'er hill and dale, by plots 'tis found ;
Go forth, then, everywhere.

mp Thou know'st not which may thrive,
The late or early sown ;
*cres*Grace keeps the precious germs alive,
When and wherever strown.

np And duly shall appear,
In verdure, beauty, strength,

The tender blade, the stalk, the ear
And the full corn at length.

mp Thou canst not toil in vain ;
Cold, heat, and moist, and dry,
Shall foster and mature the grain
For garners in the sky.

mf Thence, when the glorious end,
The day of God is come,
*cres*The angel-reapers shall descend,
And heaven cry, (*f*) "Harvest Home."

J. Montgomery.

463   8.8.

mf COME, Holy Ghost, our souls inspire,
And lighten with celestial fire.

mf Thou the anointing Spirit art,
Who dost Thy sevenfold gifts impart.

mf Thy blessèd unction from above
Is comfort, life, and fire of love.

mf Enable with perpetual light
The dulness of our blinded sight.

mf Anoint and cheer our soilèd face
With the abundance of Thy grace.

*dim*Keep far our foes ; give peace at home :   [come.
*cres*Where Thou art Guide no ill can

mf Teach us to know the Father, Son,
And Thee, of both, to be but One ;

*cres*That, through the ages all along,
Thy praise may be our endless song :

f To Father, Son, and Spirit One,
ff Be everlasting praises done.

*Latin, 9th century, tr. J. Cosin.
v. 8. l. 2. v. 9 altd.*

(3) MEETINGS OF MINISTERS.

L.M.

ORD, speak to me, that I may speak
n living echoes of Thy tone ;
As Thou hast sought, so let me seek
Thy erring children, lost and lone.

O lead me, Lord, that I may lead
The wandering and the wavering feet ;
O feed me, Lord, that I may feed
Thy hungering ones with manna sweet.

[f O strengthen me, that while I stand
Firm on the rock and strong in Thee,
dim I may stretch out a loving hand
To wrestlers with the troubled sea.]

mf O teach me, Lord, that I may teach
The precious things Thou dost impart ;　　[may reach
And wing my words, that they
The hidden depths of many a heart.

p O give Thine own sweet rest to me,
That I may speak with soothing power
A word in season, as from Thee,
To weary ones, in needful hour.]

f O fill me with Thy fulness, Lord,
Until my very heart o'erflow
In kindling thought and glowing word,
Thy love to tell, Thy praise to show.

cres O use me, Lord, use even me
Just as Thou wilt, and when, and where,
ff Until Thy blessèd face I see,
Thy rest, Thy joy, Thy glory share.

Frances R. Havergal.

465　　88.88.88

mf GIVE me the faith which can move
And sink the mountain to a pla.
Give me the child-like, prayi
love,　　[aga
Which longs to build Thy ho
cres Thy love, let it my heart o'erpow
Let it my ransomed soul devou

mp I would the precious time rede
And longer live for this alone,—
To spend and to be spent for th
Who have not yet my Savi
known ;
cres Fully on these my mission pro
And only breathe, to breathe T
love.

mp My talents, gifts, and graces, L
Into Thy blessèd hands receive
And let me live to preach Thy w
And let me to Thy glory live
cres My every sacred moment spe
In publishing the sinner's Fr

mf Enlarge, inflame, and fill my
With boundless charity divi
So shall I all my strength e
And love them with a z
Thine ;
cres And lead them to Thine o
The sheep for whom their S
died.

C. Wesley, v. 1, l.

466

mf LORD, give me light work,
For only, Lord, from
Can come the light, by
The way of work

{*mp*In plainest things I daily err,
  When walking in the light
  The wisdom of this world affords,
  However fair and bright.]

mp In word and plan and deed I err,
  When busiest in Thy work :
  Beneath the simplest\ forms of
    truth
  The subtlest errors lurk.

mp The way is narrow, often dark,
  With lights and shadows strewn ;
*dim*I wander oft. and think it Thine,
  When walking in mine own.

*cres*Yet pleasant is the work for Thee,
  And pleasant is the way ;
*dim*But, Lord, the world is dark, and I
  All prone to go astray.

*cres*Oh ! send me light to do Thy work,
  More light, more wisdom give !
mf Then shall I work Thy work indeed,
  While on Thine earth I live.

mf The work is Thine, not mine, O
    Lord !
  It is Thy race we run ;
*cres*Give light, and then shall all I do
  Pe well and truly done.
                         H. Bonar.

467   L.M.

mf POUR out Thy Spirit from on high ;
  Lord, Thine assembled servants
    bless ;
*cres*Graces and gifts to each supply,
  And clothe Thy priests with
    righteousness.

mf Within Thy temple, when we stand
  To teach the truth, as taught by
    Thee,   [hand
f Saviour, like stars in Thy right
  The angels of the churches be.

mf Wisdom and zeal and faith impart,
  Firmness with meekness from
    above,
  To bear Thy people on our heart,
  And love the souls whom Thou
    dost love ;

mf To watch and pray, and never faint;
  By day and night strict guard to
    keep ;
  To warn the sinner, cheer the saint,
  Nourish Thy lambs, and feed Thy
    sheep.

p Then, when our work is finished
    here,
  In humble hope our charge resign.
*cres*When the Chief Shepherd shall
    appear,
f O God, may they and we be Thine.
                      J. Montgomery.

468   C.M.
PART I.

f I THANK Thee, Lord, for using me
  For Thee to work and speak ;
  However trembling is the hand,
  The voice however weak.

f I thank Thee, Lord, that some true
    rays
  Of Thine from me have shone
  Into a world so dark as ours,
  However faint and wan.

f I bless Thee for each seed of truth
  That I through Thee have sowed
  Upon this waste and barren earth—
  The living seed of God.

mf For those to whom, through me,
    Thou hast
  Some heavenly guidance given,
  For some, it may be, saved from
    death,
  And some brought nearer heav'

For any hope, or light or joy,
　Imparted, Lord, through me
To one sad soul upon this earth,
　Unknown to all but Thee.

f For every note of Christian song,
　However poorly sung ;
For lips that sought to speak but
　truth,
　And for a willing tongue.

PART II.　　C.M.

f I THANK Thee, gracious God, for all
Of witness there hath been
From me, in any path of life,
Though silent and unseen.

mp For solace ministered perchance
　In days of grief and pain ;
For peace to troubled, weary souls,
　Not spoken all in vain.

mf Oh honour higher, truer far,
　Than earthly fame could bring,
Thus to be used. in work like this,
　So long, by such a King !

mp Lord, keep us still the same as in
　Remembered days of old ;
Oh, keep us fervent still in love,
　'Mid many waxing cold.

mp Help us, O Christ, to grasp each
　truth,
　With hand as firm and true,
As when we clasped it first to
　heart,
　A treasure fresh and new.

mf Thy Name to name, Thyself to own
　With voice unfaltering,
f And face as bold and unashamed,
　As in our Christian spring.

H. Bonar.

469 /　　　　　7s.

mf DAY by day, and year by year,
　Late and early. far and near,
At Thy bidding, O my Lord,
I have sown Thy precious word.

mf Give the increase, let me know
Thou hast chosen me to sow ;
Bid me come with joy again,
Bringing sheaves of ripened grain

mp For the earnest Thou hast given,
　For souls garnered safe in heaven
cres Lord, I praise Thee, and I pray
There to meet them in that day.

mp In some hearts if hid there lie ·
　Good seed slow to fructify,
This Thy power can quicken still,
And the reaper's bosom fill.

mf Cheer Thy servant's heart, O Lord
Give large blessings on Thy word
Multiply the scattered seed,
Then shall I rejoice indeed.

dim But if this I may not see,
　Lo ! my work is yet with Thee ;
cres And my day of joy shall come
f In the final harvest-home.

II. Downton

[SEE ALSO SECTION VII. 14.]

4.—ELECTION OF DEACONS.

470　　　　88.88.88.
mf LORD JESU CHRIST, by Whom alone
Is fitly placed each living stone,
Anointed with Thy Spirit free

For every task assigned by Th
Till the whole Church fulfil
　boast—
　" A Temple of the Holy Ghos

mf Choose for us men, to serve aright
In this Thy house, as in Thy sight;
Of conscience pure, and steadfast
aim, [blame ;
Of good report, and free from
And " full "—'tis this we need the
most—
" Of faith and of the Holy Ghost."

mf Grant them in wisdom to excel,
To use the deacon's office well :
That each may win " a good degree,
And boldness in the faith " in Thee;
f And praise, with all the heavenly
host,
ff The Father, Son, and Holy Ghost.
T. G. Crippen.

5.—BAPTISM.
(1) OF INFANTS.

471   88.88.88.

mf O FATHER, in Thy Father's heart
We know our children have their
part ;
We sign them in Thy threefold
Name,
And by the sprinkled water claim
Thy covenant in Christ revealed
To us and to our children sealed.

mf Name of the Father ! pledge that
we
Our inmost being draw from Thee ;
Name of the Son ! whereby we
know
The Father's love to men below ;
Name of the Spirit ! blessèd sign
That now we share the life divine.

mp Fulfil Thy covenant of love ;
Baptize our children from above !
Thy blest, Thy highest gift impart,
The blessing of a childlike heart,
cres And mould them through life's
strain and stress,
f To the full growth of perfectness.
E. S. A.

472   L.M.

mf A LITTLE child the Saviour came,
The mighty God was still His name;

And angels worshipped as He lay,
The seeming Infant of a day.

mf He Who a little child began
The life Divine to show to man,
Proclaims from heaven the message
free,
" Let little children come to Me."

p We bring them, Lord, and with the
sign
Of sprinkled water, name them
Thine :
Their souls with saving grace
endow,
Baptize them with Thy Spirit now.

mf O give Thine angels charge, good
Lord,
Them safely in Thy way to guard;
Thy blessing on their lives com-
mand,
And write their names upon Thy
hand.

f O Thou Who by an infant's tongue
Dost hear Thy perfect glory sung ;
May these, with all the heavenly
host,
Praise Father, Son, and Holy
Ghost.
W. Robertson.

3   7s.

PRAYING by the river-side,
From the heaven serenely wide,
To Thee, Saviour, came the Dove,
Fullest life of peace and love.

p And He came not as a guest,
Thou art His eternal rest,
O Thou holiest abode
Of the inmost life of God.

p Saviour, now this infant bless
As with a Divine caress ;
Make this little heart Thy home,
To it with Thy Spirit come.

p Soft as water on the brow,
Softly, gently, comest Thou ;
cres But hast gifts for every hour,
Purity and peace and power.

mf Faith and hope and holy love,
Wings and spirit of the Dove,
cres Father, on this babe bestow ;
Like the Saviour may he grow.

T. T. Lynch.

474   C.M.

mf SEE, Israel's gentle Shepherd stands
With all engaging charms ;
Hark! how He calls the tender lambs,
And folds them in His arms.

mp "Permit them to approach," He
cries,
"Nor scorn their humble name ;
For 'twas to bless such souls as these
The Lord of angels came."

mf We bring them, Lord, in thankful
hands,
And yield them up to Thee ;
f Joyful that we ourselves are Thine ;
Thine let our offspring be.

P. Doddridge.

475   S.M.

mf To Him Who children blessed,
And suffered them to come,
To Him Who took them to His brea
We bring these children home.

mf To Thee, O God ! Whose face
Their angels still behold, [gra
We bring these children, that Th
May keep, Thine arms enfold.

mf And as the blessing falls
Upon each youthful brow,
Thy Holy Spirit grant, O Lord !
To keep them pure as now.

J. F. Clarke.

476   L.M.

mf GOD of that glorious gift of gra
By which Thy people seek Thy fac
When in Thy presence we appea
Vouchsafe us faith to venture nea

mf Confiding in Thy truth alone,
Here, on the steps of Jesus' thro
We lay the treasure Thou hast gi
To be received and reared for hea

p Lent to us for a season, we
cres Lend him for ever, Lord, to T
f Assured, that, if to Thee he li
We gain in what we seem to

mf Large and abundant blessing
Warm as these prayers, up
head !
And on his soul the dews o'
Fresh as these drops upon

mf Make him and keep him
own child,
Meek follower of the Un
cres Possessor here of grace
Inheritor of heaven abo

J. S. B.

(2) OF BELIEVERS.

477   S.M.

f   STAND, soldier of the cross,
    Thy high allegiance claim,
    And vow to hold the world but loss
    For thy Redeemer's Name.

mf   Arise, and be baptized,
    And wash thy sins away :
cres Thy league with God be solemnized,
    Thy faith avouched to-day.

mf   No more thine own, but
    Christ's,—
    With all the saints of old,

Apostles, seers, evangelists,
    And martyr throngs enrolled,—
cres In God's whole armour strong,
    Front hell's embattled powers :
    The warfare may be sharp and
    long,
f   The victory must be ours.

f   O bright the conqueror's crown,
    The song of triumph sweet,
    When faith casts every trophy down
    At our great Captain's feet.

           E. H. Bickersteth.

[SEE ALSO HYMNS 450 AND 453.]

6.—THE LORD'S SUPPER.

478   8.8.8.4.

mf BY Christ redeemed, in Christ re-
    stored,
    We keep the memory adored,
dim And shew the death of our dear
    Lord
       Until He come.

mf His body broken in our stead
    Is here, in this memorial bread,
cres And so our feeble love is fed
       Until He come.

pp The streams of His dread agony,
    His life-blood shed for us, we see ;
cres The wine shall tell the mystery
       Until He come.

p And thus that dark betrayal night,
    With the last advent we unite,
cres By one blest chain of loving rite,
       Until He come.

f Until the trump of God be heard,
    Until the ancient graves be stirred,

ff And with the great commanding
    word
       The Lord shall come.

mf O blessèd hope ! with this elate
    Let not our hearts be desolate,
cres But strong in faith, in patience wait
       Until He come.

           G. Rawson.

479   10s.

mf HERE, O my Lord, I see Thee face
    to face ;
    Here would I touch and handle
    things unseen ;
cres Here grasp with firmer hand the
    eternal grace,
dim And all my weariness upon Thee
    lean.

mf Here would I feed upon the Bread
    of God ;
    Here drink with Thee the roy
    Wine of Heaven ;

p Here would I lay aside each earthly
   load,
   Here taste afresh the calm of sin
   forgiven.

mf This is the hour of banquet and
   of song,
   This is the heavenly table spread
   for me ;
*cres*Here let me feast, and, feasting,
   still prolong
   The brief bright hour of fellowship
   with Thee.

mp Too soon we rise ; the symbols
   disappear ;
   The Feast, though not the Love, is
   past and gone ;
   The Bread and Wine remove ; but
   Thou art here,
*cres*Nearer than ever ; still my Shield
   and Sun.

mf Feast after feast thus comes, and
   passes by ;
   Yet, passing, points to the glad
   Feast above,
*cres*Giving sweet foretaste of the festal
   joy,
f The Lamb's great Bridal Feast of
   bliss and love.
                           H. Bonar.

480   S.M., double.

mf JESU, we thus obey
   Thy last and kindest word,
   Here, in Thine own appointed way,
   We come to meet our Lord ;
   The way Thou hast enjoined
   Thou wilt therein appear ;
*cres*We come with confidence to find
   Thy special presence here.

mf Our hearts we open wide,
   To make the Saviour room ;

And lo ! the Lamb, the Cr[...]
The Sinner's Friend is co[...]
His presence makes the [...]
And now our spirits feel
The glory not to be expres[...]
The joy unspeakable.

f Thee, King of Saints, w[...]
For this our living Brea[...]
Nourished by Thy preservin[...]
And at Thy table fed !
We in these lower parts
Of Thy great kingdom [...]
And feel the earnest in ou[...]
Of our eternal rest.

mf Yet still a higher seat
We in Thy kingdom clai[...]
Who here began by faith t[...]
The supper of the Lamb
cres That glorious heavenly [...]
We surely shall attain,
f And in the palace of the s[...]
With Thee for ever reig[...]
            Cento from C. W[...]

481

p MY God, and is Thy table
And does Thy cup with l[...]
flow ?
*cres*Thither be all Thy childr[...]
And let them all its sweetne[...]

mf Hail ! sacred feast, whic[...]
makes,
Rich banquet of His flesh a[...]
*cres*Thrice happy he, who here
That sacred stream, that [...]
food. .

mp Why are these emblem[...]
vain
Before unwilling hearts di[...]
Was not for you the victi[...]
Are you forbid the children

mf O let Thy table honoured be,
And furnished well with joyful
  guests ; .
And may each soul salvation see,
That here its sacred pledges tastes
    P. Doddridge, v. 3, l. 1 altd.

482   6.5., 8 lines.

mf   JESUS, great Redeemer !
    Source of life Divine !
    In our souls for ever
    Grant the light to shine !
mp   Light of peace eternal,
    Prince of Peace restore ;
mf   Light of life immortal,
    Shine for evermore !

mp   Bread for sinners broken,
    Bread of life indeed !
    Manna for the hungry,
    In their sorest need ;
cres   Pledge of our salvation,
    How we thirst for Thee !
    Cup of heavenly blessing,
    Wine of charity !

mp   Thou, O holy Saviour,
    Come and enter in ;
    Cleanse away the impress
    Of our dreadful sin !
cres   Make us pure, we pray Thee,
    Thou Who art so pure !
    And O let Thy likeness
    In our heart endure.

mp   Spirit, Holy Spirit,
    Aid us with Thy love ;
    Give Thy gentle presence, ·
    Ever blessèd Dove !
cres   Father, O receive us,
    Now for Jesus' sake.
dim   And our feeble worship
    Condescend to take !
         Ada Cross.

483   10.10.10.10.

mp "THIS is My body, which is | given
  for you ;   [membering Me.
Do this," He said, and brake, "re- |
O Lamb of God, our Paschal |
  offering true,   [moment be.
To us the Bread of life each |

mp "This is My blood, for sins' re- |
  mission shed,"
He spake, and passed the cup of |
  blessing round;   [fulness fed,
cres So let us drink, and on life's |
f With heavenly joy each quicken-
  ing | pulse shall bound.

p "The hour has come!" with us in |
  peace sit down ;   [to the end:
Thine own beloved, O love us |
Serve us our banquet, ere the |
  night's dark frown
Veil from our sight the presence |
  of our Friend.

cres Girded with love, still wash Thy |
  servants' feet,   [and adore ;
While they, submissive, wonder |
Bathed in Thy blood, our spirits |
  every whit   [more and more.
Are clean : yet cleanse our goings |

mp Some will betray Thee—"Master, |
  is it I ? "   [in fear—
Leaning upon Thy love, we | ask
Ourselves mistrusting, earnest | ly
  we cry   [when | sin is near.
To Thee, the strong, for strength,

dim But round us fall the evening |
  shadows dim,   [darkening sense;
A saddened awe pervades our |
In solemn choir we sing the | part-
  ing hymn,   us go hence."
And hear Thy voice, " Arise, let,
          C. L. Ford

7.6.7.6., double.

BREAD to pilgrims given,
/ food that angels eat,
nanna sent from heaven.
For heaven-born natures meet,
ive us, for Thee long pining,
To eat till richly filled ;
ill, earth's delights resigning,
Our every wish is stilled.

O water, life-bestowing,
Forth from the Saviour's heart,
A fountain purely flowing,
A fount of love Thou art :
es O let us, freely tasting,
Our burning thirst assuage ;
Thy sweetness, never wasting,
Avails from age to age.

mp Jesus, this feast receiving,
We Thee unseen adore :
Thy faithful word believing.
We take, and doubt no more :
cres Give us, Thou true and loving,
On earth to live in Thee :
f Then, death the veil removing,
Thy glorious face to see.
Ray Palmer, adapted from
T. Aquinas.

485 L.M.

mf JESUS, Thou joy of loving hearts,
Thou Fount of life, Thou Light of
men,
From the best bliss that earth
imparts,
We turn unfilled to Thee again.

mf Thy truth unchanged hath ever
stood ;   [call ;
Thou savest those that on Thee
cres To them that seek Thee, Thou art
good,
To them that find Thee, all in all.

mf We taste Thee. O Thou Living Bre
And long to feast upon Thee sti
We drink of Thee, the Fount:
Head,   [1
cres And thirst our souls from Thee

p Our restless spirits yearn for Tl
Where'er our changeful lot is ca:
cres Glad, when Thy gracious smile
see ;   [Thee fa
Blest, when our faith can h(

p O Jesus, ever with us stay ;
Make all our moments calm a
bright ;
cres Chase the dark night of sin awe
Shed o'er the world· Thy h(
light.
Bernard of Clairvaux, tr. Ray Palm

486 C.M

mf ACCORDING to Thy gracious wc
In meek humility,
This will I do, my dying Lord
I will remember Thee.

mp Thy body, broken for my sake
My bread from heaven sha'
Thy testamental cup I take,
And thus remember Thee.

p Gethsemane can I forget ?
Or there Thy conflict see,
Thine agony and bloody sw
And not remember Thee

p When to the cross I turn m
And rest on Calvary,
cres O Lamb of God. my sacri
I must remember Thee

mf Remember Thee, and all '
And all Thy love to n
cres Yea, while a breath. remains,
f Will I remember Th

p And when these failing lips grow
   dumb,
   And mind and memory flee,
*cres*When Thou shalt in Thy kingdom
   come,
f Then, Lord, remember me.
              J. Montgomery.

487   L.M.

mp O GOD of mercy, God of might,
   How should weak sinners bear the
   sight.
   If, as Thy power is surely here,
   Thine open glory should appear?

mf For now Thy people are allowed
   To scale the mount, and pierce the
   cloud :
*cres*And faith may feed her eager view
   With wonders Sinai never knew.

p Fresh from the atoning sacrifice,
   The world's Redeemer bleeding lies,
*cres*That man, His foe, for whom He
   bled,
   May take Him for his daily bread.

p Oh! agony of wavering thought,
   When sinners first so near are
   brought :
   It is my Maker—dare I stay?
*cres*My Saviour—dare I turn away?

mp Refresh us, Lord, to hold Thee fast;
   And when Thy veil is drawn at
   last,
   Let us depart where shadows cease,
p With words of blessing and of peace.
       J. Keble, v. 1, l. 2, v. 5, l. 1 altd.

488   7.7.7.

mf JESUS, to Thy table led,
   Now let every heart be fed
   With the true and living bread.

p While in penitence we kneel,
*cres*Thy sweet presence let us feel,
f All Thy wondrous love reveal.

p While on Thy dear cross we gaze,
   Mourning o'er our sinful ways,
*cres*Turn our sadness into praise ;

p Draw us to Thy wounded side,
*cres*Whence there flowed the healing
   tide,
*dim*There our sins and sorrows hide.

mf From the bonds of sin release,
   Cold and wavering faith increase,
   Lamb of God, grant us Thy peace!

mf Lead us by Thy piercèd hand,
*cres*Till around Thy throne we stand,
f In the bright and better land.
            R. H. Baynes.

489   S.M.

f No Gospel like this feast,
   Spread for Thy Church by Thee ;
   Nor prophet nor evangelist
   Preach the glad news so free.

mf All our redemption cost,
   All our redemption won ;
   All it has won for us, the lost,
   All it cost Thee, the Son.

dim Thine was the bitter price,
   Ours is the free gift given :
*dim*Thine was the blood of sacrifice,
cres Ours is the wine of heaven.

mp For Thee the burning thirst,
   The shame, the mortal strife.
*dim*The broken heart, the piercèd side ;
cres To us the Bread of Life.

mp Here we would rest midway,
   As on a sacred height,
   That darkest and that brightest day
   Meeting before our sight.

mp From that dark depth of woes
 Thy love for us hath trod,
cres Up to the heights of blest repose,
 Thy love prepares with God ;

mf Till, from self's chains released,
 One sight alone we see,
cres Still at the cross, as at the feast,
 Behold Thee, only Thee !

Elizabeth Charles.

490   L.M.

f BEHOLD! the Eternal King and
 Priest   [wine :
 Brings forth for me the bread and
 Himself the Master of the Feast,
 His flesh and blood the food divine !

mf Jesus ! I come, for Thou dost call ;
 I eat and drink at Thy command ;
dim Low at Thy feet I humbly fall :
 O touch me with Thy piercèd hand.

mp Wash throughly clean this heart of
  mine,
 That it may beat for Thee alone ;
 O let it lose its life in Thine,
 And have no will except Thine
  own.

mp In weariness be Thou my rest,
 In loneliness be Thou my friend,
 In sorrow hold me to Thy breast,
 And keep me, Jesu, to the end.

491   C.M.

mp FOR ever here my rest shall be,
 Close to Thy bleeding side ;
 This all my hope and all my plea,
 For me the Saviour died.

f My dying Saviour and my God,
 Fountain for guilt and sin !
Sprinkle me ever with Thy blood,
 And cleanse, and keep me clean.

cres Wash me; and make me thus Thine
 own ;
 Wash me, and mine Thou art;
 Wash me, but not my feet alone,
 My hands, my head, my heart

mf The atonement of Thy blood apply
 Till faith to sight improve;
 Till hope in full fruition die,
f And all my soul be love.

C. Wesley.

492   8.7.

mf SWEET the moments, rich in
 blessing,
 Which before the cross I spend
cres Life and health and peace possessing,
 From the sinner's dying Friend

mp Here I'll sit for ever viewing
 Mercy's streams, in streams of
 blood :
p Precious drops my soul bedewing
 Plead and claim my peace with
 God.

mf Love and grief my heart dividing
 With my tears His feet I'll bathe
cres Constant still in faith abiding,
 Life deriving from His death.

mf May I still enjoy this feeling ;
cres In all need to Jesus go :
f Prove His wounds each day most
 healing,
 And Himself more deeply know

J. Allen and W. W. Shirley.

493   7s., 6 lines.

mp BREAD of heaven ! on Thee I feed
 For Thy flesh is meat indeed.
cres Ever may my soul be fed
 With this true and living bread

Day by day, with strength supplied,
Through the life of Him Who died.
mp Vine of heaven! Thy blood supplies
This blest cup of sacrifice.
'Tis Thy wounds my healing give :
To Thy cross I look, and live.
*cres*Thou my life ! O let me be
f Rooted, grafted, built on Thee.

J. Conder.

494   9.8.9.8.

mp BREAD of the world, in mercy
broken,
Wine of the soul, in mercy shed ;
*cres*By whom the words of life were
spoken.   [dead :
And in Whose death our sins are

p Look on the heart by sorrow broken,
Look on the tears by sinners shed,
*cres*And be Thy feast to us the token
f That by Thy grace our souls are
fed.

R. Heber.

495   7s.

p " TILL He come," O let the words
Linger on the trembling chords :
Let the little while between
In their golden light be seen ;
Let us think how heaven and home
*cres*Lie beyond that " Till He come."

p When the weary ones we love
Enter on their rest above,
Seems the earth so poor and vast,
All our life-joy overcast !
*dim*Hush, be every murmur dumb :
It is only "Till He come."

*cres*Clouds and conflicts round us
press ;
Would we have one sorrow less ?

. All the sharpness of the cross,
All that tells the world is loss,
*dim*Death, and darkness, and the tomb,
pp Only whisper, " Till He come."
mf See, the feast of love is spread,
Drink the wine and break the
bread :
Sweet memorials,—till the Lord
Call us round His heavenly board ;
Some from earth, from glory some:
*cres*Severed only "Till He come."

E. H. Bickersteth.

496   7s., 6 lines.

p Go to dark Gethsemane,
Ye that feel the tempter's power ;
*cres*Your Redeemer's conflict see :
Watch with Him one bitter hour :
Turn not from His griefs away ;
p Learn of Jesus Christ to pray.

p Follow to the judgment-hall ;
View the Lord of life arraigned.
*cres*O the wormwood and the gall !
O the pangs His soul sustained !
Shun not suffering, shame, or loss :
p Learn of Him to bear the cross.

p Calvary's   mournful   mountain
climb :
There, adoring at His feet,
*cres*Mark that miracle of time,—
God's own sacrifice complete.
pp It is finished ! hear Him cry :
p Learn of Jesus Christ to die.

p Early hasten to the tomb,
Where they laid His breathless clay,
*dim*All is solitude and gloom :—
Who hath taken Him away ?
f Christ is risen ;—He meets our eyes :
Saviour, teach us so to rise.

J. Montgomery.

497 L.M.

mf How rich are Thy provisions, Lord !
Thy table furnished from above !
The fruits of life o'erspread the
board, [love.
The cup o'erflows with heavenly

dim We are the poor, the blind, the lame,
And help was far, and death was
nigh ;
But at the gospel-call we came,
And every want received supply.

mp From the highway that leads to
hell,
From paths of darkness and despair,
cres Lord, we are come with Thee to
dwell,
Glad to enjoy Thy presence here.

mf What shall we render to the Son,
That left the heaven of His abode,
And to this wretched earth came
down,
To bring us wanderers back to God ?

mp It cost Him death to save our lives ;
To buy our souls it cost His own ;
And all the unknown joys He gives
Were bought with agonies un-
known.

mf Our everlasting love is due
To Him that ransomed sinners lost ;
And pitied rebels when He knew
The vast expense His love would
cost.

I. Watts, v. 4, l. 1 altd.

498 88.88.88.

mp FORTH from the dark and stormy
sky,
Lord, to Thine altar's shade we fly ;
*Forth from the world, its hope and
fear,*

Saviour, we seek Thy shelter here.
dim Weary and weak, Thy grace we
pray ; [away !
Turn not, O Lord, Thy guests

mp Long have we roamed in want and
pain ; [vain ;
Long have we sought Thy rest in
'Wildered in doubt. in darkness lost,
Long have our souls been tempest-
tost ;

dim Low at Thy feet our sins we lay,
p Turn not, O Lord, Thy guests away.

R. Heber.

499 7.6.7.6.7.7.7.6.

mp LAMB of God ! Whose bleeding
love
We now recall to mind,
Send the answer from above,
And let us mercy find :
Think on us, who think on Thee,
Every struggling soul release ;
p O ! remember Calvary,
And bid us go in peace.

p By Thine agonising pain,
And bloody sweat, we pray,
By Thy dying love to man,
Take all our sins away.
cres Burst our bonds, and set us free.
From iniquity release ;
p O ! remember Calvary,
And bid us go in peace.

mf Let Thy blood, by faith applied.
The sinners' pardon seal,
cres Speak us freely justified,
And all our sickness heal :
dim By Thy Passion on the tree,
Let our griefs and troubles cease ;
p O ! remember Calvary,
And bid us go in peace.

C. Wesley.

7.—THE COMMUNION OF SAINTS.

500 L.M.

f WE triumph in the glorious grace
That set us in this English land,
And welcome the high earthly place
Wherein our God has made us stand.

f But, oh ! to us a grace more great,
A dignity more dear is given ;
He links us to a nobler state,
He makes us citizens of heaven.

[*f* Yes, mightily our hearts are bound
This goodly fatherland to love ;
But more our own Emmanuel's
ground,
That better, dearer land above.]

f Our land's good laws we proudly
praise,   [tell ;
Our land's great tale with triumph
But, oh ! what majesty arrays
The people of Emmanuel !

[*f* Their glorious freedom how com-
plete !
How absolute His holy will !
What task divine, what tribute
sweet,   [fulfil !]
Their spirits bring, their hands

mf Dear fellow-citizens they greet,
Of every age, of every clime ;
Far dwellers in one city meet ;
Strange voices raise one song
sublime.

mf O city, where God's people dwell !
O home, where no sweet bonds are
riven !
O country of Emmanuel !
The only fatherland is heaven.

f Joy ! joy ! our King doth never die !
Our city doth for ever stand ;

We serve the Eternal Majesty,
And hold the heavenly fatherland.
T. H. Gill.

501 C.M., double.

f COME, let us join our friends above,
That have obtained the prize,
And on the eagle wings of love
To joy celestial rise ;
Let all the saints terrestrial sing
With those to glory gone ;
For all the servants of our King,
In earth and heaven, are one.

mf One family, we dwell in Him,
One Church, above, beneath,
Though now divided by the stream,
The narrow stream of death ;
One army of the living God,
To His command we bow ;
Part of His host hath crossed the
flood,
dim   And part is crossing now.

[*mp* Our old companions in distress
We haste again to see,
And eager long for our release
And full felicity ;
cres E'en now by faith we join our
hands
With those that went before,
And greet the blood-besprinkled
bands
On the eternal shore.]

mf Our spirits too shall quickly join,
Like theirs with glory crowned,
And shout to see our Captain's sign,
To hear His trumpet sound.
Oh that we now might grasp our
Guide !
Oh that the word were given !

*cres*Come, Lord of Hosts ! the waves
divide,
f And land us all in heaven !
C. Wesley.

502   6.6.6.6.4.4.4.4.

f YE holy angels bright,
Who wait at God's right hand,
Or through the realms of light
Fly at your Lord's command !
Assist our song,
For else the theme
Too high doth seem
For mortal tongue.

mp Ye blessèd souls at rest,
Who ran this earthly race,
*cres*And now, from sin released,
Behold the Saviour's face !
f God's praises sound,
As in His light.
With sweet delight
Ye do abound.

mf Ye saints, who toil below !
Adore your heavenly King,
And onward as ye go
Some joyful anthem sing :
cres Take what He gives ;
f And praise Him still,
Through good and ill,
Who ever lives !

mf My soul ! bear thou thy part ;
Triumph in God above,
And with a well-tuned heart
Sing thou the songs of love !
f Let all thy days
Till life shall end,
Whate'er He send,
ff Be filled with praise !
R. Baxter, altd. R. R. Chope.

503   C.M.

f HAPPY the souls to Jesus joined,
And saved by grace alone :
Walking in all His ways they find
Their heaven on earth begun.

f The Church triumphant in Thy
love—
Their mighty joys we know :
They sing the Lamb in hymns
above,
And we in hymns below.

f Thee, in Thy glorious realm they
praise,
And bow before Thy throne :
We, in the kingdom of Thy grace—
The kingdoms are but one.

mf The holy to the holiest leads,
From thence our spirits rise,
*cres*And he that in Thy statutes treads
f Shall meet Thee in the skies.
C. Wesley.

8.—*THE EXAMPLE, VICTORY, AND REWARD OF THE SAINTS.*

504   C.M.

mf GIVE me the wings of faith to
rise
Within the veil, and see
The saints above, how great their
joys !
How bright their glories be !

mp Once they were mourning here
below,
And wet their couch with
tears ;
They wrestled hard, as we do
now,
With sins and doubts and fears.

mf I asked them whence their victory came ?
They, with united breath,
cres Ascribe their conquest to the Lamb,
f Their triumph to His death.

mf They marked the footsteps that He trod,
His zeal inspired their breast ;
And, following their Incarnate God,
Possess the promised rest.

f Our glorious Leader claims our praise
For His own pattern given,
While the long cloud of witnesses
ff Show the same path to heaven.

I. Watts.

505   L.M., with refrain.

mf THE saints of God ! their conflict past,
And life's long battle won at last,
No more they need the shield or sword,   [Lord :—
They cast them down before their
cres O happy saints ! for ever blest,
p At Jesus' feet how safe your rest !

mf The saints of God ! their wanderings done,   [run,
No more their weary course they
No more they faint, no more they fall,
No foes oppress, no fears appal :—
cres O happy saints ! for ever blest,
p In that dear home, how sweet your rest !

[*mf* The saints of God ! life's voyage o'er,
Safe landed on that blissful shore,
No stormy tempests now they dread,
No roaring billows lift their head :—

cres O happy saints ! for ever blest,
p In that calm haven of your rest !]

mf The saints of God their vigil keep
While yet their mortal bodies sleep,
Till from the dust they too shall rise,
And soar triumphant to the skies:—
cres O happy saints ! rejoice and sing !   [King !
p He quickly comes, your Lord and

mf O God of saints ! to Thee we cry !
O Saviour ! plead for us on high :
O Holy Ghost ! our Guide and Friend,   [end .
p Grant us Thy grace till life shall
cres That with all saints our rest may be   [Thee.
f In that bright Paradise with

W. D. Maclagan.

506   8.7.8.7., double.

f HARK the sound of holy voices,
Chanting at the crystal sea,
Hallelujah ! Hallelujah !
Hallelujah ! Lord, to Thee.
p Multitude, which none can number,
Like the stars, in glory stands.
f Clothed in white apparel, holding
Palms of victory in their hands.

p They have come from tribulation,
And have washed their robes in Blood,   [Jesus ;
Washed them in the Blood of
Tried they were, and firm they stood ;
Mocked, imprisoned, stoned, tormented,
Sawn asunder, slain with sword,
cres They have conquered Death and Satan,
f By the might of Christ the Lord

[*f(unis.*) Marching with Thy cross
    their banner,
  They have triumphed, following
  Thee, the Captain of Salvation,
    Thee, their Saviour and their
    King ;
dim(har.) Gladly, Lord, with Thee
    they suffered ;   [died,
  Gladly, Lord, with Thee they
  And, by death, to life immortal
  They were born and glorified.]

ff Now they reign in heavenly glory,
  Now they walk in golden light,
(*uni.*) Now they drink, as from a river,
  Holy bliss and infinite ; [ever ;
p (*har.*) Love and peace they taste for
  And all truth and knowledge see
  In the beatific vision
  Of the Blessèd Trinity.

f God of God, the one-Begotten,
  Light of Light, Emmanuel,
  In Whose Body, joined together,
  All the Saints for ever dwell ;
p Pour upon us of Thy fulness,
  That we may for evermore
  God the Father, God the Son, and
  God the Holy Ghost adore.
          C. Wordsworth.

507   C.M.

mf YE that put on the heavenly crown
  And sing with seraphim,
  Brethren in glory, bend ye down,
  And aid our faltering hymn.

mf Come let us praise the One Great
    Head,
  The selfsame power to save,
  Ye, who in bliss are perfected,
  And we, so near the grave !

f Glory to Him Who tasted death,
  Life to us all to give !

Ye in His presence—we
  In, through, and to B
f Glory to Him, Who woi
  For you gone up on h
  The Resurrection and tl
  By Whom we never d
f Glory from us, who t
  long,
  And for His coming v
  And glory from your pal
  Within the pearly gai
mf When wilt Thou be at o
  By one Church, in on
  Hasten the time ; delay i
  Lord Jesus, quickly ci
             G.

508

mf How bright these glor
  shine !
  Whence all their whit
  How came they to the bl
  Of everlasting day ?
p Lo ! these are they from
  . great,
  Who came to realms c
cres And in the blood of C
  washed
  Those robes which
  bright.
f Now, with triumphal p
  stand
  Before the throne on
  And serve the God they l
  The glories of the sky
f His presence fills each
  joy,
  Tunes every voice to i
  By day, by night, the sa
  With glad hosannas ri

mf Hunger and thirst are felt no more,

. Nor suns with scorching ray ;

cres God is their Sun, Whose cheering beams
Diffuse eternal day.

mf The Lamb that dwells amidst the throne,
Shall o'er them still preside,

p Feed them with nourishment Divine,

cres And all their footsteps guide.

p 'Mong pastures green He'll lead His flock,
Where living streams appear ;

cres And God the Lord from every eye
Shall wipe off every tear.

Variation from I. Watts and Scripture Songs, 1745, by W. Cameron.

IX.
Public Worship.
1.—*THE LORD'S DAY.*
(a) MORNING.

509 L.M.

mf LORD of the Sabbath ! hear our vows, [house ;
On this Thy day, in this Thy
And own, as grateful sacrifice,
The songs which from the desert rise.

mf Thine earthly Sabbaths, Lord, we love ;

cres But there's a nobler rest above.
To that our labouring souls aspire,
With ardent hope and strong desire.

p No more fatigue, no more distress ;
No guilt the conscience to oppress;
No groans to mingle with the songs [tongues :
Resounding from immortal

mf No rude alarms of raging foes,
No cares to break the long repose,
No midnight shade, no clouded sun,

cres But sacred, high, eternal noon.

mf O long-expected day begin !
Dawn on these realms of woe and sin ;

dim Fain would we leave this weary road,

p And sleep in death to rest with God.
P. Doddridge, v. 2, l. 4, v. 3, ll. 2, 4 altd.

510 C.M.

mf BLEST day of God, most calm, most bright,
The first and best of days ; [light,
The labourer's rest, the saint's de-
A day of mirth and praise.

mf My Saviour's face did make thee
His rising did thee raise ; [shine.
This made thee heavenly and divine
Beyond the common days.

mf The firstfruits do a blessing prove
To all the sheaves behind ;
And they that do a Sabbath love,
A happy week shall find.

mf This day must I for God appear,
For, Lord, the day is Thine ;
O let me spend it in Thy fear !
Then shall the day be mine.
J. Mason.

C.M.

Lord, my Love, was crucified,
He all the pains did bear ;
ut in the sweetness of His rest
He makes His servants share.

low sweetly rest Thy saints above,
Which in Thy bosom lie ;
The Church below doth rest in
h ,pe
Of that felicity.

'Welcome and dear unto my soul
Are these sweet feasts of love ;
But what a Sabbath shall I keep
When I shall rest above !

nf I bless Thy wise and wondrous love,
Which binds us to be free ;
Which makes us leave our earthly
snares,
That we may come to Thee.

mf I come, I wait, I hear, I pray ;
Thy footsteps, Lord, I trace ;
cres I sing to think this is the way
Unto my Saviour's face.

mf These are my preparation days ;
And when my soul is drest,
cres These Sabbaths shall deliver me
To mine eternal rest.

J. Mason.

512   8.6.8.4.

f HAIL ! sacred day of earthly rest,
From toil and trouble free :
Hail ! day of light, that bringest
light
And joy to me.

mp A holy stillness, breathing calm
On all the world around,
Uplifts my soul, O God, to Thee,
Where rest is found.

mp No sound of jarring strife is heard,
As weekly labours cease ; [sing
No voice, but those that sweetly
p   Sweet songs of peace.

[*mf* On all I think, or say, or do,
A ray of light divine
Is shed, O God, this day by Thee,
For it is Thine.

f I hear the organ loudly peal,
And soaring voices raise
To Thee, their great Creator, hymns
Of deathless praise.

p All earthly things appear to fade
As, rising high and higher,
cres The yearning voices strive to join
The heavenly choir.]

f For those who sing with saints
below
Glad songs of heavenly love,
Shall sing—when songs on earth
have ceased—
With saints above.

f Accept, O God, my hymn of prai·
That Thou this day hast given
Sweet foretaste of that endless ‹
Of rest in heaven.

G. Thrin

513   S.

f   THIS is the day of Light !
Let there be light to-day ŀ
O Dayspring, rise upon our
And chase its gloom away

p   This is the day of Rest !
Our failing strength ren‹
dim On weary brain and ſ
breast
cres Shed Thou Thy freshen

p   This is the day of Peac
Thy Peace our spirits fiˈ

*cres*Bid Thou the blasts of discord cease,
The waves of strife be still.

p This is the day of Prayer !
Let earth to heaven draw near ;
*cres*Lift up our hearts to seek Thee there,
Come down to meet us here.

This is the First of days! [breath,
Send forth Thy quickening
f And wake dead souls to love and praise,
O Vanquisher of Death !

J. Ellerton.

514   7.6.7.6., double.

mf THE dawn of God's dear Sabbath
Breaks o'er the earth again,
As some sweet summer morning
After a night of pain.
It comes as cooling showers
To some exhausted land,
As shade of clustered palm-trees
'Mid weary wastes of sand.

mpo O day when earthly sorrow
Is merged in heavenly joy,
And trial changed to blessing
That foes may not destroy,—
*cres*When want is turned to fulness,
And weariness to rest,
And pain to wondrous rapture,
Upon the Saviour's breast!]

mf Lord! we would bring for offering,
Though marred with earthly soil,
A week of earnest labour,
Of steady, faithful toil ;
Fair fruits of self-denial,
Of strong, deep love to Thee,
Fostered by Thine own Spirit,
In our humility.

p And we would bring our burden
Of sinful thought and deed,
In Thy pure presence kneeling,
From bondage to be freed ;
Our heart's most bitter sorrow
For all Thy work undone—
So many talents wasted !
So few bright laurels won !

mf And with that sorrow mingling,
A steadfast faith, and sure,
And love so deep and fervent,
That tries to make it pure :—
*cres*In His dear presence finding
The pardon that we need ;
*dim*And then the peace so lasting—
Celestial peace indeed !

mf So be it, Lord, for ever.
O may we evermore,
In Jesu's holy Presence
His blessèd Name adore !
Upon His peaceful Sabbath,
Within His temple-walls—
Type of the stainless worship
In Sion's golden halls.

f So that, in joy and gladness,
We reach that Home at last,
When life's short week of sorrow,
And sin, and strife is past ;
*cres*When Angel-hands have gathered
The fair, ripe fruit for Thee,
ff O Father, Lord, Redeemer !
Most Holy Trinity !

Ada Cross, v. 4, l. 3 altd.

515   7.6.7.6., double.

f O DAY of rest and gladness,
O Day of joy and light,
O balm of care and sadness,
Most beautiful, most bright ;
On thee, the high and lowly,
Through ages joined in tune,

p Sing Holy, Holy, Holy,
cres To the great God Triune.

f On thee, at the Creation,
   The Light first had its birth ;
On thee, for our salvation,
   Christ rose from depths of earth;
cres On thee, our Lord victorious,
   The Spirit sent from heaven ;
And thus on thee, most glorious,
   A triple Light was given.

[*mf* Thou art a port protected
   From storms that round us rise,
A garden intersected
   With streams of Paradise ;
Thou art a cooling fountain
   In life's dry, dreary sand ;
From thee, like Pisgah's mountain,
   We view our Promised Land.]

p To-day on weary nations
   The heavenly Manna falls ;
f To holy convocations
   The silver trumpet calls,
Where Gospel-light is glowing
   With pure and radiant beams ;
And living water flowing
   With soul-refreshing streams.

mf New graces ever gaining
   From this our day of rest,
We reach the rest remaining
   To spirits of the blest :
f To Holy Ghost be praises,
   To Father and to Son ;
The Church her voice upraises
   To Thee, Blest Three in One.

                    C. Wordsworth.

516   S.M.

f WELCOME, sweet day of rest,
   That saw the Lord arise :
Welcome to this reviving breast,
And there rejoicing eyes.

mf The King Himself comes near,
   And feasts His saints to-day ;
cres Here we may sit, and see Him here,
   And love and praise and pray.

mf One day, amidst the place
   Where my dear Lord hath been,
Is sweeter than ten thousand days
   Of pleasurable sin.

p My willing soul would stay
   In such a frame as this,
cres And sit and sing herself away
   To everlasting bliss.

             I. Watts, v. 3, l. 2 altd.

517   C.M.

f THIS is the day the Lord hath made,
   He calls the hours His own ;
Let heaven rejoice, let earth be
      glad,
   And praise surround the throne.

To-day He rose and left the dead,
   And Satan's empire fell ;
To-day the saints His triumphs
      spread,
   And all His wonders tell.

ff Hosanna to the Anointed King,
   To David's Holy Son :
Help us, O Lord, descend and bring
   Salvation from the throne.

f. Blest be the Lord, Who comes to
      men
   With messages of grace : [Name
Who comes, in God His Father's
   To save our sinful race.

ff Hosanna in the highest strains
   The Church on earth can raise ;
The highest heavens in which He
      reigns
   Shall give Him nobler praise.

                    I. Watts.

518　　　　　　　　L.M.

mf THIS day at Thy creating word,
　　First o'er the earth the light was
　　　　poured,—
cres O Lord, this day upon us shine,
　　And fill our souls with light divine.

mp This day the Lord for sinners slain,
res In might victorious rose again,—
mf O Jesu, may we raisèd be
　　From death of sin, to life in Thee.

mf This day the Holy Spirit came
　　With fiery tongues of cloven
　　　　flame :—
mp O Spirit, fill our hearts this day
　　With grace to hear, and grace to
　　　　pray.

mf O day of Light, and Life, and
　　Grace !
　　From earthly toils sweet resting-
　　　place !　　　　　　　　[love,
　　Thy hallowed hours, best gift of
　　Give we again to God above.
　　　　　　　　　　W. W. How.

519　　　　　　　8.8.6.8.8.6.

f THE festal morn, O God, is come,
　　That calls us to Thy hallowed dome.

Thy presence to adore ;
With joy the summons we attend,
With willing steps Thy courts
　ascend.
And tread the sacred floor.

f Behold to our enraptured eyes
The heaven-built towers of Salem
　rise ;
　By faith with glad survey,
We view her mansions that contain
Angelic forms. a glorious train,
　And shine with cloudless day.

f Thither, from earth's remotest end,
Lo ! the redeemed of God ascend,
　Their tribute thither bring :
Here, crowned with everlasting joy,
In hymns of praise their tongues
　employ,
　And hail the Immortal King.

mp There in Thy house not made with
　hands,
May we amid these heavenly bands
　Thy holy Name adore.
cres There all Thy works of grace
　resound　　　　　　　　[found
　When of these courts no trace is
　And time shall be no more.
　　　　J. Merrick, altd. T. Cotterill.

(b) EVENING.

520　　　　　　　　L.M.

mf AT even, ere the sun was set,
　　The sick, O Lord, around Thee lay ;
p O in what divers pains they met !
cres O with what joy they went
　　away !

p Once more 'tis eventide, and we,
　　Oppressed with various ills, draw
　　near ;

What if Thy form we cannot see ?
cres We know and feel that Thou art
here.

p O Saviour Christ, our woes dispel ;
For some are sick, and some are sad ;
And some have never loved Thee
well,
And some have lost the love they
had

[*mf* And some are pressed with worldly
care ;
And some are tried with ·sinful
doubt ; [tear
And some such grievous passions
That only Thou canst cast them out.

mf And some have found the world is
vain,
Yet from the world ·they break
not free :
p And some have friends who give
them pain,
Yet have not sought a friend in
Thee.]

mf And none, O Lord, have perfect
rest,
For none are wholly free from sin ;
And they who fain would serve
Thee best, [within.
*dim*Are conscious most of wrong

p O Saviour Christ, Thou too art
Man ;
Thou hast been troubled, tempted,
tried ; [scan
Thy kind but searching glance can
The very wounds that shame would
hide ;

f Thy touch has still its ancient
power ; [fall :
No word from Thee can fruitless
*dim*Hear in this solemn evening hour,
p And in Thy mercy heal us all.

H. Twells.

521   L.M.

f MILLIONS within Thy courts have
met, [bowed ;
Millions this day before Thee
Their faces Zionward were set,
*Vows with their lips to Thee they
vowed*

[*f* People of many a tribe and tongue,
Men of strange colours, climates.
lands, [sung
Have heard Thy truth, Thy glory
*dim*And offered prayer with holy
hands.

mf Still as the light of morning broke
O'er island, continent, or deep,
Thy far-spread family awoke,
Sabbath all round the world to
keep.

mf From east to west the sun surveyed,
From north to south, adoring
throngs,
And still where evening stretched
her shade
The stars came out to hear their
songs.]

mf And not a prayer, a tear, a sigh,
Hath failed this day some suit to
gain ; [nigh,
To those in trouble Thou wert
Not one hath sought Thy face in
vain.

mp Thy poor were bountifully fed,
Thy chastened sons have kissed
the rod,
Thy mourners have been comforted,
The pure in heart have seen their
God.

mp Yet one prayer more !—and be it
one accord ;—
In which both heaven and earth
*cres*Fulfil Thy promise to Thy Son,
Let all that breathe call Jesus,
Lord.

J. Montgomery.

522   S.M.

p   OUR day of praise is done ;
'The evening shadows fall ;

*cres*But pass not from us with the sun,
  True Light that light'nest all !

mf Around the Throne on high,
  Where night can never be.
  The white-robed harpers of the sky
  Bring ceaseless hymns to Thee.

p Too faint our anthems here :
  Too soon of praise we tire ;
*cres*But oh, the strains how full and
  clear
  Of that eternal choir !

mf Yet, Lord, to Thy dear will
  If Thou attune the heart,
  We in Thine angels' music still
  May bear our lower part.

mp 'Tis Thine each soul to calm,
  Each wayward thought reclaim,
  And make our life a daily psalm
  Of glory to Thy Name.

p A little while, and then
cres Shall come the glorious end ;
  And songs of angels and of men
f In perfect praise shall blend.

                J. Ellerton.

523   L.M.

mp AGAIN, as evening's shadow falls.
  We gather in these hallowed walls ;
  And evening hymn and evening
  prayer
  Rise mingling on the holy air.

mf May struggling hearts, that seek
  release,   [peace ;
  Here find the rest of God's own
  And strengthened here by hymn
  and prayer,
  Lay down the burden and the care.

mp O God our Light, to Thee we bow ;
  Within all shadows standest Thou ;
  Give deeper calm than night can
  bring ;
  Give sweeter songs than lips can
  sing.

mf Life's tumult we must meet again,
  We cannot at the shrine remain ;
  But in the spirit's secret cell,
  May hymn and prayer for ever
  dwell.

      S. Longfellow, v. 1, l. 3 altd.

2.—THE HOUSE OF PRAYER.

524   7s., 8 lines.

mf PLEASANT are Thy courts above,
  In the land of light and love ;
  Pleasant are Thy courts below,
  In this land of sin and woe :
*cres*O my spirit longs and faints
  For the converse of Thy saints,
  For the brightness of Thy face,
  For Thy fulness, God of grace.

mf Happy birds that sing and fly
  Round Thy altars, O Most High ;
  Happier souls that find a rest
p In a Heavenly Father's breast :

  Like the wandering dove that
  found
  No repose on earth around,
*cres*They can to their ark repair,
  And enjoy it ever there.

mp Happy souls ! their praises flow
  Even in this vale of woe ;
*cres*Waters in the desert rise,
  Manna feeds them from the skies :
f On they go from strength to
  strength,
  Till they reach Thy throne
  length,

p At Thy feet adoring fall,
ff Who hast led them safe through all.

p Lord, be mine this prize to win ;
Guide me through a world of sin ;
Keep me by Thy saving grace ;
Give me at Thy side a place :
mf Sun and Shield alike Thou art,
Guide and guard my erring heart ;
cres Grace and glory flow from Thee.—
f Shower, O shower them, Lord, on me.

H. F. Lyte.

525 L.M., with refrain.

mf HOSANNA to the living Lord !
Hosanna to the incarnate Word !
To Christ, Creator, Saviour, King,
Let earth. let heaven, Hosanna sing.
f Hosanna ! Lord ! Hosanna in the
highest !

mf " Hosanna," Lord, Thine angels cry;
" Hosanna," Lord, Thy saints reply:
Above, beneath us, and around,
The dead and living swell the
sound.
f Hosanna ! Lord ! Hosanna in the
highest !

mf O Saviour, with protecting care
Return to this Thy house of prayer,
Assembled in Thy sacred Name,
Where we Thy parting promise
claim.   [highest !
f Hosanna ! Lord ! Hosanna in the

p But, chiefest, in our cleansèd breast,
Eternal, bid Thy Spirit rest ;
And make our secret soul to be
cres A temple pure, and worthy Thee.
f Hosanna ! Lord ! Hosanna in the
highest !

p So, in the last and dreadful day,
When earth and heaven shall melt

cres Thy flock, redeemed from sinful
stain,
f Shall swell the sound of praise
again.
ff Hosanna ! Lord ! Hosanna in the
highest !

R. Heber.

526 6.6.6.6.4.4.4.4.

mf LORD of the worlds above,
How pleasant and how fair
The dwellings of Thy love,
Thine earthly temples are !
cres To Thine abode,
My heart aspires
With warm desires,
To see my God.

f O happy souls that pray
Where God appoints to hear !
O happy men that pay
Their constant service there !
cres They praise Thee still ;
And happy they
That love the way
To Zion's hill.

mf They go from strength to strength
Through this dark vale of tears.
cres Till each arrives at length,
Till each in heaven appears :
O glorious seat.
f When God our King
Shall thither bring
Our willing feet !

mf God is our sun and shield,
Our light and our defence :
With gifts His hands are fill
We draw our blessings thence
cres He shall bestow
On Jacob's race
Peculiar grace
And glory too.

f The Lord His people loves ;
His hand no good withholds
From those His heart approves,
From pure and pious souls :
cres   Thrice happy he,
O God of Hosts,
Whose spirit trusts
ff   Alone in Thee.
I. Watts.

527   L.M.

f How pleasant, how divinely fair,
O Lord of Hosts, Thy dwellings are !
With long desire my spirit faints
To meet the assemblies of Thy
saints.

mf My flesh would rest in Thine abode,
My panting heart cries out for
God ;   [be
My God, my King, why should I
So far from all my joys and Thee ?

mf Blest are the saints who sit on high
Around Thy throne of majesty :
Thy brightest glories shine above,
f And all their work is praise and
love.

mp Blest are the souls that find a place
Within the temple of Thy grace ;
There they behold Thy gentler rays,
cres And seek Thy face and learn Thy
praise.

mf Blest are the men whose hearts are
set
To find the way to Zion's gate ;
cres God is their strength, and through
the road
They lean upon their helper, God.

mf Cheerful they walk with growing
strength,
Till all shall meet in heaven at
length ;

cres Till all before Thy face appear,
f And join in nobler worship there.
I. Watts.

528   C.M.

f THE Lord of glory is my light,
And my salvation too :
God is my strength, nor will I
fear
What all my foes can do.

mf One privilege my heart desires :
O grant me an abode
Among the churches of Thy saints,
The temples of my God.

mf There shall I offer my requests,
And see Thy beauty still ;
Shall hear Thy messages of love,
And there inquire Thy will.

mp When troubles rise, and storms
appear,
There may His children hide :
cres God has a strong pavilion, where
He makes my soul abide.

mf Now shall my head be lifted
high
Above my foes around ;
f And songs of joy and victory
Within Thy temple sound.
I. Watts.

529   6.6.8.6.6.8.3.3.6.6.

mf   GOD is in His temple,
The Almighty Father !
Round His footstool let us gather:--
Him with adoration
Serve, the Lord most holy,
Who hath mercy on the lowly.
cres   Let us raise
Hymns of praise,
For His great salvation :—
f   God is in His temple !

mf Christ comes to His temple :
We, His word receiving.
Are made happy in believing.
Lo ! from sin delivered,
He hath turned our sadness,
Our deep gloom to light and gladness.
cres Let us raise
Hymns of praise,
For our bonds are severed :—
f Christ comes to His temple !

mf Come and claim Thy temple,
Gracious Holy Spirit !
In our hearts Thy home inherit:—
Make in us Thy dwelling,
Thy high work fulfilling ;
Into ours Thy will instilling
cres Till we raise
Hymns of praise,
Beyond mortal telling,
f In the eternal temple !
W. T. Matson.

3.—WORSHIP.

530   7s

f SING the great Jehovah's praise ;
Trophies to His glory raise :
Say,—How wonderful Thy deeds !
Lord, Thy power all power exceeds !

mf Let the many-peopled earth,
All, of high and humble birth,
Worship our eternal King ;
f Hymns unto His honour sing.

mf We, through fire, with flames embraced,
We, through raging floods, have passed ;
f Yet, by Thy conducting hand.
Brought into a wealthy land.

mf We will to Thy house repair,
Worship, and Thy power declare :
Offerings on Thine altar lay ;
All our vows devoutly pay.

dim Fervently to Thee we cried ;
We His goodness magnified :
cres Source of mercy, be Thou blest,
f That hast granted our request.
G. Sandys.

531   L.M.

f ALL people that on earth do dwell.
Sing to the Lord with cheerful voice ;   [forth tell ;
Him serve with fear, His praise
Come ye before Him and rejoice.

mf The Lord ye know is God indeed :
Without our aid He did us make :
We are His flock, He doth us feed ;
And for His sheep He doth us take.

ff O enter, then, His gates with praise,   [unto :
Approach with joy His courts
Praise, laud, and bless His Name always,
For it is seemly so to do.

f For why ? the Lord our God is good,
His mercy is for ever sure ;
cres His truth at all times firmly stood,
And shall from age to age endure.
W Kethe.

532   L.M.

f BEFORE Jehovah's awful throne
Ye nations bow with sacred joy :

:he Lord is God alone ;
te and He destroy.

ɲn power, without our
[men ;
' clay and formed us
like wandering sheep,
ɪ,
us to His fold again.

people, we His care,
and all our mortal
[rear,
ɪɡ honours shall we
[aker, to Thy Name ?

Thy gates with thank-
[raise :
.e heavens our voices
ɼith her ten thousand
[praise.
y courts with sounding

world is Thy command;
nity Thy love : [stand,
rock Thy truth shall
g years shall cease to

ɪtts, altd. C. Wesley.

C.M.
ɔur God ! Thou shinest

ɪ this latter day : ●
adiant steps appear,
Thy glorious way.

ɪt once our flesh ; Thy

ur darkness shone ;
ɪ each age new births
!
! Thy glory known.

ɪɛu ages felt
ɪce of the Lord :

Not only with the fathers dwelt
Thy Spirit and Thy Word.

mf Doth not the Spirit still descend
And bring the heavenly fire ?
Doth not He still Thy Church
extend,
And waiting souls inspire?

mp Come, Holy Ghost ! in us arise ;
Be this Thy mighty hour !
And make Thy willing people wise
To know Thy day of power !

[*mp*Pour down Thy fire in us to glow,
Thy might in us to dwell ;
Again Thy works of wonder show,
Thy blessèd secrets tell !]

*cres*Bear us aloft, more glad, more
strong
On Thy celestial wing, [long
And grant us grace to look and
For our returning King.

mf He draweth near, He standeth by,
He fills our eyes, our ears : [cry,
*cres*Come, King of grace, Thy people
f And bring the glorious years !
T. H. Gill.

534 7s.

f To Thy temple I repair ;
Lord, I love to worship there,
When within the veil I meet
Christ before the mercy-seat.

f While Thy glorious praise is sung,
Touch my lips, unloose my tongue,
That my joyful soul may bless
Thee, the Lord, my righteousness.

mf While the prayers of saints ascend,
God of love, to mine attend ;
p Hear me, for Thy Spirit pleads;
Hear, for Jesus intercedes.

mf While I hearken to Thy law,
Fill my soul with humble awe,
Till Thy gospel bring to me
Life and immortality.

mf While Thy ministers proclaim
Peace and pardon in Thy Name,
Through their voice, by faith. may I
Hear Thee speaking from the sky.

From Thy house when I return,
May my heart within me burn,
p And at evening let me say,—
I have walked with God to-day.

J. Montgomery.

535 L.M.

f O THOU, to Whom in ancient time
The lyre of Hebrew bards was
strung ; [sublime,
Whom kings adored in song
And prophets praised with glowing
tongue ;

f Not now on Zion's height alone,
Thy favoured worshippers may
dwell,
Nor where at sultry noon Thy Son
Sat weary by the patriarch's well :

f From every place below the skies,
The grateful song, the fervent
prayer,
The incense of the heart may rise
To heaven, and find acceptance
there.

mf To Thee shall age with snowy hair,
And strength and beauty bend the
knee ; [air,
And childhood lisp, with reverent
Its praises and its prayers to Thee.

f O Thou, to Whom in ancient time,
*The lyre of prophet bard was
strung,*

To Th
Shall
sun

536

f Ho
To
Come,
Yes
We
And t
p
f Zio
Ad
And
tl
In
To
The s
f The
Ha
He s
t
He
He
And l

mp Ma
An
To bl
Th
An
cres A th

mp My
Pe
For t

cres Ar
Ma
f My s

37 7.5.7.5.7.5.7.5.8.8.

f When the weary, seeking rest,
To Thy goodness flee ;
When the heavy-laden cast
All their load on Thee ;
' When the troubled, seeking peace,
On Thy Name shall call ;
When the sinner, seeking life,
At Thy feet shall fall :
*cres*Hear then in love. O Lord, the cry.
*dim*In heaven Thy dwelling-place on
high.

f When the worldling, sick at
heart,
Lifts his soul above ;
' When the prodigal looks back
To his Father's love ;
f When the proud man. in his pride.
Stoops to seek Thy face :
When the burdened brings his
guilt
To Thy throne of grace ;
*cres*Hear then in love, O Lord, the cry.
*dim*In heaven Thy dwelling-place on
high.

f When the stranger asks a home,
All his toils to end ;
When the hungry craveth food,
And the poor a friend ;
, When the sailor on the wave
Bows the fervent knee ;
When the soldier on the field
Lifts his heart to Thee :
*cres*Hear then in love, O Lord, the cry.
*dim*In heaven Thy dwelling-place on
high.

mf When the man of toil and care
In the city crowd ;
When the shepherd on the moor
Names the Name of God ;

When the learned and the high,
Tired of earthly fame,
Upon higher joys intent,
Name the blessèd Name :
*cres*Hear then in love, O Lord, the cry.
*dim*In heaven Thy dwelling-place on
high.]

mp When the child, with grave fresh
lip,
Youth or maiden fair ;
When the aged, weak and grey,
Seek Thy face in prayer ;
dim When the widow weeps to Thee,
Sad and lone and low ;
When the orphan brings to Thee
All his orphan woe :
*cres*Hear then in love, O Lord. the cry.
*dim*In heaven Thy dwelling-place on
high.

mp When creation, in her pangs,
Heaves her heavy groan ;
When Thy Salem's exiled sons
Breathe their bitter moan :
dim When Thy widowed, weeping
Church,
Looking for a home,
Sendeth up her silent sigh—
"Come. Lord Jesus, come :"
*cres*Hear then in love, O Lord, the cry,
*dim*In heaven Thy dwelling-place on
high.
H. Bonar.

538 7s.

f Praise the Lord, His glories show.
Saints within His courts below,
Angels round His throne above,
All that see and share His love.
*cres*Earth to heaven, and heaven to
earth,
Tell His wonders, sing His worth ;

Age to age and shore to shore,
ff Praise Him, praise Him, evermore !

f Praise the Lord, His mercies trace ;
Praise His providence and grace,
p All that He for man hath done,
*cres*All He sends us through His Son :

f Strings and voices, hands and hearts,
In the concert bear your parts ;
ff All that breathe, your Lord adore,
Praise Him, praise Him, evermore !
H. F. Lyte.

539 88.88.88.

mf Lo ! God is here ! Let us adore,
And own how dreadful is this place !
p Let all within us feel His power,
And silent bow before His face !
*cres*Who know His power, His grace
who prove. [love.
p Serve Him with awe, with reverence

mf Lo ! God is here ! Him day and night
*cres*The united quires of angels sing :
ff To Him, enthroned above all
height, [bring :
Heaven's hosts their noblest praises
*dim*Disdain not, Lord, our meaner song,
Who praise Thee with a stammer-
ing tongue !

mf Gladly the toys of earth we leave,
Wealth, pleasure, fame, for Thee
alone : [give ;
To Thee our will, soul, flesh, we
O take, O seal them for Thine own !
f Thou art the God ! Thou art the
Lord !
Be Thou by all Thy works adored !

ff Being of beings, may our praise
*Thy courts with grateful fragrance
fill ;*

Still may we stand before Thy face,
Still hear and do Thy sovereign
will !
To Thee may all our thoughts arise,
Ceaseless, accepted sacrifice !
G. Tersteegen, tr. J. Wesley.

540 L.M.

f SWEET is the work, my God, my
King,
To praise Thy Name, give thanks
and sing :
To show Thy love by morning light,
And talk of all Thy truth at night.

p Sweet is the day of sacred rest,
No mortal cares shall seize my
breast ;
O may my heart in tune be found,
Like David's harp of solemn sound.

f My heart shall triumph in my Lord,
And bless His works, and bless His
word :
Thy works of grace, how bright
they shine !
How deep Thy counsels ! how
divine !

mf But I shall share a glorious part,
When grace hath well refined my
heart,
*cres*And fresh supplies of joy are shed,
Like holy oil to cheer my head.

mp Sin, my worst enemy before,
Shall vex my eyes and ears no more:
My inward foes shall all be slain,
Nor Satan break my peace again.

f Then shall I see and hear and know
All I desired or wished below ;
And every power find sweet employ
In that eternal world of joy.
I. Watts.

541 L.M.

f PRAISE, Lord, for Thee in Zion
    waits ;   [gates ;
  Prayer shall besiege Thy temple-
  All flesh shall to Thy throne repair,
  And find, through Christ, salvation
    there.

p Our spirits faint ; our sins prevail;
  Leave not our trembling hearts to
    fail :
  O Thou that hearest prayer, descend,
  And still be found the sinner's
    Friend.

mf How blest Thy saints ! how safely
    led !
  How surely kept ! how richly fed !
  Saviour of all in earth and sea,
dim How happy they who rest in Thee!

mf Thy hand sets fast the mighty hills,
  Thy voice the troubled ocean stills ;
cres Evening and morning hymn Thy
    praise,   [plays.
  And earth Thy bounty wide dis-

mf The year is with Thy goodness
    crowned ;   [around ;
  Thy clouds drop wealth the world
cres Through Thee the deserts laugh
    and sing.   [King.
  And Nature smiles, and owns her

p Lord, on our souls Thy Spirit pour:
  The moral waste within restore :
cres O let Thy love our spring-tide be,
  And make us all bear fruit to Thee.
                        H. F. Lyte.

542 7s., 6 lines.

f LORD of power, Lord of might !
  God and Father of us all ;
  Lord of day, and Lord of night,
  Listen to our solemn call :

  Listen, whilst to Thee we raise
  Songs of prayer, and songs of praise.

mf Light, and love, and life are Thine,
  Great Creator of all good ;
  Fill our souls with light divine ;
  Give us with our daily food
  Blessings from Thy heavenly store,
  Blessings rich for evermore.

mf Graft within our heart of hearts
  Love undying for Thy Name ;
  Bid us ere the day departs
  Spread afar our Maker's fame :
  Young and old together bless,
  Clothe our souls with righteousness.

mp Full of years, and full of peace,
  May our life on earth be blest ;
  When our trials here shall cease,
dim And at last we sink to rest,
cres Fountain of eternal love !
  Call us to our home above.
                        G. Thring.

543 S.M.

mf STAND up and bless the Lord,
  Ye people of His choice ;
  Stand up and bless the Lord your
    God,
  With heart and soul and voice.

mf Though high above all praise,
  Above all blessing high,
p Who would not fear His holy
    Name,
cres And laud and magnify ?

mf O for the living flame
  From His own altar brought
  To touch our lips, our minds in-
    spire,
cres And wing to heaven our thoughts !

mf There, with benign regard,
  Our hymns He deigns to hear

Though unrevealed to mortal sense,
The spirit feels Him near.

f   God is our strength and song,
And His salvation ours ; [claimed
Then be His love in Christ pro-
With all our ransomed powers.

ff Stand up and bless the Lord ;
The Lord your God adore: [Name,
Stand up and bless His glorious
Henceforth for evermore.

J. Montgomery.

544
            6.5.6.5., 8 lines.

f WITH gladness we worship,
Rejoice as we sing,
Free hearts and free voices
How blessèd to bring.
The old. thankful story
Shall scale Thine abode,
Thou King of all glory,
Most bountiful God.

f Thy right would we give Thee,
True homage Thy due,
And honour eternal
The universe through.
With all Thy creation,
Earth, heaven. and sea.
In one acclamation,
We celebrate Thee.

mf Renewed by Thy Spirit,
Redeemed by Thy Son ;
Thy children revere Thee
For all Thou hast done.
O Father, returning
To love and to light,
Thy children are yearning
To praise Thee aright.

f We join with the angels,
And so there is given
From earth, Hallelujah.
In answer to heaven.

Amen
Belc
Redeei
And

545
f SONGS of
Heaver
When Je
When H

f Songs of
When th
vurn ;
Songs of
Captive l

mf Heaven ɛ
cres Songs of
day ;
f God will
Songs of
birth.

p And can
Till that
cres No : the
Psalms. ɛ
praise.

mf Saints be
Still in sɛ
cres Learning
f Songs of

mf Borne uƥ
Songs of ƥ
cres Then, an
f Songs of ƥ

546
f SING we
stanɗ
Arounɗ

Of every kindred, clime, and land,
A multitude unknown.

mf Life's poor distinctions vanish here;
To-day the young, the old.
Our Saviour and His flock appear,
One Shepherd and one fold.

mp Toil, trial, suffering still await
On earth the pilgrim-throng ;
cres Yet learn we in our low estate
The Church triumphant's song;—

f Worthy the Lamb for sinners slain,
Cry the redeemed above,
Blessing and honour to obtain,
And everlasting love.

f Worthy the Lamb, on earth we
sing,
Who died our souls to save ;
Henceforth, O Death, where is Thy
sting ?
Thy victory, O Grave?

f Then, Hallelujah! power and praise
To God, in Christ, be given ;
May all who now this anthem raise
Renew the strain in Heaven.

J. Montgomery.

547   7.7.7.5.

mf GOD of pity, God of grace,
When we humbly seek Thy face,
Bend from heaven. Thy dwelling-
place :
p Hear, forgive, and save.

mf When we in Thy temple meet,
Spread our wants before Thy feet,
Pleading at the mercy-seat :
p Look from heaven and save.

mf When Thy love our hearts shall
fill,
And we long to do Thy will,

Turning to Thy holy hill ;
p Lord, accept and save.

p Should we wander from Thy fold
And our love to Thee grow cold,
With a pitying eye behold ;
pp Lord, forgive and save.

p Should the hand of sorrow press,
Earthly care and want distress,
cres May our souls Thy peace possess :
Jesus, hear and save.

mf And whate'er our cry may be,
When we lift our hearts to Thee,
cres From our burden set us free :
p Hear, forgive, and save.

Eliza F. Morris.

548   8.7.8.7.4.7.

mf IN Thy Name, O Lord, assembling,
We, Thy people, now draw
near ;
p Teach us to rejoice with trembling,
Speak, and let Thy servants hear;
Hear with meekness,
Hear Thy word with godly fear.

mf While our days on earth are
lengthened,
May we give them, Lord, to Thee;
cres Cheered by hope, and daily
strengthened,
May we run, nor weary be,
f Till Thy glory,
Without clouds in heaven we see.

f There, in worship purer, sweeter,
Thee Thy people shall adore ;
Tasting of enjoyment greater
Far than thought conceived
before ;
ff Full enjoyment,
Full, unmixed and evermore.

T. Kell

549 12.10.12.10.

f O WORSHIP the Lord in the beauty
of holiness, [proclaim;
Bow down before Him, His glory
With gold of obedience, and incense
of lowliness.
Kneel and adore Him, the Lord
is His Name.

mp Low at His feet lay Thy burden of
carefulness, [it for thee,
High on His heart He will bear
Comfort thy sorrows, and answer
thy prayerfulness,
Guiding thy steps as may best for
thee be.

mf Fear not to enter His courts in the
slenderness [reckon as thine:
Of the poor wealth thou would'st

Truth in its beauty, and love in its
tenderness,
These are the offerings to lay at
His shrine.

mp These, though we bring them in
trembling and fearfulness,
He will accept for the Name that
is dear; [of tearfulness,
*cres*Mornings of joy give for evenings
Trust for our trembling, and hope
for our fear.

f O worship the Lord in the beauty
of holiness, [proclaim;
Bow down before Him, His glory
With gold of obedience, and incense
of lowliness,
Kneel and adore Him, the Lord
is His Name.

J. S. B. Monsell.

4.—THE CLOSE OF WORSHIP.

550 10.10.10.10.

f SAVIOUR, again to Thy dear Name
we raise
With one accord our parting hymn
of praise; [worship cease,
We stand to bless Thee ere our
p Then lowly kneeling, wait Thy
word of peace.

mp Grant us Thy peace upon our
homeward way;
*cres*With Thee begun, with Thee shall
end the day;
mf Guard Thou the lips from sin, the
hearts from shame,
That in this house have called
upon Thy Name.

mp Grant us Thy peace, Lord, through
the coming night, [into light;
*cres*Turn Thou for us its darkness

mf From harm and danger keep Thy
children free, [to Thee.
For dark and light are both alike

mp Grant us Thy peace throughout
our earthly life,
*cres*Our balm in sorrow, and our stay
in strife; [conflicts cease,
mf Then, when Thy voice shall bid our
pp Call us, O Lord, to Thine eternal
peace.

J. Ellerton.

551 C.M.

mp THE Lord be with us as we bend
His blessing to receive;
His gift of peace upon us send,
Before His courts we leave.

mp The Lord be with us as we walk
Along our homeward road;

In silent thought or friendly talk,
  Our hearts be still with God.
mp The Lord be with us till the night
  Enfold our day of rest ;
  Be He of every heart the Light,
  Of every home the Guest.
mp And when our nightly prayers we
    say,
  His watch He still shall keep,
  Crown with His grace His own
    blest day,
  And guard His people's sleep.
             J. Ellerton.

552
         6.5., 8 lines.

f   ON our way rejoicing,
  As we homeward move,
  Hearken to our praises,
  O Thou God of love !
  Is there grief or sadness ?
  Thine it cannot be.:
  If our sky be clouded,
  Clouds are not from Thee.

nf   If with honest-hearted
  Love for God and man,
  Day by day Thou find us
  Doing all we can,
  Thou Who giv'st the seed-time,
  Wilt give large increase,
p   Crown the head with blessings,
  Fill the heart with peace.

f   On our way rejoicing,
  Gladly let us go,
  Victor is the Leader !
  Vanquished is the foe !
  Christ without—our safety !
  Christ within—our joy !
  Who, if we be faithful,
  Can our hope destroy ?

Unto God the Father !
  Joyful songs we sing ;

Unto God the Saviour !
  Thankful hearts we bring ;
Unto God the Spirit !
  Bow we and adore,
On our way rejoicing,
  Ever, evermore !
          J. S. B. Monsell.

553
      L.M., with refrain.

mf SWEET Saviour, bless us ere we go .
  Thy word into our minds instil ;
cres And make our lukewarm hearts to
    glow
  With lowly love and fervent will.
f   Through life's long day and
    death's dark night,
cres   O gentle Jesus, be our light.

[*p* The day is done, its hours have
    run,
  And Thou hast taken count of all—
  The scanty triumphs grace hath
    won,
  The broken vow, the frequent fall.
f   Through life's long day and
    death's dark night,
cres   O gentle Jesus, be our light.]

mp Grant us, dear Lord, from evil ways
  True absolution and release ;
  And bless us more than in past
    days
  With purity and inward peace.
f   Through life's long day and
    death's dark night,
cres   O gentle Jesus, be our light.

f Do more than pardon ; give us joy
  Sweet fear and sober liberty ;
  And loving hearts without alloy,
  That only long to be like Thee.
  Through life's long day and
    death's dark night,
cres   O gentle Jesus, be our light.

mf Labour is sweet, for Thou hast
    toiled ;
    And care is light, for Thou hast
    cared :
p Let not our works with self be
    soiled,·
    Nor in unsimple ways ensnared.
f   Through life's long day and
    death's dark night,
cres O gentle Jesus, be our light.

p For all we love—the poor, the sad,
    The sinful—unto Thee we call ;
cres O let Thy mercy make us glad :
    Thou art our Jesus and our All.
f   Through life's long day and
    death's dark night,
cres O gentle Jesus, be our light.

               F. W. Faber.

554   8.7.8.7.4.7.

mf LORD, dismiss us with Thy blessing,
    Fill our hearts with joy and
    peace :
    Let us all, Thy love possessing,
    Triumph in redeeming grace :
cres   O refresh us,
    Travelling through this wilder-
    ness.   ·

f Thanks we give, and adoration,
    For Thy gospel's joyful sound :
    May the fruits of Thy salvation
    In our hearts and lives abound.
    May Thy presence
    With us evermore be found.

 So, whene'er the signal's given,
    Us from earth to call away,
cres Borne on angels' wings to heaven,
    Glad the summons to obey.
f   May we ever
    Reign with Christ in endless day.
                J. Fawcett.

555

mf AND no·
    bro
    Thy c
    Here li
    nou
    But s

mf The hop
    Absor
    That g:
    pra
    For b

mf For Th
    Sar
    O'er ɛ
    And rou
    Naɪ
    There

mp O wonɔ
    dwɵ
    On eɪ
    To kno
    tell
    How

mf O Thou
    O'er t
    Thy veɪ
    To wɵ

mp For wh
    Thɵ
    A tas
    We say
    He
    And]

f All gloɪ
    All g
    All gloɪ
    Whilɵ

5.—*PRAYER MEETINGS.*

556   C.M.

mf BEHOLD us, Lord, a little space,
    From daily tasks set free,
And met within Thy holy place
    To rest awhile with Thee.

f Around us rolls the ceaseless tide
    Of business, toil, and care,
And scarcely can we turn aside
    For one brief hour of prayer.

nf Yet these are not the only walls
    Wherein Thou mayest be sought;
On homeliest work Thy blessing
      falls
In truth and patience wrought.

f Thine is the loom, the forge, the
      mart
    The wealth of land and sea ;
The worlds of science and of art,
    Revealed and ruled by Thee.

mf Then let us prove our heavenly
      birth
    In all we do and know ;
And claim the kingdom of the earth
    For Thee, and not Thy foe.

mf Work shall be prayer, if all be
      wrought
    As Thou would'st have it done ;
ad prayer, by Thee inspired and
      taught,
    Itself with work be one.

                  J. Ellerton.

557   C.M.

mp LORD, teach us how to pray aright,
    With reverence and with fear ;
Though dust and ashes in Thy sight,
    We may, we must draw near.

mp Burdened with guilt, convinced of
      sin,
    In weakness, want, and woe, [in,
Fightings without, and fears with
    Lord, whither shall we go ?

mp God of all grace, we come to Thee
    With broken, contrite hearts ;
Give, what Thine eye delights
      to see,
    Truth in the inward parts.

[*p* Give deep humility ; the sense
    Of godly sorrow give ;
cres A strong, desiring confidence
    To hear Thy voice and live ;]

mp Faith in the only sacrifice
    That can for sin atone ;
cres To cast our hopes, to fix our eyes
    On Christ, on Christ alone ;

[*mp* Patience to watch, and wait, and
      weep,
    Though mercy long delay ;
cres Courage, our fainting souls to
      keep,
    And trust Thee, though Thou
      slay ;]

mf Give these,—and then Thy will be
      done ;
    Thus strengthened with all
      might,
cres We by Thy Spirit, and Thy Son,
    Shall pray, and pray aright.

              J. Montgomery.

558   8.8.8.

mf O LORD, it is a blessèd thing
    To Thee both morn and night to
      bring
Our worship's lowly offering :—

mp And, from the strife of tongues
away,
' Ere toil begins, to meet and pray
For blessings on the coming day :—

f And night by night for evermore
Again with blended voice to pour
Deep thanks for mercies gone
before.

mp O Jesu, be our morning Light,
That we may go forth to the fight
*cres*With strength renewed and armour
bright.

mp And when our daily work is o'er,
And sins and weakness we deplore,
*cres*Oh, then be Thou our Light once
more.

uf Light of the world ! with us
abide,
And to Thyself our footsteps guide
At morn, and noon, and eventide.

W. W. How.

559
7s.

uf COME, my soul, thy suit prepare ;
Jesus loves to answer prayer :
He Himself has bid thee pray :
Therefore will not say thee, Nay.

mf Thou art coming to a King ;
Large petitions with thee bring ;
For His grace and power are such.
None can ever ask too much.

mp With my burden I begin :   '
Lord, remove this load of sin ;
Let Thy blood, for sinners spilt,
Set my conscience free from guilt.

mp Lord, I come to Thee for rest,
Take possession of my breast ;
There Thy blood-bought right
maintain,
And without a rival reign.

[*mf*As the image in the glass
Answers the beholder's face;
Thus unto my heart appear,
Print Thine own resemblance the

mp While I am a pilgrim here,
Let Thy love my spirit cheer;
As my Guide, my Guard, my Frie
Lead me to my journey's end.]

mf Show me what I have to do ;
*cres*Every hour my strength. renew;
f Let me live a life of faith ;
*dim*Let me die Thy people's death.

J. Newton.

560
C.M.

mp SHEPHERD Divine, our wa
relieve,
In this our evil day ;
To all Thy tempted followers g
The power to watch and pray.

mp Long as our fiery trials last.
Long as the cross we bear,
*cres*O let our souls on Thee be cast,
In never-ceasing prayer !

mp Thy Spirit's interceding grace
Give us in faith to claim ;
*cres*To wrestle till we see Thy face,
And know Thy hidden Name.

f Till Thou Thy perfect love imp
Till Thou Thyself bestow,
Be this the cry of every heart,—
"I will not let Thee go."

f "I will not let Thee go, unless
Thou tell Thy Name to me ;
*cres*With all Thy great salvation bl
And make me all like Thee."

f Then let me, on the moun
top,
Behold Thine open face,

*cres*Where faith in sight is swallowed up,
And prayer in endless praise.
C. Wesley.

561   C.M.

mf APPROACH, my soul, the mercy-seat,
    Where Jesus answers prayer;
There humbly fall before His feet,
    For none can perish there.

mp Thy promise is my only plea;
    With this I venture nigh:
Thou callest burdened souls to Thee,
dim And such, O Lord, am I.

p Bowed down beneath a load of sin,
    By Satan sorely pressed,
By wars without, and fears within,
    I come to Thee for rest.

mp Be Thou my shield and hiding-place,
    That, sheltered near Thy side,
*cres*I may my fierce accuser face,
f And tell him, Thou hast died.

mf O wondrous love to bleed and die,
    To bear the cross and shame,
That guilty sinners, such as I,
    Might plead Thy gracious Name!
J. Newton.

562   S.M.

mf BEHOLD the throne of grace,
    The promise calls me near:
There Jesus shows a smiling face.
    And waits to answer prayer.

mf That rich atoning blood,
    Which sprinkled round I see,
Provides for those who come to God
    An all-*prevailing* plea.

mp My soul, ask what thou wilt,
    Thou canst not be too bold:
Since His own blood for thee He spilt,
    What else can He withhold?

mf Beyond thine utmost wants,
    His love and power can bless:
To praying souls He always grants
    More than they can express.

mf Thine image, Lord, bestow,
    Thy presence and Thy love:
*cres*I ask to serve Thee here below,
f And reign with Thee above.
J. Newton.

563   L.M.

mp LORD, let me pray; I know not how
    Nor what to pray for—Thou must show;
The darkest, feeblest, need the most
    The "praying in the Holy Ghost."

mp What can man do, himself alone,
    Beyond a faithless, useless moan?
Helper of man's infirmity,
    O God the Spirit! help Thou me.

mf Descend, O purity Divine,
    And stoop to sins and wants like mine;
Humble Thyself to all my need,
    And in me, for me, with me plead.

mf Spirit of Holiness! control,
    Dilate, inspire, pervade my soul:
Make it a harp, from whose poor strings   [brings.
    Thy hand the suppliant music

f Make it a voice for heavenly thought,   [wrought;
    Spirit of power! by Thee in-
*dim*Thou tender Spirit! breathe in
    The tenderness of Deity.

mf Then God will hear ; He knows
    right well   [tell,
    The holy mind : Thy groanings
cres All interceding might is there ;
    Spirit of God ! pray Thou the
    prayer.

              G. Rawson.

564   L.M.

mf JESUS, our best-belovèd Friend,
    Draw out our souls in pure desire ;
    Jesus, in love to us descend ;
    Baptize us with Thy Spirit's fire.

mf On Thy redeeming Name we call,
    Poor and unworthy though we be ;
    Pardon and sanctify us all ;
    Let each Thy full salvation see.

mf Our souls and bodies we resign,
    To fear and follow Thy commands :
    . O take our hearts ; our hearts are
      Thine ;
    Accept the service of our hands.

f Firm, faithful, watching unto
      prayer,
    May we Thy blessèd will obey ;
    Toil in Thy vineyard here, and
      bear
    The heat and burden of the day.

mp Yet, Lord, for us a resting-place
    In heaven, at Thy right hand,
      prepare ;
cres And till we see Thee face to face,
    Be all our conversation there.

             J. Montgomery.

565   C.M.

mp LORD, when we bend before Thy
      throne,
    And our confessions pour,
    Teach us to feel the sins we own,
    And hate what we deplore.

mp Our broken spirits pitying see,
    And penitence impart ;
cres Then let a kindling glance from
      Thee
    Beam hope upon the heart.

mf When we disclose our wants in
      prayer,
    May we our wills resign,
    And not a thought our bosoms
      share,
    That is not wholly Thine.

mp Let faith each meek petition fill,
    And waft it to the skies ;
mf And teach our hearts 'tis goodness
      still,
    That grants it or denies.

             J. D. Carlyle.

566   7s.

mp LORD, we come before Thee now ;
    At Thy feet we humbly bow :
    O do not our suit disdain :
    Shall we seek Thee, Lord, in vain ?

mp Lord, on Thee our souls depend ;
    In compassion now descend :
    Fill our hearts with Thy rich
      grace :
    Tune our lips to sing Thy praise.

mp In Thine own appointed way,
    Now we seek Thee : here we stay :
    Lord, from hence we would not go,
    Till a blessing Thou bestow.

mf Send some message from Thy
      word,
    That may joy and peace afford ;
cres Let Thy Spirit now impart
    Full salvation to each heart.

p Comfort those who weep and
      mourn :
    Let the time of joy return :

*cres*Those that are cast down lift up ;
  f Make them strong in faith and hope.
mf Grant that those who seek may find
  Thee, a God supremely kind :

*cres*Heal the sick ; the captive free :
  f Let us all rejoice in Thee.

W. Hammond, v. 3, l. 3 ; v. 5. l. 4 ;
v. 6, l. 2 altd.

[SEE ALSO SECTION VII. 7, 8, 11, 13, 18.]

X.
Christian Missions.
1.—THEIR NECESSITY.

567   6.6.4.6.6.6.4.

f CHRIST for the world we sing !
  The world to Christ we bring,
    With loving zeal ;
mf The poor, and them that mourn,
  The faint and overborne,
  Sin-sick and sorrow-worn,
    Whom Christ doth heal.

f Christ for the world we sing !
  The world to Christ we bring,
    With fervent prayer ;
mp The wayward and the lost,
  By restless passions tossed,
  Redeemed at countless cost,
    From dark despair.

f Christ for the world we sing !
  The world to Christ we bring,
    With one accord :
  With us the work to share,
  With us reproach to dare,
  With us the Cross to bear,
    For Christ our Lord.

f Christ for the world we sing !
  The world to Christ we bring,
    With joyful song ;
  The new-born souls, whose days,
  Reclaimed from error's ways,
  Inspired with hope and praise,
    To Christ belong.
        S. Wolcott.

568   8.7.8f., double.

mf SAVIOUR, sprinkle many nations,
  Fruitful let Thy sorrows be,
  By Thy pains and consolations
  Draw the Gentiles unto Thee ;
*cres*Of Thy cross the wondrous story
  Be to all the nations told ;
  Let them see Thee in Thy glory,
  And Thy mercy manifold.

mf Far and wide, though all un-
    knowing,   [breast ;
  Pants for Thee each mortal
*dim*Human tears for Thee are flowing,
  Human hearts in Thee would
    rest.
  Thirsting, as for dews of even,
  As the new-mown grass for rain,
  Thee they seek, as God of heaven,
  Thee, as Man, for sinners slain.

mf Saviour, lo ! the isles are waiting,
  Stretched the hand, and strained
    the sight,
  For Thy Spirit, new creating [light;
  Love's pure flame and wisdom's
*cres*Give the word, and of the preacher
  Speed the foot, and touch the
    tongue,
f Till on earth by every creature
ff Glory to the Lamb be sung.
        A. C. Coxe.

569   P.M.

(*For Sunday Schools.*)

f MARCH on, march on, ye soldiers
true,
  In the Cross of Christ confiding,
For the field is set, and the hosts
are met,
  And the Lord His own is guiding.

mf Through the earth's wide round, we
the tidings sound   [heaven;
  Of the Lord Who came from
Of the mighty hope, that with
death can cope,
  And the love so freely given.
f   March on, etc.

[*f* We march to fight with the powers
of night
  That hold the world in sorrow;
dim And the broken heart shall be
healed of its smart,
cres And arise to a joyful morrow.
f   March on, etc.]

mf We fight against wrong, with the
weapon strong,   [banish;
  Of the Love that all hate shall
mf And the chains shall fall from the
down-trodden thrall, [vanish.
  As the thrones of the tyrant
f   March on, etc.

[*mf* O'er the realms of night, shall our
standard bright
  Arise, their darkness clearing;
cres And the souls that were dead to
the Lord Who bled,
  Shall revive at His glad
appearing.
f   March on, etc.]

mf Long, long is the fight, but the God
of light
  Is ever watching near us;

cres And prayers that rise
listening skies
  Like a song of hope a
f   March on, etc.

f Till the sunrise broad (
of God
  Shall shine on the
glory,   [
mf And earth at rest, in
cres Shall rejoice in the
story.
f   March on, marc
soldiers true,
  In the Cross of (
fiding, [host
For the field is se
  And the Lord I
guiding.

570   7.6.7.6.,

mf FROM Greenland's icy m
From India's coral str
Where Afric's sunny fo
Roll down their golde
From many an ancient i
From many a palmy p
They call us to deliver
Their land from error

mf What though the spicy
Blow soft o'er Ceylon'
Though every prospect i
And only man is vile
mp In vain, with lavish kin
The gifts of God are s
dim The heathen, in his blin
p Bows down to wood i
mf Can we, whose souls are
With wisdom from or
Can we to men benighte
The lamp of life deny

on ! O salvation ı
joyful sound proclaim,
ch remotest nation
learned Messiah's name.

waft, ye winds, His story ;
you, ye waters, roll. .

Till, like a sea of glory,
　It spreads from pole to pole ;
*cres*Till, o'er our ransomed nature,
　The Lamb for sinners slain,
ff Redeemer, King, Creator,
　In bliss returns to reign.

R. Heber.

2.—*PRAYER FOR THEIR SUCCESS.*

L.M.

ıɪᴛ of the living God,
Thy plenitude of grace,
'er the foot of man hath trod
d on our apostate race.

ongues of fire and hearts of

ach the reconciling word ;
ower and unctionfrom above,
'er the joyful sound is heard.

kness, at Thy coming, light ;
ion, order in Thy path :
　without strength inspire
ı might ;
ercy triumph over wrath.

it of the Lord, prepare
e round earth her God to
t ; 　　　　　　　[air,
ıe Thou abroad like morning
arts of stone begin to beat.

e the nations : far and nigh
iumphs of the cross record :
ıme of Jesus glorify,
ery kindred call Him Lord.

om eternity hath willed
sh shall His salvation see :
the Father's love fulfilled,
aviour's sufferings crowned
ugh Thee.

J. Montgomery.

572　　　　7s., 6 lines.

mf GOD of mercy, God of grace,
　Show the brightness of Thy face.
*cres*Shine upon us. Saviour. shine !
　Fill Thy Church with life divine ;
　And Thy saving health extend
　Unto earth's remotest end.

f Let the people praise Thee, Lord ;
　Be by all that live adored :
　Let the nations shout and sing
　Glory to their Saviour King ;
　At Thy feet their tributes pay,
　And Thy holy will obey.

f Let the people praise Thee, Lord ;
　Earth shall then her fruits afford
　God to man His blessing give ;
　Man to God devoted live :
　All below, and all above,
　One in joy and light and love.

H. F. Lyte.

573　　　　S.M.

f　COME ı kingdom of our God,
　Sweet reign of light and love,
　Shed peace and hope and joy abroad,
　And wisdom from above.

mf　Over our spirits first
　Extend Thy healing reign ;
*cres*Then raise and quench the sacred
　　thirst
　That never pains again.

mf Come! kingdom of our God,
    And make the broad earth Thine;
Stretch o'er her lands and isles the
    rod
    That flowers with grace divine.

mf Soon may all tribes be blest
    With fruit from Life's glad tree ;
And in its shade like brothers rest,
    Sons of one family.

f Come! kingdom of our God,
    And raise Thy glorious throne
cres In worlds by the undying trod,
    Where God shall bless His own.

                  J. Johns.

574   6.6.4.6.6.6.4.

mf THOU, Whose almighty word,
    Chaos and darkness heard,
cres   And took their flight,
p Hear us, we humbly pray ;
cres And where the gospel's day
    Sheds not its glorious ray,
ff   Let there be light.

mf Thou Who didst come to bring
    On Thy redeeming wing
cres   Healing and sight,
p Health to the sick in mind,
cres Sight to the inly blind,
    O now to all mankind
ff   Let there be light.

mf Spirit of truth and love,—
    Life-giving, Holy Dove,—
cres   Speed forth Thy flight,
p Move on the waters' face,
cres Bearing the lamp of grace,
    And in earth's darkest place
ff   Let there be light.

f Holy and blessèd Three !
  Glorious Trinity ;
cres   Wisdom ! Love ! Might !

---

ff Boundless as ocea
    Rolling in fullest
    Through the eartl
ff   Let there be l

575

mf LIGHT of the l
    heart,
    Star of the comi
Arise, and, with
    Chase all our gr

mf Come, blessèd Lord
    And answering
The praises of Th}
    And own Thee a

mf Bid the whole eartl
    To the bright w<
f Break forth in rap
    In memory of T

mp Lord, Lord, Thy
    groans,
    The air, the eart
cres In unison with all
f   And calls aloud :

mf Come, then, with a
    ing power,
With one awake
And bid the serpen
    Thy beauteous r<

mf Thine was the c<
    fruits
    Of grace and pe<
cres Be Thine the crow
f   The palm of vict

576

f O LORD our God
    The cause of tru

le o'er all the peopled world
d her blessèd reign.

Prince of Life, arise,
t Thy glory cease ;
ead the conquests of Thy
ce.
less the earth with peace.

Holy Ghost, arise,
d Thy quickening wing,
r a dark and ruined world
ght and order spring.

the earth arise,
d the Saviour sing ;
ore to shore, from earth to
ven,
hoing anthems ring.

R. Wardlaw.

L.M.

ITY God, Whose only Son
nd death the triumph won,
r lives to intercede
ls who Thy sweet mercy

lear Name to Thee we pray
who err and go astray,
ers, whereso'er they be,
not serve and honour Thee.

e who never yet have heard
ngs of Thy blessèd word,
in heathen darkness dwell,
one thought of heaven or

ne within Thy sacred fold
things are dead and cold,
te the precious hours of life
ease, or toil, or strife :

y a quickened soul within
rks the secret love of sin,

A wayward will, or anxious fears,
Or lingering taint of bygone years.]

mf O give repentance true and deep
To all Thy lost and wandering
sheep,
cres And kindle in their hearts the fire
Of holy love and pure desire.

f That so from angel-hosts above
May rise a sweeter song of love,
And we, with all the blest, adore
Thy Name, O God, for evermore.

H. W. Baker.

578
L.M.

mf JESUS, Thy Church with longing
eyes
For Thy expected coming waits :
When will the promised light arise.
cres And glory beam from Zion's gates ?

mf Ev'n now, when tempests round us
fall,
And wintry clouds o'ercast the sky,
Thy words with pleasure we recall,
And deem that our redemption's
nigh.

mp Come, gracious Lord, our hearts
renew,
Our foes repel, our wrongs redress,
Man's rooted enmity subdue,
And crown Thy Gospel with
success.

mf O come, and reign o'er every land ;
Let Satan from his throne be
hurled ;
All nations bow to Thy command
And grace revive a dying world !

mf Yes, Thou wilt speedily appear !
The smitten earth already reels ;
cres And not far off we seem to hear
f The thunder of Thy chariot wheels

mp Teach us in watchfulness and
prayer
To wait for the appointed hour ;

cres And fit us by Thy grace to share
f The triumphs of Thy conquering
power.

W. H. Bathurst.

3.—ANTICIPATION OF THEIR FINAL SUCCESS.

579   L.M.

f JESUS shall reign where'er the sun
Doth his successive journeys run ;
His kingdom stretch from shore to
shore,
Till moons shall wax and wane no
more.

mf For Him shall endless prayer be
made,   [head ;
And praises throng to crown His
His Name like sweet perfume shall
rise
With every morning sacrifice.

f People and realms of every tongue
Dwell on His love with sweetest
song ;
mp And infant voices shall proclaim
cres Their early blessings on His Name.

f Blessings abound where'er He
reigns ;   [chains ;
The prisoner leaps to lose his
dim The weary find eternal rest,
cres And all the sons of want are blest.

f Let every creature rise and bring
Peculiar honours to our King ;
ff Angels descend with songs again,
And earth repeat the loud Amen.

I. Watts, v. 2, l. 2 altd.

580   7s., 8 lines.

f HARK ! the song of jubilee,
Loud as mighty thunders roar,
Or the fulness of the sea.
When it breaks upon the shore :

"Hallelujah ! for the Lord
God omnipotent shall reign :
cres Hallelujah ! " let the word
ff Echo round the earth and main.

f "Hallelujah ! " Hark ! the sound
From the depths unto the skies,
Wakes above, beneath, around,
All creation's harmonies ;
See Jehovah's banner furled,
Sheathed His sword ; He speaks—
'tis done,
cres And the kingdoms of this world
ff Are the kingdoms of His Son.

f He shall reign from pole to pole
With illimitable sway ;
He shall reign when like a scroll
Yonder heavens have passed away :
Then the end ; beneath His rod
Man's last enemy shall fall ;
cres "Hallelujah ! " Christ in God,
ff God in Christ is All in all !

J. Montgomery.

581   C.M.

f BEHOLD ! the Mountain of the
Lord
In latter days shall rise
On mountain tops, above the hills,
And draw the wondering eyes.

f To this the joyful nations round,
All tribes and tongues shall
flow ;
Up to the hill of God, they'll say,
And to His house we'll go.

f The beam that shines from Zion hill
    Shall lighten every land ;
    The King Who reigns in Salem's
      towers
    Shall all the world command.

mp No strife shall vex Messiah's reign,
    Or mar the peaceful years ;
    To ploughshares men shall beat
      their swords,
    To pruning-hooks their spears.

mf No longer hosts encountering hosts
    Their millions slain deplore ;
    They hang the trumpet in the hall,
    And study war no more.

mf Come, then ! O, come, from every
      land,
    To worship at His shrine ;
cres And, walking in the Light of
      God,
    With holy beauties shine.
             M. Bruce.

582   L.M.

f From all that dwell below the skies
    Let the Creator's praise arise ;
    Let the Redeemer's Name be sung
    Through every land, by every
      tongue !

f Eternal are Thy mercies, Lord !
    Eternal truth attends Thy word :
ff Thy praise shall sound from shore
      to shore,
    Till suns shall rise and set no more.
             I. Watts.

583   S.M., double.

mf Father of boundless grace,
    Thou hast in part fulfilled
    Thy promise made to Adam's race,
    In *God Incarnate* sealed :

    A few from every land
    At first to Salem came,
cres And saw the wonders of Thy
      hand,
    And saw the tongues of flame ;

mp Yet still we wait the end,
    The coming of our Lord :
    The full accomplishment attend
    Of Thy prophetic word.
    Thy promise deeper lies,
    In unexhausted grace ;
cres And new-discovered worlds arise
    To sing their Saviour's praise.

mf Beloved for Jesus' sake,
    By Him redeemed of old,
    All nations must come in, and
      make
    One undivided fold ;
cres While gathered in by Thee,
    And perfected in one,
f They all at once Thy glory see,
    In Thine Eternal Son.
            C. Wesley.

584   7.6.7.6.7.6.7.6.

mf Awake, awake, O Zion,
    Put on thy strength divine,
    Thy garments bright in beauty,
    The bridal dress be thine :
    Jerusalem the holy,
    To purity restored ;
    Meek Bride all fair and lowly,
    Go forth to meet thy Lord.

mf From henceforth pure and spotless,
    All glorious within,
    Prepared to meet the Bridegroom.
    And cleansed from every sin ;
dim With love and wonder smitten,
    And bowed in guileless shame.
p Upon my heart be written
    The new mysterious Name.

f Jerusalem victorious
  In triumph o'er her foes ;
Mount Zion, great and glorious,
  Thy gates no more shall close.
Earth's millions shall assemble
  Around thine open door,
While hell and Satan tremble,
  And earth and heaven adore.

mf The Lamb Who bore our sorrows,
  Comes down to earth again ;
No Sufferer now, but Victor,
  For evermore to reign.

f To reign in every nation,
  To rule in every zone ;
Oh world-wide coronation,
  In every heart a throne !

mf Awake, awake, O Zion,
  Thy bridal day draws nigh ;
The day of signs and wonders,
  And marvels from on high.
*dim*Thy sun uprises slowly,
  But keep thou watch and ward ,
*cres*Fair Bride, all pure and lowly,
  Go forth to meet thy Lord.

           B. Gough.

4.—MISSIONS TO THE JEWS.

585   C.M.

f WAKE, harp of Sion, wake again,
  Upon thine ancient hill,
On Jordan's long deserted plain,
  By Kedron's lowly rill.

The hymn shall yet in Sion swell,
  That sounds Messiah's praise,
And Thy loved Name, Emmanuel
  As once in ancient days.

For Israel yet shall own her King,
  For her salvation waits,
And hill and dale shall sweetly sing,
  With praise in all her gates.

mf O hasten, Lord, these promised days,
  When Israel shall rejoice ;
*cres*And Jew and Gentile join in praise,
  With one united voice !

           J. Edmeston.

5.—COLONIAL MISSIONS.

586   7.6., 8 lines.

mf FAR off our brethren's voices
  Are borne from distant lands,
Far off our Father's children
  Reach out their waiting hands.
" Give us," they cry, " our portion ;
  Co-heirs of grace divine !
Give us the Word of promise,
  On us let glory shine."

mf Yea, though the world of waters
  Between us ever rolls,
No ocean wastes may sever
  The brotherhood of souls ;

Far from us, they are of us ;
  No bound of all the earth
May part the sons and daughters
  Who share the second birth.
[*mf*One standard floats above
  us ;
One old historic throne,
  In nearness or in distance,
One loyal faith we own ;
*cres*So in the things eternal
  Adore we at one shrine,
And with the nation's banner
  Bear we the Church's sign.

)iest homely commune,
ι sweetest songs are sung,
ι those alien echoes
acred mother-tongue.
et us praise together !
ther let us pray,
 together homeward
ι the ancient way.]

er, heavenward. homeward ;
ιver in our view
ritual city—
ιalem the New ;

For ever drawing nearer
 To One beloved, adored,
The Crucified Who bought us.
 The crowned Incarnate Lord.

mp Lord God ! Eternal Father !
 Send down the Holy Dove,
For His dear sake Who loved us,
 To quicken us in love.
cres Bless us with His compassion,
 That we, or ere we rest,
May work to bless our brethren,
f And, blessing, be more blest.

S. J. Stone, v. 1, ll. 2, 8 altd.

6.—*HOME MISSIONS.*

L.M.

'rom Thy sphere of endless

of mercy and of might ;
 look on those who stray
ted, in this land of light.

)led vale, in lonely glen,
vded mart, by stream or sea,
ιany of the sons of men
ιot the message sent from

orth Thy heralds, Lord, to
 [hardened old,
thoughtless young, the
ered homeless flock, till all
ιered to Thy peaceful fold.

hem Thy mighty word to
ι,
ith shall dawn and doubt
rt,
: the bold, to stay the weak,
ιd and heal the broken heart.

ιll these wastes, a dreary
ι,
ιake us sadden as we gaze,

cres Shall grow, with living waters,
 green,
f And lift to heaven the voice of
 praise.

W. C. Bryant.

588 7s.

f SOLDIERS of the Cross, arise !
 Gird you with your armour bright,
 Mighty are your enemies.
 Hard the battle ye must fight.

mf O'er a faithless, fallen world
 Raise your banner in the sky :
 Let it float there wide unfurled ;
 Bear it onward ; lift it high.

dim 'Mid the homes of want and
 woe,
 Strangers to the living word,
 Let the Saviour's herald go,
cres Let the voice of hope be heard.

[*mp* Where the shadows deepest lie,
 Carry truth's unsullied ray ;
 Where are crimes of blackest dye,
 There the saving sign display.]

mp To the weary and the worn
Tell of realms where sorrows cease ;
To the outcast and forlorn
Speak of mercy and of peace.
mp Guard the helpless ; seek the strayed ;
Comfort troubles ; banish grief ;

*cres*In the might of God arrayed,
Scatter sin and unbelief.
mf Be the banner still unfurled,
Still unsheathed the Spirit's sword,
*cres*Till the kingdoms of the world
ff Are the kingdoms of the Lord.

W. W. How.

7.—DEPARTURE OF MISSIONARIES.

589 8.7.8.7.4.7.

mp SOULS in heathen darkness lying,
Where no light has broken through,
Souls that Jesus bought by dying,
Whom His soul in travail knew,
cres Thousand voices,
Call us o'er the waters blue.

mp Christians, hearken ! none has taught them
Of His love so deep and dear ;
Of the precious price that bought them
Of the nail, the thorn, the spear ;
cres Ye, who know Him, [drear.
Guide them from their darkness

mf Haste, O haste, and spread the tidings
Wide to earth's remotest strand ;
Let no brother's bitter chidings
dim Rise against us, when we stand
p In the Judgment,
From some far, forgotten land.

mf Lo ! the hills for harvest whiten
All along each distant shore ;
*cres*Seaward far the islands brighten,—
Light of nations, lead us o'er ;
When we seek them,
Let Thy Spirit go before.

C. Frances Alexander.

590 S.M.

f How beauteous are their feet
Who stand on Zion's hill !
Who bring salvation on their tongue,
And words of peace reveal.

mp How charming is their voice !
How sweet the tidings are !—
*cres*Zion, behold thy Saviour-King ;
He reigns and triumphs here.

mf How happy are our ears
That hear this joyful sound !
*dim*Which kings and prophets waited for,
And sought, but never found.

mf How blessèd are our eyes
That see this heavenly light !
*dim*Prophets and kings desired it long,
But died without the sight.

cres The watchmen join their voice,
And tuneful notes employ ;
f Jerusalem breaks forth in songs,
And deserts learn the joy.

ff The Lord makes bare His arm,
Through all the earth abroad ;
Let every nation now behold
Their Saviour and their God.

I. Watts.

591   8.7.8.7.4.7.

mf SPEED Thy servants, Saviour, speed
    them !
  Thou art Lord of winds and
    waves :
  They were bound, but Thou hast
    freed them ;
  Now they go to free the slaves :
cres   Be Thou with them !
  'Tis Thine arm alone that saves.

mp Friends and home and all for-
    saking,
  Lord ! they go at Thy command ;
  As their stay Thy promise taking,
  While they traverse sea and land:
cres   O be with them !
  Lead them safely by the hand !

mf Speed them through the mighty
    ocean,
  In the dark and stormy day,
  When the waves in wild commotion
  Fill all others with dismay :
cres   Be Thou with them !
  Drive their terrors far away.

mf When they reach the land of
    strangers,
  And the prospect dark appears,
  Nothing seen but toils and dangers,
    Nothing felt but doubts and
    fears ;
cres   Be Thou with them !
  Hear their sighs, and count their
    tears.

mp When they think of home, now
    dearer
  Than it ever seemed before,
  Bring the promised glory nearer ;
  Let them see that peaceful shore,
cres   Where Thy people
  Rest *from toil*, and weep no
    more !

p Where no fruit appears to cheer
    them,
  And they seem to toil in vain.
cres Then in mercy, Lord, draw near
    them,
  Then their sinking hopes sustain:
f   Thus supported,
  Let their zeal revive again !]

mf In the midst of opposition,
  Let them trust, O Lord, in Thee ;
  When success attends their mission,
  Let Thy servants humbler be :
cres   Never leave them,
  Till Thy face in heaven they see ;

f There to reap, in joy for ever,
  Fruit that grows from seed here
    sown !
  There to be with Him, Who never
  Ceases to preserve His own,
ff   And with gladness
  Give the praise to Him alone !
                T. Kelly.

592   6.6.8.4.

mp   WITH the sweet word of peace
    We bid our brethren go ;
cres Peace, as a river to increase,
    And ceaseless flow.

mp   With the calm word of prayer
    We earnestly commend   [care,
  Our brethren to Thy watchful
    Eternal Friend !

mf   With the dear word of love
    We give our brief farewell ;
  Our love below, and Thine above,
    With them shall dwell.

f   With the strong word of faith
    We stay ourselves on Thee :
  That Thou, O Lord, in life and
    death
    Their Help shalt be.

mf Then the bright word of hope
Shall on our parting gleam,
And tell of joys beyond the scope
Of earthborn dream.

mf Farewell! in hope, and love,
In faith, and peace, and prayer;
*cres*Till He Whose home is ours above
f Unite us there!

G. Watson.

XI.
Special Occasions.

1.—MARRIAGE.

593 7.6.7.6., double.

mp O LOVE divine and golden,
Mysterious depth and height,
To Thee the world beholden.
Looks up for life and light ;
O Love divine and gentle,
The blesser and the blest !
Beneath Whose care parental
The world lies down in rest.

f The fields of earth adore Thee,
The forests sing Thy praise,
All living things before Thee
Their holiest anthems raise :
Thou art the joy of gladness;
The life of life Thou art ;
*dim*The dew of gentle sadness,
p That droppeth on the heart.

mp O Love divine and tender !
That through our homes doth move,
Veiled in the softened splendour
Of holy household love,
A throne without Thy blessing
Were labour without rest,
And cottages, possessing
Thy blessedness, are blest.

*cres*God bless these hands united ;
God bless these hearts made one ;

Unsevered and unblighted
May they through life go on :
Here in earth's home preparing
For the bright home above ;
f And there for ever sharing
Its joy where "God is love."

J. S. B. Monsell.

594 8.6.8.4.

mf ETERNAL Love, Whose law doth sway
The worlds in ordered course,
And works in human hearts its way
With sacred force ;

mp To Thee our waiting hearts we lift,
This solemn, joyful hour,
And ask Thy Spirit's perfect gift,
For marriage dower.

mf Thy hand the sacred links hath wrought
That bind two souls in one;
Thy highest mysteries thus are taught,
Thy heaven begun.

mp O hallow with Thy presence now
This sacrament of love; [vow
Breathe in the trembling human
Strength from above.

at scenes the
road
nay roam,
ne altar glowed
he home.

E. S. A.

6.7.6., double.

ting,
ıd Whose power
'es together
 hour;
y children
't renew ;—
ade blessèd,
:ept true.

nost bounteous
,
'hy presence,
wait on Thee ;
hly gladness
ıvenly wine,
n the tasting,
t is Thine.

her,
ı from above,—
.y pureness,
' love ;
'hy presence,
rife kept free,
n Thy guidance,
ruled by Thee.

 it, Father,
lt in vain ;
., sustain it,
ı to pain :

f But nought can break the union
 Of hearts in Thee made one,
And love, which Thou hast hal-
 lowed,
 Is endless love begun.

G. Thring.

596   S.M.

mf How welcome was the call,
 And sweet the festal lay,
When Jesus deigned in Cana's hall
 To bless the marriage-day.

f And happy was the bride,
 And glad the bridegroom's heart,
For He Who tarried at their side
 Bade grief and ill depart.

mf His gracious power divine
 The water-vessels knew ;
And plenteous was the mystic wine
 The wondering servants drew.

mp O Lord of life and love,
 Come Thou again to-day,
And bring a blessing from above
 That ne'er shall pass away.

mp O bless, as erst of old,
 The bridegroom and the bride ;
Bless with the holier stream that
 flowed
 Forth from Thy piercèd side.

mp Before Thine altar-throne
 This mercy we implore ;   [one,
As Thou dost knit them, Lord, in
 So bless them evermore.

H. W. Baker.

_____

2.—*BURIAL OF THE DEAD.*

7.7.7.7.8.8.

er's task is o'er :
lay is past ;

cres Now upon the farther shore
 Lands the voyager at last.
mf Father, in Thy gracious keeping
dim Leave we now Thy servant sleeping.

mf There the tears of earth are dried ; .
There its hidden things are clear ;
There the work of life is tried
By a juster Judge than here.
mf Father, in Thy gracious keeping
*dim*Leave we now Thy servant sleeping.

p There the sinful souls that turn
To the cross their dying eyes,
cres All the love of Christ shall learn
At His Feet in Paradise.
mf Father, in Thy gracious keeping
*dim*Leave we now Thy servant sleeping.

mf. There no more the powers of hell
Can prevail to mar their peace ;
Christ the Lord shall guard them well ;
He Who died for their release.
*cres*Father, in Thy gracious keeping
*dim*Leave we now Thy servant sleeping.

p "Earth to earth, and dust to dust ; "
Calmly now the words we say ;
Leaving him to sleep in trust,
Till the Resurrection-day.
*cres*Father, in Thy gracious keeping
pp Leave we now Thy servant sleeping.

J. Ellerton.

598
4.6., 8 lines.

p SLEEP thy last sleep,
Free from care and sorrow ;
Rest where none weep,
Till th' eternal morrow ;
Though dark waves roll
O'er the silent river,
Thy fainting soul
Jesus can deliver.

p Life's dream is past,
All its sin and sadness ;

cres Brightly at last
Dawns a day of gladness :
Under the sod,
Earth, receive our treasure,
p To rest in God,
Waiting all His pleasure.

p Though we may mourn
Those in life the dearest,
cres They shall return,
Christ, when Thou appearest !
Soon shall Thy voice
Comfort those now weeping,
f Bidding rejoice
All in Jesus sleeping.

E. A. Dayman.

599
6.5., 8 lines.

p LAY the precious body
In the quiet grave ;
'Tis the Lord hath taken,
'Twas the Lord that gave :
cres Till the resurrection,
Lay the treasure by ;
It will then awaken,
And go up on high !

p Farewell, blessèd body,
Till the morn arise :
Welcome, happy spirit,
Into paradise !
cres No more work or weeping ;
Gone for ever home ;
In Christ's holy keeping
Rest until He come.

p Here the casket lieth
Waiting for repair ;
There doth Christ the jewel
In His bosom wear :
cres Wait a little season,
And in Him shall be
Both again united
Through eternity !

J. S. B. Monsell.

C.M.

ιe voice from heaven

ɔious dead ;
ιvour of their names,
ɜir sleeping bed.

·sus and are blest ;
heir slumbers are !
ιgs and from sins

rom every snare.

s world of toil and

sent with the Lord ;
f their mortal life
rge reward.
I. Watts.

L.M.

ιu hast the victory ;
ɹrength are laid with
[tier.
ːh's mightiest, migh-
. hast thy Vanquisher.

ght was man forlorn ;
ιou laugh his hope to

Conqueror of Death.
ιn of Nazareth.

ween us and despair :
gave us strength to
[sealed,
ɜs of the grave un-
destiny revealed.

not this mortal clime :
ιot its bounds in time :
ɹ but a cloud that lies
soul and paradise.
Elliot's Selection.

602 P.M.

mp THOU art gone to the grave ; but
we will not deplore thee.
Though sorrows and darkness
encompass the tomb :
*cres*The Saviour hath passed through
its portal before thee,
And the lamp of His love is thy
guide through the gloom !

mp Thou art gone to the grave : we
no longer behold thee,
Nor tread the rough path of the
world by thy side ;
*cres*But the wide arms of mercy are
spread to enfold thee,
And sinners may die, for the
Sinless has died !

mp Thou art gone to the grave ; and,
its mansion forsaking,
Perchance thy weak spirit in
fear lingered long :
*cres*But the mild rays of Paradise
beamed on thy waking,
And the sound which thou
heard'st was the Seraphim's
song !

mp Thou art gone to the grave ; but
we will not deplore thee :
Whose God was thy Ransom,
thy Guardian, and Guide !
*cres*He gave thee, He took thee, and
He will restore thee ;
And death has no sting, for the
Saviour has died !
R. Heber.

603 Irregular.

mp SOON and for ever
Such promise our trust,
Though ashes to ashes,
And dust unto dust ;

cres Soon and for ever
Our union shall be
Made perfect, our glorious
Redeemer, in Thee.
When the sins and the sorrows
Of time shall be o'er,
Its pangs and its partings
Remembered no more ;
Where life cannot fail, and
where
Death cannot sever,
f Christians with Christ shall be,
Soon and for ever.

mf Soon and for ever,
The breaking of day
Shall drive all the night-clouds
Of sorrow away ;
Soon and for ever
We'll see as we're seen,
And learn the deep meaning
Of things that have been.
When fightings without us,
And fears from within,
Shall weary no more in
The warfare of sin ;
Where fears, and where tears.
and where
Death shall be never,
f Christians with Christ shall be,
Soon and for ever.

mp Soon and for ever
The work shall be done,
The warfare accomplished
The victory won ;
cres Soon and for ever
The soldier lays down
His sword for a harp, and
His cross for a crown.
Then droop not in sorrow,
Despond not in fear,
A glorious to-morrow
Is brightening and near ;

When (blessed reward o:
Faithful endeavour)
f Christians with Christ sl
Soon and for ever.
J. S. B. M

604

mp HUSH ! blessèd are the de:
In Jesu's arms who rest.
And lean their weary head
For ever on His breast.

mf O beatific sight !
No darkling veil betwee
They see the Light of Lig
Whom here they loved

mp For them the wild is past
With all its toil and car
Its withering midnight bl
Its fiery noonday glare.

mp Them the Good Shepherd
Where storms are never
In tranquil dewy meads,
Beside the Fount of Lif

p Ours only are the tears,
Who weep around their
The light of bygone year
And shadowing years t

mp Their voice, their tou
smile,
Those love - springs
o'er ;
Earth for its little while
Shall never know them

mp O tender hearts and true.
Our long last vigil kep
We weep and mourn for
Nor blame us : Jesus v

But soon, at break of day
His calm almighty voic

f Stronger than death, shall say,
ff Awake,—arise,—rejoice.

E. H. Bickersteth.

605

(*For the death of a child.*) 7.7.4.

mp LET no tears to-day be shed,
Holy is this narrow bed.
Hallelujah !

[*mf* Death eternal life bestows,
Open heaven's portal throws.
Hallelujah !

cres And no peril waits at last
Him who now away hath past.
Hallelujah !]

mp Not salvation hardly won,
Not the meed of race well run ;
Hallelujah !

p But the pity of the Lord
Gives His child a full reward ;
Hallelujah !

f Grants the prize without the course;
Crowns, without the battle's force.
Hallelujah !

God, Who loveth innocence,
Hastes to take His darling hence.
Hallelujah !

Christ, when this sad life is done,
Join us to Thy little one.
Hallelujah !

mp And in Thine own tender love,
Bring us to the ranks above.
Hallelujah !

Paris Missal, 18th century,
tr. R. F. Littledale.

606

7s., 8 lines

mp SAFELY, safely gathered in,
No more sorrow, no more sin,
No more childish griefs or fears,
No more sadness, no more tears ;
p For the life, so young and fair,
Now hath passed from earthly care:
God Himself the soul will keep,
Giving His belovèd—sleep.

mp Safely, safely gathered in,
Free from sorrow, free from sin,
Passed beyond all grief and pain,
Death, for thee, is truest gain :
cres For our loss we must not weep,
Nor our loved one long to keep
From the home of rest and peace,
Where all sin and sorrow cease.

mp Safely, safely gathered in,
No more sorrow, no more sin ;
p God has saved from weary strife,
In its dawn, this young fresh life,
Which awaits us now above,
Resting in the Saviour's love :
f Jesu, grant that we may meet
There, adoring at Thy feet.

E. O. Dobree.

[SEE ALSO SECTION VII. 20, 21, 22.]

3.—LAYING FOUNDATION STONE.
(1) OF A CHURCH.

8.7.8.7.8.7.

BLESSED city, heavenly Salem,
Vision dear of peace and love,

f Who, of living stones upbuilded,
Art the joy of heaven above,
mf And, with angel-hosts encircled,
As a bride to earth dost move.

f Christ is made the sure foundation,
  And the precious corner-stone,
mf Who, the two walls underlying,
  Bound in each, binds both in one ;
f Holy Sion's help for ever,
  And her confidence alone.

mf All that dedicated city,
  Dearly loved of God on high,
f In exultant jubilation
  Pours perpetual melody :
p God, the One in Three, adoring
cres In glad hymns eternally.

mf To this temple, where we call Thee,
  Come, O Lord of hosts, to-day ;
  With Thy wonted loving-kindness
  Hear Thy people as they pray ;
cres And Thy fullest benediction
  Shed within its walls for aye.

p Here vouchsafe to all Thy servants
  What they ask of Thee to gain,
cres What they gain from Thee for ever
  With the blessèd to retain,
f And hereafter in Thy glory
  Evermore with Thee to reign.

  *Latin, 7th century, tr. J. M.
  Neale, altd. by Compilers
  Hymns Ancient and Modern.*

608   L.M.

mf O LORD of hosts, Whose glory fills
  The bounds of the eternal hills,
  And yet vouchsafes, in Christian lands,
  To dwell in temples made with hands ;

mf Grant that all we, who here to-day
  Rejoicing this foundation lay,
  *May be in very deed Thine own,
  Built on the precious Corner-stone.*

mp The heads that guide endue with skill, [ill,
  The hands that work preserve from
  That we, who these foundations lay,
  May raise the topstone in its day.

mp Both now and ever, Lord, protect
  The temple of Thine own elect :
cres Be Thou in them, and they in Thee,
  O Ever-blessèd Trinity !
  •   *J. M. Neale.*

609   L.M.

mf THIS stone to Thee in faith we lay ;
  We build the temple, Lord, to Thee;
  Thine eye be open night and day,
  To guard this house and sanctuary.

p Here, when Thy people seek Thy face,
  And dying sinners pray to live,
cres Hear Thou in heaven, Thy dwelling-place,
  And, when Thou hearest, O forgive !

mf Here, when Thy messengers proclaim
  The blessèd gospel of Thy Son,
cres Still, by the power of His great Name,
  Be mighty signs and wonders done.

mf But will, indeed, Jehovah deign
  Here to abide, no transient guest !
  Here will the world's Redeemer reign,
  And here the Holy Spirit rest ?

f That glory never hence depart !
  Yet choose not, Lord, this house alone ;
ff Thy kingdom come to every heart,
  In every bosom fix Thy throne.
           J. Montgomery.

(2) OF A SCHOOL.

310　　　　　　　L.M.

if EXCEPT the Lord the temple build,
In vain their toil the workmen
　　yield ;　　　　　　[bounds,
Except the Lord shall guard the
In vain the watchman's voice re-
　　sounds.

ip O Lord, the Master-builder Thou,
Make us Thy fellow-workers now ;
Builders of souls here may we be,
And living shrines be raised for
　　Thee.

if Give to our teachers words of fire,
To kindle every high desire ;

And form in all the constant mind
To serve their God and serve man-
　　kind.

mp Watch Thou within, lest we should
　　spoil
Thy work, or fail in earnest toil ;
May Thine abiding presence keep
Our hearts from strife, our souls
　　from sleep.

mp Thus may we train, in Thy blest
　　will,　　　　　　[still,
Young ardent souls to serve Thee
cres To bear, in bright and eager bands,
The torch that leaves our drooping
　　hands.

　　　　　　　　　　E. S. A.

4.—OPENING AND DEDICATION OF CHURCHES.

311　　　　　　　L.M.

if JESUS, where'er Thy people meet,
There they behold Thy mercy-seat :
Where'er they seek Thee, Thou art
　　found,　　　　　　[ground.
And every place is hallowed

if For Thou, within no walls confined,
Inhabitest the humble mind :
Such ever bring Thee where they
　　come,　　　　　　[home.
And going, take Thee to their

nf Dear Shepherd of Thy chosen few,
Thy former mercies here renew ;
pres Here to our waiting hearts pro-
　　claim
　The sweetness of Thy saving name.

mp Here may we prove the power of
　　prayer,　　　　　　[care ;
To strengthen faith and sweeten

cres To teach our faint desires to rise,
And bring all heaven before our
　　eyes.

p Lord, we are few, *(cres)* but Thou
　　art near ;
Nor short Thine arm, nor deaf
　　Thine ear.
cres O rend the heavens, come quickly
　　down,
f And make a thousand hearts Thine
　　own.

　　　　　　　　　W. Cowper.

612　　　　　　　L.M.

mf ALL things are Thine : no gift
　　have we,
Lord of all gifts ! to offer Thee ;
And hence with grateful hearts
　　to-day,
Thy own before Thy feet we lay.

mf Thy will was in the builder's
thought;
Thy hand unseen amidst us
wrought;
Through mortal motive, scheme
and plan,
Thy wise eternal purpose ran.

mp In weakness and in want we call
On Thee for Whom the heavens
are small;
Thy glory is Thy children's good,
Thy joy Thy tender Fatherhood.

mp O Father! deign these walls to
bless;
Fill with Thy love their emptiness:
cres And let their door a gateway be
To lead us from ourselves to Thee!
J. G. Whittier.

613   C.M.

mf LIGHT up this house with glory,
Lord;
Enter, and claim Thine own;
Receive the homage of our souls,
Erect Thy temple-throne.

mp We ask no bright shekinah-cloud
To glorify the place;
Give, Lord, the substance of that
sign—
A plenitude of grace.

mp We rear no altar—Thou hast died;
We deck no priestly shrine;
What need have we of creature-
aid?
The power to save is Thine.

mp O Thou, Who, risen, cam'st to bless,
Gently as comes the dew,
lim Here, entering, breathe. on all
around,
p   "*Peace, peace be unto you.*"

mf No rushing, mighty wind we
ask;
No tongues of flame desire;
Grant us the Spirit's quickening
light,
His purifying fire.

f Light up this house with glory,
Lord—
The glory of that love
Which forms and saves a church
below,
And makes a heaven above.
J. Harris.

614   C.M.

mf O THOU, Whose own vast temple
stands
Built over earth and sea,
Accept the walls that human
hands
Have raised to worship Thee.

mp Lord, from Thine inmost glory
send,
Within these courts to 'bide,
The peace that dwelleth without
end,
Serenely by Thy side.

mp May erring minds that worship
here
Be taught the better way;
And they who mourn, and they
who fear,
Be strengthened as they pray.

mf May faith grow firm, and love
grow warm,
And pure devotion rise,
While round these hallowed walls
the storm
Of earth-born passion dies.
W. C. Bryant.

5.—*OPENING OF A SCHOOL.*

315 C.M., double.

mf O LORD of life, and love, and
  power,
  How joyful life might be,
If in Thy service every hour
  We lived and moved with Thee!
If youth in all its bloom and might
  By Thee were sanctified,
And manhood found its chief
  delight
  In working at Thy side.

mp 'Tis ne'er too late, while life shall
  last,
  A new life to begin ;
'Tis ne'er too late to leave the past,
  And break with self and sin
res And we this day, both old and
  young,
  Would earnestly aspire [strung,
For hearts to nobler purpose
  And purified desire.

mf In this new house our hands have
  raised,
  Thy service to pursue,
O may Thy Name henceforth be
  praised
  By work more pure and true ;
May child and teacher evermore
  Come here with earnest heart,
And those who never worked before
  Stand forth and bear their part.

mf Nor for ourselves alone we plead,
  But for all faithful souls
Who serve Thy cause by word or
  deed,
  Whose names Thy book enrols.
cres O speed Thy work, victorious King!
  And give Thy workers might,
That through the world Thy truth
  may ring,
f And all men see Thy light!
  E. S. A.

6.—*DEDICATION OF AN ORGAN.*

316 8.5.8.5.8.4.3.

f ANGEL voices, ever singing
  Round Thy throne of light,
Angel harps for ever ringing,
  Rest not day nor night ;
Thousands only live to bless Thee,
  And confess Thee,
  Lord of might !

nf Thou, Who art beyond the farthest
  Mortal eye can scan,
Can it be that Thou regardest
  Songs of sinful man ? [us
Can we know that Thou art near
  And wilt hear us ?
  Yea ! we can.

mf Yea ! we know that Thou rejoicest
  O'er each work of Thine ;
Thou didst ears and hands and
  voices.
For Thy praise design ;
Craftsman's art and music's measure
  For Thy pleasure
  All combine.

mf In Thy house, great God, we offer
  Of Thine own to Thee ;
And for Thine acceptance proffer,
  All unworthily, [voices
Hearts and minds, and hands and
  In our choicest
  Psalmody.

f Honour, glory, might, and merit,
  Thine shall ever be !
Father, Son, and Holy Spirit,
  Blessèd Trinity !

Of the best that Thou hast gi
Earth and Heaven
Render Thee.
F. P(

7.—ANNIVERSARY.
(1) OF A SUNDAY SCHOOL.

617 6.5., 12 lines.

mf JESUS, King of glory,
  Throned above the sky.
Jesus, tender Saviour,
  Hear Thy children cry.
dim Pardon our transgressions,
  Cleanse us from our sin ;
By Thy Spirit help us
  Heavenly life to win.
mf   Jesus, King of glory,
    Throned above the sky,
dim   Jesus, tender Saviour,
    Hear Thy children cry.

mf On this day of gladness,
  Bending low the knee
In Thine earthly temple,
  Lord, we worship Thee ;—
cres Celebrate Thy goodness,
  Mercy, grace, and truth :
All Thy loving guidance
  Of our heedless youth.
f   Jesus, King of glory,
    Throned above the sky,
  Jesus, tender Saviour,
    Hear our grateful cry.

mp For the little children
  Who have come to Thee ;
For the glad, bright spirits
  Who Thy glory see ;
dim For the loved ones resting
  In Thy dear embrace ;
cres For the pure and holy
  Who behold Thy face ;

f   Jesus, King of glory,
    Throned above the sky,
  Jesus, tender Saviour,
    Hear our grateful cry.

mf For Thy faithful servants
  Who have entered in ;
For Thy fearless soldiers
  Who have conquered sin ;
For the countless legions
  Who have followed Thee,
Heedless of the danger,
  On to victory ;
f   Jesus, King of glory,
    Throned above the sky,
  Jesus, tender Saviour,
    Hear our grateful cry.

mf Help us ever steadfast
  In the faith to be :
In Thy Church's conflicts
  Fighting valiantly.
cres Loving Saviour, strengthen
  These weak hearts of ours,
Through Thy cross to conquer
  Crafty evil powers.
f   Jesus, King of glory,
    Throned above the sky,
  Jesus, tender Saviour,
    Hear Thy children cry.

mp When the shadows lengthen,
  Show us, Lord, Thy way ;
Through the darkness lead us
  To the heavenly day ;

se is finished,
 strife,
the faithful
owns of life.
; of glory,
 above the sky,
er Saviour,
y children cry.
W. H. Davison.

6.5., 8 lines.

y dwelling,
neet again,
voices swelling,
 yearly strain ;
iding lowly,
igels' cry,
Holy,
l most High ! "

ll His glory—
heaven above ;
iel story
iondrous love :
ther gave us
on to die ;
, to save us,
irone on high.

t to know Him,
ive so true !
r to show Him,
ve Him too !
given,
ite His grace,
e in heaven
His Face.

 His dwelling,
yearly song ;
ies swelling
rain prolong ;
nding lowly,
igels' cry,

" Holy. Holy, Holy,
 Is the Lord most High ! "
T. A. Stowell.

619 C.M., double.

[For Children.]

f O LORD of all, we bring to Thee
 our sacrifice of praise,
To Thee with glad and thankful
 hearts our festal hymn we raise :
mf We are but children here on
 earth, and Thou art high above,
*cres*But yet we dare to come to Thee,
 because Thy Name is Love.

f We praise Thee now for life, and
 health, and earthly happiness,
For all the sacred human love that
 still our lives doth bless.
For Thy dear Son Whom Thou
 hast sent, Whose kind and tender
 voice
Bids the young children come to
 Thee, and in Thy love rejoice.

mf What shall we render Thee, O Lord ?
 what tribute shall we bring ?
O let us give our hearts, our lives,
 in thankful offering.
Although we are but children, yet
 Thou dost our service ask,
And each in Thy great work may
 find his own appointed task.

mp O make us watchful, lest by sin
 our hearts be overborne ;
O make us true in word and work,
 though all the world should
 scorn ;
O make us willing here to serve,
 in lowliness and love,
For Him Who in a servant's form
 came down from heaven above.

mp The night of sin must wane at
   last, the morn of joy begin,
When Christ in every human heart
   His royal throne must win ;
cres O let us give Him now in youth
   our ardour and our strength,
f Work for His glorious kingdom
   here, and share His joy at length !

mf Already breaks the early dawn of
   that great day of God ;
Already sounds the Master's voice
   through all the earth abroad.
f Then cast the works of night
   away, gird on the arms of light,
And on the side of Christ our King,
   stand ready for the fight.
                E. S. A.

620
             6.6.4.6.6.6.4.

mf SHEPHERD of tender youth,
   Guiding in love and truth,
      Through devious ways ;
f Christ, our triumphant King,
   We come Thy Name to sing,
   Hither our children bring,
ff   To shout Thy praise.

mf Thou art our Holy Lord,
   The all-subduing Word,

     Healer of strife :
p Thou didst Thyself abase,
   That from sin's deep disgrace
cres Thou mightest save our race,
f   And give us life.

mf Thou art the Great High Priest ;
   Thou hast prepared the feast
      Of heavenly love :
p While in our mortal pain,
   None calls on Thee in vain :
   Help Thou dost not refrain,—
f   Help from above.

mf Ever be Thou our Guide,
   Our Shepherd and our Pride,
 .   Our staff and song :
Jesus, Thou Christ of God,
   By Thy perennial word,
   Lead us where Thou hast trod ;
f .   Make our faith strong.

mf So now, and till we die,
   Sound we Thy praises high,
     And joyful sing.
Infants, and the glad throng
   Who to Thy Church belong,
cres Unite to swell the song
ff   To Christ our King.

      H. M. Dexter, from Clement
           Alexandria.

[SEE ALSO SECTION FOR CHILDREN'S SERVICES.]

(2) OF A TEMPERANCE SOCIETY OR BAND OF HOPE.

621
              6.5.

mf CHRISTIAN, work for Jesus,
   Who on earth for thee
Laboured, wearied, suffered,—
   Died upon the tree.

[*mp* Work with eye that rangeth
   Over sin's great deep :
dim Where lie thousands drifting,
   Rocked to fatal sleep.

mf Work with hands that Jesus
   Maketh strong to bring
Souls to Him their Saviour,
   Trustfully to cling.]

mf Work with feet untiring
   By the Master led,
Help to free the drunkards
   From their bondage dread.

ı lips so fervid
y words may prove
brought a message
ıe God of love.

h heart that burneth
ʒ at His Feet ;
gems to offer,
crown made meet.

mp Work with prayer unceasing,
　　Borne on faith's strong wing,
cres Earnestly beseeching
　　Trophies for the King.

mf Work while strength endureth,
　　Until death draw near ;
cres Then thy Lord's sweet welcome
　　Thou in heaven shalt hear.

M. Haslock.

8.—*HOSPITAL SUNDAY.*

C.M. double.

m, O Lord, in days of

ong to heal and save ;
hed o'er disease and death,
rkness and the grave :
hey went, the blind, the
ı,
sied and the lame,
with his tainted life,
k with fevered frame.

Thy touch brought life
ıealth,
peech, and strength, and
;
th renewed and frenzy
ʒd
Thee, the Lord of Light.
O Lord, be near to bless,
ıty as of yore,
ʒd street, by restless couch,
ʒennesareth's shore.

our great Deliverer still,
ıord of life and death,
ınd quicken, soothe and

hine almighty breath :
that work, and eyes that

isdom's heavenly lore,

cres That whole and sick, and weak
　　and strong,
f 　　May praise Thee evermore.

E. H. Plumptre.

623 8.7.8.7.7.7.

mf THOU to Whom the sick and dying
　　Ever came, nor came in vain.
　Still with healing words replying
　　To the wearied cry of pain ;
alm Hear us, Jesu, as we meet
　Suppliants at Thy mercy-seat.

mp Every care, and every sorrow,
　　Be it great, or be it small.
　Yesterday,—to-day,—to-morrow,—
　　When,—where'er it may befall,
dim Lay we humbly at Thy Feet,
　Suppliants at Thy mercy-seat.

p Still the weary, sick, and dying
　　Need a brother's, sister's care ;
cres On Thy higher help relying,
　　May we now their burden share.
f 　Bringing all our offerings meet,
　Suppliants at Thy mercy-seat.

mf May each child of Thine be willing
　Willing both in hand and heart,
　All the law of love fulfilling,
　　Ever comfort to impart,
cres Ever bringing offerings meet,
　Suppliant to Thy mercy-seat.

1ი

mp So may sickness, sin, and sadness,
　To Thy healing power yield,
　Till the sick and sad in gladness—
　Rescued, ransomed, cleansèd,
　　healèd,—
cres One in Thee together meet,
　Pardoned at Thy judgment-seat.
　　　　　　　　G. Thring.

624　　　　　　　　L.M.

mp O THOU through suffering perfect
　made,
　On Whom the bitter cross was laid ;
　In hours of sickness, grief, and pain,
　No sufferer turns to Thee in vain.

mf The halt, the maimed, the sick, the
　blind,
　Sought not in vain Thy tendance
　kind ;

Now in Thy poor Thyself w
And minister through them t

mf O loving Saviour, Thou can
　The pains and woes Tho
　endure :
cres For all who need, Physicia
　Thy healing balm we suppl

p But, O far more, let eac
　pain
And hour of woe be heaven
Each stroke of Thy chastisi
Bring back the wanderer
　God.

cres O ! heal the bruisèd heart
　O ! save our souls all sick w
Give life and health in bo
　store,
f That we may praise Thee ev
　　　　　　　　W. W.

9.—FLOWER SERVICES.

625　　　　　　11.10.11.10.

mf HERE, Lord, we offer Thee all that
　is fairest,
　Bloom from the garden, and
　flowers from the field ;
　Gifts for the stricken ones, knowing
　　Thou carest　［that we yield.
　More for the love than the wealth

mp Send, Lord, by these to the sick
　and the dying ;
　Speak to their hearts with a
　message of peace ;
　Comfort the sad, who in weakness
　are lying ;　　　［release.
　Grant the departing a gentle

cres Raise, Lord, to health again those
　who have sickened,
　*Fair be their lives as the roses
　in bloom;*

Give of Thy grace to t
　Thou hast quickened,
Gladness for sorrow, and
　ness for gloom.

mp We, Lord, like flowers, mus
　and must wither,
　We, like these blossom
　fade and must die ;
cres Gather us, Lord, to Thy B
　ever,
mf　Grant us a place in Th
　in the sky.
　　　　　　　A. G. W.

626

mf NOT only for the goodly fr
　tall
　The Master cares, Whos
　over all ;

The tiny herbs which blossom everywhere
No less His watchful toil and patience share.

mp The little ones who ᴚ the kingdom grow,   [to know ;
The weak, the tender, He delights
His Spirit loves the humble and the meek,
And 'tis the lowly whom He deigns to seek.

mp And all small flowers of fair humility,   [charity,
Sweet temper, daily patience,
Kind words and cheerfulness to Him are dear,
More than most deeds whose praise men tell and hear.

mp For these sweet virtues, meet for daily food,   [by His blood ;
Grow near His cross, are watered
Were no such' flowerets in their circle wrought,
The hero's and the martyr's crown were nought !

mf Thou, who would'st till thy garden-plot to please   [water these !
The Master's eye, oh, tend and Weave from these blossoms, wet with tears divine,
*cres*A garland meet for His most holy shrine.

E. S. A.

627

C.M.

mf IT is the Lord Himself Who tends His garden here below ;
The sunshine and the rain He sends, That it may thrive and grow.

mf Within this garden-plot are found Both *goodly cedars* tall,

And little herbs upon the ground;
The Master cares for all.

mp One thing is ever His pursuit, And fills His loving mind,
That each should grow and bring forth fruit
According to its kind.

p It is the Lord Who lays His knife Upon the tender shoot,
And though it pierce the very life, 'Tis needful for the fruit.

mf The richer is the soul He tends, The more doth He desire   [ends,
*cres*That it should serve yet nobler More nobly still aspire.

mp Withhold not, Lord, Thy pruning knife,
If dead leaves of-decay, Or overgrowth of worldly life,
In us are gaining sway.

mp We ask Thee not for gladsome lives Untouched by earthly ill ;
We ask but for the soul that strives Thy pattern to fulfil.

E. S. A.

628

6.5.6.5.

[*For Children.*]

mf IN our dear Lord's garden, Planted here below,
Many tiny flowerets In sweet beauty grow.

mp Christ, the loving Gardener. Tends these blossoms small ;
Loves the little lilies As the cedars tall.

mp Nothing is too little For His gentle care ;
Nothing is too lowly In His love to share.

mf Jesus l. res the children,
  Children such as we,
Blessed them when their mothers
  Brought them to His knee.

nf Jesus calls the children,
  Bids them come and stand

In His pleasant garden,
  Watered by His hand.

mp Lord, Thy call we answer;
  Take us in Thy care,
Train us in Thy garden,
. In Thy work to share.

E. S. A.

10.—*GENERAL CHARITIES AND ALMSGIVING.*

329 S.M.

nf WE give Thee but Thine own,
  Whate'er the gift may be;
All that we have is Thine alone,
  A trust, O Lord, from Thee.

if May we Thy bounties thus
  As stewards true receive,
And gladly, as Thou blessest us
  To Thee our firstfruits give.

up O! hearts are bruised and dead,
  And homes are bare and cold,
And lambs, for whom the Shepherd
    bled,
  Are straying from the fold.

up To comfort and to bless,
  To find a balm for woe,
To tend the lone and fatherless
  .Is angels' work below.

up The captive to release,
  To God the lost to bring,
To teach the way of life and peace,
  It is a Christ-like thing.

nf And we believe Thy Word,
  Though dim our faith may be;
res Whate'er for Thine we do, O Lord,
  We do it unto Thee.

W. W. How.

330 8.8.8.6

f O GOD of mercy, God of might,
In love and pity infinite,

Teach us, as ever in Thy sight,
  To live our life to Thee.

mp And Thou, Who cam'st on earth
    to die,
  That fallen man might live thereby,
  O hear us, for to Thee we cry,
  In hope, O Lord, to Thee.

mp Teach us the lesson Thou hast
    taught,
  To feel for those Thy Blood hath
    bought:
That every word, and deed, and
    thought
  May work a work for Thee.

mf For all are brethren, far and
    wide,
  Since Thou, O Lord, for all hast
    died:—
Then teach us, whatsoe'er betide,
  To love them all in Thee.

p In sickness, sorrow, want, or care,
  Whate'er it be, 'tis ours to share;
cres May we, when help is needed,
    there
  Give help as unto Thee.

mf And may Thy Holy Spirit move
  All those who live, to live in love,
cres Till Thou shalt greet in heaven
    above
  All those who give to Thee.

G. Thring.

8.8.8.4.

LORD of heaven and earth and sea,
Thee all praise and glory be ;
)w shall we show our love to Thee,
Giver of all ?

r peaceful homes and healthful
days,
r all the blessings earth displays,
e owe Thee thankfulness and
praise,
Giver of all.

ou didst not spare Thine only
Son,
t gav'st Him for a world undone,
id freely with that Blessèd One
Thou givest all.

ou giv'st the Spirit's blessèd
dower,
irit of life and love and power,
d dost His sevenfold graces
shower
Upon us all.

r souls redeemed, for sins forgiven,   [heaven,
r means of grace and hopes of
ther. what can to Thee be given,
Who givest all ?

lose what on ourselves we spend ;
e have as treasure without end

f Whatever, Lord, to Thee we lend,
    Who givest all.

mf Whatever, Lord, we lend to Thee,
    Repaid a thousandfold will be ;
f Then gladly will we give to Thee,
    Giver of all ;—

mf To Thee, from Whom we all derive
    Our life, our gifts, our power to give;
p Oh, may we ever with Thee live,
f Giver of all !
                C. Wordsworth.

632   7.5.

mp THINE are all the gifts, O God !
    Thine the broken bread ;
    Let the naked feet be shod,
    And the starving fed.

mp Let Thy children, by Thy grace,
    Give as they abound,
    Till the poor have breathing-space,
    And the lost are found.

mf Wiser than the miser's hoards
    Is the giver's choice ;
    Sweeter than the song of birds
    Is the thankful voice.

f Welcome smiles on faces sad
    As the flowers of spring ; •
    Let the tender hearts be glad
    With the joy they bring.
              J. G. Whittier.

XII.
Special Intercession.

1.—FOR CHILDREN AND HOME.

7.4.

INDING forth on life's rough
    way,
  Father, *guide them* ;
I we know not what of harm

    May betide them ;
  'Neath the shadow of Thy wing,
    Father, hide them ;
Waking, sleeping, Lord, we pray,
    Go beside them.

n prayer they cry to Thee,
ou wilt hear them ;
he stains of sin and shame
ou wilt clear them ;
e quicksands and the rocks,
ou wilt steer them ;
ptation, trial, grief,
  Thou near them.

hee we give them up ;
rd, receive them ;
world we know must be
ich to grieve them—
triving oft and strong
  deceive them :
il, in Thy hands of love
  ? must leave them.
                      W. C. Bryant.

                      L.M.

y Lord, content to fill
ly home the lowliest place,
ildhood's law a mother's will,
nce meek Thy brightest
?.

mp Lead every child that bears Thy
    Name   [way.
To walk in Thine own guileless
To dread the touch of sin and
    shame,
And humbly, like Thyself, obey !

mp O let not this world's scorching
    glow
Thy Spirit's quickening dew efface,
Nor blast of sin too rudely blow,
And quench the trembling flame
    of grace.

p Gather Thy Lambs within Thine
    arm,
And gently in Thy bosom bear ;
Keep them, O Lord, from hurt and
    harm,
And bid them rest for ever there !

mf So shall they, waiting here below,
Like Thee, their Lord, a little span,
In wisdom and in stature grow,
And favour both with God and man.
                      W. W. How.

2.—FOR MINISTERS AND STUDENTS.

                      L.M.

of Christ ! be earnest given
iese our prayers are heard.
;hey
:asp, this hour, the sword of
en
iel Thee on their weary way.

at morn or soothing evé
ie holy Fount they lean,
  fading garland freshly
'c,   [serene.
i them with Thine airs
of *Light* and *Truth* ! to
              [hour ;
t them in that musing

cres Till they with open heart and free
    Teach all Thy word, in all its
    power.

mp When foemen watch their tents
    by night,   [and fell,
    And mists hang wide o'er moor
cres Spirit of counsel and of might,
    Their pastoral warfare guide Thou
    well.

p And O ! when worn and tired, they
    sigh
With that more fearful war within,
cres When passion's storms are loud
    and high,
And, brooding o'er remembered sin

p The heart dies down—O Mightiest !
then
Come, ever true ; come, ever near ;
*res*And wake their slumbering love
again,
Spirit of God's most holy fear !
J. Keble, v. 1, *l.* 1 *altd.*

636   L.M.

np FATHER of mercies, bow Thine ear,
Attentive to our earnest prayer.
We plead for those who plead for
Thee ;
Successful pleaders may they be.

np How great their work ! how vast
their charge !
Do Thou their anxious souls en-
large ;   [gain ;
Their best acquirements are our
We share the blessings they obtain.

*res*Clothe, then, with energy divine
Their words, and let those words
be Thine :
To them Thy sacred truth reveal ;
Suppress their fear, inflame their
zeal.

mf Teach them to sow the precious
seed ;   [feed ;
Teach them Thy chosen flock to
*cres*Teach them immortal souls to gain,
Souls that will well reward their
pain.

mf Let thronging multitudes around
Hear from their lips the joyful
sound :   [implore,
In humble strains Thy grace
And feel Thy new-creating power.
B. Beddome.

637   7s.

f MIGHTY One, before Whose face
Wisdom had her glorious seat,
When the orbs that people space
Sprang to birth beneath Thy feet !

mf Source of truth, Whose rays alone
Light the mighty world of mind !
God of love, Who from Thy throne
Watchest over all mankind !

mf Shed on those who in Thy Name
Teach the way of truth and right,
Shed that love's undying flame,
Shed that wisdom's guiding light.
W. C. Bryant.

3.—FOR THE SORROWING AND AFFLICTED.

638   8s., 6 lines (trochaic).

np HOPE of those that have none other,
Left for life by father, mother,
All their dearest lost or taken,
Only not by Thee forsaken,
Comfort Thou the sad and lonely,
Saviour dear, for Thou canst only.

up When the glooms of night are
o'er us,
Satan in his strength before us ;
When *despair, and doubt,* and terror
Drag the blinded heart to error ;

Comfort Thou the poor and lonely,
Saviour dear, for Thou canst only.

mp By Thy days of earthly trial,
By Thy friend's foreknown denial
By Thy cross of bitter anguish,
Leave not Thou Thy lambs to
languish ;
Comforting the weak and lonely,
Lead them in Thy pastures only.

mp Sick with hope deferred, or
yearning
For the never-now-returning ;

When the glooms of grief o'ershade
us,   [aid us !
Thou hast known, and Thou wilt

To Thine own heart take the lonely
Leaning on Thee only, only.

F. T. Palgrave.

4.—FOR THOSE AT SEA.

639   L.M., with refrain.

mf ETERNAL Father, strong to save,
Whose arm doth bind the restless
wave,
Who bidst the mighty ocean deep
Its own appointed limits keep ;
p   O hear us when we cry to Thee
For those in peril on the sea.

mf O Saviour, Whose almighty word
p The winds and waves submissive
heard,
f Who walkest on the foaming deep,
dim And calm amid its rage didst
sleep ;
p   O hear us when we cry to Thee
For those in peril on the sea.

mf O Holy Spirit, Who didst brood
Upon the chaos dark and rude,
Who bad'st its angry tumult cease,
And gavest light, and life, and
peace ;   .
p   O hear us when we cry to Thee
For those in peril on the sea.

f O Trinity of love and power,
Our brethren shield in danger's
hour ;   .   [foe,
From rock and tempest, fire and
Protect them whereso'er they go ;
ff   And ever let there rise to Thee
Glad hymns of praise from land
and sea.

W. Whiting, v. 3, l. 1, v. 4,
ll. 3, 4 altd.

XIII.

𝕹ational 𝕳ymns.

1.—THE THRONE.

640   L.M.

f O KING of kings, Thy blessing
shed
On our anointed sovereign's head ;
And, looking from Thy holy
heaven,
Protect the crown Thyself hast
given.

mf Him with Thy choicest mercies
bless,
To all his counsels give success ;

In war, in peace, Thy succour
bring,
f Thy strength command, God save
the King.

mf Him may we honour and obey,
Uphold his right and lawful
sway,
Remembering that the powers
that be
Are ministers ordained of Thee.

mf Thou, ever mindful of his want,
Through all his days Thy blessing
  grant ;
And bid the golden circlet spread
Its purest splendours round his
  head.

p And oh ! when earthly thrones
  decay,
And earthly kingdoms fade away,
cres Grant him a throne in worlds on
  high,
f A crown of immortality.

Cotterill's Selection, 1819.

641
        6.6.4.

f GOD save our gracious King,
· Long live our noble King,
  God save the King.

Send him victorious,
Happy and glorious, *l*
Long to reign over us,
  God save our King.

f O Lord, our God, arise,
Scatter his enemies,
  And make them fall.
Confound their politics,
Frustrate their knavish tricks.
On Thee our hopes we fix.
  God save us all.

f Thy choicest gifts in store
On him be pleased to pour,
  Long may he reign,
May he defend our laws,
And ever give us cause
To sing with heart and voice,
  God save the King.

(?) *Henry Carey* (—1748).

2.—*THANKSGIVINGS.*

(1) GENERAL.

642
        L.M.

mf PRAISE to our God, whose bounteous
  hand
Prepared of old our glorious land ;
A garden fenced with silver sea ;
A people prosperous, bold, and free.

mf Praise to our God ; through all
  our past
His mighty arm hath held us fast,
Till wars and perils, toils and tears.
Have brought the rich and peaceful
  years.

mf Praise to our God ; the vine He
  set
Within our coasts is fruitful yet ;
On many a shore her seedlings
  grow ;   [glow.
'Neath many a sun her clusters

mf Praise to our God ; His power alone
Can keep unmoved our ancient
  throne,
Sustained by counsels wise and just,
And guarded by a people's trust.

mf Praise to our God ; Who still
  forbears,
Who still this guilty nation spares ;
Who calls us still to seek His face,
And lengthens out our day of
  grace.

f Praise to our God ; though chasten-
  ings stern
Our evil dross should throughly
  burn,
His rod and staff, from age to age,
Shall rule and guide His heritage.

J. Ellerton.

10a

643   8.7.8.7., double.

ʄ LIFT thy song among the nations,
   England of the Lord beloved !
Sing the grace for generations
   That hath kept thy lamp un-
     moved ;
Sing how vainly hosts assembled
   'Gainst the isle of His delight ;
Sing how tyrants turned and
     trembled
   When His arm upheld thy right!

mf Sing how He, the Lord, hath
     brought thee
   Onward still from height to
     height,
How the Heavenly Lustre sought
   thee   [bright
   Ere it made the world more
Let the freedom long-descended
   Gloriously uplift thy voice !
In the Good Old Cause defended
   By thy men of might, rejoice !

mf Sing how He His England crownèd
   When He loosed the yoke of
     Rome ;
Sing how He His truth enthronèd
   In this consecrated home ;
How He trusts thee with the
     treasure
Of His Word to send it forth :
Mightily fulfil His pleasure ;
   Send His word o'er all the earth !

[*f* Sing how gleamed His sword
     victorious
In the hands of heroes thine !
How His fire more sweetly glorious
   Streamèd from Thy souls divine !
Let no marvel of Thy story
   Lose its place amidst the praise!
Praise Him for Thine olden glory !
Praise Him for these latter days!]

f Sing how freedom's fire abideth
   Where it first did burn and
     shine;
How for thee the Lord provideth
   Boundless realms and tasks
     divine !
As ascends and spreads thy glory,
   So thy strain advance, prolong !
With the fulness of thy story
   Blend the fulness of thy song !
            T. H. Gill.

644   C.M.

mf SHINE, mighty God, on Britain
     shine,
   With beams of heavenly grace ;
Reveal Thy power through all our
     coasts,
   And show Thy smiling face.

mf Amidst our isle, exalted high,
   Do Thou our glory stand,
And like a wall of guardian fire,
   Surround the favoured land.

mf When shall Thy Name, from shore
     to shore,
   Sound all the earth abroad ;
And distant nations know and
     love
   Their Saviour and their God ?

f Sing to the Lord, ye distant lands,
   Sing loud, with solemn voice :
While British tongues exalt His
     praise,
   And British hearts rejoice.

mf He, the great Lord, the sovereign
     Judge,
   That sits enthroned above,
Wisely commands the worlds He
     made
   In justice and in love.

ll obey her Maker's will, | Our God will crown His chosen isle
ld a full increase ; | With fruitfulness and peace.

I. Watts.

(2) FOR PEACE.

L.M. | **646** | 6.7.6.7.6.6.6.6.

of Hosts, Thou God of | *mf*   LORD God, we worship Thee,
| Whose goodness reigneth o'er us :
st the issues of the fight, | *cres*   We praise Thy love and power
e tumult of the strife | *f*   In loud and happy chorus.
the scales of death and | To heaven our song shall soar ;
| For ever shall it be
is Thine, the night is | Resounding o'er and o'er ;
     [shine ; | Lord God, we worship Thee.
st the sun of peace to | *mf*   Lord God, we worship Thee,
of war is fled away, | For Thou our land defendest ;
of peace we hail to-day. | Thou pourest down Thy grace,
Thee, Lord, Thou Prince | And strife and war Thou endest.
e,   [cease ; | Since golden peace, O Lord.
dost bid war's fears to | Thou grantest us to see,
e the message comes | *cres*   Our land with one accord,
     [men." | *f*   Lord God, gives thanks to Thee.
e on earth, goodwill to | *mf*   Lord God, we worship Thee :
on's voice is heard no | Thou didst indeed chastise us ;
| Yet still Thy goodness spares,
the furious battle roar, | And still Thy mercy tries us.
sinks the deadly blast— | Once more our Father's hand
quake and the storm are | Has bid our sorrows flee,
| And peace rejoice our land :
we hear their echo still | Lord God, we worship Thee.
ly on the distant hill, | *mf*   Lord God, we worship Thee,
, Lord, as we rejoice, | And pray Thee, Who hast blest us,
in the still small voice. | That we may live in peace,
ou, and with the battle- | And none henceforth molest us.
| O crown us with Thy love,
and malice pass away ; | And our Defender be ;
be all hatred then, | Thou, Who hast heard our prayer,
f Jesus Christ : Amen. | Lord God, we worship Thee.

G. Moultrie. | *J Franck, tr. Catherine Winkworth.*

(3) FOR VICTORY.

647 C.M.

f GREAT God of hosts, our ears have
   heard,
   Our fathers oft have told, [them,
What wonders Thou hast done for
   Thy glorious deeds of old.

f Not by their might was safety
   wrought,
   Nor victory by their sword; [race
But Thou didst guard the chosen
   Who Thy great Name adored.

mf Great God of Hosts, their God and
   ours !
   Our only Lord and King !
Let that right arm which fought
   for them
   To us salvation bring.

mf To Thee the glory we'll ascribe,
   By Whom the conquest came,
f And, in triumphant songs of praise,
   Will celebrate Thy Name.

E. Osler.

(4) FOR REMOVAL OF PESTILENCE.

648 7s., 6 lines.

f GOD the Lord has heard our prayer,
   God has lightened all our care ;
To His glorious throne on high
   Rose His children's mournful cry :
ff   Hallelujah ! praises sing
   To our Father and our King.

mp Helpless, Lord, Thy face we sought,
   Thou hast our deliverance wrought;
   God, Who gave us faith to pray,
*cres*Gives us thankful hearts to-day :
ff   Hallelujah, Lord, to Thee
   Sing we, though unworthily.

mf Now the night of grief is gone,
   Now with joy breaks forth the
   morn ;
*cres*Trust in God, if ye would prove
   All the riches of His love :
ff   Hallelujah ! praise the Lord.
   Trust His love, and plead His
   word !

f Praise to God, Who heard our cry !
Praise to Christ, Who pleads on
   high !

And the Holy Ghost, Who gave
   Strength our Father's help to
   crave :
ff   Hallelujah ! glory be
.   To the Blessèd Trinity !

H. H. Wyatt.

649 8.7.8.7.6.6.6.6.7.

f REJOICE to-day, with one accord,
   Sing out with exultation ;
Rejoice and praise our mighty Lord
   Whose Arm hath brought salva-
   tion :
   His works of love proclaim
   The greatness of His Name ;
   For He is God alone,
   Who hath His mercy shown ;
dim   Let all His saints adore Him.

p When in distress to Him we cried
   He heard our sad complaining ;
*cres*O trust in Him, whate'er betide,
   His love is all-sustaining :
   Triumphant songs of praise
   To Him our hearts shall raise

Now every voice shall say,
"O praise our God alway;"
n Let all His saints adore Him.

r Rejoice to-day, with one accord,
Sing out with exultation;
Rejoice and praise our mighty
Lord,

Whose Arm hath brought salvation:
His works of love proclaim
The greatness of His Name;
For He is God alone,
Who hath His mercy shown;
dim Let all His saints adore Him.

H. W. Baker.

(5) FOR RAIN.

50   5.5.5.5.

O SING to the Lord,
Whose bountiful hand
Again doth accord
His gifts to the land.

His clouds have shed down
Their plenteousness here;
His goodness shall crown
The hopes of the year;

And every fold
Shall teem with its sheep,
With harvests of gold
The fields shall be deep;

The vales shall rejoice
With laughter and song,
And man's grateful voice
The music prolong.

So, too, may He pour,
The Last and the First,
His graces in store
On spirits athirst.

mp Till when the great day
Of harvest hath come,
cres He takes us away
To garner at home.

R. F. Littledale.

(6) FOR FAIR WEATHER.

51   7.6.

THE wintry time hath ended,
The rain is past and gone;
With genial glory splendid
Once more shines out the sun.

The chill and wasting showers
Yield now to radiant morn;
The earth is gay with flowers,
The fields are thick with corn.

f We praise Thee, Sun unsetting,
Whose bountiful right Hand
In mercy unforgetting
Hath blest again the land.

mp And when is closed earth's story,
And past its rain and storm,
cres Illume us with the glory
mf Of Thine all-beauteous form.

R. F. Littledale.

3.—PRAYER AND HUMILIATION.
(1) GENERAL.

52   7.6.

Now pray we for our country,
That England long may be

The holy, and the happy,
And the gloriously free.

Who blesseth her is blessèd !
So peace be in her walls,
And joy in all her palaces,
Her cottages and halls.

A. C. Coxe.

653   6.6.4.6.6.6.4.

mf GOD bless our native land !
May Heaven's protecting hand
    Still guard her shore ;
May peace her sway extend,
Foe be transformed to friend,
And Britain's power depend
    On war no more.

*mp*Through every changing scene,
    O Lord ! preserve the King ;
    Long may he reign.
His heart inspire and move
With wisdom from above ;
And in a nation's love
    His throne maintain.

mf May just and righteous laws
    Uphold the public cause,
    And bless our Isle.
Home of the brave and free,
The land of liberty,
We pray that still on thee
    Kind Heaven may smile.

mf And not this land alone,
    But be Thy mercies known
    From shore to shore.
*cres*Lord, make the nations see
That men should brothers be,
And form one family,
    The wide world o'er.

W. E. Hickson.

654   6.6.4.6.6.6.4.

mf GOD bless our native land :
    Her strength and glory stand
        Ever in Thee !

Her faith and laws be pure,
Her throne and hearths secure ;
And let her name endure—
    Home of the free.

mf God guard our sea-girt land,
    And save by Thy right hand
        From all her foes ;
The reign of peace prolong,
Till freedom's rising song
Loud tells the end of wrong
    And nature's throes !

mp God smile upon our land,
    And countless as the sand
        Her blessings be !
*cres*Arise, O Lord, Most High !
    And call her children nigh,
    Till heart and voice reply—
f   Glory to Thee.

655   7.6.7.6.8.8.8.5.

mp WHEN wilt Thou save the
        people ?
    O God of mercy, when ?
    Not kings and lords, but nations !
    Not thrones and crowns, but
        men !   [they ;
    Flowers of Thy heart, O God, are
    Let them not pass, like weeds,
        away—
    Their heritage a sunless day.
cres   God save the people !

mp   Shall crime bring crime for ever,
        Strength   aiding   still   the
            strong ?
    Is it Thy will, O Father,
        That man shall toil for wrong?
    "No," say Thy mountains ; "No,"
        Thy skies ;   [rise,
    Man's clouded sun shall brightly
    And songs ascend instead of sighs.
cres   God save the people !

np When wilt Thou save the
 people?
 O God of mercy, when?
 The people, Lord, the people!
 Not thrones and crowns, but
  men!   [are,
 God save the people; Thine they
 Thy children, as Thine angels fair;
 From vice, oppression, and despair,
cres God save the people!
     Ebenezer Elliott.

656   6.6.6.6.8.8.

mp To Thee, our God, we fly
 For mercy and for grace;
 O hear our lowly cry,
 And hide not Thou Thy face.
cres O Lord, stretch forth Thy mighty
  hand,   [land.
 And guard and bless our Father-

mp Arise, O Lord of Hosts!
 Be jealous for Thy Name,
 And drive from out our coasts
 The sins that put to shame.
cres O Lord, stretch forth Thy mighty
  hand,   [land.
 And guard and bless our Father-

f Thy best gifts from on high
 In rich abundance pour,
 That we may magnify
 And praise Thee more and more.
cres O Lord. stretch forth Thy mighty
  hand,   [land.
 And guard and bless our Father-

[*mf* The powers ordained by Thee
 With heavenly wisdom bless;
 May they Thy servants be,
 And rule in righteousness.
cres O Lord, stretch forth Thy mighty
  hand,   [land.
 And guard and bless our Father-

mf The Church of Thy dear Son
 Inflame with love's pure fire;
 Bind her once more in one,
 And life and truth inspire.
cres O Lord, stretch forth Thy mighty
  hand,
 And guard and bless our Father-
  land.]

p Give peace, Lord, in our time;
 Oh! let no foe draw nigh,
 Nor lawless deed of crime
 Insult Thy Majesty.
cres O Lord, stretch forth Thy mighty
  hand   [land.
 And guard and bless our Father-

p Though vile and worthless, still
 Thy people, Lord, are we;
 And for our God we will
 None other have but Thee.
cres O Lord. stretch forth Thy mighty
  hand,   [land.
 And guard and bless our Father-
     W. W. How.

657   C.M.

mp LORD, while for all mankind we
  pray,
 Of every clime and coast,
 O hear us for our native land,—
 The land we love the most.

mp Our fathers' sepulchres are here,
 And here our kindred dwell:
 Our children too;—how should we
  love
 Another land so well!

mf O guard our shores from every foe,
 With peace our borders bless:
 With prosperous times our cities
  crown,
 Our fields with plenteousness.

f Unite us in the sacred love
 Of knowledge, truth, and Thee;
And let our hills and valleys shout
 The songs of liberty.

mp Here may religion pure and mild
 Upon our Sabbaths smile;
And piety and virtue reign,
 And bless our native isle.

mp Lord of the nations, thus to Thee
 Our country we commend;
*crex*Be Thou her refuge and her trust,
 Her everlasting Friend.

J. R. Wreford.

658   C.M.

BEFORE A PARLIAMENTARY
ELECTION.

mf O GOD, Who holdest in Thy hand
 The islands of the sea;
Whose bounty makes our native
 land
So glorious, great, and free:

mf We bless Thee for Thy guardian
 care,
Who dost our foes restrain,

And for the freedom, larg⸱
 fair,
Our fathers died to gain.

mp Now bend our hearts to
 command;
And grant us wisdom true
To know the times, and unde⸱
 What England ought to d⸱

mp The heat of party strife abat⸱
 And teach us how to choo⸱
Good men and wise to guic
 State—
The evil to refuse.

mf Let all our chosen rulers hai
 The kingdom of Thy Son,
And strive that virtue may p⸱
 That justice may be done:

f That so the land Thou deig⸱
 bless
May flourish, all our days,
 In freedom, peace, and righ
 ness;
And Thine shall be the pr

T. G. Crip.

---

(2) TIMES OF DISTRESS.
(*a*) *War.*

659   11.10.11.9.

f GOD the All-terrible! King, Who
 ordainest
Great winds Thy clarions, the
 lightnings Thy sword;
*dim*Show forth Thy pity on high
 where Thou reignest;
pp Give to us peace in our time, O
 Lord.

*f God the Omnipotent! Mighty
 Avenger,* [heard;
Watching invisible, judging un-

*dim*Doom us not now in the h
 our danger;
pp Give to us peace in our t
 Lord.

mf God the All-merciful! eart⸱
 forsaken
Thy way of blessedness, al
 Thy word;
*dim*Bid not Thy wrath in its
 awaken;
pp Give to us peace in our t
 Lord.

od the All-righteous One ! man
  hath defied Thee ;
Yet to eternity standeth Thy
  word ;
alsehood and wrong shall not
  tarry beside Thee :
Give to us peace in our time, O
  Lord !]

od the All-wise ! by the fire of
  Thy chastening,
Earth shall to freedom and truth
  be restored ;
hrough the thick darkness Thy
  kingdom is hastening ;
Thou wilt give peace in Thy time,
  O Lord !

o shall Thy children in thankful
  devotion
Laud Him Who saved them from
  peril abhorred,
inging in chorus from ocean to
  ocean,
" Peace to the nations and praise
  to the Lord."

ꝼ. *Chorley, altd. by J. Ellerton.*

1 C.M., double.

BEAT King of nations, hear our
  prayer,
While at Thy feet we fall,
nd humbly, with united cry,
To Thee for mercy call. [Thine ;
he guilt is ours, but grace is
O turn us not away :
ut hear us from Thy lofty throne,
And help us when we pray.

ur fathers' sins were manifold,
And ours no less, we own ;
et wondrously, from age to age,
Thy *goodness* hath been shown.

660 L.M.

mf O GOD of Love, O King of Peace,
  Make wars throughout the world
    to cease ;
  The wrath of sinful man restrain ;
p Give peace, O God, give peace
    again.

mf Remember, Lord, Thy works of old,
  The wonders that our fathers told ;
dim Remember not our sin's dark stain ;
p Give peace, O God, give peace
    again.

mf Whom shall we trust but Thee, O
    Lord ? [word ?
  Where rest but on Thy faithful
cres None ever called on Thee in vain ;
p Give peace, O God, give peace
    again.

f Where saints and angels dwell
    above,
  All hearts are knit in holy love ;
  O bind us in that heavenly chain ;
p Give peace, O God, give peace again.

H. W. Baker.

(*b*) *Pestilence.*

mp When dangers, like a stormy sea,
  Beset our country round. [cried,
cres To Thee we looked, to Thee we
  And help in Thee we found.

mf Though love and might no longer
    heal
  By touch or word or look ;
  Though they who do Thy work
    must read
  Thy laws in nature's book :
cres Yet come to cleanse the sick man's
    soul,
  Come cleanse the leprous taint,
f Give joy and peace where all is strife,
  And strength where all is faint.

p With one consent we meekly bow
 Beneath Thy chastening hand,
And. pouring forth confession meet,
 Mourn with our mourning land.
cres With pitying eye behold our need,
 As thus we lift our prayer ;
mp Correct us with Thy judgments,
  Lord,
 Then let Thy mercy spare.
     J. II. Gurney.

662   C.M.

mp O LORD of life and death, we come
 In sorrow to Thy throne,
 Yet not bewildered, blind and
  dumb,
 Before some power unknown.

mp The scourge is in our Father's
 hand ;   [Thee ;
 The plague comes forth from

663   7s.

mp THOU that sendest sun and rain,
 Ruling over land and sea,
 May we ne'er of Thee complain,
 Whatsoe'er our lot may be.

mp Whether sun or rain in turn
 Ripen·or destroy the grain,
 May we still this lesson learn,
 Ne'er to murmur or complain.

mp Fewer flocks or fewer herds,
 Scanty though our store may be,
 Still we seem to hear Thy words,
cres " Trust, ye faithful, trust in
  Me."

mp All we have, we know, is Thine,
 Thine to give and take away ;
 Feed us then with food divine,
 Feed us this and every day.

Oh, give us hearts to understand,
 And faith Thy ways to see !
mp Forgive the foul neglect that
  brought
 Thy chastening to our door
The homes uncared for, souls
  untaught,
 The unregarded poor.

mp The slothful ease, the greed of
  gain,
 The wasted years, forgive ;
Purge out our sins by needful pain,
 Then turn, and bid us live.

mp So shall the lives for which we
  plead
 Be spared to praise Thee still,
cres And we, from fear and danger
  freed,
mf Be strong to do Thy will.·
     J. Ellerton.

(c) Dearth.

mp Thus as changeful seasons bring
 Wealth or want, whiche'er it be,
cres Uncomplaining still we'll sing
 Simply trusting all to Thee.
     G. Thring.

664   8.7.8.7.

mp GOD, Creator, and Preserver ;
  God. Who feedest man and beast ;
 God, Whose tender mercy careth
  For the weakest and the least ;

mp If in former times of gladness,
  In the fulness of our bread,
 Harvest gifts to Thee we offered,
  Harvest songs to Thee we said:

cres Shall we not in trustful patience
  Cast our cares upon Thee now ?
 Shall we not in meek obedience
  To Thy righteous judgments bow?

›Though the earth withhold her increase, [dew,
Though the heaven restrain its
Though his hand the reaper fill not,
Yet we know that Thou art true.

' Not in vain the mighty promise,
From beneath the bow of peace,
Told us, while the earth remaineth,
Seed-time, harvest, shall not cease.

*dim*But our sins have stayed Thy blessing,
Our rebellions drawn Thy sword;
Pity now Thy mourning people,
Think upon Thy covenant, Lord!

mf So the sunshine of Thy bounty
Once again shall dry our tears,
*cres*And Thy gracious Hand restore us
All our canker-eaten years!
J. Ellerton.

(d) Drought.

65   888.888.

› O LIFT our spirits, Lord, to Thee!
We would not earthward bend the knee
To grovel for some golden gain ;
It is for very life we plead!
O hear us, Father, in our need,
And ope Thy hand to us in rain.

› We trust our seed to the dark earth,
But only Thou canst bring it forth
In ripened fruits of smiling grain :
By Thee alone are all things fed,
To Thee alone we look for bread :
Pity us, Lord, and send the rain.

› A world of dumb things droop and die ;
For their sake hear the human cry,
O make Thy covenant once again,
And bid the bow of promise rise,
₂₈While smiling earth drinks from the skies
The life and glory of the rain.

'The world revive ; make glad the vine
That turns the water into wine ;
In the green ear enrich the grain ;
Anoint the flower and crown the fruit

All nature quicken, core and root,
And send Thy blessing, Lord, in rain.
G. Massey.

666   7s., 6 lines.

mf WHAT our Father does is well :
Blessèd truth His children tell!
*dim*Though He send, for plenty, want,
Though the harvest-store be scant,
*cres*Yet we rest upon His love,
Seeking better things above.

mf What our Father does is well :
Shall the wilful heart rebel ?
*dim*If a blessing He withhold
In the field, or in the fold,
*cres*Is it not Himself to be
All our store eternally ?

mf What our Father does is well :
Though He sadden hill and dell,
*cres*Upward yet our praises rise
For the strength His word supplies·
He has called us sons of God,
p Can we murmur at His rod ?

mf What our Father does is well :
May the thought within us dwell ;
*dim*Though nor milk nor honey flow
In our barren Canaan now ;

*cres*God can save us in our need,
  God can bless us, God can
   feed.

  Therefore unto Him we raise
  Hymns of glory, songs of praise ;

To the Father, and the Son,
And the Spirit, Three in One.
Honour, might, and glory be.
Now and through eternity.

   B. Schmolcke, tr. H. W. Baker.

(e) *Excessive Rain.*

667   7.7.6.7.7.6.

...f IN the hollow of Thy Hand,
  Maker of the sea and land,
   Thou dost hold the waters ;
*dim*Father, in our sore distress,
  Seal the opened heavens, and bless
   Sion's sons and daughters.

mf Evermore Thy words remain,
  Ne'er again shall floods and rain
   Overwhelm in sadness ;

*dim*Merciful. receive our cry,
  By Thy Covenant, Most High,
   Visit us with gladness.
f Then our land shall laugh and sing.
  Then the valleys increase bring,
   Fear no more oppress us,
  Sunlight fall on field and wold,
  On the stall and on the fold,
   God, our own God, bless us.

   W. C. Dix.

XIV.
Special Seasons.
1.—*MORNING.*

668   L.M.

f AWAKE, my soul, and with the sun
  Thy daily stage of duty run ;
  Shake off dull sloth, and joyful rise
  To pay thy morning sacrifice.

mf Thy precious time mis-spent re-
   deem ;
  Each present day thy last esteem ;
  Improve thy talent with due care ;
  For the great day thyself prepare.

[*mf*In conversation be sincere ;
  Keep conscience as the noontide
   clear ;
  Think how All-seeing God thy ways
  And all thy secret thoughts surveys.

f Wake and lift up thyself, my heart,
And with the angels bear thy part,

Who, all night long, unwearied sing
High praise to the Eternal King.]

mf All praise to Thee, Who safe hast
   kept,   [slept :
  And hast refreshed me whilst 1
  Grant, Lord, when I from death
   shall wake,
  I may of endless light partake !

p Lord, I my vows to Thee renew ;
  Disperse my sins as morning dew :
  Guard my first springs of thought
   and will,
  And with Thyself my spirit fill.

*cres*Direct, control, suggest, this day.
  All I design, or do, or say, [might.
  That all my powers, with all their
  In Thy sole glory may unite.

d, from Whom all
flow ;   [below !
n, all creatures here
n above, ye heavenly

.ther, Son, and Holy

T. Ken.

L.M.

rd of heavenly grace,
ıtness of Thy Father's

.tain of eternal light,
ms disperse the shades
;—

Sun of heavenly love,
wn Thy radiance from

inward hearts convey
Spirit's cloudless ray.

he Father's help will
          [Name ;
the Father's glorious
'ul succour we implore,
ıy stand, to fall no more.

ır actions deign to bless,
he bonds of wickedness,
en falls our feet defend,
us to a prosperous end.]

deep-rooted in the soul,
flesh, our minds control;
.epart, and discord cease,
:hin be joy and peace.

be the approaching day !
ıss be our morning ray ;
ful love our noonday

our sunset, calm and

---

mf O Christ ! with each returning
morn
Thine image to our hearts is borne ;
cres O, may we ever clearly see
Our Saviour and our God in Thee !

Ambrose, tr. J. Chandler.

670   L.M.

mf FORTH in Thy Name, O Lord, I go,
My daily labour to pursue ;
Thee, only Thee. resolved to know,
In all I think, or speak, or do.

mf The task Thy wisdom hath as-
signed,
O let me cheerfully fulfil ;
In all my works Thy presence find,
And prove Thy good and perfect
will.

mf Thee may I set at my right hand,
Whose eyes my inmost substance
see ;
And labour on at Thy command,
And offer all my works to Thee.

mp Give me to bear Thine easy yoke,
And every moment watch and pray.
cres And still to things eternal look,
f And hasten to Thy glorious day.

f For Thee delightfully employ
Whate'er Thy bounteous grace
hath given,
And run my course with even joy,
And closely walk with Thee to
heaven.

C. Wesley, v. 2, l. 4 altd.

671   8.3.3.6.

f RISE, my soul, adore thy Maker !
Angels praise,
Join thy lays ;
With them be partaker.

mf Father, Lord of every spirit,
In Thy light
Lead me right,
Through my Saviour's merit.

mp Never cast me from Thy Presence
Till my soul
Shall be full
Of Thy blessèd Essence.

mp O my Jesus, God Almighty,
Pray for me,
Till I see
Thee in Salem's city

mp Holy Ghost, by Jesus given,
Be my Guide,
Lest my pride
Shut me out of heaven.

cres Thou by night wast my Protector :
With me stay
All the day,
Ever my Director

mf Holy, Holy, Holy Giver
Of all good,
Life and food,
f Reign, adored for ever !

J. Cennick.

672   7s., 6 lines.

mf EVERY morning mercies new
Fall as fresh as early dew ;
Every morning let us pay
Tribute with the early day ;
cres For Thy mercies, Lord, are sure ;
Thy compassion doth endure.

mf Still the greatness of Thy love
Daily doth our sins remove ;
Daily, far as east from west,
Lifts the burden from the breast ;
cres Gives unbought to those who
pray
Strength to stand in evil day.

mf Let our prayers each morn prevail,
That these gifts may never fail :
And as we confess the sin,
And the tempter's power within.
cres Every morning, for the strife,
Feed us with the Bread of Life.

mf As the morning light returns,
As the sun with splendour burns.
Teach us still to turn to Thee,
Ever-blessèd Trinity,
cres With our hands our hearts to
raise,
f In unfailing prayer and praise.

G. Phillimore, v. 1, l. 1 altd.

673   L.M.

mf O TIMELY happy, timely wise,
Hearts that with rising morn
arise !
Eyes that the beam celestial view,
Which evermore makes all things
new !

mf New every morning is the love
Our wakening and uprising prove,
Through sleep and darkness safely
brought,   [thought.
Restored to life and power and

mf New mercies each returning day
Hover around us while we pray :
New perils past, new sins forgiven,
New thoughts of God, new hopes
of heaven.

mp If, on our daily course, our mind
Be set to hallow all we find,
New treasures still, of countless
price,
God will provide for sacrifice.

mf Old friends, old scenes, will lovelier
be,
As more of heaven in each we see ;

Some softening gleam of love and
   prayer
Shall dawn on every cross and care.

np The trivial round, the common
   task,
   Will furnish all we ought to ask ;
   Room to deny ourselves ; a road
   To bring us, daily, nearer God.

p Only, O Lord, in Thy dear love
   Fit us for perfect rest above ;
*cres*And help us, this and every day,
mf To live more nearly as we pray.
                    J. Keble.

674   7s., 6 lines.

f CHRIST, Whose glory fills the skies,
   Christ, the true, the only Light,
   Sun of Righteousness, arise,
   Triumph o'er the shades of night !
   Day-spring from on high, be near !
   Day-star, in my heart appear !

p Dark and cheerless is the morn
   Unaccompanied by Thee ;
   Joyless is the day's return,
*cres*Till Thy mercy's beams I see ;
   Till they inward light impart,
   Glad my eyes, and warm my heart.

mf Visit then this soul of mine,
   Pierce the gloom of sin and grief !
   Fill me, Radiancy Divine,
   Scatter all my unbelief !
*cres*More and more Thyself display,
f Shining to the perfect day.
                C. Wesley.

675   L.M.

mf MY God, how endless is Thy love !
   Thy gifts are every evening new ;
   And morning mercies from above
   Gently distil like early dew.

mp Thou spread'st the curtains of the
   night,
   Great Guardian of my sleeping
   hours ;
*cres*Thy sovereign word restores the
   light,
   And quickens all my drowsy
   powers.

mf I yield my powers to Thy command,
   To Thee I consecrate my days ;
*cres*Perpetual blessings from Thy
   hand
f Demand perpetual songs of praise.
                I. Watts.

676   7.6.7.6., double.

f THY love for all Thy creatures
   What tongue, O God, may tell ?
   The morning, noon, and evening,
   Alike our praise compel :
   The morning, noon, and evening,
   Whene'er they rise or fall,
   Unite to hymn Thy praises,
   Great Maker of them all.

f Behold the sun in splendour
   Hath lit his fires on high,
   The farther on his journey,
   The higher in the sky ;
*dim*And when again he sinketh
   Beneath the western wave,
*cres*A radiant crown of glory
   Shall kindle o'er his grave.

mf May we to whom in mercy
   A brighter light is given,
   The farther on our journey,
   The nearer be to heaven ;
*dim*And when the shades of evening
   Shall lengthen o'er our heads,
*cres*May rays of heavenly glory
   Illume our dying beds.

mf Shine ! shine ! Thou Sun Eternal,
And cast a ray divine
On those who hymn Thy praises ;
Both now and ever shine :
cres For, then, no cloud of evening
Shall gather round the past,
f But Thou, O Christ, shalt light us
Safe Home,—safe Home at last.
G. Thring.

677   C.M., or 4.4.6. .4.6.

f   My soul, awake !
Thy rest forsake,
And greet the morning light :
With song arise—
Glad sacrifice
For mercies of the night.

f   With courage drest,
Strong-hearted, blest,
Fulfil thy work abroad.
Fearless and true,
Thy way pursue,
A happy child of God.

mf   Amid the strife
Of daily life,
Amid its noontide heat,
Fear not to miss
Thy secret bliss,
The rest of sonship sweet.

In liberty
Of holy glee,
Accept thy childhood's part ;
And thou shalt find,
By faith enshrined,
The Father in thy heart.

mp   O blessèd rest,
With such a Guest
Life's duty grows divine,
Dross becomes gold,
And, as of old,
The water turns to wine.

f   Eternal praise
To Thee we raise,
Who deign'st with men to dwel
Great Word of God,
Jehovah ! Lord !
Adored Immanuel !
Jane Livoci

678   L.M

mf O GOD, Who canst not change
fail,
Guiding the hours as they roll
Brightening with beams the mo
ing pale,
And burning in the mid-day sk

mp Quench Thou the fires of hate
strife,
The wasting fever of the heart
dim From perils guard our feeble l
p And to our souls Thy peace imp

mp Grant this, O Father, only Son,
And Holy Spirit, God of grace,
cres To Whom all glory, Three
One,
mf Be given in every time and pla
Ambrose, tr. J. H. Newma:

679   7e., 6 li:

mf AT Thy feet, O Christ, we lay
Thine own gift of this new day
Doubt of what it holds in store
Makes us crave Thine aid
more :
Lest it prove a time of loss,
Mark it, Saviour, with Thy Cr

mp If it flow on calm and bright,
Be Thyself our chief delight ;
If it bring unknown distress,
Good is all that Thou canst bl
Only, while its hours begin,
Pray we, keep them clear of si

our weakness know,
discern our foe ;
, before Thine eyes
ger open lies :
om us, while we plead
ssions and our need.

we Thy Word embrace,
ioment in Thy grace,
es to Thee consign,
our wills in Thine,
speak, and do, and be,
t which pleases Thee.

rd, and that right soon ;
grant the choicest boon
ive can e'er impart,
eness of heart :
is and all our days,
God, show forth Thy

W. Bright.

C.M.
' life, Thy quickening

ny morning song ;
e words I would rejoice
Thee belong.

ght, I feel Thy wind ;
Thy uttered word ;
wakes my heart and

ince is, my Lord.

choose my highest part,
my face to Thee ;
stir my inmost heart
ip fervently.

e live and act this day.
g from the dead ;
e my spirit good and

ny daily bread.

mp Within my heart, speak, Lord,
speak on,
My heart alive to keep
dimTill the night comes, and, labour
done,
p   In Thee I fall asleep.

G. Macdonald.

681
L.M.
f LORD God of morning and of night,
We thank Thee for Thy gift of
light ;
As in the dawn the shadows fly,
We seem to find Thee now more
nigh.

mf Fresh hopes have wakened in the
heart,
Fresh force to do our daily part ;
Thy slumber-gifts our strength
restore   [more.
Throughout the day to serve Thee

mp Yet, whilst Thy will we would
pursue,
Oft what we would we cannot do ;
The sun may stand in zenith skies,
dimBut on the soul thick midnight
lies.

mf O Lord of lights, 'tis Thou alone
Canst make our darkened hearts
Thine own :
O then be with us, Lord, that we
In Thy great day may wake to
Thee.

f Praise God, our Maker, and our
Friend ;
Praise Him through time, till time
shall end ;   [adore
cresTill psalm and song His Name
ff Through Heaven's great day of
Evermore.

F. T. Palgrave.

2.—EVENING.

682   L.M.

f GLORY to Thee, my God, this night,
For all the blessings of the light ;
Keep me, O keep me, King of kings,
Beneath Thine own almighty
    wings !

.np Forgive me, Lord, for Thy dear Son,
The ill that I this day have done ;
' That with the world, myself, and
    Thee,
J, ere I sleep, at peace may be.

Teach me to live, that I may dread
The grave as little as my bed !
p To die, that this vile body may
*cres*Rise glorious at the awful day !

mp O may my soul on Thee repose ;
And may sweet sleep mine eyelids
    close ;
Sleep, that may me more vigorous
    make
To serve my God when I awake !

[*p* When in the night I sleepless lie,
My soul with heavenly thoughts
    supply !
Let no ill dreams disturb my rest,
No powers of darkness me molest !]

mf O when shall I, in endless day,
For ever chase dark sleep away,
And hymns with the supernal choir
Incessant sing, and never tire ?

ff Praise God, from Whom all bless-
    ings flow,
Praise Him all creatures here
    below !   [host !
Praise Him above, ye heavenly
Praise Father, Son, and Holy
    Ghost !

                 T. Ken.

683   L.M.

mf SUN of my soul, Thou Saviour dear,
It is not night if Thou be near ;
Oh ! may no earth-born cloud arise
To hide Thee from Thy servant's
    eyes.

[*p* When with dear friends sweet talk
    I hold,
And all the flowers of life unfold;
Let not my heart within me burn,
Except in all I Thee discern.

pp When the soft dews of kindly sleep
My wearied eyelids gently steep,
Be my last thought, how sweet to
    rest
For ever on my Saviour's breast!]

[*mf* Abide with me from morn till eve,
For without Thee I cannot live ;
Abide with me when night is nigh,
For without Thee I dare not die.

mf Thou Framer of the light and dark,
Steer through the tempest Thine
    own ark !
Amid the howling wintry sea,
We are in port if we have Thee.]

p If some poor wandering child of
    Thine
Have spurned, to-day, Thy voice
    Divine,
Now, Lord, the gracious work
    begin ;
Let him no more lie down in sin !

mp Watch by the sick ; enrich the poor
With blessings from Thy boundless
    store,
*dim*Be every mourner's sleep to-night,
pp Like infant's slumbers, pure and
    light !

near and bless us when we
:e,   [we take ;
hrough the world our way
n the ocean of Thy love,
se ourselves in Heaven above !

J. Keble.

10s.

ε with me ! fast falls the
ntide ;
arkness deepens ; Lord, with
abide !   [forts flee,
 other helpers fail, and com-
of the helpless, O abide with
!

, to its close ebbs out life's
le day !
.'s joys grow dim ; its glories
s away ;   [see,
ʒe and decay in all around I
ou, who changest not, abide
h me !

, brief glance I beg, a passing
rd ;
as Thou dwell'st with Thy
:iples, Lord,   [free,
liar, condescending, patient,
;, not to sojourn, but abide,
:h me.

, not in terrors, as the King of
ʊgs ;
:ind and good, with healing in
y wings ;   [every plea,—
; for all woes, a heart for
:,·Friend of sinners, and thus
le with me !

ı on my head in early youth
lst smile ;
though rebellious and perverse
ʌn*while,*

Thou hast not left me, oft as I left
  Thee :   [me!
On to the close, O Lord, abide with
mf I need Thy presence every passing
  hour :
  What but Thy grace can foil the
    tempter's power ?   [stay can be ?
  Who like Thyself my guide and
  Through cloud and sunshine, O
    abide with me !]
mf I fear no foe with Thee at hand to
  bless :
  Ills have no weight, and tears no
    bitterness :   [grave, thy victory?
*cres*Where is death's sting ? where,
  I triumph still, if Thou abide with
  me !

p Hold Thou Thy cross before my
  closing eyes !
*cres*Shine through the gloom, and
  point me to the skies !
f Heaven's morning breaks ! and
  earth's vain shadows flee !
  In life, in death, O Lord, abide
  with me !

H. F. Lyte, v. 8, ll. 1, 2 altd.

685   8.4.8.4.8.8.8.4.
mf GOD that madest earth and heaven,
  Darkness and light ;
  Who the day for toil hast given,
  For rest the night ;
mp May Thine angel-guards defend us,
  Slumber sweet Thy mercy send us,
  Holy dreams and hopes attend us,
  This livelong night.

mf Guard us waking, guard us sleep·
  ing ;
  And when we die,
  May we, in Thy mighty keeping,
  All peaceful lie.

mp When the last dread call shall
　　　wake us,
cres Do not Thou, our God, forsake us ;
f But to reign in glory take us
　　　With Thee on high.
　　　　R. Heber and R. Whately.

686　　　　　8.8.7.8.8.7.

mf FATHER, in high heaven dwelling,
　　May our evening song be telling
　　　Of Thy mercy large and free.
　　Through the day Thy love has
　　　　fed us,　　　　　　[us.
　　Through the day Thy care has led
　　　With divinest charity.

mp This day's sins, O pardon, Saviour,
　　Evil thoughts, perverse behaviour,
　　　Envy, pride, and vanity ;
　　From the world, the flesh, deliver,
　　Save us now, and save us ever,
　　　O Thou Lamb of Calvary !

mp From enticements of the devil,
　　From the might of spirits evil,
　　　Be our shield and panoply ;
　　Let Thy power this night defend us,
p And a heavenly peace attend us,
　　　And angelic company.

mp Whilst the night-dews are distil-
　　　ling,
　　Holy Ghost, each heart be filling
　　　With Thine own serenity ;
dim Softly let the eyes be closing,
　　Loving souls on Thee reposing,
　　　Ever blessèd Trinity.
　　　　　　　　　G. Rawson.

687　　　　　6.4.6.6.

mp THE sun is sinking fast,
　　　The daylight dies ;
cres Let love awake, and pay
　　　Her evening sacrifice.

pp As Christ upon the cros
　　In death reclined,
　　And to His Father's hai
　　His parting soul resigne

mf So now herself my soul
　　Would wholly give
　　Into His sacred charge.
　　In Whom all spirits live

mp So now beneath His eye
　　Would calmly rest,
　　Without a wish or thou;
　　Abiding in the breast,

mf Save that His will be do
　　Whate'er betide ;
　　Dead to herself ; and de
　　In Him to all beside.

mf Thus would I live ;—ye
　　Not I, but He
　　In all His power and lo
　　Henceforth alive in me

f One sacred Trinity !
　　One Lord divine !
　　May I be ever His !
　　And He for ever mine !
　　　Latin, 7th century. tr. E. C

688　　　　　　　　　i

mp THE radiant morn hath
　　　away,
　　And spent too soon her
　　The shadows of departing
　　　Creep on once more

mp Our life is but an autumn
　　Its glorious noon how
　　　past ;—
cres Lead us, O Christ, Tho
　　Safe home at last.

mf Oh ! by Thy soul-inspirin
　　Uplift our hearts to realm

ɔ look to that bright place
yond the sky ;—
·ht, and life, and joy, and
)eace
ded empire reign,
nging angels never cease
eir deathless strain ;—

ints are clothed in spot-
ess white,
,ing shadows never fall,
hou, Eternal Light of
Jight,
; Lord of all.

G. Thring.

6.5.6.5.

day is over,
ə drawing nigh,
ɔf the evening
:ross the sky.

larkness gathers,
·gin to peep,
l beasts, and flowers
ill be asleep.

· the weary
ıd sweet repose ;
tenderest blessing
r eyelids close.

little children
bright of Thee ;
: sailors tossing
deep blue sea.

very sufferer
ıg late in pain ;
o plan some evil
ıeir sin restrain.

:he long night-watches
ine angels spread
te wings above me,
ıg round my bed.

cres When the morning wakens,
Then may I arise
f Pure, and fresh, and sinless
In Thy holy eyes.

S. Baring-Gould.

690
8.7.8.7.

mp HEAR my prayer, O Heavenly
Father,
Ere I lay me down to sleep :
Bid Thine angels, pure and holy,
Round my bed their vigil keep.

mp Heavy though my sins, Thy mercy
Far outweighs them every one :
Down before Thy cross I cast them,
Trusting in Thy help alone.

mf Keep me, through this night of
peril,
Underneath its boundless shade ;
Take me to Thy rest, I pray Thee,
When my pilgrimage is made.

mf None shall measure out Thy
patience
By the span of human thought :
None shall bound the tender mercies
Which Thy holy Son hath
bought.

mp Pardon all my past transgressions,
Give me strength for days to
come ;
cres Guide and guard me with Thy
blessing,
Till Thine angels bid me home.

Harriet Parr, v. 2, l. 1 altd.

691
6.6.4.6.6.6.4.

mf FATHER of love and power,
Guard Thou our evening hour,
cres   Shield with Thy might.

For all Thy care this day
Our grateful thanks we pay,
*dim*And to our Father pray,—
p　　Bless us to-night!

mf Jesus, Immanuel!
Come in Thy love to dwell
In hearts contrite.
*dim*For all our sins we grieve,
*cres*But we Thy grace receive,
And in Thy word believe;
p　　Bless us to-night!

mp Spirit of holiness,
Gentle, transforming grace,
Indwelling light!
*dim*Soothe Thou each weary breast.
Now let Thy peace possessed
Calm us to perfect rest,
p　　Bless us to-night.
　　　　　　　　　G. Rawson.

692　　　　　　L.M.

mp THE night is come : like to the day
Depart not Thou, great God, away ;
Let not my sins, all black as night,
Eclipse the lustre of Thy light.

mf Keep Thou still in my heaven : for
　　me
The day doth need no sun but Thee ;
O Thou Whose nature cannot sleep,
O'er my closed eyelids sentry keep.

mp Guard me against those watchful
　　foes,　　　　　　　[close ;
Whose eyes are open while mine
Let no ill dreams my sleep infest,
But such as Jacob's slumbers blest ;

mp That so I may, my rest being
　　wrought,
Awake into some holy thought ;
*cres*And with an active vigour run
　*My course, as doth the unwearied
　sun.*

mp Sleep is a death : O make me try
By sleeping what it is to die ;
p And then as gently lay my head
Upon my grave, as now my bed.
　　　　　　　T. Browne, altd.

693　　　　7.6.7.6.8.8.

mf　THE day is past and over ;
All thanks, O Lord, to Thee;
dim　I pray Thee that offenceless
The hours of dark may be :
pp O Jesu, keep me in Thy sight,
And save me through the coming
　　night.

mf　The joys of day are over ;
I lift my heart to Thee ;
dim　And call on Thee that sinless
The hours of dark may be :
pp O Jesu, make their darkness light,
And save me through the coming
　　night.

mf　The toils of day are over ;
I raise the hymn to Thee ;
dim　And ask that free from peril
The hours of fear may be :
pp O Jesu, keep me in Thy sight,
And guard me through the coming
　　night.

mf　Be Thou my soul's preserver,
O God! for Thou dost know
How many are the perils
Through which I have to go.
pp Lover of men! O hear my call,
And guard and save me from them
　　all.
　　　　　Anatolius, tr. J. M. Neale.

694　　　　8.7.8.7.7.7.

mp THROUGH the day Thy love has
　　spared us,
Now we lay us down to rest ; [us
Through the silent watches guard

Let no foe our peace molest ;
mf Jesus, Thou our guardian be ;
Sweet it is to trust in Thee.

mp Pilgrims here on earth, and
strangers
Dwelling in the midst of foes,
Us and ours preserve from dangers;
In Thy love may we repose !
p And when life's sad day is past,
Rest with Thee in heaven at last.
T. Kelly.

695 L.M.

mp THOU Who hast known the care-
worn breast, [balm,
The weary need of sleep's deep
Come, Saviour, ere we go to rest,
And breathe around Thy perfect
calm.

mf Thy presence gives us childlike
trust.
Gladness, and hope without alloy,
*cres*The faith that triumphs o'er the
dust,
And gleamings of eternal joy.

mp Stand in our midst, dear Lord, and
say, [hour,"
" Peace be to you, this evening
Then all the struggles of the day
Vanish before Thy loving power.

mf Blest is the pilgrimage to heaven,
A little nearer every night ; [given,
Christ, to our earthly darkness
*cres*Till in His glory, there is light.
G. Rawson.

696 C.M., double.

p THE shadows of the evening hours
Fall from the darkening sky ;
Upon the fragrance of the flowers
The dews of evening lie ;

*cres*Before Thy throne, O Lord of
heaven,
We kneel at close of day: [high,
*dim*Look on Thy children from on
rall And hear us while we pray.

p The sorrows of Thy servants, Lord,
O do not Thou despise ;
But let the incense of our prayers
Before Thy mercy rise ;
*cres*The brightness of the coming night
Upon the darkness rolls ;
f With hopes of future glory chase
rall The shadows on our souls.

p Slowly the rays of daylight fade ;
So fade within our heart
The hopes in earthly love and joy
That one by one depart ;
*cres*Slowly the bright stars, one by one,
Within the heavens shine ;
f Give us, O Lord, fresh hopes in
heaven,
rall And trust in things divine.

p Let peace, O Lord,—Thy peace, O
God,—
Upon our souls descend :
From midnight fears and perils
Thou
Our trembling hearts defend ;
*cres*Give us a respite from our toil ;
Calm and subdue our woes ;
*dim*Through the long day we suffer,
Lord,
rall O give us now repose.
Adelaide A. Procter.

697 8.7.8.7.

mp SAVIOUR, breathe an evening
blessing,
Ere repose our spirits seal ;
Sin and want we come confessing :
Thou canst save, and Thou canst
heal.

*es*Though destruction walk around
us,
Though the arrows past us fly,
if Angel-guards from Thee surround
us;
We are safe, for Thou art nigh.

p Though the night be dark and
dreary,
Darkness cannot hide from Thee;
*cres*Thou art He Who, never weary,
Watchest where Thy people be.

p Should swift death this night
o'ertake us,
And our couch become our tomb,
*cres*May the morn in heaven awake us,
f Clad in light, and deathless
bloom.
J. Edmeston.

698 L.M.

mp O LIGHT of life, O Saviour dear,
Before we sleep bow down Thine
ear:
*cres*Through dark and day, o'er land
and sea,
We have no other hope but Thee.

mp Oft from Thy royal road we part,
Lost in the mazes of the heart !
Our lamps put out, our course
forgot, [not.
We seek for God, and find Him

mf What sudden sunbeams cheer our
sight! [night !
What dawning risen upon the
Thou giv'st Thyself to us. and we
Find guide and path and all in Thee.

mp Through day and darkness, Saviour
dear,
Abide with us, more nearly near,
Till on Thy face we lift our eyes.
The Sun of God's own Paradise.

f Praise God, our Maker and
Friend,
Praise Him, through time,
time shall end !·
*cres*Till psalm and song His N
adore,
ff Through Heaven's great da;
Evermore.
F. T. Palgra

699 8.3.3

mf ERE I sleep, for every favour
This day showed
By my God,
I will bless my Saviour.

mf O my Lord, what shall I rend
To Thy Name,
Still the same,
Gracious, good, and tende

mf Thou hast ordered all my goi
In Thy way,
Heard me pray,
Sanctified my doings.

mp Leave me not, but ever love
Let Thy peace
Be my bliss,
Till Thou hence remov

mf Visit me with Thy salvatio
Let Thy care
Now be near
Round my habitation

f Thou my rock, my guard, r
Safely keep,
While I sleep,
Me, with all Thy po

p So, whene'er in death I.
cres Let me rise
With the wise,
f Counted in their n

J

700
C.M.

nf Now from the altar of my heart
Let incense-flames arise !
Assist me, Lord, to offer up
Mine evening sacrifice.

f Awake, my love ! awake, my joy !
Awake, my heart and tongue !
Sleep not when mercies loudly
call,
Break forth into a song.

mf This day God was my sun and
shield,
My keeper and my guide ;
His care was on my frailty shown,
His mercies multiplied.

mp Minutes and mercies multiplied,
Have made up all this day ;
Minutes came quick, but mercies
were
More fleet and free than they.

mf New time, new favour, and new
joys
Do a new song require ;
cres Till I shall praise Thee as I would.
Accept my heart's desire.

mf Lord of my time, Whose hand hath
set
New time upon my score,
f Thee shall I praise for all my time,
When time shall be no more.

J. Mason.

701
4.4.7.8.7.

mp THE day departs ;
Our souls and hearts
Long for that better morrow,
cres When Christ shall set His people
free
From every care and sorrow.

mp The sunshine bright
Is lost in night ;
O Lord, Thyself unveiling,
cres Shine on our souls with beams of
love,
All darkness there dispelling.

mp Be Thou still nigh,
With sleepless eye,
While all around are sleeping ;
cres And angel-guards, at Thy com-
mand,
Afar all danger keeping.

p The land above,
Of peace and love,
No earthly beams need brighten,
cres For all its borders Christ Himself
f Doth with His glory lighten.

mp May we be there,
That joy to share,
cres Glad Hallelujahs singing :
f With all the ransomed evermore
Our joyful praises bringing.

mp Lord Jesu, Thou
Our Refuge now,
Forsake Thy servants never ;
cres Uphold and guide, that we may
stand
mf Before Thy throne for ever.

J. A. Freylinghausen, tr. H. L. L.

702
8.7.8.7., double.

p Now on land and sea descending,
Brings the night its peace pro-
found ;
Let our vesper-hymn be blending
With the holy calm around.
Soon as dies the sunset glory,
cres Stars of heaven shine out above,
f Telling still the ancient story,
Their Creator's changeless love

11

p Now our wants and burdens leaving
To His care, Who cares for all,
Cease we fearing, cease we grieving,
At His touch our burdens fall.
cres As the darkness deepens o'er us,
Lo! eternal stars arise ;
f Hope and faith and love rise
glorious,
Shining in the spirit's skies.

S. Longfellow.

703
7.7.7.5.

mf HOLY Father, cheer our way
With Thy love's perpetual ray :

· Grant us every closing day
f Light at evening-time
mp Holy Saviour, calm our fe
When earth's brightness die
. Grant us in our later year
f Light at evening-tim
p Holy Spirit, be Thou nigh
When in mortal pains we
pp Grant us, as we come to d
cres Light at evening-tim
mf Holy, Blessèd Trinity,
Darkness is not dark to. T
Those Thou keepest alwa
f Light at evening-tim

R. H. R

3.—SATURDAY EVENING.

704
8.7.8.7.

mp SOUL, thy week of toil is ended,
And a voice, whilst world-cares
fly,
With the closing hours is blended,—
Rest is coming, rest is nigh.

mf Nearing Sabbath, how I bless thee !
Let thy calmness fill my breast ;
Let me even now possess thee ;
And anticipate thy rest.

dim Is my journey full of sadness,
Through a desert wild and drear ?

Be to me a well of gladne
Bid me quite forget my

mp So when life's long week
Blessèd it will be to die
Angel's whispering, as the
" Rest is coming, rest i

mp Then the heavenly rest to
In Thy mercy, Lord, be
cres Rest of God ! the sun an
Of the bliss that is div

G. 1

4.—SPRING.

705
C.M.

f THE glory of the spring how sweet!
The newborn life how glad !
What joy the happy earth to greet
In new, bright raiment clad !

mf Divine Renewer ! Thee I bless ;
I greet Thy going forth ;
I love Thee in the loveliness
Of Thy renewèd earth.

---

f But O ! these wonders of T
These nobler works of
These marvels sweeter fa
These new-births more

mp These sinful souls Thou l
These hearts Thou mak
These mourning souls
made blest,
These faithless hearts r

Spirit, work in me
: wonders sweet of Thine !
Renewer, graciously
w this heart of mine !

; new life and strength up-
ing,
let new joy be given !
ant the glad new song to
g　　　　　[heaven !
igh the new earth and
　　　　　T. H. Gill.

4.4.6.4.4.6., or C.M.

E spring-tide hour
ngs leaf and flower,
ngs of life and love ;
d many a lay
ars out the day
y a leafy grove.

d, flower, and tree
m to agree
hoicest gifts to bring ;
t this poor heart
ars not its part,
ere is no spring.

mp　　Dews fall apace,—
　　　The dews of grace,—
Upon this soul of sin ;
　　　And love divine
　　　Delights to shine
Upon the waste within.

cres　Yet year by year
　　　Fruits, flowers appear,
And birds their praises sing ;
dim　But this poor heart
　　　Bears not its part,
Its winter has no spring.

mp　　Lord, let Thy love,
　　　Fresh from above,
Soft as the south wind blow,
cres　Call forth its bloom,
　　　Wake its perfume,
And bid its spices flow.

f　　　And when Thy voice
　　　Makes earth rejoice,
And the hills laugh and sing ;
cres　Lord, teach this heart
　　　To bear its part,
ff And join the praise of spring.
　　　　　J. S. B. Monsel

5.—SUMMER.

6.5., 8 lines.

R suns are glowing
land and sea,
light is flowing
tiful and free.
ling rejoices
e mellow rays ;
h's thousand voices
. the psalm of praise.

ree mercy streameth
all the world,
s banner gleameth
rwhere unfurled.

. Broad and deep and glorious
　　As the heaven above,
Shines in might victorious
　　His eternal Love.

p Lord, upon our blindness
cres　Thy pure radiance pour ;
mf For Thy loving-kindness
　　Make us love Thee more.
p And when clouds are drifting
　　Dark across our sky,
cres Then, the veil uplifting,
　　Father, be Thou nigh.

11*

mf We will never doubt Thee,
dim Though Thou veil Thy light :
p Life is dark without Thee ;
cres Death with Thee is bright.

f Light of Light ! shine o'er u
On our pilgrim way,
Go Thou still before us
To the endless day.

W. W. 1

6.—*AUTUMN AND HARVEST.*

708   7s., 8 lines.

f COME, ye thankful people, come,
Raise the song of Harvest-Home !
All is safely gathered in,
Ere the winter's storms begin ;
mf God, our Maker, doth provide
For our wants to be supplied ;
f Come to God's own temple, come,
Raise the song of Harvest-Home !

mf All the world is God's own field,
Fruit unto His praise to yield ;
Wheat and tares together sown,
. Unto joy or sorrow grown :
First the blade, and then the ear,
Then the full corn shall appear :
p Lord of harvest, grant that we
cres Wholesome grain and pure may be!

p For the Lord our God shall come,
And shall take His harvest-home ;
cres From His field shall in that day
All offences purge away ;
p Give His angels charge at last
In the fire the tares to cast,
cres But the fruitful ears to store
f In His garner evermore.

mf Even so, Lord, quickly come
To Thy final harvest-home ;
cres Gather Thou Thy people in,
Free from sorrow, free from sin ;
There for ever purified,
In Thy presence to abide :
f Come, with all Thine angels, come,
rall Raise the glorious Harvest-Home !

H. Alford.

709   7.6.7.6., dou

f SING to the Lord of harvest,
Sing songs of love and pra
With joyful hearts and voic
Your hallelujahs raise :
By Him the rolling seasons
In fruitful order move,
Sing to the Lord of harvest
A song of happy love.

mf By Him the clouds drop fat:
The deserts bloom and spr
The hills leap up in gladnes
The valleys laugh and sin
He filleth with His fulness
All things with large incr
He crowns the year with go
With plenty and with pea

mf Heap on His sacred altar
The gifts His goodness ga
The golden sheaves of harve
The souls He died to save
mp Your hearts lay down befor
When at His feet ye fall,
And with your lives adore
Who gave His life for all.

f To God the gracious Father,
Who made us " very good
cres To Christ, Who when we wa
Restored us with His blo
And to the Holy Spirit,
Who doth upon us pour
· His blessèd dews and sunshi
ff Be praise for evermore.

J. S. B. Mo

8.5.8.3.

ᵌE, O praise the Lord of
    harvest,
'rovidence and Love !
ᵌ Him in His earthly temples,
    And above !

e Him, every living creature,
ᵌy His goodness fed,
e rich mercy daily giveth
    Daily bread.

Him thanks for all the
    bounties
ᵗf His gracious Hand ;—
ng peace and welcome plenty,
    O'er our land.

ᵌ His Name that war's loud
    thunder
ᵌreaks not on our shore !
ᵌ of harvest, not of plunder,
    Yield their store.

:ened unto life eternal,
ᵌear we heavenly fruit ;
if barren, He reject us
    Branch and root.]

:he Church of God in patience
ᵌaits her Harvest-Home,
ᵌith angels for His reapers,
    Christ shall come.

we all be safely gathered,
t the Master's word,
ᵌ everlasting garner,
    With the Lord :—

the saints of far back ages,
rowns upon their brow :—
the army of the martyrs,
    Conquerors now :—

the flowers of strength and
    beauty,
ᵌaped before their time—

*dim*Smitten down by death's sharp
    sickle,
    In their prime :—

p With the sweet departed faces
    Missed these weary years :—
*cres*Given back in heavenly places,
    Past all fears.]

mf Speed, O speed that glorious
    harvest
    Of the souls of men ;
When Christ's members, here long
    scattered,
    Meet again.
ff Glory to the Lord of harvest !
    Holy Three in One !
To the Father, Son, and Spirit,
    Praise be done !
             J. Hamilton.

711   7.6.7.6.7.6.7.6.6.6.8.4.

mf WE plough the fields, and scatter
    The good seed on the land,
    But it is fed and watered
    By God's almighty hand ;
    He sends the snow in winter,
    The warmth to swell the grain,
    The breezes and the sunshine,
p   And soft refreshing rain.
f   All good gifts around us
    Are sent from heaven above ;
ff Then thank the Lord, O thank the
    Lord,
    For all His love.

mf He only is the Maker
    Of all things near and far ;
    He paints the wayside flower,
    He lights the evening star ;
*cres*The winds and waves obey Him,
p   By Him the birds are fed ;
    Much more to us, His children,
    He gives our daily bread.

f All good gifts around us
Are sent from heaven above ;
ff Then thank the Lord, O thank the Lord,
For all His love.

f We thank Thee, then, O Father,
For all things bright and good,
The seed-time and the harvest,
Our life, our health, our food.
mp No gifts have we to offer
For all Thy love imparts,
But that which Thou desirest,
p Our humble, thankful hearts.
f All good gifts around us
Are sent from heaven above ;
ff Then thank the Lord, O thank the Lord,
For all His love.

M. Claudius, tr. Jane M. Campbell.

712 8.7.8.7., double.

f To Thee, O Lord, our hearts we raise
In hymns of adoration,
To Thee bring sacrifice of praise
With shouts of exultation :
Bright robes of gold the fields adorn,
The hills with joy are ringing,
The valleys stand so thick with corn
That even they are singing.

f And now, on this our festal day,
Thy bounteous hand confessing,
Upon Thine altar, Lord, we lay
The firstfruits of Thy blessing ;
By Thee the souls of men are fed
With gifts of grace supernal ;
Thou, Who dost give us earthly bread,
Give us the Bread Eternal.

mp We bear the burden of the day,
And often toil seems dreary ;
cres But labour ends with sunset ray,
And rest comes for the weary ;

f May we, the angel-reaping
Stand at the last accepte
Christ's golden sheaves fo
more
To garners bright elected

mf O, blessèd is that land of G
Where saints abide for e·
Where golden fields spread broad,
Where flows the crystal :
cres The strains of all its holy ·
With ours to-day are ble
f Thrice blessèd is that :
song
Which never hath an en·

W. C

713 C.M., d

mf O THRONED, O Crowned ·
renown,
Since Thou the earth ha
Thou reignest, and by Th
down
Henceforth the gifts of
By Thee the suns of space, t
Unspent, their watches :
The hosts that turn, a
return,
Are swayed, and pois
rolled.

mf The powers of earth, for al
An endless treasure yiel·
The precious things of the hills,
Forest and fruitful field.
Thine is the health and ·1
wealth
That in our halls aboun
And Thine the beauty an
With which the ye
crowned.

mp And as, when ebbed the Flood, our
   sires
   Kneeled on the mountain sod ;
  While o'er the new world's altar-
   fires
   Shone out the bow of God ;
  And sweetly fell the peaceful spell,
   Word that shall aye avail ;
  " Summer and winter shall not
   cease,
   Seed-time nor harvest fail ; "

mp Thus in their change let frost and
   heat
  And winds and dews be given ;
  All fostering power, all influence
   sweet,   [heaven.
  Breathe from the bounteous

  Attemper fair with gentle air
   The sunshine and the rain,
  That kindly earth, with timely
   birth,
   May yield her fruits again ;
mf That we may feed Thy poor aright,
   And, gathering round Thy
   throne,
  Here, in the holy angels' sight,
   Repay Thee of Thine own.
cres That we may praise Thee all our
   days,
   And with the Father's Name,
  And with the Holy Spirit's gifts
f   The Saviour's love proclaim.
   E. W. Benson ; v. 5, ll. 5-8, B. H.
      Kennedy.

7.—WINTER.

714   7s.
mp WINTER reigneth o'er the land,
  Freezing with its icy breath ;
  Dead and bare the tall trees stand :
  All is chill and drear as death.

mp Yet it seemeth but a day   [here,
  Since the summer flowers were
  Since they stacked the balmy hay,
  Since they reaped the golden ear.

mp Sunny days are past and gone :
  So the years go, speeding fast,
  Onward ever, each new one
  Swifter speeding than the last.

dim Life is waning ; life is brief ;
  Death, like winter, standeth nigh :
  Each one, like the falling leaf,
  Soon shall fade and fall and die.

cres But the sleeping earth shall wake,
  And the flowers shall burst in
   bloom,
f And all Nature rising break
  Glorious from its wintry tomb.

mf So the saints, from slumber blest
cres Rising, shall awake and sing,
ff And our flesh in hope shall rest
  Of a never-fading Spring.
          W. How.

8.—CLOSE OF THE YEAR.

715   8.7.8.7., double.
mf HARP, awake ! tell out the story
  Of our love and joy and praise ;
  Lute, awake ! *awake our glory !*
  Join a thankful song to raise !

  Join we, brethren faithful-hearted,
   Lift the solemn voice again
dim O'er another year departed
   Of our threescore years and
   ten !

mp Lo ! a theme for deepest sadness,
  In ourselves with sin defiled ;
*cres*Lo ! a theme for holiest gladness,
  In our Father reconciled !
*dim*In the dust we bend before Thee,
  Lord of sinless hosts above ;
*cres*Yet in lowliest joy adore Thee,
  God of mercy, grace, and love !

mp Gracious Saviour ! Thou hast
    lengthened
  And hast blest our mortal span,
  And in our weak hearts hast
    strengthened
  What Thy grace alone began !
  Still, when danger shall betide us,
  Be Thy warning whisper heard ;
  Keep us at Thy feet, and guide us
  By Thy Spirit and Thy Word !

mf Let Thy favour and Thy blessing
  Crown the year we now begin ;
*cres*Let us all, Thy strength possessing,
  Grow in grace, and vanquish sin !
*dim*Storms are round us, hearts are
    quailing,   [sea ;
  Signs in heaven and earth and
*cres*But, when heaven and earth are
    failing,
f   Saviour ! we will trust in Thee !
                    H. Downton.

716   8.7.8.7 ; last verse L.M.
mf DAYS and moments quickly flying,
  Blend the living with the dead ;
p Soon will you and I be lying,
  Each within his narrow bed.

p Soon our souls to God Who gave
    them
  Will have sped their rapid flight ;
*cres*Able now by grace to save them,
  Oh. that while we can we might !

mf Jesu, Infinite Redeemer,
  Maker of this mortal frame,
*dim*Teach, O teach us to remember
  What we are and whence we
    came ;

p Whence we came, and whither
    wending :   [go,
  Soon we must through darkness
*cres*To inherit life unending,
p   Or the death of shame and woe.

p Life passeth soon ; death draweth
    near :
  Keep us, good Lord, till Thou
    appear :
  For Thee to live in Thee to die,
  With Thee to reign through eter-
    nity.
E. Caswall ; v. 5, E. H. Bickersteth.

717   7.6.7.6., double
mp O GOD, the Rock of Ages,
  Who evermore hast been,
  What time the tempest rages,
  Our dwelling-place serene.
*cres*Before Thy first creations,
  O Lord, the same as now,
  To endless generations
  The everlasting Thou !

p Our years are like the shadows
  On sunny hills that lie,
  Or grasses in the meadows
  That blossom but to die :
  A sleep, a dream, a story
  By strangers quickly told,
  An unremaining glory
  Of things that soon are old.

mf O Thou, Who canst not slumber,
  Whose light grows never pale,
  Teach us aright to number
  Our years before they fail.

On us Thy mercy lighten,
 On us Thy goodness rest,
And let Thy Spirit brighten
 The hearts Thyself hast blessed.

mf Lord, crown our faith's endeavour
 With beauty and with grace,
Till, clothed in light for ever,
 We see Thee face to face ;—
f A joy no language measures ;
 A fountain brimming o'er ;
An endless flow of pleasures ;
 An ocean without shore.

E. H. Bickersteth.

718   7s.

mf FOR Thy mercy and Thy grace,
 Constant through another year,
cres Hear our song of thankfulness,
 Father, and Redeemer, hear !

nf Lo ! our sins on Thee we cast,
 Thee, our perfect sacrifice ;
res And, forgetting all the past,
f Press towards our glorious prize.

p Dark the future ; (*cres*) let Thy
 light
Guide us, bright and morning Star:
f Fierce our foes, and hard the fight,
 Arm us, Saviour, for the war.

mf In our weakness and distress,
cres Rock of Strength, be Thou our stay;
 In the pathless wilderness
 Be our true and living Way.

p Who of us death's awful road
 In the coming year shall tread ?
With Thy rod and staff, O God,
 Comfort Thou his dying bed.

mf Keep us faithful, keep us pure,
 Keep us evermore Thine own ;
Help, oh help us to endure ;
 Fit us for the promised crown.

f So within Thy palace gate
 We shall praise, on golden strings,
Thee, the only Potentate,
 Lord of lords, and King of kings !

H. Downton.

9.—*MIDNIGHT SERVICES.*

719   C.M.

nf BREAK, new-born Year, on glad
 eyes break,
Melodious voices move ! [make
On, rolling Time ! thou canst not
The Father cease to love.

np The parted year had wingèd feet ;
 The Saviour still doth stay :
The New Year comes ! but, Spirit
 sweet,
Thou goest not away.

sp Our hearts in tears may oft run
 o'er ;
But, Lord, Thy smile still beams :

Our sins are swelling evermore ;
 But pardoning grace still
 streams.

mf Lord ! from this year more service
 win,
 More glory, more delight !
O make its hours less sad with
 sin,
 Its days with Thee more bright !

cres Then we may bless its precious
 things,
If earthly cheer should come,
Or gladsome mount on angel wings,
 If Thou should'st take us home,

11a

f O ! golden then the hours must be ;
 The year must needs be sweet ;
Yes, Lord, with happy melody
 Thine opening grace we greet.
     T. H. Gill.

720   6.5., 12 lines.

mf STANDING at the portal
 Of the opening year,
Words of comfort meet us,
 Hushing every fear ;
Spoken through the silence
 By our Father's voice,
Tender, strong, and faithful,
 Making us rejoice.
f Onward then, and fear not,
  Children of the day !
 For His word shall never,
  Never pass away !

mf I, the Lord, am with thee,
 Be thou not afraid !
I will keep and strengthen,
 Be thou not dismayed !
Yea, I will uphold thee
 With My own right hand ;
Thou art called and chosen
 In My sight to stand.
f Onward then, and fear not, etc.

mf For the year before us,
 Oh, what rich supplies !
For the poor and needy
 Living streams shall rise ;
For the sad and sinful
 Shall His grace abound ;
For the faint and feeble
 Perfect strength be found.
f Onward then, and fear not, etc.

mf He will never fail us,
 He will not forsake ;
His eternal covenant
 He will never break !

Resting on His promise,
 What have we to fear ?
God is all-sufficient
 For the coming year.
  Onward then, and fear
   Children of the day !
  For His word shall ne'
   Never pass away !
     Frances R. Har.

721   5.£

mf COME, let us anew
 Our journey pursue,
Roll round with the yeaı
 And never stand still 1
 Master appear.

mf His adorable will
 Let us gladly fulfil,
And our talents improve
 By the patience of hope, ɔ
 labour of love.

mp Our life is a dream ;
 Our time as a stream
Glides swiftly away,
 And the fugitive moment
 to stay.

mf O that each in the day
 Of His coming may say,
" I have fought my way t
 I have finished the work Th
 give me to do ! "

mf O that each from his Lo
 May receive the glad wo
" Well and faithfully do
 Enter into My joy, and s
 on My throne."
     C. Ħ

722   8.7.8.7.8.8.7.

mp ACROSS the sky the shades of
   night
   This winter's eve are fleeting;
We come to Thee the Life and
   Light,
   In solemn worship meeting.
And as the year's last hours go by
We lift to Thee our earnest cry,
   Once more Thy love entreating.

p Before the cross, subdued we
   bow,
   To Thee our prayers addressing;
Recounting all Thy mercies now,
   And all our sins confessing:
Beseeching Thee this coming year,
To hold us in Thy faith and fear,
   And crown us with Thy blessing.

mp And while we kneel, we lift our
   eyes
   To dear ones gone before us;
Safe housed with Thee in Paradise,
   Their spirits hovering o'er us;
And beg of Thee, when life is past,
To reunite us all at last,
   And to our lost restore us.

mf We gather up in this brief hour
   The memory of Thy mercies;
Thy wondrous goodness, love, and
   power,
   Our grateful song rehearses:
For Thou hast been our strength
   and stay
In many a dark and dreary day
   Of sorrow and reverses.

mf In many an hour, when fear and
   dread
   Like evil spells have bound us.
And clouds were gathering over-
   head,
   Thy providence hath found us;
In many a night when waves ran
   high,   [nigh
Thy gracious presence drawing
   Hath made all calm around us.

mf Then, O great God, in years to
   come,
   Whatever fate betide us, [home
Right onward through our journey
   Be Thou at hand to guide us;
Nor leave us till, at close of life,
Safe from all peril, toil, and strife,
   Heaven shall unfold and hide us.

J. Hamilton, v. 1, l. 3 altd.

10.—*NEW YEAR.*

723   7.6.7.6.

mp ANOTHER year is dawning;
   Dear Master, let it be,
   In working or in waiting,
   Another year with Thee.

mp Another year of leaning
   Upon Thy loving breast,
   Of ever-deepening trusting,
   Of quiet, happy rest.

mf Another year of mercies,
   Of faithfulness and grace,

cres Another year of gladness
   In the shining of Thy face.

f Another year of progress,
   Another year of praise,
   Another year of proving
   Thy presence "all the days."

mf Another year of service,
   Of witness for Thy love;
   Another year of training
   For holier work above.

mp Another year is dawning;
  Dear Master, let it be,
*cres*On earth, or else in heaven,
  Another year for Thee!
  Frances R. Havergal.

724 L.M.

mf GREAT God, we sing that mighty
  hand
  By which supported still we stand;
  The opening year Thy mercy shows,
  That mercy crowns it till it close.

mf By day, by night, at home, abroad,
  Still are we guarded by our God;
  By His incessant bounty fed,
  By His unerring counsel led.

mf With grateful hearts the past we
  own;
p The future, all to us unknown,
  We to Thy guardian care commit,
  And peaceful leave before Thy feet.

mf In scenes exalted or depressed,
  Thou art our joy, and Thou our
  rest;   [raise
  Thy goodness all our hopes shall
  Adored throughout our changing
  days.

p When death shall interrupt these
  songs,
  And seal in silence mortal tongues,
*cres*Our Helper, God, in Whom we trust,
*dim*Shall keep our souls, and guard
  our dust.
  P. Doddridge, v. 1, l. 4, v. 5,
  l. 4 altd.

725 C.M.

mf ETERNAL Father! who can tell
  The years of Thy right hand?
  Like sunbeams bright but number-
  less,
  Or as the ocean's *sand.*

mf Thine ageless age no limit knows,
  No dawn began Thy day,
  Nor evening shade shall ever fall
  Upon Thy glorious way.

mp All time is but a fleeting wave
  Upon Thy calm, deep sea,
  A fading leaf that feebly falls
  From Life's Eternal Tree.

mp Yet unto Thee our fleeting years,
  Our fading days are known,
  And every hour its message bears
  Up to the eternal throne.

[*p* Old year, farewell! Thou'rt gone
  to God,
  Gone to record our life,
  Its poor success, its wasted hours,
  Its oft unworthy strife.   •

f New year, all hail! Thou'rt come
  from God;
  Blest be thy dawning bright!
  Blest be thy swiftly-fleeting hours!
  And blest thine evening light.]

mf Into the hand of Him Who died,
  Who evermore doth live, [path
  This strange and solemn New Year's
  In trustful prayer we give.

mf Enough for us to hear His voice,
  To feel His guiding hand,
*cres*To know each step is bringing us
  Nearer the Better Land.
  R. Dawson.

726 6.5., 12 lines.

f JESUS, blessèd Saviour,
  Help us now to raise
  Songs of glad thanksgiving,
  Songs of holy praise.
  Oh, how kind and gracious
  Thou hast always been!
  Oh, how many blessings
  Every day has seen!

1s, blessèd Saviour,
ow our praises hear,
Thy grace and favour
rowning all the year.

oly Saviour,
Thou canst tell
often stumbled.
we often fell !
sins (so many !),
1r, Thou dost know ;
blood most precious,
us white as snow.
1s, blessèd Saviour,
eep us in Thy fear,
Thy grace and favour
ardon all the year.

ving Saviour,
Thou dost know
may befall us,
onward go ;
umbly pray Thee,
1s by the hand,
ever upward
Better Land.
.s, blessèd Saviour,
eep us ever near,
Thy grace and favour
uield us all the year.

ecious Saviour,
1s all Thine own,
Thine for ever,
us Thine alone.
day, each moment
1 glad New Year
sus only,
Saviour dear.
1, O blessèd Saviour,
ver need we fear ;
Thy grace and favour
own our bright New Year.

Frances R. Havergal.

727   7.5.7.5., double.

mf FATHER, let me dedicate
    This new year to Thee,
In whatever worldly state
    Thou wilt have me be.
Not from sorrow, pain, or care
    Freedom dare I claim ;
cres This alone shall be my prayer :
f   Glorify Thy Name.

mp Can a child presume to choose
    Where or how to live ?
Can a Father's love refuse
    All the best to give ?
cres More Thou givest every day
    Than the best can claim ;
Nor withholdest aught that **may**
f   Glorify Thy Name.

mp If in mercy Thou wilt spare
    Joys that yet are mine ;
If on life, serene and fair,
    Brighter rays may shine ,
cres Let my glad heart while it sings,
    Thee in all proclaim ;
And, whate'er the future brings,
f   Glorify Thy Name.

p If Thou callest to the Cross,
    And its shadow come,
Turning all my gain to loss,
    Shrouding heart and home ;
Let me think how Thy dear Son
    To His glory came,
And in deepest woe pray on,
f   Glorify Thy Name.
           L. Tuttiett.

728   C.M.

mf THE year is gone, beyond recall,
    With all its hopes and fears,
With all its bright and gladdening
      smiles,
p   With all its mourners' tears.

mf Thy thankful people praise Thee, Lord,
For countless gifts received.
And pray for grace to keep the faith
Which saints of old believed.

mf To Thee we come, O gracious Lord,
The new-born year to bless ;
Defend our land from pestilence,
Give peace and plenteousness.

mp Forgive this nation's many sins,
The growth of vice restrain,
And help us all with sin to strive.
And crowns of life to gain.

p From evil deeds that stain the past
We now desire to flee ;
cres And pray that future years may all
Be spent, good Lord, for Thee.

mf O Father, let Thy watchful eye
Still look on us in love, [year,
That we may praise Thee, year by
As angels do above.

Meaux Breviary, tr. F. Potts.

XV.
Benedictions and Doxologies.

729   8.7.8.7., double.

mf MAY the grace of Christ our Saviour,
And the Father's boundless love,
With the Holy Spirit's favour,
Rest upon us from above !
cres Thus may we abide in union
With each other and the Lord ;
And possess in sweet communion
Joys which earth cannot afford.

J. Newton.

730   7.6.7.6., double.

mf O FATHER, ever glorious,
O everlasting Son,
O Spirit all victorious,
Thrice holy Three in One :
Great God of our salvation,
Whom earth and heaven adore,
ff Praise, glory, adoration,
Be Thine for evermore.

E. H. Bickersteth.

731   8.7.8.7., double.

mf WORSHIP, honour, glory, blessing,
Lord, we offer to Thy Name ;

p Young and old, Thy praise express-ing,
Join their Saviour to proclaim.
cres As the saints in heaven adore Thee,
We would bow before Thy throne,
p As Thine angels serve before Thee,
cres So on earth Thy will be done !

E. Osler.

732   C.M.

f To Father, Son, and Holy Ghost,
The God whom we adore ;
Be glory, as it was, is now,
And shall be evermore.

N. Tate and N. Brady.

733   L.M.

f PRAISE God, from Whom all blessings flow !
Praise Him, all creatures here below ; [host,
Praise Him above, ye heavenly
Praise Father, Son, and Holy Ghost.

T. Ken.

8.7.8.7., double.

e God of all creation !
he Father's boundless

Lamb, our Expiation,

Priest and King, enthrone',
  above !
Praise the Fountain of salvation,
  Him, by Whom our spirits live !
Undivided adoration
  To the One Jehovah give.

J. Conder.

XVI.
Cbilòren's Services.

7s.

day Thy children meet
irts with willing feet ;
tʰⁱs daʸ they raise
earts in hymns of praise.

the day of rest
worship shall be blest ;
asure and our glee,
vould remember Thee.

ito Thee to pray,
· our happy day !
presence thus to win
pure and free from sin.

easures here below,
·om Thy mercy flow :
dren Thou dost love,
hearts to Thee above.

ord, our childhood shine
swly grace, like Thine :
sugh all eternity,
ive in heaven with Thee.

W. W. How.

7s.

s good, and great, and

, and is to be,
er be it new,
ather, comes from Thee.

---

mf Mercies dawn with every day,
  Newer, brighter than before,
  And the sun's declining ray
  Layeth others up in store.

mf Not a bird that doth not sing
  Sweetest praises to Thy Name ;
  Not an insect on the wing
  But Thy wonders doth proclaim.

mf Every blade and every tree,
  All in happy concert ring,
  And in wondrous harmony
  Join in praises to their King.

mf Far and near, o'er land and sea,
  Mountain-top and wooded dell,
  All, in singing, sing of Thee
  Songs of love ineffable.

mp Fill us then with love **divine**,
  Grant that we, **though** toiling here,
  May in spirit, being **Thine**,
  See and **hear** Thee everywhere.

mf May we all **with** songs of praise
  Whilst on **earth** Thy Name adore,
cres Till with angel-choirs we raise
f Songs of praise for evermore.

G. Thring.

737
8.7.8.7.

f DAY by day we magnify Thee,—
  When our hymns in school we
  raise :

Daily work begun and ended,
With the daily voice of praise.

f Day by day we magnify Thee,—
When, as each new day is born,
On our knees at home, we bless
Thee,
For the mercies of the morn.

mp Day by day we magnify Thee,—
In our hymns before we sleep ;
Angels hear them, watching by us,
Christ's dear lambs all night to
keep.

mf Day by day we magnify Thee,—
Not in words of praise alone ;
Truthful lips, and meek obedience,
Show Thy glory in Thine own.

mp Day by day we magnify Thee,—
When for Jesu's sake we try
Every wrong to bear with patience,
Every sin to mortify.

mp Day by day we magnify Thee,—
Till our days on earth shall cease,
dim Till we rest from these our labours,
p Waiting for Thy day in peace.

mf Then on that eternal morning,
With Thy great eternal host,
f May we fully magnify Thee—
Father, Son, and Holy Ghost.
J. Ellerton.

738 L.M.

mf GREAT God, and wilt Thou con-
descend
To be my Father and my Friend ?
I, a poor child, and Thou so high,
The Lord of earth, and air, and
sky ?

mp Art Thou my Father ! Canst Thou
bear
To hear my poor imperfect prayer ?

dim Or wilt Thou listen to the [
That such a little one can n

mf Art Thou my Father ? Let r
A meek, obedient child to T
And try, in word and de
thought,
To serve and please Thee as I

cres Art Thou my Father ? I'll
Upon the care of such a Fr
And only wish to do and be
Whatever seemeth good to '

f Art Thou my Father ? Then
When all my days on ea
past,
Send down and take me
To be Thy better child abov
Ann Gi

739

f OH ! let us all be glad to-d
And with the shepherds
pay :
Come, see what God to r
given,
His only Son, sent dowr
heaven.

mf Awake, my soul ! from sadr
Come, see what in the man;
Who is this smiling infant C
'Tis little Jesus, sweet and

mp Twice welcome, O Thou h
Guest,
To save a world with sin dia
Com'st Thou in lowly guise
What homage shall I give t

mp Ah ! Lord eternal, heaven!
Hast Thou become so mean
And hast Thou left Thy
seat,
To rest where colts and ox

de world much wider

d costly gems arrayed:
far too mean 'twould

ttle crib for Thee.

es surround Thy head,
ay is all Thy bed !
, a King so rich and
[state.
as in Thy heavenly

viour, come to me—
little crib for Thee :
in this heart of mine,
aye remember Thine.

my soul glad songs
—
a day I'll gaily sing ;
osannas will I raise,
:hat loves to sing Thy

Luther, tr. J. Hunt.

6.5.6.5.

'hristian children,
let us sing
voice the praises
iew-born King.

fear to seek Him,
a though we be ;
aid to children,
em come to Me.

;er lowly
he Heavenly Child,
fondly bendeth
iother mild.

that stable,
eaven so high,
t star outshineth,
ig silently.

mp Fear not then to enter,
Though we cannot bring
Gold, or myrrh, or incense,
Fitting for a king.

mf Gifts He asketh richer,
Offerings costlier still,
Yet may Christian children
Bring them if they will.

mp Brighter than all jewels
Shines the modest eye ;
Best of gifts He loveth
Childlike purity.

mf Haste we then to welcome,
With a joyous lay,
cres Christ the King of glory,
Manifest to-day.
S. C. Hamerton.

741 P.M.

mf In the fields with their flocks
abiding,
They lay on the dewy ground :
And glimmering under the star-
light
The sheep lay white around ;
When the light of the Lord
streamed o'er them,
And lo ! from the heaven above
An angel leaned from his glory,
And sang his song of love.
He sang that first sweet Christ-
mas [cease—
The song that shall never
f " Glory to God in the highest,
On earth, goodwill and
peace."

f "To you in the city of David
A Saviour is born to-day ! "
And sudden a host of the heavenly
ones
Flashed forth to join the lay

Oh, never hath sweeter message
Thrilled home to the souls of men,
. And the heavens themselves had
    never heard
A gladder choir till then.
For they sang that Christmas
    carol
    That never on earth shall
    cease—
f   " Glory to God in the highest,
    On earth, goodwill and
    peace."

mp And the shepherds came to the
    manger,
And gazed on the Holy Child,
And calmly o'er that rude cradle
The Virgin Mother smiled ;
And the sky in the starlight silence
Seemed full of the angel lay :
"To you in the city of David
A Saviour is born to-day."
    Oh they sang—and I ween that
    never
    The carol on earth shall
    cease—
f   " Glory to God in the highest,
    On earth, goodwill and
    peace."
               F. W. Farrar.

742   P.M.

mf THERE came a little Child to earth
    Long ago ;
And the angels of God proclaimed
    His birth,
    High and low.
p Out on the night, so calm and
    still,
    Their song was heard ;
*cres*For they knew that the Child on
    Bethlehem's hill
Was Christ the Lord.

mf Far away in a goodly lar
    Fair and bright,
    Children with crowns
    Robed in white ;
mf In white more pure
    spotless snow,
    And their tongues u
    In the psalm which tl
    sang long ago
p   On Christmas night.

mf They sing how the Lor
    world so fair
    A child was born ;
    And that they might a
    glory wear,
p   Wore a crown of thor
    And in mortal weaknes
    and pain,
    Came forth to die ;
*cres*That the children of ea
    for ever reign
    With Him on high.

f He has put on His king
    now,
    In that goodly land.
    And He leads to where
    of water flow
    That chosen band :
*cres*And for evermore in tl
    most fair
    And undefiled,
    Those ransomed child
    praise declare
    Who was once a chi
              Emily E. S.

743   8.

mf ONCE in royal David's c
    Stood a lowly cattle s
p Where a mother laid hei
    In a manger for His l

that mother mild,
st her little Child.

n to earth from heaven,
od and Lord of all,
lter was a stable,
radle was a stall :
poor, and mean, and

earth our Saviour holy.
;h all His wondrous
od,
honour and obey,
atch the lowly mother
gentle arms He lay.
children, all must be
lient, good as He.

ar childhood's Pattern,
ay like us He grew ;
e, weak and helpless,
smiles like us He knew ;
'eeleth for our sadness,
hareth in our gladness.

es at last shall see Him
His own redeeming love,
iild so dear and gentle
rd in Heaven above ;
eads His children on
ace where He is gone.

poor lowly stable,
oxen standing by,
e Him ; but in Heaven,
d's right hand on high ;
ce stars His children
d,
iite shall wait around.
7. *Frances Alexander.*

8.7.8.7.8.7.

> shepherds kept their

world *in darkness lay,*

Came the holy Advent Angel,
Shone the sudden glory ray ;
Then, ten thousand times ten
thousand
Radiant heralds of the day.

f Then they sang the first sweet
carol,
"Glory be to God on high,
And on earth be peace and blessing
To the nations far and nigh ! "
So our God made good His promise,
And the old prophetic cry.

f Fuller, farther o'er the wide world
Year by year that music swells ;
Year by year to some new people
Christmas-tide the story tells,
With the chanting of the children,
And the pealing of the bells.

f Louder over hill and valley
Let the towers and steeples ring !
In the hamlet and the city
Sweeter carols let us sing—
Louder peals of holy pleasure,
Sweeter carols to our King.

mp Hear Thy children, blessèd Jesus,
Once for us on earth a Child ;
Keep us in Thy great compassion,
Holy, harmless, undefiled ;
Blest through Thee by God the
Spirit,
To the Father reconciled.

mf Still we look for Thine appearing,
O Thou bright and Morning
Star !
cres Still we wait to hear the rolling
Of Thy great triumphal car ;
f We who sing Thy first glad
Advent,
Know Thy second is not far.
S. J. Stone.

745 P.M.

mf I THINK, when I read that sweet story of old,
When Jesus was here among men,
How He called little children as lambs to His fold, [them then;
I should like to have been with
I wish that His hands had been placed on my head,
That His arm had been thrown around me,
And that I might have seen His kind look when He said, [Me."

p " Let the little ones come unto

mf Yet still to His footstool in prayer I may go,
And ask for a share in His love :
And if I now earnestly seek Him below, [above,
I shall see Him and hear Him
In that beautiful place He has gone to prepare [forgiven ;
For all that are washed and
cres And many dear children are gathering there, [heaven."
" For of such is the kingdom of

p But thousands and thousands who wander and fall, [home ;
Never heard of that heavenly
cres I should like them to know there is room for them all,
And that Jesus has bid them to come.

mf I long for the joy of that glorious time, [best.
The sweetest, and brightest, and
When the dear little children of every clime
Shall crowd to His arms and be blest.

Jemima Luke.

746 6.5., 12 line

mf BRIGHTLY gleams our banner.
Pointing to the sky,
Waving on Christ's soldiers
To their home on high ;
mf Marching through the desert,
Gladly thus we pray,
f Still, with hearts united,
Singing on our way,—
ff Brightly gleams our banne
Pointing to the sky,
Waving on Christ's soldier
To their home on high !

mf Jesu, Lord and Master,
At Thy sacred feet,
Here, with hearts rejoicing,
See Thy children meet.
p Often have we left Thee,
Often gone astray ;
cres Keep us, mighty Saviour,
In the narrow way.
ff Brightly gleams, etc.

mp Pattern of our childhood,
Once Thyself a Child,
Make our childhood holy,
Pure and meek and mild.
p In the hour of danger
Whither can we flee,
cres Save to Thee, dear Saviour,
Only unto Thee ?
ff Brightly gleams, etc.

mf All our days direct us
In the way we go ;
Crown us still victorious
Over every foe :
p Bid Thine angels shield us
When the storm-clouds lour !
Pardon Thou and save us
In the last dread hour.
ff Brightly gleams, etc.

;h saints and angels
'e join above,
prayers and praises
y throne of love.
.e march is over,
:ome rest and peace, ·
His beauty !
that never cease !
;htly gleams, etc.
Potter and W. W. How.

6.5.6.5.

, holy Jesus,
ir meek and mild,
ho once wast fashioned
. little child ;

grace and meekness
manhood grew ;
human weakness,
in sorrow too :

word so holy,
ir, we can see,
us Thou sayest,
them come to Me."

come ! and render
e have to give :
ur hearts are tender,
us, Lord, to live

y young disciples,
:he world may see
taught by Jesus,
iave learned of Thee.

copy closely
ve so much love,
bear His likeness,
:ted above.
Emma Whitfield.

88.88.88.
green hills of Galilee,
nile quiet Nazareth,

What glorious vision did ye see,
When He Who conquered sin and
death   [trod,
Your flow'ry slopes and summits
And grew in grace with man and
God ?

mf We saw no glory crown His head
As childhood ripened into youth ;
No angels on His errands sped,
He wrought no sign. But meek-
ness, truth,   [trod ;
And duty marked each step He
And love to man, and love to God.

mp Jesus ! my Saviour, Master, King,
Who didst for me the burden bear,
While saints in heaven Thy glory
sing,
Let me on earth Thy likeness wear :
cres Mine be the path Thy feet have
trod ;
Duty and love to man and God.
E. R. Conder.

749   C.M.

mf O HAPPY pair of Nazareth,
Who saw the early light [world
Of Him Who dawned upon the
As dawns the day on night.

mp Within their home, they saw the
Child
That lived the perfect love,
A love like that which rules the
heart
Of the great God above.

mp His childish voice and kindly tone,
His pure and patient face,
His tender mercies, shown to all,
With never-ceasing grace ;

mp The way He bore His youthful
cross,
The reasons for His tears,

The kind of things which gave
   Him joy—
Unchanged through growing
   years,—
mf At home and in the playground
   throng,
They saw these heavenly ways,
And grew increasingly to speak
   With words of reverent praise.

mp That simple, lovely, wondrous life
   Betrayed itself from heaven ;
He was the Child that should be
   born,
The Son that should be given.

mf He grew in stature and in praise,
   By honest hearts adored, [born
Till in that home where He was
   His brothers called Him Lord.
              B. Waugh.

750   C.M.

mf As to His earthly parents' home
   Went down the Holy Child,
And found His Father's business
   there,
   Subjection meek and mild :

mp And as obedience all those years,
   In lowly Nazareth,
Forsook Him not, but bore Him on,
   Obedient unto death :

mp So by Thy mercies teach us, Lord,
   Our sacrifice to bring,   [love,
Our treasures, heart, and life, and
   To spread before our King.

mp Thy presence is our guiding star,
   We seek Thy holy hill ; [minds
cres Transform us, Lord, renew our
mf   To prove Thy perfect will.
              H. Alford.

751   7s.

mf GENTLE Jesus, meek and mild,
   Look upon a little child ;
p Pity my simplicity,
   Suffer me to come to Thee.

mf Fain I would to Thee be brought
   Dearest Lord, forbid it not :
Give me, dearest Lord, a place
   In the Kingdom of Thy grace.

p Lamb of God, I look to Thee ;
   Thou shalt my example be ;
Thou art gentle, meek, and mild,
   Thou wast once a little child.

mf Fain I would be as Thou art ;
   Give me Thy obedient heart ;
Thou art pitiful and kind,
   Let me have Thy loving mind.

mf Let me, above all, fulfil
   God, my Heavenly Father's will,
Never His good Spirit grieve,
   Only to His glory live.

Thou didst live to God alone,
   Thou didst never seek Thine own
Thou Thyself didst never please,
   God was all Thy happiness.

p Loving Jesus, Gentle Lamb,
   In Thy gracious hands I am ;
Make me, Saviour, what Thou art
cres Live Thyself within my heart.

mf I shall then show forth Thy prais
   Serve Thee all my happy days ;
dim Then the world shall always see
   Christ, the Holy Child, in me.
             C. Wesley.

752   C.M.

mf I LOVE to think, though I a
   young,
   My Saviour was a child ;

That Jesus walked this earth along,
With feet all undefiled.

mf He kept His Father's word of truth,
As I am taught to do ; [youth,
And while He walked the paths of
He walked in wisdom too.

mp I love to think that He Who spake,
And made the blind to see,
And called the sleeping dead to
wake,
Was once a child like me.

p That He Who wore the thorny
crown,
And tasted death's despair,
Had a kind mother like my own,
And knew her love and care.

mp I know 'twas all for love of me
That He became a child,
. And left the heavens, so fair to see,
And trod earth's pathway wild.

mf Then, Saviour, Who wast once a
child,
A child may come to Thee ;
And oh, in all Thy mercy mild,
f Dear Saviour, come to me !
E. Paxton Hood.

753 C.M.

mf THERE is a green hill far away,
Without a city wall,
p Where the dear Lord was crucified,
Who died to save us all.

p We may not know, we cannot tell
What pains He had to bear,
But we believe it was for us
He hung and suffered there.

mf He died that we might be forgiven,
He died to make us good,
cres That we might go at last to heaven,
p Saved by His precious blood.

mf There was no other good enough
To pay the price of sin,
He only could unlock the gate
Of heaven and let us in.

f Oh, dearly, dearly has He loved,
And we must love Him too,
And trust in His redeeming blood,
And try His works to do.
C. Frances Alexander.

754 L.M.

mp IT is a thing most wonderful,
Almost too wonderful to be,
That God's own Son should come
from heaven
And die to save a child like me.

mf And yet I know that it is true :
He chose a poor and humble lot,
dim And wept, and toiled, and mourned,
. and died, [not.
For love of those who loved Him

mp I cannot tell how He could love
A child so weak and full of sin ;
cres His love must be most wonderful,
If He could die my love to win.

mf It is most wonderful to know
His love for me so free and sure ;
But 'tis more wonderful to see
dim My love for Him so faint and poor.

mf And yet I want to love Thee, Lord ;
O light the flame within my heart,
cres And I will love Thee more and
more,
Until I see Thee as Thou art.
W. W. How.

755 6.5., 8 lines.

mf JESUS is our Shepherd,
Wiping every tear ;

Folded in His Bosom,
What have we to fear?
Only let us follow
Whither He doth lead,
To the thirsty desert,
Or the dewy mead.

mf Jesus is our Shepherd:
Well we know His voice,
How its gentlest whisper
Makes our heart rejoice;
dim Even when He chideth,
Tender is His tone:
cres None but He shall guide us;
We are His alone.

mp Jesus is our Shepherd,
For the sheep He bled;
Every lamb is sprinkled
With the blood He shed;
Then on each He setteth
His own secret sign,—
They that have My Spirit, .
These, saith He, are Mine.

cres Jesus is our Shepherd;
Guarded by His arm,
Though the wolves may ravin,
None can do us harm;
dim When we tread death's valley,
Dark with fearful gloom,
cres We will fear no evil,
f Victors o'er the tomb.
H. Stowell.

756
8.3.8.3.

mf JESUS, the children are calling,
Oh, draw near! [Bosom,
Fold the young lambs in Thy
Shepherd dear.

mp Slow are our footsteps and failing,
Oft we fall:
*Jesus, the children are calling,
Hear their call!*

mp Cold is our love, Lord, and narrow—
Large is Thine:
Faithful and stronger and tender—
So be mine!

mp Gently, Lord, lead Thou our
mothers—
Weary they;
Bless all our sisters and brothers
Night and day.

mp Fathers themselves are God's children,
Teach them still:
Let the Good Spirit show all men
God's wise will!

cres Now to the Father, Son, Spirit—
Three in One—
mf Bountiful God of our Fathers,
f   Praise be done!
Annie Matheson.

757
L.M.

mp LORD JESUS, Shepherd of mankind,
Tender and watchful, good and
kind,
List to the song Thy lambs would
raise,
Deign to accept their humble
praise.

mp Belovèd Son of God most high,
How shouldst Thou come to earth
and die,
To ransom thus Thy sinful sheep,
Who never would Thy pastures
keep!

mf O love most tender, deep, divine,
That Thou shouldst wish us to be
Thine,
Shouldst gather us into Thy fold
From this world's bleak and barren
wold!

rpassing mortal song,
  omnipotently strong,
ir defence and refuge be,
iake us safe in Thee.

y pastures let us feed,
iay know nor fear nor

ll waters let us rest,
ee content, and blest.

u before us all the

. O let us never stray ;
's sunset let us lie
ing, loving arms to die.
G. W. *Conder.*

7.6.7.6., double.
'riend for little children,
ie bright blue sky :
Vho never changeth,
ive can never die.
 friends by nature,
ige with changing years,
l is always worthy
ious Name He bears.

iet for little children,
ie bright blue sky ;
he blessèd Saviour,
iba, Father," cry ;
i every turmoil,
: and danger free ;
·y little pilgrim
t eternally.

ome for little children,
ie bright blue sky ,
is reigns in glory,
if peace and joy.
i earth is like it,
with it compare ;
ie is happy,
l be happier, there.

mf There's a crown for little children,
  Above the bright blue sky ;
  And all who look for Jesus
    Shall wear it by-and-by.
res A crown of brightest glory,
    Which He will then bestow
  On all who've found His favour
    And loved His Name below.

mf There's a song for little children
  Above the bright blue sky—
  A song that will not weary,
    Though sung continually ;
  A song which even angels
    Can never, never sing ;
  They know not Christ as Saviour,
    But worship Him as King.

f There's a robe for little children,
  Above the bright blue sky ;
  And a harp of sweetest music,
    And a palm of victory.
  All, all above is treasured,
    And found in Christ alone ;
  O come, dear little children,
    That all may be your own.
A. *Midlane.*

759   8.7.8.7., double.
f FAR above in highest heaven,
  Jesus reigns, our Lord and King ;
  He His life for us has given,
    He did life eternal bring : [ness,
  Sing, then, children, sing with glad-
    Loud let grateful anthems ring ;
  Jesus is the children's Saviour,
  Jesus is the children's King.

f Once on earth the children praised
    Him,
  And "Hosanna" was their cry ;
  Now that God to heaven has raised
    Him,
  Loud they praise Him in the sky

ff Shout, then, children, shout your
 praises,
 Loud let grateful anthems ring,
 Jesus is the children's Saviour,
 Jesus is the children's King.

mf Come, then, early, come to Jesus,
 As the children did of old ;
 He from sin and sorrow frees us,
 Never will His love grow cold :
 Daily let us learn to love Him,
 Daily let us join to sing
 Praises to our Lord and Saviour,
 Praises to the children's King.

mp Then, when life's short days are
 ended,
 If we've served our Saviour well,
 By His angels gently tended,
 In His kingdom we shall dwell ;
f There we'll shout our joyous praises,
 There the song of victory sing :
 Jesus is our Lord and Saviour,
 Jesus is the children's King.
      W. H. Scott.

760   6.5.6.5.

mp JESUS, gentlest Saviour,
 God of might and power,
 Thou Thyself art dwelling
 In us at this hour.

mp Nature cannot hold Thee,
 Heaven is all too strait,
cres For Thine endless glory,
 And Thy royal state.

mf Out beyond the shining
 Of the farthest star,
 Thou art ever stretching
 Infinitely far.

cres Yet the hearts of children
 Hold what worlds cannot,
 And the God of wonders
 Loves the lowly spot.

p Jesus, gentlest Saviour !
 Thou art in us now ;
 Fill us full of goodness
 Till our hearts o'erflow.

p Pray the prayer within us,
 That to heaven shall rise ;
 Sing the song that angels
 Sing above the skies.

cres Multiply our graces,
 Chiefly love and fear ;
 And, dear Lord, the chiefest,
 Grace to persevere.

mf O ! how can we thank Thee
 For a gift like this ?—
 Gift that truly maketh
 Heaven's eternal bliss.

mf Ah ! when wilt Thou always
 Make our hearts Thy home !
f We must wait for heaven,
 Then the day will come.
      F. W. Faber.

761   C.M.

f THY Word is like a garden, Lord,
 With flowers bright and fair ;
 And everyone who seeks may pluck
 A lovely nosegay there.

mf Thy Word is like a deep, deep mine ;
 And jewels rich and rare
 Are hidden in its mighty depths,
 For every searcher there.

mf Thy Word is like a starry host :
 A thousand rays of light
 Are seen, to guide the traveller
 And make his pathway bright.

f Thy Word is like a glorious choir,
 And loud its anthems ring ;
 Though many tongues and parts
 unite,
 It is one song they sing.

f Thy Word is like an armoury,
 Where soldiers may repair,
And find for life's long battle-day
 All needful weapons there.

p O, may I love Thy precious Word,
 May I explore the mine,
May I its fragrant flowers glean,
 May light upon me shine !

f Oh, may I find my armour there,
 Thy Word my trusty sword ;
res I'll learn to fight with every foe
f The battle of the Lord.

E. Hodder.

762
8.7.8.7.

f GRANT us, O our Heavenly Father,
 Now in these our early days,
Thee in all things to remember,
 Thee to serve, and Thee to praise.

np Drawing nearer still and nearer,
 May we close and closer cling,
To our Lord, and to His altar
 There ourselves an offering bring.

np Step by step in life advancing,
 Onward, upward, as we move
res Through the world unharmed,—
 rejoicing
 In His all-redeeming love :—

mf Blest in joy, upheld in sorrow,
 At our work as in His sight, ·
May His Presence still be with us,
 As we do it with our might.

mf Serving Thee, our Heavenly Father,
 From the dawn to set of sun,
Serving Thee in life's young morn-
 ing,—
 Till our work on earth is done :—

mp Till the shadows of the evening
 Shall for ever pass away,

cres And the Resurrection-morning
f Kindle into perfect day.

G. Thring.

763
C.M.

mp Is earth too fair, is youth too bright
 To need the smile of heaven ?
Have I no deadly foes to fight ?
 No sins to be forgiven ?

mp Am I too young to seek that Lord
 Who left His heaven for me ?
Too young to hold those sins
 abhorred
He bore upon the tree ?

cres My Father, may not this glad
 heart
Feel Thee its sovereign good,
And bless, my Saviour, its dear part
 In Thine atoning blood ?

mf Hath not Thy Word a promise sweet
 For spirits young as mine ?
May not my soul have leave to greet
 Some vision all divine ?·

cres May not I noblest pleasure win
 And still Thy servant be ?
May not I drink Thy beauty in,
 Nor miss Thy purity ?

p O awful God of holiness !
 I would be all Thine own ;
cres O God of joy ! O God of grace !
 I smile before Thy throne.

mp I pray Thee not to keep from me
 All sorrow and all smart ;
cres But now I bring my joy to Thee,
 Accept this glowing heart.

T. H. Gill.

764
C.M.

mp WITH sin I would not make abode
 While shines each golden hour

Nor keep away from Thee, my God,
Till falls my blissful bower.

mp I would not give the world my
heart,
And then profess Thy love ;
I would not feel my strength
depart,
And then Thy service prove.

[*mp*I would not with swift-wingèd zeal
On the world's errands go.
And labour up the heavenly hill
With weary feet and slow.

*dim*O ! not for Thee my weak desires,
My poorer. baser part !
O ! not for Thee my fading fires,
The ashes of my heart !]

*cres*Lord ! in the fulness of my might
I would for Thee be strong ;
While runneth o'er each dear
delight,
To Thee should soar my song.

mf O choose me in my golden time,
In my dear joys have part !
*cres*For Thee the glory of my prime,
The fulness of my heart !

mp I cannot, Lord, too early take
The covenant divine ;   [break
*cres*O ! ne'er the happy heart may
Whose earliest love was Thine.
T. H. Gill.

765   7s., 8 lines.

mf SAVIOUR! teach me, day by day,
Love's sweet lesson to obey ;
Sweeter lesson cannot be,
Loving Him Who first loved me.
Teach me, I am not my own,
I am Thine, and Thine alone ;
Thine to keep, to rule, to save
From all sin that would enslave.

mf With a child's glad heart of love,
At Thy bidding may I move ;
Prompt to serve and follow Thee,
Loving Him Who first loved me.
*dim*Though Thy will should cross my
own,
May it instantly be done ;
*cres*Thus may I rejoice to show
That I feel the love I owe.

mp Thine, Lord, was a bitter cup,
Thou didst meekly drink it up;
Thou, the Father's only Son,
Ever saidst, Thy will be done.
Teach me thus Thy steps to trace,
*cres*Strong to follow in Thy grace ;
Learning how to love from Thee,
Loving Him Who so loved me.

mf Love in loving finds employ,
In obedience all her joy ;
*cres*Ever now that joy will be,
Loving Him Who first loved me.
*dim*Though a foolish child and weak,
More than this I need not seek :
*cres*Singing, till Thy face I see,
f Of His love Who first loved me.
Jane E. Leeson.

766   7s.

mp FATHER, lead me day by day,
Ever in Thine own sweet way ;
Teach me to be pure and true,
Show me what I ought to do.

*cres*When in danger, make me brave ;
Make me know that Thou canst
save ;
Keep me safe by Thy dear side ;
Let me in Thy love abide.

p When I'm tempted to do wrong,
*cres*Make me steadfast, wise, and
strong ;
And, when all alone I stand,
Shield me with Thy mighty hand.

art is full of glee,
:emember Thee,—
of all to know
:her ioves me so.

rk seems hard and dry,
on cheerily ;
tiently to bear
rdship, toil and care.

.e good and bright,
oass before my sight ;
the heavenly veice
ire and wise rejeice.

e good I know ;
ng child below,
, go home to Thee,
1y child to be.
J. P. Hopps.

7s., 6 lines.

hildren guide and keep,
eeble steps they press
way, rough and steep,
:his weary wilderness.
:su, day by day,
in the narrow way.

ony ways to tread,
trength we sorely lack ;
ngled paths to thread,
lest we miss the track.
:su, day by day,
i in the narrow way.

ndy wastes that lie
sunless, vast and drear,
eeble faint and die ;
grace to persevere.
:su, day by day,
i in the narrow way.

ift and flowery glades
with golden - fruited

Sunny slopes and scented shades ;
 Keep us, Lord, from slothful ease.
cres Holy Jesu, day by day,
  Lead us in the narrow way.

mf Upward still to purer heights,
 Onward yet to scenes more blest,
Calmer regions, clearer lights,
 Till we reach the promised rest.
cres Holy Jesu, day by day,
  Lead us in the narrow way.
     W. W. How.

768   7.6.7.6.

mf LOOKING upward every day,
 Sunshine on our faces ;
Pressing onward every day
 Toward the heavenly places.

mp Growing every day in awe,
 For Thy Name is holy ;
Learning every day to love,
 With a love more lowly.

mp Walking every day more close
 To our Elder Brother ;
Growing every day more true
 Unto one another.

cres Leaving every day behind
 Something which might hinder ;
Running swifter every day,
 Growing purer, kinder.

mp Lord, so pray we every day,
 Hear us in Thy pity,
cres That we enter in at last
 To the Holy City.
     Mary Butler.

769   5.6.5.6.

mf God intrusts to all
 Talents few or many ;
 None so young and small
 That they have not any.

mp   Though the great and wise
      Have a greater number,
cres   Yet my one I prize,
      And it must not slumber.

mp   God will surely ask,
      Ere I enter heaven,
      Have I done the task
      Which to me was given ?

cres   Every little mite,   •
      Every little measure,
      Helps to spread the light,
      Helps to swell the treasure.

mp   Little drops of rain
      Bring the springing flowers :
cres   And I may attain
      Much by little powers.

                      J. Edmeston.

770   7.6.7.6., double.

mf THE wise may bring their learning,
     The rich may bring their wealth ;
     And some may bring their great-
        ness,   [health.
     And some bring strength and
     We, too. would bring our treasures
     To offer to the King :
     We have no wealth or learning,
     What shall we children bring ?

mf We'll bring Him hearts that love
       Him,
     We'll bring Him thankful praise,
     And young souls meekly striving
     To walk in holy ways.
     And these shall be the treasures
     We offer to the King,
     And these are gifts that ever
     The poorest child may bring.

mp We'll bring the little duties
     We have to do each day ;
cres We'll try our best to please Him
     At home, at school, at play.

mf And better are these treasures
     To offer to our King,
     Than richest gifts without them,
     Yet these a child may bring.

771   C.M.

mp GOD make my life a little light
     Within the world to glow ;
     A little flame that burneth bright,
     Wherever I may go.

mp God make my life a little flower
     That giveth joy to all,
     Content to bloom in native bower,
     Although the place be small.

cres God make my life a little song
     That comforteth the sad ;
mf That helpeth others to be strong,
     And makes the singer glad.

mp God make my life a little staff,
     Whereon the weak may rest,
     That so what health and strength
       I have
     May serve my neighbours best.

mf God make my life a little hymn
     Of tenderness and praise ;
cres Of faith—that never waxeth dim,
     In all His wondrous ways.

               Matilda B. Edwards.

772,   L.M.

mp WE are but little children weak,
     Nor born in any high estate ;
     What can we do for Jesus' sake,
     Who is so high and good and great!

mp O, day by day, each Christian child
     Has much to do, without, within,
     A death to die for Jesus' sake,
     A weary war to wage with sin.

mp When deep within our swelling
       hearts   [rise,
     The thoughts of pride and

words are on our

passion in our eyes ;

ʼ stay the angry blow,
ıy check the hasty

ınswers back again,
ıattle for our Lord.

)f peace, and looks of
[make,
ɾ dwellings we may
ıod-humour brighten

ıll for Jesus' sake.

a child so small and

ittle cross to take ;
rk of love and praise,
ʼ do for Jesus' sake.
Frances Alexander.

8.7.8.7.
little workers,
n would do Thy will :
ʼhee, Lord, to help us,
ies to fulfil.

ırchance may brighten
sorrow, care, and sin
ope's blessèd sunshine
ʒer enters in.

ʼe never weary,
ts are seldom sad ;
that Thou wouldst

ke grown people glad.

often bring them

ow not what to say :
message fresh from

)ur *lips to-day.*

mp Thou hast taught us, dearest
Saviõur,
That e'en whispered words can
fly
Straight above the clouds of
heaven,
And be heard by Thee on high.

mp Help us, then, to say to others,
Who have never learnt to know—
" God is listening still to answer
Those who watch and wait
below."

mf Grant that ᴡ⌐, Thy willing
workers,
By Thy grace may find at
length,
Even children in their weakness
May help others in Thy strength.
A. Marryat.

774 7.6.7.6., double.

mf GOD, Who hath made the daisies
And ev'ry lovely thing,
cres He will accept our praises,
And hearken while wē sing.
He says though we are simple,
Though ignorant we be,
pp " Suffer the little children,
And let them come to Me.'"

f Though we are young and simple,
In praise we may be bold ;
The children in the temple
He heard in days of old.
dim And if our hearts are humble,
He says to you and me,
pp " Suffer the little children,
And let them come to Me."

mf He sees the bird that wingeth
Its way o'er earth and sky ;
He hears the lark that singeth
Up in the heaven so high :

*dim*But sees the heart's low breathings,
   And says (well pleased to see),
pp "Suffer the little children,
   And let them come to Me."

mf Therefore we will come near Him,
   And solemnly we'll sing ;
*cres*No cause to shrink or fear Him,
   We'll make our voices ring ;
   For in our temple speaking,
   He says to you and me,
pp "Suffer the little children,
   And let them come to Me."

             E. P. Hood.

775   C.M., with chorus.

mf AROUND the throne of God in
     heaven
   Thousands of children stand ;
. Children whose sins are all forgiven,
   A holy, happy band,
f   Singing, Glory, glory, glory.

mf In flowing robes of spotless white
   See every one arrayed ;
   Dwelling in everlasting light,
   And joys that never fade,
f   Singing, Glory, glory, glory.

mp Once they were little things like
     you,
   And lived on earth below,
   And could not praise as they do now
   The Lord Who loved them so,
mf   Singing, Glory, glory, glory.

mp What brought them to that world
     above,
   That heaven so bright and fair,
   Where all is peace, and joy, and
     love :
   How came those children there,
mf   Singing, Glory, glory, glory !

mp Because the Saviour shed His blood
   To wash away their sin ;
   Bathed in that precious, purple
     flood,
cres Behold them white and clean,
f   Singing, Glory, glory, glory.

mp On earth they sought the Saviour's
     grace,
   On earth they loved His name ;
*cres*So now they see His blessèd face,
   And stand before the Lamb,
f   Singing, Glory, glory, glory.
             Anne Shepherd.

CONGREGATIONAL
CHURCH HYMNAL.

EDITED FOR

THE CONGREGATIONAL UNION OF ENGLAND AND WALES

BY

GEORGE S. BARRETT, B.A., D.D.

THE POINTING ARRANGED AND THE MUSIC SELECTED BY

JOSIAH BOOTH.

PART II.—LITANIES AND CHANTS.

PART III.—ANTHEMS.

LONDON:

MEMORIAL HALL, FARRINGDON STREET.

12

LONDON :

PRINTED BY ALEXANDER AND SHEPHEARD, LTD.

NORWICH STREET, FETTER LANE, E.C.

Medium 16mo, Brevier.—1.1907.

GENERAL TABLE OF CONTENTS.

CHANTS FOR SPECIAL OCCASIONS.

SELECTED PASSAGES OF SCRIPTURE FOR CHANTING

INDEX TO ANTHEMS.

INDEX TO ANTHEMS.

Metrical Litanies.

THE ETERNAL FATHER.

1   7.7.7.6.

PART I.

1 UNCREATED Fount of light,
Glory without shade of night,
Everlasting, infinite :
　　Holy Father, hear us.

2 Well of life that ever flows,
Life more pure than stainless
　　snows,
Life in calm, serene repose :
　　Holy Father, hear us.

3 Blessèd One, Whose Name is love,
Pleads with Thee Thy Son above ;
Broods o'er us Thy hovering
　　Dove :
　　Holy Father, hear us.

4 Round about Thy sapphire throne
Shines the rainbow's emerald zone,
Breathing heavenly peace alone :
　　Holy Father, hear us.

5 There before Thy mercy-seat
Saints in light and angels meet ;
Yet behold us at Thy feet :
　　Holy Father, hear us.

6 Thou Whose deep compassions
　　yearn
For the prodigal's return,
And his far-off steps discern :
　　Holy Father, hear us.

7 All have some great gift to seek,
Hungered, thirsty, weary, weak !
All have wants no words can
　　speak :
　　Holy Father, hear us.

PART II.

1 THOU Who sparedst not Thy Son,
Him Thine own, Thine only One,
Till Thy work by Him was
　　done :
　　Holy Father, hear us.

2 Thou, in all His sorrows nigh,
Thou Who heardest His last cry,
Thou Who sufferedst Him to die :
　　Holy Father, hear us.

3 Thou, omnipotent to save
From destruction's whelming wave,
Death and hell and vanquished
　　grave :
　　Holy Father, hear us.

4 Thou Who crownest Him with
　　grace,
Foldest Him to Thine embrace,
Him the brightness of Thy face :
　　Holy Father, hear us.

5 All the richest gifts of heaven,
Sevenfold from the Spirits Seven,
Measureless to Him are given :
　　Holy Father, hear us.

6 At His word Thy Spirit came,
Crowns of light and tongues of
　　flame :
Oh, for our Redeemer's Name ?
　　Holy Father, hear us.

7 Hear our cry, our voiceless needs :
Hear ; in us Thy Spirit pleads :
Hear, for Jesus intercedes :.
　　Holy Father, hear us.

T. B. Pollock.

JESUS CRUCIFIED.

2   7.7.7.6.

PART I.

" Father, forgive them ; for they know
not what they do."

1 JESU, in Thy dying woes,
  Ever while Thy life-blood flows,
  Craving pardon for Thy foes :
    Hear us, Holy Jesu.

2 Saviour, for our pardon sue
  When our sins Thy pangs renew,
  For we know not what we do ;
    Hear us, Holy Jesu.

3 Oh, may we, who mercy need,
  Be like Thee in heart and deed
  When with wrong our spirits bleed ;
    Hear us, Holy Jesu.

PART II.

" To-day shalt thou be with Me in
Paradise."

1 JESU, pitying the sighs
  Of the thief who near Thee dies,
  Promising him Paradise :
    Hear us, Holy Jesu.

2 May we, in our guilt and shame,
  Still Thy love and mercy claim,
  Calling humbly on Thy Name :
    Hear us, Holy Jesu.

3 Oh, remember us who pine,
  Looking from our cross to Thine ;
  Cheer our souls with hope Divine :
    Hear us, Holy Jesu.

PART III.

" Woman, behold thy son. . . . Behold
thy mother."

1 JESU, loving to the end
  Her whose heart Thy sorrows rend,
  And Thy dearest human friend
    Hear us, Holy Jesu.

2 May we all Thy sorrows share,
  And for Thee all peril dare,
  And enjoy Thy holy care :
    Hear us, Holy Jesu.

3 May we all Thy loved ones be,
  All one holy family,
  Loving for the love of Thee :
    Hear us, Holy Jesu.

PART IV.

" My God, My God, why hast
forsaken Me ?"

1 JESU, whelmed in fears unkn
  With our evil left alone,
  While no light from heaven is s
    Hear us, Holy Jesu.

2 When we vainly seem to pray
  And our hope seems far away
  In the darkness be our stay :
    Hear us, Holy Jesu.

3 Though no Father seems to h
  Though no light our spirits cl
  Tell our faith that God is nea
    Hear us, Holy Jesu.

PART V.

" I thirst."

1 JESU, in Thy thirst and pain,
  While Thy wounds Thy life
    drain
  Thirsting more our love to ga
    Hear us, Holy Jesu.

2 Thirst for us in mercy still ;
  All Thy holy work fulfil ;
  Satisfy Thy loving will :
    Hear us, Holy Jesu.

'hy love to know ;
;in and woe,
ng waters flow :
Holy Jesu.

r VI.

inished."

nsom paid,
; will obeyed,
;s perfect made :
Holy Jesu.

oul's distress ;
:heer and bless
in holiness :
Holy Jesu.

· heavenward way
)lier ray,
)erfect day :
Holy Jesu.

PART VII.

" Father, into Thy hands I commend My spirit."

1 JESU, all Thy labour vast,
All Thy woe and conflict, past,
Yielding up Thy soul at last :
Hear us, Holy Jesu.

2 When the death-shades round us lower,
Guard us from the tempter's power :
Keep us in that trial-hour :
Hear us, Holy Jesu.

3 May Thy life and death supply
Grace to live and grace to die,
Grace to reach the Home on high :
Hear us, Holy Jesu.

T. B. Pollock.

JESUS IN GLORY.

7.7.7.6.

;T I.

, throned on high ;
1st come to die ;
sanctify :
Holy Trinity.

Life and Light,
1 glory bright,
;s by Thy might :
Holy Jesus.

to heaven ascend,
nner's Friend,
to defend :
Holy Jesus.

th did death destroy,
iin didst pass to joy,
hout alloy :
Holy Jesus.

5 Thou Who must in glory reign,
Conqueror of sin and pain,
Till no enemy remain :
Hear us, Holy Jesus.

PART II.

1 JESUS, Who art glorified
In the very flesh that died,
With the piercèd hands and side :
Hear us, Holy Jesus.

2 Jesus, though enthroned on high,
Still for our infirmity
Touched with human sympathy .
Hear us, Holy Jesus.

3 Jesus, in our time of need
Our High-priest to intercede,
Living still Thy Death to plead :
Hear us, Holy Jesus.

120

4 Jesus, Who, to heaven upborne,
Didst not leave Thy Church to
mourn,
Orphaned, comfortless, forlorn :
Hear us, Holy Jesus.

5 Thou Who, still our Saviour-Friend,
Didst the Holy Spirit send
To be with us to the end :
Hear us, Holy Jesus.

PART III.

1 THOU Whose gifts of grace on all
Who to Thee for succour call,
Like the dews of evening fall :
Hear us, Holy Jesus.

2 Only Balm for souls distressed,
Happiness of all the blessed,

Peace of those who long for
Hear us, Holy Jesus.

3 Thou Who, as Thou once di(
Shalt be seen by human eye(
Coming through the parted
Hear us, Holy Jesus.

4 Thou Who on the quick and
All for whom Thy blood wa
Shalt pronounce the ju
dread :
Hear us, Holy Jesus.

5 Thou Who then shalt call t(
In the mansions of the bles(
Those who have Thy Name co
Hear us, Holy Jesus.
T. B. P(

THE HOLY GHOST.

4   7.7.7.6.

PART I.

1 SPIRIT blest, Who art adored,
With the Father and the Word,
One Eternal God and Lord :
Hear us, Holy Spirit.

2 Spirit guiding to the right,
Spirit making darkness light,
Spirit of resistless might :
Hear us, Holy Spirit.

3 Spirit falling like a dove
From the opened skies above,
With the Father's power and love :
Hear us, Holy Spirit.

4 Comforter to Whom we owe
All that we rejoice to know
Of our Saviour's work below :
Hear us, Holy Spirit.

5 Spirit showing us the way,
Warning when we go astray,

Pleading in us when we pr(
Hear us, Holy Spirit.

6 Spirit, Whom our failings (
Whom the world will not r(
Who dost help us to believe
Hear us, Holy Spirit

7 Spirit guarding us from ill.
Bending right our stubbom
Though we grieve Thee pati
Hear us, Holy Spirit.

PART II.

1 SPIRIT, strength of all the
Giving courage to the meel
Teaching faltering tongues
Hear us, Holy Spirit

2 Spirit, aiding all who yean
More of truth Divine to le(
And with deeper love to b(
Hear us, Holy Spirit

3 Spirit, Fount of faith and joy,
  Giving peace without alloy,
  Hope that nothing can destroy :
    Hear us, Holy Spirit. .

4 Source of love and light Divine,
  With that hallowing grace of Thine,
  More and more upon us shine :
    Hear us, Holy Spirit.

5 Holy, loving, as Thou art,
  Come and live within our heart,
  Never from us to depart :
    Hear us, Holy Spirit.

6 May we soon, from sin set free,
  Where Thy work may perfect be,
  Jesu's face with rapture see :
    Hear us, Holy Spirit.

T. B. Pollock.

PENITENCE.

5   7.7.7.6.

PART I.

1 FATHER, hear Thy children's call ;
  Humbly at Thy feet we fall,
  Prodigals, confessing all :
    We beseech Thee, hear us.

2 Christ, beneath Thy Cross of shame,
  All our sinful life we blame ;
  Penitent, we breathe Thy Name :
    We beseech Thee, hear us.

3 Holy Spirit, grieved and tried,
  Oft forgotten and defied,
  Now we mourn our stubborn pride :
    We beseech Thee, hear us.

4 Love that caused us first to be,
  Love that bled upon the tree,
  Love that draws us lovingly :
    We beseech Thee, hear us.

PART II.

[*To be sung with Part I.*]

1 WE Thy call have disobeyed,
  Have neglected and delayed,
  Into paths of sin have strayed :
    We beseech Thee, hear us.

2 Sick, we come to Thee for cure ;
  Guilty, seek Thy mercy sure ;
  Evil, come to be made pure :
    We beseech Thee, hear us.

3 Blind, we pray that we may see ;
  Bound, we pray to be made free ;
  Stained, we pray for sanctity :
    We beseech Thee, hear us.

4 By the nature Jesus wore,
  By the stripes and death He bore,
  By His life for evermore :
    We beseech Thee, hear us.

5 By the love that longs to bless,
  Pitying our sore distress,
  Leading us to holiness :
    We beseech Thee, hear us.

6 By the love so calm and strong,
  Patient still to suffer wrong,
  And our day of grace prolong :
    We beseech Thee, hear us.

7 By the love that bids Thee spare,
  By the heaven Thou dost prepare,
  By Thy promises to prayer :
    We beseech Thee, hear us.

PART III.

[*To be sung with Part I.*]

1 TEACH us what Thy love has
  borne,
  That, with loving sorrow torn,
  Truly contrite, we may mourn :
    We beseech Thee, hear us

2 Gifts of light and grace bestow ;
Help us to resist the foe,
Fearing what indeed is woe :
    We beseech Thee, hear us.

3 May we to all evil die,
Fleshly longings crucify,
Fix our hearts and thoughts on
   high :
    We beseech Thee, hear us.

4 Grant us Faith to know Thee near.
Hail Thy grace, Thy judgment
   fear,
And through trial persevere :
    We beseech Thee, hear us.

5 Grant us Hope from earth to rise,
And to strain with eager eyes

Towards the promised heavenly prize:
    We beseech Thee, hear us.

6 Grant us Love Thy love to own,
Love to live for Thee alone,
And the power of grace make
   known :
    We beseech Thee, hear us.

7 All our weak endeavours bless,
As we ever onward press,
Till we perfect holiness :
    We beseech Thee, hear us.

8 Lead us daily nearer Thee,
Till at last Thy Face we see,
Crowned with Thine own purity :
    We beseech Thee, hear us.
        T. B. Pollock.

THE CHRISTIAN LIFE.

6   7.7.7.6.

1 JESU, God's Incarnate Son,
By Thy work for sinners done,
By the gifts for sinners won :
    We beseech Thee, hear us.

2 That, with faithful hearts, we may
Love the things which are for aye
More than those which pass away :
    We beseech Thee, hear us.

3 That while pilgrims toiling here,
We Thy Name may love and fear,
And to death may persevere :
    We beseech Thee, hear us.

4 That Thy grace our lusts may kill,
That we may subdue our will,
All Thy pleasure to fulfil :
    We beseech Thee, hear us.

5 That, all holy as Thou art,
Thou wouldst dwell within our
heart,

Never from us to depart :
    We beseech Thee, hear us.

6 That our love may stronger grow,
And our faith more clearly show
What we hope to see and know :
    We beseech Thee, hear us.

7 That, when earthly toil is o'er,
We, in rest for evermore,
May enjoy Thee and adore :
    We beseech Thee, hear us.

8 That in mercy Thou wouldst come,
Seeking those who careless roam,
Bringing wanderers safely home :
    We beseech Thee, hear us.

9 That we soon may welcome Thee,
And may hear Thee say that we
Where Thou art shall ever be :
    We beseech Thee, hear us.
        T. B. Pollock.

FOR EVERY NEED.

7   7.7.7.6.

﹖ GOD the Father, throned on high ;
Saviour Who didst come to die :
Spirit Who dost sanctify :
    Lord, in mercy hear us.

﹖ We would hope in Thee alone ;
May our hopes be all Thine own,
And in fuller peace be shown :
    Lord, in mercy hear us.

3 Lord, we love Thee ; we deplore
That we do not love Thee more ;
Warm our coldness, we implore :
    Lord, in mercy hear us.

4 At Thy feet our thoughts we lay ;
Make Thine own the words we say ;
Make our lives more pure each day :
    Lord, in mercy hear us.

5 What Thou willest may we will,
Nor our own desires fulfil,

For we know not good from ill ·
    Lord, in mercy hear us.

6 May our lips our faith confess ⁚
Teach us, when reviled, to ble﹖ .
Conquering by gentleness :
    Lord, in mercy hear us.

7 Make us wise to do the right,
Calm in trouble, brave in fight.
Humble when our path is bright :
    Lord, in mercy hear us.

8 May we live that, free from fear,
We the angels' call may hear,
And before Thy throne appear :
    Lord, in mercy hear us.

9 May we then, from sin set free,
Rise to heaven to dwell with Thee,
Safe for all eternity :
    Lord, in mercy hear us.
               T. B. Pollock.

FOR THE YOUNG.

8   7.7.7.6.
       PART I.

1 JESU, from Thy Throne on high,
Far above the bright blue sky,
Look on us with loving eye :
    Hear us, Holy Jesu.

2 Little children need not fear
When they know that Thou art near;
Thou dost love us, Saviour dear :
    Hear us, Holy Jesu.

3 Little lambs may come to Thee ;
Thou wilt fold us tenderly,
And our careful Shepherd be :
    Hear us, Holy Jesu.

4 Little lives may be Divine,
Little deeds of love may shine,

Little ones be wholly Thine :
    Hear us, Holy Jesu.

5 Little hearts may love Thee well,
Little lips Thy love may tell,
Little hymns Thy praises swell :
    Hear us, Holy Jesu.

6 Jesu, once an Infant small,
Cradled in the oxen's stall,
Though the God and Lord of all :
    Hear us, Holy Jesu.

7 Once a Child so good and fair,
Feeling want and toil and care,
All that we may have to bear :
    Hear us, Holy Jesu.

8 Jesu, Thou dost love us still,
And it is Thy holy will

That we should be safe from ill,
Hear us, Holy Jesu.

9 Fold us to Thy loving breast ;
There may we, in happy rest,
Feel that we indeed are blest :
Hear us, Holy Jesu.

PART II.

1 JESU, from Thy Throne on high,
Far above the bright blue sky,
Look on us with loving eye :
Hear us, Holy Jesu.

2 Be Thou with us every day,
In our work and in our play,
When we learn and when we
pray :
Hear us, Holy Jesu.

3 When we lie asleep at night,
Ever may Thy angels bright
Keep us safe till morning's light :
Hear us, Holy Jesu.

4 Make us brave without a fear,
Make us happy, full of cheer,
Sure that Thou art always near :
Hear us, Holy Jesu.

5 May we grow from day to day
Glad to learn each holy way,

Ever ready to obey :
Hear us, Holy Jesu.

6 May we prize our Christian name
May we guard it free from blame
Fearing all that causes shame:
Hear us, Holy Jesu.

7 May we ever try to be
From our sinful tempers free,
Pure and gentle, Lord, like Thee :
Hear us, Holy Jesu.

8 May our thoughts be undefiled:
May our words be true and mild,
Make us each a holy child:
Hear us, Holy Jesu.

9 Jesu, Son of God most high,
Who didst in a manger lie,
Who upon a cross didst die :
Hear us, Holy Jesu.

10 Jesu, from Thy heavenly throne
Watching o'er each little one,
Till our life on earth is done:
Hear us, Holy Jesu.

11 Jesu, Whom we hope to see,
Calling us to come to Thee,
Happy evermore with Thee:
Hear us, Holy Jesu.

T. B. Pollock.

Ancient hymns of the Church.

9, 10, 11* TE DEUM LAUDA-
MUS.

1 WE praise . |Thee, O|God ||
We acknowledge|Thee to|be the|
Lord.

2 All the earth . doth|worship|Thee||
The . |Father|ever-|lasting.

3 To Thee all angels|cry a-|loud |
The heavens, . and|all the
powers there-|in.

4 To Thee Cherubin . and|Sera
phin ||
Con- . |tinual-|ly do|cry,

5 Holy,|holy,|holy ||
Lord . |God of|Saba-|oth;

6 Heaven and earth are full . |of the|majesty ||
Of . | ... Thy|glo- ... |ry.

7 The glorious company . |of the a-|postles ||
Praise . |... ...| ... ... |Thee.

8 The goodly fellowship . |of the| prophets ||
Praise . |... ...| ... ... |Thee.

9 The noble|army of |martyrs ||
Praise . |... ...| ... ... |Thee.

10 The holy Church . throughout|all the|world ||
Doth . | ... ac-|knowledge|Thee :

11 The Father . of an|infi - nite| majesty ||
Thine honourable, . |true, and| only|Son ;

12 Also . the|Holy|Ghost ||
The . |Com-...|...|for-|ter.

13 Thou art . the|King of |Glory ||
O . |... ...|... ... |Christ.

14 Thou art the ever-|lasting |Son |
Of . |... the|Fa-...|ther.

15 When Thou tookest upon Thee . to de-|liver|man ||
Thou didst not . ab-|hor the| Virgin's|womb.

16 When Thou hadst overcome . the| sharpness of |death ||
Thou didst open the Kingdom . of |Heaven to|all be-|lievers.

17 Thou sittest at the right . |hand of |God ||
In . the|glory|of the|Father.

18 We believe . that|Thou shalt|come||
To . |be ...|our ... |Judge.

19 We therefore pray Thee, . |help Thy|servants ||
Whom Thou hast redeemed |with Thy|precious|blood.

20 Make them to be numbered |with Thy|saints ||
In . |glory|ever-|lasting.

21 O Lord, . |save Thy|people ||
And . |bless Thine|heri-|tage.

22 Go-| .. vern|them ||
And . |lift them|up for|ever.

23 Day . |by ... |day ||
We . |magni-|fy ... |Thee ;

24 And . we|worship Thy|Name ||
Ever|world with-|out ... |end.

25 Vouch-. |safe, O|Lord ||
To keep us . this|day with-|out ...|sin.

26 O Lord, . have|mercy up-|on us ||
Have . |mercy up-|on ...|us.

27 O Lord, let Thy mercy |lighten up-| on us ||
As . our|trust ...|is in|Thee.

28 O Lord, in Thee . |have I |trusted ||
Let . me|never|be con-|founded.

12 BENEDICTUS.
Luke i. 68—79.

1 BLESSED be the Lord . |God of| Israel ||
For He hath visited . |and re-| deemed His|people,
And hath raised up an horn . of sal-|vation|for us ||
In the house . |of His |servant| David ;

2 As He spake by the mouth . of His|
holy| prophets ||
Which have been . |since the|
world be-|gan :
That we should be saved . |from
our|enemies ||
And from . the|hand of |all that|
hate us ;

3 To perform the mercy promised . |
to our|fathers ||
And ₁ to re-|member His|holy|
covenant,
The oath which He sware . to our|
father|Abraham ||
That He . would|grant ...|unto|
us,

4 That we, being delivered out of the
hand . |of our|enemies ||
Might .|serve Him|without|fear,
In holiness and righteous-|ness be-|
fore Him ||
All . the|days ...|of our|life.

5 And thou, child, shalt be called the
Prophet . |of the|Highest ||
For thou shalt go before the face
of the Lord, . |to pre-|pare His|
ways ; •
To give knowledge of salvation|
᠂ unto His|people ||
By . the re-|mission |of their|sins,

3 Through the tender mercy|of our|
God ||
Whereby the day-spring from .|
on| high hath|visited|us,
To give light to them that sit in
darkness and in . the|shadow
of|death ||
To guide our feet . |into the|way
of |peace.

*Glory be to the Father, . and|to
the|Son ||*

And . |to the|Holy'Ghost,
As it was in the beginning. s now,·
and|ever|shall be ||
World |without|end. A-. men.

13, 14 MAGNIFICAT.

Luke i. 46—55.

1 MY soul doth magni-|fy the|Lord'
And my spirit hath . re-|joiced
in|God my|Saviour.

2 For He . |hath re-|garded ||
The low . es-|tate of |His hand-|
maiden :

3 For, . be-|hold, from|henceforth|
All . gener-|ations shall |call me|
blessed.

4 For He that is mighty hath done .
to |me great|things ||
And . |holy|is His|Name.

5 And His mercy . is on |them that|
fear Him ||
From gener-|ation to|gener|
ation.

6 He hath shewed strength . |with
His|arm ||
He hath scattered the proud in
the imagi-|nation|of their|
hearts.

7 He hath put down the mighty|
from their|seats ||
And exalted|them of|low de-|
gree.

8 He hath filled the hungry with|
good ...|things ||
And the rich . He hath|sent ...|
empty a-|way.

9 He hath holpen . His|servant|
Israel, ||
In . re-|membrance |of . His|
mercy ;

:e . |to our|fathers ‖
ham, . and|to his|seed
er.

)RY BE, ETC.

IC DIMITTIS.

ke ii. 29—32.

lettest Thou Thy ser-
le-|part in|peace ‖
ding|to Thy|word :

eyes have|seen ‖
... | ... sal-|vation,

ou|hast pre-|pared ‖
1e|face of|all ...|people;

|lighten the|Gentiles ‖
be the glory|of Thy|
Israel.

.OBY BE, ETC.

ATOR MUNDI.

R of the world, . the|
rd|Jesus ‖
Thy strength, and help
e|humbly be-|seech ...|

oss and precious blood .
1ast re-|deemed us ‖
nd help us. . we|humbly
ch ...|Thee.

. save Thy disciples .
:eady to|perish ‖
nd save us, . we|humbly
ch ...|Thee.

fulness . of|Thy great|

from our sins, . we|
r be-|seech ...|Thee.

pear that Thou art our
. and | mighty De-|
‖

Oh, save us, that we may praise
Thee, . we|humbly be-|seech...|
Thee.

6 Draw near, according to Thy
promise, from the throne . | of
Thy|glory ‖
Look down and hear our crying, .
we| humbly be-|seech ...|Thee.

7 Come again, and dwell with us, ·
O|Lord Christ|Jesus ‖
Abide with us for ever, . we|
humbly be-|seech ...|Thee.

8 And when Thou shalt appear with
power . and|great ...|glory ‖
May we be made like unto Thee .
|in Thy|glorious|kingdom.

9 Thanks . be to|Thee, O|Lord ‖
Halle-|lujah !| A- ...|men.

17 GLORIA IN EXCELSIS.

1 Glory . be to|God on|high ‖
And in earth . |peace, good-|will
towards|men.

2 We praise Thee, we bless Thee, ,
we|worship|Thee ‖
We glorify Thee, . |we give|
thanks to|Thee,

3 For Thy great glory, . |O Lord|
God ‖
Heavenly King, God . the|
Father|Al- ...|mighty.

4 O Lord, the only-begotten Son, . |
Jesus|Christ ‖
O Lord God, Lamb of God, . |
Son ...|of the|Father,

5 That takest away the sins . |of
the|world ‖
Have . \mercy up-\on ...\us.

6 Thou that takest away the sins . |
of the|world ‖ ·
Have . |mercy up-|on ...|us.

7 Thou that takest away the sins . |
of the|world ‖
Re- . |ceive ... |our ...|prayer.

8 Thou that sittest at the right
hand . of|God the|Father ‖
Have . |mercy up-|on ...|us.

9 For Thou . |only art|holy ‖
Thou . |only|art the|Lord ;

10 Thou only, O Christ, . with the |
Holy|Ghost ‖
Art most high in the glory of
God . the|Father.| A-...|men.

18   SURSUM CORDA.

I. *Unis.*
1 Lift . |up your|hearts ‖
II. *Unis.*
We lift . them|up un-|to the Lord.

I. *Unis.*
2 Let us give thanks . unto the|Lord
our|God ‖
II. *Unis.*
It is meet .and|right ...|so to|do.

Full.
3 It is very meet, right, . and our|
bounden|duty ‖
That we . |should at|all ...|times

4 And . in|all ...|places ‖
Give . | thanks unto | Thee, O|
Lord,

5 Ho-|.. ly|Father ‖
Almighty, |Ever-|lasting|Father.

6 Therefore, with angels . |and arch-|
angels ‖
And all . the|compa-|ny of|
heaven,

7 We laud and magnify . Thy|
glorious|Name ‖
Evermore . |praising|Thee and|
saying,

•8 Holy,|Holy,|Holy ‖
Lord|God ...|... of|Hosts.

9 Heaven and earth are full . |of
Thy|glory ‖ ·
Glory be . to|Thee, O|Lord most|
high.

19   THE STRAIN UPRAISE.

"All Thy works shall praise Thee,
. O Lord."

1 THE strain upraise of joy and
praise, Alle-|lu- . ia ‖
To the glory of their King shall the
ransomed|people sing
Al- ... le-|lu- . ia ! ‖ Al-... le-|
luia !

2 And the choirs . that|dwell on
high ‖
Shall re-echo . |through the sky.
Al- ... le-|lu- . ia ! ‖ Al-... le-|
luia !

3 They in the rest . of|Paradise who
dwell ‖
The blessed ones, with joy . the|
chorus swell,
Al- ... le-|lu- . ia ! ‖ Al- ... le-|
luia !

4 The planets, glittering on . their|
heavenly way ‖
The shining constellations,|join
and say
Al- ... le-|lu- . ia ! ‖ Al- ... le-|
luia !

5 Ye clouds that onward sweep, Ye
winds . on|pinions light ‖
Ye thunders, echoing loud and deep,

Ye lightnings, | wildly bright,
In sweet . con- | sent unite ||
Your Al- ... le- | luia !

6 Ye floods and ocean billows, Ye
  storms and | winter snow ||
  Ye days of cloudless beauty, Hoar
  frost . and | summer glow,
  Ye groves that wave in spring,
  And glorious | forests, sing ||
  Al- ... le- | luia !

7 First let the birds, with painted |
  plumage gay ||
  Exalt their great Creator's | praise,
  and say   o
  Al- ... le- | lu- . ia ! || Al- ... le- |
  luia !

8 Then let the beasts of earth, . with |
  varying strain ||
  Join in creation's hymn . and | cry
  again
  Al- ... le- | lu- . ia ! || Al- ... le- |
  luia !

9 Here let the mountains thunder
  forth . so- | nor- . ous ||
  Al- ... le- | lu- . ia !
  There let the valleys sing in gen-
  tler | cho- . rus ||
  Al- ... le- | luia !

10 Thou jubilant abyss . of | ocean,
   cry ||
   Al- ... le- | lu- . ia ʔ
   Ye tracts of earth and conti- | nents,
   reply ||
   Al- ... le- | luia !

11 To God, Who all . cre- ation made ||
   The frequent hymn . be | duly
   paid,
   Al- ... le- | lu- .. ia ! || Al- ... le- |
   luia !   .

12 This is the strain, th' eternal strain,
   the Lord . Al- | mighty loves, ||
   Al- ... le- | lu- . ia !
   This is the song, the heavenly song,
   that Christ . the | King approves ||
   Al- ... le- | luia !

13 Wherefore we sing, both heart and
   voice . a- | waking ||
   Al- ... le- | lu- . ia !
   And children's voices echo, answer |
   making ||
   Al- ... le- | luia !

14 Now from all men . | be outpoured ||
   Alleluia | to the Lord,
   With Alleluia | evermore ||
   The Son and Spirit . | we adore.

15 Praise be done . to the | Three in
   One ||
   Al- ... le- | lu- . ia !
   Al- ... le- | lu- . ia ! || Al- ... le- |
   luia ! Amen.

20 BENEDICITE, OMNIA
         OPERA.

1 O ALL ye works . of the . | Lord, ||
  bless | ye the | Lord ||
  Praise Him, and | magnify | Him
  for ev- | er.

2 O . ye | heavens, || bless | ye the |
  Lord ||
  Praise Him, and | magnify | Him
  for ev- | er.

3 O ye angels . of the | Lord, || bless |
  ye the | Lord ||
  Praise Him, and | magnify | Him
  for ev- | er.

4 O sun, moon, . and | stars, || bless |
  ye the | Lord ||
  Praise Him, and | magnify | Him
  for ev- | er.

5 O ye **winter** . and | summer, ‖ bless |
ye the | Lord ‖
Praise Him, and | magnify | Him
for ev- | er.

6 O ye **nights** : and | days, ‖ bless | ye
the | Lord ‖
Praise Him, and | magnify | Him
for ev- | er.

7 **O** . let the | earth ‖ bless . (... the |
Lord ‖
Praise Him, and | magnify | Him
for ev- | er.

8 O all ye green things upon . the |
earth, ‖ bless | ye the | Lord ‖
Praise Him, and | magnify | Him
for ev- | er.

9 O ye **seas** . and | floods, ‖ bless | ye
the | Lord ‖
Praise Him, and | magnify | Him
for ev- | er.

10 O all ye that **move** . in the | waters,
‖ bless | ye the | Lord ‖
Praise Him, and | magnify | Him
for ev- | er.

11 O ye **fowls** . of the | air, ‖ bless | ye
the | Lord ‖
Praise Him, and | magnify | Him
for ev- | er.

12 O ye **beasts** . and | cattle, ‖ bless | ye
the | Lord ‖
Praise Him, and | magnify | Him
for ev- | er.

13 O ye **children** . of | men, ‖ bless | yc
the | Lord ‖
Praise Him, and | magnify | Him
for ev- | er.

14 O ye **servants** . of the | Lord, ‖
bless | ye the | Lord ‖
Praise Him, and | magnify \Him
for ev- | er.

15 O ye **souls** . of the | rig]
bless | ye the | Lord |
Praise Him, and | magn
for ev- | er.

16 O ye holy and humble ■
heart, ‖ bless | ye the | L
Praise Him, and | magn
for ev- | er.

21 DIES IRÆ.

1 DAY of wrath! oh day of mc
See fulfilled the prophet's w
Heaven and earth in ashes b
Oh, what fear man's bosom
When from heaven the Ju
scendeth,
On Whose sentence all depe

2 Wondrous sound the
flingeth ;   [1
Through earth's sepulc]
All before the throne it bri
Death is struck, and natur
ing ;
All creation is awaking,
To its Judge an answer ma]

3 Lo, the Book, exactly word
Wherein all hath been reco1
Thence shall judgment be s
When the Judge His seat a!
And each hidden deed arrai
Nothing unavenged remain

4 What shall I, frail man, be ¡
Who for me be interceding,
When the just are mercy n◦
King of Majesty tremendo◦
Who dost free salvation se1
Fount of pity, then befrien

5 Think, good Jesu, my salv:
Caused Thy wondrous inca
Leave me not to reprbatio

weary Thou hast sought

℔ of suffering bought me ;
grace be vainly brought

Judge, for sin's pollution
gift of absolution
ty of retribution.
ℓ I pour my moaning,
me with anguish owning:
od, Thy suppliant groan-

inful woman savedst ;
ying thief forgavest ;
a hope vouchsafest.
are my prayers and

.ord, in grace complying,
from fires undying.

8 With Thy favoured sheep, oh,
place me,
Nor among the goats abase me.
But to Thy right hand upraise
me.
While the wicked are confounded,
Doomed to flames of woe unbounded,
Call me with Thy saints surrounded.

9 Low I kneel with heart-submission ;
See, like ashes, my contrition ;
Help me in my last condition.
Ah, that day of tears and mourning !
From the dust of earth returning,
Man for judgment must prepare
him ;
Spare, O God, in mercy spare him.
Lord, all-pitying, Jesu blest,
Grant them Thine eternal rest.
Amen.

elections from the Book of Psalms.

PSALM I.

:he | man ‖
ılketh **not** . in the |
l | of the un- | godly.

ɔth in . the | way of |
‖
:th in . the | seat ... | of
ɔrnful :

.ight is in the law . ! of
rd ‖
Iıs **law** . doth he | medı -
ıy and | nıght.

ll be lıke a tree planted .
rivers of | water ‖

That bringeth forth . his | fruit... |
in his | season ;

5 His **leaf** . also | shall not | wither ‖
And whatso- | ever he | doeth shall |
prosper.

6 The ungodly | are not | so ‖
But are like the **chaff** . which
the | wind ... | driveth a- | way.

7 Therefore the ungodly shall not
stand . | in the ; judgment ‖
Nor sinners in the congre- | gation |
of the | righteous.

8 For the Lord knoweth the **way** . |
of the | righteous ‖
But the **way** . of the un- | godly |
shall ... | perish.

GLORIA PATRI.

GLORY be to the **Father**, . | and to
the | Son ‖
And . | to the | Holy | Ghost ;
As it was in the beginning, is **now**, .
and | ever | shall be ‖
World . without | end, ... | A- ... |
men.

or,

Glory be to the **Father**, . and | to
the | Son ‖
And ₑ | to the | Holy | Ghost ;
As it was in the beginning, is **now**, .
and | ever | shall be ‖
World . | without | end, A- | men.

23   PSALM II.

1 **Why** . do the | heathen | rage ‖
And the **people** . im- | agine a |
vain ... | thing ?
The kings of the earth set them-
selves, and the **rulers** . take |
counsel to- | gether ‖
Against the **Lord** . and a- | gainst
His an- | ointed, | saying,

2 Let us **break** . their | bands a- | sunder ‖
And **cast** . a- | way their | cords ... |
from us.
He that **sitteth** . in the ' heavens
·shall | laugh ‖
The **Lord** . shall | ha··e them | in
de- | rision.

3 Then shall He speak unto **them** . |
in His | wrath ‖
And **vex** . them | in His | sore dis- |
pleasure.
Yet . have I | set My | King ‖
Upon . My | holy | hill of | Zion.

4 I will declare the decree : the Lord
hath said unto **Me**, . | Thou art
My | Son ‖

This . | day have | I be- | gotten
Thee.
Ask of **Me**, and I shall give Thee
the **heathen** . for | Thine in- |
heritance ‖
And the uttermost **parts** . of the |
earth for | Thy pos- | session.

5 Thou shalt **break** them . with a |
rod of | iron ‖
Thou shalt dash them in | **pieces** . |
like a | potter's | vessel.
Be wise now, **therefore**, . | O ye ;
kings ‖
Be **instructed**, . ye | judges | of
the | earth.

6 Serve the Lord with **fear**, . and re- |
joice with | trembling ‖
Kiss the Son, lest He be **angry**, .
and ye | perish | from the | way,
When His **wrath** is **kindled** . | but
a | little ‖
Blessed are all **they** . that | put
their | trust in | Him.

GLORY BE, ETC.

24   PSALM IV.

1 **HEAR** me when I call, O **God** . | of
my | righteousness ‖
Thou hast enlarged me when I was
in distress ; have **mercy** . up- |
on me, and | hear my | prayer.
O ye sons of men, how long will ye
turn my **glory** | into | shame ‖
How long will ye love **vanity**, .
and | seek ... | after | leasing ?

2 But know that the Lord hath **set**
apart him that is **godly** | for
Him- | self ‖
The Lord will **hear** . | when I |
call unto | Him.

ve, and | sin not ||
 with your own heart
 your | bed, ... | and be |

cri- | fices of | righteous-

. your | trust ... | in the |

ıny that say, Who will
s | any | good ||
Thou up the **light** . of
ınte- | nance up- | on us.

; **gladness** | in my | heart ||
 in the time that their
 | and their | wine in- |

ay me **down** . in | peace,
ıp ||
ı, Lord, **on**ly | makest
ll in | safety.

ıBY BE, ETC. .

SALM V.

to my | words, O | Lord ||
der my | medi- | tation.

ıto the voice of my **cry**, .
ng, and my | God ||
o | Thee ... | will I | pray.

ıalt Thou **hear** . in the |
ıg, O | Lord ||
orning will I direct my
. unto | Thee, and | will
p.

 art not a **God** . that
leasure in | wickedness ||
 shall | evil | dwell with |

ı shall not **stand** . | in
ght ||
test . all | workers | of
ity.

6 Thou shalt destroy **them** . that |
 speak ... | **leasing** ||
 The Lord will abhor the **bloody** . |
 and de- | ceitful | man.

7 But as for me, I will come into
 Thy house in the **multitude** . |
 of Thy | mercy ||
 And in Thy fear will I **worship** |
 toward Thy | holy | temple.

8 Lead me, O Lord, in Thy **righteous-
 ness** . be- | cause of mine |
 enemies ||
 Make Thy **way** . | straight be- |
 fore my | face.

9 For there is no **faithfulness** . | in
 their | mouth ||
 Their inward | part is | very |
 wickedness ;

10 Their **throat** . is an | open | sepul-
 chre ||
 They . | flatter | with their | tongue.

11 **Destroy** . Thou | them, O | God ||
 Let them **fall** . | by their | own ... |
 counsels ;

12 Cast them out in the **multitude** .
 of | their trans- | gressions ||
 For . they | have re- | belled a- |
 gainst Thee.

13 But let all those that put their
 trust . in | Thee re- | joice ||
 Let them ever shout for joy.
 because . | Thou de- | fendest |
 them.

14 Let them also that love Thy **Name** .
 be | joyful in | Thee ||
 For Thou, Lord, wilt bless the
 righteous ; with favour wilt
 Thou **compass** | him as | with a |
 shield.
 GLORY BE, ETC.

26 PSALM VIII.

1 O Lord, our Lord, how excellent is
    Thy **Name** . in|all the|earth ‖
    Who hast **set** . Thy|glory a-|
    bove the|heavens.

2 Out of the **mouth** . of|babes and|
    sucklings ‖
    Hast . | Thou   or- | dain - ed |
    strength,

3 Because . | of Thine|enemies ‖
    That Thou mightest **still** . the|
    en-emy|and   the a-|venger.

4 When I consider **Thy** heavens, the
    work . |of Thy|fingers ‖
    The moon and the **stars**, . |which
    Thou|hast or-|dained ;

5 What is man, that **Thou** . art|
    mindful of|him ‖
    And the son of **man**, . |that
    Thou|visitest|him ?

6 For Thou hast made him a little
    lower|than the|angels ‖
    And hast **crowned**|him with|
    glory and|honour.

7 Thou madest him to have dominion
    over the **works** . |of Thy|
    hands ‖
    Thou **hast** . put|all things|under
    his|feet :

8 **All** . |sheep and|oxen ‖
    Yea, . and the|beasts ...|of the|
    field ;

9 The fowl of the **air**, . and the|
    fish of the|sea ‖
    And whatsoever passeth **through** .
    the paths ...|of the|seas.

10 **O** . |Lord, our|Lord ‖
    How excellent **is** . Thy|Name
    in|*all* the|earth |
    GLORY BE. ETC.

27 PSALM XV.

1 Lord, who shall **abide** .
    tabernacle ‖
    Who shall **dwell** . |in ?
    hill ?

2 He that walketh **upright**
    worketh|righteousne
    And **speaketh** . the | t
    his|heart.

3 He that backbiteth **not** .
    tongue ‖
    Nor doeth evil to his ?
    nor taketh **up** . a ?
    a-|gainst his|neighb‹

4 In whose eyes a vile pe
    con-|temned ‖
    But he **honoureth** . |t‹
    fear the|Lord.

5 He that **sweareth** . to |
    hurt ‖
    And . |chang- ...| ... eth

6 He that putteth not **out** .
    to|usury ‖
    Nor **taketh** . re-|ward
    the|innocent.

7 **He** . that|doeth|these th‹
    Shall . |ne- ...|ver be|r
    GLORY BE, ETC.

28 PSALM XVI.

1 **Preserve** . |me, O|God ‖
    For in **Thee** . |do I|put
    O my soul, thou hast sai‹
    Lord, . |Thou art my
    My **goodness** . ex-|t‹
    to|Thee ;

2 But to the **saints** . that ‹
    earth ‖
    And to the **excellent**,
    is\all my de-\light.

. | shall be | multi-

|after an- | other | god :

ferings of **blood** . will |
: ||

. their | names ... | into

the portion of mine
:e . and | of my | cup ||
· | tainest | my ... | lot.

fallen unto **me** . in |
)laces ||
e a | goodly | heritage.
ie **Lord** , . Who hath |
counsel ||
) **instruct** . me | in the |
seasons.

e **Lord** . | always be- |

s at my right **hand** , . |
t be | moved.
leart is **glad** , . and my |
joiceth ||
lso shall | rest in | hope.

; not **leave** . my | soul

t Thou suffer Thine
to | see cor- | ruption.
w me . the | path of |

ence is fulness of joy ;
ght **hand** . there are |
for | ever- | more.

Y BE, ETC.

,M XVIII.
;ES 1—20.)

Thee, . O | Lord, my |
||
; **my reck** , . and my |
md / my de- | liverer ;

My God, my **strength**, . in | Whom
I will | trust ||
My buckler, and the horn of my
salvation, | and my | high ... |
tower.

2 I will call upon the Lord, Who is
worthy | to be | praised ||
So shall I . be | sa - ved | from
mine | enemies.
The sorrows of **death** . | com-passed |
me ||
And the floods of **ungodly** | men
made | me a- | fraid.

3 The sorrows of hell **compassed** | me
a- | bout ||
The . | snares of | death pre- |
vented me.
Iu my distress I called upon the
Lord, and **cried** . | unto my |
God ||
He heard my voice out of His
temple, and my cry came be-
fore Him, . | even | into His |
ears.

4 Then the **earth** . | **shook** and |
trembled ||
The foundations also of the hills
moved and were **shaken**, . be- |
cause ... | He was | wroth.
There went **up a smoke** . | out o'
His | nostrils ||
And fire out of His mouth **devour**
ed ; | coals were | kindled | by it.

5 He bowed the **heavens also**, . and |
came . | down ||
And . | **darkness was** | under His |
feet.
And He rode upon a **cherub**, . |
and did | fly ||
Yea, He did **fly** . up- | on the |
wings of the | wind.

6 He made **darkness** . His | secret | place ‖
His pavilion round about Him were dark waters and **thick** . | clouds ... | of the | skies.
At the brightness that was before Him, His **thick** . | clouds ... | passed ‖
Hail- | stones and | coals of | fire.

7 The Lord also thundered in the heavens, and the **Highest** | gave His | voice ‖
Hail- . | stones and | coals of | fire.
Yea, He sent out His **arrows,** . and | scatter - ed | them ‖
And He shot out **light**nings, | and dis- | comfit - ed | them.

8 Then the **channels** . of | waters were | seen ‖
And the **foundations** . of the | world ... | were dis- | covered
At **Thy** . re- | buke, O | Lord ‖
At the **blast** . of the | breath ... | of Thy | nostrils.

9 He **sent**. from a- | bove. He | took me ‖
He **drew** . me | out of | many | waters.
He delivered me **from** . my | strong ... | enemy ‖
And from them which hated me : **for** . they | were too | strong for | me.

10 They prevented me in the **day** . of | my ca- | lamity ‖
But . the | Lord ... | was my | stay.
He brought me forth also into . a | large ... | place ‖
He delivered me, **because** . | He *de-* | *lighted* | in me.

GLORY BE, ETC.

30   PSALM XIX.

1 THE heavens **declare** . th God ‖
And the **firmament** His | handy- | work.
Day unto **day** . | utter-ε
And **night** . unto sheweth | knowledge

2 There is **no** . | speech nor **Where** . their | voice heard.
Their line is gone **out** . the | earth ‖
And their **words** . to of the world.

3 In them hath He set a tε for the | sun ‖
Which is **as a** bridegrε out of his chamber, a as a **strong** . | man race.
His going forth is frε of the heaven, and **unto** . the | ends of |
And there is nothing the | heat there- | of.

4 The law of the Lord con- | verting the | sε
The testimony of t **sure** . | making | simple :
The statutes of the Lord re- | joicing the | hea
The commandment oː is | pure, en- | ligh eyes :

5 The fear of the Lord is during for | ever ‖
The **judgments of** t true . and (right gether.

e desired are they **than**
yea, . than | much fine|

also than **honey** . |and
)ney-|comb.

by **them** . is Thy|servant|
d ||
keeping of **them** . |there
at re-|ward.
.nder-|stand his|errors ||
. Thou|me from|secret|
.

. Thy servant **also** . from
umptuous|sins ||
n **not** . have do-|minion|
ne :
ll|I be|upright ||
hall be **innocent** . |from
:reat trans-|gression.

)rds . |of my|mouth ||
nedi-|tation|of my|heart,
ble . |in Thy|sight ||
. my|strength and|my
)emer.
LORY BE, ETC.

PSALM XX.

hear thee . in the|day of|
e ||
ne of the **God** . of|Jacob
nd ...|thee.

help . |from the|sanctu-

trengthen thee | out of|

|all thy|offerings ||
:- | cept ... | thy burnt|
)e.

according . to|thine own|
||
:-|fil ... |all my|counsel.

5 We will rejoice in thy salvation, and
in the name of our God we will
set . |up our|banners ||
The **Lord** . ful-|fil all | thy pe-|
titions.

6 Now know I that the Lord **saveth**|
His an-|ointed ||
He will hear him from His holy
heaven with the **saving** |
strength of|His right|hand.

7 Some trust in **chariots,** . and | some
in|horses ||
But we will remember the **Name** .|
of the|Lord our|God.

8 They are **brought** .|down and |fallen||
But **we** . are | risen, and | stand
up-|right.

9 **Save,** . |...|Lord ||
Let the **King** . |hear us|when we|
call.
GLORY BE, ETC.

32 PSALM XXIII.

1 THE **Lord** . |is my|Shepherd ||
I . |shall ...|not ...|want.

2 He maketh me to lie **down** · in|
green ...|pastures ||
He leadeth **me** . be-|side the|
still ...|waters.

3 **He** . re-|storeth my|soul ||
He leadeth me in the paths of
righteousness . | for His |
Name's ...|sake.

4 Yea, though I walk through the
valley . of the | shadow of |
death ||
I . | ... will|fear no|evil :

5 For . |Thou art|with me ||
Thy **rod** . |and Thy|staff they|
comfort me.

6 Thou preparest . a|table be-|fore
  me ‖
  In . the|presence|of mine | ene-
  mies :
7 Thou anointest . my|head with|oil ‖
  My . |cup ...|runneth|over.
8 Surely|goodness and|mercy ‖
  Shall follow me all . the|days...|
  of my|life ;
  And . |I will|dwell ‖
  In the house . |of the|Lord for|
  ever.
      GLORY BE, ETC.

33   PSALM XXIV.
1 THE earth is the Lord's, . and the|
  fulness there·|of ‖
  The world, . and|they that|dwell
  there-|in :
  For He hath founded it . up-|on
  the|seas ‖
  And established . |it up-|on the|
  floods.
2 Who shall ascend into the hill . |
  of the|Lord ‖
  Or who shall stand . |in His|
  holy|place ?
  He that hath clean hands, . and
  a|pure ...|heart ‖
  Who hath not lifted up his soul
  unto vanity, . |nor ...|sworn
  de-|ceitfully.
3 He shall receive the blessing|from
  the|Lord ‖
  And righteousness from . the|
  God of|his sal-|vation.
  *This is the generation . of|them
  that|seek Him ‖
  That . |seek Thy|face, O|Jacob.*

4 Lift up your heads, O ye gates ; and
  be ye lift up, ye ever-|lasting|
  doors ‖
  And the King . of|glory|shall
  come|in.
  Who is . this|King of|glory ‖
  The Lord strong and mighty, .
  the|Lord ...|mighty in|battle
5 Lift up your heads, O ye gates,
  even lift .them up, ye ever-|
  lasting|doors ‖
  And the King . of|glory|shall
  come|in.
  Who is . this|King of|glory ‖
  The Lord of hosts, . |He is the|
  King of|glory.
      GLORY BE, ETC.

34   PSALM XXV.
1 UNTO Thee, O Lord, do I lift . |up
  my|soul ‖
  O . my|God, I|trust in|Thee :
  Let me not . |be a-|shamed ‖
  Let not mine enemies . |triumph|
  over|me.
2 Yea, let none that wait on Thee . |
  be a-|shamed ‖
  Let them be ashamed which .
  trans- | gress with- | out ...|
  cause.
  Shew me . Thy|ways, O|Lord ‖
  Teach . |me ...|Thy ...|paths.
3 Lead me in . Thy|truth, and|teach
  me ‖ ·
  For Thou art the God of my
  salvation ; on Thee . do I |
  wait ...|all the|day.
  Remember, O Lord, Thy tender
  mercies and . Thy|loving-|
  kindnesses ‖
  For . they|have been|ever of|
  old.

4 Remember not the sins of my
youth, . nor|my trans- |gres-
sions ‖
According to Thy mercy re-
member Thou me, for . Thy|
goodness'|sake, O|Lord.
Good and upright .|is the|Lord ‖
Therefore will He |teach .|sin-
ners|in the|way.

5 The meek . will He|guide in|judg-
ment ‖
And the meek . |will He | teach
His|way.
All the paths of the Lord . are|
mercy and|truth ‖
Unto such as keep . His | cove-
nant|and His|testimonies.

6 For Thy Name's . |sake, O|Lord ‖
Pardon mine iniquity ; . |for ...|
it is|great.
What man is he . that|feareth the|
Lord ‖
Him shall He teach . in the|way
that|He shall|choose.

7 His soul . shall|dwell at|ease ‖
And . his | seed shall in-| herit
the|earth.
The secret of the Lord . is with|
them that|fear Him ‖
And He . will| shew ... |them
His|covenant.

8 Mine eyes are ever . |toward the|
Lord ‖
For He shall pluck . my | feet
out|of the|net.
Turn Thee unto me, . |and have |
mercy up-|on me ‖
For I . am|deso - late|and af- |
flicted.

9 The troubles of my heart . |are
en-/larged ‖

Oh, bring Thou me . |out of|my
dis-|tresses.
Look upon mine affliction, . |and
my|pain ‖
And . for-|give ... |all my|sins.

10 Consider mine enemies ; . for|they
are|many ‖
And . they|hate me with|cruel|
hatred.
Oh, keep my soul, . and de- |liver|
me ‖
Let me not be ashamed ; for . I|
put my|trust in|Thee.

GLORY BE, ETC.

35 PSALM XXVI.

1 JUDGE me, O Lord ; for I have
walked . in|mine in-|tegrity ‖
I have trusted also in the Lord ; .|
therefore I|shall not|slide.

2 Examine me, . O|Lord, and|prove
me ‖
Try . my|reins ... |and'my|heart.

3 For Thy loving-kindness . is be-|
fore mine|eyes ‖
And I . have|walk-ed|in Thy|
truth.

4 I have not sat . with|vain .. |per-
sons ‖
Neither will . I|go in|with dis-|
semblers.

5 I have hated the congregation .
of|evil-|doers ‖
And will not . |sit ... |with th ·|
wicked.

6 I will wash . mine | hands in |
innocency ‖
So will I compass .Thine|altar:
O ...|Lord :

7 That I may publish with the
voice . | of thanks- | giving ‖
And tell . of | all Thy | wondrous |
works.

8 Lord, I have loved the habitation |
of Thy | house ‖
And the place . | where Thine |
honour | dwelleth.

9 Gather not . my | soul with | sin-
ners ‖
Nor . my | life with | bloody | men ;

10 In whose . | hands is | mischief ‖
And their right . | hand is | full
of | bribes.

11 But as for me, I will walk . in |
mine in- | tegrity ‖
Redeem me . and be | merci- ful |
unto | me.

12 My foot standeth . in an | even |
place ‖
In the congregations | will I |
bless the | Lord.

GLORY BE, ETC.

36   PSALM XXVII.

1 THE Lord is my light and my salva-
tion; . | whom shall I | fear ‖
The Lord is the strength of my
life ; . of | whom   shall I | be
a- | fraid ?
When the wicked, even mine
enemies . | and my | foes ‖
Came upon me to eat up . my |
flesh, they | stumbled and | fell.

2 Though an host . should en- |
camp a- | gainst me ‖
My | heart ... | shall not | fear ;
Though war . should | rise a- | gainst
me ‖
In . | this will | I be | confident.

3 One thing have I desired . | of the |
Lord ‖
That . | will I | seek ... | after ;
That I may dwell in the house of the
Lord . all the | days of my | life |
To behold the beauty of the Lord,
and . to in- | quire ... | in His |
temple.

4 For in . the | time of | trouble ‖
He . shall | hide me in | His
pa- | vilion :
In the secret of His tabernacle . |
shall He | hide me ‖
He shall set . me | up up- | on
a | rock.

5 And now shall mine head . be |
lifted | up ‖
Above . mine | ene-mies | round
a- | bout me :
Therefore will I offer in His taber-
nacle sacri- | fices of | joy ‖
I will sing, yea, I will sing . |
praises | unto the | Lord.

6 Hear, O Lord, . when I | cry with
my | voice ‖
Have mercy also . up- | on me,
and | answer | me.
When Thou saidst, . | Seek ye My
face ‖
My heart said unto Thee, . Thy
face, Lord, | will I | seek.

7 Hide not . Thy | face far | from me
Put not . Thy | servant a- | way
in | anger :
Thou . hast | been my | help ‖
Leave me not, neither forsake
me, O | God of | my sal- | vation.

8 When my father . and my | mother
for- | sake me ‖
Then . the | Lord will | take me |
up.

Teach me . Thy|way, O|Lord ‖
And lead me in a plain path, .
be-|cause ... |of mine|enemies.

9 Deliver . |me not|over ‖
Unto . the | will ... |of mine |
enemies ;
For false witnesses are risen|up
a-|gainst me ‖
And . | such as | breathe out |
cruelty.

10 I had fainted, unless I had believed
to see the goodness|of the|
Lord ‖
In the|land ... |of the|living.
Wait on the Lord ; be of good
courage, and He . shall |
strengthen thine|heart ‖
Wait, . I|say, ... |on the|Lord.

GLORY BE, ETC.

37   PSALM XXIX.

1 GIVE unto the Lord, . | O ye |
mighty ‖
Give unto the Lord . | glory |
and ... |strength.

2 Give unto the Lord the glory
due . |unto His|Name ‖
Worship the Lord . in the |
beauty of|holiness.

3 The voice of the Lord . is up-|on
the|waters ‖
The God of glory thundereth;
the Lord . |is up- on|many|
waters.

4 The voice . of the|Lord is|power-
ful ‖
The voice . of the|Lord is|full
of|majesty.

5 The voice of the Lord . |breaketh
the|cedars ‖

Yea, the Lord . |breaketh the|
cedars of|Lebanon.

6 He maketh them also to skip . |
like a|calf ‖
Lebanon and Sirion . |like a|
young ... |unicorn.

7 The voice . |of the|Lord ‖
Di- . |videth the|flames of|fire.

8 The voice of the Lord . |shaketh
the|wilderness ‖
The Lord shaketh . the|wilder-|
ness of|Kadesh.

9 The voice of the Lord maketh the
hinds to calve, . and dis- |
covereth the|forests ‖
And in His temple doth every
one . |speak of|His ... |glory.

10 The Lord sitteth . up- | on the |
flood ‖
Yea, the Lord . |sitteth | King
for|ever.

11 The Lord will give strength . |
unto His|people ‖
The Lord . will|bless His|people
with|peace.

GLORY BE, ETC.

38   PSALM XXX.

1 I WILL extol Thee, O Lord ; for
Thou . hast|lifted me|up ‖
And hast not made my foes . to
re-|joice ... |over|me.
O Lord my God, . I|cried unto|
Thee ‖
And . |Thou hast|healed|me.

2 O Lord, Thou hast brought up my
soul . |from the|grave ‖
Thou hast kept me alive, that I
should not . go down ... |to
the|pit.

Sing unto the **Lord**, . O ye|saints
of | His ||
And give **thanks** . at the re-|
membrance|of His|holiness.

3 For His **anger** endureth | but a |
moment ||
In . His|fa- ... |vour is|life :
Weeping may endure . | for a |
night ||
But joy . |cometh|in the|morn-
ing.

4 And in my prosperity I said, I .
shall|never be|moved ||
Lord, by Thy favour Thou hast
made . my | mountain to |
stand ... |strong :
Thou didst hide Thy **face**, . and|I
was|troubled ||
I cried to Thee, O Lord ; and unto
the **Lord** . I|made ... |suppli-|
cation.

5 What profit is there in my blood.
when I . go|down to the|pit ||
Shall the dust praise Thee ? . shall|
it de-|clare Thy|truth ?
Hear, O **Lord**, . and have|mercy
up-|on me ||
O . |Lord, be|Thou my|Helper.

6 Thou . hast|turn-ed|for me ||
My . |mourning|into|dancing :
Thou hast . put|off my|sackcloth ||
And . |girded|me with|gladness ;

7 To the end . |that my|glory ||
May sing **praise** . to|Thee. and|
not be|silent.
O . |Lord my|God ||
I **will** . give|thanks unto|Thee
for|ever.

GLORY ᴺᴿ ETC.

---

39 PSALM XXXII.

1 BLESSED is he whose transgression|
is for-|given ||
Whose . |sin ... |is ... |covered.
Blessed is the man unto whom the
Lord imput- . eth | not in- |
iquity ||
And in whose . |spirit there|is
no|guile.

2 **When** . |I kept|silence ||
My bones waxed old, **through** .
my|roaring|all the day|long.
For day and night Thy **hand** .
was|heavy up-|on me ||
My moisture is **turned** . | into
the|drought of|summer.

3 I acknowledged my sin . | unto |
Thee ||
And mine **iniquity** . | have I!
not ... |hid.
I said, I will confess my trans-
gressions|unto the|Lord ||
And Thou forgavest . the in-|
iquity|of my|sin.

4 For this shall every one that is godly
pra . unto Thee in a **time** . when
Thou|mayest be|found ||
Surely in the floods of the great
waters **they** . shall|not come|
nigh unto|him.
Thou **art** my hiding-place ; Thou
shalt preserve . | me from|
trouble ||
Thou shalt compass me **about** .
with|songs ... |of de-|liverance.

5 I will instruct thee, and teach thee in
the **way** . which |thou shalt|go|
I . will |guide thee|with Mine|eye.
Be ye not as the horse, or as the
mule, which have **no** , |under-|
standing ||

Whose mouth must be held in
with bit and bridle, lest . they|
come ... |near unto|thee.

6 Many **sorrows** . shall|be to the|
wicked ‖
But he that trusteth in the Lord,
mercy . shall | compass | him
a-|bout.
Be glad in the Lord, . and re-|joice,
ye|righteous ‖
And shout for joy, all **ye** . that
are|upright|in ... |heart.

GLORY BE, ETC.

40 PSALM XXXIII.

1 REJOICE in the Lord, . |O ye|
righteous ‖
For **praise** . is|comely|for the|
upright.
Praise . the|Lord with|harp ‖
Sing unto Him with the **psaltery** .
and an|instru - ment|of ten |
strings.

2 Sing unto **Him** . a|new ... |song ‖
Play **skilfully** . |with a|loud ... |
noise.
For the **word** . of the|Lord is |right‖
And all . His | works are|done
in|truth.

3 He loveth **righteous**- |ness and|
judgment ‖
The earth is **full** . of the|good-
ness|of the|Lord.
By the **word** of the **Lord** were
the|heavens|made ‖
And all the host of them **by** .
the|breath ... |of His|mouth.

4 He gathereth the **waters** of the sea
together . |as an|heap ‖
He **layeth** | up the | depth in |
storehouses.

Let all the **earth** . |fear the|Lord ‖
Let all the inhabitants of the
world . |stand in |awe of |Him.

5 For He **spake**, . and|it was|done ‖
He **commanded**, . and it |
stood ... |fast.
The Lord bringeth the **counsel** . of
the|heathen to|nought ‖
He maketh the **devices** of . the|
people of |none ef-|fect.

6 The counsel of the **Lord** . |standeth
for|ever ‖
The thoughts of His **heart** . to|
all ... |gener- |ations.
Blessed is the nation whose **God** . |
is the|Lord ‖
And the people whom He hath
chosen|for His | own in-|heri-
tance.

7 The **Lord** . |looketh from|heaven ‖
He beholdeth|all the|sons of|
men.
From the **place** . of His | habi-|
tation ‖
He looketh upon all . the in-|
habitants|of the|earth.

8 He **fashioneth** . their|hearts a-|
like ‖
He . con-|sider - eth|all their|
works.
There is no king saved by the
multitude . |of an|host ‖
A mighty man is **not** . de-|
livered by|much ... |strength.

9 An horse is a **vain** . |thing for|
safety ‖
Neither shall he deliver any |
by his|great ... |strength.
Behold, the eye of the Lord is
upon them that fear Him
Upon them that hope
His|mercy ;

13

10 To deliver . their|soul from|death‖
And . to|keep them a-|live in|
famine.
Our soul waiteth|for the|Lord ‖
He is . our|help ... |and our|
shield.

11 For our heart . shall re-|joice in|
Him ‖
Because we have trusted|in His|
holy|name.
Let Thy mercy, O Lord, . |be up- |
on us ‖
According|as we|hope in|Thee.
GLORY BE, ETC.

41 PSALM XXXIV.

1 I WILL bless . the | Lord at | all
times ‖
His praise shall continually . |
be ...|in my|mouth.
My soul shall make her boast . |in
the|Lord ‖
The humble shall hear . there-|
of, ...|and be|glad.

2 Oh, magnify . the|Lord with|me ‖
And let us . ex-|alt His|name
to-|gether.
I sought the Lord, . |and He |
heard me ‖
And delivered|me from|all my|
fears.

3 They looked unto Him, . | and
were|lightened ‖
And . their|faces were|not a-|
shamed.
This poor man cried, . and the |
Lord ...|heard him ‖
And saved . him|out of|all his|
troubles.

4 The angel of the Lord encampeth
round . about|them that|fear
Him ‖

And . | ... de-|liver - eth|them.
Oh, taste and see . that the|Lord is|
good ‖
Blessed . is the | man that|
trusteth in|Him.

5 Oh, fear the Lord, . |ye His|saints‖
For there is no want . to|them
that|fear ...|Him.
The young lions do lack . and|
suffer|hunger ‖
But they that seek the Lord .
shall | not want | any good|
thing.

6 Come, ye children, hearken|unto|
me ‖
I will teach you . the|fear ...|of
the|Lord.
What man is he . that de-|sireth|
life ‖
And loveth many days, . that|
he may|see ...|good?

7 Keep . thy|tongue from|evil ‖
And . thy|lips from|speaking|
guile.
Depart from evil, . and | do ...|
good ‖
Seek . |peace, ...|and pur-|sue it.

8 The eyes of the Lord . are up-|on
the|righteous ‖
And His ears . are|open|unto
their|cry.
The face of the Lord is against
them . |that do|evil ‖
To cut off the remembrance|of
them|from the|earth.

9 The righteous cry, . and the|
Lord ...|heareth ‖
And delivereth . them|out of|
all their|troubles.
The Lord is nigh unto them that
are . of a|broken|heart ‖

And saveth such . as | be of a |
contrite | spirit.

Many are the afflictions . | of the |
righteous ‖
But the Lord delivereth him . |
out ... | of them | all.
He keepeth | all his | bones ‖
Not . | one of | them is | broken.

Evil . shall | slay the | wicked ‖
And they that hate . the | right-
eous | shall be | desolate.
The Lord redeemeth the soul . | of
His | servants ‖
And none of them that trust .
in | Him ... | shall be | desolate.

GLORY BE, ETC.

2 PSALM XXXVI.

THE transgression of the wicked
saith . with- | in my | heart ‖
That there is no fear . of | God
be- | fore his | eyes.
For he flattereth himself . in his |
own ... | eyes ‖
Until his iniquity . be | found ... |
to be | hateful.

The words of his mouth are in-
iquity . | and de- | ceit ‖
He hath left off to be wise, . |
and to | do ... | good.
He deviseth mischief . up- | on his |
bed ‖
He setteth himself in a way that
is not good; he ab- | horreth |
not ... | evil.

Thy mercy, O Lord, . is | in the |
heavens ‖
And Thy faithfulness . | reacheth |
unto the | clouds.

Thy righteousness is like the great
mountains; Thy judgments . |
are a great | deep ‖
O Lord, Thou . pre- | servest | man
and | beast.

4 How excellent is Thy loving- |
kindness, O | God ‖
Therefore the children of men
put their trust under . the |
shadow | of Thy | wings.
They shall be abundantly satisfied
with the fatness . | of Thy |
house ‖
And Thou shalt make them drink .
of the | river | of Thy | pleasures.

5 For with Thee . is the | fountain of |
life ‖
In Thy light . | shall we | see ... |
light.
Oh, continue Thy loving-kindness
unto | them that | know Thee ‖
And Thy righteousness . | to the |
upright in | heart.

6 Let not the foot of pride . | come
a- | gainst me ‖
And let not . the | hand of the |
wicked re- | move me.
There are the workers . of in- |
iquity | fallen ‖
They are cast down, . and shall |
not be | able to | rise.

GLORY BE, ETC.

43 PSALM XXXVII.

1 FRET not thyself because . of |
evil- | doers ‖
Neither be thou envious against .
the | workers | of in- | iquity :
For they shall soon be cut down . |
like the | grass ‖
And wither . | as the | green .
herb.

18*

2 Trust in the Lord, . and | do ... |
good ‖
So shalt thou dwell in the land, .
and | verily thou | shalt be |
fed.
Delight thyself also . | in the |
Lord ‖
And He shall give thee . the de- |
sires of | thine ... | heart.

3 Commit Thy way . | unto the |
Lord |
Trust also in Him, . and | He
shall | bring it to | pass :
And He shall bring forth thy
righteousness . | as the | light ‖
And . thy | judgment | as the |
noon-day.

4 Rest in the Lord, and wait patient- |
ly for | Him ‖
Fret not thyself because of him
who prospereth in his way,
because of the man who
bringeth | wicked de- | vices to |
pass.
Cease from anger, and . for- |
sake ... | wrath ‖
Fret not thyself . in | any wise |
to do | evil.

5 For evil-doers . shall | be cut | off ‖
But those that wait upon the
Lord, . | they shall in- | herit
the | earth.
Nor yet a little while, and the
wicked . | shall not | be ‖
Yea, thou shalt diligently con-
sider his place, . | and it | shall
not | be.

6 But the meek . shall in- | herit
the | earth ‖
And shall delight themselves . |
in the a- | bundance of | peace.

The wicked plotteth . a- | gainst the |
just ‖
And gnasheth . up- | on him | with
his | teeth.

7 The Lord . shall | laugh at | him ‖
For He seeth . | that his | day is |
coming.
The wicked have drawn out the
sword, . and have | bent their |
bow ‖
To cast down the poor and needy,
to slay such as be . of | upright |
conver - | sation.

8 Their sword shall enter into their |
own ... | heart ‖
And . their | bows ... | shall be |
broken.
A little that a righteous | man ... |
hath ‖
Is better than . the | riches of |
many | wicked.

9 For the arms of the wicked . | shall
be | broken ‖
But . the | Lord up- | holdeth the |
righteous.
The Lord knoweth the days . | of
the | upright ‖
And their inheritance . | shall ... |
be for | ever.

10 They shall not be ashamed . in the |
evil | time ‖
And in the days . of | famine
they | shall be | satisfied.
For such as be blest of Him .
shall in- | herit the | earth ‖
And they that be cursed of
Him . | shall be | cut ... | off.

11 The steps of a good man are
ordered . | by the | Lord ‖
And He . de- | lighteth | in his |
way.

Though he fall, he shall not be
utterly . |cast ... |down ||
For the Lord . up-|holdeth him|
with His|hand.

I have been **young**, . and|now am|
old ||
Yet have I not seen the right-
eous forsaken, **nor** . his |
seed ...|begging|bread.
He is ever **merci**-|ful, and |lendeth||
And . his|seed ...|is ...|blessed.

Depart from **evil** . and|do ...|good||
And . |dwell for|ever-|more.
For the Lord loveth judgment, and
forsaketh nut His saints;
they . are pre-|served for|ever||
But the seed of the **wicked** . |
shall be|cut ...|off.

The righteous **shall** . in-|herit
the|land ||
And . |dwell there-|in for|ever.
The mouth of the **righteous** . |
speaketh|wisdom ||
And . his|tongue ...|talketh of|
judgment.

The law of his **God** . is|in his|
heart ||
None . of his|steps ...|shall ...|
slide.
The **wicked** . |watcheth the|right-
eous ||
And . |seek- ...|eth to|slay him.

The Lord will not **leave** him . |in
his|hand ||
Nor . con-|demn him|when he
is|judged.
Wait on the Lord, and keep His
way, and He shall **exalt** thee .
to in-|herit the|land ||
When the wicked are **cut** . |
off ...|thou shalt|see it.

17 Mark the perfect man, **and** . be-|
hold the|upright ||
For the **end** . of|that ...|man
is|peace.
But the transgressors shall **be** .
de-|stroyed to-|gether ||
The end of the **wicked** . |shall
be|cut ...|off.

18 But the salvation of the **righteous** .
is|of the|Lord ||
He is their **strength** . |in the|
time of|trouble.
And the Lord shall help them,
and . de-|liver|them ||
He shall deliver them from the
wicked, and **save** them, . be-|
cause they|trust in|Him.

GLORY BE, ETC.

44 PSALM XXXIX.

1 I SAID, I will take heed to my ways,
that I **sin** not . |with my|
tongue ||
I will keep my mouth with a
bridle, **while** . the|wicked | is
be-|fore me.
I . was|dumb with|silence ||
I held my peace, even from **good**; .|
and my|sorrow was|stirred.

2 My heart was hot within me ; while
I was **musing** . the | fire ... |
burned ||
Then . |spake I|with my|tongue,
Lord, make me to know mine end,
and the measure of my **days**, . |
what it|is ||
That **I** . may|know how|frail
I|am.

3 Behold, Thou hast made my days .
as an|handbreadth |

And mine **age** . |is as|nothing
be-|fore Thee :
Verily every **man** . at|his best|state||
Is . |alto-|gether|vanity.

4 Surely every man **walketh**|in a
vain|shew ||
Surely they **are** . dis-|quiet-|ed
in|vain :
He .|heapeth up|riches ||
And **knoweth** not . |who shall|
gather|them.

5 And now, **Lord**, . what|wait I|for ||
My . |hope ...|is in|Thee.
Deliver me from **all** . |my trans-|
gressions ||
Make me **not** . the re-|proach ...|
of the|foolish.

6 I was dumb, I **opened**|not my|
mouth ||
Be- . |cause ...|Thou ...|didst it.
Remove Thy **stroke** . a-|way from|
me ||
I am con**sumed** . by the|blow ...|
of Thine|hand.

7 When Thou with rebukes dost
correct man for iniquity, Thou
makest his beauty to consume
away . |like a|moth ||
Surely|every|man is|vanity.
Hear my prayer, O Lord, and give
ear . |unto my|cry ||
Hold **not** . Thy|peace ...|at my|
tears :

8 For I am . a|stranger|with Thee ||
And a **sojourner**, . as|all my|
fathers|were.
Oh, spare me, that I **may** . re-|cover|
strength ||
Before I go . |hence, and|be no|
more.
GLORY BE, ETC.

45   PSALM XL.

1 I **WAITED** **patiently** . | for the|
Lord ||
And He **inclined** . unto|me, and|
heard my|cry.
He brought me up also **out** . of
an|horri - ble|pit ||
Out . |of the|miry|clay,

2 And set my **feet** . up-|on a|rock||
And . es-|tablish-|ed my|goings.
And He hath put a new **song** .|
in my|mouth ||
Even|praise ...|unto our|God :

3 **Many** . shall|see it, and|fear ||
And . shall | trust ... | in the|
Lord.
Blessed is the man that **maketh** .
the|Lord his|trust ||
And respecteth not the proud,
nor **such** . as|turn a-|side to|
lies.

4 Many, O Lord my God, are the
wonderful **works** . which |
Thou hast|done ||
And . Thy|thoughts which|are
to|us-ward :
They cannot be reckoned up in
order . |unto|Thee ||
If I would declare and speak of
them, **they** . are|more than|
can be|numbered.

5 Sacrifice and offering Thou didst
not desire ; mine **ears** . |hast
Thou|opened ||
Burnt - offering and sin-**offer-
ing** . | hast Thou | not re-|
quired.
Then said I, . |Lo, I|come ||
In the volume of the **book** . |it
is|written of|me,

I delight to do Thy will, . |O my|
God ‖
Yea, . Thy|law is with-|in
my|heart.
I have published righteousness in
the great . |congre-|gation ‖
Lo, I have not refrained . my|
lips, O|Lord, Thou|knowest.
I have not hid Thy righteousness .
with-|in my|heart ‖
I have declared Thy faithful-
ness . |and ...| Thy sal-|va-
tion :
I have not concealed Thy loving-
kindness . |and Thy|truth ‖
From . the|great ...|congre-|ga-
tion.
Withhold not Thou Thy tender
mercies . from|me, O|Lord ‖
Let Thy loving-kindness and
Thy truth . con-|tinual-|ly
pre-|serve me.
For innumerable evils have com-
passed . |me a-|bout ‖
Mine iniquities have taken hold
upon me, so that I am . not|
able to|look ...|up :
They are more than the hairs . |
of mine|head ‖
Therefore . my|heart ..|faileth|
me.
Be pleased, O Lord, . |to de-|liver
me ‖
O . |Lord, make | haste to|help
me.
Let them be ashamed . and con-|
founded to-|gether ‖
That seek after . my|soul ...|to
de-|stroy it ;
Let them . be|driven|backward ‖
And put . to|shame, that|wish
me|evil.

11 Let all those that seek Thee
rejoice . and be|glad in|Thee ‖
Let such as love Thy salvation
say continually, The . |Lord
be|magni-|fied.
But I am poor and needy ; yet the
Lord . |thinketh up-|on me ‖
Thou art my help and my de-
liverer ; make . no|tarry - ing,|
O my|God.
GLORY BE, ETC.

46 PSALM XLII.

1 As the hart panteth after . the|
water-|brooks ‖
So panteth my soul . |after|Thee,
O|God.
2 My soul thirsteth for God, . for
the|living|God ‖
When shall I come . and ap-|
pear be-|fore ...|God ?
3 My tears have been my meat . |
day and|night ‖
While they continually say unto
me, . |Where ...|is thy|God?
4 When I . re-|member|these things‖
I pour . |out my|soul ...|in me :
5 For I had gone . |with the|multi-
tude ‖
I went with them . |to the|house
of|God,
6 With the voice . of|joy and|praise‖
With a multitude . |that kept|
holy-|day.
7 Why art thou cast down, . |O
my|soul ‖
And why art thou . dis-|quiet-|
ed in|me ?
8 Hope thou in God; . for I|shall
yet|praise Him ‖

For . the | help ... | of His| countenance.

9 Deep ealleth unto deep at the noise .|of Thy|water-spouts ‖ All Thy **waves** . and Thy | billows|are gone|over me.

10 Yet the Lord will command His **loving-kindness** . |in the|day-time ‖·
And in the night His song shall be with me, and my prayer unto . the|God ...|of my|life.

11 I will say unto God my rock, **Why** . hast|Thou for-|gotten me ‖
Why go I mourning because . of the op- | pression | of the | enemy?

12 As with a sword in my **bones,** . mine|enemies re-|proach me‖
While they say daily unto me, . | Where ...|is thy|God?

13 Why art thou cast **down,** . |O my| soul ‖
And why art thou . dis-|quiet-|ed with-|in me?

14 Hope thou in **God;** . for I|shall yet|praise Him ‖
Who is the **health** . of my| countenance,|and my|God.

GLORY BE, ETC.

47 PSALM XLIII.

1 JUDGE me, O God, and plead my cause against . an un-|godly| nation ‖
Oh, deliver me from . the de-|ceitful and|unjust|man.

2 *For Thou art the God of my strength: why . dost Thou|cast me|off ‖*

Why go I mourning because . of the op-|pression|of the|enemy?

3 Oh, send out Thy light and Thy truth: .|let them|lead me ‖
Let them bring me unto Thy holy| hill, and|to Thy|tabernacles.

4 Then will I go unto the altar of God, unto **God** . my ex-|ceeding|joy‖
Yea, upon the harp will I **praise.**| Thee, O|God, my|God.

5 Why art thou cast **down,** . |O my| soul ‖
And why art thou . dis-|quiet-|ed with-|in me?

6 Hope thou in **God;** . for I|shall yet|praise Him ‖
Who is the **health** . of my |counte-nance,|and my|God.

GLORY BE, ETC.

48 PSALM XLV.

1 MY heart is inditing . a|good ...| matter ‖
I speak the things which I . have| made ...|touching the|King;
My **tongue** .|is the|pen ‖
Of .| ... a|ready|writer.

2 Thou art fairer **than** . the|children of|men ‖
Grace is poured into thy lips: therefore **God** . hath|bless-ed| thee for|ever.
Gird thy sword upon thy **thigh,** . | O most|mighty ‖
With . thy | glory | and thy | majesty.

3 And in thy majesty ride on prosperously because of **truth** . and| meekness and|righteousness‖

And thy right hand . shall | teach thee | terrible | things.
Thine arrows are sharp in the heart . of the | King's ... | enemies ||
Whereby . the | people | fall ... | under thee.

4 Thy throne, O **God**, . is for | ever and | ever ||
The sceptre of Thy **kingdom** . | is a | right ... | sceptre.
Thou lovest **righteousness**, . and | hatest | wickedness ||
Therefore God, Thy God. hath anointed thee with the oil . of | gladness a- | bove thy | fellows.

5 All thy garments smell of myrrh, and aloes. and cassia, out . of the | ivory | palaces ||
Whereby . | they have | made thee | glad.
Kings' daughters are among . thy | honour - able | women ||
Upon thy right hand did **stand** the | queen in | gold of | Ophir.

6 Hearken, O daughter, and consider, and . in- | cline thine | ear ||
Forget also thine own **people** . | and thy | father's | house ;
So shall the King greatly . de- | sire thy | beauty ||
For He is thy **Lord** ; . and | worship | thou ... | Him.

7 And the daughter of Tyre shall be **there** . | with a | gift ||
Even the rich among the people | shall en- | treat thy | favour.
The King's daughter is all glori- | ous with- | in ||
Her clothing . | is in- | wrought *with | gold.*

8 She shall be brought unto the **King**. in | raiment of | needle-work ||
The virgins her companions that follow her **shall**. be | brought ... | unto | thee.
With gladness and rejoicing . shall | they be | brought ||
They shall **enter** . | into the | King's ... | palace.

9 Instead of thy **fathers** . shall be thy | children ||
Whom thou mayest **make** . | princes in | all the | earth.
I will make thy name to be remem- bered in all . | gener- | ations ||
Therefore shall the people **praise**. | thee for | ever and | ever.

GLORY BE, ETC.

49 PSALM XLVI.

1 **God** . is our | refuge and | strength ||
A **very** | present | help in | trouble.
Therefore will not we **fear**, . though the | earth be re- | moved ||
And though the mountains be carried **into** . the | midst ... | of the | sea ;

2 Though the waters thereof **roar** . | and be | troubled ||
Though the mountains **shake** . | with the | swelling there- | of.
There is a river, the streams whereof shall make glad . the | city of | God ||
The holy place of the **taber- nacles** . | of the | Most ... | High.

3 God is in the midst of her ; **she** shall | not be | moved ||
God . shall | help her, and | it right | early.

The heathen **raged**, . the|kingdoms
were|moved ‖
He **uttered** . His|voice, the|
earth ...|melted.

4 The Lord . of|hosts is|with us ‖
The God . of|Jacob|is our|refuge.
Come, behold the **works** . | of
the|Lord ‖
What desolations **He** . hath|
made ...|in the|earth.

5 He maketh|wars to|cease ‖
Unto . the|end ...|of the|earth ;
He breaketh the bow. and **cutteth** .
the|spear in|sunder ‖
He **burneth** . the | chariot | in
the|fire.

6 Be still, and **know** . that|I am|God ‖
I will be exalted among the
heathen, I will **be** . ex-|alted|
in the|earth.
The Lord . of|hosts is|with us ‖
The God . of|Jacob|is our|refuge.
GLORY BE, ETC.

50 PSALM XLVII.

1 OH, clap your **hands**, . |all ye|
people ‖
Shout unto God . |with the|
voice of|triumph.

2 For the Lord . most|high is|ter-
rible ‖
He is a great **King** . |over|all
the|earth.

3 He shall **subdue** . the|people|
under us ‖
And . the|nations|under our|
feet.

4 He shall **choose** . our in-|herit -
ance/for us ‖
The excellency . of |Jacob|whom
He/loved.

5 God is gone **up** . |with a|shout ‖
The **Lord** . with the|sound ...|
of a|trumpet.

6 Sing **praises** . to | God, sing |
praises ‖
Sing **praises** . |unto our|King,
sing |praises.

7 For God is the **King** . of|all the|
earth ‖
Sing . ye|praises with|under-|
standing.

8 God **reigneth**|over the|heathen ‖
God sitteth upon . the|throne ...|
of His|holiness.

9 The princes of the **people** . are|
gathered to-|gether ‖
Even the people|of the|God of|
Abraham :

10 For the shields of the **earth**
belong . |unto|God ‖
He . is|great-...|ly ex-|alted.
GLORY BE, ETC.

51 PSALM XLVIII.

1 GREAT is the Lord, and **greatly**|
to be|praised ‖
In the city of our **God**, . in the|
mountain|of His|holiness.
Beautiful for situation, the joy of the
whole **earth**, .|is mount|Zion|
On the sides of the north, the
city|of the|great ...|King.

2 God is known in her **palaces** . for
a|refuge ‖
For lo, the kings were **assembled**, .
they|pass - ed|by to-|gether.
They **saw** it, . and | so they|
marvelled ‖
They . were | troubled, and|
hasted a-|way.

3 Fear took **hold** . up- | on them | there||
  And **pain** . | as of a | woman in |
    travail.
  Thou **breakest** . the | ships of |
    Tarshish ||
  With ... | ... an | east ... | wind.

4 As we have **heard**, . | so have we |
    seen ||
  In the **city** | of the | Lord of | hosts.
  In the **city** | of our | God ||
  God . will es- | tablish | it for | ever.

5 We have thought of Thy **loving-** |
    kindness, O | God ||
  In . the | midst ... | of Thy | temple.
  According to Thy Name, O God,
    so is Thy praise unto the
    ends . | of the | earth ||
  Thy . right | hand is | full of |
    righteousness.

6 Let mount Zion rejoice, let the
    daughters . of | Judah be | glad||
  Be- . | cause ... | of Thy | judgments.
  Walk about Zion and **go** . | round
    a- | bout her ||
  Tell . | ... the | towers' there- | of.

7 **Mark** ye well her **bulwarks**, . con- |
    sider her | palaces ||
  That ye may **tell** it . to the |
    gener- | ation | following.
  For this God is our **God** . for | ever
    and | ever ||
  He will be our **guide** . | even |
    unto | death.
        GLORY BE, ETC.

52   PSALM LI.

1 **HAVE mercy** . up- | on me, O | God]|
  According . | to Thy | loving- |
    kindness :
  According unto the **multitude** . of
    Thy | tender | mercies ||
  Blot. | out ... | my trans- | gressions.

2 Wash me **throughly** . from | mine
    in- | iquity ||
  And . | cleanse me | from my | sin.
  For I **acknowledge** . | my trans- |
    gressions ||
  And . my | sin is | ever be- | fore me.

3 Against Thee, Thee **only,** | have I |
    sinned ||
  And **done** . this | evil | in Thy | sight:
  That Thou mightest be **justified** . |
    when Thou | speakest ||
  And . be | clear ... | when Thou |
    judgest.

4 Behold, I was **shapen** | in in- | iquity||
  And in **sin** . | did my mother con- |
    ceive me.
  Behold, Thou desirest **truth** . in
    the | inward | parts ||
  And in the hidden part **Thou** .
    shalt | make me to | know ... |
    wisdom.

5 Purge me with hyssop, **and** . I | shall
    be | clean ||
  Wash me, **and** . I | shall be | whiter
    than | snow.
  Make me to **hear** . | joy and | glad-
    ness ||
  That the bones which **Thou** . hast |
    broken | may re- | joice.

6 Hide Thy **face** . | from my | sins ||
  And **blot** out . | all ... | mine in- |
    iquities.
  Create in me a **clean** . | heart, O |
    God ||
  And **renew** . a | right ... | spirit
    with- | in me.

7 Cast me not **away** . | from Thy |
    presence ||
  And **take not** . Thy | Holy | Spirit |
    from me.

Restore unto me the joy .·of|Thy
sal-|vation ‖
And uphold . me | with Thy|
free ...|spirit.

8 Then will I teach . trans-|gressors
Thy|ways ‖
And sinners shall be . con-|verted|
unto|Thee.
O Lord, open|Thou my|lips‖
And my mouth . shall|shew ...|
forth Thy|praise.

9 For Thou desirest not sacrifice; . |
else would I|give it ‖
Thou delightest|not in|burnt- ...|
offering :
The sacrifices of God . are a|broken|
spirit ‖
A broken and a contrite heart, O
God, . |Thou wilt|not de-|spise.
GLORY BE, ETC.

53 PSALM LVII.

1 BE merciful unto me, O God, be
merciful . |unto|me ‖
For . my|soul ...|trusteth in|
Thee.
Yea, in the shadow of Thy wings .
will I|make my|refuge ‖
Until these . ca-|lamities be|
over-|past.

2 I will cry . unto|God most|high ‖
Unto God, . that per-|formeth|
all things|for me.
He shall send from heaven, and
save me from the reproach of
him . that would|swallow me|
up ‖
God shall send forth . His|mercy|
and His|truth.

3 My soul . is a-|mong ...|lions ‖
I lie among them . |that are|set
on|fire,

Even the sons of men, whose
are|spears and|arrows ‖
And . their|tongue a|sh
sword.

4 Be Thou exalted, O God, .
the|heavens ‖
Let Thy glory|be a - bove|
earth.
They have prepared a net
my|steps ‖
My . |soul is|bowed|down

5 They have digged . a|pit]
me ‖
Into the midst whereof
are|fallen them-|selves.
My heart is fixed, O God
heart is|fixed ‖
I . will|sing and|give ...|

6 Awake up, my glory; aw
psaltery and|harp ‖
I myself . |will a-|wake ..
I will praise Thee, O Lor
mong the|people ‖
I will sing . unto|Thee a
the|nations.

7 For Thy mercy is great .
the|heavens ‖
And . Thy|truth ...|unt
clouds.
Be Thou exalted, O God, .
the|heavens ‖
Let Thy glory|be a-]
the|earth.
GLORY BE, ETC.

54 PSALM LXI.

1 Hear . my|cry, O|God ‖
At- . |tend un-|to my|pra

2 From the end of the earth .
cry unto|Thee ‖
When . my | heart is
whelmed.

3 Lead me to the **rock** . that is|
 higher than|I ‖
 For Thou hast been a shelter
 for me, and a **strong** . |tower|
 from the|enemy.

4 I will abide in Thy **taber-**|nacle
 for|ever ‖
 I will **trust** . in the|covert|of
 Thy|wings.

5 For Thou, O **God**, . hast|heard
 my|vows ‖
 Thou hast given me the **heritage** .
 of|those that|fear Thy|Name.

6 Thou wilt prolong . the|king's ...|
 life ‖
 And his **years** . as|many|gener-|
 ations.

7 He shall **abide** . before|God for|
 ever ‖
 Oh, prepare mercy and | truth
 which|may pre-|serve him.

8 So will I sing **praise** . unto Thy|
 Name for|ever ‖
 That **I** . may|daily per-|form
 my|vows.
 GLORY BE, ETC.

55   PSALM LXII.

1 TRULY my soul **waiteth** . up-|
 on ...|God ‖
 From **Him** . |cometh|my sal-|
 vation.
 He **only** is my **rock** . and | my
 sal-|vation ‖
 He is my defence ; I . shall|not
 be|greatly|moved.

2 How long will ye imagine **mis-**
 chief . a-|gainst a|man ‖
 Ye shall be slain, all of you : **as** a
 bowing wall shall ye **be,** . and|
 as a|totter - ing|fence.

They only consult to **cast** him
 · **down** . |from his|excellency ‖
 They delight in lies : they bless
 with their **mouth,** . |but they|
 curse ...|inwardly.

3 My soul, wait thou only up-|on ...|
 God ‖
 For my **expec-**|tation | is from|
 Him.
 He only is my **rock** . and|my sal-|
 vation ‖
 He is my **defence** ; . | I shall|not
 be|moved.

4 In God is my **salvation**| and my|
 glory ‖
 The rock of my strength, **and** .
 my|refuge,|is in|God.
 Trust . in|Him at|all times ‖
 Ye people, pour out your **heart**
 before **Him** : . | God is a |
 refuge|for us.

5 Surely men of low degree are vanity,
 and men of **high** degree . |are
 a|lie ‖
 To be laid in the balance they are
 alto- | gether | lighter than |
 vanity.
 Trust not in oppression, and **become** .
 · not|vain in|robbery ‖
 If riches increase, set . |not your|
 heart.up-|on them.

6 God hath spoken once, **twice** . have
 I|heard ...|this ‖
 That **power** . be-|longeth|unto|
 God :
 Also unto Thee, O **Lord,** . be-|
 longeth|mercy ‖
 For Thou renderest to every **man** .
 ac-|cording|to his|work.
 GLORY BE, ETC.

56 PSALM LXIII.

1 O **God**, . Thou art|my ...|God ‖
Early|will I|seek ...|Thee :
My soul thirsteth for Thee, my
flesh . |longeth for|Thee ‖
In a dry and thirsty **land**, . |
where no|water|is,

2 To see Thy **power** . |and Thy|
glory ‖
So as I . have|seen Thee|in the|
sanctuary :
Because Thy loving-**kindness** . is|
better than|life ‖
My . |lips shall|praise ...|Thee.

3 Thus will I **bless** Thee . | while I
live ‖
I will **lift** up . my|hands ...|in
Thy|Name.
My soul shall be satisfied as . with|
marrow and|fatness ‖
And my mouth shall **praise** . |
Thee with|joyful|lips ;

4 When I remember **Thee** . up-|on
my|bed ‖
And meditate on **Thee** . |in the|
night- ...|watches.
Because **Thou**. hast|been my|help‖
Therefore in the **shadow** . of
Thy|wings will|I re-|joice.

5 My soul followeth **hard** . |after|
Thee ‖
Thy **right** . | hand up-|holdeth|
me.
But those that seek my **soul**, . |to
de-|stroy it ‖
Shall go into the **lower**|parts ... |
of the|earth. ·

6 They shall **fall** . |by the|sword ‖
They . shall|be a|portion for|
foxes.

But the King shall rejoice in God:
everyone that **sweareth** . by|
Him shall|glory ‖
But the mouth of them that
speak . |lies ...|shall be|stopped.
GLORY BE, ETC.

57 PSALM LXV.

1 PRAISE waiteth for **Thee**, . O|
God, in|Zion ‖
And unto **Thee** . shall the|
vow ...|be per-|formed.
O **Thou** . that|hearest|prayer ‖
Unto|Thee shall|all flesh|come.

2 **Iniquities** . pre-|vail a-|gainst me‖
As for our transgressions, **Thou** .
shalt|purge ...|them a-|way.
Blessed is the **man** .|whom Thou|
choosest ‖
And causest to approach unto
Thee, that **he** . may|dwell ...|
in Thy|courts :
We shall be satisfied with the **good**-
ness|of Thy|house ‖
Even|of Thy|holy|temple.
By terrible things in **righteous**-
ness .|wilt Thou|answer us ‖
O . |God of|our sal-|vation :

4 Who art the confidence of all the
ends . |of the|earth ‖
And of them that are **afar** . |off
up-|on the|sea :
Which by His **strength** . setteth|
fast the|mountains ‖
Being|gird- ...|ed with|power :

5 Which stilleth the **noise** . |of the|
seas ‖
The noise of their **waves**, and .
the|tumult|of the|people.
They also that **dwell** . in the|
utter-most|parts ‖
Are . a-|fraid ...|at Thy|tokens :

6 Thou makest the outgoings|of the|
 morning ‖
 And . |even - ing|to re-|joice.
Thou **visitest** . the | earth, and|
 waterest it ‖
 Thou greatly enrichest it with
 the river of **God,** . |which is|
 full of|water.

7 **Thou** . pre-|parest them|corn‖
 When **Thou** . hast|so pro-|vided|
 for it.
Thou waterest the **ridges** . there-|
 of a-|bundantly ‖
 Thou . | settlest the | furrows
 there-|of :

8 Thou **makest** . it|soft with|showers‖
 Thou . | blessest the | springing
 there-|of.
Thou crownest the **year** . |with
 Thy|goodness ‖
 And . |Thy ...|paths drop|fatness.

9 They drop upon the **pastures**|of
 the|wilderness ‖
 And the little **hills** . re-|joice on|
 every|side.
The pastures are clothed with
 flocks ; the valleys also are
 covered|over with|corn ‖
 They **shout** . for|joy, they|also|
 sing.

 GLORY BE, ETC.

58 PSALM LXVI.

1 MAKE a joyful noise unto **God,** . |
 all ye|lands ‖
 Sing **forth** . the|honour|of His|
 Name :
 Make . His|praise ...|glorious ‖
 Say unto God, How **terrible** . |
 art Thou|in Thy|works |

2 Through the **greatness** | of Thy|
 power ‖
 Shall Thine **enemies** . sub-|mit
 them - selves|unto|Thee.
All the earth shall worship Thee,
 and shall **sing** . |unto|Thee ‖
 They . shall | sing ... | to Thy |
 Name.

3 Come and **see** . the|works of |God‖
 He is terrible in His **doing** . |
 toward the|children of|men.
He turned the sea into dry land :
 they went **through** . the|flood
 on|foot ‖
 There . did|we re-|joice in|Him.

4 He ruleth by His power for ever ;
 His **eyes** . be- | hold the | na-
 tions ‖
 Let **not** . the re-|bellious ex-|alt
 them-|selves.
Oh, **bless** . our|God, ye|people ‖
 And make the **voice** . of His|
 praise ...|to be|heard :

5 Which **holdeth** . our|soul in|life ‖
 And suffereth **not** . our|feet ...|
 to be|moved.
For Thou, O God, . hast|prov - ed|
 us ‖
 Thou . hast|tried us, as|silver
 is|tried.

6 Thou **broughtest** us . |into the |
 net ‖
 Thou **layedst** . af-|fliction up-|
 on our|loins.
Thou hast caused men to ride over
 our heads ; we went through
 fire . |and through|water ‖
 But Thou broughtest us **out** . |
 into a|wealthy |place.

7 I will go into Thy house . |with
 burnt-|offerings ‖

I . will | pay … | Thee my | vows
Which . my | lips have | uttered ‖
And my mouth hath **spoken**, . |
    when I | was in | trouble.

8 I will offer unto Thee burnt sacri-
    fices of fatlings, **with** . the |
    incense of | rams ‖
I . will | offer | bullocks with |
    goats.
Come and hear, all **ye** . that |
    fear … | God ‖
And I will declare what **He** .
    hath | done … | for my | soul.

9 I cried unto **Him**. | with my | mouth ‖
And **He** was ex- | tolled | with my |
    tongue.
If I regard **iniquity** . | in my |
    heart ‖
The . | Lord … | will not | hear me.

10 But **verily** . | God hath | heard me ‖
He hath attended **to** . the |
    voice … | of my | prayer.
Blessed be God, which hath not
    turned . a- | way my | prayer ‖
Nor . His | mercy | from … | me.
    GLORY BE, ETC.

59 PSALM LXVII.

1 GOD be merciful **unto** | us, and |
    bless us ‖
And **cause** . His | face to | shine
    up- | on us ;

2 That Thy way may be **known** .
    up- | on … | earth ‖
Thy **saving** | health a- | mong all |
    nations.

8 Let the people **praise** . | Thee, O |
    God ‖
Let all . the | people | praise … |
    Thee.

4 Oh, let the nations be **glad** . and |
    sing for | joy ‖
For Thou shalt judge the people
    righteously, and **govern** . the |
    nations up- | on … | earth.

5 Let the people **praise** .. | Thee, O |
    God ‖
Let all . the | people | praise … |
    Thee.

6 Then shall the earth . | yield her |
    increase ‖
And God, **even** . our | own … |
    God, shall | bless us.

7 **God** . | shall … | bless us ‖
And all the · **ends** . of the | earth
    shall | fear … | Him.
    GLORY BE, ETC.

60 PSALM LXVIII.

1 LET God arise, let His **ene-** | mies
    be | scattered ‖
Let them **also** . that | hate Him |
    flee be- | fore Him ;
As **smoke** . is | driven a- | way ‖
So . | drive … | them a- | way.

2 As wax melteth . be- | fore the | fire ‖
So let the wicked **perish** . | at
    the | presence of | God.
But let the righteous be glad ;
    let them **rejoice** . be- | fore … |
    God ‖
Yea, let **them** . ex- | ceeding- | ly
    re- | joice.

3 Sing unto God, sing **praises** | to
    His | Name ‖
Extol Him that rideth upon the
    heavens by His Name **Jah**, . |
    and re- | joice be- | fore Him.

A Father of the fatherless, and
　a Judge . | of the | widows ‖
Is God . in His | holy | habi- |
　tation.

4 God setteth the solitary in families,
　He bringeth out those . that
　are | bound with | chains ‖
　But the rebellious | dwell　in a |
　dry … | land.
　O God, when Thou wentest forth .
　be- | fore Thy | people ‖
　When Thou . didst | march … |
　through the | wilderness,

5 The earth shook, the heavens also
　dropped . at the | presence of |
　God ‖
　Even Sinai itself was moved at
　the presence . of | God, the |
　God of | Israel.
　Thou, O God, didst send . a |
　plenti-ful | rain ‖
　Whereby Thou didst confirm
　Thine inheritance . | when … |
　it was | weary.

6 Thy congregation . hath | dwelt
　there- | in ‖
　Thou, O God, hast prepared . of
　Thy | goodness | for the | poor.
　The Lord . | gave the | word ‖
　Great was the company . of |
　those that | published | it.

7 Kings of armies . did | flee a- | pace‖
　And she that tarried . at | home
　di- | vided　the | spoil.
　Though ye have lien among the
　pots, yet shall ye be as the
　wings of a dove . | covered
　with | silver ‖
　And . her | feathers with | yellow |
　gold.

8 When the Almighty scattered . |
　kings … | in it ‖
　It . was | white as | snow in |
　Salmon.
　The hill of God . is as the | hill
　of | Bashan ‖
　An high hill . | as the | hill of |
　Bashan.

9 Why leap ye, ye high hills? This
　is the hill which God . de- |
　sireth to | dwell in ‖
　Yea, the Lord . will | dwell in | it
　for | ever.
　The chariots of God are twenty
　thousand, even | thousands of |
　angels ‖
　The Lord is among them as in
　Sinai, . | in the | holy | place.

10 Thou . hast as- | cended on | high ‖
　Thou . hast | led cap- | tivi-　ty |
　captive ;
　Thou hast received . | gifts for | men‖
　Yea, for the rebellious also, that
　the Lord . | God might | dwell
　a- | mong them.

11 Blessed be the Lord, Who daily
　loadeth | us with | benefits ‖
　Even . the | God of | our sal- |
　vation.
　He that is our God . is the | God of
　sal- | vation ‖
　And unto God the Lord . be- |
　long the | issues　from | death.

12 Sing unto God, ye kingdoms . | of
　the | earth ‖
　O . sing | praises | unto the | Lord,
　To Him that rideth upon the
　heavens of heavens, . which |
　were of | old ‖
　Lo, He doth send out His voice,
　and | that a | mighty | voice.

13 Ascribe ye . |strength unto|God ‖
His excellency is over Israel,
and . His|strength is|in the|
clouds.
O God, Thou art terrible out . of
Thy|holy|places ‖
The God of Israel is He that
giveth strength and power
unto His people . | Blessed |
be ...|God.
GLORY BE, ETC.

61 PSALM LXXI.

1 IN Thee, O **Lord**, . do I|put my|
trust ‖
Let . me|never be|put to con-|
fusion.
Deliver me in Thy righteousness,
and **cause** . me|to es-|cape ‖
Incline Thine **ear** . |unto | me,
and|save me.

2 Be Thou my strong habitation,
whereunto I may continual-|
ly re-|sort ‖
Thou hast given commandment
to save me ; for **Thou** . art my |
rock ...|and my|fortress.
Deliver me, O my God, out of the
hand . |of the|wicked ‖
Out of the **hand** . of the un-|
righteous and|cruel|man.

3 For Thou art my **hope**, . O |
Lord ...|God ‖
Thou . art my|trust...|from my|
youth.
By Thee have I been holden **up** . |
from the|womb ‖
My praise shall **be** . con-|tinual-|
ly of|Thee.

4 I am as a **wonder**|unto|many ‖
But Thou . |art my | strong...|
refuge.

Let my mouth be **filled** . |with
Thy|praise ‖
And **with** . Thy|honour|all the|
day.

5 Cast me not off in the **time** . of|
old ...|age ‖
Forsake me **not** . |when my |
strength ...|faileth.
For mine **enemies** . |speak a- |
gainst me ‖
And they that lay **wait** . for my|
soul take|counsel to-|gether,

6 Saying, God hath forsaken him;
perse-|cute . and|take him,
For there is **none** . |to de-|liver|
him.
O **God**, . be|not far|from me ‖
O my **God**, . make|haste ...|for
my|help.

7 Let them be confounded and con-
sumed that are **adversaries** . |
to my|soul ‖
Let them be covered with re-
proach . and dis-|honour that|
seek my|hurt.
But **I** . will|hope con-|tinually ‖
And will **yet** . |praise Thee|more
and|more.

8 My mouth shall shew forth Thy
righteousness and Thy **salva-**
tion|all the|day ‖
For . I|know not the|number
there-|of.
I will go in the **strength** . of the|
Lord ...|God ‖
I will make mention of Thy
righteousness, . |even of |
Thine ...|only.

9 O God, Thou hast **taught** . me
from my|youth ‖

And hitherto have I . de-|clared
Thy|wondrous|works.
Now also. when I am old and grey-
headed, O God, . for-|sake me|
not ||
Until I have shewed Thy strength
unto this generation, and Thy
power to every|one that|is to|
come.

10 Thy righteousness also, O God, is
very high ; Who hast done . |
great ...|things ||
O God, . | who is |like... | unto
Thee ?
Thou, which hast shewed me great
and sore troubles, shalt
quicken|me a-|gain ||
And shalt bring me up again .
from the | depths ...|of the |
earth.

11 Thou shalt . in-|crease my|great-
ness ||
And comfort|me on|every|side.
I will also praise Thee with the
psaltery, even Thy truth, . |O
my|God ||
Unto Thee will I sing with the
harp, O . Thou|Holy|One of|
Israel.

12 My lips shall greatly rejoice when
I sing . |unto|Thee ||
And my soul, . which|Thou ...|
hast re-|deemed.
My tongue also shall talk of Thy
righteousness . |all the day|
long ||
For they are confounded, for
they are brought . unto|shame,
that|seek my|hurt.

GLORY BE, ETC.

62 PSALM LXXII.

1 GIVE the king . Thy|judgments,
O|God ||
And Thy righteousness . |unto
the|king's ... |son.
He shall judge . Thy|people with|
righteousness ||
And . |... Thy|poor with|judg-
ment.

2 The mountains shall bring peace .|
to the|people ||
And . the|little|hills by|right-
eousness.
He shall judge the poor of the
people, He shall save the
children|of the|needy ||
And shall break . in|pieces|the
op-|pressor.

3 They shall fear Thee as long as the
sun . and|moon en-|dure ||
Throughout . | all ...| genera- |
tions.
He shall come down like rain
upon . the|mown ...|grass ||
As . |showers that|water the|
earth.

4 In His days . shall the|righteous|
flourish ||
And abundance of peace, . so|
long as the|moon en-|dureth.
He shall have dominion also .
from|sea to|sea ||
And from the river . unto the|
ends ... |of the|earth.

5 They that dwell in the wilderness .
shall| bow be-|fore Him ||
And . His|ene - mies shall|lic
the|dust.

The kings of Tarshish and of the
isles . shall|bring ...|presents ||
The kings of **Sheba** . and|Seba
shall|offer|gifts.

6 Yea, all **kings** . shall fall | down
be-|fore Him ||
All . |nations shall | serve ...|
Him.
For He shall deliver the **needy**|
when he|crieth ||
The poor **also**, . and|him that|
hath no|helper.

7 He shall **spare** . the | poor and |
needy ||
And shall **save** . the|souls ...|of
the|needy.
He shall redeem their **soul** . from
de-|ceit and|violence ||
And **precious** . shall their|blood
be|in His|sight.

8 **And** . | He shall | live ||
And to Him shall be given|of
the|gold of|Sheba :
Prayer also shall be **made** . for |
Him con-|tinually ||
And . |daily shall|He be|praised.

9 There shall be an handful of **corn** .|
in the|earth ||
Upon . the|top ...|of the|moun-
tains ;
The fruit thereof . shall | shake
like|Lebanon ||
And they of the **city** . shall|
flourish like | **grass** of the |
earth.

10 His **Name** . shall en-|dure for|ever||
His name shall be continued .
as|long ...|as the|sun :
And **men** . shall be|blessed in|
Him ||
All . *|nations* shall|call Him |
blessed.

11 Blessed be the Lord **God**, . the|God
of|Israel ||
Who **only**. | doeth | wondrous |
things :
And blessed be His glorious|Name
for|ever ||
And let the whole earth be filled
with His glory. **A** -. | men,
and|A- ...|men.

GLORY BE, ETC.

63 PSALM LXXIII.

1 TRULY **God** . is|good to|Israel ||
Even to **such** . as|are of a|
clean ...|heart.
But as for me, my **feet** . were|
almost|gone ||
My . |steps had | well nigh|
slipped.

2 For I was envious|at the|foolish ||
When I **saw** . the pros-|peri- ty|
of the|wicked.
For there are no **bands** . |in their|
death ||
But . |their ...|strength is|firm.

3 They are not in **trouble** . as|other|
men ||
Neither are **they** . |plagued
like|other|men.
Therefore pride compasseth them
about . |as a|chain ||
Violence .|covereth them|as a|
garment.

4 Their **eyes** . stand | out with |
fatness ||
They . have|more than|heart
could|wish.
They are corrupt, and speak **wicked-**
ly . con-|cerning op-|pression|
They . |speak ...|loftä-|ly.

5 They set their mouth . a-|gainst
the|heavens ‖
And their tongue . |walketh|
through the|earth.
Therefore His people . re-|turn ...|
hither ‖
And waters of a full cup . are|
wrung ...|out to|them.

6 And they say, How . doth|God ...|
know ? ‖
And is there knowledge|in the|
Most ...|High ?
Behold, these .|are the un-|godly‖
Who prosper in the world; .|
they in-|crease in|riches.

7 Verily I have cleansed . my|heart
in|vain ‖
And . |washed my|hands in|
innocency ;
For all the day long . have|I
been|plagued ‖
And.|chasten- ed|every| morn-
ing.

8 If I say, . I will|speak ...|thus ‖
Behold, I should offend against
the gener- | ation | of Thy |
children.
When I thought . to|know ...|this‖
It . was|too ...|painful|for me ;

9 Until I went into the sanctuary|
of ...|God ‖
Then under-|stood ...|I their|
end.
Surely Thou didst set them . in|
slipper- y|places ‖
Thou castedst . them|down ...|
into de-|struction.

10 How are they brought into deso-
lation|as in a|moment ! ‖
They are utter-|ly con-|sumed
with|terrors.

As a dream.|when one a-|waketh‖
So, O Lord, when Thou awakest
Thou . |shalt de-|spise their|
image.

11 Thus . my|heart was|grieved ‖
And I . was | pricked | in my|
reins :
So foolish . was|I. and|ignorant ‖
I . was|as a|beast be-|fore Thee.

12 Nevertheless, I am continual-|ly
with|Thee ‖
Thou hast holden me .|by my|
right ...|hand.
Thou shalt guide . me|with Thy|
counsel ‖
And afterward . re-|ceive ...|me
to|glory.

13 Whom have I . in|heaven but|
Thee ? ‖
And there is none upon earth
that I . de-|sire be-|side ...|
Thee.
My flesh .and my|heart ...|faileth|
But God is the strength of my
heart . |and my|portion for|
ever.

14 For lo, they that are far . from|
Thee shall|perish ‖
Thou hast destroyed all them .
that|go a-|whoring from|
Thee.
But it is good for me . to draw|
near to|God ‖
I have put my trust in the Lord
God, that I may . de-|clare ...|
all Thy|works.
GLORY BE, ETC.

64 PSALM LXXVI.

1 IN Judah . is|God ...|known ‖
His . |Name is|great in|Israel.

In Salem also|is His|tabernacle ‖
And . His | dwelling-|place in |
Zion.

2 There brake He the **arrows** . |of
the|bow ‖
The **shield**, . and the|sword, ...|
and the|battle.
Thou **art** . more|glorious and |
excellent ‖
Than . the | moun- ...| tains of|
prey.

3 The stout-hearted are spoiled, **they** .
have|slept their|sleep ‖
And none of the **men** . of|might
have|found their|hands.
At Thy rebuke, . O|God of|Jacob ‖
Both the chariot and horse are
cast . |into a|dead ...|sleep.

4 Thou, even **Thou**, . art|to be|feared ‖
And who may stand in Thy **sight** .
when|once ...|Thou art|angry?
Thou didst cause **judgment** . to be|
heard from|heaven ‖
The **earth** . |feared, |and was|still,

5 When **God** . a-|rose to|judgment ‖
To **save** . all the|meek ...|of the|
earth.
Surely the **wrath** . of|man shall|
praise Thee‖
The **remainder** . of|wrath shalt|
Thou re-|strain.

6 Vow, and **pay** . unto the|Lord your |
God ‖
Let all that be round about Him
bring presents unto **Him** . that|
ought ...|to be|feared.
He shall cut **off** . the | spirit of|
princes ‖
He is terrible . to the|kings ...|
of the|earth.
GLORY BE, ETC.

65 PSALM LXXVII.

1 I CRIED unto **God** . |with my|
voice ‖
Even unto God with my **voice**, .
and|He gave|ear unto|me.
In the day of my **trouble** . I |
sought the|Lord ‖
My sore ran in the night, and
ceased not; my **soul** . re-|
fused|to be|comforted.

2 I remembered **God**, . | and was |
troubled ‖
I **complained**, . and my|spirit
was|over- |whelmed.
Thou **holdest** . mine|eyes ...|wak-
ing ‖
I am so **troubled** . |that I|can-
not|speak.

3 I have **considered** . the|days of|
old ‖
The . |years of|ancient|times.
I call to remembrance my song in
the night : I **commune** . with
mine|own ...|heart ‖
And . my|spirit made|diligent|
search.

4 Will the **Lord** . cast|off for|ever‖
And will He . be|favoura- ble|
no ...|more ?
Is His **mercy** . clean | gone for|
ever ‖
Doth His promise|fail for|ever-|
more ?

5 Hath God **forgotten** | to be | gra-
cious ‖
Hath He in anger . shut|up His|
tender|mercies ?
And I said, **This** . is|my in-|firmity‖
But I will remember the years
of the right **hand** . |of the|
Most ...|High.

I will remember the **works** . | of
the | Lord ‖
Surely I . will re- | member Thy |
wonders of | old.
I will meditate **also** . of | all Thy |
work ‖
And . | talk ... | of Thy | doings.

Thy way, O **God**, . is | in the | sanc-
tuary ‖
Who is so **great** . a | god as |
our ... | God?
Thou art the **God** . that | doest |
wonders ‖
Thou hast declared . Thy |
strength a- | mong the | people.

Thou hast with Thine **arm** . re- |
deemed Thy | people ‖
The . | sons of | Jacob and | Joseph.
The waters saw Thee, O **God** ; . the |
waters | saw Thee ‖
They were **afraid** ; . the |
depths ... | also were | troubled.

The clouds poured out water ; the
skies . sent | out a | sound ‖
Thine **arrows** . | also | went a- |
broad.
The voice of Thy thunder was in
the heaven ; the **lightnings** |
lightened the | world ‖
The . | earth ... | trembled and |
shook.

Thy way is in the sea, and Thy
path . in the | great ... | waters ‖
And . Thy | footsteps | are not |
known.
Thou leddest Thy **people** | like a |
flock ‖
By . the | hand of | Moses and |
Aaron.

GLORY BE, ETC.

66   PSALM LXXX.
1 GIVE ear, O Shepherd of Israel,
Thou that leadest **Joseph** | like
a | flock ‖
Thou that dwellest **between** . the |
cherubims, | shine ... | forth.

2 Before Ephraim and **Benjamin** . |
and Ma- | nasseh ‖
Stir **up** . Thy | strength, and |
come and | save us.

3 **Turn** us . a- | gain, O | God ‖
And cause Thy face to **shine**, . |
and we | shall be | saved.

4 O **Lord** . | God of | hosts ‖
How long wilt Thou be angry
against . the | prayer ... | of
Thy | people ?
Thou feedest them **with** . the |
bread of | tears ‖
And givest them **tears** . to |
drink in | great ... | measure.

5 Thou makest us a **strife** . | unto
our | neighbours ‖
And our **enemies** . | laugh a- |
mong them- | selves.
Turn us **again**, . O | God of | hosts ‖
And cause Thy face to **shine**, . |
and we | shall be | saved.

6 Thou hast brought a **vine** . | out
of | **Egypt** |
Thou hast **cast out** . the | heathen
and | planted | it.
Thou preparedst | room be- | fore it ‖
And didst cause it to take deep
root, . | and it | filled the | land.

7 The hills were **covered** . with the |
shadow | of it ‖
And the boughs thereof . were |
like the | goodly | cedars.

She sent out her **boughs** . | unto the | sea ||
And . her | branches | unto the | river.

8 Why hast Thou then **broken** | down her | hedges ||
So that all they which **pass** . | by the | way do | pluck her ?
The **boar out** . of the | wood doth | waste it ||
And the wild **beast** . of the | field ... | doth de- | vour it.

9 Return, we **beseech** Thee, . O | God of | hosts ||
Look down from heaven, **and** . be- | hold, and | visit this | vine,
And the vineyard which **Thy** . right | hand hath | planted ||
And the branch that Thou **mad-** est | strong ... | for Thy- | self.

10 It is burned with fire, **it** . is | cut ... | down ||
They perish **at** . the re- | buke ... | of Thy | countenance.
Let Thy hand be upon the **man** . of | Thy right | hand ||
Upon the son of man whom Thou **madest** | strong ... | for Thy- | self.

11 So will not **we** . go | back from | Thee ||
Quicken Thou us, and **we** . will | call up- | on Thy | Name.
Turn us again, O **Lord** . | God of | hosts ||
Cause Thy face to **shine**, . | and *we | shall be | saved.*

GLORY BE. ETC.

67 **PSALM LXXXIV.**

1 How **amiable** . | are Thy | taber-nacles ||
O . | Lord ... | of ... | hosts !
My soul longeth, yea, even fainteth for the **courts** . | of the | Lord |
My heart and my flesh crieth **out** . | for the | living | God.

2 Yea, the **sparrow** . hath | found an | house ||
And the **swallow** . a | nest ... | for her- | self,
Where . she may | lay her | young ||
Even Thine altars, O Lord of **hosts**, . my | King ... | and my | God.

3 Blessed are they that **dwell** . | in Thy | house ||
They . will be | still ... | praising | Thee.
Blessed is the man whose **strength** . | is in | Thee ||
In whose **heart** . | are the | ways of | them.

4 Who passing through the valley of **Baca** . | make it a | well ||
The **rain** . | also | filleth the | pools.
They **go** . from | strength to | strength ||
Every one of them in **Zion** . ap- | peareth be- | fore ... | God.

5 O Lord God of **hosts**, . | hear my | prayer ||
Give . | ear, O | God of | Jacob.
Behold, . O | God our | shield ||
And look upon . the | face of | Thine an- | ointed.

6 For a **day** . | in Thy | courts ||
Is . | better | than a | thousand.
I had rather be a doorkeeper in the **house** . | of my | God ||

)|dwell in the|tents of|
lness.

ord **God** . is a|sun and|
ll
.. | will give|grace and|

:hing will He withhold
them . that|walk up-|
r ||
of hosts, blessed **is** . the|
1at|trusteth in|Thee.
,OBY BE, ETC.

ALM LXXXV.

1 hast been **favourable** . |
Thy|land ||
1st brought **back** . the
vi-|ty of|Jacob.
forgiven the **iniquity** . |
|people ||
ast|cover- ed|all their|

taken away . |all Thy|
||
st turned Thy**self** . from
rceness|of Thine|anger.
) **God** . of|our sal-|va-

1se Thine **anger** | to-
..|us to|cease.

be **angry** . with|us for|

1u draw out Thine **anger** .
..|gener-|ations?
not **revive** . |us a-|gain||
y **people**|may re-| joice
e ?

'hy|mercy, O|Lord ||
:ant us|Thy sal-|vation.
r what **God** . the|Lord
reak ||

For He will speak peace **unto** .
His|people, and|to His|saints.
5 **But** . |let them|not ||
Turn . | ... a-|gain to|folly.
Surely His salvation is **nigh** . |them
that|fear Him ||
That **glory** . may|dwell ...|in our|
land.
6 Mercy and **truth** . are | met to-|
gether ||
Righteousness . and|peace have|
kissed each|other.
Truth shall **spring** . |out of the |
earth ||
And **righteousness** . shall|look...|
down from|heaven.
7 Yea, the Lord shall **give** . | that
which is|good ||
And . our|land shall|yield her|
increase.
Righteousness . shall | go be-|fore
Him ||
And shall set us **in** . the|way ...|
of His|steps.
GLORY BE, ETC.

69 PSALM LXXXVI.

1 Bow down Thine **ear**, . O|Lord, ... |
hear me ||
For . |I am|poor and|needy.
Preserve my **soul** ; . for|I am|holy ||
O Thou my God, **save** . Thy|ser-
vant that|trusteth|in Thee.
2 Be **merciful** . unto|me, O|Lord ||
For . I|cry unto|Thee ...|daily.
Rejoice the **soul** . |of Thy|servant ||
For unto Thee, **O Lord,** . do I|
lift ...|up my|soul.
3 For Thou, Lord, art good, and
ready|to for-|give ||
And plenteous in mercy unto **all** .|
them that|call up-|on Thee.

Give ear, O Lord, . |unto my|
  prayer ‖
And attend unto the voice . |of
  my|suppli-|cations.

4 In the day of my trouble . I will|
  call up- on|Thee ‖
For . |Thou wilt|answer|me.
Among the gods there is none like .
  unto|Thee, O|Lord ‖
Neither are there any works . |
  like unto|Thy ...|works.

5 All nations whom Thou hast made
  shall come and worship before .|
  Thee, O|Lord ‖
And . shall|glo-ri-|fy Thy|Name.
For Thou art great, and doest|won-
  drous|things ‖
Thou . |...art|God a-|lone.

6 Teach me Thy way, O Lord; I will
  walk . |in Thy|truth ‖
Unite . my|heart to|fear Thy|
  Name.
I will praise Thee, O Lord my God, .
  with|all my|heart ‖
And I will glorify . Thy|Name
  for|ever-|more.

7 For great . is Thy|mercy|toward
  me ‖
And Thou hast delivered my
  soul . | from the|lowest|hell.
O God, the proud . are|risen a-|
  gainst me ‖
And the assemblies of violent
  men have sought after my soul,
  and . have|not set|Thee be-|
  fore them.

8 But Thou, O Lord, art a God full .
  of com-|passion and|gracious‖
Longsuffering, . and | plenteous
  in|mercy and|truth.

Oh, turn unto me, . and have
  up-|on me ‖
Give Thy strength unto T
  vant, and save . the|sc
  Thine|handmaid.

9 Shew me . a|token for|go
  That they which hate me
  see it, and|be a-|sham
Because . |Thou, O|Lord ‖
  Hast holpen | me and | c
  ed|me.
    GLORY BE, ETC.

70   PSALM LXXXVII.
1 HIS foundation is in . th
  mountains ‖
The Lord loveth the gates
  more . than|all the|d
  of|Jacob.

2 Glorious things . are|spo
  thee ‖
O . |city|of ...|God.

3 I will make mention of Ra
  Babylon . to|them th
  me ‖
Behold Philistia and Ty
  Ethiopia : this . | ma
  born ...|there.

4 And of Zion it shall be s
  and that man . was|t
  her ‖
And the Highest . Him-|s
  es-|tablish|her.

5 The Lord shall count, w
  writeth|up the|people
That this . |man was|
  there.

6 As well the singers as the pl
  instruments . |shall be
All . my|springs ...|are i
   GLORY BE, ETC.

ORDER NUMBER
40327900700000
ORDER DATE **08/09/2021**

SHIPPING ADDRESS:
amela Danielson
02 Douglas Drive
uffalo, MN 55313 9243
nited States

SHIPPING METHOD:
usps postal bpm parcels

Description	QTY
Textbook 6x9 Softcover BW	1

4 0 3 2 7 9 0 0 7 0 0 0 0 0

TO REORDER YOUR UPS DIRECT THERMAL LABELS:

1. Access our supply ordering web site at **UPS.COM**® or contact UPS at 800-877-8652.

2. Please refer to label #02774006 when ordering.

71 PSALM LXXXIX., vv. 1-18.

1 I WILL sing of the mercies of the|
Lord for | ever ||
With my mouth will I make
known Thy faithfulness . to |
all ... | gener- | ations.
For I have said, Mercy shall be
built . | up for | ever ||
Thy faithfulness shalt Thou
establish | in the | very | heavens.

2 I have made a covenant . | with My |
chosen ||
I . have | sworn unto | David My |
servant,
Thy seed . will I es- | tablish for |
ever ||
And build up thy throne, . to |
all ... | gener- | ations.

3 And the heavens shall praise . Thy |
wonders, O | Lord ||
Thy faithfulness also in the
congre- | gation | of the | saints.
For who in the heaven can be com-
pared . | unto the | Lord ||
Who among the sons of the
mighty . can be | likened | unto
the | Lord ?

4 God is greatly to be feared in the
assembly | of His | saints ||
And to be had in reverence of
all . | them that | are a- | bout
Him.
O Lord God of hosts, who is a strong
Lord . | like unto | Thee ||
Or . to Thy | faithful-ness | round
a- | bout Thee ?

5 Thou rulest the raging | of the | sea ||
When the waves thereof arise, . |
Thou ... | stillest | them.

Thou hast broken Rahab in pieces,
as | one that is | slain ||
Thou hast scattered Thine ene-
mies . | with Thy | strong ... | arm.

6 The heavens are Thine, the earth . |
also is | Thine ||
The world and the fulness there-
of, . | Thou hast | founded | them.
The north and the south, Thou . hast
cre- | ated | them ||
Tabor and Hermon shall . re- |
joice ... | in Thy | Name.

7 Thou hast . a | mighty | arm ||
Strong is Thy hand, . and | high is
Thy | right ... | hand.
Justice and judgment are the habi-
tation | of Thy | throne ||
Mercy and truth . shall | go be- |
fore Thy | face.

8 Blessed is the people that know .
the | joyful | sound ||
They shall walk, O Lord, . in the |
light ... | of Thy | countenance.
In Thy Name shall they rejoice . |
all the | day ||
And in Thy righteousness . | shall
they | be ex- | alted.

9 For Thou art the glory | of their |
strength ||
And in Thy favour . our | horn
shall | be ex- | alted.
For the Lord . is | our de- | fence ||
And the Holy One . of | Israel | is
our | King.

GLORY BE, ETC.

72 PSALM XC.

1 LORD, Thou . hast (been our (
· dwelling-place ||
In . | all ... | gener- | ations.

Before the mountains | were
brought | forth ||
Or ever Thou hadst formed . the |
earth ... | and the | world,

2 Even . from | ever- | lasting ||
To ever- | lasting, | Thou art | God.
Thou turnest man . | to de- | struc-
tion ||
And sayest, . Re- | turn, ye |
children of | men.

3 For a thousand years in Thy sight
are but as yesterday . | when
it is | past ||
And as . a | watch ... | in the | night.
Thou carriest them away as with a
flood ; they . are | as a | sleep ||
In the morning they are like . |
grass which | groweth | up.

4 In the morning it flourisheth, .
and | groweth | up ||
In the evening . it is | cut ... |
down, and | withereth.
For we are consumed . | by Thine |
anger ||
And by . Thy | wrath ... | are we |
troubled.

5 Thou hast set our iniquities . be- |
fore ... | Thee ||
Our secret sins . in the | light ... |
of Thy | countenance.
For all our days are passed away . |
in Thy | wrath ||
We spend our years . as a |
tale ... | that is | told.

6 The days of our years are three-
score . | years and | ten ||
And if by reason of strength . |
they be | fourscore | years,
Yet is their strength . | labour
and | sorrow ||
For it is soon cut off, . | and we |
fly a- | way.

7 Who knoweth the power
Thine | anger ||
Even according to Thy fe
so is | Thy ... | wrath.
So teach us . to | number our |
That we may apply .
hearts ... | unto | wisdom.

8 Return, . O | Lord ; how | long
And let it repent Thee .
cerning | Thy ... | servant
Oh, satisfy us early | with
mercy ||
That we may rejoice . an
glad ... | all our | days.

9 Make us glad according to the
wherein Thou hast .
flicted | us ||
And the years . where- | ir
have | seen ... | evil.
Let Thy work appear . | unto
servants ||
And . Thy | glory | unto
children.

10 And let the beauty . of the
our | God ||
Be . | ... up- | on ... | us :
And establish Thou the wor
our | hands up- | on us |
Yea, the work . of our |
e- | stablish Thou | it.
GLORY BE, ETC.

73 PSALM XCI.

1 HE that dwelleth in the
place . of the | Most ... | Hi
Shall abide . under the | sl
of the Al- | mighty.
I will say of the Lord, He
refuge | and my | fortress |
My God ; . in | Him ... | w
trust.

2 Surely He shall deliver thee from
the snare . | of the | fowler |
And . | from the | noisome | pesti-
lence.
He shall cover thee with His
feathers, and under His wings . |
shalt thou | trust ||
His truth . shall | be thy | shield
and | buckler.

Thou shalt not be afraid . for the |
terror by | night ||
Nor . for the | arrow that | flieth
by | day.
Nor for the pestilence . that | walk-
eth in | darkness ||
Nor for the destruction . that |
wasteth at | noon- ... | day.

A thousand shall fall at thy side,
and ten thousand . at | thy
right | hand ||
But . it shall | not come | nigh ... |
thee.
Only with thine eyes . shalt | thou
be- | hold ||
And see . the re- | ward ... | of the |
wicked.

Because thou hast made the Lord, .
which | is my | refuge ||
Even the Most . | High, thy |
habi- | tation,
There shall no . | evil be- | fall thee ||
Neither shall any | plague come |
nigh thy | dwelling.

For He shall give His angels
charge . | over | thee ||
To keep . | thee in | all thy | ways.
They shall bear thee up . | in their |
hands ||
Lest thou dash . thy | foot a- |
gainst a | stone.

7 Thou shalt tread upon . the | lion
and | adder ||
The young lion and the dragon .
shalt thou | trample | under | feet.
Because he hath set . his | love up- |
on Me ||
Therefore . will | I de- | liver | him :

8 I . will | set him on | high ||
Because . | he hath | known My |
Name.
He . shall | call up- | on Me ||
And . | I will | answer | him ;

9 I will . be | with him in | trouble ||
I will . de- | liver | him, and |
honour him ;
With long life . will I | satis- fy | him ||
And . | shew him | My sal- | vation.

GLORY BE, ETC.

74   PSALM XCII.

1 IT is a good thing to give thanks . |
unto the | Lord ||
And to sing praises . unto Thy |
Name, ... | O Most | High :
To shew forth Thy loving-kindness |
in the | morning ||
And . Thy | faithful- ness | every |
night,

2 Upon an instrument of ten strings,
and . up- | on the | psaltery ||
Upon the harp . | with a | solemn |
sound.
For Thou, Lord, hast made me
glad . | through Thy | work ||
I will triumph . in the | works ... |
of Thy | hands.

3 O Lord, how great . | are Thy | works ||
And . Thy | thoughts are | very |
deep.

A brutish man . | knoweth | not ‖
Neither doth a fool . | under- |
stand ... | this :

4 When the wicked spring as the grass,
and when all the workers . of
in- | iquity do | flourish ‖
It is that they . shall | be de- |
stroyed for | ever :
But . | Thou, ... Lord ‖
Art . most | high for | ever- | more.

5 For, lo, . Thine | enemies, O | Lord ‖
For, lo, . Thine | ene- | mies shall |
perish ;
All . | ... the | workers ‖
Of . in- | iqui- ty | shall be |
scattered.

6 But my horn shalt Thou exalt like
the horn . | of an | unicorn ‖
I shall be . a- | nointed | with
fresh | oil.
Mine eye shall also see my desire . |
on mine | enemies ‖
And mine ears shall hear my
desire of the wicked . that |
rise ... | up a- | gainst me.

7 The righteous shall flourish | like
the | palm-tree ‖
He shall grow . | like a | cedar in |
Lebanon.
Those that be planted in the
house . | of the | Lord ‖
Shall flourish . in the | courts ... |
of our | God.

8 They shall still bring forth fruit .
in | old ... | age ‖
They . | shall be | fat and | flourish-
ing :
To shew . that the | Lord is | upright ‖
He is my rock, and there is no .
un- | righteous- | ness in | Him.
GLORY BE, ETC.

75 PSALM XCIII.

1 THE Lord reigneth ; He . is | clothed
with | majesty ‖
The Lord is clothed with
strength, . where- | with He
hath | girded Him- | self.

2 The world . | also is | stablished ‖
That . it | cannot | be ... | moved.

3 Thy throne . is e- | stablished of | old ‖
Thou . | art from | ever- | lasting.

4 The floods have lifted up, O Lord,
the floods have lifted | up their |
voice ‖
The . | floods lift | up their | waves.

5 The Lord on high is mightier than
the noise . of | many | waters ‖
Yea, than the mighty | waves ... |
of the | sea.

6 Thy testimonies . are | very | sure ‖
Holiness becometh . Thine | house,
O | Lord, for | ever.
GLORY BE, ETC.

76 PSALM XCV.

1 OH, come, let us sing . | unto the |
Lord ‖
Let us make a joyful noise . to
the | rock of | our sal- | vation.

2 Let us come before His presence |
with thanks- | giving ‖
And make a joyful noise . | unto |
Him with | psalms.

3 For the Lord . is a | great ... | God |
And a great . | King a- | bove
all | gods.

4 In His hand are the deep places |
of the | earth ‖
The strength . of the | hills is |
His ... | also.

The sea is **His**, . |and He|made it ‖
And His **hands** . |formed the|
dry ... |land.

Oh, come, let us **worship** |and bow|
down ‖
Let us **kneel** . be-|fore the|
Lord our|Maker :

For . |He is our|God ‖
And we are the people of His
pasture. **and** . the|sheep of|
His ... |hand.

To-day if **ye** . will|hear His|voice‖
Hard- . |... en|not your|heart,

As **in** . the|provo-|cation ‖
And as in the **day** . of temp-|
tation|in the|wilderness,

When your **fathers**|tempted|Me ‖
Proved|Me, and|saw My|work.

Forty|years...|long ‖
Was . I | grieved with | this
gener-|ation,

And said, It is a people that do
err . |in their|heart ‖
And . they | have not | known
My|ways :

Unto whom I **sware** . |in My|
wrath ‖
That they **should** not. |enter|
into My|rest.
GLORY BE, ETC.

7   PSALM XCVI.

OH, sing unto the **Lord** . a|new ...|
song ‖
Sing . unto the|Lord, ...|all the|
earth.
Sing unto the **Lord**, . |bless His|
Name ‖
Shew **forth** . His sal-|vation
from|day to|day.

2 Declare His **glory** a-|mong the|
heathen ‖
His . |wonders a-|mong all |people.
For great is the Lord, and **greatly** |
to be|praised ‖
He is . to be|feared a-|bove all|
gods.

3 For all the **gods** . of the|nations
are|idols ‖
But . the|Lord ... | made the
heavens.
Honour and **majesty** |are be-|fore
Him ‖
Strength . and | beauty are|in
.   His|sanctuary.

4 Give unto the Lord, O ye **kindreds**|
of the|people ‖
Give unto the **Lord** . | glory |
and ...|strength.
Give unto the Lord the glory **due** .|
unto His|Name ‖
Bring an **offering**, . and|come ...|
into His|courts.

5 Oh, worship the **Lord** . in the|beauty
of |holiness ‖
Fear . be-|fore Him, |all the|
earth.
Say among the **heathen** . that the|
Lord ... |reigneth ‖
The world also shall be established
that it shall not be moved :
He . shall|judge the|people|
righteously.

6 Let the heavens rejoice, and **let** .
the|earth be|glad ‖
Let the sea roar, . |and the|ful-
ness there-|of ;
Let the field be joyful, and **all** .
that|is there-|in ‖
Then shall all the **trees** of the
wood . re-|joice be-|fore the|
Lord :

7 For . |He ... |cometh ||
  For . He|cometh to|judge the|
    earth :
  He shall judge . the|world with|
    righteousness ||
  And . the|people|with His|truth.

  GLORY. BE, ETC.

78   PSALM XCVII.

1 THE Lord reigneth ; let . the|earth
    re-|joice ||
  Let the multitude . of|isles be|
    glad there-|of.
  Clouds and darkness are|round a-|
    bout Him ||
  Righteousness and judgment are
    the habit-|ation|of His|throne.

2 A fire ; |goeth   be-|fore Him ||
  And burneth up . His|ene-mies|
    round a-|bout.
  His lightnings . en-|lightened the|
    world ||
  The   . | earth ... | saw, and |
    trembled.

3 The hills melted like wax at the
    presence|of the|Lord ||
  At the presence of the Lord . |of
    the|whole ... |earth.
  The heavens . de- | clare His |
    righteousness ||
  And all . the | people | see His |
    glory.

4 Confounded be all they that serve
    graven images, that boast .
    them-|selves of |idols ||
  Worship|Him, ... |all ye|gods.
  Zion heard, . |and was|glad ||
  And the daughters of Judah
    rejoiced, . be-|cause of Thy|
    judgments, O|Lord.

5 For Thou, Lord, art high .
    all the|earth ||
  Thou art exalted|far a-|b
    gods.
  Ye that love the Lord, . |l
    evil ||
  He preserveth the souls
    saints ; He delivereth th
    of the|hand ... |of the|

6 Light is sown . |for the|rigl
  And gladness | for the |
    in|heart.
  Rejoice . in the|Lord, ye|rig
  And give thanks . at tl
    membrance|of His|holi

  GLORY BE, ETC.

79   PSALM XCVIII.

1 OH, sing unto the Lord . a|l
    song ||
  For He . hath|done ... |n
    ous|things :
  His right hand, . and Hi
    arm ||
  Hath . |gotten|Him the|v

2 The Lord hath made known
    sal-|vation ||
  His righteousness hath He
    shewed . in the|sight ...|
    heathen.
  He hath remembered His mei
    His truth . toward the
    of|Israel ||
  All the ends of the eart
    seen . the sal-|vation|o
    God.

3 Make a joyful noise unto the I
    all the|earth ||
  Make a loud noise, . and re
    and|sing ...|praise.

Sing unto the **Lord** . | with the |
harp ‖
With the harp . |and the|voice
of a|psalm.

4 With **trumpets** . and | sound of |
cornet ‖
Make a joyful **noise** . be- | fore
the|Lord, the|King.
Let the sea roar, . and the|fulness
there-|of ‖
The **world**, . and|they that|dwell
there-|in ;

3 Let the **floods** . |clap their|hands ‖
Let the hills be joyful . to-|gether
be-|fore the|Lord,
For He **cometh** . to|judge the|earth‖
With righteousness shall He judge
the **world**, . |and the|people
with|equity.
GLORY BE, ETC.

80 PSALM XCIX.

1 THE Lord reigneth ; let . the|people|
tremble. ‖
He sitteth upon the **cherubims** ; . |
let the|earth be|moved.

2 **The Lord** . is|great in|Zion ‖
And He . |is|high a- bove|all
the|people.

3 Let them praise Thy **great** and|
terri - ble|Name ‖
For . |it ... |is ... |holy.

4 The King's **strength** . also|loveth|
judgment ‖
Thou dost establish equity ; Thou
executest **judgment** . and|right-
eous-|ness in|Jacob.

5 Exalt ye the Lord our God, and
worship|at His|footstool ‖
For . |He ... |is ... |holy.

6 Moses and Aaron among His priests
and Samuel among them the
call . up-|on His|Name ‖
They called upon the **Lord,** .
and He|answer- ed|them.

7 He spake unto **them** . in the|cloudy|
pillar ‖
They kept His testimonies, and .
the|ordi - nance|that He|gave
them.

8 Thou answeredst **them,** . O|Lord
our|God ‖
Thou wast a God that forgavest
them, though Thou **tookest**|
vengeance of|their in-|ven-
tions.

9 Exalt the Lord our God, and **wor-**
ship . at His|holy|hill ‖
For . the|Lord our|God is|holy.

GLORY BE, ETC.

81 PSALM C.

1 MAKE a joyful **noise** **unto** the
Lord, . |all ye|lands ‖
Serve the Lord with gladness ;
come . be-|fore His|presence
with|singing.

2 Know ye that the **Lord** . |He is|
God ‖
It is He that hath made us, and
not we ourselves ; we are His
people, . and the | sheep of |
His ... |pasture.

3 Enter into His gates with **thanks**|
giving, and **into** . His|courts
with|praise ‖
Be **thankful** unto|Him . and|
bless His|Name.

4 For the Lord is good ; His mercy
is|ever-|lasting ||
And His truth endureth . to|
all ...|gener-|ations.
GLORY BE, ETC.

82   PSALM CII.

1 Hear . my|prayer, O|Lord ||
And let my cry . |come ...|unto|
Thee.
Hide not . Thy|face from|me ||
In the day . |when I|am in|
trouble ;

2 Incline Thine ear . |unto|me ||
In the day when I call . |answer|
me ...|speedily.
For my days . are|consumed like|
smoke ||
And my bones . are|burned|as
an|hearth.

3 My heart is smitten . and|withered
like|grass ||
So that I . for-|get to|eat my|
bread.
By reason of the voice . |of my|
groaning ||
My bones . |cleave ...|to my|
skin.

4 I am like a pelican . | of the |
wilderness ||
I am like . an|owl ...|of the|
desert.
ɪ watch, . and am|as a|sparrow ||
A- . |lone up-|on the|housetop.

5 Mine enemies reproach . me|all
the|day ||
And they that are mad . a-|
gainst me   are | sworn a-|
gainst me,

For I have eaten|ashes lik
And . | mingled   my
with|weeping.

6 Because of Thine indigna
Thy|wrath ||
For Thou hast lifted
and|cast me|down.
My days are like a shac
de-|clineth ||
And . I am|wither- ei
grass.

7 But Thou, O Lord, . shalt
for|ever ||
And Thy remembran
all ...|gener-|ations.
Thou shalt arise, and ha
up-|on ...|Zion ||
For the time to favour
the|set ...|time, is|cɑ

8 For Thy servants take pl
her|stones ||
And . |favour the|dust
So the heathen shall
Name .|of the|Lord
And all the kings . |of
Thy|glory.

9 When the Lord shall builc
He shall appear .
glory ||
He will regard the pra
destitute, . and|not
their|prayer.
This shall be written
gener-|ation to|cor
And the people which
cre- | ated shall | pra
Lord.

10 For He hath looked di
the height . (of I
tuary ||

From **heaven** . did the|Lord be-|
hold the|earth ;
To hear the **groaning** | of the |
prisoner ||
To loose **those** . that|are ap-|
pointed to|death ;

11 To declare the **Name** . of the|Lord
in|Zion ||
And . His|praise ... | in Je-|rusa-
lem ;
When the **people** . are | gathered
to-|gether || .
And . the|kingdoms, to|serve
the|Lord.

12 He weakened **my strength** . |in
the|way ||
He . |shorten - ed|my ... |days.
I said, O my God, take me not
away in the **midst** . |of my|
days|| .
Thy years are through**out** . |
all ... |gener-|ations.

13 Of old hast Thou laid the founda-
tion|of the|earth ||
And the **heavens** . are the|work
of |Thy ... |hands.
They shall perish, but **Thou** . |
shalt en-|dure ||
Yea, all of them shall **wax** old
as a garment ; as a vesture
shalt Thou **change** them, . |
and they|shall be|changed.

14 But **Thou** . |art the|same ||
And Thy **years** . |shall have|
no ... |end.
The children of Thy **servants**|shall
con-|tinue ||
And their **seed** . shall|be e-|stab-
lished be-|fore Thee.
GLORY BE, ETC,

---

83 PSALM CIII.

1 BLESS the **Lord,** . |O my|soul ||
And all that is within me, . |
bless His|holy|Name. '
Bless the **Lord,** . |O my|soul ||
And . for-| get not |all His |
benefits :

2 Who forgiveth **all** . | thine in-|
iquities ||
Who **healeth** | all ... | thy dis-|
eases ;
Who redeemeth thy **life** . | from
de-|struction ||
Who crowneth thee with **loving-**|
kindness and|tender|mercies ;

3 Who satisfieth thy **mouth** . with|
good ... |things ||
So that thy **youth** . is re-|newed|
like the|eagle's.
The Lord executeth **righteous-**|
ness and|judgment ||
For . |all that|are op-|pressed.

4 He made known His **ways** . |unto|
Moses ||
His **acts** . | unto the|children
of |Israel.
The **Lord** . is | merciful and |
gracious ||
Slow . to|anger, and|plenteous
in|mercy.

5 He **will** . not|always|chide ||
Neither **will** . He | keep His (
anger for|ever.
He hath not **dealt** . with us|after
our|sins ||
Nor **rewarded** us . ac-|cording
to|our in-|iquities.

6 For as the heaven is high . a-¡bove
    the|earth ‖
    So great is His mercy|toward...|
    them that|fear Him.
    As far as the east . is|from the|
    west ‖
    So far hath He removed|our
    trans-|gressions|from us.

7 Like as a father|pitieth his|
    children ‖
    So the Lord . |piti- eth|them
    that|fear Him.

8 For . He|knoweth our|frame ‖
    He . re-|membereth that|we
    are|dust.

9 As for man, his days . | are as|
    grass ‖
    As a flower . of the|field, ... |so
    he|flourisheth.

10 For the wind passeth over it, . |
    and it is|gone ‖
    And the place . there-|of shall|
    know it no|more.

11 But the mercy of the Lord is from
    everlasting to everlasting .
    upon|them that|fear Him ‖
    And His righteousness . |unto|
    children's|children ;
    To such . as|keep His|covenant ‖
    And to those that remember|His
    com-|mandments to|do them.

12 The Lord hath prepared His
    throne . |in the|heavens ‖
    And His kingdom|ruleth|over|
    all.
    Bless the Lord, ye His angels,
    that . ex-|cel in|strength ‖
    That do His commandments,
    hearkening unto . the|voice...|
    of His|word.

13 Bless ye the Lord, . all
    hosts ‖
    Ye ministers . of|His
    His|pleasure.
    Bless the Lord, all ye His
    all places . of | His do-
    Bless . the|Lord, ...|0
    GLORY BE, ETC.

84 PSALM CIV.

1 BLESS the Lord, . |0 my
    O Lord my God, . | 7
    very|great ;
    Thou art clothed . wit
    and|majesty ‖
    Who coverest Thyself
    light as|with a|gar

2 Who stretchest out the 1
    like a|curtain ‖
    Who layeth the beams
    chambers|in the|wa
    Who maketh . the|clo
    chariot ‖
    Who walketh upon
    wings ... |of the|win

3 Who maketh . His|angel
    His . |minis- ters a|fla
    Who laid the foundation
    earth ‖
    That it should . no
    moved for|ever.

4 Thou coveredst it with
    as|with a|garment ‖
    The waters|stood a-|
    mountains.
    At Thy . re-|buke they|f
    At the voice . of Th;
    they|hasted a-|wa

5 They go up by the mount
    go down . |by the|v
    Unto the place . wh
    hast|founded|for t

Thou hast set a bound that they .
may | not pass | over ‖
That they turn not . a- | gain to |
cover the | earth.

⸎ He sendeth the springs . | into
the | valleys ‖
Which . | run a- | mong the | hills:
They give drink to every beast . |
of the | field ‖
The wild . | asses | quench their |
thirst.

7 By them shall the fowls of the
heaven have . their | habi- |
tation ‖
Which . | sing a- | mong the |
branches.
He watereth the hills . | from His |
chambers ‖
The earth is satisfied . with the |
fruit ... | of Thy | works.

8 He causeth the grass to grow for
the cattle, and herb . for the |
service of | man ‖
That he may bring forth . |
food ... | out of the | earth :
And wine that maketh glad . the |
heart of | man ‖
And oil to make his face to shine,
and bread . which | strengthen-
eth | man's ... | heart.

9 The trees of the Lord . are | full
of | sap ‖
The cedars of Lebanon, . |
which ... | He hath | planted ;
Where the birds . | make their |
nests ‖
As for the stork, . the | fir trees |
are her | house.

10 The high hills are a refuge . for
the | wild ... | goats ‖
And . the | rocks ... | for the |
conies.

He appointed . the | moon for |
seasons ‖
The sun . | knoweth his | going |
down.

11 Thou makest darkness, . | and it
is | night ‖
Wherein all the beasts . of the |
forest do | creep ... | forth.
The young lions roar . | after their |
prey ‖
And . | seek their | meat from |
God.

12 The sun ariseth, they gather .
them- | selves to- | gether ‖
And lay . them | down ... | in
their | dens.
Man goeth forth . | unto his | work ‖
And to his labour | un- ... | til
the | evening.

13 O Lord, how manifold . | are Thy |
works ‖
In wisdom hast Thou made
them all : . the | earth is | full
of Thy | riches.
So is this great . and | wide ... | sea ‖
Wherein are things creeping
innumerable, . both | small
and | great ... | beasts.

14 There . | go the | ships ‖
There is that leviathan, whom
Thou . hast | made to | play
there- | in.
These wait . | all up- on | Thee ‖
That Thou mayest give them
their | meat in | due ... | season.

15 That Thou givest | them they |
gather ‖
Thou openest Thine hand, . |
they are | filled with | good.

Thou hidest Thy face, . |they are|
troubled ||
Thou takest away their breath,
they die, . and re-|turn ...|
to their|dust.

16 Thou sendest forth Thy Spirit, .
they|are cre-|ated ||
And Thou renewest . the|
face ... |of the|earth.
The glory of the Lord . shall en-|
dure for|ever ||
The Lord . shall re-|joice ... |in
His|works.

17 He looketh on the earth, . |and
it|trembleth ||
He toucheth . the|hills, ... |and
they|smoke.
I will sing unto the Lord . as|
long as I|live ||
I will sing praise to my God . |
while I|have my|being.

18 My meditation of Him . |shall be|
sweet ||
I . will be|glad ... |in the|Lord.
Let the sinners be consumed out
of the earth, and let the
wicked . |be no|more ||
Bless thou the Lord, O my
soul . |Praise ... |ye the|Lord.

GLORY BE, ETC.

85 PSALM CV.

1 OH, give thanks unto the Lord;
call . up-|on His|Name ||
Make known . His | deeds a- |
mong the|people.
Sing unto Him, . sing | psalms
unto|Him ||
Talk ye . of|all His|wondrous|
works.

2 Glory ye in . His|holy|Nan
Let the heart of them . r
that|seek the|Lord.
Seek the Lord, . |and His|sti
Seek . His|face ...|ever-|i

3 Remember His marvellous '
that|He hath|done ||
His wonders, and . the
ments|of His|mouth,
O ye seed of Abra-|ham I
vant ||
Ye . |children of|Jacot
chosen.

4 He is . the|Lord our|God ||
His judgments | are in|a
earth.
He hath remembered His
nant for|ever ||
The word which He comm
to a|thousand|gener-|s

5 Which covenant . He|made
Abraham ||
And . His|oath ... |unto|I
And confirmed the same
Jacob|for a|law ||
And to Israel for . an |eve:
ing|covenant ;

6 Saying, Unto thee will I
the|land of|Canaan ||
The . |lot of|your in-|her:
When there were but a few
in|number ||
Yea, . very|few, and|stra
in it.

7 When they went from one i
to an-|other ||
From one kingdom|to an-|
people ;

He suffered **no** man . to|do them|
wrong ‖
Yea, He reproved | kings for |
their ... |sakes ;

8 Saying, **Touch** not . |Mine an-|
ointed ‖
And . |do My|prophets no|
harm.
Moreover. He called for a **famine** .
up-|on the|land ‖
He **brake** . the|whole ... |staff of |
bread.

9 He **sent** . a|man be-|fore them ‖
Even **Joseph,** . |who was | sold
for a|servant :
Whose **feet** . they | hurt with |
fetters ‖
He . |... was|laid in|iron :

10 Until the **time** . that his|word ...|
came ‖
The **word** . |of the|Lord ... |tried
him.
The **king** . |sent and|loosed him ‖
Even the ruler of the **peo** . **ple,**
and|let him|go ... |free.

11 He made him **lord** . |of his|house‖
And . |ruler of | all his | sub-
stance :
To bind his **princes** |at his |pleasure‖
And . |teach his|senators|wis-
dom.

12 Israel also **came** . |into|Egypt ‖
And Jacob **sojourned**'| in the|
land of |Ham.
And He **increased** . His | people|
greatly ‖
And **made** . them|stronger|than
their |enemies.

13 He turned their **heart** . to | hate
His|people ‖
To **deal** . |subtil- ly|with His|
servants.

He **sent** . |Moses His|servant ‖
And . |Aaron,|whom He had|
chosen.

14 They **shewed** . His|signs a-|mong
them‖
And **wonders**|in the|land of|
Ham.
He sent **darkness,** . and|made it|
dark ‖
And they **rebelled** . |not a-|
gainst His|word.

15 He turned their **waters**|into|blood‖
And . |slew ... |their ... |fish.
Their land brought forth **frogs** . |
in a-|bundance ‖
In . the | chambers | of their |
kings.

16 He spake, and there came **divers**|
sorts of |flies ‖
And . |lice in|all their|coasts.
He **gave** . them|hail for|rain ‖
And **flaming** | fire ...|in their |
land.

17 He smote their **vines** also, . |and
their |fig trees ‖
And **brake** . the | trees ... | of
their |coasts.
He spake, and the locusts came,
and **caterpillars,** . and | that
with- out|number ‖
And did eat up all the herbs in
their land, **and** . de-|voured
the|fruit of their|ground.

18 He smote also all the **firstborn** . |
in their|land ‖
The . | chief **of** | all their |
strength.
He brought them forth **also** . with|
silver and|gold ‖
And there was not one . feeble|
person a-|mong their|tribes

19 Egypt was glad . when|they de |
    parted ||
    For . the|fear of them|fell up-|
    on them.
    He spread a cloud ، |for a|cover-
    ing ||
    And fire . to give | light ... | in
    the|night.

20 The people asked, . and He |
    brought ...|quails ||
    And satisfied . them|with the|
    bread of|heaven.
    He opened the rock, and the
    waters|gushed|out ||
    They ran . in the|dry places|like
    a|river.

21 For He remembered . His|holy|
    promise ||
    And . |Abra-|ham His|servant.
    And He brought forth . His|people
    with|joy ||
    And . His|cho- ...|sen with|glad-
    ness :

22 And gave them the lands . |of
    the|heathen ||
    And they inherited . the|labour|
    of the|people ;
    That they might observe His
    statutes, . and|keep His|laws||
    Praise . |... ...|ye the|Lord.
    GLORY BE, ETC.

86   PSALM CVII.

1 OH, give thanks unto the Lord, .
    for|He is|good ||
    For . His | mercy en-|dureth
    for|ever.

2 Let the redeemed . of the|Lord
    say|so ||
    Whom He hath redeemed from
    the|hand ...|of the|enemy ;

3 And gathered . them|out of the|
    lands ||
    From the east, and from the
    west : from . the|north, and|
    from the|south.

4 They wandered in the wilderness .
    in a|solitary|way ||
    They . |found no|city to|dwell
    in.

5 Hungry|and ...|thirsty ||
    Their . |soul ...|fainted|in them.

6 Then they cried unto the Lord . |
    in their|trouble ||
    And He delivered . them|out
    of|their dis-|tresses.

7 And He led them forth . by the|
    right ...|way ||
    That they might go . to a|
    city of|habi-|tation.

8 Oh, that men would praise the
    Lord . |for His|goodness ||
    And for His wonderful works .|
    to the|children of|men !

9 For He satisfieth . the|longing|
    soul ||
    And filleth . the|hungry|soul
    with|goodness.

10 Such as sit in darkness and in .
    the|shadow of|death ||
    Being bound . | in af-|fliction
    and|iron ;

11 Because they rebelled against .
    the|words of|God ||
    And contemned the counsel|of
    the|Most ...|High.

12 Therefore He brought down .
    their|heart with|labour ||
    They fell down, . and | there
    was|none to|help.

Then they cried unto the **Lord** . |
in their | trouble ‖
And He **saved** . them | out of |
their dis- | tresses.

He **brought** them out of **darkness** .
and the | shadow of | death ‖
And . | brake their | bands in |
sunder.

Oh, that men would praise the
Lord . | for His | goodness ‖
And for His wonderful **works** . |
to the | children of | men !

For He hath **broken** . the | gates
of | brass ‖
And cut . the | bars of | iron in |
sunder.

Fools because . of | their trans- |
gression ‖
And because of their . in- |
iquai- ties, | are af- | flicted.

Their soul abhorreth . all | manner
of | meat ‖
And they draw **near** . | unto the |
gates of | death.

Then they cry unto the **Lord** . | in
their | trouble ‖
And He **saveth** . them | out of |
their dis- | tresses.

He **sent** . His | word, and | healed
them ‖
And **delivered** . | them from |
their de- | structions.

Oh, that men would praise the
Lord . | for His | goodness ‖
And for His wonderful **works** . |
to the | children of | men !

And let them sacrifice the **sacri-
fices** . of | thanks- ... | giving ‖
And **declare** . His | works ... |
with re- | joicing.

23 They that go **down** . to the | sea
in | ships ‖
That **do** . | business in | great ... |
waters :

24 These see the **works** . | of the |
Lord ‖
And . His | wonders | in the | deep.

25 For He commandeth, and **raiseth** .
the | stormy | wind ‖
Which **lifteth** | up the | waves
there- | of.

26 They mount up to the heaven,
they go **down** . a- | gain to
the | depths ‖
Their **soul** . is | melted be- | cause
of | trouble.

27 They reel to and fro, and stagger
like . a | drunken | man ‖
And . are | at their | wits' ... | end.

28 Then they cry unto the **Lord** . |
in their | trouble ‖
And He **bringeth** . them | out
of | their dis- | tresses.

29 He **maketh** . the | storm a | calm ‖
So . that the | waves there- | of
are | still.

30 Then are they **glad** . be- | cause
they be | quiet ‖
So He bringeth them unto |
their de- | sired ... | haven.

31 Oh, that men would praise the
Lord . | for His | goodness ‖
And for His wonderful **works** . |
to the | children of | men !

32 Let them **exalt** -Him also in the
congregation | of the | people ‖
And praise Him **in** . the as- |
sembly | of the | elders.

SELECTIONS FROM THE BOOK OF PSALMS.

33 He turneth rivers . | into a |
wilderness ‖
And the watersprings . | into |
dry ... | ground,

34 A fruitful land . | into | barrenness‖
For the wickedness . of | them
that | dwell there- | in.

35 He turneth the wilderness into .
a | standing | water ‖
And dry ground . | into | water- |
springs.

36 And there He maketh . the |
hungry to | dwell ‖
That they may prepare . a | city
for | habi- | tation ;

37 And sow the fields, . and | plant ... |
vineyards ‖
Which . may | yield ... | fruits of |
increase.

38 He blessed them also, so that they
are multi- | pli - ed | greatly ‖
And suffereth not . their | cattle |
to de- | crease.

39 Again, they are minished . and |
brought ... | low ‖
Through . op- | pression, af- |
fliction, and | sorrow.

40 He poureth . con- | tempt up- on |
princes ‖
And causeth them to wander in
the wilderness . | where there |
is no | way.

41 Yet setteth He the poor on high . |
from af- | fliction ‖
And maketh . him | fami- lies |
like a | flock.

42 The righteous shall see it, . | and
re- | joice ‖
And all iniqui- | ty shall | stop
her | mouth.

43 Whoso is wise, and will . ob-
these | things ‖
Even they shall understa
loving- | kindness | of the

GLORY BE, ETC.

87   PSALM CXI.

1 PRAISE ye the Lord. I will
the Lord . with | my ᵥ
heart ‖
. In the assembly of the uᵖ
and | in the | congre- | gat

2 The works . of the | Lord are |
Sought out of all them
have | pleasure there- |.

3 His work is honourable . | ₐ
glorious ‖
And His righteousness .
dur- ... | eth for | ever.

4 He hath made His woɾ
works . to | be re- | memb
The Lord is gracious .
full ... | of com- | passion

5 He hath given meat . untₑ
that | fear Him ‖
He will ever . be | minᵈ
His | covenant.

6 He hath shewed His peoᵖ
power . | of His | works
That He may give then
heri - tage | of the | heat

7 The works of His han
verity . | and ... | judgm
All . | His com- | mandmeᵣ
sure.

8 They stand fast . for | eve
ever ‖
And are done . in | truth
up- | rightness.

9 He sent **redemption** | unto His |
people ||
He hath commanded His cove-
nant for ever : **holy** . and|
rever- end|is His|Name.

10 The fear of the Lord **is** . the be-|
ginning of|wisdom ||
A good understanding have all
they that do His command-
ments : **His** . | praise en- |
dureth for|ever.

GLORY BE, ETC.

88 PSALM CXII.

1 PRAISE ye the Lord. Blessed is
the **man** . that|feareth the|
Lord ||
That delighteth|greatly in|His
com-|mandments.

2 His seed shall be **mighty** . up- |
on ...|earth ||
The generation **of** . the|upright|
shall be|blessed.

3 Wealth and **riches** . shall|be in
his|house ||
And his **righteousness** . en- |
dur-...|eth for|ever.

4 Unto the upright there ariseth
light . |in the|darkness ||
He is **gracious**, . and|full of
com-|passion, and|righteous.

5 A good man **sheweth** | favour,
and|lendeth ||
He will **guide** . his af-|fairs ... |
with dis-|cretion.

6 Surely he shall **not** . be|moved for|
ever ||
The righteous shall **be** . in |
ever-|lasting re-|membrance.

7 He shall not be **afraid** . of|evil|
tidings ||
His heart is **fixed**,|trusting|in
the|Lord.

8 His heart is established ; he **shall** .
not|be a-|fraid ||
Until he **see** . his de-|sire up-|on
his|enemies.

9 He hath dispersed, he hath given
to the poor ; his **righteous-
ness** . en-|dureth|for|ever ||
His **horn** . shall | be ex-|alted
with||honour.

10 The wicked shall see it, and be
grieved ; he shall gnash with
his **teeth**, . and|melt a-|way ||
The **desire** . | of the | wicked
shall|perish.

GLORY BE, ETC.

89 PSALM CXIII.

1 PRAISE ye the Lord. Praise, O ye
servants|of the|Lord ||
Praise . the | Name ... | of the|
Lord.

2 Blessed be the **Name** . |of the|Lord||
From this time **forth** . |and for|
ever-|more.

3 From the rising of the sun unto the
going **down** . |of the|same ||
The **Lord's** . |Name is | to be |
praised.

4 The Lord is **high** . a- | bove all |
nations ||
And . His | glory a- | bove the |
heavens.

5 Who is like unto the Lord our **God**, .
Who|dwelleth on|high ||
That humbleth Himself to behold the things that are . in
heaven and|in the|earth |

6 He raiseth up the **poor** . |out of
the|dust ||
And **lifteth** . the | needy|out of
the|dunghill ;

7 That He may **set** . | him with |
princes ||
˜ Even with the princes of His
people, .|Praise ... |ye the|Lord.

GLORY BE, ETC.

90   PSALM CXIV.

1 WHEN Israel **went** . | out of |Egypt||
The house of Jacob **from** . a|
people of |strange ... |language,

2 **Judah**|was his|sanctuary ||
And . |Isra- el|his do-|minion.

3 The **sea** . |saw it, and|fled ||
Jor- .|... dan was|driven|back.

4 The **mountains**|skipped like|rams ||
And . the|little|hills like|lambs.

5 What ailed thee, O thou **sea,** . |that
thou|fleddest ||
Thou **Jordan,** . that|thou wast|
driven|back?

6 Ye **mountains,** . that ye | skipped
like|rams ||
And . ye|little|hills, like|lambs ?

7 Tremble,thou earth, at the **presence** |
of the|Lord ||
At the **presence**|of the|God of|
Jacob ;

8 Which turned the **rock** . into a|
standing | water ||
The **flint** . |into a|fountain of|
waters.

GLORY BE, ETC.

91   PSALM CXV.

1 NOT unto us, O Lord, no
but unto **Thy** Name, .
glory ||
For Thy **mercy** . and|
truth's ... |sake.

2 Wherefore **should** . the|
say ||
Where . | ... is|now th

3 But our **God** . is|in the|h
He hath done **whatso-**
hath|pleased.

4 Their **idols** . are|silver
The . |work of |men's ..

5 They have **mouths,** . | t
speak not ||
Eyes . |have they,|but
not :

6 They have **ears,** . |but
not ||
Noses|have they, |but t
not :

7 They have hands, but th
not : feet **have** the
they | walk not ||
Neither | speak they |
their|throat.

8 They that **make** them .
un- |to them ||
So is **every**|one that|
in them.

9 O Israel, trust **thou** . |in t
He is . their|help ...|a
shield.

10 O house of **Aaron,** . |trus
Lord ||
He is . their|help ...|a
shield.

11 Ye that 'fear the Lord, . | trust in the | Lord ||
He is . their | help ... | and their | shield.

12 The Lord hath been mindful of us : . | He will | bless us ||
He will bless the house of Israel ;
He . will | bless the | house of | Aaron.

13 He will bless them . that | fear the | Lord ||
Both . | small ... | and ... | great.

14 The Lord shall increase . you | more and | more ||
You . | and ... | your ... | children.

15 Ye are blessed | of the | Lord ||
Which . | made ... | heaven and | earth.

16 The heaven, even the heavens, . | are the | Lord's ||
But the earth hath He given | to the | children of | men.

17 The dead praise . | not the | Lord ||
Neither any that go . | down ... | into | silence.

18 But we . will | bless the | Lord ||
From this time forth and for ever-more . | Praise ... | ... the | Lord.

GLORY BE, ETC.

92   PSALM CXVI.

1 I . | love the | Lord ||
Because He hath heard my voice . | and my | suppli- | ca- tions.

2 Because He hath inclined . His | · ear unto | me ||
Therefore will I call upon Him . as | long ... | as I | live,

3 The sorrows of death compassed me, and the pains of hell . gat | hold up- | on me ||
I . | found ... | trouble and | sorrow.

4 Then called I upon the Name . | of the | Lord ||
O Lord, I beseech . | Thee, de-' liver my | soul.

5 Gracious is . the | Lord, and ' righteous ||
Yea, . | our ... | God is | merciful.

6 The Lord . pre- | serveth the : simple ||
I was brought low, . | and He | helped | me.

7 Return unto thy rest, . | O my | soul ||
For the Lord hath dealt . | bounti- | fully | with thee.

8 For Thou hast delivered . my | soul from | death ||
Mine eyes from tears, . | and my | feet from | falling.

9 I will walk . be- | fore the | Lord ||
In . the | land ... | of the | living.

10 I believed ; therefore . | have I ! spoken ||
I . was | great- ... | ly af- | flicted.

11 I said . | in my | haste ||
All . | ... ... | men are | liars.

12 What shall I render | ... the | Lord ||
For all . His | bene - fits | toward | me ?
I will take the cup . | of sal- | vation ||
And call upon . the | Name . of the | Lord.

13 I will pay my **vows** . |unto the|
Lord ||
Now . in the|presence of|all
His|people.
Precious in the **sight** . | of the |
. Lord ||
Is . the|death ...|of His|saints.
14 O Lord, truly|I am Thy|servant ||
I am Thy servant, and the son
of Thine **handmaid**; . |Thou
hast|loosed my|bonds.
I will offer to Thee the **sacrifice** . |
of thanks-|giving ||
And will call upon . the |
Name ...|of the|Lord.
15 I will pay my **vows** . |unto the|
Lord ||.
Now . in the|presence of|all
His|people :
In the **courts** . of the|Lord's ...|
house ||
In the midst of thee, O Jcru-
salem, . | praise ... | ye the|
Lord.
GLORY BE, ETC.

93   PSALM CXVII.
1 OH, praise the **Lord,** . | all ye|
nations ||
. **Praise** . |... Him,|all ye|people.
2 For His merciful **kindness** . is|
great ...|toward us ||
And the truth of the Lord en-
dureth for **ever**. . | Praise ... |
ye the|Lord.
GLORY BE, ETC.

94   PSALM CXVIII.
1 OH, give thanks unto the **Lord**; .
for|He is|good ||
Because His **mercy** . en-|dur- ...|
eth for|ever.

Let **Israel** . |now ...|say ||
That His **mercy** . en-|dur- ...,|eth
for|ever.
2 Let the house of **Aaron** . |now ...|
say ||
That His **mercy** . en-|dur-...|eth
for|ever.
Let them now . that | fear the
Lord|say ||
That His **mercy** . en-|dur- ...|
eth for|ever.
3 I called upon the **Lord** . |in dis-|
tress ||
The Lord answered me, and **set** .
me|in a|large ...|place.
The Lord is on my **side**; . I|will
not|fear ||
What . can|man ...|do unto|me?
4 It is **better** . to|trust in the|Lord|
Than to **put** . |confi-|dence in|
man.
It is **better** . to|trust in the|Lord|
Than to **put** . |confi-|dence in|
princes.
5 The **Lord** . is my|strength and|
song ||
And **is** . be-|come ...|my sal-|
vation.
The voice of rejoicing and salva-
tion is in the **tabernacles** . |of
the|righteous ||
The right **hand** . of the|Lord...|
doeth|valiantly.
6 The right hand of the **Lord** . is
ex-|alted ||
The right **hand** . of the|Lord...|
doeth|valiantly.
I shall not . |die, but|live|
And **declare** . the|works ...|of
the|Lord.

7 The **Lord** . hath|chastened me|
  sore ‖
  But He hath not given . me |
  over|unto|death.
  Open to **me** . the|gates of |right-
  eousness ‖
  I will go into **them,** . and|I will|
  praise the|Lord :

8 This **gate** . |of the|Lord ‖
  Into **which** . the | righteous |
  shall ... |enter.
  I will praise **Thee,** . for|Thou hast|
  heard me ‖
  And art . be-|come ... |my sal-|
  vation.

9 The **stone** . which the|builders re-|
  fused ‖
  Is **become** . the | head stone | of
  the|corner.
  This . is the|Lord's ... |doing ‖
  It . is|marvel- lous|in our |eyes.

10 This is the **day** . which the|Lord
  hath|made ‖
  We will rejoice . |and be|glad
  in|it.
  Save **now,** . I be-|seech Thee,   O|
  Lord ‖
  O **Lord,** . I be- | seech Thee,
  send|now pros-|perity.

11 Blessed is he that cometh in the
  Name . |of the|Lord ‖
  We have blessed you **out** . of
  the|house ... |of the|Lord.
  God is the **Lord,** . which hath|
  shewed us|light ‖
  Bind the sacrifice with cords,
  even **unto** . the | horns ... | of
  the|altar.

12 Thou art my **God,** . and|I will|
  praise Thee ‖
  Thou art . my|God, I|will ex-|
  alt Thee,

O give thanks unto the **Lord ;** .
  for|He is|good ‖
  For His **mercy** . en-|dur- ... |eth
  for|ever.
  GLORY BE, ETC.

95   PSALM CXXI.

1 I WILL lift up mine **eyes** . |unto
  the|hills ‖
  From . |whence ... |cometh my|
  help.

2 My help cometh|from the|Lord ‖
  Which . |made ... |heaven and|
  earth.

3 He will not suffer thy **foot** . |to be|
  moved ‖
  He . that | keepeth thee | will
  not|slumber.

4 Behold, **He** . that|keepeth|Israel ‖
  Shall . | neither | slumber nor |
  sleep.

5 The **Lord** . |is thy|Keeper ‖
  The Lord is thy **shade** . up-|on
  thy|right ... |hand.

6 The sun shall not **smite** . |thee by|
  day ‖
  Nor . the|moon ... |by ... |night.

7 The Lord shall **preserve** thee .
  from |all ... |evil ‖
  He . |shall pre-|serve thy|soul.

8 The Lord shall preserve thy going
  out . and thy|coming |in ‖
  From this time **forth,** . and |
  even for|ever-|more.
  GLORY BE, ETC.

96   PSALM CXXII.

1 I WAS glad when they **said** . |
  unto|me ‖
  Let us go **into** . the|house ... |of
  the|Lord.

2 **Our** . | feet shall | stand ||
Within . **thy** | **gates,** ... | O Je- |
rusalem.

3 Jerusalem is **builded** | as a | city ||
That . | is com- | pact to- | gether :

4 Whither the tribes go **up,** . the |
tribes of the | Lord ||
Unto the testimony of Israel, to
give **thanks** . unto the |
Name ... | of the | Lord.

5 For there are **set** . | thrones of |
judgment ||
The **thrones** . | of the | house of |
David.

6 Pray for the **peace** . | of Je- |
rusalem ||
They . shall | prosper that |
love ... | thee.

7 **Peace** . be with- | in thy | walls ||
And pro**sperity** . with- | in thy |
pala- | ces.

8 For my **brethren and** . com- |
panions' | sakes ||
I will now **say,** . | Peace ... | be
with- | in thee.

9 Because of the **house** . of the | Lord
our | God ||
I . | ... will | seek thy | good.

GLORY BE, ETC.

97 PSALM CXXV.

1 THEY that trust in the **Lord** . shall
be | as Mount | Zion ||
Which cannot be **removed,** . | but
a- | bideth for | ever.

2 As the mountains are **round** . a- |
bout Je- | rusalem ||
So the Lord is round about His
people . from | henceforth \ even
for | ever.

3 For the rod of the wicked **shall not**
rest upon the lot . | of the |
righteous ||
Lest the righteous put **forth** .
their | hands ... | unto in- |
iquity.

4 Do good, O Lord, unto **those** . |
that be | good ||
And to **them** . that are | upright |
in their | hearts.

5 As for such as turn aside unto their
crooked ways, the Lord shall
lead them forth with the
workers | of in- | iquity ||
But **peace** . shall | be up- | on ... |
Israel.

GLORY BE, ETC.

98 PSALM CXXX.

1 **Out** . | of the | depths ||
Have I **cried** . | unto | Thee, O |
Lord.
Lord, . | hear my | voice ||
Let Thine ears be attentive to the
voice . | of **my** | suppli- | cations.

2 If Thou, **Lord,** . **shouldest** | mark
in- | iquities ||
O . | Lord, ... | who shall | stand ?
But there **is** . **for-** | giveness with |
Thee ||
That . | Thou... | mayest be | feared.

3 I wait for the **Lord,** . my | soul doth |
wait ||
And in . His | word ... | do I | hope.
My soul waiteth for the Lord **more**
than they that **watch** . | for
the | morning ||
I say, more than **they** . that |
watch ... | for the | morning.

4 **Let Israel hope** . | in the | Lord ‖
For with the Lord there is mercy,
and . with | Him is | plenteous
re-; demption.
And **He** . shall re- | deem ... | Israel ‖
From . | all ... | his in- | iquities.
GLORY BE, ETC.

99 PSALM CXXXII.

1 **Lord**, . re- | member | David ‖
And . | all ... | his af- | flictions,
How he **sware** . | unto the | Lord ‖
And vowed **unto** . the | mighty |
God of | Jacob,

2 Surely I will not come unto the
tabernacle . | of my | house ‖
Nor . | go up | into my | bed,
will not give **sleep** . | to mine |
eyes ‖
Or . | slumber | to mine | eyelids,

3 Until I find out a **place** . | for the |
Lord ‖
An habitation **for** . the | mighty |
God of | Jacob.
Lo. we **heard** . of | it at | Ephratah ‖
We found it **in** . the | fields ... | of
the | wood.

4 We will **go** . | into His | tabernacles ‖
We . will | worship | at His | foot-
stool.
Arise, O **Lord**, . | into Thy | rest ‖
Thou, . and the | ark ... | of Thy |
strength.

5 Let Thy **priests** . be | clothed with |
righteousness ‖
And **let**. Thy | saints ... | shout for |
joy.
For Thy **servant** | David's | sake ‖
Turn not **away** . the | face of |
Thine an- | ointed.

6 The Lord hath sworn in truth unto
David, **He** . will | not turn | from
it ‖
Of the fruit of thy body **will** . I |
set up- | on thy | throne.
If thy children will keep My
covenant and My **testimony** .
that | I shall | teach them ‖
Their children shall also sit upon .
thy | throne for | ever- | more.

7 For the **Lord** . hath | chosen | Zion ‖
He hath **desired** . it | for His |
habi- | tation.
This . is My | rest for | ever ‖
Here will I **dwell** ; . | for I | have
de- | sired it.

8 I will abundantly **bless** . | her pro- |
vision ‖
I will satis- | fy her | poor with |
bread.
I will also clothe her **priests** . | with
sal- | vation ‖
And her **saints** . shall | shout a- |
loud for | joy.

9 There will I make the **horn** . of |
David to | bud ‖
I have **ordained** . a | lamp for |
Mine an- | ointed.
His enemies **will** . I | clothe with |
shame ‖
But upon **himself** . | shall his |
crown ... | flourish.
GLORY BE, ETC.

100 PSALM CXXXIII.

1 BEHOLD, how **good** . and how |
pleasant it | is ‖
For **brethren** . to | dwell to- | gether |
in | unity |

2 It is like the precious ointment upon the head, that ran down upon the **beard**, . even | Aaron's | beard ‖
That went **down** . to the | skirts ... | of his | garments ;

3 As the dew of Hermon, and as the dew that descended upon . the | mountains of | Zion ‖
For there the Lord commanded the blessing, even | life for | ever- | more.
GLORY BE, ETC.

101 PSALM CXXXIV.

1 BEHOLD, bless ye the Lord, all ye **servants** | of the | Lord ‖
Which by night **stand** . in the | house ... | of the | Lord.

2 Lift up your **hands** . | in the | sanctuary ‖
And . | bless ... | ... the | Lord.

3 The Lord that **made** . | heaven and | earth ‖
Bless . | thee ... | out of | Zion.
GLORY BE, ETC.

102 PSALM CXXXV.

1 PRAISE ye the Lord. Praise ye the **Name** . | of the | Lord ‖
Praise Him, O . ye | servants | of the | Lord.
Ye that stand in the **house** . | of the | Lord ‖
In the **courts** . of the | house of | our ... | God,

2 Praise the Lord ; . for the | Lord is | *good* ‖
Sing praises **unto** . His | Name ; for | it is | pleasant.

For the Lord hath chosen **Jacob** . | unto Him- | self ‖
And **Israel** . for | His pe- | culi- ar | treasure.

3 For I **know** . that the | Lord is | great ‖
And that our **Lord** . | is a- | bove all | gods.
Whatsoever the Lord pleased, that did He in **heaven** . | and in | earth ‖
In . the | seas, and | all deep | places.

4 He causeth the vapours to ascend from the **ends** . | of the | earth ‖
He maketh lightnings for the rain ; He **bringeth** . the | wind ... | out of His | treasuries.
Who **smote** . the | first- born of | Egypt ‖
Both . of | man ... | and ... | beast.

5 Who sent tokens and wonders into the **midst** . of | thee, O | Egypt ‖
Upon **Pharaoh,** . | and up- on | all his | servants.
Who . | smote great | nations ‖
And . | slew ... | mighty | kings :

6 Sihon king of the Amorites, and **Og** . | king of | Bashan ‖
And . | all the | kingdoms of | Canaan ;
And gave their **land** . | for an | heritage ‖
An **heritage** . | unto | Israel His | people.

7 Thy Name, O **Lord,** | en- | dureth for | ever ‖
And **Thy** memorial, O Lord, . through- | out all | gener- | ations.

For the **Lord** . will|judge His|
people ‖
And He will **repent** . Him-|self
con-|cerning His|servants.

8 The idols of the **heathen** . are|
silver and|gold ‖
The . |work of |men's ... |hands.
They have **mouths**, . |but they|
speak not ‖
Eyes . |have they,|but they'see
not ;

9 They have **ears,** . |but they|hear
not ‖
Neither is there any|breath ... |
in their|mouths.
They that **make** them . are | like
un-|to them ‖
So is **every** |one that|trusteth|in
them.

10 Bless the **Lord**, . O|house of |Israel‖
Bless . the|Lord, O|house of |
Aaron :
Bless the **Lord**, . O|house of |Levi‖
Ye that **fear** . the|Lord, ... |bless
the|Lord.

11 Blessed be the Lord out of Zion,
which **dwelleth** | at Je- | ru-
salem ‖
Praise . |... ... |ye the|Lord.
GLORY BE, ETC.

103 PSALM CXXXVI.

1 O GIVE thanks unto the **Lord**; .
for|He is|good ‖
For His **mercy** . en-|dur- ... |eth
for|ever.
O give **thanks** . unto the|God of |
gods ‖
For His **mercy** . en-|dur- ... |eth
for|ever.

2 O give **thanks** . to the|Lord of |
lords ‖
For His **mercy** . en-|dur- ... |eth
for|ever.
To Him Who alone . |doeth great|
wonders ‖
For His **mercy** . en-|dur- ... |eth
for|ever.

3 To Him that by **wisdom** . | made
the|heavens ‖
For His **mercy** . en-|dur- ... |eth
for|ever.
To Him that stretched out the
earth . a-|bove the|waters ‖
For His **mercy** . en-|dur- ... |eth
for|ever.

4 To **Him** . that|made great|lights ‖
For His **mercy** . en-|dur- ... |eth
for|ever.
The **sun** . to|rule by|day ‖
For His **mercy** . en-|dur- ... |eth
for|ever.

5 The moon and **stars** . to|rule by|
night ‖
For His **mercy** . en-|dur- ... |eth
for|ever.
To Him that smote **Egypt** . | in
their|firstborn ‖
For His **mercy** . en-|dur- ... |eth
for|ever.

6 And brought out **Israel** . |from a-|
mong them ‖
For His **mercy** . en-|dur- ... |eth
for|ever.
With a **strong** hand, and with . a
stretched-out|arm ‖
For His **mercy** . en-|dur- ... |eth
for|ever.

¶ Who remembered us . in our|low
es-|tate ‖
For His mercy . en-|dur-...|eth
for|ever.

And hath redeemed . us|from our|
enemies ‖
For His mercy . en-|dur-...|eth
for|ever.

8 Who giveth food . to|all ...|flesh ‖
For His mercy . en-|dur-...|eth
for|ever.

O give thanks . unto the|God of|
heaven ‖
For His mercy . en-|dur-...|eth
for|ever.
GLORY BE, ETC.

104 PSALM CXXXVIII.

1 I WILL praise Thee . with my |
whole ...|heart ‖
Before the gods will I sing . |
praise ...|unto|Thee.

2 I will worship toward Thy holy
temple, and praise Thy Name
for Thy loving-kindness . and|
for Thy|truth ‖
For Thou hast magnified Thy
word . a- | bove ...| all Thy|
Name.

3 In the day when I cried . Thou|
answer- edst|me ‖
And strengthenedst me . with|
strength ...|in my|soul.

4 All the kings of the earth shall
praise . |Thee, O|Lord ‖
When they hear . the|words...|
of Thy|mouth.

5 Yea, they shall sing in the ways . |
of the|Lord ‖
*For great . is the|glory|of the|
Lord.*

6 Though the Lord be high, yet hath
He respect . |unto the|lowly‖
But the proud . He | knoweth
a-|far ...|off.

7 Though I walk in the midst of
trouble, . Thou|wilt re-|vive
me ‖
Thou shalt stretch forth Thine
hand against the wrath of mine
enemies, and . |Thy right|hand
shall|save me.

8 The Lord will perfect that . which
con-|cerneth|me ‖
Thy mercy, O Lord, endureth for
ever : forsake not the works .|
of Thine|own ...|hands.
GLORY BE, ETC.

105 PSALM CXXXIX.

1 O LORD, Thou hast searched|me
and|known me ‖
Thou knowest my down- . |sitting
and|mine up-|rising ;
Thou . |under-|standest ‖
My . |thought a-|far ...|off.

2 Thou compassest my path . and my|
lying|down ‖
And art . ac-|quainted with|all
my|ways.
For there is not a word . |in my|
tongue ‖
But, lo, O Lord, . Thou|knowest
it|alto-|gether.

3 Thou hast beset me behind . |and
be-|fore ‖
And . |laid Thine|hand up-|on
me.
Such knowledge is too . |wonder-
ful|for me ‖
It is high, . I|cannot at-|tain ..|
unto it.

Whither shall I go . |from Thy|
  spirit ‖
Or whither . shall I|flee ... |from
  Thy|presence ?
If I ascend up into heaven, . |Thou
  art|there ‖
If I make my bed in hell, . be-|
  hold, ... |Thou art|there.
If I take the wings . |of the|morn-
  ing ‖
And dwell in the uttermost . |
  parts ... |of the|sea,
Even there . shall|Thy hand|lead
  me ‖
And . |Thy right|hand shall|hold
  me.
If I say, Surely . the | darkness
  shall|cover me ‖
Even the night . |shall be|light
  a-|bout me.
Yea, the darkness hideth not from
  Thee; but the night shineth|
  as the|day ‖
The darkness and the light . are|
  both a-|like to|Thee.
How precious also are Thy thoughts .
  unto|me, O|God ‖
How great . |is the|sum of|them!
If I should count them, they are
  more in number|than the|sand‖
When I awake, . |I am|still with|
  Thee.
Search me, O God, . and|know my|
  heart ‖
Try . | me, and | know my |
  thoughts :
And see if there be any wicked . |
  way ... |in me ‖
And lead me . in the|way ...|
  ever-|lasting.
    GLORY BE, ETC.

106   PSALM CXLII.
1 I CRIED unto the Lord . |with my|
  voice ‖
With my voice unto the Lord.
  did I|make my|suppli-|cation.
I poured out my . com-|plaint be-|
  fore Him ‖
I shewed . be-|fore ... |Him my|
  trouble.
2 When my spirit was overwhelmed
  within me, then . Thou |
  knewest my|path ‖
In the way wherein I walked
  have they privily . | laid a |
  snare for|me.
I looked on my right hand, and
  beheld, but there was no man.|
  that would|know me ‖
Refuge failed me; no man . |
  cared ... |for my|soul.
3 I cried unto Thee, . |O ... |Lord ‖
  I said, Thou art my refuge and
  my portion . in the|land ...|of
  the|living.
Attend unto my cry; for I am
  brought . |very|low ‖
Deliver me from my persecutors;.
  for|they are|stronger than|I.
4 Bring my soul . |out of|prison ‖
  That . |I may|praise Thy|Name :
The righteous shall compass|me
  a-|bout ‖
For Thou shalt deal . | bounti- |
  fully|with me.
    GLORY BE, ETC.

107   PSALM CXLIII.
1 HEAR my prayer, O Lord, give ear .
  to my|suppli-|cations ‖
In Thy faithfulness answer me, |
  and ...|in Thy|righteousness.

And enter not into judgment|with
Thy|servant ‖
For in Thy sight . shall|no man|
living be|justified.

2 For the enemy hath persecuted my
soul ; he hath smitten my life .|
down to the|ground ‖
He hath made me to dwell in
darkness, as those . that|have
been|long ...|dead.
Therefore is my spirit over- |
whelmed with-|in me ‖
My heart . with-|in ...|me is|
desolate.

3 I remember . the|days of|old ‖
I meditate on all Thy works ; I
muse . on the|work ...|of Thy|
hands.
I stretch forth . my|hands unto|
Thee ‖
My soul thirsteth after Thee, .|
as a|thirsty|land.

4 Hear me speedily, O Lord: . my|
spirit|faileth ‖
Hide not Thy face from me, lest
I be like unto them . that go|
down ...|into the|pit.
Cause me to hear Thy loving-kind-
ness|in the|morning ‖
For . in|Thee ...|do I|trust.

5 Cause me to know the way . where-
in|I should|walk ‖
For I lift up . my|soul ...|unto|
Thee.
Deliver me, O Lord, . |from mine|
enemies ‖
I . |flee unto|Thee to|hide me.

6 Teach me . to|do Thy|will ‖
For . |Thou ...|art my|God.
Thy . |spirit is|good ‖
*Lead me into . the|land...|of up-|
rightness.*

7 Quicken me, O Lord, . |for Thy|
Name's sake ‖
For Thy righteousness' sake . !
bring my|soul out of|trouble.
And of Thy mercy cut off mine
enemies, and destroy all them.
that af-|flict my|soul ‖
For . |I am|Thy ...|servant.
GLORY BE, ETC.

108 PSALM CXLV.

1 I WILL extol Thee, . my|God, O|
King ‖
And I will bless . Thy|Name
for|ever and|ever.
Every day . |will I|bless Thee|
And I will praise . Thy|Name
for|ever and|ever.

2 Great is the Lord, and greatly|to
be|praised ‖
And . His | greatness | is un-|
searchable.
One generation shall praise Thy
works . |to an-|other|
And shall . de- | clare Thy |
mighty|acts.

3 I will speak of the glorious
honour|of Thy|majesty ‖
And . |of Thy|wondrous|works.
And men shall speak of the might.
of Thy|terri- ble|acts|
And I . will de-|clare ...|Thy...|
greatness.

4 They shall abundantly utter the
memory . of|Thy great|good-
ness ‖
And . shall | sing of | Thy ... |
righteousness.
The Lord is gracious, . and|full
of com-|passion|
Slow to anger,|and of|great ...|
mercy.

5 The **Lord** . is|good to|all ‖
  And His tender **mercies** . are|
  over|all His|works.

6 All Thy works shall **praise** .|Thee,
  O|Lord ‖
  And . Thy | saints ... | shall ... |
  bless Thee.

7 They shall speak of the glory|of
  Thy|kingdom ‖
  And . |talk ...|of Thy|power ;

8 To make known to the sons of
  men . His|mighty|acts ‖
  And the **glorious**|majes- ty|of
  His|kingdom.

9 Thy kingdom is an ever-|lasting|
  kingdom ‖
  And Thy dominion **endureth** .
  through- | out all | gener- |
  ations.

10 The Lord **upholdeth**|all that|fall‖
   And raiseth up all **those** . |that
   be|bowed|down.
   The eyes of **all** . |wait up-on|
   Thee ‖.
   And Thou givest them . their|
   meat in|due ...|season.

11 Thou **openest** . |Thine ... |hand ‖
   And satisfiest the de**sire** . of |
   every |living |thing.
   The Lord is **righteous** . in|all His|
   ways ‖ .
   And . |holy in|all His|works.

12 The Lord is nigh unto all **them** .
   that|call up-|on Him ‖
   To **all** . that|call up-|on Him
   in|truth.
   He will fulfil the de**sire** . of|them
   that|fear Him ‖
   He also will **hear** . their|cry,...|
   and will|save them.

13 The Lord pre**serveth** . all|them
   that|love Him ‖
   But **all** . the|wicked will|He
   de-|stroy.
   My mouth shall speak the **praise** .|
   of the|Lord ‖
   And let all flesh bless His holy|
   Name for|ever and|ever.
   GLORY BE, ETC.

109 PSALM CXLVI.

1 PRAISE ye the Lord. Praise the
  Lord, . |O my|soul ‖
  While I live . |will I|praise the|
  Lord.
  I will sing pra**:**ses|unto my|God ‖
  While . I|have ...|any|being.

2 **Put** not . your|trust in|princes ‖
  Nor in the son of **man**, . in|whom
  there|is no|help.
  His breath goeth forth, he **return-**
  eth|to his|earth ‖
  In that **very**|day his|thoughts...|
  perish.

3 Happy is he that hath the God of
  Jacob . |for his|help ‖
  Whose **hope** . is|in the|Lord his|
  God :
  Which made heaven and earth, the
  sea. and all . that|therein|is ‖
  Which . |keepeth|truth for|ever.

4 Which executeth **judgment**|for the
  op-|pressed ‖
  Which **giveth** | food ... | to the |
  hungry :
  The **Lord** . |looseth the|prisoners ‖
  The Lord **openeth** . the|eyes ...|
  of the|blind ;

5 The Lord raiseth **them** . that are|
  bowed|down ‖
  The . |Lord ...|loveth the|right-
  eous ;

The Lord . pre-|serveth the|stran-
gers ‖
He relieveth . the|father-|less
and|widow ;

3 But the way . |of the|wicked ‖
He . |turneth|upside|down.
The Lord . shall|reign for|ever ‖
Even thy God, O Zion, unto all
generations . |Praise ... |ye the|
Lord.

GLORY BE, ETC.

110   PSALM CXLVII.

1 PRAISE ye the Lord : for it is good
to sing praises|unto our|God‖
For . it is|pleasant ; and|praise
is|comely.
The Lord doth build . | up Je-|
rusalem ‖
He gathereth together . the |
out- ...|casts of|Israel.

2 He healeth . the|broken in|heart‖
And.|bindeth|up their|wounds.
He telleth the number|of the|
stars ‖
He calleth them . | all ... | by
their|names.

3 Great is our Lord, . and of |
great ...|power ‖
His . | under-| standing is |
infinite.
The Lord lifteth|up the|meek ‖
He casteth the wicked . |
down ...|to the|ground.

4 Sing unto the Lord . | with
thanks-|giving ‖
Sing praise . upon the|harp ...|
unto our|God :
Who covereth the heavens with
clouds, Who prepareth rain . |
for the |earth ‖

Who maketh grass . to |grow
up-|on the|mountains.

5 He giveth. to the|beast his|food|
And . to the|young ... | ravens
which|cry.
He delighteth not in the strength .|
of the|horse ‖
He taketh not pleasure . | in
the|legs of a|man.

6 The Lord taketh pleasure . in|
them that|fear Him ‖
In those . that|hope ...|in His|
mercy.
Praise the Lord, . |O Je-|rusalem|
Praise . |thy ...|God, O|Zion.

7 For He hath strengthened the
bars . |of thy|gates ‖
He . hath|blessed thy|children
with-|in thee.
He maketh peace . | in thy |
borders ‖
And filleth thee . with the |
finest|of the|wheat.

8 He sendeth forth His command-
ment . up-|on ...|earth ‖
His word . | runneth | very |
swiftly.
He giveth|snow like|wool ‖
He scattereth . the | hoar ...|
frost like|ashes.

9 He casteth forth . His|ice like|
morsels ‖
Who . can|stand be-|fore His|
cold ?
He sendeth out . His|word, and|
melteth them ‖
He causeth His wind to blow, .|
and the|waters|flow.

10 He sheweth His word . |unto|
Jacob ‖
His statutes and . His |judg-
ments|unto|Israel.

He hath not dealt so with any nation : and as for His judg-ments, . they | have not | known them ||
Praise . | ... ... | ye the | Lord.
GLORY BE, ETC.

111 PSALM CXLVIII.

1 PRAISE ye the Lord. Praise ye the Lord . | from the | heavens ||
Praise . | ... Him | in the | heights.
Praise ye Him, . | all His | angels ||
Praise . ye | Him, ... | all His | hosts.

2 Praise ye Him, . | sun and | moon ||
Praise Him, . | all ye | stars of | light.
Praise Him, . ye | heavens of | heavens ||
And ye waters . that | be a- | bove the | heavens.

3 Let them praise the Name . | of the | Lord ||
For He commanded, | and they | were cre- | ated.
He hath also established them . for | ever and | ever ||
He hath made . a de- | cree which | shall not | pass.

4 Praise the Lord . | from the | earth ||
Ye . | dragons, and | all ... | deeps :
Fire and hail, . | snow and | vapours ||
Stormy | wind, ful- | filling His | word :

5 Mountains . and | all ... | hills ||
Fruitful | trees and | all ... | cedars :
Beasts . and | all ... | cattle ||
Creeping | things and | flying | fowl:

6 Kings of the earth . and | all ... | people ||
Princes and all . | judges | of the | earth :

Both young men and maidens, | old men and | children ||
.Let them praise . the | Name ... | of the | Lord :

7 For His Name . a- | lone is | excellent ||
His glory is a- | bove the | earth and | heaven.
He also exalteth the horn of His people, the praise . of | all His | saints ||
Even of the children of Israel. a people near unto Him.
Praise . | ... ... | ye the | Lord.

GLORY BE, ETC.

112 PSALM CL.

1 PRAISE ye the Lord. Praise God . | in His | sanctuary ||
Praise Him . in the | firma- ment | of His | power.

2 Praise Him . for His | mighty | acts ||
Praise Him according | to His | ex-cel - lent | greatness.

3 Praise Him with the sound . | of the | trumpet ||
Praise Him . | with the | psaltery and | harp.

4 Praise Him . with the | timbrel and | dance ||
Praise Him with stringed . | instru- | ments and | organs.

5 Praise Him upon . the | loud ... | cymbals ||
Praise Him upon . the | high- ... | sounding | cymbals.

6 Let everything that hath breath . | praise the | Lord ||
Praise . | ... ... | ye the | Lord.

GLORY BE, ETC.

Chants for Special Occasions.

113 THE BURIAL OF THE
DEAD.

1 BLESSED are the dead . which | die
in the | Lord ||
From . | hence-... | ...... | forth :
Yea, saith the Spirit, that they may
'rest . | from their | labours ||
And . their | works do | follow |
them.—*Rev.* xiv. 13.

2 I am the resurrection, . | and the |
life ||
He that believeth in Me, though
he were dead, . | yet ... | shall
he | live :
And whosoever liveth . and be- |
lieveth in | Me ||
Shall . | ne- ... | ... ver | die.—
John xi. 25, 26.

3 I know. that my . Re- | deemer |
liveth ||
And that He shall stand at the
latter | day up- | on the | earth :
And though, after my skin, worms .
de- | stroy this | body ||
Yet . in my | flesh shall | I see | God :

4 Whom I shall see for myself, and
mine eyes shall behold, . and |
not an- | other ||
Though my reins . | be con- |
sumed with- | in me.—*Job* xix.
25—27.
For we brought nothing . | into
this | world ||
And it is certain . we can | carry |
nothing | out.—1 *Tim.* vi. 7.

5 Naked came I out . of my | mother's |
womb ||
And naked . shall | I re- | turn ... |
thither :

The Lord gave, and the Lor
taken a- | way ||
Blessed . be the | Name ..
Lord.—*Job* i. 21.

GLORY BE, ETC.

114 1 CORINTHIANS XV

1 BEHOLD, I shew you a
we . shall | not all | slee
But . | we shall | all be | c:
In a moment, in the twi
an | eye ||
At . | the ... | last ... | trun

2 For the trumpet shall so
the dead shall be r
incor- | ruptible ||
And . | we ... | shall be | ch
For this corruptible must
incor- | ruption ||
And this mortal . must
immor- | tality.

3 So when this corruptible s
put on . | incor- | rupti
And this mortal shall .
on | immor- | tality,
Then shall be brought t
saying . | that is | writ
Death . is | swallowed
victory.

4 O death, where is thy
grave, . | where is thy
The sting of death is sin
strength . of | sin ... | is
But thanks . | be to | God ||
Which giveth us the
through . our | Lord
Christ.

GLORY BE, ETC.

15   CHRISTMAS.

REJOICE greatly, . O | daughter
of | Zion ‖
Shout, . O | daughter | of Je- |
rusalem :
Behold, thy King . cometh | unto |
thee ‖
He . is | just, and | having sal- |
vation.

And the battle-bow . shall | be cut |
off ‖
And He shall speak . | peace ... |
unto the | heathen :
And His dominion shall be from
sea . | even to | sea ‖
And from the river even . to
the | ends ... | of the | earth.—
Zech. ix. 9, 10.

But thou, Bethlehem Ephratah,
though thou be little among .
the | thousands of | Judah ‖
Yet out of thee shall He come
forth unto Me that is to be . |
Ruler | in ... | Israel ;
Whose goings forth have been . |
from of | old ‖
From . | ev- ... | ... er- | lasting.—
Micah v. 2.

Therefore . the | Lord Him- | self ‖
Shall . | give ... | you a | sign :
Behold, a virgin shall conceive, ·
and | bear a | Son ‖
And . shall | call His | Name Im- |
manuel.—*Isa.* vii. 14.

5 For unto us a Child is born, unto
us . a | Son is | given ‖
And the government . shall | be
up- | on His | shoulder :

And His Name shall be called
Wonderful, Counsellor, . The |
Mighty | God ‖
The Everlasting Father, . The |
Prince ... | ... of | Peace.

6 Of the increase of His government
and peace . there shall | be no |
end ‖
Upon the throne of David, · |
·   and up- | on His | kingdom ;
To order it, and to establish it,
with judgment | and with |
justice ‖
From . | henceforth, | even for |
ever.—*Isa.* ix. 6, 7.

7 Say to them that are of a fearful
heart, Be strong, . | fear ... |
not ‖
Behold, . your | God will | come
with | vengeance,
Even God . | with a | recompense ‖
He . | will ... | come and | save you.

8 Then the eyes of the blind . | shall
be | opened ‖
And the ears . of the | deaf shall |
be un- | stopped ;
Then shall the lame man leap . |
as an | hart ‖
And the tongue . | of the |
dumb ... | sing :

9 For in the wilderness . shall |
waters break | out ‖
And . | streams ... | in the | desert :
And a highway shall be there, · |
and a | way ‖
And it shall be called . the | way
of | holi- | ness.

10 And the ransomed of the Lord · |
shall re- | turn ‖
With songs, and everlasting | joy
up- | on their | heads ·

They shall obtain . | joy and | gladness ||
And sorrow . and | sighing shall |
flee a-/way.—*Isa.* xxxv. 4—6,
8, 10.
GLORY BE, ETC.

116 EASTER, OR THE LORD'S
SUPPER.

1 CHRIST our **Passover** . is | sacrificed | for us ||
Therefore | let us | keep the | feast,

2 Not with old leaven, neither with
the **leaven** . of | malice and |
wickedness ||
But with the unleavened **bread** .
of sin-|ceri-|ty and | truth.—
1 *Cor.* v. 7, 8.

3 Christ, being raised from the
dead, . | dieth no | more ||
Death hath no **more** . do-|minion |
over | Him.

4 For in that He died, He died .
unto | sin ... | once ||
But in that He **liveth,** . He |
liveth | unto | God.

5 Likewise reckon ye also yourselves
to be dead indeed . | unto | sin ||
But alive unto **God** . through |
Jesus | Christ our | Lord.—
Rom. vi. 9—11.

6 Now is Christ **risen** . | from the |
dead ||
And become the **first-** . | fruits
of | them that | slept.

7 For **since** . by | man came | death ||
*By man came also the resur-\
rection | of the | dead.*

8 For as in **Adam** . | all ... | die
Even so in **Christ** . shall
made a-|live.—1 *Cor.* x1
GLORY BE, ETC.

117 THE OPENING OF
CHURCH.

2 CHRONICLES VI. 14, 18—

1 O **Lord** . | God of | Israel ||
There is no god like T
the | heaven nor | in the |
Which keepest covenant, an
est mercy | unto Thy | s
That **walk**. be-|fore Thee
all their | hearts.

2 But will **God** . in | very | deed
Dwell . with | men ... | c
earth ?
Behold, heaven and the he
heavens . | cannot co
Thee ||
How much **less** . this
which | I have | built !

3 Have respect, therefore,
prayer . | of Thy | serva1
And . | to his | suppli-|cat
O Lord my God. to heark
the **cry** . | and the | pray
Which Thy **servant** |
be-|fore ... | Thee,

4 That Thine eyes may be op
this **house** . | day and | n
Upon the place wherec
hast said that **Thou** . v
put Thy | Name .. | ther
To hearken | unto the | pra1
Which Thy **servant** | pra
ward this | place.

5 Hearken, therefore, unto th
cations of Thy servan1
Thy . | people | Israel |

Which **they** . shall|make... | to-
ward this|place.
Hear Thou from Thy **dwelling-
place,** . |even from|heaven ||
And **when** . Thou|hear-...|est
for-|give.

6 Now therefore arise, O Lord God,
into **Thy** . |resting-|place ||
Thou . and the|ark ...|of Thy|
strength :
Let Thy priests, O Lord God, be
clothed . |with sal-|vation ||
And let . Thy|saints re-|joice in|
goodness.
GLORY BE, ETC.

118 BAPTISM.

1 JESUS said, Suffer little children,
and forbid them **not** . to|come
unto|Me ||
For . of | such is the | kingdom
of|heaven.—*Matt.* xix. 14.

2 He shall feed His **flock** . |like a|
shepherd ||
He shall gather the lambs with
His **arm,** . and|carry them|in
His|bosom.—*Isa.* xl. 11.

3 Lo, children are a heritage of the
Lord ; and the fruit of the
womb . is|His re-|ward ||
As arrows are in the hand of a
mighty man, **so** . are|children|
of the|youth.—*Psalm* cxxvii.
3, 4.

4 I will pour My Spirit upon thy seed,
and My **blessing** . up-|on thine|
offspring ||
And they shall spring up as
among the grass, as **willows** . |
by the | water- | courses.—*Isa.*
xliv. 3, 4.

5 Go ye, **therefore,** . and|teach all|
nations ||
Baptising them in the Name of
the Father, and of the **Son,** .
and|of the|Holy|Ghost,

6 Teaching them to observe all things
whatsoever . I | have com- |
manded you ||
And lo, I am with you always,
even **unto** . the|end ...|of the|
world.—*Matt.* xxviii. 19, 20.
GLORY BE, ETC.

𝕾elected 𝕻assages of 𝕾cripture for 𝕮hanting.

119 EXODUS XV. 1—13, 17—18.

1 I WILL sing unto the Lord, for **He** .
hath|triumphed|gloriously ||
The horse and his rider **hath** .
He|thrown in-|to the|sea.
The **Lord** . is my|strength and|
song ||
And **He** . **is** be- | come ... | my
sal-|vation.

2 He is my God, and I will prepare
Him . an|habi-|tation ||
My father's **God,** . |and I|will
ex-|alt Him.
The **Lord** . is a|man of|war ||
The . |Lord ...|is His|Name.

3 Pharaoh's chariots and his host hath
He **cast** . |into the|sea ||
His chosen captains also are
drowned|in the|Red ...|Sea.

The **depths** . have | covered | them ‖
They **sank** . into the | bottom | as
a | stone.

4 Thy right hand, O Lord, is
become . | glorious in | power ‖
Thy right hand, O **Lord,** . hath |
dashed in | pieces the | enemy ;
And in the **greatness** | of Thine |
excellency ‖
Thou hast overthown **them** . that |
rose .. | up a- | gainst Thee.

5 Thou sentest forth Thy wrath,
which con**su**med | them as |
stubble ‖
And with the blast of Thy **nostrils**
the | waters were | gathered
to- | gether.
The floods stood **upright** . | as an |
heap ‖
And the depths were congealed
in . the | heart ... | of the | sea.

6 The enemy said, I will pursue, I
will overtake, I **will** . di- | vide
the | spoil ‖
My **lust** . shall be | satis- | fied up- |
on them :
I . will | draw my | sword ‖
My . | hand ... | shall de- | stroy
them.

7 Thou didst blow with Thy **wind,** .
the | sea ... | covered them ‖
They sank as . **lead** . | in the |
mighty | waters.
Who is like unto Thee, O **Lord,** . a- |
mong the | gods ‖
Who is like Thee, glorious in
holiness, **fearful** . in | praises, |
doing | wonders ?

8 Thou stretchedst out Thy right
hand, . the | earth ... | swallowed
them ‖

Thou in Thy mercy hast led fórth
the **people** . which | Thou ... |
hast re- | deemed.
Thou hast guided **them** . | in Thy |
strength ‖
Unto . Thy | holy | habi- | tation.

9 Thou shalt bring them in, and
plant them in the **mountain** .
of | Thine in- | heritance ‖
In the place, O Lord, which
Thou . hast | made for | Thee to |
dwell in,
In the sanctuary, O Lord, which
Thy **hands** . | have es- | tablished ‖
The **Lord** . shall | reign for | ever
and | ever.

GLORY BE, ETC.

120 DEUTERONOMY XXII. 1—4,
7, 9—12 ; XXXIII. 26, 27.

1 GIVE ear, O ye **heavens,** . and | I
will | speak ‖
And hear, O **earth,** . the |
words ... | of my | mouth ;
My doctrine shall **drop** . | as the |
rain ‖
My **speech** shall dis- | til ... | as the |
dew,

2 As the small rain upon . the | tender |
herb ‖
And **as** . the | showers up- | on the |
grass :
Because I will publish the **Name** . |
of the | Lord ‖
Ascribe . ye | greatness | unto our |
God.

3 He is the **Rock,** . His | work is | .
perfect ‖
For . | all His | ways are | judgment.
A God of **truth** . and with- | out in- |
iquity ‖
Just . and | right ... | is ... | He.

4 Remember . the|days of|old ‖
   Consider the **years** . of | many |
     gener-|ations :
   Ask thy **father,** . and|he will|shew
     thee ‖
   Thy . |elders, and|they will|tell
     thee.

5 For the Lord's **port**ion | is His |
     people ‖
   Jacob . is the|lot of|His in-|
     heritance.
   He found him in a desert land, and
     in the **waste,** . | howling |
     wilderness ‖
   He led him about, He instructed
     him, He kept him **as** . the |
     apple|of His|eye.

6 As an eagle stirreth up her nest,
     fluttereth . |over her|young ‖
   Spreadeth abroad her wings, **tak-
     eth** them, . |beareth them|on
     her|wings :
   So the **Lord** . a-|lone did|lead him‖
   And **there** . was | no strange |
     God ...|with him.

7 There is none like unto the **God** . |
     of Jes-|hurun ‖
   Who rideth upon the heaven in
     thy help, and in **His** . |excellen-
     cy|on the|sky.
   The Eternal **God** . |is thy|refuge ‖
   And underneath **are** . the|ever-|
     lasting | arms.

   GLORY BE, ETC.

121 1 SAMUEL II. 1—3, 6—10.

1 M**y** heart rejoiceth|in the|Lord ‖
   Mine **horn** . is ex-|alted|in the|
     Lord :
   My mouth is enlarged . |over **mine**|
     enemies

Because **I** . re-|joice in|Thy **sal-**|
     vation.

2 There is none **holy**|as the|Lord ‖
   For . |there is|none be-|side Thee :
   For the **Lord** . is a|God of|know-
     ledge ‖
   And by **Him** . |actions|are ...|
     weighed.

3 The Lord **killeth,** . and|maketh a-|
     live ‖
   He bringeth **down** . to the|grave,
     and|bringeth|up.
   The Lord maketh **poor,** . and |
     maketh|rich ‖
   He bringeth | low, and | lifteth |
     up.

4 He raiseth up the **poor** . |out of
     the|dust ‖
   And lifteth **up** . the|beggar|from
     the|dunghill,
   To **set** them . a-|mong ...|princes ‖
   And to **make** them . in-|herit
     the|throne of|glory.

5 For the **pillars** of the **earth** . |are
     the|Lord's ‖
   And **He** . hath|set the|world up-|
     on them.
   He will keep the feet of His saints,
     and the **wicked** · shall be |
     silent in|darkness ‖
   For by **strength** . shall|no ...|
     man prevail.

6 The adversaries of the **Lord** . shall
     be|broken to|pieces ‖
   Out of **heaven** . shall He|thun-...|
     der up-|on them :
   The Lord shall **judge** . the|ends of
     the|earth ‖
   And He shall give strength unto
     His King, and exalt . the|horn
     of|His An-|ointed.
       GLORY BE, ETC.

122 1 CHRONICLES XXIX.
10—13.

1 BLESSED be Thou, Lord God . of|
Israel our|Father ‖
For . |ev- ...|er and|ever.

2 Thine, O Lord, is the greatness, and
the power, . |and the|glory ‖
And . the|victo- ry,|and the|
majesty.

3 For all . that is|in the|heaven ‖
And . |in the|earth is|Thine ;

4 Thine . is the|kingdom, O|Lord ‖
And Thou art exalted . as|head
a-|bove ...|all.

5 Both riches and honour . |come of|
Thee ‖
And Thou . |reignest|over|all ;

6 And in Thine hand . is|power and|
might ‖
And in Thine hand it is to make
great, and to give . |strength...|
unto|all.

7 Now therefore, . our | God, we|
thank Thee ‖
And . |praise Thy|glorious|Name.
GLORY BE, ETC.

123 PROVERBS III. 5—7,
9—18 ; II. 2—11.

1 TRUST in the Lord . with |all
thine|heart ‖
And lean not unto . thine|
own ...|under-|standing.
In all thy ways . ac-|knowledge|
Him ‖
And He . |shall di-|rect thy|
paths.

2 Be not wise . in thine|own ...|
eyes ‖
*Fear the Lord, . | and de-|part
from |evil.*

Honour the Lord with thy substance, and with the first-
fruits . of|all thine|increase|
So shall thy barns be filled with
plenty, and thy presses shall
burst. |out with|new ...|wine.

3 My son, despise not the chasten-
ing|of the|Lord ‖
Neither . be|weary of|His cor-|
rection :
For whom the Lord loveth . | He
cor-|recteth ‖
Even as a father the son . in
whom ...|he de-|lighteth.

4 Happy is the man . that|findeth|
wisdom ‖
And the man . that|getteth|
under-|standing :
For the merchandise of it is better
than the merchan-|dise of|
silver ‖
And the gain . there-|of than|
fine ...|gold.

5 She is more . | precious than|
rubies ‖
And all the things thou canst
desire are not . to|be com-|
pared unto|her.
Length of days . is|in her|right
hand ‖
And in . her|left hand|riches
and|honour.

6 Her ways . are|ways of|pleasant-
ness ‖
And . |all her|paths are|peace.
She is a tree of life to them that
lay . |hold up-|on her ‖
And happy is every one . |that
re-|taineth|her.

So that thou incline thine ear . |
  unto | wisdom ‖
And apply . thine | heart to |
  under- | standing :
Yea, if thou criest . | after | know-
  ledge ‖
And liftest up . thy | voice for |
  under- | standing ;
If thou seekest | her as | silver ‖
And searchest for her . | as for |
  hid ... | treasures ;
Then shalt thou understand the
  fear . | of the | Lord ‖
And . | find the | knowledge of |
  . God.
For the Lord giveth wisdom : out
  of His mouth cometh know-
  ledge . and | under- | standing ‖
He layeth up sound . | wisdom |
  for the | righteous :
He is a buckler to them . that |
  walk up- | rightly ‖
He keepeth the paths of judg-
  ment, and preserveth . the |
  way ... | of His | saints.
Then shalt thou understand
  righteousness, . and | judg-
  ment, and | equity ‖
Yea, . | every | good ... | path.
When wisdom entereth into thine
  heart, and knowledge is
  pleasant . | unto thy | soul ‖
Discretion shall preserve thee, . |
  under- | standing shall | keep
  thee.
    GLORY BE, ETC.

24 JOB XXVIII. 12—15, 18—28.
BUT where . shall | wisdom be |
  found ‖
And where . is the | place of |
  under- | standing ?

Man knoweth not . the | price there- '
  of ‖
Neither is it found . in the
  land ... | of the | living.
2 The depth saith, . It is | not in | me ‖
And the sea saith, . | It is | not
  with | me.
It cannot . be | gotten for | gold ‖
Neither shall silver be weighed . |
  for the | price there- | of.
3 No mention shall be made of
  coral, . | or of | pearls ‖
For the price of wisdom . | is a- |
  bove ... | rubies.
The topaz of Ethiopia . | shall not |
  equal it ‖
Neither shall it . be | valued with |
  pure ... | gold.
4 Whence then . | cometh | wisdom ‖
And where . is the | place of |
  under- | standing ?
Seeing it is hid from the eyes . of |
  all ... | living ‖
And kept close . | from the | fowls
  . of the | air.
5 Destruction and death say, We have
  heard the fame thereof . | with
  our | ears ‖
  God understandeth the way
  thereof. and He . | knoweth the |
  place there- | of.
For He looketh to the ends . | of
  the | earth ‖
And seeth . | under the | whole ... |
  heaven,
6 To make the weight . | for the |
  winds ‖
And He weigheth . the | waters |
  by ... | measure.

When He made a decree . |for the|
  rain ||
And a way . for the|lightning|
  of the|thunder :

7 Then did He see it, . |and de-|clare
  it ||
He prepared it, . |yea, and|
  searched it|out.
And unto man He said, Behold, the
  fear of the **Lord,** . |that is|
  wisdom ||
And to depart . from|evil is|
  under-|standing.

    Glory be, etc.

125 PROVERBS VIII. 1, 4,
      10—20, 32—36.

1 **Doth** . not| wisdom |cry ||
  And under-|standing put|forth
  her|voice ?
Unto **you,** . O|men, I|call ||
  And my voice . is|to the|sons of|
  man.

2 Receive my **instruction,** . |and not|
  silver ||
And **knowledge** . | rather than |
  choice ...|gold.
For **wisdom** . is | better than |
  rubies ||
And all the things that may be
  desired are **not** . to|be com-|
  pared ...|to it.

3 I **wisdom** . |dwell with|prudence ||
  And **find** out . |knowledge of|
  witty in-|ventions.
The fear of the **Lord** . is to|hate ...|
  evil ||
Pride, **and** arrogancy, and the
  evil **way,** and the **froward** . \
  mouth ... |do I|hate.

4 Counsel is **mine,** . | and
  wisdom ||
  I am under-|standing ;
  strength.
By me kings reign, and
  de-|cree ...|justice ||
By me princes rule, an
  even all . the|judge
  earth.

5 I love them that love me,
  that **seek** . me|earl
  find me ||
Riches and honour are
  yea, **durable** . | rich
  righteous-|ness.
My fruit is better than g
  than|fine ...|gold ||
And **my** . re- | venue
  choice ...|silver.

6 I lead in the **way** . of|ri
  ness ||
In . the|midst of the|
  judgment :
Now therefore hearken ur
  O ye|children ||
For **blessed** . are|they
  my |ways.

7 Hear instruction, and b
  and re-|fuse it|not ||
Blessed . is the | ma
  heareth|me,
Watching **daily** |at my|ga
  Waiting . at the|posts .
  doors.

8 For whoso findeth me . |find
  And shall obtain . | f
  the|Lord ;
But he that sinneth ag
  wrongeth . his|own ..
All **they** . that|hate ...
  death.

    Glory be, etc.

126 ISAIAH XI. 1—6, 9, 10.

1 THERE shall come forth a rod . out
of the|stem of|Jesse ‖
And a Branch . shall|grow ...|
out of his|roots.
And the spirit of the Lord . shall|
rest up-|on Him ‖
The spirit . of | wisdom and /
under-|standing,

2 The spirit . of|counsel and|might‖
The spirit of knowledge . and of
the|fear ... |of the|Lord ;
And shall make Him of quick
understanding in the fear . |of
the|Lord ‖
And He shall not judge after the
sight.of His eyes, neither re-
prove after . the|hearing|of
His|ears :

3 But with righteousness shall . He|
judge the|poor ‖
And reprove with equity . |for
the|meek of the|earth :
And He shall smite the earth . with
the|rod of His|mouth ‖
And with the breath of His lips . |
shall He|slay the|wicked.

4 And righteousness shall be the
girdle|of His|loins ‖
And faithfulness . the|girdle|of
His|reins.
The wolf also shall dwell with the
lamb, and the leopard shall lie
down . |with the|kid ‖
And the calf and the young lion
and the fatling together ; and .
a|little|child shall|lead them.

5 They shall not hurt . |nor de-|stroy‖
In . |all My|holy|mountain :

For the earth shall be full of the
knowledge . |of the|Lord ‖
As . the|waters|cover the|sea.

6 And in that day there shall be . a|
root of |Jesse ‖
Which shall stand . for an |
ensign|of the|people ;
To it . shall the|Gentiles|seek ‖
And . His|rest ...|shall be|glori-
ous.

GLORY BE, ETC.

127 ISAIAH XII.

1 O LORD, I will praise Thee : though
Thou . wast|angry|with me ‖
Thine anger is turned away, . |
and Thou|comfort- edst|me.

2 Behold, God . is|my sal-|vation ‖
I . will|trust, and |not be a-|fraid.

3 For the Lord Jehovah is my
strength . |and my|song ‖
He also ، is be-|come ...|my sal-|
vation.

4 Therefore with joy . shall|ye draw|
water ‖
Out . of the|wells ...|of sal-|
vation.

5 And in that day . |shall ye|say ‖
Praise the Lord, . |call up-|on
His|Name.

6 Declare His doings . a-|mong the|
people ‖
Make mention that His . /
Name ...|is ex-|alted.

7 Sing unto the Lord ; for He hath
done . |excel- lent|things ‖
This . is|known in|all the|earth

15*

8 Cry out and shout, thou inhabi-|tant
of |Zion ||
For great is the Holy One of
Israel . |in the|midst of|thee.

GLORY BE, ETC.

128 ISAIAH XXV. 1—9.

1 O Lord, . |Thou art my|God||
I will exalt Thee, . |I will|praise
Thy|Name ;
For Thou hast done . |wonder- ful|
things ||
Thy counsels of old . are|faith-
ful-|ness and|truth.

2 For Thou hast made . of a|city an|
heap ||
Of . a de-|fenced|city a|ruin :
A palace of strangers . to|be no|
city ||
It . shall|ne- ... |ver be|built.

3 Therefore shall the strong people
glorify Thee, the city of the
terrible nations . |shall ... |fear
Thee ||
For Thou hast been a strength to
the poor, a strength . to the|
needy in|his dis-|tress.
A refuge from the storm, a shadow .|
from the|heat ||
When the blast of the terrible
ones is as . a|storm a-|gainst
the|wall.

4 Thou shalt bring down . the|noise
of |strangers ||
As . the|heat ... |in a dry|place,
Even the heat with the shadow . |of
a/cloud ||
The branch of the terrible ones .|
shall be|brought ... |low.

5 And in this mountain
Lord of Hosts make
all|people ||
A feast of fat things, a
wines ... |on the|lees
Of fat things . |full of|m
Of wines . on the|l
re-|fined.

6 And He will destroy .
mountain ||
The face of the cover
over|all ... |people,
And the veil . |that is|sp
O- . |... ver|all ... |nati
7 He will swallow up . |
victory ||
And the Lord God
away . | tears from
faces ;
And the rebuke of His p
He take away from
the|earth ||
For . the|Lord ... |hath
it.

8 And it shall be said in
Lo, . |this is our|G
We have waited . for|
He will|save us :
This is the Lord ; . we ha
for|Him ||
We will be glad . an
in|His sal-|vation.

GLORY BE, ETC.

129 ISAIAH XXVI.

1 WE have . a|strong ... |ci
Salvation will God .
for|walls and|bulwa
Open|ye the|gates ||
That the righteous na
keepeth . the|truth
in.

Thou wilt keep him in perfect peace
  whose **mind** . is | stayed on |
  Thee ‖
Be- . |cause he|trusteth|in Thee.
Trust **ye** . in the|Lord for|ever ‖
  For in the Lord **Jehovah** . is|
  ever-|lasting|strength :

For He bringeth down **them** . that|
  dwell on|high ‖
  The **lofty**|city, He|layeth   it|
  low ;
He layeth it low, **even** | to the |
  ground ‖
  He **bringeth** it . |even|to the|
  dust.

The **foot** . shall|tread it|down ‖
  Even the feet of the **poor,** . and
  the|steps ... |of   the|needy.
The way of the **just** . | is up- |
  rightness ‖
  Thou, most **upright,** . dost|weigh
  the|path of the|just.

Yea, in the **way** · . of Thy|judg-
  ments,   O|Lord ‖
Have . we|waited|for ... |Thee ;
The desire of our **soul** . is|to Thy|
  Name ‖
  And . to the re-|membrance|
  of ... |Thee.

With my soul have I **desired**
  "Thee . |in the|night ‖
  Yea, with my spirit with**in** me . |
  will I|seek Thee|early :
For when Thy **judgments** . are|in
  the|earth ‖
  The in**habitants** . of the|world
  will|learn ... |righteousness.

Let favour be **shewed** . | to the |
  wicked ‖
  Yet . | will he   not | learn ... |
  righteousness :

In the land of uprightness **will** ·
  he|deal un-|justly ‖
  And will not be**hold** . the |
  majes- ty|of the|Lord.

8 Lord, when Thy **hand** . is|lifted|up‖
  They . |will ... |not ... |see :
  But they shall see, and be ashamed
  for their **envy**|at the|people ‖
  Yea, the fire of **Thine** . | ene-
  mies|shall de-|vour them.

9 Lord. Thou wilt or**dain** . | peace
  for|us ‖
  For Thou also hast **wrought** . |all
  our|works ... |in us.
O Lord our God. other lords beside
  Thee have **had** . do-|minion|
  over us ‖
  But by Thee only will we **make** . |
  mention|of Thy|Name.
  GLORY BE, ETC.

130   ISAIAH XXXV.

1 THE wilderness, and the solitary
  place. **shall** . be|glad for|them‖
  And the desert shall **rejoice** . and|
  blossom|as the|rose.
  It shall blossom **abundantly** . |and
  re-|joice ‖
  Even . with|joy ... |and ... |sing-
  ing :

2 The glory of Lebanon **shall** . be|
  given|unto it ‖
  The **excellency** . of | Carmel |
  and ... |Sharon,
  They shall see the **glory**|of the|
  Lord ‖
  And . the|excellen- cy|of our|
  God.

3 Strengthen ye the weak hands, and
confirm . the|feeble|knees ‖
Say to them that are of a fearful
heart, Be . |strong,…|fear ..|
not :
Behold, your God . will|come with|
vengeance ‖
Even God with a recompense ; . |
He will|come and|save you.
4 Then the eyes of the blind . |shall
be|opened ‖
And the ears . of the|deaf shall|
be un-|stopped ;
Then shall the lame man leap . |as
an|hart ‖
And the tongue . |of the|dumb…|
sing :
5 For in the wilderness . shall|waters
break|out ‖
And . |streams…|in the|desert.
And the parched ground . shall be-|
come a|pool ‖
And the thirsty|land …|springs
of|water.
6 In the habitation of dragons, . |
where each|lay ‖
Shall . be|grass with|reeds and|
rushes.
And an highway shall be there, . |
and a|way ‖
And it shall be called . the|way
of|holi-|ness ;
7 The unclean shall not pass over it ;
but . it shall|be for|those ‖
The wayfaring men, though
fools, . |shall not|err there-|in.
No lion shall be there, nor any
ravenous beast . shall go|up
there-|on ‖
*It shall not be found there ; but .
the re-|deemed shall|walk…|
there :*

8 And the ransomed of the Lord . |
shall re-|turn ‖
And come to Zion with songs,
and everlasting | joy up- | on
their|heads :
They shall obtain . |joy and|glad-
ness ‖
And sorrow . and|sighing shall|
flee a-|way.

GLORY BE, ETC.

131 ISAIAH XL. 1—11, 28—31.

1 COMFORT ye, comfort ye My
people, |saith your|God ‖
Speak ye comfortably . |to Je-|
rusa-|lem,
And cry unto her that her warfare
is accomplished. that her . in-|
iquity is|pardoned‖
For she hath received of the
Lord's hand . |double for|all
her|sins.
2 The voice of him that crieth | in
the|wilderness ‖
Prepare ye . the|way …|of the|
Lord,
Make straight . |in the|desert ‖
A . |highway|for our|God.
3 Every valley . shall|be ex-|alted ‖
And every mountain . and|hill
shall be|made …|low :
And the crooked . shall be|made…|
straight ‖
And . the|rough . |places|plain.
4 And the glory of the Lord . shall|
be re-|vealed
And all . |flesh shall|see it
to-|gether :
For the mouth . |of the|Lord |
Hath . |spo- …|ken …|it.

5 The voice . |said, ... |Cry ‖
   And he said, . |What ... |shall I|
   cry ?
All . |flesh is|grass ‖
   And all the goodliness thereof is
   as . the|flower|of the|field.

6 The grass withereth, . the|flower|
   fadeth ‖
   Because the spirit of the Lord
   bloweth upon it ; . |surely
   the|people is|grass.
   The grass withereth, . the|flower|
   fadeth ‖
   But the word . of our|God shall|
   stand for|ever.

7 O Zion, . that|bringest good|tid-
   ings ‖
   Get thee up . |into the|high...|
   mountain ;
   O Jerusalem, . that|bringest good|
   tidings ‖
   Lift . | up thy | voice with |
   strength.

8 Lift it up, . |be not a-|fraid‖
   Say unto the cities . of|Judah,
   Be-|hold your|God !
   Behold, the Lord God will come
   with strong hand, and His
   arm . shall|rule...|for Him ‖
   Behold, His reward is with
   Him, . |and His|work be-|fore
   Him.

9 He shall feed His flock . |like a|
   shepherd ‖
   He shall gather . the|lambs ...|
   with His|arm,
   And carry them . |in His|bosom ‖
   And shall gently lead . |those
   that|are with|young.

10 Hast thou not known ? . |hast thou
   not|heard ‖
   That the everlasting God, the
   Lord, the Creator . of the|
   ends ... |of the|earth,
   Fainteth not, . |neither is|weary ‖
   There is no searching|of His|
   under-|standing.

11 He giveth power . |to the|faint ‖
   And to them that have no
   might . | He in- | creaseth |
   strength.
   Even the youths shall faint . |and
   be|weary ‖
   And the young . | men shall |
   utter- ly |fall.

12 But they that wait upon the Lord .
   shall re-|new their|strength ‖
   They shall mount . |up with|
   wings as |eagles ;
   They shall run, . and | not be |
   weary ‖
   And they . shall|walk, and|
   not ... |faint.
    GLORY BE, ETC.

132 ISAIAH XLI. 10, 17, 18, 20 ;
      XLIII. 1—3 ; LIV. 7, 8, 10, 17.

1 FEAR thou not; . for|I am|with
   thee ‖
   Be not dismayed ; . for | I am |
   thy ... |God :
   I will strengthen thee ; yea, . |I
   will|help thee ‖
   Yea, I will uphold thee . with
   the|right hand|of My|right-
   eousness.

2 When the poor and needy seek
   water, . and|there is|none ‖
   And . their|tongue ... |faileth for|
   thirst,

I . the|Lord will|hear them ‖
I the **God** . of|Israel will|not
for-|sake them.

3 I will open **rivers** . | in high |
places ‖
And **fountains** . in the|midst ...|
of the|valleys :
I will make the **wilderness** . a|pool
of | water ‖
And . the|dry land|springs of|
water :

4 That **they** . may|see, and|know ‖
And consider, . and|under-|stand
to-|gether,
That the **hand** . of the|Lord hath|
done this ‖
And the **Holy** One . of|Israel|
hath cre-|ated it.

5 Fear not ; for **I** . |have re-|deemed
thee ‖
I have called thee **by** . thy |
name ; ... |thou art|Mine.
When thou passest through the
waters, . I|will be|with thee ‖
And through the **rivers,** . they|
shall not|over-|flow thee :

6 When thou walkest through the
fire, . thou | shalt not be |
burned ‖
Neither . shall the | flame ... |
kindle up-|on thee.
For **I** . am the|Lord thy|God ‖
The **Holy** One . of|Israel,|thy ...|
Saviour.

7 For a small moment have **I** . for-|
saken|thee ‖
But with **great** . |mercies|will I|
gather thee.
In a little **wrath** *I hid My face*
from thee . |for a|moment ‖

But with everlasting **kindness**
will I have mercy on thee,
saith . the|Lord ...|thy Re-|
deemer.

8 For the mountains shall depart, and
the **hills** . |be re-|moved ‖
But My **kindness** . shall|not de-|
part from|thee,
Neither shall the covenant of My
peace . |be re-|moved ‖
Saith the **Lord** . |that hath|mercy|
on thee.

9 No weapon that is formed **against** .|
thee shall|prosper ‖
And every tongue that shall rise
against **thee** . in | judgment
thou|shalt con-|demn.
This is the heritage of the **servants**|
of the|Lord ‖
And their righteousness **is** . of|
Me, ...|saith the|Lord.

GLORY BE, ETC.

133 ISAIAH LII. 7—10.

1 How **beautiful** . up-|on the|moun-
tains ‖
Are the feet of **him** . that|bring-
eth|good ...|tidings,
That publisheth peace ; that **bring-
eth** . good|tidings of|good ‖
That publisheth **salvation** ; that
saith . unto | Zion, | Thy God |
reigneth !

2 The watchmen shall **lift** . |up the|
voice ‖
With the **voice** . to-|gether|shall
they|sing :
For they shall **see** . |eye to|eye ‖
When the **Lord** . shall|bring a-|
gain ...|Zion.

3 Break forth . |into|joy ‖
   Sing together, ye **waste** . |places|
   of Je-|rusalem :
   For the Lord hath comfort-|ed His|
   people ‖
   He . | hath re- | deemed Je- | rusa-
   lem.

4 The Lord hath laid **bare** . His |
   holy|arm ‖
   In . the|eyes of|all the|nations ;
   And all . the|ends of the|earth ‖
   Shall **see** . the sal-|vation|of
   our|God.
   GLORY BE, ETC.

134 ISAIAH LIII. 3—12.

1 HE is despised, . and re-|jected
   of|men ‖
   A Man of **sorrows**, . | and ac- |
   quainted with|grief :
   And we hid as it **were** . our|faces|
   from Him ‖
   He was despised, . and|we es-|
   teemed Him|not.

2 Surely **He** . hath|borne our|griefs ‖
   And . |carried|our ... |sorrows ;
   Yet we **did** . es- | teem Him |
   stricken ‖
   Smitten . of | God ... | and af- |
   flicted.

3 But He was **wounded** . for | our
   trans-|gressions ‖
   He . was|bruised for|our in-|
   iquities ;
   The chastisement of our **peace** . |
   was up-|on Him ‖
   And with **His** . |stripes ... | we
   are|healed.

4 All we like **sheep** . have|gone a-|
   stray ‖
   We have **turned** . every|one to|
   his *own*|*way ;*

And the **Lord** . hath|laid on|Him ‖
   The . in-|iquity|of us|all.

5 He was oppressed, and **He** . |was
   af-|flicted ‖
   Yet . He | open - ed | not His |
   mouth :
   He is brought as a **lamb** . |to the|
   slaughter ‖
   And as a sheep before her
   shearers is dumb, **so** . He |
   open- eth|not His|mouth.

6 He was taken from **prison** . |and
   from | judgmen⌣ ‖
   And **who** . shall de-|clare His|
   gener-|ation ?
   For He was cut off out of the
   land . |of the living ‖
   For the transgression of **My** . |
   people|was He|stricken.

7 And He made His **grave** . |with
   the|wicked ‖
   And **with** . the|rich ... |in His|
   death :
   Because **He** . had | done no | vio-
   lence ‖
   Neither was **any** . de-|ceit ... |in
   His|mouth.

8 Yet it **pleased** . the|Lord to|bruise
   Him ‖
   He . hath|put ... |Him to|grief.
   When Thou shalt make His **soul** .
   an|offering for|sin ‖
   He shall see His seed, **He** . |
   shall pro-|long His|days.

9 And the **pleasure** . |of the|Lord ‖
   Shall . |prosper|in His|hand.
   He shall see of the travail . \⌁
   His\soul ‖
   And . \shall be\satis-\fied.
   ٦๖4

10 By His knowledge shall My right-
eous servant | justi- fy | many ‖
For He . shall | bear ... | their in- |
iquities :
Therefore will I divide Him a
portion | with the | great ‖
And He shall divide . the |
spoil ... | with the | strong ;

11 Because He hath poured out His
soul . | unto | death ‖
And He was numbered | with
the | trans -... | gressors ;
And He bare . the | sin of | many ‖
And made intercession . | for the |
trans- ... | gressors.

GLORY BE, ETC.

135 ISAIAH LV. 1, 2, 6—13.

1 Ho, every one that thirsteth, come .
ye | to the | waters ‖
And he that hath no money ; . |
come ye, | buy and | eat ;
Yea, come, . buy | wine and | milk ‖
Without . | money and | without |
price.

2 Wherefore do ye spend money for
that . which | is not | bread ‖
And your labour for that . which |
satis- | fieth | not ?
Hearken diligently unto me, and
eat ye that . | which is | good ‖
And let your soul . de- | light it- |
self in | fatness.

3 Seek ye the Lord while . He | may
be | found ‖
Call ye . up- | on Him | while He
is | near :
Let the wicked . for- | sake his |
way ‖
And . the un- | righteous | man his |
thoughts :

4 And let him return . | unto the |
Lord ‖
And He . | will have | mercy up- |
on him ;
And . to | our ... | God ‖
For He . | will a- | bundant- ly |
pardon.

5 For My thoughts . | are not | your
thoughts ‖
Neither are your ways . | My
ways, | saith the | Lord.
For as the heavens are higher than
the earth, so are My ways . |
higher than | your ways ‖
And . | My ... | thoughts than |
your thoughts.

6 For as the rain cometh down, .
and | the | snow from | heaven ‖
And returneth not thither, . but |
water- | eth the | earth,
And maketh it bring . | forth and |
bud ‖
That it may give seed to the
sower, . and | bread ... | to the |
eater :

7 So shall My word be that goeth
forth . | out of My | mouth ‖
It shall not . re- | turn unto |
Me ... | void,
But it shall accomplish | that which
I | please ‖
And it shall prosper . in the |
thing where- | to I | sent it.

8 For ye shall go . | out with | joy ‖
And . be | led ... | forth with | peace :
The mountains and the hills shall
break forth before . you | into |
singing ‖
And all the trees . of the | fields
shall | clap their | hands.

) Instead of the **thorn** . shall come|
up the|fir tree ‖
And instead of the **brier** . shall|
come ... |up the|myrtle tree :
And it shall be to the **Lord** . |for a|
name ‖
For an everlasting **sign** . that|
shall not|be cut|off.

GLORY BE, ETC.

136 ISAIAH LX. 1—5, 11, 18—22.

1 ARISE, **shine**, . for thy|light is|
come ‖
And the **glory** . of the|Lord is|
risen up-|on thee.
For, behold, the **darkness** . shall|
cover the|earth ‖
And . |gross ...|darkness the|
people :

2 But the **Lord** . shall a-|rise up-|on
thee ‖
And His **glory** |shall be|seen up-|
on thee.
And the **Gentiles** . shall|come to
Thy |light ‖
And **kings** . to the|brightness|
of Thy|rising.

3 Lift up thine eyes **round** . a-|bout'
and|see ‖
All they gather them**selves** . to-|
gether, they|come to|thee :
Thy **sons** . shall|come from|far ‖
And thy **daughters** . shall be |
nursed|at thy |side.

4 Then thou|shalt **see**, . and|flow to-|
gether ‖
And thine **heart** . shall | fear,
and|be en-|larged ;

Because the abundance of the **sea**
shall be converted|unto|thee‖
The forces of the **Gentiles** .
shall|come ... |unto|thee.

5 Therefore thy **gates** . shall be |
open con-|tinually ‖
They **shall** not . be|shut ...|day
nor|night ;
That men may bring unto thee
the forces|of the|Gentiles ‖
And that **their** . |kings ...|may
be|brought.

6 Violence shall no more be **heard** . |
in thy|land ‖
Wasting . nor de- | struction
with-|in thy|borders ;
But thou shalt **call** . thy|walls
Sal-|vation ‖
And . | ... thy|gates ...|praise.

7 The sun shall be no **more** . thy|
light by|day ‖
Neither for brightness **shall** .
the|moon give|light unto|
thee ;
But the Lord shall be unto thee
an ever-|lasting |light ‖
And . |thy ...|God thy|glory.

8 Thy **sun** . shall no|more go|down‖
Neither **shall** . thy |moon with-|
draw it-|self ;
For the Lord shall be thine **ever**-|
lasting |light ‖
And the **days** . of thy|mourn-
ing|shall be|ended.

9 Thy people **also** . shall be|all ...|
righteous ‖
They . shall in-|herit the|land
for|ever,
The **branch** . |of My |planting‖
The work of My **hands**, . |that
I|may be|glorified.

10 A little one shall . be-|come a |
thousand ‖
And . a|small one a|strong ...|
nation.
I . | ... the|Lord ‖
Will . |hasten it|in His|time.
GLORY BE, ETC.

137 LAMENTATIONS III. 22—27,
31—33, 39—41.

1 It is of the Lord's mercies that we .
are|not con-|sumed ‖
Because . | His com- | passions |
fail not.
They are new . |every|morning ‖
Great . |is Thy|faithful-|ness.

2 The Lord is my portion,|saith my|
soul ‖
Therefore|will I|hope in|Him.
The Lord is good unto them . that|
wait for|Him ‖
To . the|soul that|seeketh|Him.

3 It is good . |that a|man ‖
Should both hope and quietly
wait for . the sal- | vation | of
the|Lord.
It is good . |for a|man ‖
That he bear . the|yoke ...|in his|
youth.

4 For the Lord will not cast . |off for|
ever ‖
But . |though He|cause ...|grief,
Yet will He have compassion, ac-
cording to the multitude . |of
His|mercies ‖
For He doth not afflict willingly, .
nor|grieve the|children of|
men.

5 Wherefore doth a living |man com-|
plain ‖
A man . for the|punish- ment\
of his|sins ?

Let us search and try our ways,
and turn again . |to the|Lord ‖
Let us lift up our heart with our
hands . unto | God ... | in the |
heavens.
GLORY BE, ETC.

138 HABAKKUK III. 2—6, 10,
11, 13, 17, 18.

1 O Lord, I have heard Thy speech,
and|was a-|fraid ‖
O Lord, revive Thy work . in
the|midst ...|of the|years ;
In the midst . of the|years make|
known ‖
In . |wrath re-|member|mercy.

2 God . |came from|Teman ‖
And the Holy One . |from . |
Mount ...|Paran.
His glory|covered the|heavens ‖
And the earth . was | full ... | of
His|praise.

3 And His brightness . was|as the|
light ‖
He had horns coming out of His
hand ; and there was . the|
hiding|of His|power.
Before Him . |went the|pestilence ‖
And burning coals . went |
forth ...|at His|feet.

4 He stood, . and | measured the |
earth ‖
He beheld, . and|drove a-|sunder
the|nations ;
And the everlasting mountains were
scattered ; the perpetual | hills
did|bow ‖
His . |ways are|ever-|lasting.

5 The mountains saw Thee, . | and
they|trembled ‖
The overflowing . of the|water|
passed|by ;

The **deep** . |uttered his|voice ‖
And **lifted**|up his|hands on|high.

6 The sun and moon stood **still** . in
their|habi-|tation ‖
At the light of Thine arrows
they went, and at the **shining**|
of Thy|glitter- ing|spear.
Thou wentest forth for the **salva-**
tion|of Thy|people ‖
Even for salvation|with ...|Thine
an-|ointed.

7 Although the **fig** tree . |shall not|
blossom ‖
Neither . shall|fruit be|in the|
vines ;
The **labour** . of the|olive shall|
fail ‖
And . the|fields shall|yield no|
meat ;

8 The flock shall be cut **off** . |from·
the|fold ‖
And **there** . shall|be no|herd in
the|stalls :
Yet I will rejoice . |in the|Lord ‖
I will **joy** . in the|God of|my
sal-|vation.

GLORY BE, ETC.

139 ROMANS VIII. 31—39.

1 **If** . |God be|for us ‖
Who . |can be a-|gainst ...|us ?
He that spared not His own Son,
but **delivered** . Him|up for
us|all ‖
How shall He not with Him also|
freely|give us|all things ?

2 Who shall lay anything to the
charge . of |God's e-|lect ‖
It is God that justifieth. **Who** .
is|he ...|that con-|demneth?

It is Christ that died, yea **rather** .
that is|risen a-|gain ‖
Who is even at the right hand of
God, Who also **maketh**|inter-|
cession|for us.

3 Who shall separate us **from** . the|
love of|Christ ‖
Shall **tribu-**|lation,|or dis-|tress,
Or **perse-**|cution, or|famine ‖
Or **nakedness,** . or|peril,|or ...|
sword ?

4 As it is written, For Thy **sake** we
are **killed** . |all the day|long‖
We are **accounted** . as|sheep ...|
for the|slaughter :
Nay, in all these things **we** . are|
more than|conquerors ‖
Through . |Him that|loved|us.

5 For I . |am per-|suaded ‖
That . |neither|death, nor|life,
Nor angels, nor **princi-**|palities,
nor|powers ‖
Nor **things** . | present, nor |
things to|come,

6 **Nor** . |height, nor|depth ‖
Nor . |any|other|creature,
Shall be able to separate us **from** .
the|love of|God ‖
Which is in **Christ** . | Jesus |
our ...|Lord.

GLORY BE, ETC.

140 REVELATION I. 5—8 ;
IV. 8, 11.

1 **Unto**|Him that|loved us ‖
And washed us from our **sins** . |
in His|own ...|blood,

2 And hath made us kings and
priests unto **God** . |and His|
Father ‖
To Him be glory and dominion .
for|ever and|ever. A-|men

3 Behold, . He|cometh with|clouds‖
And . |every|eye shall|see Him,

4 And they also . which | pierced |
Him ‖
And all kindreds of the earth .
shall|wail be-|cause of|Him.

5 I . am|Alpha and|Omega ‖
The beginning and . the |
ending,|saith the|Lord,

6 Which is, . |and which!was ‖
And which is . to|come, ...|the
Al-|mighty.

7 Holy,|Holy,|Holy ‖
Lord . |God ...|Al- ...|mighty,

8 Which was, . |and ...|is ‖
And . |is ...|to ...|come.

9 Thou . art|worthy, O|Lord ‖
To receive . |glory and|honour
and|power ;

10 For Thou . hast cre- | ated | all
things ‖
And for Thy pleasure . they|
are and|were cre-|ated.

GLORY BE, ETC.

141 REVELATION V. 2, 9, 10,
12, 13.

1 WHO is worthy . to |open the |
book ‖
And . to|loose the|seals there-|of ?

2 Thou art worthy, . for|Thou wast|
slain ‖
And hast redeemed us . to|God
by|Thy ...|blood.

3 Out . of|every|kindred ‖
And . |tongue, and|people, and|
nation,

4 And hast made us unto our God. |
kings and|priests ‖
And we . shall|reign ...|on the|
earth ‖

5 Worthy is the Lamb . |that was|
slain ‖
To . re-|ceive ...|power, and|
riches,

6 And . |wisdom, and|strength‖
And . |honour, and|glory, and|
blessing.

7 Blessing, and honour, . and|glory,
and|power ‖
Be unto Him . that|sitteth up-|
on the|throne,

8 And . |unto the|Lamb ‖
For ever . and|ever.| A-...|men.

GLORY BE, ETC.

142 REVELATION VII.
10, 12—17.

1 SALVATION to our God, which
sitteth . up-|on the|throne ‖
And . |un- ...|to the|Lamb.

2 A-.|... ...|men ‖
Blessing, and glory, . and|wis-
dom, |and thanks-|giving,

3 And honour, . and | power, and |
might ‖
Be unto our God . for|ever and|
ever. A-|men.

4 What are these which are arrayed .
in|white ...|robes ‖
And.|whence ...|came ...|they?

5 These are they which came out of
great . |tribu-|lation ‖
And have washed their robes,
and made them white . in the|
blood ...|of the|Lamb.

6 Therefore are they before . the|
throne of|God ‖
And serve Him day . and |
night ...|in His|temple :

7 And He that sitteth . |on the|
throne ‖
Shall . |dwell a-|mong ...|them.

8 They . shall|hunger no|more ‖
Neither|thirst ...|any|more ;

9 Neither shall the sun . |light ...|
on them ‖
Nor . |a- ...|... ny|heat.

10 For the Lamb which is in the
midst . of the|throne shall|
feed them ‖
And shall lead them . unto |
living|fountains of|waters :

11 And God . shall|wipe a-|way ‖
All . |tears ...|from their|eyes.

GLORY BE, ETC.

143 REVELATION XI. 17 ; XII.
10—12 ; XIV. 13.

1 WE give Thee thanks, O Lord . |
God Al-|mighty ‖
Which art, . and|wast, and|art
to|come,

2 Because Thou . hast|taken to|
Thee ‖
Thy great . |power, ...|and hast|
reigned.

3 Now is come . sal-|vation and|
strength ‖
And the kingdom of our God, . and
the|power ...|of His|Christ :

4 For the accuser of our brethren .
is|cast ...|down ‖
Which accused them before .
our|God ...|day and|night.

5 And they overcame him by the .
blood|of the|Lamb ‖
And by . the|word ...|of their|
testimony ;

6 And they loved not their lives . |
unto the|death ‖
Therefore rejoice, ye heavens, . .
and|ye that|dwell in|them.

7 Blessed are the dead which die in
the Lord . |from ...|henceforth‖
Yea, . |saith ...|the ...|Spirit,

8 That they may rest . |from their|
labours ‖
And . their | works do | follow |
them.

GLORY BE, ETC.

144 REVELATION XV. 3, 4 ;
XI. 15.

1 GREAT and marvellous . |are Thy|
works ‖
Lord . |God ...|Al- ...|mighty ;

2 Just and true . |are Thy|ways ‖
Thou . |King ...|of ...|saints.

3 Who shall not fear Thee, O Lord,
and glori-|fy Thy|Name ‖
For Thou . |only|art ...|holy :

4 For all nations shall come . and|
worship be-|fore Thee ‖
For Thy . |judgments|are made|
manifest.

5 The kingdoms of this world are
become the kingdoms|of our|
Lord ‖
And . |of ...|His ...|Christ :

6 And . |He shall|reign ‖
For . |ever|and ...|ever.

GLORY BE, ETC.

145 REVELATION XIX. 1, 2,
5, 6, 7, 9.

1 Alle-|lu- ...|ia ‖
Salvation, . and | glory, and |
honour, and|power,

2 Unto . the|Lord our|God ‖
For true . and | righteous | are
His|judgments.

3 Alle-|lu- ...|ia ‖
Praise . our | God, all | ye His |
servants,

4 And ye . that|fear ...|Him ‖
Both . |small ...|and ...|great.

5 Alle-|lu- ...|ia ‖
For the Lord God . om-|nipotent|
reign- ...|eth.

6 Let us be glad . |and re-|joice ‖
And give . |honour|to ...|Him ;

7 For the marriage . of the|Lamb is|
come ‖
And His wife . hath|made her-|
self ...|ready.

8 Blessed are they . | which are |
called ‖
Unto the marriage | supper | of
the|Lamb.

GLORY BE, ETC.

146 REVELATION XXI. 3, 4 ;
XXII. 3—5, 17.

1 BEHOLD, the tabernacle of God . |
is with|men ‖
And He will dwell with them, .
and|they shall|be His|people ;

2 And God Himself shall be with
them, . and|be their|God ‖
And God shall wipe away all . |
tears ...|from their|eyes ;

3 And there shall be . | no more |
death ‖
Neither|sorrow,|nor ...|crying,

4 Neither shall there be any |
more ...|pain ‖
For the former | things are |
passed a-|way.

5 And there shall be . | no more |
curse ‖
But the throne of God . and of
the|Lamb shall|be ...|in it.

6 And His servants . shall|serve ...|
Him ‖
And they shall see His face, and
His .|Name shall be|in their|
foreheads.

7 And there shall be . | no night |
there ‖
And they need no candle, . |
neither|light of the|sun ;

8 For the Lord God . |giveth them|
light ‖
And they shall reign . for |
ev- ...|er and|ever.

9 And the Spirit and . the | bride
say,|Come ‖
And let him . that | heareth |
say, ...|Come ;

10 And let him . that is a-|thirst ...|
come ‖
And whosoever will, let him
take . of the | water of |
life ...|freely.

GLORY BE, ETC.

147 REVELATION XXI. 1, 2, 10,
11, 18, 19, 21—27.

1 I SAW a new **heaven** . and a |
new ... | earth ‖
For the first heaven and the first
earth were passed away, and
there . was | no ... | more ... |
sea.

2 And I saw the holy **city,** . | new
Je- | rusalem ‖
Descending **out** . of | heaven |
from ... | God,

3 **Having** . the | glory of | God ‖
And her light was like . unto a |
stone ... | most ... | precious ;

4 And the building of the . **wall** of
it | was | of jasper ‖
And the foundations of the wall
of the city were garnished
with **all** . | manner of |
precious | stones.

5 And the twelve **gates** . were |
twelve ... | pearls ‖
Every several **gate** . | was of |
one ... | pearl ;

6 And the street of the **city** . was |
pure ... | gold ‖
As . it | were trans- | parent | glass.

7 And I saw no . | temple there- | in ‖
For the Lord God almighty
and . the | Lamb are the |
temple of | it :

8 And the city had no need of the
sun, neither of the **moon,** . to |
shine in | it ‖
For the glory of God did lighten
it, **and** . the | Lamb is the |
light there- | of.

9 And the nations of them that are
saved shall **walk** . in the | light
of | it ‖
And the kings of the earth do
bring their **glory** . and |
honour | into | it.

10 And the gates of it shall not be
shut . at | all by | day ‖
For there . shall | be no | night ... |
there.

11 And they shall bring the glory
and **honour** . of the | nations |
into it ‖
And there shall in no wise enter
into it . | anything | that de- |
fileth,

12 Neither whatsoever worketh abom-
ination, . or | maketh a | lie ‖
But they that are written **in** .
the | Lamb's ... | book of | life.
GLORY BE, FTC

ANTHEMS.

peated in singing are printed in italics, and words sung in other voices than the treble are enclosed in brackets.

ORSHIP THE LORD.
i. 9, 6.

ip the Lord, *O worship the worship the Lord* in the f holiness, *the beauty of* fear before Him all the *ar before Him, all the earth.* nd majesty are before Him ; and beauty are in His sanc- *O worship the Lord,) O ic Lord, O worship the Lord, v the Lord in the beauty of he beauty of holiness.*

ILL EXTOL THEE.
r. 1, 2, 8-10.

Lowell Mason.

tol Thee, my God, O King ; l bless Thy Name for ever Every day will I bless d I will praise Thy Name nd ever. *Every day, every ll bless Thee; and I will l Name for ever and ever.* rd is gracious, and full of n ; slow to anger, and of :cy, *slow to anger, and of cy.* The Lord is good, *is* l; and His tender mercies all His works, *His tender e over all His works.*

All Thy works shall praise Thee, O Lord, and Thy saints shall bless Thee, *Thy saints shall bless Thee. All Thy works shall praise Thee, O Lord, and Thy saints shall bless Thee, Thy saints shall bless Thee. All Thy works shall praise Thee, shall praise Thee, O Lord, and Thy saints shall bless Thee, Thy saints shall bless Thee.*

3 O PRAISE GOD IN HIS HOLINESS.

Ps. cl.   *J. Weldon.*

O PRAISE God in His holiness ; praise Him in the firmament of His power. Praise Him in His noble acts, *praise Him in His noble acts ;* praise Him according to His excellent greatness. Praise Him in the sound of the trumpet : Praise Him upon the lute and harp ; praise Him in the cymbals and dances ; Praise Him upon the strings and pipe. Let everything that hath breath praise the Lord, *let everything that hath breath praise the Lord.*

4 BLESSING, GLORY, WISDOM AND THANKS.

J. S. Bach.

BLESSING, glory, wisdom and thanks, *blessing, glory, wisdom and thanks,* power and might, *power and might,* power and might be unto our God, *be unto our God, be unto our God,* for evermore, *for evermore.*

Blessing, glory, wisdom and thanks, blessing, glory, wisdom and thanks, power and might, power and might, power and might be unto our God for evermore, for evermore, for evermore, for evermore. Amen.

5 **THEY THAT WAIT UPON THE LORD.**

Isa. xl. 31.　　*G. J. Elvey, Mus. Doc.*

THEY that wait upon the Lord shall renew their strength; they shall mount up with wings, *shall mount up with wings, with wings* as eagles. *(They that wait upon the Lord,) they that wait upon the Lord shall renew their strength, shall renew their strength; they shall mount up with wings, shall mount up with wings, shall mount up with wings, with wings as eagles.* They shall run and not be weary; they shall walk and not be faint, *they shall run and not be weary, shall walk and not be faint, they shall walk and not be faint.*

Trust ye in the Lord, in the Lord for ever, for in the Lord Jehovah is everlasting strength. *Trust ye in the Lord, in the Lord for ever, for in the Lord Jehovah is everlasting strength. Trust ye in the Lord, in the Lord Jehovah, for in the Lord Jehovah is everlasting strength, everlasting strength.*

6 **TEACH ME THY WAY.**

Ps. lxxxvi. 11, 16.　　*From Spohr.*

·TEACH me Thy way, O Lord, I will *walk in Thy truth.* O knit my heart *to Thee, that I may fear Thy Name.*

Teach me Thy way, O Lord, I will walk in Thy truth. O knit my heart to Thee, that I may fear Thy Name. O turn Thou unto me; have mercy upon me. *Teach me Thy way, O Lord, I will walk in Thy truth. O turn Thou unto me ; have mercy upon me. Teach me Thy way, O Lord, I will walk in Thy truth, I will walk in Thy truth.* Amen.

7 **GOD, MY HELP.**

M. Hauptmann.

(GOD, my help, unto Thee I lift my eyes: hear, O hear, O Lord, my prayer;) *unto Thee I lift my eyes, God, my help: hear, O God, my prayer;* leave me not in trouble, *God, my help : hear, O Lord, my prayer;* leave me not, *(and leave me not, and leave me not,) and leave me not, and leave me not* in days of grief, *of grief, not in days of grief, and leave me not in trouble, in days of grief.* O God, my help, show Thy mercy, *God, leave me not in days of grief, O God, O God, my help.*

8 **LOOK UP TO GOD.**

M. Hauptmann.

LOOK up to God and bless His Name, thy broken heart will then find peace; His streams of mercy never cease, and hosts on high His powers, *His powers* proclaim. *Look up to God and bless His Name, thy broken heart will then find peace ; His streams of mercy never cease, and hosts on high His powers, His powers proclaim.*

O trust Him, *O trust Him;* soon He'll hear thy cry, *soon He'll hear thy cry, and send thee comfort, peace, and*

. His justice like the hills reins ; His providence the world
tains, *His providence sustains, His
vidence sustains, His providence the
rld sustains.* Look up to God and
ss *His Name, thy broken heart will
n find peace ; His streams of mercy
er cease, and hosts on high His
vers proclaim.*

THE HEAVENS PROCLAIM HIM.

Beethoven.

E heavens proclaim Him with
iseless devotion, the Eternal's Name
r all is heard ; His praise is echoed
earth and by ocean, receive, O
n, their Godlike word.
He holds the stars in the firmament
wing, (He bids) *He bids* the sun in
endour rise ; in songs of gladness
join to adore Him, our God all-
d, all-great, all-wise, *our God all-
d, all-great, all-wise.*

THY GOODNESS SPREADS.

Beethoven.

GOD, Thy goodness spreads around,
ke o'er all extended ; by Thee we
with mercy crowned, in danger's
ur defended, *in danger's hour
ended.* O Lord, my tower, my
uge here, receive my tears, receive
r prayer, for I will pray before
ee, *for I will pray before Thee.*

COME UNTO ME.

Matt. xi. 28-30. *J. S. Smith.*

ME unto Me, all ye that labour and
heavy-laden, and I will give you
t.

Take My yoke upon you, and learn
of Me ; (for I am lowly.) meek and
lowly in heart, *take My yoke upon
you, (and learn of Me, learn of Me ;)*
and ye shall find rest unto your souls,
find rest unto your souls. For My
yoke is easy, and My burden is light,
*My yoke is easy, My burden is light,
My yoke is easy, and My burden is
light, My yoke is easy, and My burden
is light, and My burden is light, My
yoke is easy, and My burden is light.*

12   I WILL ARISE.

Luke xv. 18, 19. *R. Cecil.*

I WILL arise, *I will arise* and go to
my Father, and will say unto Him,
Father, *Father,* I have sinned, *have
sinned, I have sinned* against Heaven
and before Thee, and am no more
worthy to be called Thy son.
*I will arise, I will arise and go to
my Father, my Father.*

13   LIKE AS THE HART.

Ps. xlii. *V. Novello.*

LIKE as the hart desireth the water-
brooks, so panteth my soul after
Thee, O God. *Like as the hart desireth
the water-brooks, so panteth my soul
after Thee, O God.*
Why art thou so full of heaviness,
so full of heaviness, O my soul, and
why art thou so disquieted within
me?
O put thy trust, thy trust in God,
*O put thy trust, thy trust in God, O
put thy trust, thy trust in God, O put
thy trust, thy trust in God.*

14 AS THE HART PANTETH.

Ps. xlii. 1, 2.   *L. Mason.*

As the hart panteth after the water-brooks, *as the hart panteth after the water-brooks*, so panteth my soul, *so panteth my soul* after Thee, O God, *so panteth my soul after Thee, O God.* My soul thirsteth, *my soul thirsteth, thirsteth* for God, for the living God, *for the living God.* When shall I come, *when shall I come* and appear before God? *When shall I come, when shall I come and appear before God?*

As the hart panteth after the water-brooks, as the hart panteth after the water-brooks, so panteth my soul, so panteth my soul after Thee, O God, so panteth my soul after Thee, O God.

15 O LORD, MY STRENGTH.

Auber.

O Lord, my strength, to Thee I pray; turn not Thou Thine ear away. *O Lord, my strength, to Thee I pray; turn not Thou Thine ear away.* Grant me, Lord, Thy love to share; feed me with a shepherd's care. Thou my rock and fortress art, Thou the refuge of my heart.

O Lord, my strength, to Thee I pray.

16 WHEN MY HEART IS OVERWHELMED.

Ps. lxi. 2; xlii. 5.

W. B. Bradbury.

When my heart is overwhelmed, *when my heart is overwhelmed*, lead me to the rock, *lead me to the rock*, *lead me to the rock* that is higher than I, *lead me to the rock that is higher than I.* Why art thou cast down, O my soul, and why art thou disquieted within me?

Hope thou in God, *hope thou in God, hope thou in God*, for I shall yet praise Him, *I shall yet praise Him*, Who is the health of my countenance and my God, *Who is the health of my countenance and my God.*

17 ENTER NOT INTO JUDGMENT.

Ps. cxliii. 2.   *T. Attwood.*

Enter not into judgment with Thy servant, O Lord, for in Thy sight shall no man living be justified. *Enter not into judgment with Thy servant, O Lord, for in Thy sight shall no man living be justified, (for in Thy sight,) for in Thy sight shall no man living be justified, (for in Thy sight,) for in Thy sight shall no man living be justified, shall no man living be justified, for in Thy sight shall no man be justified, shall no man be justified.*

18 TURN THY FACE FROM MY SINS.

Ps. li. 9-11.   *T. Attwood.*

Turn Thy face from my sins, and put out all my misdeeds. Make me a clean heart, O God, and renew a right spirit within me, *renew, renew, (renew,) renew, renew a right spirit within me, renew a right spirit within me.*

Cast me not away, *away* from Thy presence, and take not Thy Holy Spirit from me, *and take not Thy Holy Spirit from me, Thy Holy Spirit from me. Cast me not away, away from*

resence, and take not Thy Holy
from me, and take not Thy Holy
from me, Thy Holy Spirit from

AVE VERUM.
Mozart.

Word of God incarnate, of the
Mary born, on the Cross Thy
body for us men with nails
orn. Cleanse us by the blood
water streaming from Thy
1 side ; be through life our
nanna, and in death's lone path
uide, *in death's lone path, in
: lone path our Guide.*

HOW LOVELY ARE THE MESSENGERS.
ı. x. 15, 18. *Mendelssohn.*

lovely are the messengers that
. us the Gospel of peace, *how
are the messengers that preach
Gospel of peace, the Gospel of
the messengers that preach us
spel of peace.* How lovely are
:hat preach us the Gospel of
) To all the nations is gone
:he sound of their words, *to all
tions is gone forth the sound of
vords, is gone forth the sound of
words. (How lovely are the
gers that preach us the Gospel,)
rvely are the messengers that
. us the Gospel of peace, they
reach us the Gospel of peace.
: the nations is gone forth the
of their words, (to all the nations
forth the sound of their words,)
the nations is gone forth the
of their words, is gone forth the
of their words. to all the nations*

is gone forth the sound of their words,
throughout all the lands their glad
tidings. *(How lovely are the messengers that preach us the Gospel of
peace,) how lovely they that preach us
the Gospel of peace, they that preach
us the Gospel of peace.*

21 TEACH ME, O LORD.
Ps. cxix. 33. *T. Attwood.*

TEACH me, O Lord, the way of Thy
statutes, *teach me, teach me the way of
Thy statutes,* and I shall keep it, *and
I shall keep it* unto the end, *(and I
shall keep it,) and I shall keep it, and
I shall keep it unto the end, (and I
shall keep it unto the end.)*
   *Teach me, O Lord, teach me, O
Lord, the way of Thy statutes, (and I)
shall keep it, (and I) shall keep it,
and I shall keep it unto the end,
(and I) shall keep it unto the end,
unto the end.*

22 ALL YE NATIONS, PRAISE THE LORD.
W. F. Müller.

ALL ye nations, praise the Lord, all
ye lands, your voices raise ; heaven
and earth with one accord, praise the
Lord, *praise the Lord, praise the Lord,*
for ever praise. *All ye nations, praise
the Lord, all ye nations, praise the
Lord, all ye nations, praise the Lord,
all ye nations, praise the Lord, all ye
lands your voices raise ; heaven and
earth,* with loud accord, *heaven and
earth, with loud accord,* praise the
Lord, for ever praise, *praise the Lord,
for ever praise, praise the Lord, praise
the Lord, praise the Lord, for ever
praise, praise the Lord. All ye lands*

praise the Lord, praise the Lord, for ever praise. For His truth and mercy stand, past and present and to be, like the years of His right hand, like His own eternity. *For His truth and mercy stand, past and present and to be, like the years of His right hand, like His own eternity. All ye nations, praise the Lord, all ye lands, your voices raise ; heaven and earth, with loud accord, praise the Lord, for ever praise, for ever praise, for ever praise.*

23 O DEATH, WHERE IS THY STING?

1 Cor. xv. 55-57.   *A. H. Brown.*

O DEATH, where is thy sting ? *where is thy sting ?* O grave, where is thy victory? *where is thy victory, thy victory?* The sting of death is sin, *sin,* and the strength of sin is the law. But thanks, *but thanks* be to God, *thanks, thanks, thanks be to God,* Who giveth us the victory, *Who giveth us the victory* through our Lord Jesus Christ, *thanks be to God, thanks be to God, to God, Who giveth us the victory through our Lord Jesus Christ, through our Lord Jesus Christ.*

24 WORTHY IS THE LAMB.

Rev. v. 12, 13.   *C. Darnton.*

WORTHY is the Lamb that was slain. and hath redeemed us to God, *to God* by His blood, to receive power, and riches, and wisdom, and strength, and honour, and glory, and blessing. *Worthy is the Lamb that was slain, and hath redeemed us to God, to God by His blood, to receive power, and riches, and wisdom, and strength, and*

honour, and glory, and blessing. Blessing and honour, glory and power, be unto Him, *be unto Him* that sitteth upon the throne and unto the Lamb for ever and ever, *and ever.* *Blessing and honour, glory and power, be unto Him, be unto Him that sitteth upon the throne and unto the Lamb for ever and ever, and ever.* Amen.

25 WHAT SHALL I RENDER?

Ps. cxvi. 12-14.   *A. H. Brown.*

WHAT shall I render unto the Lord for all His benefits toward me, *for all His benefits toward me, toward me ?* I will take the cup of salvation, and call upon the Name of the Lord, *and call upon the Name of the Lord, the Name of the Lord.* I will pay my vows, *I will pay my vows, my vows* unto the Lord, *unto the Lord,* now in the presence of all His people, *now in the presence of all His people.* Praise ye the Lord, *praise ye the Lord, praise ye the Lord.*

26 CREATE IN ME A CLEAN HEART, O GOD.

E. Pr. t

CREATE in me a clean heart, O God, and renew a right spirit within me. Cast me not away from Thy presence, and take not Thy Holy Spirit from me, *take not Thy Holy Spirit from me.*
Restore unto me the joy of Thy salvation, and uphold me. *and uphold me* with Thy free Spirit, *and uphold me with Thy free Spirit.*
Then will I teach transgressors Thy ways, and sinners shall be converted, *and sinners shall be converted,*

ncerted unto Thee. *Then will I uch transgressors Thy ways, and mers shall be converted, converted to Thee.*

7 THINE, O LORD, IS THE GREATNESS.

1 Chron. **xxix**. 11.

J. Kent (adapted by W. Shore).

HINE, O Lord, *O Lord*, is the great- ss, (*Thine, O Lord, O Lord, is the eatness,*) *Thine, O Lord, O Lord, is e greatness*, and the power, and the ory, and the victory, and the ajesty, *the victory and majesty. hine, O Lord,*) *Thine, O Lord, (is e greatness, and the power,) is the eatness and the power, (and the ry,) and the victory, and the jesty the majesty;* for all that is the heaven, *in the heaven* and the rth are Thine. (Thine is the king- m,) *Thine is the kingdom*, O Lord, d Thou art exalted as Head over , *as Head over all, as Head, as ead over all.*

8 LIFT UP YOUR HEADS.

Ps. **xxiv.** 7, 8, 10.

J. L. Hopkins, Mus. Doc.

FT up your heads, O ye gates, and ye lift up, ye everlasting doors, *'t up your heads, O ye gates, and be lift up, ye everlasting doors,* and e King of glory shall come in, *and e King of glory shall come in, and r King of glory shall come in.*

(Who is the King?) *who is the King, the King* of glory? (*Who is the King?*) *who is the King, the King of glory? Who is the King of glory? Who is the King of glory?* (The Lord strong and mighty, mighty in battle, *the Lord strong and mighty,*) *the Lord mighty in battle.* (The Lord of hosts,) He is the King of glory, *He is the King of glory, He is the King of glory, of glory. The Lord of hosts, He is the King of glory, He is the King of glory, He, He is the King, the King of glory.* (*The Lord of hosts,*) *He is the King of glory, He is the King of glory, He is the King of glory, of glory. The Lord of hosts, He is the King of glory, He is the King of glory, He, He is the King, the King of glory.* The Lord of hosts, He is the King of glory.

29 COMFORT THE SOUL OF THY SERVANT.

Ps. **lxxxvi.** 4.

W. Crotch, Mus. Doc.

COMFORT, O Lord, the soul of Thy servant, for unto Thee do I lift up my soul. *Comfort, O Lord, the soul of Thy servant, for unto Thee do I lift up my soul. Comfort, O Lord, the soul of Thy servant, for unto Thee do I lift up my soul, do I lift up my soul. Comfort, O Lord, the soul of Thy servant, for unto Thee do I lift up my soul. Comfort, O Lord, the soul of Thy servant, for unto Thee do I lift up my soul, do I lift up my soul. Comfort, O Lord, the soul of Thy servant, for unto Thee do I lift up my soul, do I lift up my soul.*

30 CHRIST IS RISEN.

1 Cor. xv. 20 ; Rev. v. 13.

J. Goss, Mus. Doc.

CHRIST is risen, *is risen*, from the dead, *Christ is risen, is risen from the dead*, and become the first-fruits of them that slept.

Blessing, and honour, and glory, and power be unto Him that sitteth upon the throne and unto the Lamb. *Christ is risen, Christ is risen, and become the first-fruits of them that slept. Blessing, and honour, and glory, and power be unto Him that sitteth upon the throne and unto the Lamb for ever and ever.* Amen.

31 SLEEPERS, WAKE: A VOICE IS CALLING.

Matt. xxv. 1. *Mendelssohn.*

SLEEPERS, wake: a voice is calling; it is the watchman on the walls, thou city of Jerusalem. For lo, the Bridegroom comes! Arise, and take your lamps. Hallelujah! Awake! His kingdom is at hand. Go forth, *go forth* to meet your Lord.

32 THE LORD IS MY STRENGTH.

Ps. cxviii. 14, 19, 22, 24.

W. H. Monk, Mus. Doc.

THE Lord is my strength, *my strength* and my song, and is become my salvation, *and is become my salvation, and is become, become my salvation.* Open me the gates of righteousness, that I *may go into* them, and give thanks, *give thanks, give thanks* unto the Lord. *The same stone* which the builders refused, *the same stone which the builders refused* is become the head stone in the corner, *is become the head stone in the corner.* This is the day which the Lord hath made ; we will rejoice and be glad in it, *we will rejoice and be glad in it, we will rejoice and be glad in it.* Hallelujah! Amen.

33 O LOVE THE LORD.

Ps. xxxi. 23, 24.

Arthur Sullivan.

O LOVE the Lord, all ye His saints, for the Lord preserveth them that are faithful, and plenteously rewardeth the proud doer, *and plenteously rewardeth the proud doer, rewardeth the proud doer.* (Be strong, and He,) *be strong, and He* shall establish your heart, all ye that put your trust in the Lord, *(and He) and He shall establish your heart, be strong, and He shall establish your heart, be strong, be strong, (be strong, and He shall establish your heart.) O love the Lord, all ye His saints, for the Lord preserveth them that are faithful, and plenteously, and plenteously rewardeth the proud doer. (O love,) O love the Lord, all ye His saints, O love the Lord.* Amen.

34 WHAT ARE THESE THAT ARE ARRAYED?

Rev. vii. 13-17.

J. Stainer, Mus. Doc.

HALLELUJAH! *Hallelujah! Hallelujah!* What are these, *what are these* that are arrayed in white robes, and whence come they? *whence come they?* These are they which came great tribulation, and have their robes and made them the blood of the Lamb, *the the Lamb. These are they ıme out of great tribulation, washed their robes and made te in the blood of thc Lamb, made them white in the blood mb. Hallelujah! Hallelujah! ah!* Therefore are they, *are* ore the throne of God, and im day and night, *day and* His temple. They shall no more, neither thirst any either shall the sun light on or any heat. *They shall no more, neither thirst any* 'or the Lamb which is in the the throne shall feed them, d them, and shall lead them ing fountains of waters; and ıll wipe away all tears, *all* m their eyes, *and God shall ay all tears, all tears from es, all tears from their eyes, from their eyes.*

AVE VERUM.

C. Gounod.

'ord of God incarnate, of the Mary born, on the Cross Thy ody for us men with nails a. Cleanse us by the blood er streaming from Thy piercèd ed us with Thy body broken, l in death's agony. O Jesu, ; O Jesu, spare us; Jesu, n of Mary, O grant us, Lord, rcy, *O grant us, Lord, Thy grant us, O grant us, Lord, rcy.* Amen. *Amen. Amen.*

36 O LORD, MY GOD.

1 Kings viii. 28, 30.

S. S. Wesley, Mus. Doc.

O LORD my God, *O Lord my God,* hear Thou the prayer Thy servant prayeth; have Thou respect unto his prayer, *respect unto his prayer.* Hear Thou in heaven Thy dwelling-place, and when Thou hearest, Lord, forgive. *Hear Thou in heaven Thy dwelling-place, and when Thou hearest, Lord, forgive, and when Thou hearest, Lord, forgive, forgive, forgive, and when Thou hearest, Lord, forgive, forgive, forgive, and when Thou hearest, Lord, forgive.*

37 O LORD, HOW MANIFOLD ARE THY WORKS.

Ps. civ. 24; lxv. 14; ciii. 2.

J. Barnby.

O LORD, how manifold, *how manifold* are Thy works; in wisdom, *in wisdom* hast Thou made them all. *O Lord, how manifold, how manifold are Thy works; in wisdom hast Thou made them all, in wisdom hast Thou made them all.* The earth is full, *the earth is full* of Thy riches. The valleys stand so thick with corn, that they laugh and sing, *they laugh and sing, they laugh and sing, (they laugh and sing, they laugh and sing.) The valleys stand so thick with corn, that they laugh and sing, (they laugh and sing.) they laugh and sing. O Lord, how manifold, how manifold are Thy works; in wisdom, in wisdom hast Thou made them all. O Lord, how manifold, how manifold are Thy works; in wisdom hast thou made* them all, *in wisdom hast thou made them all. The earth is full, the earth is full of Thy riches.* Praise the Lord, O my soul, *Praise the Lord, O my soul,* and forget not all His benefits. *Praise the Lord, O my soul, praise the Lord, O my soul, and forget not all His benefits. Praise the Lord, praise the Lord.*

38 BLESSED ARE THE MERCIFUL.

Matt. v. 7, 3, 8.

H. Hiles, Mus. Doc.

BLESSED are the merciful, for they shall obtain mercy. (O blessed,) *blessed* are the poor in spirit, for theirs is the kingdom, *is the kingdom* of heaven. *Blessed, blessed, blessed are the merciful. Blessed, blessed, blessed, blessed, blessed are the merciful.* Blessed are the pure in heart, *blessed are the pure in heart,* for they shall see God, *they shall see God, God, they shall see God, God, they shall see God ; blessed are the pure in heart, blessed are the pure in heart, blessed are the pure in heart, for they shall see God, for they shall see God, for they shall see God.*

39 IT IS HIGH TIME TO AWAKE OUT OF SLEEP.

Rom. xiii. 11, 12.   *J. Barnby.*

(IT is high time to awake, *to awake* out of sleep,) for now is our salvation nearer than when we believed, *is nearer, nearer. (It is high time to awake, to awake out of sleeep,) for now is our salvation nearer than when we believed; it is high time to awake, to awake out of sleep, it is high time to awake, to*

awake out of sleep, for now is our salvation nearer than when we believed, *now is our salvation nearer than when we believed. It is high time to awake out of sleep.*

The night is far spent, *far spent;* the day is at hand, *the day is at hand.* Let us therefore cast off the works, *the works* of darkness, and let us put on the armour, *the armour* of light. *Let us put on the armour, the armour of light. Let us cast off, cast off the works of darkness, and let us put on the whole armour of light.*

40 REJOICE IN THE LORD.

Ps. xxxiii. 1, 2.

G. J. Elvey, Mus. Doc.

REJOICE, *rejoice, rejoice* in the Lord, *rejoice, rejoice, rejoice, rejoice in the Lord,* O ye righteous ; for it becometh well the just, *for it becometh well the just, the just* to be thankful.

Praise the Lord with harp, *praise the Lord with harp;* sing praises unto Him, *sing praises unto Him, sing praises unto Him, unto Him* with the lute and instrument of ten strings. *Praise the Lord with harp, praise the Lord with harp; sing praises unto Him with the lute, (with the lute,) with the lute and instrument of ten strings. Rejoice, rejoice, rejoice in the Lord, O ye righteous.*

41 HE THAT SHALL ENDURE

Mendelssohn.

HE that shall endure to the end shall be saved. He *that shall endure to the end (shall, shall) shall be saved,* shall be saved, shall be saved, shall be saved, shall be saved. He that shall endure to the end shall be saved. (*He that, he that*) he that shall endure to the end shall be saved, shall be saved, shall be saved, shall be saved.

42 CAST THY BURDEN.

Mendelssohn.

CAST thy burden upon the Lord, and He shall sustain thee ; He will never suffer the righteous to fall ; He is at thy right hand. Thy mercy, Lord, is great, and far above the heavens. Let none be made ashamed that wait upon Thee.

43 O TASTE AND SEE.

Ps. xxxiv. 8, 9, 10.

J. Goss, Mus. Doc.

O TASTE and see how gracious the Lord is ; blessed is the man that trusteth in Him. *O taste and see taste and see, taste and see how gracious the Lord is ; blessed is the man that trusteth in Him. O taste and see how gracious the Lord is ; blessed is the man that trusteth in Him. O taste and see, taste and see, taste and see how gracious the Lord is ; blessed is the man that trusteth in Him.* O fear the Lord, ye that are His saints, for they that fear Him, *that fear Him* lack nothing.

(The lions do lack and suffer hunger ;) but they who seek the Lord, *they who seek the Lord* shall want no manner of thing that is good, *shall want no manner of thing that is good, shall want no manner of thing that is good, no manner of thing that*

is good. *The lions do lack and suffer hunger, and suffer hunger, but they who seek the Lord, they who seek the Lord shall want no manner of thing that is good, shall want no manner of thing that is good, shall want no manner of thing that is good, no manner of thing that is good. O taste and see how gracious the Lord is ; blessed is the man that trusteth in Him.*

44 I WILL LIFT UP MINE EYES.

Ps. cxxi.

J. Clarke-Whitfield, Mus. Doc.

I WILL lift up mine eyes unto the hills, from whence cometh my help. *I will lift up mine eyes unto the hills, from whence cometh my help.* My help cometh even from the Lord, (*my help cometh even from the Lord,*) Who hath made heaven and earth, *Who hath made heaven and earth.*

(The Lord Himself is thy Keeper, *the Lord Himself is thy Keeper;* the Lord is Thy defence upon thy right hand, *the Lord is thy defence upon thy right hand;*) so that the sun shall not burn thee by day, neither the moon by night, *so that the sun shall not burn thee by day. neither the moon by night, neither the moon by night.*

The Lord shall preserve thee from all evil ; yea, it is He that shall keep thy soul. The Lord shall preserve thy going out, (*thy going out,*) and coming in, from this time forth for evermore. *The Lord shall preserve thee from all evil; yea, it is He that shall keep thy soul. Hallelujah!* Amen.

45 O LOVE THE LORD.

Ps. xxxi. 23, 24.

O LOVE the Lord, *O love the Lord, O love the Lord,* all ye His saints; for the Lord preserveth, *preserveth* the faithful, and plentifully rewardeth the proud doer.

Be of good courage, *be of good courage,* and He shall strengthen, *shall strengthen* your heart, all ye that hope, *that hope* in the Lord, *all ye that hope, that hope in the Lord, all ye that hope, that hope in the Lord.*

46 O WORSHIP THE LORD.

Ps. xcvi. 9, 10.   *T. Smith.*

O WORSHIP the Lord in the beauty of holiness, *worship the Lord in the beauty of holiness.* Let the whole earth, *let the whole earth, let the whole earth* stand in awe of Him. *Worship the Lord in the beauty of holiness, worship the Lord, worship the Lord, worship the Lord in the beauty of holiness. Let the whole earth, let the whole earth, let the whole earth, let the whole earth stand in awe of Him.*

(Tell it out among, *tell it out among,*) tell it out among the heathen, *tell it out, tell it out among the heathen* that the Lord, *the Lord* is King. *Tell it out, tell it out among the heathen that the Lord, the Lord is King. Tell it out, tell it out, tell it out, tell it out among the heathen that the Lord, the Lord is King. Tell it out among the heathen that the Lord is King.*

47 O LORD, BOW DOWN.

Ps. xxxi. 1, 2, 16.

Adapted from Himmel.

O LORD, bow down, *bow down* Thine ear to me, *bow down, bow down,* bow down Thine ear to me; make haste make haste to deliver me. *O Lord bow down, bow down Thine ear to me* make haste, make haste to deliver me O save me for Thy mercies' sake, *save me, save me for Thy mercies' sake. O save me for Thy mercies' sake, save me, save me for Thy mercies' sake.*

48 NOW UNTO HIM.

Jude 24, 25.   *L. Mason.*

Now unto Him that is able to keep you, *unto Him that is able to keep you* from falling, and to present you faultless before the presence of His glory with exceeding joy, to the only wise God our Saviour, *to the only wise God our Saviour,* be glory and majesty, dominion and power, *both glory and majesty, dominion and power, both* now and ever, Amen, *both now and ever, Amen.*

49 THE DAY IS GENTLY SINKING.

H. Smart.

THE day is gently sinking to a close,
Fainter and yet more faint the setting light glows;
O brightness of Thy Father's glory, Thou,
Eternal Light of light, be with us now
Where Thou art present, darkness cannot be,
Midnight is glorious noon, O Lord, with Thee.

geful lives are ebbing to an

o darkness and to death we

ror of the grave, be Thou
ide,
 our Light, in death's dark
e ;
ou mortal hour will be no

 in death, no terror in the

o, in darkness walking, didst

e waves, and Thy disciples

rd, in lonesome days, when
assail,
hly hopes and human suc-
ail ;
is dark, may we behold Thee

Thy voice, "Fear not, for it

ry world is mouldering to

s wane, its pageants fade

last sunset, when the stars
ll,
rise, awakened by Thy call,
e, O Lord, for ever to abide
lest day which has no even-
Amen.

ABIDE WITH ME.
J. Barnby.

ith me, fast falls the even-
 darkness deepens, Lord,
abide ; When other helpers
comforts flee, *when other*

helpers fail and comforts flee, Help of
the helpless, *help of the helpless, help
of the helpless*, O abide with me.
(Swift to its close ebbs out life's
little day ; Earth's joys grow dim, its
glories pass away ; Change and decay
in all around I see ; O Thou Who
changest not, abide with me, *O Thou
Who changest not, abide with me.*
I need Thy presence every passing
hour ; What but Thy grace can foil
the tempter's power ? Who like
Thyself my guide and stay can be ?
Through cloud and sunshine, Lord
abide with me.
I fear no foe, with Thee at hand to
bless ; Ills have no weight, and tears
no bitterness ; Where is death's sting ?
where, grave, thy victory ? I triumph
still, if Thou abide with me, *I triumph
still, if Thou abide with me.*)
Hold Thou Thy Cross before my closing eyes ; Shine through the gloom,
and point me to the skies ; Heaven's
morning breaks, and earth's vain
shadows flee, *heaven's morning breaks,
and earth's vain shadows flee, heaven's
morning breaks, and earth's vain
shadows flee ;* In life, in death, abide
with me, *in life, in death,* O Lord,
abide with me. Amen. *Amen.*

51 THE RADIANT MORN HATH
PASSED AWAY.
H. H. Woodward.

THE radiant morn hath passed away,
And spent too soon her golden store ;
The shadows of departing day Creep
on once more, *the shadows of departing day creep on once more.* Our life
is but a fading dawn, Its glorious
noon, *its noon now quickly past ;*

Lead us, O Christ, when all is gone, Safe home at last (*safe home at last*). *Lead us, O Christ, when all is gone, safe home at last, safe home at last.* Where saints are clothed in spotless white, And evening shadows never fall, Where Thou, *where Thou*, Eternal Light of light, Art Lord of all, *art Lord of all. Where saints are clothed in spotless white, and evening shadows never fall, where Thou, Eternal Light of light, art Lord of all, art Lord of all, art Lord of all.*

52 ARISE, SHINE, FOR THY LIGHT IS COME.

Isa. lx. 1-3. *G. J. Elvey, Mus. Doc.*

ARISE, *arise*, shine, for thy light is come, *shine, for thy light is come*, and the glory of the Lord is risen upon thee, *is risen upon thee.*

For, behold, **darkness** shall cover the earth, and gross darkness, *and gross darkness, gross darkness* the people, *gross darkness the people ;* but the Lord shall arise, *the Lord shall arise, the Lord shall arise* upon thee, and His glory shall be seen, *His glory shall be seen, His glory shall be seen* upon thee. And the Gentiles shall come, *shall come* to thy light, and kings to the brightness of thy rising, *and kings to the brightness, the brightness of thy rising. Arise, arise, shine, for thy light is come, shine, for the light is come, thy light is come.*

53 LET US NOW GO.

Luke ii. 15, 10, 11.

E. J. Hopkins, Mus. Doc.

LET us now go even unto Bethlehem, *and see this thing which is come to*

pass, which the Lord hat known, *hath made known* which the Lord hath made made known unto us, which t *hath made known, hath mad unto us. Let us now go ei Bethlehem, and see this thin is come to pass, which the Li made known, hath made known which the Lord hath made made known unto us, which t hath made known unto us.* angel said unto us, Fear i behold, I bring you good ti great joy, which shall be to a people, (*I bring you*) *good ti bring you*) *good tidings, which to all, to all people.* (For un *for unto you* is born this day city of David a Saviour, w Christ the Lord. *I bring tidings of great joy, which sha all people. For unto you is b day, is born in the city of 1 Saviour, which is Christ the Saviour, which is Christ the L*

54 THERE WERE SHEP!

Luke ii. 8-11, 13, 14.

C. Vincent, Mu

THERE were shepherds abidin field, keeping watch, *keepin* over their flocks by night. *were shepherds abiding in tl keeping watch over their fl night.* And, lo ! the angel Lord came upon them, *and, angel of the Lord came upon tl* the glory, *and the glory, and t* of the Lord shone r^{o}und abou and they were sore afraid. *A angel said unto them, Fear n* not, for, behold, I bring you good tidings, *good tidings* of great joy, *good tidings of great joy*, which shall be, *which shall be* to all, *to all* people. For unto you is born this day, *this day* in the city of David, a Saviour, *a Saviour*, which is Christ, *which is Christ* the Lord. And suddenly there was with the angel a multitude of the heavenly host, praising God, *praising God* and saying, Glory to God, *Glory, Glory to God, Glory, Glory to God, Glory to God* in the highest, (and peace on earth, goodwill towards men, *and peace on earth, goodwill towards men, goodwill, goodwill towards men, and peace on earth, goodwill towards men,) and peace on earth, goodwill towards men, goodwill, goodwill towards men, goodwill, goodwill towards men, Glory to God, Glory, Glory to God, Glory, Glory to God, Glory to God* in the highest, *Glory, Glory to God, Glory to God, Glory to God in the highest, Glory to God.*

ADVENT ANTIPHONS.

55 O WISDOM WHICH CAMEST.

J. Kinross.

O WISDOM which camest out of the mouth of the Most High, reaching from one end to another, mightily and sweetly ordering all things, come and show us the way of understanding. Come, Lord Jesus, *Lord Jesus*, come!

56 O LORD AND RULER.

E. Prout.

O LORD and Ruler of the house of Israel, Who *didst appear to Moses* in *a flame of fire in* the bush, (and

gavest him the law,) *and gavest him the law* in Sinai, come, *come* and redeem us, *come and redeem us, come come, come and redeem us* with an outstretched arm, *come and redeem us with an outstretched arm.* Come, Lord Jesus! *come, Lord Jesus!* Come! *come!*

57 ROOT OF JESSE.

M. B. Foster.

O ROOT of Jesse, which standeth for an ensign of the people, at Whom kings shall shut their mouths, *at Whom kings shall shut their mouths*, to Whom the Gentiles shall seek, Come! come and deliver us! Come. and tarry not! Come, Lord Jesus! *Come, Lord Jesus! Come!*

58 O KEY OF DAVID.

M. B. Foster.

O KEY of David and Sceptre of the house of Israel, Thou that openest and no man shutteth, and shuttest and no man openeth, come and bring the prisoner out of his prison-house, who sitteth in darkness and in the shadow of death, *come and bring the prisoner out of his prison-house, who sitteth in darkness and in the shadow of death.*

O Key of David and Sceptre of the house of Israel, come, Lord Jesus! *come, Lord Jesus! come! come, Lord Jesus! come, Lord Jesus! come!*

59 O DAYSPRING.

J. Stainer, Mus. Doc.

O DAYSPRING, O Dayspring, brightness of the everlasting Light,

16

Sun of Righteousness, O Dayspring, *O Dayspring*, come and enlighten them that sit in darkness, *come and enlighten them that sit in darkness* and in the shadow of death. Come, Lord Jesus! *Come, Lord Jesus!* Lord Jesus, come! *come! come!*

60 O KING AND DESIRE.

J. Stainer, Mus. Doc.

O KING and Desire of all nations, Thou Corner-stone, Who hast made both one, come and save man, whom Thou formedst from the clay, *come and save man, whom Thou formedst from the clay, come and save man, whom Thou formedst from the clay.* Come, Lord Jesus, come! *Come, Lord Jesus, come! Come, Lord Jesus, come! Come, Lord Jesus, come!*

61 O EMMANUEL.

J. M. Coward.

O EMMANUEL, *O Emmanuel*, our King and Lawgiver, *King and Lawgiver, O Emmanuel, O Emmanuel, O Emmanuel*, Hope of all nations and their Saviour, come and save us, *come and save us*, O Lord our God, *O Lord our God, come and save us, O Lord our God, (Hope of all nations and their Saviour, come and save us, come and save us, O Lord our God, O Lord our God,) O Lord our God, O Lord our God, our God, (our God,) our God, (come and save us, come and save us,) save us*, O God. Come, Lord Jesus! *Come, Lord Jesus!* Come! *come! come!*

62 O HOLY OF HOLIES.

J. M. Coward.

O HOLY of holies, *O. Holy of holies*, unspotted mirror, *unspotted mirror* of the majesty of God, *of the majesty of God* and image of His bounty, (come and take away, *take away, come and take away,) come and take away* iniquity, *iniquity, iniquity,* (and bring, *and bring, and bring,) and bring, and bring* in everlasting, *and bring in everlasting, and bring in everlasting, everlasting* righteousness. Come, come. Lord Jesus! *Come, come, Lord Jesus! Come, come, Lord Jesus! Come, Lord Jesus! Come, Lord Jesus! Come!*

63 O SHEPHERD OF ISRAEL.

G. A. Macfarren, R.A.M.

(O SHEPHERD of Israel,) *O Shepherd of Israel* and Lord over the house of David, Whose goings forth, *Whose goings forth have been, have been* of old, (*of old,) of old* from everlasting, come and feed Thy people in Thy strength, and rule over them with justice and judgment, *come and feed Thy people in Thy strength, and rule over them in justice and judgment.* (O come,) Lord Jesus! (*O come,) Lord Jesus! (come,) come, (come,) come, (come,) Lord Jesus! come, Lord Jesus! come, come, come, Lord Jesus! come, come, come!*

64 GLORY TO GOD IN THE HIGHEST.

W. Tidd Matson.

GLORY, glory to God in the highest! Angels in chorus joyfully cry;

Glory, glory to God in the highest!
Trembling and weak our voices reply.
Fain would we echo their anthem
above,
Fain would we sing to the Fountain
of love,
Glory to God in the highest!
What though but feebly our accents
arise!
Deigning to hearken, He bends from
the skies—
Glory to God in the highest!

Glory, glory to God in the highest!
Bright-beaming stars of midnight
proclaim;
Glory, glory to God in the highest!
All nature peals forth in praise to
His Name.
Warbles the woodland and whispers
the breeze,
Roar out the torrents and tempest-
tossed seas,
Glory to God in the highest!
Loud His creation, still ceaseless, pro-
longs
Praise to her Maker in all her glad
songs—
Glory to God in the highest!

Glory, glory to God in the highest!
Joining the choir, our tribute we
bring;
Glory, glory to God in the highest!
Mortals, break silence, gratefully sing.
Reigning in majesty, thronèd above,
Yours is the royalest gift of His
love—
Glory to God in the highest!
Spread through creation, His grandeur
we trace,
Only in man He revealeth His grace—
Glory to God in the highest!

65 LORD OF ALL POWER AI
MIGHT.

E. Minshall

LORD of all power and might, W
art the Author and Giver of all g
things, graft in our hearts the love
Thy Name, *graft in our hearts
love of Thy Name*, increase in us t
religion, nourish us with Thy go
ness, and of Thy great mercy keep
in the same, through Jesus Christ
Lord. Amen.

66 PREVENT US, O LORD.

W. Couchman

PREVENT us, O Lord, in all our doin
with Thy most gracious favour, a
further us with Thy continual he
that in all our works, begun, c
tinued, and ended in Thee, we n
glorify Thy holy Name, and fina
by Thy mercy, obtain everlasting li
through Jesus Christ our Lord. Am

67 LET THY MERCIFUL EA
B. Vine Westbrook, F.C.O

LET Thy merciful ear, O Lord,
open.) *be open* to the prayers of T
humble servants, *let Thy merci
ear, O Lord, (be open,) be open to
prayers, the prayers, to the prayers
Thy humble servants;* (and that
may obtain our petitions,) *and t
we may obtain our petitions, and t
we may obtain our petitions.* make
to ask such things as shall ple
Thee, *make us to ask such thing
shall please Thee, make us to ask
16

things as shall please Thee, such things as shall please Thee, through Jesus Christ our Lord, through Jesus Christ our Lord. Amen.

68 GRANT, WE BESEECH THEE.

J. Booth.

GRANT, we beseech Thee. merciful Lord. to Thy faithful people, pardon and peace, *pardon and peace. pardon and peace, to Thy faithful people pardon and peace, pardon and peace, pardon and peace,* (that they may be cleansed from all their sins,) *that they may be cleansed from all their sins, that they may be cleansed from all their sins, be cleansed, be cleansed from all their sins,* and serve Thee with a quiet mind, *and serve thee with a quiet mind,* through Jesus Christ our Lord, *through Jesus Christ our Lord.* Amen. *Amen.*

69 LORD, FOR THY TENDER MERCIES' SAKE.

R. Farrant.

LORD, for Thy tender mercies' sake, lay not our sins to our charge ; but forgive that is past, and give us grace to amend our sinful lives : to decline from sin and incline to virtue : (that we may walk, *that we,) that we may walk* with a perfect heart. *that we may walk with a perfect heart* before Thee now and evermore. *(that we may walk; that we,) that we may walk with a perfect heart, that we may walk with a perfect heart before Thee now and evermore.*

70 ALMIGHTY GOD, UNTO WHOM.

J. Kinross.

ALMIGHTY God, unto Whom all hearts are known, all desires manifest. and from Whom no secrets are hid. cleanse the thoughts of our hearts by the inspiration of Thy Holy Spirit. that we may perfectly love Thee and worthily magnify Thy holy Name. through Christ our Lord, *through Christ our Lord.* Amen. *Amen.*

71 WE BOW IN PRAYER.

W. B. Bradbury.

WE bow in prayer before Thy throne, O God. Help us to worship Thee, *to worship Thee* in spirit and in truth. Help us to pray, help us to praise, and hear Thy word. Look down, O Lord, in mercy upon us, and blot out all our transgressions. O hear our prayer, accept our praise, forgive and bless us, for Jesus' sake, *forgive and bless us, for Jesus' sake.* Amen.

72 THOU KNOWEST, LORD.

H. Purcell.

THOU knowest, Lord. the secrets of our hearts. Shut not, *shut not* Thy merciful ears unto our prayer, but spare us, Lord, *spare us, Lord* most holy. O God, *O God* most mighty. O holy and most merciful Saviour, Thou most worthy Judge eternal, suffer us not, *suffer us not* at our last hour, for any pains of death, *for any pains of death, to fall, to fall from Thee* Amen.

73 TE DEUM LAUDAMUS.

H. Smart.

WE praise Thee, O God ; we acknowledge Thee to be the Lord. All the
earth doth worship Thee, the Father
everlasting. To Thee all angels cry
aloud, the heavens and all the powers
therein. To Thee cherubin and sera-
phin continually do cry, Holy, holy,
holy, Lord God of Sabaoth ! Heaven
and earth are full of the majesty of
Thy glory. (The glorious company
of the apostles) praise Thee ; (the
goodly fellowship of the prophets)
praise Thee ; (the noble army of
martyrs) praise Thee ; the holy
Church throughout all the world
doth acknowledge Thee, the Father
of an infinite majesty, Thine honourable, true, and only Son, also the
Holy Ghost, the Comforter.

Thou art the King of Glory, O
Christ ; Thou art the everlasting Son
of the Father. When Thou tookest
upon Thee to deliver man, Thou
didst not abhor the Virgin's womb.
When Thou hadst overcome the sharpness of death, Thou didst open the
kingdom of heaven to all believers.
Thou sittest at the right hand of
God, in the glory of the Father. We
believe that Thou shalt come to be
our Judge. We therefore pray Thee,
help Thy servants, whom Thou hast
redeemed with Thy precious blood.
Make them to be numbered with Thy
saints in glory everlasting. O Lord,
save Thy people, and bless Thine heritage. Govern them, and lift them up
forever. Day by day we magnify
Thee, and we worship Thy Name ever
world *without* end. Vouchsafe, O

Lord, to keep us this day without sin.
O Lord, have mercy upon us ; *have
mercy upon us.* O Lord, let Thy
mercy lighten upon us, as our trust
is in Thee. O Lord, in Thee, *in Thee*
have I trusted ; let me never be
confounded.

74 TE DEUM LAUDAMUS.

G. M. Garrett, Mus. Doc.

WE praise Thee, O God ; we acknowledge Thee to be the Lord. All the
earth doth worship Thee, the Father
everlasting. To Thee all angels cry
aloud, the heavens and all the powers
therein. To Thee cherubin and sera-
phin continually do cry, Holy, holy,
holy, Lord God of Sabaoth ! Heaven
and earth are full of the majesty of
Thy glory ; the glorious company of
the apostles praise Thee ; the goodly
fellowship of the prophets praise
Thee ; the noble army of martyrs
praise Thee ; the holy Church throughout all the world doth acknowledge
Thee, the Father, of an infinite majesty,
Thine honourable, true, and only Son,
also the Holy Ghost, the Comforter.
Thou art the King of Glory, *the King
of Glory*, O Christ ; Thou art the
everlasting Son of the Father. When
Thou tookest upon Thee to deliver
man, Thou didst not abhor the
Virgin's womb. When Thou hadst
overcome the sharpness of death,
Thou didst open the kingdom of
heaven, *of heaven* to all believers.
Thou sittest at the right hand of
God, in the glory of the Father.

We believe that Thou shalt come
be our Judge. We therefore

Thee, help Thy servants, whom Thou hast redeemed with Thy precious blood. Make them to be numbered with Thy saints in glory everlasting. O Lord, save Thy people and bless Thine heritage. Govern them and lift them up, *lift them up* for ever. Day by day, *day by day* we magnify Thee, and we worship Thy Name, *Thy Name* ever world without end. Vouchsafe, O Lord, to keep us this day without sin. O Lord, have mercy upon us; *have mercy upon us.* O Lord, let Thy mercy lighten, *lighten* upon us, as our trust is in Thee. O Lord, in Thee have I trusted; let me never be confounded.

75 JUBILATE DEO.

G. M. Garrett, Mus. Doc.

O BE joyful in the Lord, all ye lands, serve the Lord with gladness, and come before His presence with a song. Be ye sure that the Lord, He is God; it is He that hath made us, and not we ourselves; we are His people, (*we are His people,*) and the sheep of His pasture, *and the sheep of His pasture.* O go your way into His gates with thanksgiving, and into His courts, *His courts* with praise. Be thankful unto Him, *be thankful unto Him,* and speak good of His Name. For the Lord, *the Lord* is gracious. His mercy is everlasting, and His truth endureth, *His truth endureth* from generation to generation. Glory be to the Father, and to the Son, and to *the Holy Ghost,* · as it was in the *beginning, is* now, and ever shall be, *ever shall be,* world without end. *Amen.*

76 MAGNIFICAT.

J. Baptiste Calkin.

MY soul doth magnify the Lord. and my spirit hath rejoiced in God my Saviour, for He hath regarded the lowliness, *the lowliness, the lowliness* of His handmaiden. (For behold, from henceforth, *for behold, from henceforth,*) *for behold, from henceforth* all generations, *all generations* shall call me blessed. For He that is mighty hath magnified me, and holy, *holy* is His Name. And His mercy is on them that fear Him throughout all generations. He hath shewed strength with His arm, *He hath shewed strength with His arm,* He hath scattered the proud in the imagination of their hearts. He hath put down the mighty from their seat, and hath exalted the humble and meek. He hath filled the hungry with good things, (and the rich He hath sent empty away).

He, remembering His mercy, hath holpen His servant Israel, as He promised our forefathers, Abraham and his seed for ever, *for ever, for ever.* Glory be to the Father, and to the Son, and to the Holy Ghost, as it was in the beginning. is now, and ever shall be, *as it was in the beginning, as it was in the beginning, is now, and ever shall be,* world without end. Amen.

77 NUNC DIMITTIS.

J. Baptiste Calkin.

LORD, now lettest Thou Thy servant depart in peace, according to Thy word, *according to Thy word.* For mine eyes have seen, *have seen* Thy salvation, which Thou hast prepared before the face of all people, to be a light to lighten the Gentiles, and to be the glory, *the glory* of Thy people Israel.

Glory be to the Father, and to the Son, and to the Holy Ghost, as it was in the beginning, is now, and ever shall be, world without end. Amen, *world without end. Amen. Amen.*

78　　MAGNIFICAT.

E. Bunnett, Mus. Doc.

MY soul doth magnify the Lord, and my spirit hath rejoiced in God my Saviour, *for He hath regarded the lowliness, *the lowliness* of His handmaiden. For, behold, from henceforth all generations shall call me blessed. For He that is mighty hath magnified me, and holy, *holy* is His Name. And His mercy is on them that fear Him throughout all generations. He hath shewed strength, *shewed strength* with His arm. He hath scattered the proud in the imagination of their hearts. · He hath put down the mighty from their seat, and hath exalted the humble and meek. He hath filled the hungry with good things, and the rich He hath sent empty away. He, remembering His mercy, hath holpen His servant Israel, as He promised to our fore-fathers, Abraham and his seed for ever. Glory be to the Father, and to the Son, and to the Holy Ghost, as it was in the beginning, is now, and ever shall be, world without end. Amen.

79　　NUNC DIMITTIS.

E. Bunnett, Mus. Doc

LORD, now lettest Thou Thy serv depart in peace, *in peace*, accord to Thy word. For mine eyes h seen, *have seen* Thy salvation, wh Thou hast prepared before the f of all people, to be a light to ligh the Gentiles and to be the glory Thy people Israel.

Glory be to the Father, and to Son, and to the Holy Ghost, as it v in the beginning, is now, and e shall be, world without end. Ame

80　　CANTATE DOMINO.

E. Bunnett, Mus. Doc

O SING unto the Lord a new so: for He hath done, *hath done* marv lous things. With His own rig hand and with His holy arm hath gotten Himself the victory. 1 Lord declared His salvation; l righteousness hath He openly shev in the sight of the heathen. He h remembered His mercy and tru toward the house of Israel, and the ends of the world have seen, h *seen* the salvation of our God. Sh yourselves joyful unto the Lord, ye lands, sing, rejoice, and give than Praise the Lord upon the harp; si to the harp with a psalm of than giving, with trumpets also a shawms, *with trumpets also a shawms.* O shew yourselves jo before the Lord the King. Le sea make a noise, and all that therein is, the round world and they that dwell therein. Let the floods clap their hands, and let the hills be joyful together before the Lord, *before the Lord*, for He cometh to judge the earth; with righteousness shall He judge the world, and the people with equity, *the people with equity, the people, the people with equity.*

Glory be to the Father, and to the Son, and to the Holy Ghost, as it was in the beginning, is now, and ever shall be, world without end. Amen.

81 DEUS MISEREATUR.

E. Bunnett, Mus. Doc.

GOD be merciful unto us, and bless us, and shew us the light of His countenance, and be merciful unto us, that Thy way may be known upon earth, Thy saving health among all nations. Let the people praise Thee, *praise Thee*, O God; yea, let all the people praise Thee. O let the nations rejoice and be glad, for Thou shalt judge, *shalt judge* the folk righteously, and govern the nations upon earth. *Let the people praise Thee, praise Thee, O God; yea, let all the people praise Thee.* Then shall the earth bring forth her increase, and God, even our own God, shall give us His blessing. God shall bless us, *God shall bless us*, and all the ends of the world shall fear, *shall fear* Him.

Glory be to the Father, and to the Son, and to the Holy Ghost, as it was *in the beginning*, is now, and ever *shall be, world* without end. Amen.

82 LIFT UP YOUR HE

J. i

(LIFT up your hearts.) We up unto the Lord. (Let thanks unto the Lord our is meet, *meet* and right so to is very meet, right, and our duty, that we should at and in all places give thar Thee, O Lord, holy Father everlasting God,) *holy Fati lasting God.*

Therefore, with angels a angels and all the company o we laud and magnify Thy Name, *we laud and magn glorious Name, therefore, wi and archangels and all the co heaven, (we magnify Thy Thy glorious Name,) we mag glorious, Thy glorious Name, nify Thy glorious,) we maqi glorious Name, therefore, wit and archangels and all the of heaven, we laud and magn and magnify Thy glorious Na* more, *evermore* praising Th *more, evermore praising, prais evermore praising Thee* and sa

Holy, holy, holy, Lord God heaven, and earth, *heaven a* are full of Thy glory. Glo Thee, O Lord, *to Thee, O Lord. Amen. Amen.*

83 SANCTUS.

T. L. I

HOLY, holy, holy, Lord God c heaven and earth are full

majesty, *the majesty* of Thy glory.
Glory be to Thee, *glory be to Thee*, O
Lord most high. Amen.

84 SANCTUS.
J. Camidge, Mus. Doc.

HOLY, holy, holy, Lord God of hosts,
heaven and earth are full of Thy
glory. Glory be to Thee, O Lord
most high. Amen.

85 SANCTUS.
T. Attwood.

HOLY. holy, holy, Lord God of hosts,
heaven and earth are full of the
majesty, *the majesty* of Thy great
glory. Glory be to Thee, *glory be to
Thee*, *glory be to Thee*, O Lord most
high. Amen.

86 REJOICE GREATLY.
Zech. ix. 9 ; St. Matt. xxi. 9 ;
Malachi iii. 2 ; Ps. xx. 9.
H. H. Woodward, M.A.

REJOICE greatly, O daughter of Sion :
behold, thy King cometh unto thee,
*rejoice, rejoice, behold thy King cometh
unto Thee.* He is just, and having
salvation, *He is just, and having salvation,* Hosanna to the Son of David.
Blessed is He that cometh in the
name of the Lord. But who may
abide the day of His coming ? and
who shall stand when He appeareth ?
Save, Lord, and hear us, O King of
Heaven, when we call upon Thee.

87 SING AND REJOICE.
Zech. ii. 10-13. *J. Barnby.*

SING and rejoice, O daughter of Sion,
sing, sing, *O sing and rejoice, sing and*
rejoice, O daughter of Sion, sing, sing,
O sing and rejoice, (for lo, lo, I come,
saith the Lord), *lo, lo, I come, saith
the Lord,* (and I will dwell in the
midst of thee), *will dwell in the midst
of thee,* saith the Lord thy God, (*lo, I
come, and I will dwell in the midst of
thee*), *saith the Lord thy God,* Sing
and rejoice, O daughter of Sion, *sing,
sing, O sing and rejoice, sing and
rejoice, O daughter of Sion, sing, sing,
O sing and rejoice.* Be silent, silent,
O all flesh, before the Lord, *before the
Lord,* for He is raised up, *is raised up*
out of His holy habitation, *Be silent,
silent, O all flesh, before the Lord,
before the Lord,* (*for He is raised up,
is raised up*), *out of His holy habitation, out of His holy habitation.* Sing
and rejoice, O daughter of Sion, *sing,
sing, O sing and rejoice, sing and
rejoice, O daughter of Sion, sing, sing,
O sing and rejoice,* (*for lo, lo, I come
saith the Lord*), *lo, lo, I come, saith the
Lord, I will dwell in the midst of thee,
will dwell in the midst of Thee, saith
the Lord thy God.* O come all ye
faithful, joyful and triumphant ; O
come ye, *O come ye* to Bethlehem ;
Come and behold Him, Born the King
of angels ; O come let as adore Him,
*O come let us adore Him, O come let us
adore Him,* Christ the Lord. Amen.

88 O ZION, THAT BRINGEST GOOD TIDINGS.
J. Stainer, Mus. Doc.

ALLELUIA, *Alleluia, Alleluia.* O
Zion, that bringest good tidings, get
thee up, *get thee up* into the high
mountain. *Alleluia, Alleluia, Alleluia.* O Jerusalem that bringes
good tidings, lift up thy voice,

voice with strength ; *lift up thy voice,* be not afraid, *lift up thy voice, be not, be not afraid :* Say to the cities of Judah, Behold your God, *your God, Behold your God. Alleluia, Alleluia, Alleluia. Lift up thy voice, be not afraid, lift up thy voice, be not afraid. Alleluia, Alleluia, Amen.* O that birth for ever blessed, when the Virgin, full of grace, By the Holy Ghost conceiving, Bare the Saviour of our race, And the Babe, the worlds Redeemer, first reveal'd His sacred face, evermore and evermore. (Of the Father's Love begotten ere the world s began to be, He is Alpha and Omega, He the source, the ending He, of the things that are, that have been, and that future years shall see, *evermore and evermore.) Alleluia,* etc.

89 CHRISTIANS, AWAKE.

J. Barnby.

CHRISTIANS, awake, salute the happy morn, whereon the Saviour of mankind was born ; Rise to adore the mystery of love, which hosts of angels, *hosts of angels, which hosts of angels* chanted from above ; with them the joyful tidings first begun of God incarnate, *God incarnate, God incarnate* of the Virgin's Son, *the Virgin's Son.*

Oh ! may we keep and ponder in our mind, *Oh ! may we keep and ponder in our mind* God's wondrous love in saving lost mankind, *God's wondrous love in saving lost mankind, saving lost mankind ;* Trace we the *babe, who* hath retrieved our loss, *race we the babe, who hath retrieved*

our loss, from the poor manger to the bitter Cross, *from the poor manger to the bitter Cross, bitter bitter Cross ;* Tread in His steps assisted by His grace, *His grace,* Till man's first heavenly state again takes place. Then may we hope, th' angelic hosts among, to join redeemed, a glad triumphant throng. He that was born upon this joyful day around us all His glory shall display, *around us all His glory shall display ;* Saved by His love, incessant we shall sing, eternal praise to heaven's *to heaven's* Almighty King, *saved by His love, incessant we shall sing, incessant we shall sing, incessant we shall sing, shall sing, eternal praise, eternal praise to heaven's, to heaven's Almighty King.* Amen.

90 SING, O HEAVENS.

Isa. xlix. 13 ; St. Luke ii. 11 ; St. Matt. xxi. 9 ; &c.

Berthold Tours.

SING, O heavens, *sing, O heavens,* and be joyful, O earth, *sing, O heavens, sing, O heavens, and be joyful, O earth ;* and break forth into singing, *and break forth into singing,* O mountains, O mountains, O mountains, *Sing, O heavens, sing, O heavens, and be joyful, O earth, O earth, O earth, and be joyful, O earth, sing, O heavens, and be joyful, O earth, sing, O heavens, and be joyful, be joyful, be joyful, be joyful, O earth.*

For unto us is born this day in the city of David a Saviour, which is *Christ the Lord, which is Christ the*

Lord. Hosanna, *Hosanna, Hosanna* to the Son of David. Blessed is He, *blessed is He, blessed is He* that cometh in the name *in the name* of the Lord, *in the name of the Lord.* (*Blessed is He that cometh,*) *Blessed is He that cometh, is He that cometh, blessed is He, is He, is He, He that cometh in the name of the Lord.* Hosanna, *Hosanna, Hosanna* in the highest, To God on high be glory, *to God on high be glory, to God be glory, to God be glory,* and peace on earth to men, *to God on high be glory, to God on high be glory, to God, to God on high, to God to God on high, to God on high, to God on high, to God on high, to God be glory.* O come all ye faithful, joyful and triumphant, O come ye, O come ye to Bethlehem; Come and behold Him born the King of Angels : O come let us adore Him, O come let us adore Him, O come let us adore Him, Christ the Lord. Amen.

91 CHRIST BEING RAISED FROM THE DEAD.

Sir G. Elvey.

CHRIST being raised from the dead, *Christ being raised from the dead, Christ being raised from the dead,* dieth no more, *dieth no more, dieth no more, dieth no more, dieth no more, no more,* Death hath no more dominion over Him, *death hath no more dominion over Him, death hath no more dominion over Him, death hath no more, no more dominion over Him, death hath no more dominion over Him, no more dominion over Him.*

92 I WILL SING OF THE MERCIES OF THE LORD.

J. Booth.

I WILL sing of the mercies of the Lord, *I will sing of the mercies of the Lord, of the mercies of the Lord for ever, I will sing, I will sing, I will sing, I will sing,* with my mouth will I make known Thy faithfulness, *Thy faithfulness to* all generations, *to all generations.* And the heavens shall praise Thy wonders, O Lord, *and the heavens shall praise Thy wonders, O Lord, the heavens shall praise Thy wonders, O Lord,* (O Lord God, Lord God of Hosts, who is a strong Lord like unto Thee ?) *who is a strong Lord like unto Thee ?* Thou rulest the raging of the sea, *Thou rulest the raging of the sea* when the waves thereof arise, *when the waves thereof arise, when the waves thereof, the waves thereof arise,* Thou stillest them, *Thou stillest them, Thou stillest them.*

I will sing of the mercies of the Lord, I will sing of the mercies of the Lord, with my mouth will I make known Thy faithfulness, with my mouth will I make known Thy faithfulness, Thy faithfulness to all, to all generations.

For the Lord is our defence, *for the Lord is our defence,* and the Holy One of Israel is our King, *and the Holy One of Israel is our King.*

93 AWAKE UP, MY GLORY.

Ps. lvii. 9 ; Ps. cxviii. 24 ;
1 Cor. xv. 20 and 57.

J. Barnby.

AWAKE up, my glory, awake late my harp, awake up, my glory, awake and harp, awake up, my glory, awake, lute and harp, awake up, my glory, awake, lute and harp. I myself will awake right early, *I myself will awake right early, I myself will awake right early, I will awake right early.* (This is the day which the Lord hath made,) *this is the day which the Lord hath made,* we will rejoice and be glad, *we will rejoice and be glad, be glad* in it ; *This is the day the Lord hath made, this is the day the Lord hath made, we will rejoice, we will rejoice, this is the day the Lord hath made, we will rejoice.* Awake up, my glory, awake, lute and harp, awake up, my glory, awake, lute and harp, *I myself will awake right early, I myself will awake right early, I myself will awake right early, I myself will awake right early.* (For now is Christ risen from the dead, and become the first fruits of them that slept, *now is Christ risen from the dead, and become the first fruits of them that slept*) ; *Christ is risen from the dead.* Thanks, thanks be to God, *thanks be to God, thanks be to God, thanks be to God,* which giveth us the victory, *giveth us the victory, which giveth us the victory* through our Lord Jesus Christ. All praise be Thine, O risen Lord, from death to endless life restored, all praise to God the Father be. and Holy Ghost eternally. Amen. *Amen.*

94 THEY HAVE TAKEN AWAY MY LORD.

St. John xx. 13, 15, 16.
1 Cor. xv. 55, 57.

J. Stainer, Mus. Doc.

THEY have taken away my Lord, and know not where they have laid Him.

(Woman, why weepest thou?) Because *they have taken away my Lord, and I know not where they have laid Him.* (*Woman, why weepest thou? whom* seekest thou?) Sir, if thou have borne Him hence, tell me where thou hast laid Him, *tell me where thou hast laid Him.* (Mary!) Master! O Death. where is thy sting? O Grave, where is thy victory? Thanks be to God. *thanks be to God,* Hallelujah, *thanks be to God,* who giveth us the victory. *who giveth us the victory* through our Lord Jesus Christ. O death, where is thy sting? O death, where is thy sting! O death, O grave, where is thy victory. where is thy victory? Thanks be to God, Hallelujah, thanks be to God. who giveth us the victory, who giveth us the victory through our Lord Jesus Christ. Amen. Hallelujah, Hallelujah, Hallelujah. Amen.

95 BREAK FORTH INTO JOY.

Isa. lii. 9-10.   *J. Barnby.*

BREAK forth into joy, *break forth into joy ;* sing together. ye waste places of Jerusalem, *break forth into joy, break forth into joy ; sing together, ye waste places of Jerusalem :* for the Lord hath comforted His people. *for the Lord hath comforted His people.* Break forth into joy, break forth into joy, He hath redeemed Jerusalem. (*He hath redeemed Jerusalem,*) *sing together ye waste places of Jerusalem : for He hath redeemed Jerusalem.* (The Lord hath made bare His holy arm in the sight of all His people,) *Break forth into joy, break forth into joy; sing together ye waste places of Jerusalem, (The Lord hath made bare His* *holy arm, The Lord hath made bare His holy arm, The Lord hath made bare His holy arm), The Lord hath made bare His holy arm in the sight of all the people.* Break forth into joy, break forth into joy ; sing together, ye waste places of Jerusalem, break forth into joy, break forth into joy, the Lord hath comforted and redeemed His people, und hath made bare His holy arm in the sight of all people.* Hymns of praise then let us sing, Alleluia, unto Christ, our heavenly King, Alleluia, Who endured the Cross and grave, Alleluia, Sinners to redeem and save, Alleluia. Amen.

96 IF WE BELIEVE THAT JESUS DIED.

1 Thess. iv. 14-18.

Edward Bunnett, Mus. Doc.

IF we believe that Jesus died and rose again, *if we believe that Jesus died and rose again,* even so them also, *even so them also* which sleep in Jesus, *which sleep in Jesus* will God bring with Him, *will God bring with Him.* For this we say unto you by the word of the Lord, that we which are alive and remain unto the coming of the Lord, shall not prevent them, *shall not prevent them* which are asleep, *shall not prevent them which are asleep, which are asleep.* For the Lord Himself shall descend from heav'n with a shout, with the voice of the Archangel, and with the trump of God : and the dead in Christ shall rise first, *the dead in Christ shall rise first.* Then we which are alive and remain shall be caught up together *with them in the clouds,* to meet the

Lord in the air, *to meet the Lord in the air :* so shall we ever be with the Lord, *so shall we ever be with the Lord.*

Wherefore comfort, *comfort* one another with these words, *with these words, wherefore comfort, comfort one another with these words, wherefore comfort one another with these words, with these words, wherefore comfort, comfort one another with these words, with these words, comfort one another with these words.*

97 THE EYES OF ALL WAIT ON THEE.

Ps. cxlv. 15, 16 ; cxlvii. 14 ; cxlv. 1.

G. J. Elvey.

(THE eyes of all wait on Thee, O Lord, and Thou givest them their meat in due season.) *The eyes of all wait on Thee, O Lord, and Thou givest them their meat in due season.* Thou openest Thine hand, *Thou openest Thine hand,* and fillest all things living with plenteousness, *Thou openest Thine hand, Thou openest Thine hand, and fillest all things living with plenteousness, and fillest all things living with plenteousness, the eyes of all wait on Thee. O Lord, and Thou givest them their meat, Thou givest them their meat in due season. Thou openest Thine hand, Thou openest Thine hand. and fillest all things, and fillest all things, and fillest all things living with plenteousness, fillest all things living with plenteousness.*

He maketh peace, peace in thy borders, and filleth thee with the flour of wheat, filleth thee with th flour of wheat. He maketh peace, peace, peace, peace, He maketh peace, peace in thy borders, and filleth Thee with the flour of wheat, He maketh peace, p'ace, peace, He maketh peace, peace, peace. I will magnify Thee, O Lord, and will praise Thy Name for ever and ever, *I will magnify Thee, O Lord, and praise Thy Name for ever and ever, I will praise Thy Name, will praise Thy Name for ever and ever, I will magnify Thee, O Lord, Hallelujah, Hallelujah, Hallelujah, Hallelujah, Hallelujah, Hallelujah, Hallelujah, Amen, Hallelujah, Amen, Hallelujah, Amen, Hallelujah, Amen.*

98 PRAISE THE LORD, O JERUSALEM.

Ps. cxlvii. 12, 13 ;
cxlv. 8-10 ; lxv. 14.

J. H. Maunder.

PRAISE the Lord, O Jerusalem, praise thy God. O Zion, *praise the Lord, praise the Lord, praise thy God, O Zion, praise the Lord, O Jerusalem, praise thy God, O Zion, praise thy God, O Zion.* For He hath made fast the bars of thy gates, and hath blessed thy children within thee, *He hath made fast the bars of thy gates, and hath blessed thy children within thee. Praise the Lord, O Jerusalem, praise thy God, O Zion, praise thy God, O Zion.* The Lord is gracious, and full of compassion, slow to anger, and of great goodness. The Lord is good, *is good* to all, and His tender mercies, *His tender mercies* are over *all, are over all* His works. All Thy works praise Thee, *praise Thee, O Lord, all Thy works praise Thee,*

praise Thee, O Lord, and Thy saints give thanks, *give thanks* unto Thee, *all Thy works praise thee, all Thy works.* The valleys stand so thick with corn, that they laugh and sing. *(the valleys stand so thick with corn, that they laugh and sing, that they laugh and sing), the valleys stand so thick with corn, that they laugh and sing, the valleys stand so thick with corn, the valleys stand so thick with corn, the valleys stand so thick with corn, that they laugh and sing, they laugh and sing, they laugh and sing, they sing. Praise the Lord, O Jerusalem, praise thy God, O Zion, praise the Lord, praise the Lord, praise thy God, O Zion, praise the Lord, O Jerusalem, praise thy God, O Zion, praise thy God, O Zion, praise the Lord, praise the Lord,* Amen.

99 OH! FOR A CLOSER WALK WITH GOD.

Myles B. Foster.

OH ! for a closer walk with God, a calm and heavenly frame ! A light to shine upon the road that leads me to the Lamb ! *Oh! for a closer walk with God, a calm and heav'nly frame! A light to shine upon the road that leads me to the Lamb.* What peaceful hours I once enjoyed ! How sweet their mem'ry still ! But they have left an aching void, *an aching void the world can never fill, the world can never fill.* Return, O holy Dove ! *return, return,* sweet messenger of rest ! I hate the sins *that made* Thee mourn, and drove Thee from my breast. The dearest idol I have known, whate'er that idol be, Help it from Thy throne, *to tear y throne,* and worship only *ate the sins that made Thee ! drove Thee from my breast. holy Dove, return, return, :enger of rest return.* So walk be close with God, serene .ny frame, so purer mark tne road that leads Lamb. *So shall my walk :h God, calm and serene my purer light shall mark the leads me to the Lamb. So valk be close with God, So walk be close with God, be God.* Amen.

)ME, HOLY GHOST.

T. Attwood.

ly Ghost, our souls inspire, n with celestial fire, Thou ting Spirit art, Who dost nfold gifts impart. Thy iction from above, Is com- nd fire of love, *Is comfort, fire of love.* Enable with light, The dulness of our ;ht; Anoint and cheer our e, With the abundance of :. Keep far our foes, give . home, Where Thou art il: can come; *Where Thou no ill can come.* s to know the Father, Son, of both to be but one, That the ages all along, This our endless song; Praise ternal merit, Father, Son. . Spirit, *Father, Son, and 'it.*

101 IF YE LOVE ME, KEEP MY COMMANDMENTS.

St. John xiv. 15, 16. *T. Tallis.*

IF ye love Me, keep My command- ments, and I will pray the Father, and He shall give you another Com- forter, that He may abide with you for ever. Ev'n the Spirit of Truth, *Ev'n the Spirit of Truth, that He may abide with you for ever, Ev'n the Spirit of Truth, Ev'n the Spirit of Truth.*

102 SWEET IS THY MERCY.

J. Barnby.

SWEET is Thy mercy, Lord! Before Thy mercy seat, My soul adoring pleads Thy word, and owns Thy mercy sweet, Where'er Thy name is blest, Where'er Thy people meet, There I delight in Thee to rest, And find Thy mercy sweet, *and find Thy mercy sweet, Thy mercy sweet,* Light Thou our weary way, our wand'ring feet; That while we stay on earth we may Still find Thy mercy sweet. Thus shall the heav'nly host Hear all our songs repeat, To Father, Son, and Holy Ghost, *to Father, Son, and Holy Ghost; Thy mercy sweet, Our joy, our joy, Thy mercy sweet. Amen, Amen.*

103 REMEMBER NOW THY CREATOR.

Eccles. xii. 1, 2, 3, 4, 7, 8.

C. Steggall, Mus. Doc.

REMEMBER now thy Creator in the days of thy youth, *Remember now thy Creator in the days of thy youth. re- member now thy Creator in the days of thy youth*, while the evil days come not, nor the years draw nigh, when thou shalt say, I have no pleasure in them, *I have no pleasure in them, no pleasure, I have no pleasure in them. Remember, remember, remember now thy Creator in the days of thy youth, remember now thy Creator in the days of thy youth, while the evil days come not, nor the years draw nigh when thou shalt say, I have no pleasure in them, I have no pleasure in them, no pleasure, no pleasure, I have no pleasure in them, no pleasure in them, I have no pleasure in them.* While the sun, or the light, or the moon, or the stars, be not darkenèd, Nor the clouds return after the rain : In the day when the keepers of the house shall tremble, and the strong men shall bow themselves, and the grinders cease because they are few, and those that look out of the windows be darkenèd, And the doors shall be shut in the streets, when the sound of the grinding is low, and he shall rise up at the voice of the bird, *of the bird*, and all the daughters of music shall be brought low. (Then shall the dust return to the earth as it was, and the spirit shall return unto God who gave it.) Vanity, *vanity*, vanity of vanities, saith the preacher. All, *all is vanity, all, all is vanity, vanity, all is vanity, all is vanity, is vanity, (all is vanity), all, all is vanity, all, all is vanity, all is vanity, all is vanity, all is vanity, all is vanity, saith the preacher, vanity of vanities, all is vanity. Remember now thy Creator in the days of thy youth, remember now thy Creator in the days of thy youth.*

104 TEACH ME, O LORD.

Ps. cxix. 33-36, 40. *G. J. Elvey.*

TEACH me, O Lord, the way of Thy statutes, and I shall keep it unto the end, *teach me, O Lord, the way of Thy statutes, and I shall keep it unto the end.* Give me understanding, *give me understanding, and I shall keep* Thy law, yea, I shall observe it with my whole.heart. Make me to go in the path of Thy commandments, for therein do I delight, Incline my heart. *incline my heart* unto Thy testimonies, and not to covetousness. Behold, I have longed after Thy precepts. quicken me in Thy righteousness, *Thy righteousness, (quicken me) quicken me in Thy righteousness, Thy righteousness, quicken me, quicken me, in Thy righteousness.*

105 LEAD ME, LORD.

Ps. v. 8 ; iv. 9. *S. S. Wesley.*

(LEAD me, Lord, lead me in Thy righteousness, make Thy way plain before my face.) *Lead me, Lord, (Lord) lead me in Thy righteousness, make Thy way plain before my face.* (For it is Thou, Lord, *Lord*, only, that makest me dwell in safety.) *Thou, For it is Thou, Lord, Thou, Lord, only, that makest me dwell in safety.*

106 BELOVED, IF GOD SO LOVED US.

1 John iv. 11, 21. • *J. Barnby.*

BELOVED, if God so loved us, we ought also to love one another, *we ought also to love one another, Beloved, if God so loved us, Beloved, if God so loved us, we ought also to love, also to*

love, *also to love one another.* And
this commandment have we from
Him, *this commandment have we from
Him,* That he who loveth God, *he
who loveth God,* love his brother also,
*love his brother also, Beloved, if God
so loved us, we ought also to love one
another.*

107 O PRAISE THE LORD.

Ps. cxxxv. 1, 2, 3, 19, 20.

Sir J. Goss.

O PRAISE the Lord, laud ye the name
of the Lord ; praise it, O ye servants of
the Lord. (Ye that stand in the
house of the Lord), *Ye that stand in
the house of the Lord,* in the courts of
the house of our God. *O praise the
Lord,* for the Lord is gracious, O sing
praises, *sing praises, sing praises, sing
praises* unto His Name, *sing praises,
sing praises unto His Name,* for it is
lovely, *is lovely. Praise the Lord, ye
house of* Israel : *Praise the Lord, ye
house of* Aaron : *Praise the Lord, ye
house of* Levi : Ye that fear *the Lord,
praise the Lord, praise the Lord.*

108 O THAT I KNEW.

Job xxiii. 3, 8, 9 ; John xx. 29.

Sir W. S. Bennett.

O THAT I knew where I might find
Him ! that I might come even to His
seat ! *O that I knew where I might
find Him ! that I might come even to
His seat !* Behold I go forward,
(but He is not there), and backward,
but I cannot perceive Him, *Behold I
go forward, but He is not there ; and
backward, but I cannot perceive Him,*

I cannot perceive Him : (On the left
hand) where He doth work, *on the
left hand where He doth work,* but I
cannot behold Him, *I cannot behold
Him :* He hideth Himself on the right
hand, *He hideth Himself on the right
hand, hideth Himself, Himself on the
right hand.* Blessed are they, *are
they* that have not seen, *that have not
seen,* and yet have believed, *Blessed,
blessed are they that have not seen,
that have not seen, not seen, and yet
have believed. Blessed are they that
have not seen, that have not, not seen,
that have not seen, and yet have believed, Blessed, blessed are they that
have not seen, that have not seen, and
yet have believed, that have not seen,
that have not, have not seen, and yet
have believed, that have not seen, not
seen, and yet, and yet have, yet have
believed.*

109 SEE WHAT LOVE HATH THE FATHER.

1 John iii. 1.   *Mendelssohn.*

(SEE what love hath the Father
bestow'd on us in His goodness, *bestow'd on us in His) See what love
hath the Father bestow'd on us in His
goodness,* that we should be called
God's own children, *God's own children. (See what love hath the) See
what love hath the Father bestow'd on
us, love in His goodness, yea in His
goodness, that we should be called God's
own children, (that we should be) that
we should be called God's own children.
(See what love hath the Father), See
what love hath the Father, see what
love hath the Father, see what love
hath the Father bestow'd on us in His*
goodness.

17

them, I am the bread of life, *I am the bread of life*, he that cometh to Me shall never hunger, he that believeth on Me shall never thirst, *he that cometh to Me shall never hunger, and he that believeth on Me shall never, never thirst, shall never thirst, shall never thirst.* Amen. Amen.

111 O SAVIOUR OF THE WORLD.

Sir J. Goss.

O SAVIOUR of the World, *O Saviour of the world*, Who by Thy Cross and precious Blood hast redeemèd us, Save us, and help us, *Save us, and help us. O Saviour of the World, O Saviour of the world. O Saviour, Who by Thy Cross and precious Blood hast redeemèd us, Save us, and help us*, we humbly beseech Thee, O Lord, we

in ev'ry place incense sha up unto My name : for M be great among the heat *name shall be great among* thus saith the Lord ! *th Lord ! From the rising unto the going down of name shall be great, sh among the Gentiles ; a place, and in ev'ry place be offer'd up unto My nan the Lord.*

113 THE DAY THOU LORD, IS EN

H. H. Woodward,

THE day Thou gavest, Lo the darkness falls at Thy Thee our morning hym Thy praise shall hallow n We thank Thee that ' unsleeping, While earth into light, Through all th watch is keeping, And re

Thy throne shall never, Like earth's proud empires, pass away; But stand, and rule, and grow for ever, Till all Thy creatures own Thy sway, *Stand and rule and grow for ever, Till all Thy creatures own Thy sway.* Amen

114 I WILL LAY ME DOWN IN PEACE.

Ps. iv. 9 ; cxxi. 2, 3, 7,

A. C. Edwards.

I WILL lay me down in peace, and take my rest, for it is Thou, Lord, only, that makest me dwell in safety, *I will lay me down in peace, lay me down, and take my rest, for it is Thou, Lord, only. that makest me dwell in safety.* My help cometh even from the Lord, who hath made heaven and earth. He will not suffer thy foot to be moved. *He will not suffer thy foot to be moved,* and He that keepeth thee will not sleep, *and He that keepeth thee will not sleep.* The Lord shall preserve thee from all evil, *The Lord shall preserve thee from all evil,* yea, it is even He, *even He* that shall keep thy soul, *even He that shall keep thy soul. I will lay me down in peace, and take my rest, for it is Thou, Lord, only, that makest me dwell in safety, I will lay me down in peace, lay me down and take my rest, for it is Thou, Lord, only, that makest me dwell in safety, I will lay me down in peace, and take my rest, for it is Thou, Lord, only, that makest me dwell in safety, I will lay me down in peace, and take my rest. in peace, in peace, in peace.*

115 I HEARD A VOICE FROM HEAVEN.

J. Goss.

I HEARD a voice from heaven, sayii unto me, Write, From hencefor blessed are the dead which die in t Lord. *Blessed are the dead which a in the Lord:* (Even so saith t spirit); *Even so saith the spirit; f* they rest from their labours, *th rest, they rest from their labou Blessed, blessed are the dead which d in the Lord, for they rest from the labours.*

116 NOW IS COME SALVATIOI

E. Bunnett.

Now is come salvation, salvation an strength, and the kingdom of o God, and the power of His Chris *Now is come salvation, salvation an strength, and the kingdom of our Go and the power of His Christ*; Then fore rejoice, rejoice ye heavens, an ye that dwell, *that dwell* in then *Therefore rejoice, rejoice ye heaven and ye that dwell, that dwell in them* For the kingdoms of this world, *th kingdoms of this world,* are becom the kingdom of our Lord, and of H Christ, and He shall reign for ev and ever. *The kingdoms of this worl are become the kingdom, the kingdo of our Lord, and of His Christ, t kingdom of our Lord, of our Lor and of His Christ, and He sha reign for ever and ever, and He sh reign for ever and ever.* Amen

117 VESPER HYMN, No. 1.

Adapted from Beethoven.

LORD, keep us safe this night,
Secure from all our fears,
May angels guard us while we sleep
Till morning light appears. Amen.

118 VESPER HYMN, No. 2.

B. Steane.

LORD, keep us safe this night,
Secure from all our fears,

May angels guard us while we s
Till morning light appears. A

119 THE SEVENFOLD AMI

J. Stain

AMEN, *Amen, Amen, Amen, A*
Amen, Amen.

120 THE DRESDEN AMEN

AMEN.

LONDON: ALEXANDER AND SHEPHEARD, LTD., PRINTERS, NORWICH STREET, I